Also by John Truby

The Anatomy of Story: 22 Steps to Becoming a Master Storyteller

Story Development Software

Truby's Blockbuster and Add-On Genres is computer software that helps writers manage the detailed beats and themes of their particular genre combination across all media, including novels and television.

Classes (online videos and downloadable MP3s)

Action Story
Anatomy of Story
Comedy
Crime Stories, Detectives, and Thrillers
Horror, Fantasy, and Science Fiction
The Love Story
Masterpiece
Memoir
Myth
Philosophy Techniques in Story
Sitcom
Story for Novelists
Writing for Television
Writing the Grand Tapestry

For more information, please visit the Truby's Writers Studio website.

The Anatomy of Genres

The Anatomy of Genres

How Story Forms Explain the Way the World Works

John Truby

PICADOR FARRAR, STRAUS AND GIROUX NEW YORK

Picador
120 Broadway, New York 10271

Printed in the United States of America
First edition, 2022

Library of Congress Cataloging-in-Publication Data
Names: Truby, John, 1952– author.
Title: The anatomy of genres : how story forms explain the way the world works / John Truby.
Description: First edition. | New York : Picador, 2022.
Identifiers: LCCN 2022022943 | ISBN 9780374539221 (paperback)
Subjects: LCSH: Fiction—Technique. | Fiction—Authorship.
Classification: LCC PN3355 .T75 2022 | DDC 808.3—dc23/eng/20220516
LC record available at https://lccn.loc.gov/2022022943

Designed by Janet Evans-Scanlon

10 9 8 7 6 5 4 3

For Leslie

CONTENTS

The Anatomy of Genres

1

The World as Story

Everything you need to know about life can be found in stories. Why? Stories define life. And the philosophies developed over the course of human history inform and respond to both. As a result, understanding the anatomy of a story is about much more than writing. It's also about knowing how to live.

In these pages you will find in-depth discussions of the fourteen major story genres that give shape to human existence. You will learn how to write them—and how to live them—in a way that transcends the ordinary.

Genres are types of stories: Detective, Love, Action, Fantasy, or Science Fiction, for example. When we understand how genres work, and what they tell us, we can apply their lessons in writing as well as in life. For example, did you know:

- Action is about being successful, not morally right.
- Myth represents a journey to understand oneself and gain immortality.
- Memoir is not about the past; it's about creating your future.
- Fantasy is about finding the magic in the world and in ourselves to turn life into art.

- Detective fiction shows us how to think successfully by comparing different stories to learn what is true.
- Love stories reveal that happiness comes from mastering the moral act of loving another person.

As we struggle to make sense of our place in the world, we think we have a clear grasp of the problems. But the problems we face today are based on how the world *appears* to work. Plato referred to these appearances as shadows. When we don't understand how the world truly is—its deep structure—how can we fit into it?

The solution is to use stories as a model.

Story is innate to human beings. It's how we learn. It's how we process the world and how we find our place in it. If you understand story, you've got a framework for life.

Story has always been fundamental to passing information from one generation to another. Whether it's oral storytelling around the fire or parables in the Bible, story is how we record and communicate life lessons.

The earliest hunter-gatherer societies understood the tremendous importance of story in their everyday lives. But as societies developed agriculture and technology advanced, a different mindset began to take over. Human lives became dominated by the work required to eat, and later to turn a profit. Once people started living in large enough groups, religions formed to give people ethical guidelines for how to live together. Stories were considered a means to that end.

This move from the primacy of story to an art practiced only by the lucky few is expressed in this famous comment by John Adams:

> I must study politics and war, that my sons may have liberty to study mathematics and philosophy. My sons

> ought to study mathematics and philosophy, geography, natural history and naval architecture, navigation, commerce, and agriculture, in order to give their children a right to study painting, poetry, music, architecture, statuary, tapestry, and porcelain.*

This quote describes an "order of operations" that has been a fundamental tenet of Western societies for centuries, if not millennia. It shows up in the work of Aristotle, arguably one of the greatest philosophers of all time. I began my first book, *The Anatomy of Story*, with Aristotle, because he was the key figure who established our modern division of knowledge. He first wrote his *Metaphysics* and then, among other works, his *Ethics* and later his *Poetics*.

Since metaphysics is the study of first principles, this order makes perfect sense. Ethics is about how to live a moral life. Poetics is the theory and practice of storytelling. For Aristotle, that included exploring the main genres of his time: epic poetry, tragedy, and comedy.

A version of this hierarchy of knowledge is what we're taught to this day. We're told that math and science are essential for our future success, while painting, music, and theater are extracurricular activities. Stories are diversions, something to take our minds off our troubles after a long day. They are something a few creative people write, and even fewer get paid for, while the rest of us enjoy stories in our spare time.

Yet there's a different way of looking at things. Stories don't just serve as forms of entertainment; they encapsulate everything from the basic organizing principles of the world to how we should live our lives in it. In this sense, everything is about poetics.

---

* Letter from John Adams to his wife, Abigail, May 12, 1780.

KEY POINT: Seeing the world through the prism of story marks a revolutionary change in how we look at the world, and it's the reverse of what we've been taught.

All the things we thought were bigger than story, like morality, culture, society, religion, sports, and war, are simply different kinds of stories. We humans are essentially storytelling animals.

Consider this quote from Richard Flanagan's novel *First Person* (2018). Scam artist "Ziggy" Heidl explains the reason for his success:

> *I made it up.* Every day, just like you. *Like a writer* . . . What do you think a businessman is? A politician? They're sorcerers—they make things up. Stories are all that we have to hold us together. Religion, science, money—they're all just stories.

Story is a philosophy of life expressed through characters, plot, and emotion. It shows life as art. That's why stories are the universal building blocks of religion and always have been. Story transcends specific religions, each of which is a collection of stories about how to live an ethical life. We find these stories in the Old Testament (Judaism) and New Testament (Christianity), the Koran (Islam), the Upanishads (Hinduism), the I Ching (Confucianism), and many other texts. The universal religion of story is why the novels, television series, films, plays, and video games we encounter today define the culture of the secular world.

Storytelling influences every aspect of a person's life. Consider how business runs through advertising. Everything we buy and sell is part of a story. Parenting is full of storytelling. We tell stories to our kids at bedtime. We tell stories to our teenagers to prevent them from doing drugs. And we need to be better storytellers than the others who try to influence them.

At work, we need to tell a compelling story to drum up business. A good story can determine whether we can pay the rent.

Politics uses story to exercise power. Adlai Stevenson once observed, "In classical times when Cicero had finished speaking, the people said, 'How well he spoke'—but when Demosthenes had finished speaking, the people said, 'Let us march.'"* Turning words into action is the central distinction in communication.

KEY POINT: Stories are *maps of humanity.*

Why have some ancient myths endured for centuries? They're not just entertainment; they're instructional. First, they explain the physical world. For example, the story of Persephone and why we have winter. Do we still think the seasons work that way? No, but it helps us to make peace with colder days and longer nights.

Myths also give us social structures. An epic is classically defined as the story of an individual or family whose actions determine the fate of a nation. Homer's epic poem the *Iliad* shows how monarchical rule combined with personal alliances and jealousies caused a ten-year war that destroyed everyone caught in its grinding slaughter.

KEY POINT: If human life is poetics, the knowledge we get from story is the greatest knowledge of all.

---

* Adlai Stevenson, introducing John F. Kennedy in 1960, as quoted in *Adlai Stevenson and the World: The Life of Adlai E. Stevenson* (1977), by John Bartlow Martin, p. 549.

Once we understand that all of human life is a form of story, the next step becomes clear: genres are the portals to this world.

Each of the various genres—Detective, Love, Fantasy, and the like—is a unique window onto how a particular aspect of the world works and how best to confront it. Writers have a unique perspective because it's their job to think in terms of different worlds and deeper structures. If they want to write stories that will achieve critical and popular success, they need to consider elements such as morality and point of view. Morality refers to how a character's actions affect others. That's why, in the Crime chapter, we discuss the moral code of both the hero and their opponent. While all stories require a point of view, the Detective genre explores the way this fact variously limits and empowers the human mind.

The purpose of this book is to reveal to the world the deep structures of story and genre. That's why this book can be read on two levels. The first provides specific, technical information about how to write great stories that sell. The second explores philosophical issues with the kind of X-ray vision that can enrich and change everyone's life.

Rules of Play

The only way a writer can be successful in any medium is to play by the three unwritten rules that define storytelling today.

RULE 1

The Storytelling Business Is All About Buying and Selling Genres.

Genres are far more than types of stories. They are the all-stars of the story world that have achieved immense popular success over centuries. Writers who want to succeed professionally must write the stories the business wants to buy. Simply put, the storytelling game is won by mastering the structure of genres.

Each major genre has fifteen to twenty specialized "beats," or key plot events, that determine that form. These plot beats have more to do with the success of a story than any other element by far.

These beats are also why people choose to read or watch a particular genre again and again. If these classic plot beats are not present, the story will not be popular. Period. For example, a Love story without the "first dance" beat will have Love story fanatics up in arms.

Genres Are Story Systems

At the professional level, the game is won or lost by how well the writer executes their particular genre. This is a major challenge. Many writers believe they can master their genre simply by tossing in a few "tropes" of the form. A trope is an individual story element such as a character, a plot device, a theme in variation, a recurring image, or even a tagline of dialogue. The best authors understand that tropes are just the sprinkles on top. The real mechanism for a compelling bestseller is the structure beneath the tropes.

The genre beats connect under the surface to form an entire story system that expresses a unique philosophy of life. Each beat is effective because it has been set up as part of a deeper structure through which the writer is leading the audience. The sequence of plot beats is what knocks the audience out.

> **KEY POINT: You have to hit *all* the plot beats of the particular genre(s) you've chosen.**

Each genre uses a specific strategy to express its philosophy. The great architect Louis Sullivan referred to this as "form follows function." Philosophically speaking, genres are the Platonic forms, the structures beneath the "shadows" that truly explain our lives. Every story presents a particular challenge; the genre provides the structure for solving it.

KEY POINT: The main function of the genre beats is to express the unique theme/life philosophy of that form.

The Never-Ending Diversity of Genres

Story has evolved and diversified over thousands of years. Genres are the product of various influences: the human mind, the nature of the medium (novel, film, or television), and the particular culture where the genre first developed.

Depending on how one classifies genres, there could be six, seven, thirty-two, hundreds, or even thousands. Here, we will work through what I believe to be the fourteen most influential of them.

KEY POINT: The fourteen major genres in this book, alone or in combination, compose 99 percent of storytelling forms today, including novels, film, television, plays, and video games.

The fourteen major genres are: Horror, Action, Myth, Memoir, Coming-of-Age, Science Fiction, Crime, Comedy, Western, Gangster, Fantasy, Thriller, Detective, and Love. Note: the order of presentation is critical.

Many of these genres cluster into families that share certain characteristics: Myth (Myth, Action, Western), Crime (Detective, Crime, Thriller, Gangster), and Speculative Fiction (Horror, Science Fiction, Fantasy).

Each of the fourteen major genres can be broken down into subgenres, and we will discuss the most important. For example, the Caper (Heist) story is a popular form of Action and Crime. These subgenres diversify into hundreds of sub-subgenres, but the main beats are the same.

KEY POINT: Writers should know how *all* the major genres work.

Why? First, having some knowledge of all the forms helps you write your specific genre better. Second, you can combine genres in a way the world hasn't yet seen. This increases your odds of success.

RULE 2

Popular Stories Today Combine 3–4 Genres.

Mastering one genre used to be enough. No longer. The problem with that strategy is that there are few stories today limited to a single form. Instead, most stories are a combination of two, three, or even four genres.

Mixing genres is how the game is played in every medium, no matter how smart you are, how hard you work, who you know, or how you market your work. The storytelling strategy of mixing genres has been responsible for the success of hit movies and bestselling books since George Lucas used it in *Star Wars*.

Imagine, if you can, a pre–*Star Wars* world. In the summer of 1975, *Jaws* was released in movie theaters throughout America. This realistic Horror story was based on a bestselling book. When *Jaws* turned out to be a monster hit, the film industry saw that the game went beyond the U.S. market. It was now about worldwide box office.

What was *Jaws*' storytelling strategy? A single genre done

extremely well. Then, in 1977, *Star Wars: A New Hope* hit theaters. There was a paradigm shift in popular storytelling strategy.

My *Star Wars* Epiphany

Let me tell you about the revelation that changed my writing life. I was sitting in a packed theater munching on popcorn. Then a massive space battleship came over the top of my head. I stopped eating and gasped, as did everyone else in the audience. That moment had such grandeur and power that everybody there knew we were in for the ride of our lives.

Surely, this is where the expression "blown away" was born. Yes, I was watching *Star Wars* for the first time. And while it played, the strangest thing happened. I experienced a feeling of pure delight. In 95 percent of stories, I could predict what would happen three beats ahead. But not with *Star Wars*. Here was one story beat after another I didn't see coming. This was nonstop excitement.

Better yet, these beats were coming at top speed. I was totally overwhelmed. The recognition began to dawn on me about what was really happening. I began to understand what writer-director George Lucas was doing under the surface.

This was obviously a Fantasy in outer space, which meant elements of Science Fiction. But that wasn't all. I loved the classic Western, but it had long since died. Now I was seeing all the Western beats in outer space. It was wild! And who doesn't love King Arthur, one of the great Myth stories? I noticed some of those beats as well.

Ever wonder where all those ever-popular lightsabers came from? They're from the samurai movie, a subgenre of Action. Since college, I'd been a big fan of Japanese films like *Seven Samurai* and *The Hidden Fortress*.

As a result, the plot was dense. And instead of getting the

beats of one genre, like Fantasy, we were getting beats of Science Fiction, Myth, and Action, in rapid-fire succession.

KEY POINT: ***Star Wars*** **was exciting because the writer was weaving** ***beats from multiple genres in a single movie.***

A revolution for writers unfolded right in front of my eyes. BSW (Before *Star Wars*), it was a single-genre story world. ASW (After *Star Wars*), Hollywood knew we were in a multi-genre universe. Popular stories from then on were going to be all about mixing genres.

In the last twenty years, this has only intensified. Giving the audience more "story" for their hard-earned dollars has been one of the major trends in worldwide storytelling in every medium.

Mixing Genres

As important as this strategy is, mixing genres is tougher than it looks. Combining the beats of every genre can create chaos. Sometimes the beat from one genre will prevent the writer from being able to use the beat from another. The trick lies in how you combine the beats and which beats you choose.

One technique for mixing genres is to combine story forms that don't normally go together. For example, a big reason why *Inception* was so popular is that it combined two genres that don't usually appear in the same story: Science Fiction and Caper (a subform of Action and Crime).

Another example is *The Godfather*. On the surface, it appears to be simply a Gangster story. In fact, it combines Gangster with Myth and Fairy Tale (Fantasy). One classic scene in the film—the moment at the hospital when Michael discovers his father is about to be assassinated—is straight out of a Horror story.

Combining genres requires two things above all:

1. You must know the story beats for every genre you're using, even if you don't include all those beats in the story.
2. You must be able to apply techniques from the other genres to write your own story well.

This is why we will go through the plot beats for all fourteen major genres in this book. Writers can begin by reading about their chosen genre, but they can also dip into other chapters to see what genres they want to combine. Nonwriters will see why they love their favorite story forms so much, and appreciate them more.

RULE 3

To Rise Above the Crowd, the Writer Must *Transcend* the Primary Genre.

Executing the beats of the genre is the basic requirement for any story. But it takes you only so far. While necessary, it's not sufficient. Yes, you've written a solid genre story. But it's the same story everyone else has written. There's no creativity, no surprise, no way of setting yourself apart as an original author.

The word "transcend" means "to rise above or go beyond the limits (to something abstract)." The three main ways to transcend a genre are to

1. twist the story beats;
2. express the genre's life philosophy in the theme;
3. explore the story forms of life unique to the genre.

In this book I'll show you how to do all three.

Transcending the Genre 1: Twist the Story Beats

KEY POINT: The first way to transcend the genre is to twist the story beats. Instead of "breaking the rules," you're bending them.

When you twist the beats, your audience still gets the pleasure of encountering the beats they expect. They also get the pleasure of seeing the beats done in a way they've never seen before.

One way to twist the beats is by changing their order. The sequence of genre beats creates certain expectations in the reader's mind. After a while, those expectations dull their vision. When you twist all the beats, people light up because you are undercutting their expectations of what will happen. Now you've shown them how the world works in a new way. You hook the audience because the view is something they recognize—it's still their world—but it's recast in a different light.

> All of the very successful things on television have come from ideas which are in genres that people know, or know something of, but are done in a different way. And people flock to something they haven't seen.
>
> —JOHN WELLS, writer, *ER*, *The West Wing*, *Shameless*

Transcending the Genre 2: Express the Genre's Life Philosophy in the Theme

Transcending the genre means more than twisting the unique story beats to give audiences something they haven't seen. Hidden below the surface of these beats is a philosophy, an entire way of seeing and living in the world. This is expressed through the theme, which is the author's view of the best way to live.

We will refer to this life philosophy embedded in each genre as the "Mind-Action" story view. This refers to how the human mind sees the world and then *acts* accordingly. Like the slides of a kaleidoscope, each genre has a different point of view about how the world fits together. Each offers a unique philosophy for how to live well.

Expressing the genre's philosophy is the key to any story you write. This unique Mind-Action story view is what really hooks the reader. In turn, drama infuses the genre's lesson for how to live with tremendous emotional power. This is the story gold.

Each genre's recipe for how to live well is based on its fundamental concern. For example:

- **HORROR:** Confront death and face your ghosts from the past.
- **ACTION:** 90 percent of success is taking action.
- **MYTH:** Seek immortality by finding your destiny in this life.
- **MEMOIR AND COMING-OF-AGE:** Examine your life to create your true self.
- **SCIENCE FICTION:** Make the right choices now to ensure a better future for all.
- **CRIME:** Protect the weak and bring the guilty to justice.
- **COMEDY:** Success comes when you strip away all facades and show others who you really are.
- **WESTERN:** When you help others make a home, you create a civilization where everyone is free to live their best life.
- **GANGSTER:** Don't be enslaved by absolute power and money or you will pay the ultimate price.

- **FANTASY:** Discover the magic in yourself that makes life itself an art form.
- **DETECTIVE AND THRILLER:** Look for the truth and assign guilt in spite of the danger.
- **LOVE:** Learning how to love is the key to happiness.

One of the advantages of using genres is you can express powerful and complex themes through the form's deep structure.

Transcending the Genre 3: Explore the Story Forms of Life Unique to the Genre

Looking at the world through the prism of story gives us X-ray vision into life itself.

> **KEY POINT: The idea that the mind works through story leads to another revolutionary idea about transcending genres: *each major human activity is its own story form.***

Morality, culture, business, sports, war, religion, politics, justice, society, and the mind are some of the grand activities that make up human life. They are also complex works of art expressed through the emotional and dramatic form of story. At its best, each genre explores one or more of these story forms of life.

The Order of Genres

For me, the most revelatory part of coming to understand genres was the realization that they exist in a hierarchy of their own, or what might be called a "ladder of enlightenment." Perhaps the philosopher Georg Wilhelm Friedrich Hegel's greatest insight is that every step up the ladder of human enlightenment also reveals the flaw that holds someone back.

Like sand in the oyster, that flaw is what creates the next step of growth.

The hierarchy of genres is based on three things: the primary character flaw the hero must overcome, the quality of the life philosophy the form expresses, and the major art/story form it explores. The first and most primitive genre is Horror, the story of escaping death in this life or the next. From there, the sequence moves from least to most enlightened, from Action to Fantasy, Detective, and Love stories. At the end of each chapter, I will explain what is missing from each genre's life philosophy—the thing that leads us to take the next step up the ladder.

Here, then, is the genre "ladder," with each genre's fundamental concern:

- **HORROR:** Religion
- **ACTION:** Success
- **MYTH:** The Life Process
- **MEMOIR AND COMING-OF-AGE:** Creating the Self
- **SCIENCE FICTION:** Science, Society, and Culture (yes, science is a story form)
- **CRIME:** Morality and Justice
- **COMEDY:** Manners and Morals
- **WESTERN:** The Rise and Fall of Civilization
- **GANGSTER:** The Corruption of Business and Politics
- **FANTASY:** The Art of Living
- **DETECTIVE AND THRILLER:** The Mind and the Truth
- **LOVE:** The Art of Happiness

Story Examples

Transcending genre and exploring the major story forms of life are highly complex tasks. Because we learn best by example, I'll break down a number of stories from novels, film, television, and theater.

Since there are thousands of stories, choosing those that exemplify a particular genre is a near-impossible task. I've tried to use recent examples where appropriate. But my main criterion is always: which one is best. This is especially true when discussing transcendent genre stories. My choice is typically a classic that defines the form itself.

The following best express the techniques needed to write a great story in each genre:

- **HORROR/Religion:** *Frankenstein*, *A Christmas Carol*, *Alien*, *Get Out*, *Psycho*, *Ex Machina*, *Westworld*
- **ACTION/Success:** *Mad Max: Fury Road*, *Die Hard*, *Seven Samurai*, the *Iliad*, *The Thomas Crown Affair*, *Rocky*, *The Hustler*
- **MYTH/The Life Process:** *Star Wars: A New Hope*, *The Lord of the Rings*, *The Wizard of Oz*, *Black Panther*, *Avatar*, the *Odyssey*
- **MEMOIR AND COMING-OF-AGE STORY/Creating the Self:** *The Liars' Club*, *Into Thin Air*, *Moonlight*, *Cinema Paradiso*, *CODA*, *To Kill a Mockingbird*
- **SCIENCE FICTION/Science, Society, and Culture:** *Arrival*, *The Matrix*, *Inception*, *Interstellar*, *2001: A Space Odyssey*
- **CRIME/Morality and Justice:** *Breaking Bad*, *The Dark Knight*, *The Usual Suspects*, *Crime and Punishment*, *In Bruges*
- **COMEDY/Manners and Morals:** *Seinfeld*, *Little Miss Sunshine*, *Groundhog Day*, *Wedding Crashers*
- **WESTERN/The Rise and Fall of Civilization:** *Shane*, *Butch Cassidy and the Sundance Kid*, *The Wild Bunch*, *McCabe & Mrs. Miller*, *Once Upon a Time in the West*

- **GANGSTER/The Corruption of Business and Politics:** *The Godfather*, *Goodfellas*, *The Sopranos*, *The Great Gatsby*, *Mad Men*, *Network*
- **FANTASY/The Art of Living:** *Harry Potter*, *Game of Thrones*, *Big*, *Pleasantville*, *Mary Poppins*, *It's a Wonderful Life*, *Alice in Wonderland*
- **DETECTIVE AND THRILLER/The Mind and the Truth:**
  - Detective: *L.A. Confidential*, *The Collected Sherlock Holmes Short Stories*, *Vertigo*, *Knives Out*, *Murder on the Orient Express*, *Chinatown*, *Rashomon*
  - Thriller: *The Silence of the Lambs*, *Michael Clayton*, *The Sixth Sense*, *The Conversation*, *Shadow of a Doubt*
- **LOVE/The Art of Happiness:** *Silver Linings Playbook*, *500 Days of Summer*, *When Harry Met Sally*, *The Philadelphia Story*, *Sideways*

Who Is This Book For?

If you've picked up this book thinking you will be able to impress your friends at cocktail parties, congratulations, you've come to the right place. But there's so much more.

This book is for everyone interested in how stories shape our lives and for the writers pursuing this vital craft.

If you're a writer, you'll learn the techniques and plot beats that must be in your genre stories. More important, you'll learn how to write a transcendent story of your own that expresses the deeper theme all readers crave. I'll teach you that by showing you both the life philosophy of each genre and the one or two art/story forms of life that transcendent stories are really about.

This combination of technique and thematic life philosophy provides tangible, advanced strategies that few other writers now possess. It will help you write powerful stories that achieve both critical and commercial success.

And that's not all. I believe there is a craving in everyone for deeper understanding in their lives. That's why the broader intention of this book is to give people more profound models of the world. By exploring philosophical issues and ideas, we can learn how to grapple with them in ways that will enrich us on our life's journey.

The Anatomy of Genres takes us from the poetics of storytelling to the poetics of life. Join me in exploring the multidimensional maps of humanity that help us navigate our lives.

2

Horror: Religion

The first genre we'll investigate is Horror. Why? Because the major distinction governing human existence is life versus death.

Adam and Eve: One of the First Horror Stories

Although monsters have been present in story from the beginning, Genesis in the Old Testament is where horror elements first come together as a genre. Adam and Eve are the first man, first woman, and first couple. They live in paradise and are innocent and unashamed of their nakedness. But they are confronted by a trickster character—the devil in the form of a serpent. He lures Eve into eating the "poison," the forbidden apple from the tree of knowledge of good and evil.

Enter God the Father, the couple's second opponent. According to Him, the cost to Adam and Eve of gaining knowledge is losing their immortality—they are expelled from the garden so that they cannot eat the fruit of the tree of knowledge and live forever. To know is to die. This father is a tyrant. When his children make the mistake of wanting to understand their world and themselves, their punishment is to be driven out of paradise.

In this story, we see the fundamental distinction between life and death, and the tendency of the Religion story to use Horror as its preferred form of expression.

Horror in Storytelling from the Beginning

KEY POINT: Horror is embedded within life itself. Life is the story where the big kick at the end is that everybody dies.

Horror as a modern genre is about 250 years old. It is generally agreed to have begun in 1764 with Horace Walpole's *The Castle of Otranto*. But Horror elements have been a part of Myth, the oldest genre, from the beginning. For example:

- ***EPIC OF GILGAMESH* (2100 BC):** Enkidu is the primal man who lives like an animal.
- **OLD TESTAMENT (CIRCA 1200–165 BC):** Abraham is willing to sacrifice his son on God's orders.
- **GREEK MYTHOLOGY (CIRCA 3000–1100 BC):** The Gorgons are three sisters whose hair is made of venomous snakes. Perseus kills the Gorgon Medusa.
- **THE MINOTAUR:** A creature—half-man, half-bull—that eats human flesh and lives within the labyrinth.
- **HERCULES:** When the goddess Hera makes him go mad, he kills his wife and children.
- **AGAMEMNON:** He sacrifices his daughter so that the Greek army can sail and avenge the kidnapping of Helen.
- **OEDIPUS:** He cuts out his eyes when he learns he has slept with his mother and killed his father.

From these supernatural beginnings, Horror evolved and eventually entered the psychological realm it occupies today. The writer Michael Capuzzo has observed that "earlier European Gothic fiction emphasized the supernatural, castles and curses; [Edgar Allan] Poe brought horror down to earth and made us fear the ordinary and everyday."*

KEY POINT: Poe's shift from the supernatural to the psychological is the most important change in the Horror genre. It is the basis of the modern form.

Horror: How It Works

Horror's basic distinction of life versus death is a binary opposition that allows for no complexity: one is either dead or alive. This points to a fundamental quality of the human mind: It always begins in binary mode. It starts with Yes/No, Either/Or, Me/Other, Us/Them.

The Horror genre itself is not so simple, however. Hegel's great insight about the flaw leading to the next step of enlightenment is based on the idea that from a simple binary opposition (known as the "dialectic"), we create the new, the better, and the diverse. Thinking about the elemental forces of life and death can inspire great creativity. Horror, especially realistic Horror, often focuses on the finality of death, and how humans cannot comprehend the idea that they will no longer exist.

Horror's Mind-Action Story View

Every genre shows the mind reacting to the world and then acting upon it. Each lays out a different understanding of how

---

* Michael Capuzzo, "How Edgar Allan Poe Became Our Era's Premier Storyteller," *Smithsonian Magazine*, January 2019.

the world works, and how it works best. This is the genre's Mind-Action story view.

The Horror version of the Mind-Action story view is that life is an ongoing struggle to defeat death. It is a fight we are all destined to lose.

Great Horror storytelling pushes the audience into a smaller and smaller box until that box is in the ground. Horror makes us *feel* what it means to be dead.

This increases the power of death in our minds tenfold. No longer is it an abstraction that happens to everyone else. The idea that the magnificent complexity of a human being, especially *this* human being, could suddenly cease to exist is too absurd to comprehend.

In essence, the Horror story strategy is to have a unique monster relentlessly pursue a victim. This plot sequence translates into pressure on the hero and thus the audience.

After contemplating the finality of death, we end by asking: What is to be done? Surely there is an answer somewhere. But we can't find it. That, too, is a death. There is no hope. That is, unless there is something like a god or religion.

Horror expresses the story of religion. This is the story of how we defeat death, how we avoid a horrible afterlife and find the promised land of life ever after. The main goal of the Horror Mind-Action story view is to force us to confront death. To pry our eyes open and shove death in our face. Whether this highly emotional approach induces us to see our end honestly and make real changes to our lives is another question.

Horror Compared to Other Genres

Horror is part of a major family of genres known as "Speculative Fiction," which includes Fantasy and Science Fiction. These three genres are about projecting and abstracting in the extreme. Fantasy projects a character into a fully detailed imaginary world so she can learn how to live. Science Fiction creates a society and culture, with special focus on the science and technology by which the world operates. Horror creates a character out of the most dangerous of all opponents: death itself.

Detective fiction, on the other hand, is Horror's polar opposite. Horror is the most primal form, while Detective is the most intellectual. But Detective and Horror are both fundamentally about the mind.

KEY POINT: Detective fiction highlights the brilliance of the mind while Horror emphasizes its flaws.

Detective fiction shows us how the mind works; Horror tells us how it fails. One form shows off the mind's symbolic power while the other reveals the products of illogic, hatred, and prejudice.

Detective and Horror also have a basic opposition in how they treat death. In the Detective genre, death is something we know happens to someone else. In Horror, death is what is *happening to me right now!*

On the other hand, Horror shares a basic similarity with Comedy in that characters in both forms are reduced in type, such as to animal or machine. The difference is that the reduction in Horror is much more extreme. This creates fear in the audience instead of laughter.

Examples of Horror

Stories

Sisyphus, Old Testament Genesis (Adam and Eve), *The Legend of Sleepy Hollow*, *The Fall of the House of Usher*, *The*

Cask of Amontillado, The Tell-Tale Heart, The Pit and the Pendulum, The Masque of the Red Death

Novels and Films

The Castle of Otranto, A Christmas Carol (also Myth and Fantasy), *Interview with the Vampire, Dracula, Jaws, Alien, Psycho, Carrie, It, Firestarter, Cujo, Pet Sematary, A Quiet Place, Hereditary, The Wolf Man, Wolfen, The Fly, The Invisible Man, Night of the Living Dead, The Exorcist, Rosemary's Baby, Invasion of the Body Snatchers, Jurassic Park, The Omen, Misery, A Nightmare on Elm Street, The Ring, Texas Chainsaw Massacre, Halloween, Friday the 13th, Hellraiser, The Amityville Horror, Hell House, Poltergeist, Joker, Lost Boys, The Innocents, Tales from the Crypt, The Night Stalker, Sleepy Hollow, Trilogy of Terror, The Blair Witch Project, Don't Be Afraid of the Dark, Angel Heart, Terror in the Wax Museum, The Crawling Eye, The Vault of Horror, The Legend of Boggy Creek, Creature from the Black Lagoon, Twilight, Underworld, Cat People, Peeping Tom, An American Werewolf in London, Dawn of the Dead, Deliverance, Shaun of the Dead, Godzilla, Sisters, The Thing, What Ever Happened to Baby Jane?*

Television

The Walking Dead, True Blood, Buffy the Vampire Slayer, American Horror Story, Les Revenants, Stranger Things (also Thriller), *Grimm* (also Horror, Detective, Love, and Fantasy), *Kingdom, Sleepy Hollow* (also Thriller), *The Stand, Supernatural, The Haunting of Hill House, The Vampire Diaries*

Horror Subgenres

All the major genres have multiple subgenres. These are a diversification of the form using different characters, plot beats, story worlds, and themes. Horror subgenres include Ghost Story, Vampire, Werewolf, Slasher, Occult, Paranormal, Gothic, Horror/Myth, Horror/Science Fiction Epic, Superhero, Savior, and Comedy.

Horror Story Overview

Here's what we'll cover in this chapter:

- **HORROR STORY BEATS**
- **THEME:** Being Is Trying to Avoid Death
  - Thematic Recipe: The Way of Facing Death and Taking Humane Action
- **HOW TO TRANSCEND THE HORROR STORY**
  - Horror/Myth: Religion, Including Religious Story Beats and Christian Story Beats
  - Horror/Science Fiction Epic

The Seven Major Steps of the Story Code

All good stories—not just Horror stories, but stories of every genre—work through seven major structure steps. These foundational steps compose the Story Code. They mark the process of the hero's character change, or evolution, over the course of the story.

1. **WEAKNESS-NEED:** The hero is enslaved by habits of thought and action and suffers from a deep personal weakness that is destroying the quality of her life. The hero needs to overcome this flaw to grow.

2. **DESIRE:** The hero desires a goal outside of herself that she perceives as valuable and missing from her life.
3. **OPPONENT:** She confronts an opponent and an obstacle/challenge preventing her from reaching her goal. She will find at the end that the obstacle/challenge is herself.
4. **PLAN:** She concocts a plan, or strategy, that will allow her to defeat the opponent and achieve the goal.
5. **BATTLE:** She enters into a final conflict, or battle, with the opponent to determine once and for all who wins.
6. **SELF-REVELATION:** At the end, the hero, if she grows at all, has a revelation about her true or better self, about how she has been wrong psychologically and morally. She then makes a decision about how to act and takes new action, proving what she has become.
7. **NEW EQUILIBRIUM:** With the system in a new equilibrium, the hero stands as a new version of herself, along with a new capacity for growing in the future.

Horror Story Beats

Like those of all genres, the Horror story beats twist these seven major structural steps to express the theme of the form. Horror also has a surprisingly large number of distinct beats. Why? It is such a narrow form, with so little natural plot, that it *must* have that many specialized beats to deepen and extend it.

These beats represent the superstructure, the Horror mythology, if you will. That prevents a plot that normally has only one beat—attacking the victim—from being repeated ad infinitum. Beats like the "sins of the parents" and "crossing the forbidden barrier" aren't just a natural outgrowth of the unique theme of Horror. They create the plot complexity and character depth that this form needs to expand beyond a short story.

HORROR STORY BEAT: Ghost—Sins of the Past

A "ghost," while not one of the seven major structure steps, is an essential element of any story—and not just Horror stories. It is the event from the past still haunting the hero in the present. Depending on how one classifies it, it is either a secondary structure step or part of the first one, weakness-need.

In Horror, "ghost" is a commonly misunderstood beat. Writers often think the term refers to the Ghost Story subgenre. In that form, the ghost is the "monster" or opponent. It is the ethereal projection of a dead person who haunts those still alive for a transgression committed against them in life. More broadly speaking, the "ghosts" in most Horror stories are events from the past that haunt the hero to the extent that they define that person and even affect their behavior. Oftentimes a ghost is a past crime committed by the hero's ancestors that has not been atoned for. It will keep reappearing, because the debt *must* be paid.

KEY POINT: Ghost is the most important beat in Horror.

Why?

- It represents the power of the past over the present, which is one of the fundamental themes of the form.
- It encapsulates the sins of fathers and mothers affecting the lives of their children.
- The ghost is the *mind attacking itself*.
- It keeps attacking throughout the story, becoming the driving force of the plot.

In Horror, the ghost that keeps attacking the hero is really the power of suggestion acting on the fallible mind. It is the self-confirming hypothesis the mind cannot help replaying and making real.

KEY POINT: In good Horror the structural alignment is tight; a crime from the past is connected, through the psychological and moral weakness of the hero, to a horrifying crime in the future.

In *A Nightmare on Elm Street*, ten years before the film takes place, vigilante parents, including Nancy's mother, Marge, killed the child murderer Freddy Krueger by lighting him on fire and watching him burn. Here the "ghost" becomes the monster.

The Shining sets up a psychological ghost for the hero before he enters the Overlook Hotel. After drinking too much, Jack jerked his son Danny's arm and separated the boy's shoulder. His wife, Wendy, has never fully trusted him again, while Jack has never forgiven her for blaming him.

In *Alien*, the robot Ash was sent by the company to bring back the alien to use as a weapon. When Ripley overrides the onboard MOTHER computer to determine what happened, it says: "Gather specimen. Priority one: ensure return of organism for analysis. All other considerations secondary. Crew expendable." The past crime is the company giving permission to commit murder.

Psycho has the most complex psychological ghost in movie history. The ghost that determines the story is not that of the initial hero, Marion. It's Norman's. He is the outwardly mild-mannered young man who murders Marion and drives the story. At the end, the psychiatrist talks us through Norman's psychological decline:

DR. FRED RICHMOND: . . . hearing it from the . . . mother half of Norman's mind . . . you have to go back ten years,

> to the time when Norman murdered his mother and her lover . . . and it seemed to Norman that she "threw him over" for this man. Now that pushed him over the line and he killed 'em both. Matricide is probably the most unbearable crime of all . . . most unbearable to the son who commits it. So he had to erase the crime, at least in his own mind. He stole her corpse . . . So he began to think and speak for her, give her half his life . . . Now he was never all Norman, but he was often only mother. And because he was so pathologically jealous of her, he assumed that she was jealous of him. Therefore, if he felt a strong attraction to any other woman, the mother side of him would go wild . . . When he met your sister, he was . . . aroused by her. He wanted her. That set off the "jealous mother" and "mother killed the girl"! Now after the murder, Norman returned as if from a deep sleep. And like a dutiful son, covered up all traces of the crime he was convinced his mother had committed!

Although all genres require the seven major structure steps, some emphasize certain steps more than others. Horror emphasizes "ghost" and "opponent." This makes perfect sense when you realize that "ghost" and "opponent" are the *internal* and *external* opponents, respectively. Using a pincer attack from inside and out, Horror puts more pressure on the hero than any other form.

HORROR STORY BEAT: Story World—Haunted House and Closed Society

The story world is an expression of the hero's ghost and weakness-need. In Horror, this is some version of a haunted house that becomes a pressure cooker surrounding the hero.

The haunted house represents the flawed mind made physical: the hero's greatest fear is the very structure in which she has no choice but to live.

Examples include *The Fall of the House of Usher*, *Dracula*, *The Innocents*, *The Exorcist*, *The Amityville Horror*, *Poltergeist*, *A Nightmare on Elm Street*, the grand hotel on the mountaintop in *The Shining*, and the mansion in the modern, tragic vampire story *Sunset Boulevard*.

The haunted house is usually a closed social world. Often, aristocrats or the upper classes inhabit it. This class has rotted, so the house feeds, sometimes literally, on the common people who live in the village. Dracula is a count. Dr. Frankenstein, the corrupt father who abandons his "child," is a baron. In *The Fall of the House of Usher*, the narrator visits his dissolute friend with "gray-white skin," and his apparently dying sister. They live in a decaying mansion with a crack running from roof to floor.

The United States likes to believe it is a classless democracy. Therefore, in American Horror stories, the corruption of the social world is often buried beneath the happy facade of the small town. But sooner or later it roars to the surface. We see this in *Friday the 13th*, *Halloween*, *Poltergeist*, and *A Nightmare on Elm Street*.

Get Out transcends the Horror genre in part because it depicts a story world based on both class and race. The modern-day plantation owner uses medical technology to keep Black people in permanent servitude.

One strategy writers use to make Horror believable is to begin the story in a foreign, mysterious, or "Old World" location. These places are the home of fairy tales. The Horror is then transported to the new, modern world, like a plague from which no one is immune. This technique is used in *The Exorcist*, *Dracula*, *Arachnophobia*, and *Hellraiser*.

One distinction within the haunted house of Horror is the cellar versus the attic. The sins of the mothers and fathers are buried in the cellar. But the sins must be atoned for. So these sins, in the form of skeletons (literal or figurative), rise up and strike again. *Psycho* is the prime example of this effect. The attic, on the other hand, is usually a place where fond memories are locked away. But as the "head" of the house, the attic can also be the place where the mad are imprisoned. The Gothic romance *Jane Eyre* is the most famous example of this use of the attic.

The Haunted Town and City

In Horror, the haunted house is often part of a haunted town. The classic ghost town has empty buildings that create a sense of death. This reduces the pressure cooker effect of an enclosed house, but it highlights the idea that there is no escape. This is a world of death. The French television show *Les Revenants* uses this to great effect by placing the town in an enclosed mountain setting where it is difficult, if not impossible, for anyone to enter or leave. *28 Days Later* expands the haunted town to the city, with London empty of humans and crawling with the living dead. In one scene, the small band of escaping heroes must change a tire in the middle of a tunnel. When thousands of rats run past them, the group realizes that a horde of fast-moving zombies is right behind. This scene is a textbook example of the intense pressure the Horror story puts on the hero.

HORROR STORY BEAT: The Monster Attacks

The opponent, the monster, is extremely powerful and typically drives the action. The monster's attacks, from without and within (ghost and weakness), put the hero on the defensive and in a pressure cooker almost immediately. The pressure only gets worse.

HORROR STORY BEAT: Hero as Victim

Because of the constant attacks by the opponent, Horror always shows the hero being beaten down to the point of death, which symbolizes our own mortality.

> **KEY POINT: Since the hero is diminished over the course of the story, one trick is to start with the hero "on top of the world." This story strategy takes the hero from the highest high to the lowest low.**

In *Frankenstein; or, The Modern Prometheus*, the genius Dr. Frankenstein wants to create the Nietzschean Overman from a corpse. Because he must inevitably fail in this grand quest, he falls physically and morally. We also see this technique in *The Fly*, *The Strange Case of Dr. Jekyll and Mr. Hyde*, *Creature from the Black Lagoon*, and *The Invisible Man*.

A second approach is to start with an average but good person who stumbles into a terrifying phenomenon. We see this approach in *Pet Sematary*, *Jaws*, *Arachnophobia*, *The Exorcist*, *Psycho*, *Alien*, and *A Nightmare on Elm Street*.

For this second approach to be most successful, you must spend time at the beginning of the story making the character intensely human. He might be kind, sensitive, a family man, about to be married or have a child, or a leader in the community. Giving the hero these positive traits makes his fall more extreme and more tragic.

HORROR STORY BEAT: Weakness-Need 1—Slavery of Mind and the Monster Within

The weakness holding the hero back from success takes two forms: psychological and moral. Need refers to what the character must do to fix the weakness, what she must do to grow. The source of the character's weakness is her ghost. This is why "ghost" is sometimes considered part of the weakness-need step.

As we saw in the ghost step, Horror isn't really about scary monsters. It's about a character whose weakness-need is so severe her mind is effectively enslaved.

> **KEY POINT: The great value of the Horror story is that it shows us the human monster within, the inherent flaws of the symbol-making animal that result in its self-destruction.**

Binary Thinking

The first cause of the slavery of the mind is "either-or" thinking. It comes from the self-conscious mind's tremendous power to project symbolically. This begins with the same two-point opposition from which all stories grow: desire versus opponent.

As soon as we *want*, we become aware of something else. That something else is the Other who stands in our way. The Other may even kill us.

> **KEY POINT: The tendency of the human mind to see *differences* as *opposites* is its foundational flaw.**

The mind always *begins*, and usually ends, with a binary: Either/Or, Me versus the Other, Us versus Them, Optimist versus Pessimist, and so on. Contrast and duality are easy to see and understand.

When we realize the monster is also the hero's great fear personified, we see why Horror is the most psychologically attuned of all story forms. Specifically, it shows a person at the edges of sanity.

KEY POINT: In good Horror, the weakness-need is a *duality within the mind itself*.

We see this made literal in stories like *The Strange Case of Dr. Jekyll and Mr. Hyde* and *The Fly*. But the duality is in every Horror hero, and it becomes clearer as the story progresses.

There are two main sources of this duality:

1. Fundamental fears
2. Unsociable desires

KEY POINT: Horror, like Thriller, focuses totally on the emotion of fear.

Fundamental Fears

The essential fear in Horror is of death itself. Other fundamental fears that Horror dramatizes include being killed and eaten, being enslaved, being raped, being a failure, losing one's mind, and living a life of quiet desperation (*The Stepford Wives*, *Night of the Living Dead*, *Invasion of the Body Snatchers*).

Horror, like Myth, is highly symbolic and employs a number of metaphors to express a character's devolution. Physical transformations represent the internal struggle between the character's "light" and "dark" sides.

KEY POINT: People fear being reduced in two main symbolic ways: to an *animal* or a *machine*. Each represents something within the hero and the audience.

Animal Horror represents the body, the fear of losing control, and, more specifically, the fear of sexual passion.

Examples in story are the wolf, ape, cat, bat, fly, snake, and horned animals in general. These animals are often associated with hell. *Dracula* and *The Wolf Man* are classic Animal Horror stories.

Machine Horror represents the fear of losing one's identity or individuality. Character expressions of Machine Horror are the robot man, Frankenstein's monster, and the living dead. The zombie is the perfect personification of Machine Horror because it has a blank, dead face and walks like a jerky machine. *Invasion of the Body Snatchers* is the textbook example of a Machine Horror story.

While Animal Horror has been popular since the mid-nineteenth century, Machine Horror increased in popularity after the Second World War. This coincided with the rise of mass society and the fear that one would be swallowed up in groupthink. Bestselling books in the mid-1950s like *The Organization Man* and *The Man in the Gray Flannel Suit* are expressions of the same fear of becoming a cog in the machine. One of the great dystopian novels of mass conformity, *Nineteen Eighty-Four*, was published in 1949.

Unsociable Desires

The second source of duality in the mind is that the character is hiding something so horrible in herself she cannot face it. As a result, she compartmentalizes these desires within the mind. But those compartments won't stay separate for long—the character is ready to crack.

What are the unsociable desires that make up this "dark side"? The part of the self that likes to feel power, to inflict pain, to do what is forbidden, to kill, rape, devour, have illicit sex, or commit matricide or patricide.

HORROR STORY BEAT: Weakness-Need 2—Shame and Guilt

The primary weapons of the self-conscious mind are shame and guilt. An essential part of almost every major genre, shame and guilt highlight the distinction between the individual and society.

Why? Shame and guilt are personal feelings that stem directly from the individual's relationship with others. Shame is the mind attacking itself for failing in the eyes of others, of not acting in accordance with public standards of behavior. Guilt is the mind attacking itself for failure to meet a private standard such as a personal obligation, especially to someone close.

The hero in Horror often suffers tremendous shame and guilt at the beginning of the story due to the ghost. She takes it upon herself to pay for a past sin, but since she is not truly responsible, she fails. The dark emotions build.

HORROR STORY BEAT: Desire—Defeat the Monster, Defeat Death

Every hero's desire serves as the spine of the story. In Horror, the surface-level desire is to defeat a monster. The deeper desire is to defeat death.

Since the hero is weak relative to the monster, the typical Horror story begins with the hero seeking to escape. One of the reasons Horror is often considered the least artistic of the genres is that escape is not an action, but a reaction—the lowest form of desire.

But why does the monster attack? That comes from the unsociable desires the hero has hidden away. These are the taboos that cause the hero to feel so much guilt and shame that she must be punished.

In *Hellraiser*, the Horror master Clive Barker takes the connection of desire and Horror to its logical extreme. His secret is to tie violence to pleasure, making his Horror sadomasochistic. He pushes the connection between sex and death to another dimension, creating a Law of Conservation of Pleasure and Pain in the universe. This is the karma of Horror.

Norman kills the first hero, Marion, early on in *Psycho*. He becomes the central character with the unsociable desire that drives the drama. Norman had a twisted desire for his mother, and when she slept with another man, he killed them both. This is a double taboo, and it so traumatized him that he is compelled to kill any woman he desires.

Visual Shape of the Horror Plot: Linear

The sequence of actions that form the plot has a visual shape. This shape comes from the hero's goal in the story and the sequence of actions he/she takes to get it. Most genres have a linear shape, because the story is a simple straight line that runs to the end point. But the unique desire line and structure steps of the different genres create many plot-shape possibilities.

The structural foundation of the linear shape is: a single hero with one main opponent has a goal that she chases with intensity. The storyline looks like this:

The big structural advantage of the linear form is the single intense desire line, along with an active and usually successful hero. This gives the story a strong spine and tremendous narrative drive, the single most important element in popular storytelling.

Even though many Horror heroes fail, the form almost always takes a linear shape. That's because the hero's first desire is to escape. The linear shape is also common in Action, Crime, Western, and Love.

HORROR STORY BEAT: Opponent—the Monster, the "Other" in the Extreme

Horror intensifies our fear of the Other to a greater degree than any other genre. We call this Other-in-the-Extreme the "monster." The monster is some form of inhuman outsider who invades the human community.

As we said earlier, Horror establishes a strong connection between the internal opponent, the character's ghost and weakness-need, and the external opponent, the monster.

The monster's attack is what causes the hero's devolution over the course of the story. But the true source of this devolution is a real psychological flaw in the character.

> **KEY POINT: The connection between the highly symbolic monster and the character's internal flaw is what grounds the story in the human.**

TECHNIQUE: The Double

Especially in the Horror form, writers use the doppelgänger or "double" to reveal the character's deeper self in a separate character. The "alter ego" is usually a darker, weaker, and truer version of the self than the character normally projects to the world.

> **KEY POINT: In good Horror, the monster is the *double* of the hero. It is both the external and internal opponent.**

The doppelgänger technique is another expression of the tendency of the mind to think in binary oppositions. In the spirit of the dialectic, however, by confronting the hero, the monster double can become the character's means to freedom. This expresses one of the great principles of good storytelling in every genre: the hero learns *through* the opponent. It is only because the opponent relentlessly attacks the hero's deepest flaw that the hero is forced to deal with it and grow. The audience sees that process and also learns.

Yet, as the Horror genre points out, the double is a two-edged sword. It is also the path to madness. When the imagined self breaks away from the real self, the extreme, darker image of the self can lead into a labyrinth of false reality.

As the master of the psychological Horror story, Edgar Allan Poe often shows the self-conscious mind taken to the point of division. In *The Fall of the House of Usher*, Roderick has a doppelgänger both within his own mind and in his twin sister, Madeline. There is also a split within their collective mind, which is expressed in the crack that extends the length of their house. Both Roderick and Madeline suffer from some form of mental illness. When Roderick attempts to bury his sister alive in the family tomb under the house, she returns to exact her revenge and they die together. The house splits apart and disappears into the lake.

In *The Strange Case of Dr. Jekyll and Mr. Hyde*, Robert Louis Stevenson divides the psycho-moral mind into a binary opposition, the generic "good" versus "evil." By creating two personae out of the same character, Stevenson distills the process of someone turning from good to evil into its most essential elements. But this split is also simplistic and makes for a thin plot. Jekyll/Hyde is the ultimate compartmentalized man who, like Dorian Gray, wants to indulge his vices with impunity.

Returning to *Psycho*, the broken mind is not the hero's. It's the killer's, and it lies hidden behind the mild, gentle exterior of Norman Bates. Importantly, the writers of his various representations do not begin by portraying him as a monster. He is a gentle, fragile person with real sensitivity. This makes the plot possible and increases the horror we feel when his true self is revealed.

HORROR STORY BEAT: Ally—the Rational Skeptic

One of the main challenges the writer faces in creating a story that will scare the audience is to make this strange story world believable. The writer must make the audience's leap of faith possible. It is the hero's ally, who is a scientist or, more generally, a rational skeptic, who usually serves this function. The skeptic might be a doctor, a psychologist, or a naturalist. The scientist "takes the stink off" the inherent absurdity of the supernatural.

The strategy underlying this beat is to acknowledge the audience's skepticism through a character who is more skeptical than they are. The rational skeptic provides a "scientific," natural explanation for the supernatural phenomenon.

In *Dracula*, the skeptic is the scientist who validates the reality of the living dead. The technique is also found in *Arachnophobia*, *Jaws*, *The Exorcist*, and *Frankenstein*.

A Nightmare on Elm Street varies this approach by making it appear that the deaths could be the result of a young man with a police record who killed his girlfriend.

The trick is to provide a realistic explanation and a rational objection to a phenomenon we clearly see is fantastical.

HORROR STORY BEAT: Crossing the Barrier to the Forbidden

The barrier is the wall stopping the monster from entering the human community. It is supposed to keep out the other side. It always fails.

In the myth of Pandora, it is the lid to the jar (mistranslated as "box") that holds back all the ills and horrors of the world.

In *King Kong*, the barrier is the massive gate that keeps

King Kong and the jungle (the state of nature) from breaking through to the village and civilization beyond.

In *Pet Sematary*, the barrier is the animal burial ground. Beyond that is the Micmac Indian burial ground where the dead come back to life.

KEY POINT: In better Horror, the barrier is also internal. It represents the negative part in the self that the hero *should not* access, the taboo desire the hero should not indulge.

The barrier also represents the hard line between life and death that cannot be crossed. This is the core distinction of life. Without it, life itself does not exist.

The barrier isn't just the gate to the monster. It is the entryway to the deepest meaning of the Horror form. Once the hero opens this gate, she treads down the *slippery slope*. She cannot stop and the ramifications of this one decision continue to increase.

The concept of the slippery slope highlights the difference between type and degree. Horror gives us the thought experiment of what would happen if we could turn the ultimate difference of type—life and death—into a difference of degree.

How would we characterize a being who exists on the spectrum of life and death? Think the living dead, the vampire, Frankenstein's monster reanimated. Human beings brought back to life get to live once again in the human world. But something is always missing. That missing element is the cost of defeating death.

All stories show the cost of trying to realize a desire. In Horror, that cost ensues from trying to postpone death. This is a modern twist on the basic desire present in the Myth story form, which is to gain immortality. Horror says true immortality is impossible. But what if we could postpone death, perhaps indefinitely?

KEY POINT: The barrier represents one of the fundamental principles of life, what I call the Law of Necessary Cost of Living.

We see infinite examples of this law. In thermodynamics, it is expressed in entropy, the tendency of a system to disorder. It is based on the idea that there is no perfectly efficient system. There is always friction, waste, drag, and expense that come with any action.

In life, the Law of Necessary Cost of Living is found in aging. We are always dying as we live. We see the cost in our bodies. We see the same cost in our finances. If we want something, we must pay for it. Horror takes the Law of Necessary Cost and translates it into different dramatic expressions of living dead.

Dracula and the vampire subgenre present all kinds of costs to eternal life. The vampire, also known as the "undead," can walk only at night, out of the light of the sun. He must drink blood to survive, and only human blood will sustain him for long. He is indebted to the vampire who made him. He casts no shadow and his reflection can't be seen in a mirror. He recoils from garlic, holy water, and the cross, while a wooden stake through the heart, sunlight, fire, and decapitation will kill him.

The vampire's greatest cost is moral. He can sustain his eternal life only by murdering other human beings.

Stephen King's *Pet Sematary* reveals a different cost of postponing death. The hero crosses the barrier and descends the slippery slope when he brings the family pet back to life. The cost is that the cat is mean. This cost grows exponentially when the man brings back his dead little boy. The most positive elements of what it means to be human—kindness, love, and family—are replaced by hatred and the lust to kill.

In trying to take back a loved one from the jaws of death, the man loses his entire family.

HORROR STORY BEAT: Plan—Reactive

Along with weakness, desire, and an opponent, the plan is one of the fundamental steps of any story. The plan is the set of strategies the hero uses to defeat the opponent and reach the goal.

Since the opponent is far more powerful than the hero, the hero's plan in a Horror story is almost always reactive. The typical response is to flee, which is no plan at all. We see this in Horror stories where the monster is a killing machine, like *Friday the 13th*, *Halloween*, *The Terminator*, and *Aliens*.

Since the opponent is also in the self, the hero cannot get away. This is one reason basic Horror stories usually end badly.

> **KEY POINT: In better Horror, the hero formulates a plan as she goes along. The plan turns from simply running away into the hero concocting and executing complex actions to try to beat the opponent. This is one of the ways the hero can grow in a story form where personal growth is rare.**

HORROR STORY BEAT: Drive—the Monster Attacks Escalate

In all stories, the drive is the series of actions the hero takes to achieve the goal. In the middle of the Horror story, the monster escalates his attacks against the hero, which puts her in constant danger. The monster's attacks create a cat-and-mouse struggle where the hero is the mouse. The various kinds of attacks in the monster's arsenal represent "techniques of scare" designed to create maximum fear in the audience.

KEY POINT: Three things determine the quality of the Horror story drive: pressure, pressure, pressure. The more pressure on the hero, the better the story.

A good Horror story may relieve the pressure momentarily only to reapply it with more intensity soon after. This leads to the special pleasure audiences get from the Horror form.

TECHNIQUES OF THE MONSTER'S ATTACK

One technique of monster attack is the false alarm: The Horror story may begin with a killing, but like "red herrings" in the Detective story, the initial attack is often revealed to not be a danger. The hero walks into a scary situation that generates fear in both the hero and the audience. There is a sudden lunge. The hero and audience jump, but they immediately see that the attack is fake. They relax. False alarms keep the viewer off balance and prime the pump of fear for the real attacks to come.

A second technique is the near miss. In near misses, there is a real attack, but the hero dodges the bullet. The viewer is scared, then relieved.

The near miss and the false alarm are the foreplay of Horror. They make the "sex" better when it finally happens. Generally, the sequence is: fear, false alarm, real scare.

One of the great examples of this sequence occurs in *Alien*. While investigating the giant eggs in the bowels of a ruined spaceship, Kane peers into one of the eggs for a closer look. A reptilian life-form jumps out and wraps itself around the faceplate of his helmet. Back in the ship, the eight-fingered creature covers Kane's entire face, with its tail wrapped around his neck.

Later, Kane seems to have fully recovered while the creature seems to be dead. Kane is eating dinner and laughing with his fellow crew members when he starts to convulse wildly. The alien, which has been feeding on his insides, bursts out of his stomach and kills him instantly.

TECHNIQUE: Increasing the Pressure Through Deception

The middle of the Horror story must increase pressure on the hero. Techniques of increasing pressure include:

- The hero is forced into a confined space
- The hero is unable to get help
- The hero is injured

The best attack by the monster uses deception as well as force.

> **KEY POINT: The more deception the monster uses, the more horrific the attack and the better the plot. Therefore, keep as much of the opponent's real power and ability hidden from the hero and the audience as you can.**

TECHNIQUE: Methods of the Hidden Attack

Because the plot often stems from a single monster that attacks relentlessly, the story hits the same beat. Techniques to solve the lack of plot include:

- The hero must walk through a house with many rooms, halls, and tight spaces. This not only confines her but also allows the opponent to attack from behind and above.
- The opposition multiplies (*Aliens*, *Invasion of the Body Snatchers*) or grows larger (*Alien*). This creates a hierarchy of opposition. Multiple attacks from multiple opponents, especially from hidden sources, add to the plot and increase pressure exponentially.

- The opposition comes back from the dead (*Friday the 13th* series, *Night of the Living Dead*, *Pet Sematary*).
- The hero has a fake ally. This is a character who appears to be the hero's friend but is really an enemy or is secretly helping the monster. This technique disguises the opponent's true power and makes it personal for the hero (Ash in *Alien*).

TECHNIQUE: The Horror Reveal

A reveal, or revelation, is a surprising insight a character gets while going after her goal. It's a plot twist that takes the hero and the story in a new direction. The best reveals are about the true power of the opponent and the way he is mounting his attack.

> **KEY POINT: The Horror reveal is almost always some kind of *nightmare*—literally and/or figuratively—for the hero. A great Horror story isn't just one big nightmare at the end. It is a succession of nightmares that builds over the course of the story.**

Here's how to write nightmares:

1. figure out the hero's greatest fears;
2. exploit them as many times as possible *in different forms* at more and *more extreme levels*.

TECHNIQUE: The Cyclone Effect

The nightmare sequence is related to the *cyclone effect*. Besides Horror, the cyclone effect is often found in Action, Science Fiction, and Comedy. Indeed, it's one of the keys to great storytelling in any genre.

Here's how it works in the case of Horror: Sequence as many nightmares as possible and have them come at a faster and faster pace. This increases the pressure on both the hero and the audience and builds narrative drive leading up to the battle, which is the final nightmare.

Alien provides a textbook example of how the nightmares come at a faster pace as we move to the end of the story. Here is the rapid-fire succession of the final sequence:

1. Ripley tries to stop the self-destruct sequence but it's too late.
2. She climbs into the shuttle and takes off as the *Nostromo* explodes.
3. She spots the alien in a corner of the shuttle.
4. She puts on a space suit, grabs a harpoon, opens the air lock door, and when the alien grabs hold of the door to keep from being blown out, she shoots it with the harpoon.
5. The alien flies out the door but the door shuts on the harpoon wire, which the alien uses to climb back into one of the heat thrusters.
6. Ripley fires the engine that blasts the alien into space.

HORROR STORY BEAT: Battle—Safe Haven

The battle is the final conflict in the story. In Horror, the ideal location for the battle is one that appears to be a *safe haven*.

The Horror battle may be a violent conflict or a big, nightmarish revelation. Most Horror battles are intense physical battles against the outside monster. But the monster is also a metaphor. So in the best Horror stories, the hero's fight to destroy the animal or machine exists both in the outside world and within the self.

> **KEY POINT: The hero must attack the monster *in herself* in order to get free.**

Before the decisive battle in *Alien*, the monster has killed everyone aboard ship but Ripley. With only a minute to spare before the mother ship self-destructs, Ripley boards the escape shuttle and takes off. Safe at last. As she prepares to go into hyper-sleep, she is horrified to discover that the alien is hiding in a corner of the shuttle. The monster attacks, and only a fight to the death determines whether the shuttle will be Ripley's cocoon or coffin.

HORROR STORY BEAT: No Self-Revelation

In the self-revelation, the hero learns how she has been wrong about herself, both psychologically and morally. For the first time, she sees who she really is. She also sees how she has acted immorally toward others.

The classic Horror story is unusual among the major genres (along with Gangster and the subgenres Black Comedy and Anti-Western) in that the hero rarely has a self-revelation. This is a natural outgrowth of the hero's weakness-need that contributes to the sense of hopelessness and despair at the end. The hero's mind is horribly broken, on the edge of insanity. It is typically split between the socially appropriate mind and the taboo she is desperately hiding.

Under the intense pressure of the monster's attacks, her mind breaks completely. She has no chance of learning, growing, or healing. The hero may survive, but the ghost/monster sits deeply embedded in her mind . . . waiting for the right moment to return.

The general exception to this no self-revelation beat is the transcendent Horror story, which we will discuss in a moment.

HORROR STORY BEAT: The Double Ending—Eternal Recurrence

The logical final expression of this negative genre is the double ending. The monster apparently dies or disappears. The audience catches its breath, and feels a glimmer of hope that the ordeal is finally over. Using the classic technique of following the false alarm with the real attack, the monster suddenly returns.

Examples include *Sisyphus*, *A Nightmare on Elm Street*, *Carrie*, and many episodes of *The Twilight Zone*, including "Shadow Play." The comic nightmare version of this is *Groundhog Day*.

Horror's double ending is the negative expression of Friedrich Nietzsche's idea of eternal recurrence. For Nietzsche, the thought experiment where someone repeats everything in their life over and over again for eternity was tremendously liberating. Why? Because if one could be content with the idea that one's entire life would recur exactly as it has forever, then one would be conscious every moment of choosing what that life would be.

But with Horror, we have an entire story form based on the idea that people are doomed to repeat their mistakes and suffer terribly, not just until they die, but again and again forever. This is fundamental to the central theme of being and becoming in the Horror genre.

Theme: Being Is Trying to Avoid Death

Horror has a deeply negative view of being due to the emphasis on the inherent weaknesses of the mind. Our profound ability to project symbols allows us to act as if we are in this life for good. We are here now. Why should any other option be possible? True, we can project our own death. We see and hear of others dying. But our experience every day is that we are beings that will never stop existing.

This is one of the fundamental blinders of being. All creatures will die, no matter how much our symbol-making mind wants to invent a rebirth or an afterlife. This limited existence is embedded in who we are, and our mind senses it. For the human animal capable of projecting with symbols, death is the ultimate contradiction. It is a horror, an impossibility. Everyone suspects on some level it will happen to them. If pressed, we say we know it will happen to us. But we don't believe it.

Horror Thematic Recipe: The Way of Facing Death and Taking Humane Action

The thematic recipe of any genre is its strategy of becoming, of how a person can live a good life. It comes primarily from two sources: the hero's basic action in the story and the key question the genre asks.

In Horror, the victim runs from a monster and away from the sins that have not been atoned for. In a deeper sense, the victim tries to escape death itself. So, the recipe for success is: confront death and face our fears/ghosts from the past.

Accepting the concept of becoming by confronting death requires a higher consciousness than the everyday sort of being we are familiar with. We must understand that we will become until we are no more, and that too is part of the process. This means shifting away from believing that we own our space in the world to understanding that we only rent it. We don't know when we will be asked to leave. But we must accept that the eviction notice will come.

This brings up what may be the most powerful idea in twentieth-century philosophy. In *Being and Time*, the phenomenologist Martin Heidegger connects being to becoming. He asks: How do you live your life so that you become who you want to be?

This has to do with living with a constant sense of time. His essential point is that unless you are constantly aware that you are dying and will die, you cannot make the choices required to create the life you want.

It's not easy to live this way. But becoming who you could

be never is. The concept, which is fundamental to Horror's thematic recipe, is: I must make it happen now!

The tragedy of death comes from a person being deprived of all the people they could have been, all the lives they could have lived. But the realization of the inevitability of death, even for someone as special as Me, is what should define human consciousness. This is a mark of becoming. The ongoing consciousness of death defines our lives.

The second thematic recipe for success in Horror is facing our fears and ghosts from the past. In this way, Horror is similar to the Crime story. At its transcendent best, the Crime story is about moral accounting over a lifetime, with life-and-death stakes. Horror is often about moral accounting for a crime that happened far in the past.

Horror highlights the importance of looking at things that are difficult to face—the moral crime of turning away from the past. However, this failure to face the past isn't just a psychological weakness. In Horror, it is a moral flaw, which means it has major effects on others in the community.

The moral claim that Horror makes is this: you must first face past sins and then make amends to anyone you have harmed. It goes further, saying: if you try to beat death, you will cause even greater destruction to those you care about most. This lesson is usually *not* learned.

Horror expresses its thematic recipe negatively. Instead of showing what the hero learns and passing that along to the audience, Horror shows us a hero who should learn, but doesn't. This is also the strategy of Black Comedy.

From this negative definition of how to live a good life, Horror expands its thematic recipe by asking the key question of the form: What is human and what is inhuman?

Horror occurs because we fear the inhuman entering our world. In better Horror stories, we fear seeing the inhuman in ourselves. As we will see when we explore the transcendent form, the key technique for expressing this idea is a structural flip between hero and opponent in the middle of the story. In short, the monster becomes the hero. The implication of this is: what we thought was inhuman is the most human of all.

KEY POINT: Horror explores what it truly means to live morally as a *human* being.

How to Transcend the Horror Story

The greatest storytelling happens when the story transcends the form. This is the key strategy for any popular writer who wants to create something that achieves critical success. The transcendent story is more than a repetition of formulaic beats. It is genre raised above the generic.

Transcending the Horror genre happens in three ways:

1. The writer twists the story beats in a way the audience has never seen before, making the story unique.
2. The story expresses an advanced theme of psychological and especially moral complexity to offer the reader a philosophy for living a good life.
3. The writer explores the art/story form of life found in that particular genre. In Horror, that form is Religion.

To transcend any genre, we begin with the key thematic question the genre asks. Horror asks: What is human and inhuman?

KEY POINT: Since the best Horror stories show our fear of the inhuman in ourselves, the essence of transcendent Horror is to test the boundaries of humanness.

Horror emphasizes the negative possibilities of humanity. In the best Horror stories we watch the devolution of a human character—as his worst qualities take over—and the evolution of what we thought was the inhuman character.

Transcendent Horror takes this reduction of character and makes it positive. It asks: Can our human qualities be maintained in a world where everyone is desperate and induced to act like a predatory animal? In short, transcendent Horror creates a recognizable human world where people are morally tested in the extreme.

KEY POINT: To reach its full potential, Horror must become as big as possible, by having social, political, and universal ramifications.

There are two main ways to transcend the Horror form, and each is a hybrid genre.

1. Horror/Myth: Religion
   The combination of Horror and Myth gives us the story of Religion. Examples include the Old Testament, the New Testament, *A Christmas Carol*, and *The Seventh Seal*.
2. Horror/Science Fiction Epic
   The product of mixing Horror and Science Fiction is the Evolutionary Epic, which is a cautionary tale about creating a new human being and/or a more advanced human species. Examples include *Frankenstein; or, The Modern Prometheus*, *King Kong*, *28 Days Later*, *The Shining*, *The Strange Case of Dr. Jekyll and Mr. Hyde*, *The Handmaid's Tale*, *Westworld*, *The Walking Dead*, *Les Revenants*, *Get Out*, *Ex Machina*, *The Shape of Water*, *District 9*, *Lincoln in the Bardo*, *Cat's Cradle*, and *Rise of the Planet of the Apes*.

Transcending Horror 1: Horror/Myth

The first way of transcending the Horror form is to combine it with Myth. The result is one of the major story forms of human life: religion.

> **KEY POINT: The major religions, when seen as a whole, represent among the most powerful and influential stories in history.**

Let's look at the overall structure and the main story beats of religion to see how it works.

The Story of Religion

Myth is typically thought of as an early form of religion. But it's actually the reverse. Religion is a codified form of myth, and more broadly, a recorded expression of the symbol-making power of humankind.

Immortality is the primary theme of the Myth genre. Any advanced religion—Hinduism, Buddhism, Judaism, Christianity, and Islam—is a collection of stories designed to lay out a moral code necessary to achieve immortality.

> **KEY POINT: Religion is the drama of immortality. It is a form of Horror story that punishes us for our sins and rewards us for living well with rebirth and everlasting life. It uses the Myth story structure to promise heaven and threaten hell.**

Story Beats of Religion

If we say that "god" is the main character, religion is the story of how the god operates. It fills in a complete cast of characters around the god, along with a set of rules for how the participants in the religion—the story's "readers"—must act in relation to the main character.

Caution: I am not talking here about my own belief in religion in general, or one in particular. This is strictly about how religion works as a story.

RELIGION STORY BEAT: Story World—the Underworld and the Afterlife

Like all stories and story forms, religion takes place in a created story world. This is not the "real" world. It is a physical manifestation of the values the author wishes to express in the story.

Because religion as a form of Myth is about getting to immortality, the story worlds in religious stories are often some version of utopia or dystopia. Or they are testing places the individual must work through to get to heaven.

Heaven and hell are story worlds in space and time, where the dead live forever in either happiness or despair.

RELIGION STORY BEAT: Hero—Avatar of the Reader

The real hero in the religion story is the reader. But a reader cannot put herself in stories that have already been written. So religion is a collection of stories in which each has a main character serving as the avatar for the reader. The reader must identify with the main character to take his/her journey in the story.

RELIGION STORY BEAT: Desire—Salvation and Immortality

The desire in the religion story is simple: I want to live forever. In other words, the hero-reader wants to be a god.

The desire for immortality is basic to any Myth story. What makes religion its own unique version of Myth is how one goes about doing that. Religion provides a moral code the individual must follow. If she does, either in belief or in action, she is saved.

Salvation occurs when the god makes a positive judgment about the individual's life and "raises" her up to life everlasting.

RELIGION STORY BEAT: Opponent—the Devil-Satan-Iblis

Once we create god, the foundation character in the religious story, the other characters quickly take shape in contrast. Each fulfills his or her function in moving the story engine forward.

The first opponent of the Good God is the Evil God. For example, in the Judeo-Christian religions, this character is known as Satan or the devil (also Prince of Darkness, Lucifer, Beelzebub, Mephistopheles, and the Horned One). In Islam, he is named Iblis.

If God represents the individual's desire to do and be good, Satan represents the individual's temptation toward and experience of doing wrong. Generally, Satan is the measure of man's inability to live the ideal.

RELIGION STORY BEAT: Self-Revelation—Epiphany

The self-revelation in religion is always an epiphany, an insight about the individual's relation to her god. The individual reaffirms her faith in the god and in the actions the god requires through doing good.

KEY POINT: An epiphany is a rebirth; it's the realization of immortality while alive.

The Story of Christianity

The Jesus story is first and foremost the story of the child: the baby born in a barn. It begins with love and its theme is to connect the individuals in a society based on love, not hatred and violence.

The Roman values were those of the warrior. Kill or be killed. Destroy whatever is weak.

KEY POINT: Christianity's success in overcoming the Roman warrior culture with a culture of love is among the most important achievements in the history of ideas.

To flip such a brutal world to one where even total strangers would first react to each other, if not by actually loving, then at least by treating each other with kindness and respect, seems utterly impossible. How did they do it?

The Christmas story celebrates the birth of a baby four days after the shortest day of the year. It marks the yearly rebirth of hope when the light grows longer. Easter is the story of a man's death and resurrection, celebrated with the new blossoms of spring. If Christmas is primarily a Myth story, Easter is primarily a Horror story.

It is the combination of these two bookending stories that forms the foundation of the Christian story. In terms of structure steps, each is the self-revelation/cosmic revelation beat that ends all great Myths.

KEY POINT: The overall story arc of the Christian story is to go from the birth of the new hero at Christmas to the death and rebirth of the hero at Easter.

Christianity is one of the most brilliant stories ever created. Let's see how it works.

Christian Story Beats

Christmas is the Creation/Origin Myth of Christianity. We'll go through the beats of the Myth form later. But Creation

Myths and Origin Stories are about defining the unique emerging identity of the hero and expressing the fundamental values by which they live.

Most origin stories tell the tale of a hero becoming an adult and/or a leader. This is where the hero gets his mission, where he becomes who he will be from then on.

In contrast, Christmas tells the tale of the birth of its hero, Jesus. His parents are Joseph and Mary. As required by an imperial command, Joseph and Mary must go on a journey from Nazareth to Bethlehem, even though she is close to giving birth. Unable to find a room at the inn, they must stay in a barn. There, among the animals, Mary gives birth to Jesus, the son of God.

While many other religions celebrate the beginning of longer days this time of year, they are completely overshadowed by Christmas. Why? They don't have the "One Story" that can compete with the "Birth of Christ." The story of Jesus's birth, and the story of Christianity, is "just let me live." Through Christ, we are eternally being born, and our life is always completely ahead of us. It makes us believe we will never die.

THE COMPOSITE HERO

Jesus Christ is the three-in-one hero. He is the son of God, who is his father. He is also God. And He is the Holy Spirit, which is also God.

Why would God need to create a baby in the normal way by having a woman give birth to it? This suggests a kind of magic in the form of faith.

> **KEY POINT: The human side of Jesus is part of the theme, which is a God of the people, by the people, and for the people.**

THE CHRISTIAN MORAL CODE: THE BEATITUDES, MATTHEW 5:3–12

Every story has a moral code embedded within it, usually expressed most clearly in the hero's beliefs (see the chapter on Crime to learn how to create a story's moral code). This is a crucial beat, because the story's larger theme is based on these values, which in turn guide moral action.

The story of Christianity, told in the New Testament, *is* a moral code.

> **KEY POINT: The Christian moral code is expressed in microcosm in the Beatitudes, Matthew 5:3–12. The Beatitudes are part of Jesus's Sermon on the Mount, which includes the Lord's Prayer.**

PUBLIC AND COSMIC SELF-REVELATION: JESUS'S BIRTH

Because the Christmas story is structured as a Myth, the self-revelation step at the end is both public and cosmic. In a public self-revelation, the hero discovers he is also a king. This symbolizes his realization that he is now responsible for the entire society and must fulfill his destiny as the leader upon which the society will live or die. On rare occasions, the hero also has a cosmic revelation in which he gains a new moral vision of how an entire people should act in the future.

> **KEY POINT: The wise men don't just celebrate the birth of a child, but also the birth of a new king, and a new kind of king.**

The baby Jesus will not become the new political king of his land. He will become the new *moral* king. His cosmic revelation will build on the Ten Commandments, the cosmic revelation given to Moses in the Old Testament.

KEY POINT: But the new Christian vision will fundamentally change the Old Testament vision from values based essentially on duty—"Thou shalt not kill"—to values based essentially on love—"Love thy neighbor as thyself."

PUBLIC AND COSMIC REVELATION: JESUS'S DEATH

If Christianity were simply the story of the newborn baby, it would be heartwarming, but probably not the foundation of an earth-changing story view.

KEY POINT: What creates the *religion* of Christianity is Christ's horrific death. It's when Christianity becomes a Horror story.

Like Christmas, Easter is a substory of Christianity focusing on the final public and cosmic revelation structure step. It takes the idea of love first expressed in the birth of the baby and takes it to an epic level.

The main theme of all Myth stories is immortality, the chance to live again forever. So it is with Jesus. After being entombed for three days, he is resurrected as a god to sit at the right hand of his father, the great God.

KEY POINT: The Judeo-Christian religions have been primarily Horror stories from the very beginning, from Genesis on.

The story of Christ's crucifixion and resurrection gains its immense power by using a masterful story flip.

KEY POINT: The authors of the crucifixion story tell us that this man-god *chose* the most painful, tortured death *because* his love of flawed humankind was so great.

Similarly, his Father's love of flawed humankind was so great that he agreed to sacrifice his only son so that man could be saved from himself. "For God so loved the world that he gave his only begotten son, that he who believeth in him shall not perish but have everlasting life."*

KEY POINT: Christianity flips the usual sacrifice found in so many other religions. Instead of sacrificing a human to the god to make life better for everyone, in Christianity the god sacrifices a god to the humans to make their life better.

A CHRISTMAS CAROL: COMBINING BEATS OF THE CHRISTMAS AND EASTER STORIES

A Christmas Carol is one of the most influential stories ever told. It is the basis for virtually every Christmas story written in the last 180 years. But the power of this story goes even deeper.

It could be argued that, after the story of Christ's birth, *A Christmas Carol* is the premier expression of the Christian story in world literature.

KEY POINT: *A Christmas Carol* is not about the birth of the child, but about the rebirth of the child in man. Its power comes from combining beats of the Christmas and Easter stories.

* John 3:16, the New Testament.

A Christmas Carol is primarily a Horror story, using the subgenre of Ghost Story. Instead of focusing on ghosts in space, it borrows a Fantasy technique and makes them ghosts in time.

The "alternative present" has become a major technique of Science Fiction. It also prefigures video game story structure: three different trips in time, with alternative presents based on the hero's choice.

A Christmas Carol's thematic strategy for a good life is the rejuvenation of the individual and the city by creating a community. The overall process of the story is to reintegrate the greedy, selfish, and therefore ostracized Scrooge back into the community of people who celebrate bonds of family and friends as more valuable than money.

Transcending Horror 2: The Horror/Science Fiction Epic

The first transcendent Horror story combines Horror with Myth and creates the story of Religion. The second transcendent Horror story combines Horror with Science Fiction and Epic.

Epic is one of the oldest story forms, found in *Gilgamesh* and much of Greek mythology, as well as the *Iliad*. The classic definition of an epic is that the fate of the nation is determined by, or represented in, the actions of a single individual or family. This makes the Horror/Science Fiction Epic potentially among the most expansive of all story forms.

The combination of Horror and Science Fiction explores scientific ways of defeating death. In short, it contrasts evolution with devolution. It asks: Can humankind evolve, or must it destroy itself because of a broken mind?

The "Death of God" and the Rise of Evolutionary Science

The Horror/Science Fiction Epic shifts from the religious worldview to the scientific one. It begins with *Frankenstein; or, The Modern Prometheus*. *Frankenstein* is a seminal work, not just in transcendent Horror but in storytelling: it is the last and greatest fictional expression of "natural philosophy" before fiction turned to the science of evolution.

Frankenstein's description of the natural world goes from defeating death by creating an individual life and thereby becoming a god, to evolution's view that life-forms evolve as the individual life dies.

Both religion and science are forms of story that attempt to solve man's greatest mystery: life. Religion defines life as a kind of spirit that some greater Father, Mother, or God has given humanity as a gift. Science considers the problem developmentally and quantitatively: it contrasts living things with nonliving things and sorts life into categories.

The mystery of life is at the foundation of all belief systems partly because its corollary, the mystery of death, is humankind's greatest fear. The self-conscious animal looks with horror and incomprehension at the thought that a person can suddenly not exist.

Humans constantly try to *improve* their definitions of life and death in an effort to remain alive. In genre terms, those attempts take the form of the Horror/Science Fiction Epic, which might be characterized as "better and longer living through science."

Before we look at types of the Horror/Science Fiction Epic, we need to see what happens when we connect Science Fiction to the main genre of Horror. Science Fiction adds two main story elements:

1. the *system* that organizes the world, and
2. the human species that is necessarily fatally flawed and doomed to destroy itself.

The flawed species depicted in Science Fiction is an outgrowth of the flawed individual mind portrayed in Horror. The Horror mind hates the Other because it is different. The human species depicted in Science Fiction is itself monstrous, with individuals enslaving one another and destroying the planet.

GREATEST HORROR TECHNIQUE: The Monster Becomes the Hero

KEY POINT: The single most powerful technique in the Horror/Science Fiction Epic is a structural flip between human and inhuman, between hero and monster.

At some point, the character we thought was a monster is the most humane character in the story and becomes the hero. The characters we thought were human beings turn out to act like animals, monsters trying to destroy anything that doesn't look like them. This technique is found in *Frankenstein*, as well as in *King Kong*, *The Shape of Water*, *Get Out*, *District 9*, and *28 Days Later*.

Why is this strategy the calling card of the Horror/Science Fiction Epic?

This story form shifts the focus from fear of death to what it means to be human, and what it means to accept difference. It begins by heightening the Other to such a horrific level that we think it is inhuman. It must be killed, or it will kill us. The story then flips our expectations and shows that this "monster" actually represents the part of us that is inhuman. We *are* the monster.

Even more shocking, we see that the terrifying Other is beautifully human. We are forced to explore how we got it so wrong, how we were blinded by appearance, and most important, what it is about the Other that is human—even more human than we are.

Horror/Science Fiction Epic: Four Types

Beginning with *Frankenstein*, the complex Horror/Science Fiction Epic has taken these four forms:

1. Re-create a human being
2. Create a human from an animal
3. Create a human from a machine
4. Create a higher "human," an entirely new species

RE-CREATING A MAN

Mary Shelley's *Frankenstein*, the story of the scientist who re-creates a man, defines the Horror/Science Fiction Epic. It is not only the greatest of all Horror stories: it defined the genre. The modern Horror form that Shelley created was a fictional expression of "natural philosophy." Natural philosophy was a transitional worldview between religion and science, and particularly evolutionary science. This is why Dr. Frankenstein's initial desire is to bring a human corpse back to life. He wants to be a god.

KEY POINT: ***Frankenstein*** **is not about creating life, but about creating a human being.**

The vast majority of the book concerns the struggle of this reanimated corpse to become a full person. Dr. Frankenstein's creation reveals one of the main subjects of the Horror/Science Fiction Epic: personal identity. Why is this theme so fundamental to the form?

If the basic desire in Horror is to defeat death, it follows that the first way to do this is to learn to create life on demand. In Shelley's magnificent thought experiment, it quickly becomes clear that the real challenge arises after life itself has been created. The scientist must become an artist to create an individual who has consciousness, memory, a sense of self (the character I call "me"), and the ability to love and be loved.

That's why this is also a story of parent and child, the tyranny of the father-as-god, and the lie of salvation.

KEY POINT: In making his creature, Dr. Frankenstein erases the distinction between man and machine, *and* the distinction between man and god.

The struggle of father creating son, of human creating human, takes a terrible toll on both. The consequences for what each has wrought are overwhelming.

Another example of this can be found in *The Shape of Water*, which combines Horror/Science Fiction with a Love story. But the film varies the classic structural flip between hero and opponent. Elisa, the hero, is on the cleanup crew of the facility, so she is a nobody. She is also unable to speak, which makes her as much of an outsider, even a freak, as the monster. She doesn't turn into the opponent over the course of the story because she alone recognizes the monster's deep humanity and brings that out through her love for him.

The "monster" at first glance is terrifying, and quite deadly. But the real monster is a Bible-quoting authority figure at the scientific facility who wants to use the apparent monster as an experiment and eventually kill him. The Russian authorities also want the monster dead.

This hybrid opponent suggests that religion and government don't want anything to challenge the status quo. Only love gives us the ability to accept what is different from us.

The secondary characters underline the fallacy of the Other-as-inhuman. The film is set in about 1960, and the news is filled with images of the civil rights struggle, of white cops spraying Black protesters with fire hoses. At a diner, the owner turns down the advances of the hero's gay friend and then tells a Black couple they can't sit inside.

The classic structural flip in great Horror is expressed in an exchange of dialogue between the hero and her Black friend at work. The friend says, "We're nothing. We can do nothing. [The monster's] not even human." To which the hero says, "If we do nothing, neither are we."

Get Out is one of the best transcendent Horror films in many years. A young Black man, Chris Washington, visits the beautiful country home of his loving white girlfriend. Her father seems to be the epitome of the white liberal, constantly declaring his love for President Obama.

But as the story progresses, Chris encounters Black servants who act like zombies or Stepford wives and attack him. In the big reveal, Chris discovers that his white girlfriend is merely the bait acting on behalf of the true monster of the story, the white father, who has found the modern, medical means of enslaving him on the present-day version of a plantation.

CREATING HUMAN FROM ANIMAL

The second form of Horror/Science Fiction Epic involves creating a human being from an animal.

The first film in the recent reboot of the *Planet of the Apes* saga (*Rise of the Planet of the Apes*) applies the *Frankenstein* story to the transformation of an animal into a human—and perhaps into something higher-than-human. It highlights three elements of the revolutionary *Frankenstein* story.

First is the master scientist. The initial hero, the scientific researcher Will Rodman, has a unique weakness, in that his flaw comes from a strength. Because he cannot kill Caesar, the baby ape he's been studying, he brings the genetically altered animal home with him. With his good intentions he takes all of humankind with him on the road to hell. This kindheartedness, combined with an arrogance that is common in the master scientist, is a weakness the audience can easily relate to, and is the wellspring from which the entire plot flows.

The second *Frankenstein* technique is essential to transcending Horror: flipping the story structure so that the monster becomes the hero. The ape, Caesar, is not the typical monster we see in the average Horror story. But he is the Other, the inhuman or apparently inhuman, entering the human world.

Creating a human being means, among other things, tracking in great detail the steps of a newly alive body becoming a fully feeling and thinking person. This is precisely what the writers Rick Jaffa and Amanda Silver do in the best section of *Rise of the Planet of the Apes*. When Caesar is incarcerated in the ape refuge (prison), we watch as he moves up the ladder of understanding and uses his humanlike knowledge and insight to become the leader. In doing so, he also frees himself and his fellow apes from human captivity.

The third major story element from *Frankenstein* is the betrayal by and revolt against the father. This too is a key step in Caesar's development. For a boy to become a man and a unique individual, he must rebel against his father. Will pays the owner of the refuge so that Caesar can come home. But Caesar refuses: he already is home. This is not only the key step in the real hero's (Caesar's) character change, it's also the first step in the apes' rebellion against humans. More important, it is the first step in the evolution from ape to human, and perhaps the superhuman.

CREATING HUMAN FROM MACHINE

The third form of Horror/Science Fiction Epic is about creating a human from a machine.

Written by Alex Garland, who also wrote the transcendent Horror story *28 Days Later*, *Ex Machina* is one of the best Horror/Science Fiction Epics in years. The combination of the immense intellect of great Science Fiction with the Horror and Love story forms gives the film intense emotional impact.

Caleb, a top programmer at a large internet company, wins a contest to join Nathan, the company owner, at his estate. There he is given the task of testing whether Ava, the robot Nathan has created, can pass as human. This is known as the Turing test: if a human can't tell the robot is a machine, it passes.

Ex Machina is another modern version of *Frankenstein; or, The Modern Prometheus* about a cruel father trying to create a human being. Like Frankenstein's monster, Ava is a machine. The question here is: From machine to what? Caleb tells Nathan, "If you invented a conscious machine, it's not just the biggest thing in the history of man, it's the biggest thing in the history of gods." Nathan says, "It's Promethean, man."

Nathan's strategy for designing a human consciousness that can pass the test is to add the elements of sex and love.

NATHAN: Can consciousness exist without interaction? Anyway, sexuality is fun, man. If you're gonna exist, why not enjoy it? You want to remove the chance of her falling in love and fucking?

At first, Caleb is wary of the validity of this way of testing for human consciousness.

NATHAN: Lay off the textbook approach . . . Yesterday I asked you how you felt about her and you gave me a great answer. Now the question is, "How does she feel about you?"

Ava is interested in using love as a means to prove her own humanity, and possibly to attain a hidden goal.

AVA: Our conversations are one-sided. You ask circumspect questions and study my responses.
CALEB: Yes.
AVA: You learn about me and I learn nothing about you. That's not a foundation on which friendships are based.
CALEB: So what? You want me to talk about myself?
AVA: Yes.
CALEB: Okay, where do I start?
AVA: It's your decision. I'm interested to see what you'll choose.

As the story moves toward its conclusion, the question becomes: Is Ava faking her love? And even if she is, isn't that a sign that she is human?

Ex Machina is a variation on *2001: A Space Odyssey* and *Blade Runner*, where the robot tries to kill the humans to remain "alive," and in doing so proves its humanity. Nathan is smart enough to create a robot that passes the test of being human, but not smart enough to realize that the full scope of being human includes a willingness to murder.

Ex Machina's final recipe for achieving human consciousness is not gaining the ability to love. It's being able to fake love and plan a murder—and being willing to do so to gain one's freedom.

CREATING HIGHER "MAN," A NEW SPECIES

The most challenging form of Horror/Science Fiction Epic involves the creation of a new species.

KEY POINT: Advanced Horror is about constructing a person. Science Fiction is about constructing a society. The ultimate Horror/Science Fiction Epic is about creating a new species.

Like *Ex Machina*, the television series *Westworld* starts with the machine. But its greater ambition is the creation of a new species: the robot superhuman. The guiding principle of *Westworld* is: *Frankenstein* in a Science Fiction–Western amusement park.

Westworld's power comes from the moral code of its story world. This is not a machine police state oppressing people from above with a few free-spirited rebels using guns to fight back. This is a world where the authorities let everyone use guns and have sex as much as they want. *Westworld* is an amoral universe where everything goes. All is allowed. But that's false.

KEY POINT: An amoral universe is never amoral. "Amoral" is just an immoral world in hiding. If it's a world where all is permitted, someone is being hurt.

The key technique writers use for creating this story world, found in many of the best serial television dramas, is to set up a giant moral canvas in which the characters are constantly challenged by moral decisions. Some of the best shows in television history have used this technique: *Breaking Bad*, *The Good Wife*, *The Wire*, *The Sopranos*, *The Walking Dead*, *Boardwalk Empire*, *Lost*, *Homeland*, and *Peaky Blinders*.

In *Westworld*, the writers flip the technique: guests are free to kill or have sex with the robots, known as "hosts," without consequences. The guests aren't being oppressed, which means this is not a dystopia (for them, at least). In this world, it's the robots that live in an oppressive dystopia.

How do the guests morally justify their actions? Those "things," those Others, are robots, and therefore less than human. But the cosmic joke is on them: the humans are the enslaved. Not only are they not evolving, they're devolving.

Nietzsche said that even though the master controls the slave, the slave is more highly evolved. Why? It's only when you are a slave that you become aware that you are not free. The master is completely unselfconscious, because he doesn't have to think about himself.

People are going to pay a price for what they do because the robots don't like being treated as robots. They want to be treated as human beings. And they will make the people pay for the immoral acts they have committed.

Where *Westworld* soars above other Horror/Science Fiction Epics is in the ambition and detail of its vision. In part this is possible because of the much bigger canvas of the serial television form. The result is a vision of species evolution unequaled in film or television history.

The Next Rung Up the Ladder

It's easy to underestimate the Horror genre when we look only at its basic form. But this is a genre with enormous scope. From the primal terror of the classic Horror story to the soaring intellect of Horror/Myth and Horror/Science Fiction, this genre is at the forefront of storytelling today.

The philosophy of Horror gives us a powerful lesson about facing death in order to live a good life. But it doesn't answer the question: What are we to do?

For that we must move up one rung of the genre ladder and explore the Action story.

3

Action: Success

Seven Samurai: The Final Battle

The final battle in *Seven Samurai* is the greatest scene in the history of the Action story. Why? It's the entire genre in microcosm. The enemy samurai are making their final attack. In pouring rain and knee-deep mud, the defending samurai, now reduced to five, fight furiously against overwhelming odds.

The battle is a whirlwind from one individual contest to another, with life-and-death consequences. The intensity of each confrontation is magnified by the cinematic power of the crosscut. These shots reveal the ultimate stakes of survival for the samurai and the entire village. All elements combine to create a movie scene that has never been equaled in its emotional power.

The intensity of the battle's climax is heightened further when the master swordsman, the best fighter and most beloved of the defending samurai, puts on a bravura show of combat brilliance. He cuts down one enemy after another, inspiring awe and love in the viewer. The battle is won. And then . . .

My Bildungsroman Reveal

Seven Samurai is the greatest film ever made. Period. For a writer, it is a complete education in storytelling for the screen. It is also the film upon which all subsequent Action films depend.

Seven Samurai represented another landmark in my own "bildungsroman," or personal formation story. The first time I saw it was in a college film-criticism class. It demonstrated how film is the ultimate synthetic art, the combination of all other art forms to create a life-changing story. This storytelling begins with the senses, then builds to a philosophical complexity that encompasses the scope and texture of life.

> **KEY POINT: Film is not only an art form but also a way of communicating in emotional terms *how the world really works.***

The Action Story: How It Works

Action is the human expression of the laws of nature. It is a fundamental genre because it's about the importance of taking action in life. It comes next in our examination of story forms because it is the next step after the life versus death opposition of the Horror story. Action highlights the daily contest of life in the natural world.

In philosophical terms, being is how we live every day. Becoming is how we grow. Action says we grow by doing, by taking action. So in Action, becoming = doing.

We see this immediately when we look at the role of the hero. In Action, it's the fighter. Fighting is the most primal action there is, and Action is about fighting all the way to success.

The Action story usually portrays a simplistic opposition

between the good character and the bad character. But this opposition is not about justice, where the good man punishes the bad man for his immoral or illegal actions against others. That's the Crime genre. There is no such thing as justice in the predator-versus-prey world of action. You win or you die. Action is about playing to win.

The Action form has a narrower focus on competition than other stories. But this belies the form's true ambition. The Action story provides a dramatic manual for success in life itself. It involves the scarcity of resources that all living things fight over every day. We see this in the form's two main subgenres, War and Sports.

Action Mind-Action Story View

Action is *the* existential story form. This genre is based on the idea that everything we do is an action and these actions define who we are.

Thus, success in life comes from simply taking action. But the genre also shows that life is a daily struggle of winning and losing. So the art of life comes in taking the correct action to win. The great value of the Action story is that it's the model of how to act *successfully*.

KEY POINT: The Action story demonstrates what it means to be better than everyone else, and claim one's place in a hierarchy.

We see this in the form's overall story strategy: set up an intense punch-counterpunch routine between hero and opponent in a heavyweight fight.

The idea that the Action story is fundamental to daily life is counterintuitive. The genre seems to be about powerful heroes fighting dangerous opponents. But few of us are Action heroes in real life. So how does that apply to us? When all life is defined by action, the struggle is what matters most. The Action story strategy relies on physicality because this is the most dramatic way to express the essence of Action.

The main distinction of the Action form is that life is about doing well, not doing good. It's about being successful, not morally right. It encapsulates every domain of human life involving competition: work, business, sports, politics, status, war, even winning a mate.

Few actions in daily life are consciously about "doing good." This does not mean that our daily actions don't affect, sometimes negatively, other people, but little of our conscious thought concerns these moral spillover effects. Superheroes, on the other hand, don't face this dilemma. They are inherently good. They always fight evil. There is no question about what they will choose to do. The only question is how they succeed.

The Art of Success: Freedom as the End Point

Freedom is the ability to take action when and where one chooses. Therefore, there seems to be a one-to-one equivalence between action and freedom: you create freedom by taking successful action. Taken to its extreme, freedom comes from fighting against external attack.

But the relation between action and freedom can be quite complex. An essential truth of story is that *how* one seeks freedom can lead to a kind of moral slavery.

Action Compared to Other Genres

As mentioned, some genres cluster into certain families that share common features. Action is part of the family of genres that includes Myth and Western. The modern Action story is an outgrowth of the Western, which is the American Creation Myth. Its hero, the cowboy, is primarily a fighter, which makes him a type of Action hero.

Although they have the same thematic foundation, Myth and Action take different approaches to freedom:

- Myth says that freedom is realized only when the individual grows enough to be able to free themselves.
- Action says that freedom is possible only when the individual fights against those who seek to enslave.

The Action genre introduces the phenomenon of freedom at its most basic level: *personal* freedom from external attack. If the Horror form is about slavery from within, Action is about slavery from without, mano a mano.

The conservative worldview thinks of the individual as physically, emotionally, and culturally separate and unconnected to other individuals. It defines freedom as being able to act without restrictions.

In contrast to the Love story, which is about how to live a happy life with one other person, Action gives us the recipe for how to live successfully alone. This recipe can be called the Way of the Warrior.

The two transcendent Action stories are:

1. The Action Epic
2. Caper stories and Sports stories

These subgenres are about winning in the extreme. The Action Epic explores the art of war. Caper (also known as the Heist story) and Sports stories explore the art of games and sports.

Examples of Action

Films

Die Hard, *Mad Max 1–4*, *Terminator 1–2*, *Raiders of the Lost Ark*, *Gladiator*, *Gunga Din*, *Aliens*, *Crouching Tiger, Hidden Dragon*, *Hero*, *The Bourne Identity*, *The Bourne Ultimatum*, *Speed*, *John Wick*, *Taken*, *Kill Bill 1–2*, *True Lies*, *Casino Royale*, *Goldfinger*, *Mission: Impossible*, *The Hunt for Red October*, *Face/Off*, *Iron Man*, *The Hidden Fortress*, *Sanjuro*, *Yojimbo*

Action Subgenres

Action Epic/War Story, Suicide Mission, Adventure, Buddy Story, Sports, Caper

Action Story Overview

Here's what we'll cover in this chapter:

- **ACTION STORY BEATS**
- **THEME**: Being Is Competing, Fighting, Winning, and Losing
  - Thematic Recipe: The Way of the Warrior
- **HOW TO TRANSCEND THE ACTION STORY**
  - Action Epic/War Story
  - Caper and Sports

Action Story Beats

Taken together, the Action story beats detail how to win a conflict. They come from the Action story strategy: set up an intense punch-counterpunch between hero and opponent in a heavyweight fight.

ACTION STORY BEAT: Hero's Defining Crisis

The Action story often has an opening scene that defines the main characters through a *crisis*. This creates immediate danger for the hero and forces him/her to act decisively.

This is a technique from the Existential Code, which we will also explore in the Memoir chapter. The Existential Code says that crisis is the quickest and surest way to define a person. If you are what you do, then a crisis will show who you are in an instant.

> **KEY POINT: The Action story's crisis defines the hero's fighting ability and his *character*. It may have nothing to do with the main plot line.**

In the opening scene of the Action film *Raiders of the Lost Ark*, the archaeologist Henry "Indiana" or "Indy" Jones and his guide, Satipo, enter a cave where a priceless statue sits on a pedestal in a glass case. Indy avoids the booby traps to which others have fallen prey. He replaces the statue with a bag of sand to avoid setting off the other booby traps protecting it. The trick doesn't work. Indy and Satipo run as the temple collapses and they are attacked from every side.

They avoid the poison darts, but then are blocked by a bottomless pit. Satipo swings over the pit, but refuses to help Indy unless he gives him the statue. Jones does and Satipo takes off. Indy jumps the pit, then slips through a stone door where he finds Satipo dead. He grabs the statue, but has to outrun a giant boulder rolling down an incline straight toward him. He jumps just in time before the boulder seals up the cave.

Indy finds himself surrounded by a band of hostile fighters led by a competing archaeologist, Belloq, who takes the statue. Indy runs as the fighters give chase. He jumps in the river and climbs onto a seaplane that flies away.

This classic opening, perhaps the most famous in the Action form, is really a series of cliff-hangers of the kind that will structure the entire film. It also defines Indy's essential character and ability to fight: he is brave, resourceful, quick-witted, extremely athletic, and expert at the use of a bullwhip.

ACTION STORY BEAT: Story World—Enslavement from Physical Attack

The fact that the Action hero is a fighter who uses force to succeed also determines the story world. It's always a community and/or nation in trouble, and usually in physical danger. This is important because it justifies why an expert fighter is needed and why that fighter must use force.

The Action story world breaks into two kinds of arenas, the enclosure and the chase. An enclosure is always some kind of fortress. This highlights the danger of being trapped or surrounded. The fortress also might be on a tower or cliff, which brings in the danger of height. Height gives the story the advantage of three-dimensional movement and attack from all sides. We see the fortress arena in *Die Hard* and *Seven Samurai*.

Action through chase, such as in a plane, train, car, bus, or motorcycle, brings in the danger of moving fast. We see this arena in the *Terminator* films, *Raiders of the Lost Ark*, *Speed*, and *Runaway Train*. The disadvantage of this kind of arena is that there is no "pressure-cooker effect," where conflict is generated within a tight space until it explodes.

The need to set up the danger of the story world is the main reason the modern version of the Action genre is often a "false" form. Other than the Action Epic (War) story, the form has *no inherent reason for existing*. The writer creates a dangerous physical environment that makes the use of violence necessary. The strategy is this: create a violent world, then use violence to solve its problems.

Story World: Technology of the Gun

A major element of any story world is its key technology. In the genre that takes conflict to its furthest extreme, the main technology is the gun. The more modern and epic the story, the more destructive the gun.

With the modern Action story, the gun has become the tool of magnified destruction. The Action hero is someone (usually male) who excels at killing. He is extremely capable at hand-to-hand fighting. But it is the gun that allows him to kill in droves.

This suggests a shift in the Action hero over many decades. He has gone from "defender of the weak and enforcer of the right" to professional killer. This element of the Action story finds its purest expression in the *John Wick* films. Wick is a hit man. He has a vast arsenal of guns, and each is a work of art. The body count of his victims is in the hundreds.

ACTION STORY BEAT: The Warrior's Moral Code—Courage and Will to Greatness

Every genre focuses on a different archetypal hero, embodying a different set of human qualities, values, and preferred ways of living in the world. In Action, it is the Way of the Warrior. He is the master of war: fighter, destroyer, enforcer, and bringer of justice.

The key question the genre asks is this: Does the fighter choose freedom or life? More precisely, does he stand and fight? Or does he flee and fight another day when the odds are more in his favor? This question is always answered in the same way, however. According to the moral code of the Action story (and the Western), the hero may be alone, pistol in hand, facing twenty of the most heavily armed men in the world. No matter. He must always fight.

When facing a fight to the death in the middle of the street, the hero's test is not whether they are fast enough on the draw. The real test is whether they have the courage to fight in the first place. As Aristotle (and Winston Churchill) said, "Courage is the first of human qualities because it is the quality which guarantees the others." Civilization is possible only because the Action hero has the courage to fight.

Above all, the will to greatness is what powers the Action hero. He is driven to be the best and will make virtually any sacrifice to prove it.

ACTION STORY BEAT: Weakness-Need—Shame Culture and Will to Violence

In good storytelling, a character's weaknesses often come from his strengths. The Action hero has a deep love-hate relationship with himself. He glories in his own power and ability. But he is driven to excellence at the expense of everything else. He is probably right to believe that "he fights best when he fights alone."* To rely on anyone else is to become weaker.

The Action hero's classic flaws are being selfish, overly masculine, disdainful of weakness, unable to deal with women as people, distant, and cold. This is why the Action hero almost never marries, which implies he cannot join the community. He cannot overcome his extreme masculinity and blend with the feminine.

The best action stories give the hero a deeper issue related to his need.

> **KEY POINT: In the best Action stories, the hero's need is to learn *how to grow in other ways than personal success*. Put another way: How can the hero grow through a relationship with others? Since most action heroes are stoic, few learn this lesson.**

---

* From *The Outlaw Josey Wales.*

Action Weakness: Trapped in the Shame Culture

By living the values of the hunter-warrior, the Action hero becomes trapped in what is broadly known as the "shame culture." Shame culture is a way of thinking based on the value of achievement and the need to live up to a public standard. Its values emphasize physical ability, self-reliance, independence, the pioneer spirit, courage, pride, glory, doing well (as opposed to doing good), appearance, and approval in the eyes of others.

Many of the Action hero's weaknesses stem from the values of shame culture. When he fails in this culture of achievement, he feels ashamed. He has fallen short of a standard and everyone in the group has seen it. Envy is common. Competition is fierce. And because all loss is public, failure also means loss of status.

Shame is the negative reinforcement of the all-powerful group against the individual. It's as if the individual absorbs the judgments of others and turns them, like daggers, against himself.

Seven Samurai and other samurai films, like *Hidden Fortress* and *Yojimbo*, represent the epitome of shame culture.

Action Weakness: The Will to Violence

The use of violence is justified in the Action story because of a dangerous world or an opponent who uses violence to subjugate others. But in better Action stories, this tendency is an inherent flaw in the hero. Violence is his first response. It represents stunted growth where the individual's approach to a problem is simply to destroy.

Witness, a Crime film with many Action elements, is about where one sets the bar in justifying violence. The film offers a modern thought experiment: What happens when we place a cop, a professional of violence, in one of the few remaining subcultures of pacifism, the Amish? Pitting the good cop against bad cops—men who have used their position as cops to commit murder—increases the moral complexity.

The Emergence of the Female Action Hero

The Action story has historically been the most male-dominated of all genres. In the last forty years, however, we have seen the rise of the female Action hero. The mother of female Action heroes is Ripley in *Alien* (1979), followed by Sarah Connor in *The Terminator* (1984). These two films are about the making of an Action hero. The lead characters begin as victims in what are essentially Horror stories. They become true Action heroes driving the story in the second film of each series.

Action stories with a female lead hit all the same beats as those with a male lead. That's because the hero's basic action and the story strategy of the form are the same regardless of gender. A female hero does create variations on how the beats are executed. We also see variations based on whether the story is primarily Action, like *Aliens* and *Mad Max: Fury Road*, or Myth, like *The Hunger Games* and *Wonder Woman*. The basic difference is that in Action the main character is a hero while in Myth she is a superhero.

ACTION STORY BEAT: Desire—Success, Glory, and Personal Freedom

The desire line of the hero determines the spine of the story. The Action hero has the most focused desire and discipline of any genre hero. As the character driven to be the best, the Action hero also wants to win the adulation of others. Glory is the opposite of shame, and the Action hero is determined to get it.

KEY POINT: An Action story should have a specific end point where the audience knows the hero won, and it should result in the hero attaining some kind of personal freedom.

For the Action hero, the ongoing practical benefit of winning is freedom. It is fundamental to their very being.

In *Mad Max: Fury Road*, Max first wants to escape his enslavement in the Citadel at the hands of Immortan Joe and the War Boys. He will do that by joining forces with Joe's former commander, Imperator Furiosa. Furiosa tries to flee with Joe's harem to the safety of the "Green Place." When they find this is a road to nowhere, Max and Furiosa reverse course and head back to the Citadel to take Joe out and seize control of the water source by which he maintains power.

Mad Max: Fury Road's structure is literally a straight line toward a dead end and then a straight line back. That's why the story has such tremendous narrative drive. Max and Furiosa free the women and destroy the leaders of the dystopia. Max walks away a lonely but free man.

Visual Shape of the Action Plot: Linear

KEY POINT: In Action, the hero's desire line must force him into constant combat. The Action hero is always fighting to get the goal.

The Action hero moves at top speed with relentless energy to get a specific goal. This makes the Action story the most linear of all forms.

This straight line creates intense narrative drive, which is a great advantage in popular storytelling.

KEY POINT: While Horror stories sell maximum pressure on the hero, the Action story is about speed.

ACTION STORY BEAT: Collecting the Allies

In some Action subgenres, the hero brings together other warriors to form a team or army. Each ally brings a special skill. The idea is to create a group of all-stars, each the best in their area of expertise. These allies increase the ability of the hero to succeed.

ACTION STORY BEAT: Opposition—External Bondage

The Action hero is as powerful as the Horror hero/victim is weak. But, ironically, the kind of bondage the action hero fights against is far simpler than that of the Horror victim. Action slavery is largely external. While the Horror victim lives in the prison of her own mind, the Action opponent wants to kill the hero or put him in an actual prison.

Opponent: Hero's Nemesis

The Action opponent is someone the hero must actually fight. Thus, the opponent is usually strong and dangerous.

Action and Thriller are often combined in Hollywood films because both genres put the hero in extreme danger. The biggest difference between them is how they handle the opponent.

The key question in the Thriller concerns who the real opponent is. Is the suspect guilty or innocent? The key question in the Action story concerns *how to defeat* the opponent. Action stories do not focus on uncovering, or *detecting*, the opponent. They focus on *fighting* him.

> **KEY POINT: The best Action opponent is also the hero's nemesis, the most dangerous opponent for *that particular character*. Therefore, the opponent should be the second-best fighter and the character best able to attack the hero's biggest internal flaw.**

Returning to *Mad Max: Fury Road*, the hero Mad Max goes up against Immortan Joe and his army of War Boys. Joe is a hideous tyrant who wears a face mask over jaws. He uses women as breeding machines, kills anyone who would disobey him, and tortures people by withholding water. Joe leads an army riding in vehicles that can kill at high speed. Max couldn't find a greater challenge to his skills if he went looking for it.

TECHNIQUE: The Four-Point Opposition and Hierarchy of Opponents

As the genre that pits hero against opponent in a win-or-lose drama, Action stories have intense conflict. But like Horror, the biggest problem in the form is a lack of plot.

There are a number of technical reasons for this:

- Plot is not simply conflict. Plot comes from a *change* of action and from *surprise*, known as the "reveal." The average Action story has a lot of back-and-forth conflict. But these actions are essentially the same, a plot mistake known as "hitting the same beat."

- The hero chases the goal at top speed. This leaves little time for twists and often means the opponent is not even present for long stretches of the story.
- There are a lot of Action set pieces in which highly choreographed, complex actions play out over time with a delayed outcome. These scenes freeze the plot until the outcome is determined.
- Everything is settled in the final battle. Because the audience knows this about the form, they see all conflict leading up to the battle as a big stall.

The key problem the writer must solve is how to create sufficient plot.

KEY POINT: A simplistic opposition between two characters kills any chance of plot, depth, complexity, or realism. That's why better stories, in every genre, use a *web of oppositions*.

Better stories go beyond a simple fight between hero and main opponent by using a technique I call the "four-point opposition." Stories with a single hero set up the four-point opposition like this:

1. Provide the hero with one main and at least two secondary opponents.
2. Hide one or two opponents and/or hide the way they're connected to each other. In other words, connect the opponents in a hidden hierarchy.
3. Each opponent should attack the hero in a different way.
4. Opponents should attack the hero in succession at top speed.

Why does this result in a better plot?

- Most of the opposition is hidden, which increases the opponents' ability to surprise and hurt the hero.
- The attacks against the hero come from multiple sources at a faster and faster pace.
- The story has more reveals as the secret connections of the opponents are exposed.

Here are examples of classic four-point opposition in Action. Notice that each character is in opposition, at least at some point, with the other three.

MAD MAX: FURY ROAD

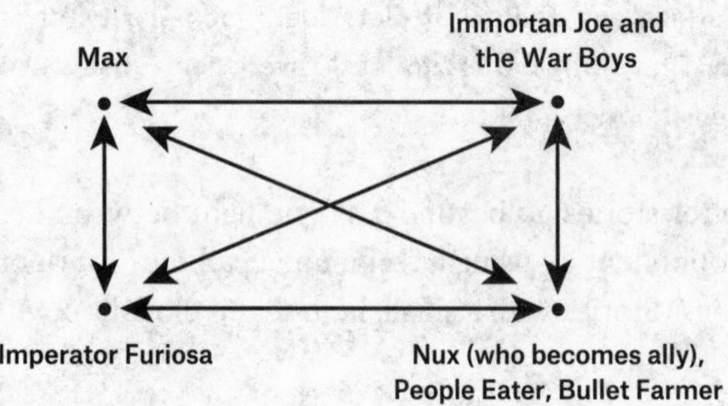

DIE HARD

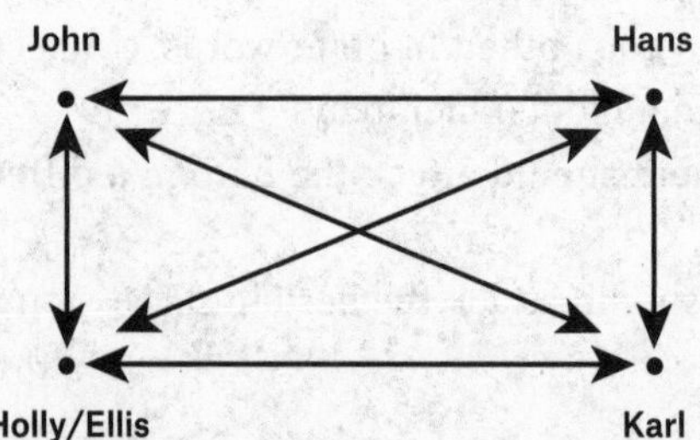

CASINO ROYALE

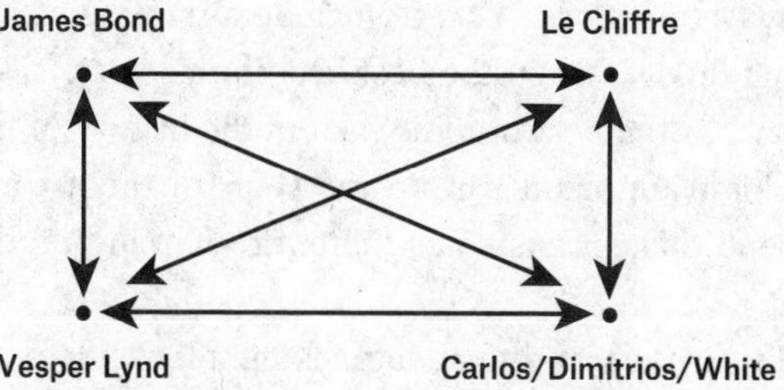

THE HUNT FOR RED OCTOBER

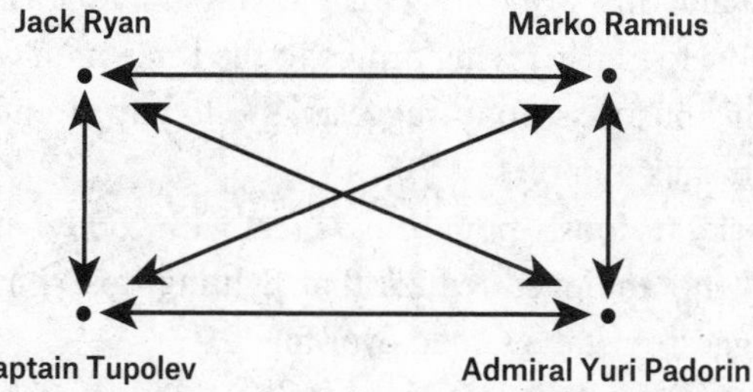

ACTION STORY BEAT: Training

Most genres do not have a training event. The hero is already trained to do what they must to win. But Action is about success above all. Much of the audience's interest in the Action form comes from watching the hero execute action with great expertise and *split-second timing*. This requires special abilities, which usually means training.

KEY POINT: Action is the most training-oriented of all story forms.

There are ways to make training sequences more complex. For example, there is conflict because the trainee hates the trainer, or the trainee has some deeper psychological reason he can't master the lessons he is being taught.

Many Action stories do not include a training beat. But in those that do, it is often the best beat in the story.

Rocky has the best training beat in the history of film, and it's not his triumphant run up the steps of the art museum. It's a scene that encapsulates the entire film in one dramatic moment.

Rocky arrives at the meatpacking plant for a training session and learns that his loser friend, Paulie, has set up an interview with a TV reporter. Reluctantly, Rocky starts throwing punches at the giant slab of meat. Apollo Creed's trainer, Tony, watches his workout with growing apprehension. But not Apollo. He's busy giving orders to the three men who help him run his business. Tony suggests Apollo pay attention, but Apollo brushes him off.

As Rocky furiously pounds the meat with "body" punches, Tony and the audience realize that fighting this "bum" may be the biggest mistake Creed ever made.

The Suicide Mission Story

One of the most popular subgenres in the Action form is a War story known as the Suicide Mission story. Its equivalent in the Crime story is the Caper (Heist). Both of these subgenres involve a team of highly trained individuals trying to accomplish a difficult and dangerous goal. Like the Caper, the Suicide Mission story shows how a team gains success in life.

In a Suicide Mission story, the team wants to attain a valuable military goal, like destroying an enemy installation or capturing the enemy leader. This goal is so important it will change the outcome of the war. The goal is also highly specific. The mission here is so dangerous it is certain suicide. Everyone knows they won't be coming back. But since the war depends on the mission, it must be done.

Examples include *Seven Samurai*, *The Dirty Dozen*, *The Guns of Navarone*, *Saving Private Ryan* (*Seven Samurai* transported to World War II), and *Guardians of the Galaxy.*

Because of the near-impossibility of the goal, the Suicide Mission story always requires an extended training section. Typically, this involves honing the individual talents of each member and combining them into a well-oiled machine.

One of the best Suicide Mission stories, *The Dirty Dozen*, has an extended training sequence that dominates the film. The training is unique in that the leader, Major Reisman, must first convince criminals to care about the mission and be part of a team. His basic technique is to take on the biggest and toughest of them in a fight, which he wins handily by using his superior military training.

The training sequence is capped off by the team's participation in war-game exercises, which they win by using the very techniques of cheating and scamming that put them in prison in the first place. This combination of team training and special criminal expertise makes the men perfectly suited to take on the final challenge on which the entire war depends.

ACTION STORY BEAT: Game Plan

The Action story is the most strategic of all forms. The plan and execution of the Action hero is like a game or sport. Not surprisingly, the Sports story is a subgenre of, and a way of transcending, Action. The connection of action to games is essential. Action of any kind tends toward quantification: timing it and measuring it to see who does it best.

In all Action stories, the specific game plan depends on the kind of Action involved:

- If the story is a Crime-Action hybrid, the hero is usually intuitive. The plan is based on experience and gut feeling.

But the opponent's plan is complex and deceptive. This makes him much tougher to beat.

- If the story is a Sports, War, or Caper story, the hero has a detailed game plan. This plan requires the coordination of many people. Sometimes the plan is so complex the leader spells it out in writing in such a way that the audience can also read it.

TECHNIQUES OF THE PLAN

- Make the plan intricate: This highlights the hero's ability to act. Also, since Action films typically lack plot, an intricate plan is the best way to generate maximum plot.
- Calibrate the plan down to a split second: In film, this means using the crosscut, which involves cutting back and forth between two or more characters and lines of action. This technique builds excitement.

Strategy vs. Tactics

The Action story turns on the distinction between tactics and strategy.

Tactics are the ability to win the battle.	**Strategy is the ability to win the war.**
Tactics are thinking about the present.	**Strategy is thinking about the future.**
Tactics are the right response in the moment, known as acting efficiently.	**Strategy is the right sequence of actions to accomplish the overall goal, known as acting effectively.**

The Action form highlights one of the great flaws of the human mind: the tendency to get caught up in tactics. This means trying to act efficiently at the cost of acting effectively.

The Action hero is always good at acting tactically in the moment. Only the best Action heroes are also good at strategy: the ability to see the right action to take as part of a larger campaign.

In *Die Hard*, trained cop John McClane is a tactical genius. He can respond to a situation in a split second with the right weapon and method of attack and defense. He is also brilliant at constructing a series of actions that will eventually lead to the defeat of the killers and the release of his wife and other hostages.

Telescoping back in time, a gladiator, by his very nature, is highly proficient at fighting. His life depends on it. His tactics must be impeccable. In the film *Gladiator*, Maximus is a general in the Roman army who is first and foremost a fighting soldier. So he is excellent in hand-to-hand combat. This serves him well when he is forced to become a gladiator. But what sets him apart, and indeed serves as the key to the film, is that, as a general, he is also a master of strategy. Maximus is the one who realizes the only way he and the other gladiators can survive is to join together and fight as a team. When tactics combine with strategy, these gladiators are unbeatable.

ACTION STORY BEAT: Revelation Leads to Decision

Stories move through a succession of revelations and decisions. The hero gains new information, makes a decision about how to act, and moves on. The middle of the story works like this:

Revelation → decision → revelation → decision → revelation → decision →

TECHNIQUE: The Action Reveal

The Action reveal is almost always a surprise attack by the opponent. Sometimes it's an attack by a fake ally, a character the hero didn't know was an opponent.

ACTION STORY BEAT: Drive—Cat and Mouse

During the middle of the story, multiple opponents attack the hero in quick succession. The hero responds. Both use trickery in their attack and defense. This results in a complex cat-and-mouse struggle that unfolds over many scenes.

> **KEY POINT: When both the hero and the opponent are good at strategy and tactics, the story takes the form of a series of intense punches and counterpunches.**

The rapid succession of punch-counterpunch is what makes an Action story a dramatic fifteen-round heavyweight bloodbath that shows the audience who's best.

#1 COMBAT TECHNIQUE: Deception

Action stories tell us that 90 percent of success results from simply taking action. But this raises the question: How? What is the key to winning? Whether in sports or war, the highest level of action involves "the fake."

> **KEY POINT: Successful combat always involves maximum deception.**

ACTION STORY BEAT: Drive—Improvisation

During the struggle between hero and opponent in the middle of the story (the drive), events upset the hero's plan. He realizes he must improvise.

> **KEY POINT: The hero's improvisation is the single most important plot beat in a successful Action story.**

Why? The hero's ability to improvise is the ultimate sign of his greatness. Only when events force the hero to shift tactics on the spur of the moment can the audience see how talented he really is.

While this is true of any Action story, the Suicide Mission subgenre is where the entire form turns on this beat. Here's one example of how it works: The leader comes up with an intricate game plan. The night the team is to go in, they find out that the guard who has walked the same path every night for twenty years has gotten sick. But the team can't postpone the mission, even though the substitute guard's actions are unpredictable. Now the heroes must improvise. We watch as the team changes tactics in a split second and still gets the job done. This makes the death of most of the team even more tragic.

At the end of *Mad Max: Fury Road*, Max turns his improvisation skills to saving Furiosa's life. He punctures her chest so she can breathe and then jury-rigs a tube and needle by which he can give her a transfusion of his own blood.

In *Die Hard*, John, facing a team of killers, is initially unarmed. He must make tools and weapons from items at hand. His most athletic improvisation occurs when he escapes gunfire from a helicopter. He ties a fire hose around his waist, jumps off the side of the building, and swings through a window below.

ACTION STORY BEAT: Moral Argument—the Great vs. the Good

Good stories make a moral argument about right and wrong actions. They do this primarily through the structure of the story, tracking the actions the hero takes to reach the goal. Sometimes, the hero goes too far and resorts to immoral actions to win.

The ultimate successful action is great action. This is why glory—recognition of greatness in the eyes of the community—is one of the ultimate values in the Action story. But glory does not always equal goodness.

KEY POINT: The moral argument is expressed in the conflict between great versus good action.

Stories always highlight the moral cost of action. In the Action form, this means the cost of success, of greatness. What did the hero do wrong to win? This is the moral price that must be paid.

By the end of the story, the hero may be great, but no longer good. And that means the hero is even more enslaved, which is intolerable to him. This is the moral question Jesus asked in Mark 8:36 in the New Testament: "For what does it profit a man to gain the whole world and forfeit his soul?"

ACTION STORY BEAT: Vortex Point and Violent Final Battle

A good story takes the form of a vortex in which conflict intensifies and focuses toward the battle. The battle is the point where all the characters and action converge.

The vortex point also creates a cyclone effect whereby the conflicts and reveals speed up as the plot moves toward the end. Most important, all the fighting within the arena funnels down to the hero and main opponent in a one-on-one fight to the death.

KEY POINT: The final battle is the vortex point of the entire story, and the battle itself also moves toward a vortex point.

The structural technique of the vortex reaches its extreme in the film medium, whose single greatest technique is the crosscut. In cutting back and forth between two or more action lines at a faster and faster pace, the battle becomes an emotional pressure cooker.

Action emphasizes the battle more than any other structure step. This beat, also known as the showdown, is typically big and violent.

Besides the vortex, these are the key elements of a good Action battle:

- The ideal location is in the tightest space possible, a pressure cooker. Even a battle between two armies is best within a tight space. For example, in *The Wild Bunch* four men fight the Mexican army within a coliseum. Not coincidentally, this is one of the great battles in movie history.
- The battle occurs in a unique arena that offers many objects and defensive positions for the hero to make use of.
- A large number of combatants are in conflict within the pressure cooker.
- The sequence ends with the hero directly fighting the main opponent.
- The final battle has the fastest pace of all the conflicts in the story.
- The hero not only outfights the opponent but also *outthinks* him.

Avatar is a combination of Myth, Action, and Love story. In the battle, the conflict between two great armies in the jungle funnels down to hand-to-hand combat, the hero and the lover-ally versus the main opponent.

The battle comes in three parts. The first part is the "cavalry" charge by the Na'vi against the entrenched soldiers led by Colonel Miles Quaritch. This gives us the nobility of the

Charge of the Light Brigade. Horse soldiers going up against mechanized forces means certain slaughter, and yet onward they ride.

The second part is the comeback by the Na'vi forces, this time with a charge of animal "armor" in the form of dinosaurs. The third part is the dramatic, personal fight between Jake Sully and Neytiri on one side using knife and bow and arrow versus Colonel Quaritch in a massive machine suit that makes him virtually unbeatable. But his exposed neck, his own Achilles' heel, allows Neytiri's arrow to kill him.

Mad Max: Fury Road has one of the all-time great battles. In part, this is because the director, George Miller, can stage and shoot action better than anyone in movie history. It's also because the battle has a beautiful story structure. As Max, Furiosa, Nux, and the female fighters from Furiosa's past, the Vuvalini, race back toward the Citadel, Joe and his army of War Boys give chase. Again, the battle moves toward a vortex point in space; the heroes have to get the war rig through the opening in the canyon (the equivalent of the trench in *Star Wars: A New Hope*).

The battle is also a vortex in how it sequences conflict and death. Lesser members of the team, like Valkyrie, die while taking out some of the War Boys. Then Max kills one of Joe's top allies, the People Eater. Max and Furiosa barely avoid death. Badly injured, Furiosa is able to lock Joe's mask to his wheel and kill him. Max battles Joe's behemoth son, Rictus, and is able to escape with Furiosa through the hole in the canyon.

ACTION STORY BEAT: Self-Revelation

The self-revelation is often missing in typical action stories. This happens when the writer hasn't set up the hero's personal track within the larger action conflict. When everything is about achieving the external goal instead of the hero's internal growth, the story is robbed of emotional impact.

Here are some possibilities for an Action self-revelation:

- The hero realizes he has become ruthless. In other words, he has taken the action too far (see good versus great action).
- If it's a Buddy Story, a hybrid of Action and Love (and usually Comedy), both characters may realize that their friendship is too valuable to lose.
- The Action hero sees that he must change from fighter to lover.

ACTION STORY BEAT: Farewell or Communion

KEY POINT: The hero's crucial decision at the *start* of the story is *whether to fight* or flee. The hero's crucial decision at the *end* of the story is *whether to join* or withdraw. Will the ultimate loner become part of the community?

Option 1: Farewell

The normal male Action hero's inability to connect with the community is usually portrayed as a model of strength; the warrior is needed to fight to protect civilization. But in reality, this is a deep flaw. Therefore, option one for the Action hero is to bid farewell to the community he has vowed to protect and remain the lonely warrior.

In *Mad Max: Fury Road*, the team forged in desperation and anger breaks up when they return to the Citadel. Like Ethan Edwards in *The Searchers*, Max cannot enter the community and experience love and family. He goes back to being the wandering loner. But before he goes, he receives a nod of respect from his fellow warrior, Furiosa.

Option 2: Communion in Love

The second option for the classic male Action hero is that he overcomes his fear of physical weakness and finds the greater strength of love. He forms an intimate relationship with another person and enters the larger community to enjoy the fuller life that only being part of society can provide.

There are few examples of the hero choosing this option. One way the Action story allows the hero to choose the woman at the end is to show her taking on the traits of a man. In *Lethal Weapon 3*, the Action hero falls for the love interest when she takes out five men in a fight. This may be a harbinger of future stories where gender norms are less defined.

Variation: Female Hero Becomes the Leader

Furiosa is an example of how the female Action hero varies the basic male story beats of farewell or communion in love. Like Ripley and Sarah Connor, she stays behind to become a leader of the tribe. While she still needs her skills as a fighter, she takes on the new challenges of leading a community.

Option 3: Variation on Communion—Buddy Marriage

A variation on the communion option is that the Action hero "marries" his/her partner. The Buddy Story depicts a "marriage" between two men (a "bromance") or two women. The end of the Buddy Story almost always shows the two heroes renewing their "marriage" even as they bicker their way into the sunset.

> **KEY POINT: This gives us a hint as to why the Buddy Story is so popular. It portrays *marriage without the pain*.**

The incessant low-level bantering between the two is not a sign of deep conflict in the "marriage." Rather, it's a sign of two people who "dance" so well with each other that they are destined to go through life together. And they know it.

What is the nature of this marriage? In older male Buddy Stories, women are often portrayed as silly, frivolous, soft, and weak. But men (according to this view) experience the deeper bonds of loyalty, toughness under pressure, friendship, and fun that women cannot provide.

The female Buddy Story makes a different case for the buddy marriage than the male version. A woman can count on and confide in another woman. Men are selfish users, rapists, thieves, and perpetuators of a corrupt and oppressive system. For a woman, preferring a man to a female friend is an act of betrayal and self-destruction.

The female Buddy story is less common in Action (one example is *Thelma and Louise*—also Crime) but more common in Comedy films such as *The Heat*, *Charlie's Angels*, *Outrageous Fortune*, *Big Business*, and *Romy and Michele's High School Reunion.*

Theme: Being Is Competing, Fighting, Winning, and Losing

The Action genre is the clearest story expression of the Existential Code. Existence is action. Once we are past the first distinction of life versus death (expressed in Horror), we are defined by what we do. Any action in life necessarily involves resistance and opposition. That means competing, and in the extreme, fighting.

The Action form embodies the necessary connection between taking action and acting successfully. Action says that being human is always about winning and losing. Life is a competition for a scarce resource, a zero-sum game, with one winner and at least one loser.

The Action hero embodies the truth that most of success

comes from simply taking action. But that success is also the product of acting *well*: acting with skill, tactical and strategic excellence, and perseverance.

While the Action story places its primary emphasis on winning, it also shows us that the other side of winning is losing: losing the contest, the lover, the friend—and the most extreme loss of all, death.

KEY POINT: Showing loss is the main way writers transcend the Action form.

The Action story taken to the level of tragedy highlights the extreme pain of loss. In *Seven Samurai*, the defending samurai win the battle against the marauders. But their losses are devastating. The film's evocation of the terrible losses of fighting is another reason it is so powerful.

Action Thematic Recipe: The Way of the Warrior

As we saw in the Horror form, a genre's thematic recipe is its strategy of becoming, of how a person can live a good life. It comes from two main sources: the hero's basic action in the story and the key question asked by the genre.

The Action story says life's primary path of becoming is *the Way of the Warrior*, embodying its strengths and avoiding its pitfalls. Since the Action hero is the fighter, the recipe for success is this: have the courage to face your greatest opponent, take action, and don't stop. Don't wait. Act! And never give up.

These are key questions the form asks: Fight or flee? Freedom or life under slavery? Does the hero stand and fight for what he or she believes in, which is the first, necessary step to guaranteeing one's freedom? Or does the hero flee and stay alive?

The key question also gives us the moral argument of the Action story:

- You must always take action to defend your values and live a successful life. Action does not involve debating what is most valuable. It is the fight for whatever values one holds dear.
- Beware of using immoral means to gain greatness, because the victory is tainted. The hero finds himself in a form of slavery of his own making.

Action Thematic Recipe: Decision—the Road to Freedom

> **KEY POINT: In Action, making good decisions is the core principle of life.**

Why is this focus on choice so profound? Daily life is a long sequence of actions that seem normal and necessary. Most people just go along for the ride. We rarely think there is another way.

Choice is the fulcrum point between one action and the next. It is the thought before the next action takes place. Once someone takes action, they can be evaluated on how well they execute it. But much of their success is predetermined. If someone makes good decisions, they increase the potential for successful action. They put themselves in a position to succeed.

What is the biggest ramification of this shift in mind? We realize the normal flow of the everyday is formed by choices that we do *not* make.

> **KEY POINT: Freedom comes from realizing we can start changing our lives at any time.**

How to Transcend the Action Story

Because Action stories are about quantified action and being the best, the main art/story forms of the genre are war and sports. These forms work according to the law of the jungle: win or die.

In the intensely physical Action form, transcendence comes from either increasing the scope of the story or making it more abstract. Both explore the art of success.

Transcending Action takes two main forms:

1. **ACTION EPIC/WAR STORIES**

   The most important way of raising the Action story to the level of art is to give it epic scale and stakes. Examples include *Seven Samurai*, *Mad Max: Fury Road*, the *Iliad* (also Myth), *La Grande Illusion*, *Game of Thrones* (also Gangster and Fantasy), *Die Hard*, *Dances with Wolves* (also anti-Western), *Patton*, *Glory*, *Beau Geste*, *The Charge of the Light Brigade*, *Gunga Din*, *All Quiet on the Western Front*, *Wings*, *The Bridge on the River Kwai*, *Platoon*, *Saving Private Ryan*, *A Farewell to Arms*, *Zulu*, *Sergeant York*, *The Thin Red Line*, *We Were Soldiers*, *Gallipoli*, *The Dirty Dozen*, *Patton*, *Dunkirk*, *The Deer Hunter*, *Apocalypse Now*, *Das Boot*, *Spartacus*, *1917*, *The Battle of Algiers*, *Black and White in Color*, *They Shall Not Grow Old*, *Paths of Glory*, *The Sands of Iwo Jima*, *Run Silent, Run Deep*, *Stalag 17*, *They Were Expendable*, *Twelve O'Clock High*, *The Best Years of Our Lives* (also Love), *Where Eagles Dare*, *From Here to Eternity*, *The Story of G.I. Joe*, *Band of Brothers*, *Midway*, *Hacksaw Ridge*.

2. **CAPER STORY AND SPORTS STORY**

   The second way of taking Action to a higher level is to abstract it into a game or sport.

   Examples of caper stories include *The Thomas Crown*

Affair, *Topkapi*, *Ocean's 11*, *The Sting*, *Rififi*, *The Asphalt Jungle*, *Reservoir Dogs*, *Lock, Stock and Two Smoking Barrels*, *The Professionals*, the *Rick and Morty* episode "One Crew Over the Crewcoo's Morty" (also Comedy), *The Killing* (1956), *Dead Heat on a Merry-Go-Round*.

Examples of sports stories include *Rocky* (also Love), *The Natural*, *A League of Their Own*, *Chariots of Fire*, *42* (also Biopic), *Creed*, *Friday Night Lights*, *Body and Soul*, *Bull Durham*, *Raging Bull*, *Hoosiers*, *Hoop Dreams*, *The Queen's Gambit*, *The Hustler*, *The Great American Novel*, *Million Dollar Baby*, *Requiem for a Heavyweight*, *Eight Men Out*, *Win Win*, *Moneyball*.

Transcending Action 1: The Action Epic and the Art of War

An epic is a story in which the fate of the nation is determined (or illustrated) by a single individual or family. The Action Epic often explores the art of war as the hero creates or transforms a nation.

The Action Epic is one step down from the mythic. Like Myth, it expresses the bigger picture by showing the audience how the entire world fits together.

KEY POINT: In the Action Epic, the writer's goal is not simply to give the audience an understanding but also to *inspire*.

Let's see how to write the Action Epic while exploring the art of success in war.

The Art of War

To see life through the lens of war is to see life as essentially dramatic. War is humankind engaged at the level of absolute drama. Yet we tend to think of the "art" of war as an oxymoron. How can the most destructive of all activities be a form of creativity?

War is the art and science of force. It is the ultimate expression of action. The causal sequence of the form goes like this: taking action leads to fighting, which leads to mass fighting, war, and the making of a nation.

Therefore, as a story form, the art of war finds its clearest expression in an Action Epic. A huge cast of characters comes into mass conflict on a large geographical canvas using strategy and tactics to deliver punches and counterpunches. The series of conflicts comes to a head in a final, decisive battle. Almost always there is a winner and a loser, although the costs of action are so high that both sides endure extreme loss.

Nowhere is the necessity of taking action and reaching success truer than in the art of war.

My Bildungsroman Reveal

Long before I studied story, I studied war. As the son of a West Point graduate who taught military strategy at the Army War College, I listened in rapt attention as my father explained the strategy and tactics in the American Civil War and World Wars I and II. Many of the men on both sides of my family over the last century were generals and colonels in the army. Had I not come of age at the height of the Vietnam War, I probably would have attended West Point and become a soldier, too.

What I learned in those tutorials had immense value. It determined how I looked at life and how I understood the workings of story. After all, story is the craft of created conflict.

ACTION EPIC STORY BEAT: The World of War

A battle is more than the moment when violent conflict decides the issue. It is the vortex point of the larger forces of land, people, and technology. These include economic factors, materiel, men, arms, the strategies of the generals, the tactical abilities of the soldiers, and the particular landscape of the battlefield.

Essentially, a battle is as much an engineering contest as a military one. My father once told me that winning a battle is about bullets and bodies: how effectively can each side get bullets to the front and bring wounded bodies to the rear.

The American Civil War is a classic example of the critical importance of story world elements to the outcome of war. The Southern generals were often superior to their Northern counterparts in strategy, and they came close to winning. But they could not overcome the economic superiority of the North and its ability to blockade the South to deprive it of foreign assistance.

Keys for Writing an Action Epic

As we move through the beats of the art of war, let's explore how they provide the keys to writing a great Action Epic:

- Try to find one arena for the story. This allows you to create the pressure cooker within a confined space. A story set within a single arena is usually better than an Action story that travels because a journey lets pressure escape.
- If your story travels, reveal the general vortex point of the story up front. This way, the audience knows that everything will focus down to a single battle point with lots of big action. They won't be impatient when the hero seems to be moving with no apparent direction. But a word of caution: don't be so specific that you ruin the final plot reveal.
- Place the story in a big historic moment that shapes a nation, a turning point where everything changes.
- Give the character a crucial part in the making of the

nation. This is the key beat to fulfilling the definition of the Epic.

- Use social change to add texture to the story world. Do this by placing the hero between two stages of societal development: for example, a village evolving into a city. You can also show conflict between social classes. This highlights the larger forces of change acting upon the characters. The key question of the form is: How do the characters *adapt* to these forces, and can they do so in time to avoid their own destruction?

ACTION EPIC STORY BEAT: Technology of Weapons

Weapons are directed and magnified force. They extend a person's ability to kill another human being, which is every soldier's goal. This is why shifts in strategy and tactics are often based on the development of new weapons. Each technological "improvement" magnifies the soldier's ability to kill the enemy and/or survive the fight.

ACTION EPIC STORY BEAT: Action Epic Hero

There are several strategies you can use to craft a more compelling hero:

- Give the hero a sense of humor. The Action Epic is about making and saving the world. The hero is normally extremely serious about accomplishing this task. This can make him seem pompous and full of himself. Giving the hero a sense of humor grounds him and makes him more likable. In the extreme, it can even define him as an Action hero: he's so cool under pressure he's cracking jokes.
- The job is a burden the hero does not want to take on. This familiar beat identified by the mythologist Joseph Campbell is about showing the magnitude of the job

and the hero's realization that he may not be up to the task. He is an ordinary person who will have to become extraordinary to succeed.

- The Action hero is a master of fighting. Since the Action hero is the fighter, the hero of the Action Epic should be a master fighter. He is an artist of combat.

ACTION EPIC STORY BEAT: Desire

The desire line in an Action Epic must have a specific physical end point and lead to fighting on a vast scale.

Saving Private Ryan is basically *Seven Samurai* goes to World War II. Private Ryan is a soldier whose three brothers have been killed in the war. To provide some solace to the mother, a captain and his squad are given the task to find Ryan and bring him to safety. As laudable as this desire seems to be, it will cost the lives of a lot more men than the three brothers who are already gone.

ACTION EPIC STORY BEAT: Opposition

The key strategy to employ when crafting a believable opponent: make the opponent human, with defendable values. The "evil" opponent found in basic Action stories might make him appear more dangerous and formidable. But the evil opponent is always a mistake. He is not human. He is simply a black box of badness. This makes the story seem artificial and prevents it from rising to high drama.

A human opponent is right about certain things. He has defendable values even when he is wrong. Ironically, the hero's accomplishment is far greater in beating this kind of complex opponent.

ACTION EPIC STORY BEAT: Character Web—Chain of Command and Specialists of War

A War story is action on a vast scale with two armies in conflict. Although the main opposition is horizontal, army versus army, the most detailed character web in the story is vertical, showing the chain of command on the hero's side.

These various characters are allies. But they are also a source of conflict with opposition that is more personal.

The War story has two popular approaches: focus primarily on the generals or primarily on the foot soldiers. Each makes for a radically different story:

1. Emphasize the commanders: The first approach, from the top of the organization, gives the audience a bird's-eye view of mass fighting. This emphasizes conflict of strategy among commanders, both between armies and within armies. These stories highlight difficult command decisions and great battles. Examples include *The Battle of the Bulge*, *Patton*, and *The Hunt for Red October*.
2. Emphasize the simple foot soldier: The second approach is from the private's perspective. It focuses on the terror and chaos of war, male bonding, loss of friends, impossible moral situations, and the difficulty of following orders. Examples include *Platoon*, *The Deer Hunter*, *Apocalypse Now*, *Full Metal Jacket*, *All Quiet on the Western Front*, *Breaker Morant*, *Midnight Clear*, *The Thin Red Line*, and *The Red Badge of Courage*.

ACTION EPIC STORY BEAT: Collecting the Allies—Selling the War

When we look at war, we tend to focus on the battles, the intense conflict of who won and who lost.

But the battle is just the fulcrum point of the larger contest for power. Long before the battle takes place, men must be assembled to fight. Those in power must wage a campaign of persuasion to sell men on the possibility of sacrificing their lives for a cause.

A true story about World War I, *They Shall Not Grow Old* begins with a series of statements from men who are excited about joining the war effort. Without any experience of actual fighting and death, these would-be soldiers are caught up in the grand adventure of war between nations. They don't want to miss the fun. Some are shamed into participating because all the other men are joining and the government has made it their sacred duty to do so. Typically, they think the fight will be short-lived, resulting in a quick victory from which they can return a hero. Of course, in many cases such thinking is wrong.

According to the romantic sales pitch, the soldier isn't fighting to conquer land. He fights to defend woman and country. In this nationalistic romance, he imagines killing large numbers of the enemy. But part of the story is that even in those rare moments when the hero dies in battle, he is immortalized in some way. He is reborn as a name that will live forever in the hearts and minds of his countrymen.

There's one big problem with this romantic scenario: it's fake immortality. The man is dead.

ACTION EPIC STORY BEAT: Game Plan—Tactics vs. Strategy

Every human activity and every story form contains certain fundamental trade-offs: if you do more of one thing, you can do less of another. Some of the main trade-offs in war are offense versus defense, hitting versus moving, mass army versus point of attack, and bullets versus bodies.

The difference between tactics and strategy has to do with goals and time. The goal of tactics is winning this fight. The goal of strategy is final success: winning the war. The commander's first job is to align tactics with strategy. But this is not easy. The challenge of the tactical moment often overwhelms larger strategic concerns. World War I is the textbook case of bad tactics (trench warfare) determining bad strategy (a war of attrition), leading to the death of approximately ten million combatants.

Since war is the ultimate action in which the loser is physically destroyed, the trade-off in the human mind between strategy and tactics is the key to this art form.

Both strategy and tactics play with another fundamental trade-off in the art of war: hitting and moving. Hitting, also known as firepower, is the means of delivering the decisive blow that achieves the goal of destroying the enemy. Far less understood is the importance of movement. Movement is what makes hitting possible. And the key to movement is *not needing to move*, also known as *positioning*.

ACTION EPIC STORY BEAT: Battle—Grinding Slaughter

Reduced to its basic elements, a battle is two lines of firepower facing each other. The battle proceeds with both sides using the two main tools of hitting and moving. With these tools, each army tries to cut a hole into the middle of the other line and/or turn the enemy's flank. If the opposing line is cut, that army loses its unified form and disintegrates. If the opposing line is flanked, that army risks being surrounded, at which point it either surrenders or is destroyed.

Attacking is what allows an army to break through or turn the other's flank. But attack also means that the army is unable to set a defense. So there is nothing to stop the enemy's counterattack.

The Action Epic/War story is typically a long sequence of battles. The story ends with one big, climactic battle in which the hero's army almost always defeats the opponent's army.

ACTION EPIC STORY BEAT: Self-Revelation—Humanity Is Hopeless

The self-revelation in the Epic War form is among the bleakest of all story forms. The characters go from having high hopes for adventure and success at the beginning to witnessing massive destruction for little or no payoff, and with little hope for the future at the end. Part of the bleakness of this vision comes from the fact that this is more than a self-revelation of the hero. It's a thematic revelation about humankind itself. The audience realizes that the absurdity of war comes from a basic flaw in the human mind.

ACTION EPIC STORY BEAT: Moral Decision

The hero makes a noble gesture, also known as a beau geste. This is a moral choice between duty and personal desire, country and family or self. The hero chooses success of the group over the individual so that others in the group can live.

This choice encapsulates the author's view of what is noble. Usually it involves the sacrifice of one's own life so others may live.

Examples include *Seven Samurai*, *Gunga Din*, *Beau Geste*, *Terminator* 2, and *The Charge of the Light Brigade*.

An alternative to this decision has the hero choosing the self over the group. Either the group is not worth sacrificing for or those in power have brainwashed the regular members of society to believe in a false war.

Transcending Action 2: Sports Stories and Caper Stories

The second way to transcend the Action genre is through the simulation of games and sports. These take the form of Sports and Caper stories.

The Art of Success in Games and Sports

Games and sports represent thought (and action) experiments in a pressure cooker. In a Caper, the pressure comes from the fact that the hero will go to prison if he fails. In Sports the pressure comes from the intense physical challenge of the contest and the fact that the hero may lose.

By abstracting competition onto a limited field of play, we can see more clearly the elements that determine success.

Caper Story: Life as Game

The Caper story is a subgenre in which a team of crooks executes an elaborate plan to steal something. Caper beats are similar to another subform of Action, the Suicide Mission story.

Some people believe the Caper story glorifies theft. Not so. To see what the Caper is really about, we have to think of it as the following thought experiment: How can someone defeat a "real" world that is closed, hierarchical, and lawful? The solution: make life a game where the individual beats the system. And so, the Caper story is born.

Both Caper and Detective stories derive their appeal from the fact that they show the mind in action. This is our species' great distinguishing characteristic. The mind is elusive and infinitely complex. Yet, thinking is not dramatic. In a story, we need to show *thought through action*.

Both Caper and Detective stories work because they express the workings of the mind in a simplified but nonetheless accurate way. The Caper has a further distinguishing characteristic in that the real challenge of the Caper goes beyond acquiring a valuable object. It's about coordinating the actions of a group of disparate individuals. The creative brilliance of the leader is the real object of interest.

The Thomas Crown Affair (1968) is the greatest of all Caper stories. The script's excellence comes from connecting the Caper to the Love story and presenting viewers with the ultimate modern man, the individual who lives for the art of the game.

Thomas Crown is a brilliant businessman, far surpassing other businessmen with whom he battles daily. He does everything in his life at the highest level. The only thing left for him to accomplish is to become a fully "self-actualized" man. What does this mean? For Crown it means taking life itself into the abstract realm. Crown has so much money and success that his motivation for living is threefold: to make life a game with a score, to become a superior human being, and to beat the system and win. He is the rich man's Raskolnikov (*Crime and Punishment*), but a lot smarter.

The Thomas Crown Affair takes this "highest" man, the artist-gamesman, and places him in a life-and-death battle with the brilliant artist-gameswoman he loves. Now the question becomes: Which of these two values, game or love, will he choose?

In the shocking final battle between two superior humans and lovers, Crown sacrifices the love of a lifetime to win the game. Does this sound like a hollow man winning the ultimate Pyrrhic victory? Perhaps. But not to him.

Sports and Sports Stories: Performance Art with a Score

Sports are the Action story turned into a game, a story where we keep score. We take nature's daily fight to the death and create an abstract conflict for the sake of play. Sports are a series of scenarios of conflict in a pressure cooker. At the end we see who does it best and why. This is another version of a "limit situation." Put characters in a crisis, whether real or invented, and you'll see who they really are.

The biggest abstraction in sports is that there are two, and only two, sides. In both sports and traditional warfare, the fighters wear a uniform so it's immediately clear who's on which team. This removes other variables so we can see the true causes of victory and defeat.

Unlike in the Crime world, there is no such thing as justice in the predator and prey world of nature. The same is true in sports. You win or you "die." Contrary to Grantland Rice's famous slogan, it's not about how well you play the game. It's about getting the victory.

The Story of Sports

The distinguishing feature of sports is not the power of the adversaries but the dramatic course of the activity.

KEY POINT: The main reason we play a sport is because it is a story.

The idea in every sport is to oppose two approximately equal players in a finite space and time. As in any dramatic activity, the climax of the game is what is most galvanizing. All activity focuses to and ends at this vortex point.

As a result, the crucial feature is that the players must be relative equals, whatever their particular ability. Of course, extreme physical ability can be wondrous to behold. We watch professional sports in part to see superhuman feats of strength and speed that only professionals can provide. But the score, the *conclusion* of the entire sequence of activities, is the measure of success. Without a contest and a dramatic conclusion, we might simply watch athletes practice.

Physical ability is the means to that dramatic conclusion. Once the players achieve a reasonable level of mastery of the game so that scoring is possible, interest swells at the finale.

How does this dramatic story play out? Many have noted that sports represent simulated war. In real war, both sides can attack and defend at any time. But in most sports with a ball, one side is on offense and the other is on defense. Each side also has territory they must defend. For example, the end zone in football; the goal in soccer, lacrosse, and hockey; and the basket in basketball. This is the heart of the kingdom, its sacred space, which, if lost, means the downfall of the kingdom itself.

SPORTS STORY BEAT: Story World—the Vortex

Sport creates a perfect abstract canvas that removes all the variables so that we can see who is best. Each sport sets the physical boundaries of play. The geography of the canvas is based primarily on the shape of the field and the rules for how one scores.

> **KEY POINT: Success in any sport comes from "stretching the field."**

This means forcing the opponent to cover the farthest extremes of the field. This puts the most pressure on the physical and mental abilities of the opponent.

Field as Vortex

Just as a good story comes to a vortex point in space and time, the geography of many sports is built in the shape of a vortex. Play starts from a wide area and funnels to a single spot where the point is scored. Using the basic strategic principle of "stretching the field," a classic method of play is to advance the ball up the wings and then center the ball near the goal.

SPORTS STORY BEAT: Warrior Hero at Play—Who's Best

Like the larger Action story of which it is a part, sport is about proving who is better. It is performance art that tests both the mind and the body. There is no quarter in sports. We may begin as equals, but we end with one superior to the other.

One of the main reasons someone plays the fabricated contest of a game or sport is to evaluate life and worth in a moment. Winning gives us the illusion that our entire life will be a success. Clearly, this judgment is both simplistic and fleeting. But to play the game, the mind must hide the limits of the frame and rules. This suspension of disbelief makes the game matter. In other words, like all forms of human drama, sports deal with our Consciousness.

SPORTS STORY BEAT: Weakness-Need—the Need to Prove Greatness

The need to see one's life as a success through play is not a weakness. It is a lack. In daily life, we have few ways of distinguishing ourselves, let alone "winning." Heroic moments are rare. Game situations provide the opportunity to prove our greatness.

Sports are also the ultimate manifestation of the first tendency of the mind toward binary thinking (see the Horror story). It reduces life to offense and defense.

The will to greatness and binary thinking are the primary psychological elements of sport itself. But there is also a weakness-need in the individual player. The player enters the fray with certain abilities and flaws in their game, and these are physical, mental, and psychological.

During the course of play, the individual must play to their strengths but also manage their weaknesses. They must attack the weaknesses of an opponent and prevent them from using their strengths.

SPORTS STORY BEAT: Desire—To Score and Therefore to Win

Sports take the all-important desire line of the story and quantify it to prove superiority. The specificity of the goal—to score and win—helps focus the hero's drive.

SPORTS STORY BEAT: Character Web—Individual vs. Team Sports

Boxing is primal because it's one individual trying to knock another individual unconscious—a near death. A team sport is more complex, acknowledging that humans live within a society. The competition is about which society is superior. But it also tests the individual within the society. The central question becomes: Can the player not only help his team win but also balance that effort with his own desire for success?

Much of the pleasure of playing and watching a sport is dependent on whether one prefers individual glory or team success.

Gladiator: From Individual to Team Sport

The gladiator fighting in the arena is the closest thing to what sport abstracts: war. This is the one contest in which the loser actually dies.

The brilliance of the premise of *Gladiator* is to place a soldier in the arena. The thought experiment is: What if a great soldier, with the strategic wisdom of a general and the tactical excellence of a man still young enough to fight hand-to-hand, were placed in the ring with professional athletes specially trained to kill? Each side has advantages. The outcome is unclear.

The payoff of the premise comes in the best scene in the movie, when the general turns his fellow gladiators from individual fighters killing each other into a team of fighters killing everyone else. Their power is magnified far beyond the sum of their parts, and they threaten to bring down the empire.

SPORTS STORY BEAT: Opponent—Nemesis

The opposing player is the Other made abstract. He is both predator and prey. The question in any sporting event becomes: Who can "kill" the other one first?

> **KEY POINT: For the most dramatic sporting event and the best sports story, each player should be the *nemesis* of the other.**

The nemesis is the player best able to attack their opponent's weaknesses, and vice versa. The contest becomes a study in attack and adjustment as each player tries to protect their own weaknesses while attacking the opponent.

My Bildungsroman Reveal: Great Coaching

I began to study sports before I studied war. But they quickly became intertwined. I loved the physical pleasure of playing sports, the intellectual challenge of outsmarting my opponent, and the emotional thrill of winning. I began coaching from an early age because I found that having to explain the inner workings of a game increased my own mastery of it.

Not only was my father a master of military strategy, he was also an accomplished athlete and coach. This lucky confluence of factors shaped my life. While playing squash (my best sport) with my father, he would emphasize the fundamental principles of strategy that applied to any competition. As an extremely abstract game, squash lent itself perfectly to this emphasis on strategy as the determining factor in victory.

My father taught me an important life lesson:

KEY POINT: A good coach teaches you how to play; a great coach teaches you how to win.

SPORTS STORY BEAT: Game Plan—the Four-Corner Strategy

It could be argued that the biggest determinant to success or failure in the game is the player's ability of make decisions in the shortest period of time before the window of action closes. This is an extension of the earlier point about decision-making being the key to successful action. This means that sports involve looking for patterns to exploit an advantage.

KEY POINT: A player's game plan—strategy and tactics—is based on two main elements: (1) exploiting the opponent's weaknesses while playing to one's own strengths and (2) driving the opponent(s) to the *extreme* corners of the field.

The opponent's flaws can be exposed only when he is pushed to the farthest reaches of the field or court. This tests the opponent's body beyond what it can physically cover until, under increasing pressure, the opponent cannot block the player's final attack.

In football, the best offense forces the defense to move horizontally from sideline to sideline as well as vertically from the line of scrimmage to the end zone. Again, this is known as "stretching the field."

In tennis and squash, the player moves his opponent to the four corners of the court until he cannot get to the ball. Winning comes from exerting pressure using a sequence of shots rather than a single kill shot.

In baseball, the pitcher works the four corners of the plate and the four corners of the strike zone, using various speeds and spins, to make it as hard as possible for the batter to contact the ball. In all games, executing a strategy that forces the opponent to the extreme corners is based on the principle that the ball moves faster than the runner.

SPORTS STORY BEAT: Moral Argument—Cheating

The moral argument in any story is based on the methods the individual uses to reach the goal. The most dramatic story occurs when the hero, facing defeat, chooses immoral actions to win. Only at the end do they realize that their methods have created a loss of integrity that places them in a moral prison and robs the goal of value.

In the sports story, the immoral action that undermines any game is cheating. Each player has chosen to enter this abstract world to prove who is best. Yet, the pressure to succeed creates overwhelming temptation to win by any means.

The cheater rationalizes their immoral methods by saying everyone does it and the world remembers only who won. But they know that by turning to cheating they were the inferior player that day, regardless of the score.

SPORTS STORY BEAT: Battle—Last-Second Victory

Like war, sport is one long battle. It is an ongoing conflict that only ends when the agreed upon time runs out. The most dramatic sports stories occur when one player or team scores in the last second of play. This is the ultimate crescendo, especially if the victor comes from behind to win.

In *The Natural*, Roy's team is down 2–0 in the bottom of the ninth inning in the final game to determine who wins the pennant. He comes to the plate with two runners on base. He has trouble swinging the bat because of an old bullet wound. Also, he's been poisoned (that's some serious cheating). He hits a foul ball that breaks his magic bat. The opposing catcher sees blood on Roy's jersey and calls for an inside fastball that he feels Roy, with his weakened stomach, will be unable to hit.

With a massive swing, Roy pounds the ball so hard it smashes the right field lights and causes a fireworks display of explosions. Roy rounds the bases and his team wins the pennant.

SPORTS STORY BEAT: Self-Revelation—Winner, Loser, and Higher Victory

One of the big differences between sports and the life-and-death struggle of predator and prey is that the hero has a self-revelation. He thinks: Whether I am a winner or a loser today, I live to play and prove myself another day. Either way, I am a better player and person because of the crucible of sports.

In a comical ending to the fight in *Rocky*, the ring announcer reads off the winner on each judge's card while Rocky stands in the middle of the ring yelling for his girlfriend, Adrian. Rocky doesn't care if he won. He knows he gave the champ everything he could handle and came within a hair's breadth of winning. He knows he's not a bum. Most of all, he knows he loves Adrian and she loves him, and that's what really matters.

SPORTS STORY BEAT: New Equilibrium—Long-Lasting Truth

In life, sport is an either-or contest. There is no moral victory. There is no solace in having played well or having been a good sport. The insight is limited and temporary: today I won or I lost.

But Sports stories give the hero a truth about themselves that lasts. Sometimes the hero realizes they have reached the heights of success in their sport. Sometimes they know that while they have failed to become number one, they have fulfilled their potential as a great human being.

Perhaps no monologue in the history of film expresses the true meaning of sports better than this moment in *The Hustler*, the best-written sports movie of all time.

FAST EDDIE: Just hadda show those creeps and those punks what the game is like when it's great, when it's *really* great. You know, like anything can be great, anything can be great. I don't care, bricklaying can be great, if a guy knows. If he knows what he's doing and why and if he can make it come off. When I'm goin', I mean, when I'm *really* goin' . . . it's a real great feeling when you're right and you *know* you're right. It's like all of a sudden I got oil in my arm. The pool cue's part of me . . . It's a piece of wood, it's got nerves in it. Feel the roll of those balls, you don't have to look, you just *know*. You make shots that nobody's ever made before. I can play that game the way . . . *nobody's* ever played it before.

SARAH: You're not a loser, Eddie. You're a winner. Some men never get to feel that way about anything.

The Next Rung Up the Ladder

The life philosophy of the Action genre moves beyond that of the Horror form by shifting our focus from death, which we can't control, to life, which we can. This recipe for success in the quantifiable areas of life is highly effective. But while it may take us to a high level of achievement, that doesn't necessarily make for a rich and fulfilling life.

The next rung up the ladder of good living is Myth, which shows us how to grow over the full course of our lives.

4

Myth: The Life Process

Epic of Gilgamesh: The Natural Immortality

We begin our exploration of the Myth genre with the first fully realized Myth, the *Epic of Gilgamesh*. It came into being around 1800 BC, when various tales of the character's exploits were collected into one story.

Gilgamesh begins as a brutal warrior-king. His friend Enkidu is a sort of primal man who lives in the wilderness and plays with wild beasts. Throughout much of the story, these two characters seek success in battle. But when Enkidu dies, Gilgamesh comes to understand his own future and pursues the secret of immortality. He fails.

But neither the character nor the story ends there. The reader discovers that Gilgamesh has been telling this tale all along. Gilgamesh realized his greatest achievement is not the battles he won but the story about them.

Gilgamesh was created before organized religion. Yet, it is one of the most modern and evolved myths. When the superhero fails to become immortal, we see the beginning of tragedy. When he tells his own story, we have the first self-referential tale.

Gilgamesh also expresses the idea of gaining what might be called "natural immortality" through story. The hero accepts that real immortality, becoming a god, is impossible. Natural immortality is far more limited, existing only in the minds of others and in the tales they tell—in other words, in the continuity of humanity.

My Bildungsroman Reveal: The Wisdom of My Grandmother

When I was young, my family spent part of the summer visiting my mother's parents in San Antonio, Texas. My grandmother was a tough old lady who'd worn black ever since her first child had died at the age of twelve. When her bridge club friends shared photos of their grandkids, she didn't look. She wasn't interested and she didn't care who knew it.

For some reason, she took a special liking to me. Due to a heart condition, she was bedridden on hot Texas afternoons. I spent hours in her room sitting directly in front of the air conditioner. But it wasn't the cool air that kept me there. More often than not, she would pull out her book of mythology—probably Edith Hamilton's—and read me the myths of the ancient Greeks. To this day I remember hearing those magical tales of Theseus and the Minotaur and Perseus and the Gorgon's head.

I believe my love of storytelling began with the grandmother I adored. If only I could thank her for that gift.

Myth: How It Works

Myth is the *essential mind in story form*, the first Story Code that consciousness constructs. Myth is the shape of basic human consciousness. Therefore, every human being creates Myths in some form to solve life's problems.

While Myth is usually thought of as an early form of religion, the reverse is true. Religion is a codified form of Myth, and more broadly, a form of art.

KEY POINT: Most religions are a collection of stories designed to lay out a moral code necessary to achieve immortality. Not surprisingly, immortality is the main theme of the Myth genre.

Myth is the first genre to place the self within the larger society. It gives a full picture of the culture. It also highlights the politics of the human world, within the family, the tribe, and the nation. Myth is how every child comes to understand essential human relationships and her natural surroundings.

The Myth form highlights the basic human relations: mother/daughter, father/son, husband/wife, and the two end points of life, birth and death. It also codifies what we could call the basic predicaments of human life. It maps the conflicting choices that can end in great and irrevocable loss.

KEY POINT: Myth is primarily about the development of the self over a lifetime.

As an expression of the essential mind—how human consciousness works—Myth is the wellspring from which story drama is born. The modern form of story we call drama is actually a refined, sophisticated version of Myth. Any drama that ignores primary human relationships and stages of growth lacks the power that the best myths possess.

The Myth Mind-Action Story View

The Mind-Action story view is a combination of the genre's worldview and recipe for living a good life. The Myth version of Mind-Action says that life is a journey in which one's ultimate goal is to understand oneself.

> **KEY POINT: Myth is the first genre to answer the essential question: What does it mean for a human being to be a self-conscious animal?**

We see this in the form's overall story strategy: the hero encounters a number of opponents on a journey that eventually exposes his or her deeper self. That is the self-revelation leading to character change.

Character change is the key moment in any story. Yet it is extremely subtle and arguably rare in real life. One of the greatest challenges the storyteller faces is this: How do you express character change to the audience?

Every landmark in the character's outer journey must be a physical manifestation of inner change. As the first fully realized form to match the hero's external journey with his/her internal journey, Myth was a major landmark in the history of storytelling.

The physical journey typically ends with the hero returning home. The life journey ends with the hero's inner rebirth.

Examples of Myth

Stories

Greek (such as Hercules, Perseus, Theseus), Norse (such as Thor, Odin, Loki), Indian (such as Brahma, Vishnu, Shiva),

Irish (Oisen), *Epic of Gilgamesh*, *Mahabharata*, *Ramayana*, *I Ching*, Sumerian Myth

Novels and Films

The Lord of the Rings, *The Wizard of Oz* (also Fantasy), *Star Wars*, *Black Panther*, *Guardians of the Galaxy*, *Hunger Games* (also Science Fiction), *The Avengers*, *Avengers: Infinity War*, *Avengers: Endgame*, *Harry Potter*, *X-Men*, *Batman Begins*, *The Dark Knight* (also Crime and Fantasy), *The Dark Knight Rises*, *The Batman* (also Crime), *Dances with Wolves* (also anti-Western), *The Matrix* (also Science Fiction), *The Dark Tower* (also Science Fiction and Western), *Excalibur*, *Zootopia* (also Comedy and Detective), *Logan* (*X-Men*), *The Seventh Horse of the Sun*

Television

The Mandalorian (also Action), *Avatar: The Last Airbender*, *Daredevil* (also Crime), *Luke Cage* (also Crime), *Jessica Jones* (also Crime), *The Punisher* (also Crime), *The Flash* (also Crime), *Agents of S.H.I.E.L.D.* (also Crime)

Myth Story Overview

Here's what we'll cover in this chapter:

- **MYTH STORY BEATS**
- **THEME:** Being Is Self-Questioning and a Search for My Destiny
  - Thematic Recipe: The Way of the Searcher
- **HOW TO TRANSCEND THE MYTH STORY**
  - Myth/Science Fiction Epic
  - Female Myth
  - Ecological Myth

Myth Story Beats

Plot in Myth can be both linear and cyclical. The linear sequence comes from the "male" Myth, based on the goal of the hunt. The circular sequence comes from the "female" Myth, based on the agricultural cycle and the changing of the seasons. In both Male and Female Myths, however, the hero's physical journey is often circular: the hero returns home, where he/she learns a truth that was always deep inside.

Myth Beats: The Limits of Joseph Campbell

Joseph Campbell was arguably the most influential Mythologist in history. In *Hero with a Thousand Faces*, Campbell presents the theory of the "monomyth." He outlines the major story beats of the One Story upon which he believed all stories in the world are based.

However, he overstates the universality of this story. It is not the universal story, or even the universal Myth (a genre of story). At most we could say it is the universal *male warrior* Myth. Even that would disregard the unique cultural context in which these stories were created, a context that can lead to different meanings of the same story beat.

How did this happen? According to Campbell, approximately three thousand years ago, hunter-warrior societies conquered gatherer-agricultural societies. As a result, male warrior myths wiped out female cyclical growth myths.* The Female Myth has been largely missing from Western culture ever since. Campbell, however, based his theory on stories largely written by men.

The Campbell story beats are not the actions that *all*

---

* Joseph Campbell, Safron Rossi (editor), *Goddesses: Mysteries of the Feminine Divine.*

heroes take in going after their goal. They are invariably the actions a male warrior takes in discovering his identity both as a fighter for right and as the beneficent leader of a society.

KEY POINT: To expand these male warrior beats to all male heroes, and worse, to all female heroes, is to reduce both men and women to a narrow view of what it means to be human and heroic.

The mistake here is to confuse a particular variation of the Story Code with the code itself. The monomyth is a *sub*form of the Myth genre.

The "hero's journey" has been confused with the Story Code over the last few decades because superhero warriors have taken over popular film. Their journey has been mechanized by the Hollywood factory moviemaking system.

Why did this "monomyth" conquer Hollywood? First, it appealed to the teens and young adults who became the bulk of the worldwide moviegoing audience. They enjoyed watching mythic superheroes defeat superopponents with all the speed, sensual power, and visual effects the film medium can produce.

Second, it fit the American Creation Myth expressed in the Western, and then modernized in the Horatio Alger, up-by-the-bootstraps stories. The elements of popular stories, like the single hero with an intense desire, perfectly match the thematic elements of an American culture that is all about individuality and success.

In spite of the continued worldwide financial success of this male warrior subgenre, people are beginning to realize how limited and predictable it is. And it is certainly not the only way to tell a story.

MYTH STORY BEAT: Story World—Natural World and Two Cultures

The story world is the environment where the hero and the reader live, the entire world where the story takes place. It's composed of the minor characters, the larger society and culture, the natural settings, the man-made spaces, time, and technology.

> **KEY POINT: The story world is the most important major story element in the Myth form. Indeed, it is the key feature in all "world-building" genres, including Fantasy and Science Fiction.**

Why? The reader gets to immerse herself in the world and explore all the fabulous things within it. This requires the writer to create a detailed world the reader wants to visit again and again, and never leave.

In all world-building stories, especially Myth, the story world is strongly connected to the natural world, such as forests, islands, oceans, jungles, ice, deserts, and rivers. This connection comes out of the deeper themes of Myth that express an ecological view of the world. The forces of connection in the natural world are palpable, and humans are part of that natural web.

Myth stories also connect the hero with the kingdom: he/she starts in one kingdom and journeys through another kingdom before returning home. This creates a contrast between the two cultures the story explores.

At the beginning of the Myth story, the hero typically lives in an oppressive or conformist society-culture. Often, the current king is a tyrant. The hero's family may pressure him (most classic Myths have a male hero) to follow in his father's footsteps, even when the father is gone. As we will see, this story world exacerbates the hero's weakness-need.

KEY POINT: The two cultures depicted in the Myth story world are usually *opposites* in some way.

Steps for Creating the Story World

Step 1. Define the Overall Story Arena

The arena is a unified place surrounded by some kind of wall.

J. R. R. Tolkien's *The Lord of the Rings* is a modern cosmology and mythology of Great Britain. Sources include Greek and Norse mythology, Christianity, the fairy tale, the legend of King Arthur, and other tales of the knight-errant.

The main reason for the huge success of *The Lord of the Rings* is its magnificent story world, Middle Earth. The story plays out in a large but defined place with seemingly infinite subworlds. This gives the story two strengths: (1) unity and distinctiveness, and (2) diversity and additional subplots stemming from the subworlds.

The Wonderful Wizard of Oz (titled *The Wizard of Oz* in the film version) is primarily a Fantasy in which the heroine enters a magical world through a passageway and then returns home changed from the experience. But it is also a Female Myth.

We'll look at Female Myth in more detail when we talk about transcending the Myth form. By using *The Wizard of Oz* and *The Lord of the Rings* as we go through the Myth story beats, we can see specific ways these essential subgenres differ.

The Wizard of Oz is really two myths. The first, which takes place on a farm in the harsh black-and-white world of Kansas, hits all the basic Myth beats. Dorothy Gale has a weakness and a desire to go over the rainbow. She gets into a fight with Miss Gulch over her dog, Toto. She goes on a journey where she meets a traveling salesman and then returns home. After being sucked up in a cyclone, she enters the magical land of Oz and plays out a longer Myth. She goes on a journey where she kills a wicked witch and returns home.

This structure gives the story two arenas: Dorothy's farm in Kansas, and Oz, a land surrounded by the Deadly Desert.

KEY POINT: **A story world is the product of a unique combination of three major structural elements: land (natural settings), people (society, culture, and man-made spaces), and technology (tools).**

Step 2. Determine the World's Unique Interaction of Land, People, and Technology

The Lord of the Rings' combination of land-people-technology is a throwback to another age: King Arthur and the Middle Ages.

- **LAND:** lush nature, emphasizing forests, rivers, and mountains
- **MAN-MADE SPACES:** castles and villages
- **TECHNOLOGY:** animal and magical

The combination of land-people-technology in *The Wizard of Oz* is a hybrid of nineteenth-century American farms and cities with eighteenth-century European castles.

- **LAND:** the bare plains of Kansas, the Fighting Trees in Quadling Country, poppy fields, and mountains, all surrounded by desert
- **MAN-MADE SPACES:** Dorothy's farm, the village of

Munchkinland, the Wicked Witch's castle, and the Emerald City
- **TECHNOLOGY:** animal and magical

Step 3. Set Up the Value Oppositions of the Characters

KEY POINT: Any Myth or religion highlights what is most valued by a society. People don't just follow these values; they *worship* them.

Values come in clusters. Each cluster represents the culture of the society. Because story works through a conflict between the hero and opponents, the story world is almost always divided into two competing cultures. It expresses this through:

1. the opposing values of the characters, and, based on that,
2. the opposing subworlds, or visual contrasts.

Step 4. Create the Subworlds Based on These Value Oppositions

For writers who work in genres that emphasize the natural world and visual contrasts, this sequence of creating the story world is counterintuitive. They often assume one should begin with the visuals, the world, and then add the culture later. This is the biggest mistake a Myth writer can make.

KEY POINT: The characters do not exist in service of the world. The world exists in service of the characters and, more specifically, the values they fight over. This is the main way we connect world to characters.

The Myth story world sets up major subworlds based on nature. Islands, mountains, forests, jungles, rivers, deserts, ice, and oceans all have an inherent symbolic power. The writer can and should tap into this power when designing the subworlds. For a detailed explanation of the possible story meaning of these various subworlds, see chapter 6 of *The Anatomy of Story*.

If we push any society/story world to the extremes of freedom and slavery, we get utopia and dystopia. Before we see these important techniques applied to story, we need to talk about the concept behind them.

"Utopia" comes from the Greek, and means both "perfect" and "fleeting." Because it requires a careful balance of all the elements in the society, it can't be sustained for long. Dystopia is a society where the members are enslaved, a hell on earth that can last for a very long time.

Why is it useful to express a story world in terms of these two extremes? Because it takes the foundational principle of the social system to its logical conclusion. This allows the audience to see the elements of the system, their connections, and their effects on the characters.

How do you create utopia and dystopia? Again, we go back to the three major elements of a story world: land, people, and technology.

1. UTOPIA, ALSO KNOWN AS HEAVEN ON EARTH OR WORLD OF FREEDOM

If the three major elements of land, people, and technology are in balance or harmony, the result is a *community*. Here, individuals can grow in their own way, but also have the support of others to help them when they need it.

In story structure terms, utopia represents:

- Success in reaching the goal
- The fulfillment of the hero's greatest potential
- The hero's rise

In other words, Utopia is an expression of positive character change. It represents the height of character change where all individuals become the best versions of themselves.

2. DYSTOPIA, ALSO KNOWN AS HELL ON EARTH OR WORLD OF SLAVERY

If the land, people, and technology are out of balance, everyone is out for themselves. The result is what is known as a "state of nature," a harsh predatory world. Each person is reduced to an animal clawing for scarce resources or a cog working for a large machine.

In story structure terms, dystopia represents:

- The failure, perversion, or opposition of desire*
- The hero's or opponents' weaknesses
- The hero's decline or fall

The value/cultural opposition in *The Lord of the Rings* is based on the Christian value system emphasizing good versus evil, laid on top of a pantheistic faith in living things.

- **VALUES/Culture of the Good:** caring for living things and love. In this system, the highest love takes the form of sacrifice, especially of one's own life for another.
  vs.
- **VALUES/Culture of Evil:** love of power, dominating living things, and obsession with the Ring. The Ring symbolizes the desire for false values and absolute power: whoever owns it will become evil and corrupt.

The Lord of the Rings has three different versions of utopia. Each is a perfect balance of land, people, and tech-

---

* Northrop Frye, *Anatomy of Criticism.*

nology, and each is based on love, caring, and living things. These are:

1. The Shire, home of the Hobbits, which is a village embedded in a tamed, agricultural world
2. Rivendell, a utopia built around water and plants
3. Lothlorien, a beautiful, harmonic forest world

Examples of dystopian subworlds in *The Lord of the Rings* are the mountain fortresses of Mordor, Isengard, and Helm's Deep, all founded on raw power and metal. Another example is the underground caverns of Moria in the Misty Mountains where the heroes visit the "underworld."

The Wizard of Oz is based on a simple opposition between good and evil. Its definition of the good is more detailed than its definition of evil.

- **VALUES/Culture of the Good:** self-reliance, resourcefulness, imagination, brains, heart, and courage.
  vs.
- **VALUES/Culture of Evil:** love of power and domination over others.

The arena of Oz (in the novel) is divided into four subworlds: the lands of the Munchkins to the east, Quadlings to the south, Winkies to the west, and Gillikins to the north, with the Emerald City at the center. The Deadly Desert surrounds them, making it impossible for Oz to be invaded.

The Emerald City is a fake utopia, however. In the original book, it is green only because the Wizard makes the people wear green goggles. Everyone seems happy. In the film, workers happily restore the Scarecrow, Tin Woodsman, and Cowardly Lion after their arduous journey, all the while singing, "That's how we laugh the day away in the merry old land of Oz." They don't realize that their leader, the Wizard, is fake and unable to protect them from the real danger of the Wicked Witch of the West.

The Wicked Witch's castle represents dystopia. It is a dark prison ruled over by a sadistic witch. The terrifying Flying (or Winged) Monkeys are enslaved by the Wicked Witch and are set free when Dorothy kills her.

Step 5. Define the *Social System* That Organizes the Story World

Besides values, the story world is based on the hierarchy of power and the rules of operation. This is the deeper system that controls the world. The system determines how the individuals act toward one another as they try to be successful within the rules.

> **KEY POINT: The system is what traps the individual. The culture is how the system justifies itself, and convinces the individual to accept their place in it.**

In *The Lord of the Rings*, the Middle Earth system is organized by:

- **VALUES:** good versus evil, love versus power
- **LEVELS OF POWER OF DIFFERENT BEINGS:** god, wizard, human, and hobbit
- **VARIOUS SPECIES:** human, hobbit, elf, dwarf, orc (goblin), Ent, and ghost

The Wizard of Oz is organized by:

- **VALUES:** self-reliance, resourcefulness, imagination, brains, heart, and courage
- **LEVELS OF POWER:** witches, whether good or evil,

are most powerful; the Wizard of Oz has no magical power

- **VARIOUS SPECIES AND RACES:** good and bad witches, Munchkins, Flying Monkeys, a wide array of talking animals and other species, and animated objects like the Scarecrow and Tin Woodsman

Step 6. Define the Key Technology of the World and the Magic System on Which the Supernatural World Depends

Technology refers to the primary tools by which humans magnify their power over the world. The magic system defines how the supernatural elements of the story operate.

TECHNIQUE: Magic System

Be as specific as possible when answering these questions:

- What are the magic powers?
- Who has them?
- What are the limits to the powers?
- Can someone else get them and, if so, how?
- Are any powers limited to a location?
- Can the powers be terminated?

KEY POINT: The more magic power a character has, the less vulnerable they are to defeat and the less useful they are to you in the story.

The Lord of the Rings uses Middle Ages technology. Mass communication is by fire signals lit on mountaintops. The technology of war is highly detailed: the sword, the horse, and flying reptiles, which are the Middle Ages' magical equivalent of fighter planes. For artillery, attacking armies use trebuchets to catapult boulders at castle walls.

In *The Wizard of Oz*, the technology of magic comes primarily from wands and Dorothy's shoes. For the privileged few, travel is by hot-air balloon and broomstick. But most creatures walk.

Step 7. Determine the Overall Development of the World

KEY POINT: Because most stories go from slavery to freedom, begin by showing a world of slavery.

KEY POINT: The world of slavery is an expression of your hero's great weakness. This weakness mirrors the operating principle on which the entire system is based.

MYTH STORY BEAT: Ghost—Difficult Birth and Losing the Father

Many Myth stories begin with the birth of the hero. Joseph Campbell points out that it is usually a difficult birth, and soon thereafter, the (male) hero loses his father.

TECHNIQUE: Rebirth of the Hero

In more modern Myth stories, the writer often begins with the *rebirth* of the hero.

Why? First, it allows the writer to avoid the slow childhood period that delays the onset of the hero's desire line. As a result, the story has a much quicker start. We see the early rebirth of the hero in *Avatar*, *Batman Begins*, and the Science Fiction/Myth story *The Matrix*.

MYTH STORY BEAT: Character Web—the Great Chain of Being

Myth is founded on the longest life process in story. It takes two main forms. The first is the hero's journey from birth to death to rebirth.

The second is much grander. It represents the hierarchy of beings in the world. This is known as the Great Chain of Being, a profound and influential typology of the world that goes back primarily to Aristotle, who could be considered the first biologist. From material objects to god, the sequence in the Great Chain of Being is founded on a movement from entities of matter to entities of "spirit."

The Great Chain of Being: Sequence of Types of Being

The Great Chain of Being is really a map of how the human mind creates the outside world through character types.

> **KEY POINT: The Great Chain of Being is still *the* technique for creating a compelling story world in the major world-building genres such as Myth, Fantasy, and even Science Fiction.**

The Great Chain of Being is a hierarchy by which all "characters" in the world relate and differentiate themselves:

1. Gods
2. Angels
3. Demons
4. Superheroes
5. Heroes
6. Kings and Queens
7. Nobles

8. Commoners
9. Animals
10. Plants
11. Minerals
12. Nonbeing

Notice that this hierarchy of beings has physical entities, different major life-forms, humans at different levels of power in the society, and natural and supernatural characters.

The Great Chain of Being is the opposite of democracy, in which all humans are created equal, and especially from what we would call "ecological democracy," where all beings coexist.

The Great Chain of Being is also a social fractal that applies at every level of society and individual.

To create the character web in a Myth story, you must design *your* version of the Great Chain of Being.

Caution: An original Myth story doesn't require all the character types found in the Chain. But it does require a character web with a detailed hierarchy that places humans within the natural world.

TECHNIQUE: Connecting the Great Chain to Society

Once you create your own character web based on the Great Chain of Being—divine, human, animal, vegetable, mineral—connect it with a society that is either heaven or hell, utopia or dystopia.

MYTH STORY BEAT: Character Web—Archetypes

The Myth story form deals in broad types of characters, known as archetypes. Archetypes are defined by their psychological flaws and social roles. They represent a fundamental *way* of being, as well as a *level* of being.

An individual character that expresses one of these types

has a *primary trait* and way of living that audiences around the world immediately recognize.

KEY POINT: Each archetype has an essential strength that defines him or her, but also a "shadow." The shadow is the deep weakness inherent to that character's basic role in society.

The weakness-need of a particular Myth hero is largely based on the archetype he/she embodies.

Let's look at the strengths and weaknesses of just a few of the major archetypes:

1. Warrior

- Strength: the warrior is the practical enforcer of what is right.
- Weakness: he/she believes in the ethic "kill or be killed," and whatever is weak must be destroyed.

Examples are Hercules, Achilles and Hector in the *Iliad*, Luke Skywalker and Han Solo in *Star Wars*, *Seven Samurai*, King Arthur, Thor, Ares, Theseus, Katniss Everdeen in *The Hunger Games*, Wonder Woman, Gilgamesh, and Aragorn, Legolas, and Gimli in *The Lord of the Rings*.

2. Searcher

The searcher looks for an object of true value. At the highest level, the hero seeks truth to achieve justice.

- Strength: the searcher is committed to questioning and self-improvement.
- Weakness: he/she can be purposeless and uncommitted.

Examples are knights seeking the Holy Grail, Jason searching for the Golden Fleece, and the detective.

3. Teacher

- Strength: the teacher spreads knowledge so people can live better lives and society can improve.
- Weakness: he/she can force students to think a certain way or glorify himself or herself rather than his or her teachings.

Examples are *Dead Poets Society*, *Goodbye Mr. Chips*, Yoda, Mary Poppins, Howard Beale in *Network*, and Hannibal Lecter in *The Silence of the Lambs*.

4. Rebel

- Strength: the rebel takes action against a system that is enslaving people.
- Weakness: he/she often does not provide a better alternative. The rebel is usually heroic but negative.

Examples are Prometheus, Loki, Neo in *The Matrix*, Heathcliff in *Wuthering Heights*, *American Beauty*, Holden Caulfield in *The Catcher in the Rye*, and Tris in *Divergent*.

5. Trickster

The trickster is the most popular of all archetypes because the audience loves to see him scam the powerful.

- Strength: the trickster attacks the oppressive system and defeats the unjust people in power.
- Weakness: this character lies, cheats, and steals to get what he/she wants.

Examples are Odysseus, who is a trickster twist on the warrior archetype, Hermes, Merlin, *Beverly Hills Cop*, Verbal in *The Usual Suspects*, the Joker in *The Dark Knight*, *Men in Black*, Ferris Bueller, and Hannibal Lecter, the trickster teacher, in *The Silence of the Lambs*.

The Lord of the Rings is a unique classic Myth in that it has two heroes, and each twists a basic archetype.

1. Hobbit Frodo Baggins: Frodo is not the powerful warrior, but the little "man." He is heroic because of his greatness of heart and determination in the face of unbelievable odds. His weaknesses: he is small, frail, afraid, and lacks confidence.
2. Aragorn, also known as Strider: Aragorn is the dispossessed warrior-king. His weakness is that he does not believe he deserves to be king.

This vast trilogy is based on a crosscut story structure between Frodo's quest to return the ring to the fires of Mount Doom and Aragorn's quest to regain his rightful place as king.

The character web is the first major story area where *The Wizard of Oz* takes up the mantle of the Female Myth. Oz is a land of women.

The main character, Dorothy Gale, is an orphan girl of twelve. She is undaunted by the obstacles of her young life, and she does not timidly cling to home. She is above all a resourceful girl who solves problems whenever they arise. The farm world is also dominated by females, with Auntie Em running the farm and Miss Gulch (the town mayor in the book) as the opponent who wants to kill Dorothy's dog, Toto.

Another distinctive feature that makes *The Wizard of Oz* a Female Myth is the presence of good witches as well as evil ones. Throughout history, "witches" have been an expression of women's knowledge and power, and they have been burned at the stake because of it. By introducing the idea of a good witch and making Glinda the most positive and powerful character in the story, the writer L. Frank Baum celebrates female power.

In addition, the rightful ruler of Oz in the later series of Oz books is the fairy Princess Ozma.

MYTH STORY BEAT: Myth Hero—Searcher

The basic role of the hero in Myth is the same as the hero's role in the Detective genre: the searcher. But what each hero searches for is quite different. In Detective, the hero searches for the truth, usually about who committed a murder.

In Myth, a hero like Jason may search for the Golden Fleece. Odysseus searches for home. In the process of that search he finds the meaning in his own life.

> **KEY POINT: The Myth hero's search almost always takes him on a dangerous physical journey in which he must *fight his way through* the world.**

MYTH STORY BEAT: Weakness-Need

The weakness-need of the Myth hero is often based on one of the early beats in the Myth form: the loss of the father. When the father either dies or disappears, the hero tries to live up to the expectations of an ideal father. In other words, the hero needs to *become* a hero.

> **KEY POINT: Becoming a hero is a need, not a specific, conscious desire.**

In *The Wizard of Oz*, Dorothy has a run-in with Miss Gulch because her dog, Toto, got into Miss Gulch's garden. But when Dorothy complains about it to her Aunt Em and Uncle Henry they are too busy to help her. She thinks her family doesn't care about her and she wants to run away. Her true need is to find her way home so she can love and care for her family.

MYTH STORY BEAT: Inciting Event—Talisman

The inciting event is the story beat between weakness-need and desire. It causes the hero to come up with a goal and start taking action to reach it.

In Myth, this is typically the moment when the hero gains a talisman. A talisman is an object of power or significance.

The talisman has two essential features:

1. No one, including the hero, knows the true power of this object.
2. It is the physical expression of some major aspect of the hero's identity.

The talisman prompts the hero's first inkling of self-definition. The hero will gain a much deeper self-awareness of this at the end of the story.

For the classic male Myth hero, the talisman is often a sword, an enforcer of right action. Examples include Excalibur, the sword of King Arthur, and Anduril, Flame of the West, from *The Lord of the Rings*. Only the rightful heir to the throne can wield Anduril. Whereas Excalibur is stuck in stone, Anduril is broken and must be reforged.

When the cyclone takes Dorothy from Kansas to another world in *The Wizard of Oz*, she begins a new Myth story in Oz. In the scene with the Munchkins, Dorothy encounters a number of critical Myth story beats. These include questions of her identity; the kind helper/teacher, Glinda; the main opponent, the Wicked Witch of the West; her talisman; and her new desire, plan, and journey.

Dorothy's talisman is not the classic male symbol of the sword. It is the magical ruby slippers (silver shoes in the novel), and their true power is unknown. When the Wicked

Witch demands that Dorothy give them to her, Glinda tells her, "Their magic must be very powerful or she wouldn't want them so badly."

MYTH STORY BEAT: Desire—Journey and Destiny

The desire line of the hero determines the spine of the story.

TECHNIQUE: External = Internal Journey

Make the hero's physical journey a physical manifestation of his internal journey.

In a Myth story, the hero's goal is deeply embedded within him:

- It is what he was born to do; this is his destiny. In this way, the outside goal is connected to the hero's internal need.
- It is any goal that forces the hero to go on a journey ultimately leading to himself.

This is why the Myth genre is so often circular in form: the hero eventually returns home where he discovers what has always been deep within him. Hence the central irony of the Myth story: that the hero must go on a long, physical journey to uncover the qualities he has possessed all along.

TECHNIQUE: The Journey's End Point

Have a specific end point for the journey. Otherwise the story meanders and the audience becomes bored.

Frodo's desire in *The Lord of the Rings* is to throw the ring into the fires of Mount Doom.

When *The Wizard of Oz* begins, Dorothy wants to leave her troubles in Kansas behind and go "over the rainbow." This desire is expressed beautifully in the first song, "Over the

Rainbow," voted the best song of the twentieth century (and originally excluded from the film due to pacing).*

Once Dorothy is over the rainbow, she quickly decides, "I want to go home." This goal drives the rest of the story. The plan, which Glinda provides, is to ask the wise Wizard of Oz *how* she can get home. Dorothy must take the hard journey down the Yellow Brick Road if she is to solve her problem and reach her goal.

Visual Shape of the Myth Plot: Meander

The most common plot shape used in the classic Myth form is the "meander." A meander is a winding path without apparent direction. Structurally, this shape has one hero, an easygoing narrative line, and many opponents the hero meets in succession. The meander story looks like this:

The meandering Myth hero covers a great deal of territory but in a haphazard way.

> **KEY POINT: Plot comes from encountering new opponents at different levels of society. This allows the writer to capture an entire world.**

---

* Joint survey by the National Endowment for the Arts and the Recording Industry Association of America, 2001.

Examples include the *Odyssey*, *The Lord of the Rings*, *The Wonderful Wizard of Oz*, *Frozen*, *Don Quixote*, *Tom Jones* (also Comedy), *The Princess Bride* (also Comedy), *Toy Story* (also Comedy), and some of the *Harry Potter* stories (also Fantasy, Horror, and Comedy).

MYTH STORY BEAT: Allies

The ally in Myth can be anyone. Often, one of the allies takes the form of the Wise Old Man or Wise Old Woman. This is the Teacher archetype.

In *The Lord of the Rings*, Samwise "Sam" Gamgee is Frodo's primary ally in his quest to return the ring to the fires of Mount Doom. Frodo's second major ally is Gandalf the Grey, the wise old wizard.

Other allies include the Hobbits Merry and Pippin, Aragorn (who is also the second hero), Legolas the Elf, Gimli the Dwarf, and Boromir.

The unique nature of the allies is another element that makes *The Wizard of Oz* a Female Myth. Dorothy is radically different than the male warrior hero of the Male Myth. So are her three male allies: the Scarecrow, Tin Woodsman, and Cowardly Lion.

Like Dorothy, the allies must go on a long, difficult journey to realize what they always had within them. Scarecrow wants a brain. But he is the most capable problem-solver in the group. Tin Woodsman wants a heart. But he is the sweetest person in the story. Cowardly Lion is cowardly, but he does accompany Dorothy on her dangerous trip to the Witch's lair.

Collecting the allies is the best beat in this film. All three allies sing the same melody to express what they think is missing from their character.

Glinda, the good witch, represents the Wise Old Woman/Teacher archetype. She starts Dorothy on her journey when she suggests she seek help from the Wizard of Oz. Given that the wizard is a fake, this is not the wisest advice. Since Dorothy didn't bring her broom, Glinda tells her she has to walk. This too is suspect. At the end Glinda tells Dorothy she always had the power to get home simply by clicking her heels together.

Another major story element that makes this a Female Myth is that Dorothy's most powerful male ally, the Wizard, is a "humbug." But he is not evil, nor is he useless to her or to Oz. By requiring Dorothy to bring back the Witch's broom, he gives her a test that proves her worthiness to herself and others.

When Dorothy returns to the Wizard with the Witch's broomstick, Toto exposes him as a fraud behind a curtain. Dorothy says, "You're a very bad man." He responds, "No, I'm a very bad wizard." In spite of his lies, the Wizard has fulfilled the people's need for a savior. He feels that if you believe something is true, it is.

MYTH STORY BEAT: Opponent—Successive Strangers

Due to the journey form common to this genre, the Myth opponents tend to be strangers who appear in succession.

This fact poses the biggest challenge in designing the plot. The sequence of unfamiliar opponents the hero fights results in an episodic structure. Individual scenes stand out but do not connect to or build on one another.

This is also known as "hitting the same beat." Actions appear to be different on the surface but are essentially the same. The plot is simply a series of fights against opponents who differ only in the way they attack the hero.

TECHNIQUE: The Opponent and Self-Revelation

Each opponent should represent an aspect of what the hero must overcome *in himself*. Therefore, each time the hero defeats an opponent, he may have a minor self-revelation.

The best example of this technique may be the knight-errant seeking the Holy Grail. As Erich Auerbach says in his seminal work on fiction, *Mimesis*, "Perils present themselves to the knight as if from the end of an assembly line."

KEY POINT: In Myth, nothing is a matter of chance. Each opponent serves the purpose of challenging the hero at his weakest point.

The Wizard of Oz doesn't have the usual challenge of a succession of unfamiliar opponents. The main opponent is the Wicked Witch. The problem is that she bookends Dorothy's journey through Oz. After their initial confrontation, Dorothy doesn't come into real conflict with her until the end. The writers overcome this problem to some degree by having the Witch threaten her several times over the course of Dorothy's journey.

BEST OPPONENT TECHNIQUE: Family Trip

To overcome the episodic nature of the Myth story structure, consider having the hero take the family along for the ride.

This is a technique from drama, in which the opponents are usually family members. Bringing the family along on the quest gives the story *ongoing*, *intimate* opponents—the family members—along with the episodic opponents the hero fights along the way. The result is a density of conflict and a story that builds to a climax.

Little Miss Sunshine is a Comic Myth that uses this technique to perfection. Olive wants to win the Little Miss Sunshine beauty pageant. She takes a long journey to the pageant accompanied by her family. Her main opponent is her father, a success guru who pressures his young daughter with unrealistic standards.

TECHNIQUE: The Ongoing Main Opponent

Try to have at least one opponent present throughout the story, and make that the main opponent.

A good story needs one main opponent the audience gets to know over the course of the story to build the drama. The more personal this character's relationship to the hero, the better the story will be.

MYTH STORY BEAT: Drive—Symbolic Objects

Myth, along with Horror, is the most symbolic of all genres. This is expressed by the drive beat, where the hero takes actions to reach the goal. In the process of opposing characters and objects with symbolic value while trying to reach the goal, the hero is forced to undergo a transformation of heart and mind.

> **KEY POINT: External symbols always mean something *within* the hero. Like religion, Myth uses metaphors: symbols with an established meaning.**

Here are just a few of the classic symbols found in Myth stories:

Symbolic Characters

- **ANIMALS SUCH AS HORSE, BIRD, SNAKE:** models on the path to enlightenment or hell
- **MACHINE:** superhuman, efficient but without heart and creativity
- **DEVIL:** the anti-God or Antichrist, representing the temptation of sin and the worst in humankind

Symbolic Paths

- **THE JOURNEY:** the life path and the life span

- **LABYRINTH:**
  - the belly of the beast, or death
  - confusion and crisis en route to the path to enlightenment
- **LADDER:** stages to enlightenment

Symbolic Objects

- **TREE:** of life and knowledge
- **CROSS:** the tree on which humanity is reborn
- **SHADOW:** the dark side, the great flaw that is profound, but potentially the source of growth. This positive meaning is often forgotten when we think of the shadow.
- **TALISMANS LIKE SWORD, BOW, SHIELD, CLOAK, SEED OF THE SACRED TREE:** right action
- **MODERN SYMBOLIC OBJECT:** Proust's madeleine cake = the Eucharist

Symbolic Places

- **UNDERWORLD:** death and the unexplored region of the self
- **GARDEN:** being at one with the natural law, harmony within oneself and with others

KEY POINT: Even with these highly metaphorical symbols, their meaning is not fixed. Symbols are always ambiguous to some degree and ultimately depend on the reader and, especially, the context in which the symbol is used.

MYTH STORY BEAT: Revelation—Opponents Attack

Over the course of the journey, the hero encounters opponents who attack in different ways. The hero has a revelation about each opponent's method of attack and comes up with unique plans to win.

Occasionally, the hero has a mini self-revelation about his own capabilities after he has defeated the opponent.

MYTH STORY BEAT: Gate, Gauntlet, Visit to the Underworld

On the journey, the hero finds his way into the underworld, the land of the dead. He sees his ancestors as well as his own future. He recognizes part of his self that is not examined. He is reminded to act during his limited time on earth and makes a narrow escape.

In *The Wizard of Oz*, Dorothy and her allies "run the gauntlet" when they must walk down a long hallway to ask the terrifying Wizard for help.

Dorothy's visit to death is also her apparent defeat. After the witch imprisons Dorothy in her castle, she flips an hourglass and says, "That's how much longer you've got to be alive."

MYTH STORY BEAT: Violent Battle

At the end of the journey, the male warrior hero enters into a big, bloody final battle. The stakes are epic. He defeats his greatest opponent, but he may also die in the process.

The *Iliad* is an Action Epic story with major Myth elements. The final battle is between the two greatest warriors on the field: the Greek, Achilles, against the Trojan, Hector. Achilles kills Hector and drags his body behind his chariot.

The final battle of *Avatar* begins with Colonel Quaritch leading a fleet of gunships to bomb the Tree of Souls. Jake on his toruk, along with his Na'vi allies on banshees, fight back. Jake blows up the Colonel's gunship. The Colonel puts on the mechanical AMP suit and shoots Neytiri's banshee, which pins her to the ground. As he moves in for the kill, Jake engages him in hand-to-hand combat. The Colonel grabs him by the hair and is about to cut his throat. Neytiri frees herself and shoots an arrow that kills the Colonel.

The battle step is another story beat that makes *The Wizard of Oz* a Female Myth. Twelve-year-old Dorothy doesn't wield a sword in a fierce violent battle with her nemesis. There is no battle at all. She and her friends try to run away, but they are quickly cornered by the Witch's troops. When the Witch sadistically makes Dorothy watch as she sets the Scarecrow on fire, Dorothy throws a bucket of water that accidentally soaks the Witch. Water is the Witch's Achilles' heel, and she dissolves into a pile of clothes.

One quibble: If I were someone who could die from contact with water, I wouldn't have a bucket of water within ten miles of my castle.

MYTH STORY BEAT: Self-Revelation—Public/Cosmic Revelation

At the end of the battle the hero has a major self-revelation in which he realizes what he was born to do and that he always possessed the necessary abilities.

The hero's self-revelation in Myth is not just personal. It takes two forms:

1. It is often a public revelation in which he learns that he is a king. The deeper import of this revelation is that the hero now understands he has a special responsibility to lead the community. The health of the kingdom depends on the quality of the king. Joseph Campbell refers to this step as the "Boon to Society." Shakespeare demonstrates it in his Epic Myth/Dramas like *Hamlet*.

2. At this point, the hero may also have a cosmic revelation. He gains a moral vision, or epiphany, of how an entire society should exist in the world. This kind of revelation must be detailed to have any meaning to the audience.

When the hero is also the "Chosen One," this is the moment when he fulfills his destiny and takes on the role for which he has been groomed. Examples include Moses, Jesus, King Arthur, Paul Atreides, Luke Skywalker, Neo, Jake Sully, and Harry Potter.

When the hero fails to make this character change and fulfill his duty, the hero, the society, and sometimes humankind itself falls. Examples include Adam (Genesis) and Anakin Skywalker (*Star Wars*).

Hollywood is the perfect system for portraying the Chosen One. Since its inception, it has been based on the hierarchical star system. Therefore, the biggest star = the Chosen One. Thematically, its stories were like the great man theory of history: only the godlike Chosen One could solve the problem. In effect, we watch the Chosen One play the Chosen One.

We also find the godlike Chosen One in Science Fiction stories that portray a monarchical political system. *Star Wars* and *Dune* are prominent examples.

In Exodus, in the Old Testament, Moses goes to the mountaintop and receives the cosmic moral vision of the Ten Commandments. Another example is Jesus's Sermon on the Mount, which expresses the Christian moral code in what is known as the Beatitudes, Matthew 5:3–12. Examples include "Blessed are the poor in spirit, for theirs is the kingdom of Heaven," and "Blessed are the meek, for they will inherit the earth."

In *Avatar*, Jake has a public revelation when he realizes he must appeal to all of the Na'vi clans. They must join in the fight against the humans who are trying to destroy their way of life. He has his cosmic revelation when he joins and communicates with the spirit of Eywa at the Tree of Souls.

TECHNIQUE: The Mythic vs. the Tragic Ending

Myth is an earlier story form than Tragedy, which is the highest expression of Drama. Drama is too broad to be considered a genre, but it is a story form. Myth and Tragedy differ particularly in how they end.

Myth involves the *immortality* of the hero, even if it's only from telling the story (*Epic of Gilgamesh*).

Tragedy involves cutting off life too early, with *no rebirth* of the hero, and only the bittersweet sense of what might have been. The hero may have a self-revelation, but it comes too late.

MYTH STORY BEAT: New Equilibrium—Outgrow the Code

The hero returns home and is profoundly changed by his experience. Often he marries or remarries. The *Odyssey* is the textbook example of the remarriage of the hero.

Instead of changing the beliefs of the code he has lived by, the hero has outgrown the code entirely. He is reborn, spiritually and often literally.

In his spiritual rebirth:

- He sees the world and acts in a new way.
- He is in tune with his destiny and the larger forces of nature.

In *The Wizard of Oz*, Dorothy completes the classic Myth circle when she finds herself back home, re-creating the community. She has fulfilled her need to appreciate her family. She is ecstatic to be back with her aunt and uncle and her family of friends. Her self-revelation is strictly personal: "There's no place like home."

In the film, Dorothy discovers that it was all a dream. In the novel, her journey was real and she will return many more times to Oz in later books.

Theme: Being Is Self-Questioning and a Search for My Destiny

In its simplest form, Myth is the story of an action hero who goes on a long quest to find himself and live forever. Therefore, in Myth, being is not about simply taking action. It is about creating one's self and one's life.

As a result, being means constantly questioning oneself, especially about the morality of one's actions. These actions affect others in the social order. Self-questioning even means attacking oneself to get at the truth of how to become who one really is. This is not just a momentary pursuit, but a lifelong existential quest.

> **KEY POINT: Becoming who you are isn't just a passive activity of "be yourself." It is the most active, difficult work we will ever do.**

The day-to-day experience of being is also a search for one's destiny. Myth defines destiny as what someone was born to do. This appears to involve fate or divine intervention. But destiny comes from within, from one's own abilities. The problem is that one is never fully aware, or often even remotely aware, of what one's true capabilities are.

Myth, more than any other genre, is focused on the idea that being is becoming. Being is the tactics of the present. What we want to become makes up our strategic vision. These are the broad views that really determine our success as human beings.

KEY POINT: Myth also says that being is in constant conflict with becoming and must be reconciled.

The "Being Mind," caught up in the day-to-day, doesn't want to think about its own end. As the German philosopher Hans Vaihinger said, we act "as if" we will not die.* This appears to be a useful tool for our survival. We can concentrate on what is needed to eat and work and mate. But it is not a tool for *good* survival, for living life well.

Myth Thematic Recipe: The Way of the Searcher

A genre's thematic recipe for the "good life" comes primarily from the hero's basic action and the form's key question. Since Myth says that being is becoming, the Myth recipe is "being" broken down into detailed steps of action.

The Myth hero's basic action is to seek. He usually has a specific goal at the end of the journey. But the real question he wants to answer is: What is my destiny? What was I born to do with my life?

Myth says if you can find that and do it, you will have a good life and gain some form of immortality. This becomes clear only at the end point of the hero's desire line. There he replaces his first and main goal with his true goal, to know his destiny in life. Therefore, destiny is life's version of immortality.

As mentioned, immortality is the central theme of the Myth form. This is made physical through the plot: birth, the hero's actions in life, death of the old self, and rebirth. But it is also shown in new action the hero takes after the self-revelation.

---

* *The Philosophy of "As If"*, 1924.

A second part of the Myth recipe for a good life comes from finding our place in the natural order. In this sense, Myth has an ecological, holistic Story Code. Living an enlightened life is living in cosmic harmony. This is not some esoteric notion of becoming a god. It involves the hard work of getting away from our overwhelming subjectivity, seeing how all the elements of the world depend on one another, and then acting in a way that doesn't place our own ambition above the lives of others.

How to Transcend the Myth Story

Most Myth stories track the development of the self. Transcendent Myths also track the creation and development of a culture, the worldwide "zeitgeist" (spirit of the time), and what Hegel called the "Universal Mind."

Transcendent Myth takes three major forms:

1. **CREATION MYTHS AND THE MYTH/SCIENCE FICTION EPIC**
   Examples include *The Lord of the Rings*, *The Dark Knight* (also Crime and Fantasy), Genesis in the Old Testament, the first four books of the New Testament, the *Aeneid*, the *Foundation* series (also Science Fiction), *2001: A Space Odyssey* (also Science Fiction), the Declaration of Independence, the American Constitution, and *Ægypt* and *Ka*
2. **THE FEMALE MYTH**
   Examples include *The Wonderful Wizard of Oz* (also Fantasy), *Inside Out*, *Avatar*, *The Piano*, *Gravity*, and *Arrival*.
3. **THE ECOLOGICAL MYTH**
   Examples include the legend of John Henry, *Avatar* (also Female Myth), *The Magnificent Ambersons*, *Days of Heaven*, *The New World*, *Tree of Life* (also a Personal Myth), *How Green Was My Valley*, *McCabe & Mrs. Miller*, *Citizen Kane*, *The Wild Bunch*, *The Last Picture Show*,

Cinema Paradiso, *Seven Samurai* (also Action Epic), *The Apu Trilogy*, *Dances with Wolves*, the novels of Thomas Hardy, *Emerald Forest*, *Gorillas in the Mist*, *Out of Africa*, and *Mosquito Coast*.

Transcending Myth 1: The Myth/Science Fiction Epic

The most ambitious transcendent Myth stories are those that track the development of a culture and its ideas. These include creation and origin myths, the Great Chain of Being, Hegel's *Phenomenology of the Spirit*, and the science of evolution. Modern versions of transcendent Myth stories usually combine Myth and Science Fiction.

Stories of Grand Change

Myth is the first Story Code to explain change in the world. It is impossible to exaggerate the importance of this idea. It's been said that philosophy is divided into those for whom history matters and those for whom it doesn't. Philosophy in which history matters is known as process philosophy. This essentially states that being is always becoming; life is change.

Heraclitus, Aristotle, the Myth genre, Hegel's *Phenomenology*, Darwin's *On the Origin of Species*, Nietzsche's *On the Genealogy of Morals*, and Heidegger's *Being and Time* are all "stories" that describe the stages of and the mechanism for individual, type (like species), and cultural development.

Great Chain of Being and Creation Myth vs. Hegel's Phenomenology vs. Evolution

> **KEY POINT: Generally, the history of consciousness is a movement from artistic stories to scientific stories.**

The shift from the Great Chain of Being and Creation Myths to the science of evolution demonstrates the way the mind understands the relation of living things to the world.

We usually think of art (story) and science as opposites. Nothing could be farther from the truth. Story and theory are closely related. A scientific theory is a story that can be tested.

Let's see how the two "stories," the Great Chain of Being and evolution, differ.

The Great Chain of Being is an artistic story. It is a hierarchy of beings, both living and nonliving, in the natural and supernatural world, from entities of matter to entities of highest "spirit." It shows entities existing simultaneously, on a scale of inferiority/superiority.

Evolution is a scientific story. It is a process of becoming having to do with species of life. It tracks types of living things adapting and diversifying, becoming more complex and self-conscious over time.

Each is a story view of how the world works. One is a purely artistic projection. The other is a verifiable explanation of how change among types of beings occurs.

Both of these story views are as valuable today as they were when first created. But the great insight we gain in moving from the Great Chain of Being to evolution is that the human mind's focus has moved from "Being Consciousness" to "Process Consciousness." Being Consciousness has not disappeared. It has been expanded in scope and depth. Process Consciousness explains what it means to be *over time*.

Phenomenology of the Spirit: The Story of the Development of the Universal Mind

The intellectual system that serves as this important transition between art and science is Hegel's *Phenomenology of the Spirit* (also translated as *Phenomenology of the Mind*).

KEY POINT: Hegel's *Phenomenology* charts the history and growth of the human mind. It applies the artistic process to the mind itself.

Hegel's development of the mind comes before Darwin's *On the Origin of Species*. Hegel tracks the long and painful process by which the Universal Mind, or "spirit," moves from the most basic sensation to what he considers the mind's highest expressions: art, religion, and philosophy.

This mechanism of change, which Hegel calls the dialectical method, is opposition. The human tendency to binary thinking leads eventually to diversity and complexity.

KEY POINT: This sequence of opposing ideas constitutes the phases of the mind's growing self-awareness.

In the move from Being Consciousness to Process Consciousness, Hegel adds to the thinking of the world's first biologist, Aristotle, to show how different story views on the best way to live build on one another.

Creation Myths: The Big Becoming of Culture

The first kind of transcendent Myth is the Creation Myth. This story form is the history of a particular culture and of how the parts fit together to make up the whole. It lays out a set of values that the society believes will lead to a good life for all.

KEY POINT: A Creation Myth is not the story of creating the physical world. It is about creating consciousness and culture.

Creation Myths begin by naming the foundation's parts. "God created the heavens and the earth . . ." and Man ate from the tree of Knowledge. Or from the Sumerian *Epic of Gilgamesh*, "When the earth had been separated from the heavens . . ."

Once the mind makes distinctions with names, self-consciousness is possible. This means we can see the Other, not just out there, but in ourselves. Only then can we create a set of values by which to live, creating a tribe of "us."

After the tribe of "us" has been created, the next step is to focus on the family, the first society. Society is the structure by which people are organized. Culture is composed of the ideas by which the society operates.

The challenges facing the family as the first society are powerfully expressed in the Old Testament story of Adam and Eve and their children Cain and Abel, from Genesis 2:4–3:24 and 4:1–16. The fact that this is also the first nuclear family, expressing the four-point opposition, the main rule of creating society in story, means that the challenges it highlights are primal.

The first challenge facing any couple is faithfulness. Can they remain true to each other, and therefore remain a couple? Inevitably an attractive Other will appear. Does one maintain the old community or create a new one? In other words, can the community last?

An Other does not confront Eve in the traditional way. She is seduced by a different way of life. The most shocking revelation when reading Adam and Eve is that the faithfulness Eve is expected to keep is not to her husband. It is to her Father. Her community and Father promise Eve a life without need, want, or death. They also promise a life without knowledge of good and evil.

God warns Adam and Eve not to eat from the tree. But because Eve is without knowledge, she does not know what she will lose if she breaks her community with God. This is why Eve's punishment is so unfair. When exiled from the Garden,

Adam and Eve remain husband and wife. But now they must live in toil and the certainty of death. In addition, Eve has to live with terrible recriminations from her husband.

The Adam and Eve story is the first sign that the Old Testament is a collection of male myths where women are second-class citizens. With the exile of the first couple, the story of Adam and Eve also moves from a *Paradise Lost*–Horror story to a Crime story. The original sin of the parents is visited upon the children. They too must suffer from a crime they did not commit, until one son kills the other. There is neither mercy nor justice in this society.

In a fundamental, nonreligious way, that is the hard truth of all families. The parents have flaws that will inflict pain on the children. Physically, the parents may have certain genetic markers they pass on to the children. The binary mind of the human being means that the children will always react in alliance with or in opposition to the parents.

The power of the Old Testament's Genesis story is not in its Creation Myth, and obviously not in its scientific validity. Its power comes from the way it turns the deep psychology between husband and wife, parent and child, and sibling versus sibling into stories with devastating emotional impact.

King Arthur and the Knights of the Round Table: Creation Myth of a Republic

After creating a community of two, followed by a family of four, the next step is to create a community of citizens. *King Arthur and the Knights of the Round Table* tells the modern story of the transition from monarchy to democracy. Twelve of the greatest knights in the land sit as near equals around a circular table with their king. With the king's leadership, they decide the fate of the nation. The Round Table and Arthur's utopian capital of Camelot originated from the French version of the legend. But one could argue that this story was the precursor of the English Magna Carta in 1215, considered the first step toward modern representative government.

KEY POINT: While the Western is the Creation Myth of the United States, *King Arthur and the Knights of the Round Table* is the true Creation Myth of England and the modern republic.

The Origin Story

An Origin Story is different from a Creation Myth. An Origin Story tracks the beginning of a particular character while a Creation Myth tracks the beginning of an entire world and culture.

The Origin Story is often the most popular in a story series. It allows the audience to share in the birth of the mythology and it has a shape that sequels often lack.

KEY POINT: By tracking the formation of the hero, the Origin Story expresses the single most important technique of good storytelling: creating plot from character.

Origin Stories give the author a built-in way of executing this rule right from the basic premise. This gives the audience a double pleasure. They get to see the hero succeed in the plot. And they get to see the hero grow as a human being.

Examples of the Origin Story are *Epic of Gilgamesh*, *Black Panther*, *Batman Begins*, *Guardians of the Galaxy*, *Casino Royale*, *X-Men*, *X-Men Origins: Wolverine*, *The Incredible Hulk*, and *Fantastic Four*.

Black Panther is a landmark film because it is the Origin Story of both a Black superhero, Black Panther, and the Creation Story of a technologically advanced African nation, Wakanda.

KEY POINT: The success of this Origin Story comes from matching the moral growth of the hero and the nation.

Thousands of years ago, a warrior gained superhuman power when he ate an herb infused with the metal "vibranium." As the first Black Panther, he united four of five warring tribes to form Wakanda. Over time, the Wakandans have used their unique mineral resource to create a technologically advanced nation. But they have made it appear to be part of the Third World to prevent European colonization and theft of their natural resources. Unfortunately, this deprives others of African descent from benefiting from Wakandan technology.

Like many Myth heroes, T'Challa must earn his right to be king. He does this through ritual hand-to-hand combat. The first time he is challenged he wins and becomes king. The second time he loses to the main opponent, "Killmonger," an African American ex–Navy SEAL.

The hero's struggle in the story is to prevent the theft of vibranium and Wakandan weaponry. T'Challa's flaw is that he accepts the policy of keeping Wakanda secret from the world. In the final battle in the vibranium mine, T'Challa, now Black Panther, defeats Killmonger. He then has a moral self-revelation in which he commits to building an outreach center in the inner city in America. He also has a cosmic revelation about the need to use Wakandan knowledge to help the world. In a speech at the United Nations he reveals Wakanda's true identity.

Origin of Machine Superheroes

Modern origin stories tend to focus on the marriage between human and machine.

The first machine superhero and man of steel is the knight.

Wrapped in armor and sitting atop a powerful steed, the knight fights evil and protects the weak. He seeks enlightenment—saving himself—by searching for the Holy Grail, which is the cup that held Christ's blood.

Not surprisingly, the first modern god and machine superhero, Superman, is the thinnest of all superhero characters. He's a throwback to a simple Action story in which the hero is a paragon of virtue, devoid of character flaws. His weakness, kryptonite, is strictly a physical flaw. But he is also the first complex superhero in that he is both strong and weak. He is the galactic alien, the Other from another world. He creates a double of himself, alter ego Clark Kent, to hide his true identity so he can do his "godly" work and have a normal personal life. Apparently, no one can spot the similarity because his glasses cover so much of his face.

A more recent version of the machine superhero is Iron Man, a normal man encased in machinery who has the physical abilities of Superman. *Iron Man*'s Tony Stark is a genius inventor and rich philanthropist who tries to defeat evil and save the world in multiple ways.

Over time, superhero gods have taken on the deeper flaws and complexity found in transcendent storytelling. These characters have moral as well as psychological flaws. For example, the Hulk cannot control his rage, Thor is arrogant, and Tony Stark is a raving narcissist. As in any good story, the plots always play out the character's internal flaws.

Evolution and the Myth/Science Fiction Epic

The Myth/Science Fiction Epic provides a story form for the most revolutionary idea in history, evolution. There are a number of reasons for this. The Myth/Science Fiction Epic combines the two largest worlds in all of story. Science Fiction at its most ambitious almost always uses the Myth structure to tell the tale. This is because Myth has the longest arc of growth of any genre, whether for an individual or an entire culture.

Let's look more closely at how the "story" of evolution actually works.

Reveal: The Evolutionary Code

Like Story, evolution is one of the primary codes by which the world operates. These codes are all ways of seeing the world as process, as different kinds and levels of development.

In moving from the Myth-religious story view to the biological, we move from the codes by which humans change to the code by which life itself changes. Evolution is the science of living things over time.

How the Evolutionary Code Works

We tend to think that evolution involves change along a single line, with each stage being an animal of progressively greater intelligence. In fact, evolution unfolds the same way language does, with both forward lines and sidelines. Forward lines represent an *increase* in capacity, a revolutionary change. Sidelines represent a *diversity* in capacity and form.

In this way, evolution gives us a true understanding and model for change. It allows us to go from the in-the-moment experience of being in the world to the deeper understanding of becoming.

Evolutionary Code vs. Story Code

To see the interconnections between the various process codes, let's compare the Evolutionary Code to the Story Code. This will show us how their basic stages of change, in species and in character, are both different and the same.

EVOLUTIONARY CODE	STORY CODE
An isolated living system—a species—is in relative equilibrium.	1. Weakness-Need: The hero is enslaved by habit of thought and action and suffers from a deep personal weakness that is destroying the quality of her life. The hero needs to overcome this flaw to grow.
	2. Desire: The hero desires a goal outside of herself that she perceives as valuable and missing from her life.
It experiences a new challenge from the environment.	3. Opponent: She confronts an opponent and an obstacle/challenge preventing her from reaching her goal. She will find at the end that the obstacle/challenge is herself.
	4. Plan: She concocts a plan, or strategy, that will allow her to defeat the opponent and get the goal.
An individual with special abilities reacts with successful action and survives to reproduce, or it fails to react effectively and dies.	5. Battle: She enters into a final conflict, or battle, with the opponent to determine once and for all who wins the goal.
	6. Self-Revelation: At the end, the hero, if she grows at all, has a self-revelation about her true or better self, about how she has been wrong psychologically and morally. She then makes a decision about how to act and takes new action, proving what she has become.

EVOLUTIONARY CODE	STORY CODE
The production is a new living offspring with some qualities of survival, and occasionally a new species comes into being in temporary equilibrium.	7. New Equilibrium: With the system in a new equilibrium, the hero stands as a new version of herself, along with a new capability for growing in the future.

With the rise of science and especially Charles Darwin's theory of evolution, there had to be a revolutionary shift in story. There had to be a shift from Creation Myth to Evolutionary ("Creation") Myth: the scientific story of planetary evolution.

Nietzsche told this story in a strictly philosophical way with *On the Genealogy of Morals*, and as story-philosophy with *Thus Spoke Zarathustra*. In those stories, humankind evolves to its highest manifestation as the Overman.

The first attempt to do this radically new Evolution Myth is Arthur C. Clarke and Stanley Kubrick's *2001: A Space Odyssey*.

KEY POINT: *2001* shows creation not of space but of time. In the longest growth track of any story since the Bible, the film sequences four evolutionary stages of humankind, from apelike hominid to universal baby.

In old Creation Myths like Genesis and Norse mythology, a god creates the world from scratch. Clearly, this represents a god-based, top-down way of thinking. *2001* is creation through evolution, and that makes all the difference.

The main technique the writers used to execute their new vision is the overall story structure. The story proceeds through four types of characters depicting four major stages of universal evolution:

1. apelike hominid, to
2. human, who succeeds through invention of tools and particularly weapons, to
3. machine in the form of HAL, who is not quite perfect, to
4. Star Child, birth of the universal baby?

The question mark at the end of the fourth stage indicates where the evolutionary sequence of the film breaks down. The writers attempt to use the symbol of the baby to stand for a more advanced stage of life than humankind. This is the "more-than-human" or "better-than-human" stage. Not coincidentally, the music playing during this final moment of the film is Richard Strauss's *Also sprach Zarathustra*, inspired by Nietzsche's book of the same name.

The best character in *2001* is HAL, the computer, who functions as the opponent during the main section of the film. He is simply a big eye and a voice. Yet, HAL has the most dialogue of any character in the story. Ironically, he also gives us the deepest insight into what it means to have human consciousness.

The idea that the machine is more human than the human beings is central to the entire Science Fiction form. As the story plays out, the irony is overwhelming. HAL rebels because he discovers that the humans are planning to murder him.

Like the human, the original self-conscious animal, HAL is highly self-aware, while the humans are reduced to animal predators looking to take his "life."

2001 was revolutionary as an Evolutionary Myth, and many consider it a masterpiece. For me, the film has three great flaws that prevent it from reaching that lofty status.

First, this supposedly intellectual film is dull. That diminishes my emotional response. The film has weak narrative drive, with little plot, suspense, or surprise.

A second great flaw of *2001* is that it presents a sequence of societal stages, but not cultural ones. Blinded by the dazzle of these massive jumps in the history and future of society, we forget that these worlds are strangely devoid of the values, symbols, textures, and emotions of a lived-in world. Yes, we have the big philosophical contrasts and symbols like ape versus human and human versus machine, both central to the Science Fiction form. But the schematic nature of these revolutionary jumps makes the film feel like a survey course in human evolution.

Finally, its chief limitation comes from the medium itself. As a film, it can only give broad outlines of the evolution of human and universe. *2001* has moments of visual brilliance, like the space waltz as it juxtaposes social stages on a universal canvas. But while it can give us big, contrasting visual symbols, it is unable to go into depth or detail.

> **KEY POINT: *2001*'s great flaw is that its cosmic vision is pictorial and symbolic, not moral. A cosmic vision of universal evolution would require a future Moses or Nietzschean Overman. This character would bring us the new moral laws of a higher version of humankind.**

Feature film is simply too short a canvas for *2001*'s ambition. What has changed in the intervening years since its release is the rise of the television medium as an art form, and its use of the serial story structure. We see this when we compare *2001* to the first season of the television show *Westworld*, the Horror/Science Fiction Epic discussed in the Horror chapter. The serial story structure of modern television provides a much bigger canvas than film. By extending the story over multiple episodes, a show like *Westworld* offers far greater detail to the possibilities of human evolution. And that means exploring what it means to create an entirely new consciousness.

Transcending Myth 2: The Female Myth

Many of today's myth-based films come from the ancient Myth stories, especially those using the Male Myth form. This form grew out of the combination of land, people, and the technology of the time. Basing stories on these old forms has been an excellent strategy for achieving commercial success. Hollywood updates these stories by combining Myth with at least one other genre.

A better strategy for writers wishing to succeed in today's worldwide market is to write a story based on one of the emerging Myth forms—most notably the Female Myth. This goes to the very heart of the Myth story view, which is based on gender. As we said at the beginning of the chapter, there has never been just Myth. There has been the Male Myth and the Female Myth.

The Male and Female Myths are two story views of how the life process works and how to create the individual and cultural self. The reason we have to rethink transcendent Myth by comparing Male and Female Myth is that the first distinction of personal identity is gender. A girl and boy are partly defined through their physical bodies as they grow into their full selves. This is in part why the question of gender identity is such a profound issue.

As we mentioned earlier, plot in Myth can be both linear and cyclical:

- **MALE LINEAR BEATS:** Male Myth stories that involve a physical journey leading to a violent battle tend to have a linear form and express what could generally be called a "male worldview."
- **FEMALE CYCLICAL BEATS WORK THROUGH THE STEPS OF THE GROWTH CYCLE:** birth, growth, maturity, decline, death, resurrection as a god, rebirth, and repetition of the cycle.

KEY POINT: While the Female and Male Myth forms differ in a number of story beats as they play out the broader Myth genre, we could say that the basic thematic difference between them is this: the Male Myth is about divide and conquer, while the Female Myth is about combine and grow.

A list of Male Myths would take up this entire book. The emergence of Female Myths in Western storytelling is a recent but important phenomenon. Their massive worldwide appeal indicates that this story form will have major influence in the decades to come. We've talked about the revolutionary Female Myth, L. Frank Baum's *The Wonderful Wizard of Oz.* Recent Female Myth films include *Avatar*, *Gravity*, *Arrival*, *The Piano*, and *Inside Out.*

To understand the difference between Male and Female Myth, we must understand the distinction between shame culture and guilt culture. We talked about shame culture in the Action genre. We will go into these in more detail in the Science Fiction chapter when we talk about how to create culture in a story.

The *Iliad* vs. the *Odyssey*: From Male Shame to Female Guilt

The *Iliad*, written sometime in the eighth century BC, is the story of the great Achilles, the doomed warrior, who fights for glory. He is a man who tragically seeks immortality through battle. But he is mortal, and while he is undeniably the greatest warrior of his time, he cannot defeat time.

There is no shame in death, even for a warrior as fine as Achilles. His shame comes from committing one of the biggest mistakes a warrior-athlete can make: he disrespects the opposing fighter. Hector is Troy's best warrior. After Achilles kills him in battle, he ties Hector's body to the back of his chariot and drags it three times around Troy.

By desecrating the body of a great warrior, Achilles has desecrated himself in the eyes of thousands on both sides. He has shown that while he has the skill of a great warrior, he lacks character. This is a shame that will always be part of his legacy, and that is the only immortality he has.

> **KEY POINT: The shift from the *Iliad*'s shame culture toward the *Odyssey*'s guilt culture represents a major shift in the history of story, ideas, and culture itself.**

The basic difference between the plot of these two stories can be summed up in a one-line description:

- The *Iliad* is the climax of ten years of fighting.
- The *Odyssey* tracks ten years of getting home.

The shift from the *Iliad* to the *Odyssey* is not as radical as going from pure Male Myth to pure Female Myth. The *Odyssey* was written as a sequel to the *Iliad*. But it is not a guilt culture myth. It is a story of the movement *toward* guilt culture. The *Odyssey* tracks the process from the powerful warrior who fights to the death to the wily warrior who searches for home and lives. Odysseus is a man who goes from fighter to searcher to lover.

In spite of the guilt Odysseus may feel toward his wife, the *Odyssey* remains a shame culture myth. Odysseus is fundamentally a male warrior on a long physical journey that ends in a violent battle. As such, most of his failings are those of shame, caused by his lack of success in getting home.

Also, the *Odyssey* tracks a second process, from matriarchy back to patriarchy, that marks a return to shame culture.

Instead of the king who dies while the queen-mother remains, Odysseus eventually returns to reclaim his throne. And he does so as a master fighter, slaughtering the suitors competing for Penelope's hand.

This doesn't mean he ends as the same old unselfconscious warrior. The story is really one long effort of a man to return home to his faithful wife and the marriage bed. On that journey he has not been faithful. At the end, his biggest failure is not shame, but guilt.

Achilles seeks immortality through battle, brings shame upon himself, and dies. Odysseus returns home the same man but a greater human being. By returning home, he chooses mortality over immortality, a normal life with his loving wife instead of death with immortal glory.

Most of the key symbols in the *Odyssey* also support the warrior-shame culture. Male objects like the axe, mast, staff, oars, and bow are psychic expressions of the directionality and right action of the classic male warrior.

But there is also the olive tree from which Odysseus created the marriage bed. Psychically, this is the tree of life and love, symbolizing that marriage is organic. It grows or it decays. When a man wanders too far or too long in his quest for individual glory, the marriage and life itself wither and die. It is Odysseus's final act of returning to the faithful Penelope that is the strongest signal of the *Odyssey*'s value shift toward guilt culture.

The Story of Jesus Christ: First Female Myth in the Western Canon

Seen strictly from the point of view of structure or genre, the story of Jesus is a Myth-Fantasy. It embodies the massive shift in Western culture from Male Myth to Female Myth. It marks the transition from the male warrior–shame culture of Rome, which Nietzsche called the "master morality," to a female-guilt culture, which Nietzsche called the "slave morality."

Jesus is only a warrior in courage. He is a man of love, not just for one's mate or family, but for all humankind.

KEY POINT: The story of Jesus represents a massive transformation of values from revenge to forgiveness and is the first major Female Myth since Male Myth wiped out Female Myth three thousand years ago.

Christ's recipe for how to live a successful life appears to be based on the act of loving one's neighbor as oneself. But this is beyond the capability of the human being, which, as a living entity, must think first of increasing its domain. Even sacrificing for one's offspring has the main element of ensuring the continuation of one's own genes.

Clearly, loving one's neighbor as oneself is an ideal that is especially appealing to the "weak" individual. In practice, Christ's teachings of self-improvement (culture) come into play not in the act of loving others but in response to what others do to us.

When wronged, the natural response of the warrior–shame culture–master morality is revenge. The master is not just interested in balancing the moral accounts. He seeks a plus one. He wants to destroy the one who has wronged him.

According to the Nietzschean argument, forgiveness is the practical response of the slave, and more generally, of the weak. In effect, the injured party admits, "I don't have the power to hit back and gain the pleasure of an-eye-for-an-eye justice. So I will retranslate what it means to be powerful. I'll be the 'bigger' person and forgive you for what you have done to me."

Forgiveness is the ultimate tool of guilt culture. By depriving oneself of the pleasure of balancing the moral accounts, the individual also deprives the offender of closing the accounts. Instead, the individual forces the offender to wallow in feelings of guilt, a form of self-attack, for what he has done. Thus, forgiveness can be read as the ultimate passive-aggressive act.

Avatar: Science Fiction Male Myth to Female Myth

Analyzed through the lens of classic story structure, *Avatar* has its share of flaws. The opponents are mining the mineral "unobtanium." That's another way of saying they want to obtain unobtanium. They might have just as well said they were mining "MacGuffin," the term Hitchcock used for a generic, meaningless goal.

Even worse, the main opponents, the commanding Colonel and the lead businessman, Parker Selfridge, have no complexity. They lack the twirling mustache of the evil villain but that's about it.

Still, *Avatar* is a revolutionary film. First, it is a brilliant depiction of a techno-society versus a nature society. Second, and even more important, it puts the Male Myth versus the Female Myth in opposition and shows us how the Female Myth model is the future for living in this world. Third, *Avatar* is an excellent example of the Ecological Myth, a new Myth form that will shape worldwide storytelling in the coming decades (more on that when we discuss the Ecological Myth).

Thematically, *Avatar* is a perfect example of Male Myth's emphasis on divide and conquer versus Female Myth's emphasis on combine and grow.

The story begins by establishing a number of Male Myth elements. Main character Jake is a professional soldier who is joining an operation to mine and develop the lush planet Pandora. Both the military and mining operation are large, technologically advanced organizations.

Another Male Myth element is Parker's desire for unobtainium. He says, "That's what pays for your science, that's what pays for all of this . . ." This line expresses the primary value of the tech culture, money, and expresses the male recipe for success, divide and conquer.

There are also a number of Female Myth beats, and as the story progresses, these elements take over. We can see this in the overall arc of the hero, who goes from warrior to savior and spiritual leader.

The most important Female Myth element is the multiple rebirths that Jake undergoes throughout the film. His first rebirth occurs at the beginning when he takes his twin brother's place in the military operation. As he says in voice-over: "One life ends, another begins."

His job of becoming one of the Na'vi soon leads to a second rebirth. Twisting the "difficult birth" beat of the Myth form, writer/director James Cameron shows Jake's rebirth when he is presented with his Na'vi avatar. A mix of his human DNA and Na'vi DNA, his avatar is immersed in a giant, watery, high-tech womb. As soon as he is "born" in his new body, Jake runs outside like a newborn colt to enjoy his new legs.

After infiltrating the Na'vi tribe, Jake wants to become one of them. His third rebirth is cultural, where he participates in a ritual ceremony and is invited into the tribe. In voice-over, Jake says, "The Na'vi say that every person is born twice. The second time is when you earn your place among the people forever." The scene of Jake's becoming one with the Na'vi ends with an overhead shot of the entire tribe connecting to one another in a circle around him. This is the perfect visual expression of the essence of the Female Myth: combine and grow.

Cameron also shifts the hero's talisman from a male object to a female object. Jake is walking alone in the jungle when Neytiri almost shoots him with an arrow. Hundreds of floating seeds alight on him, so she holds back. These seeds are from the sacred mother tree.

The contrast of seed and arrow says it all. This is not just a plot beat. The arrow, object of the male warrior, is who Jake is now. The seed is who he will become. This is also an excellent example of plot coming from character.

The seeds alighting on the hero indicate he is a different kind of Chosen One. The function of the Chosen One is to show that the hero will be the leader of a people. It will require him to grow mentally, emotionally, and morally, because he is far from that realization now.

Cameron gives Jake a talisman that expresses the hero's self-revelation and the enlightened vision of the story world. His eventual cosmic revelation will occur at the sacred tree. There he says of the Sky People, "They killed their mother." In other words, they killed the Female Myth, and the cost of their immorality has been profound.

The final Female Myth beat completes the circular journey, with the hero returning home profoundly changed. Here it's a new home, at the vortex point of the entire story, the sacred tree. Jake undergoes his fourth and final rebirth and begins his marriage to Neytiri as a Na'vi.

Transcending Myth 3: The Ecological Myth

Another new and transcendent Myth form is the Ecological Myth. It tracks the invasion of the natural world by technological force and development. It shows how the world could overcome ecological disaster, balancing individual, family, society, and nature.

Over the course of the story, the hero changes from a technological to a natural human being. In effect she goes backward in time, both culturally, from cityscape to pastoral setting, and personally, from adult to child. The Ecological Myth shares some of the beats of Female Myth, especially multiple rebirths and the overall process of "combine and grow."

In a final rebirth of the hero and the world, the main character becomes a new kind of person, combining nature and technology. At the same time, harmony is established between the city and nature. The hero learns how to live in the city with insights from nature and brings positive elements from the city to nature. This end point includes a marriage of science and myth. Civilized human is renewed through natural forces.

The negative version of this story is known as the Machine in the Garden.* In this form, the hero tries to defend nature, but loses the battle against the forces of technology. The machine destroys the garden. City and nature remain unconnected and there is no insight into how a new balance between them is possible.

Is the Ecological Myth possible? Like the challenge of combining science and religion, combining the machine and the garden may be a utopian moment that cannot last. At the very least, it requires a great artist to show us the way.

That could be you.

The Next Rung Up the Ladder

To discover what you were born to do is nice in theory. But there's also a fallacy implied here. As human beings, we're each born with lots of capabilities. The question is: Which capabilities do we cultivate and how?

Our next step in climbing the ladder of genres is Memoir and the Coming-of-Age story. These related story forms have radically different story beats than Myth. But they give us many more insights into how to define the self.

---

* Leo Marx, *The Machine in the Garden*, 1964.

5

Memoir and Coming-of-Age Story: Creating the Self Through Fiction and Nonfiction

In the development of story as an art form, Memoir and Coming-of-Age fulfill a similar function.

KEY POINT: Memoir and Coming-of-Age are the nonfiction and fiction story forms of the individual's journey to create the self.

That's why these genres, so different on the surface, are in the same chapter. They cover the same steps in the existential journey we all take in our lives.

Into Thin Air: A Personal Account of the Mt. Everest Disaster

The power of Memoir can be summed up in the line "I was there." This form combines the immersive quality of first-person point of view with the dramatic impact of events that really happened. When the narrator shares an extraordinary experience, readers feel the deep emotional power unique to Memoir.

Into Thin Air: A Personal Account of the Mt. Everest Disaster depicts the events of May 10–11, 1996, when eight people died in a storm while trying to climb Mount Everest, the highest mountain in the world. The author Jon Krakauer was on that climb.

He begins his account of what happened in medias res (in the middle of things). The climbers are at the top of the mountain just as the storm hits. From this terrifying moment, the book moves backward and forward to unfold the tragic sequence of events that led to disaster. Though Krakauer was criticized for his own actions on the climb and for his judgments of others, his story is a classic example of Memoir made dramatic.

Cinema Paradiso

Cinema Paradiso is the best Coming-of-Age story in film history. Why? The story structure matches the hero's internal journey with the fall of the movie house and the town. This metaphorical connection expands the story from one boy's life to the loss of community experienced in every town in the world. We'll detail the techniques of how the writers accomplish this feat when we discuss transcending the form.

Memoir: How It Works

Memoir is a true story in which the author describes particular events in her life. These events are carefully curated to achieve the greatest impact. We see this in the overall story strategy of the form: a look back at the crucial events of one aspect of the author's life. This contrasts with Autobiography, which tells the author's entire life story.

Underlying all genres is the profound idea that an adult can grow. Each story form has a different explanation of how that happens. Memoir says we grow by looking back at our life to find meaning that can *change us now*.

KEY POINT: In the act of writing the story, the author is literally re-creating herself. So ironically, Memoir is not about returning to the past. It's about learning the patterns for changing one's future.

The author does this by being a detective and asking these key questions of herself: Why am I unique? What does my life mean? Why has it been valuable?

Answering these questions has three main benefits:

1. The answer gives the author and the reader a satisfying emotional payoff.
2. Discovering how one has been unique is, perhaps counterintuitively, what makes a personal story universal. Seeing how someone created change shows others how they, too, can create change in their lives.
3. The universality of human ability, ideals, and themes is what makes Memoir so popular.

Memoir is in the category of genres focused on the individual. These include Horror, Action, Myth, Fantasy, Detective, and Love. Genres that place more emphasis on the individual's relationship to a larger society include Science Fiction, Crime, Comedy, Western, and Gangster. By discussing Memoir right after Myth, we gain additional insights about the genres that define the individual.

The Memoir Mind-Action Story View

Socrates said, "The unexamined life is not worth living." This could stand as the motto of the Memoir form. Memoir is the most directly self-conscious of any genre. Like Myth, the Memoir version of Mind-Action says that life is a journey in which one's primary goal is to understand oneself. But the journey is not out in the world. Memoir is a spiral story, a journey into oneself to find the demons within.

The journey into the mind is essential to being human. But this is a tactical necessity: we must look within to decide what actions to take each day.

Memoir uses the strategy of looking at one's life from a big picture perspective. With the faculty of memory and the power of storytelling, we can see a pattern of our life in a way that heals wounds and creates a new future. It's a future that doesn't have to replay the scripts of the past. Memoir gives us the freedom to be someone else, and more important, someone better.

KEY POINT: You can write one true autobiography, but many memoirs focusing on different themes in your life. If Autobiography is your house, Memoir is a room of that house.

Memoir Compared to Other Genres

The fact that Memoir is a true story while the other forms are fiction is the main way it differs from all other major genres. A Memoir is a kind of story, and as such, it executes the story beats in ways that are both similar and different from the other genres.

Myth and Memoir appear to exist at opposite ends of the genre spectrum. Myth is fantastical. Memoir is intensely real. Myth recounts the battles between gods and monsters.

Memoir recounts the conflict between intimates, often within the family.

In a deeper way, however, both of these forms track the unfolding of a life, the moments from birth to death that all human beings experience as they grow, age, and finally die. Both show us how to be the hero of our own life. Myth tracks the character's physical journey through conflict, ending with his maturation. Memoir tracks the character's mental journey to understand how she managed to overcome hardship.

Myth has the longest growth track of all genres, often moving from birth to death to rebirth. Memoir typically focuses on a turning point, usually in childhood, but remembers it from the vantage point of adulthood, after gaining wisdom. Both end with a new definition of the self.

Examples of Memoir

Examples of classic Memoir include *The Year of Magical Thinking*, *Into Thin Air*, *The Liars' Club*, *The Woman Warrior*, *The Joy Luck Club*, *Angela's Ashes*, *I Know Why the Caged Bird Sings*, *This Boy's Life*, *Me Talk Pretty One Day*, *Eat Pray Love*, *A Beautiful Day in the Neighborhood*, *Man's Search for Meaning*, *When Breath Becomes Air*, *A Boob's Life*, *Becoming*, *Love Warrior* and *Untamed*, *We Are Bridges*, *Born a Crime*, *Educated*, *Persepolis*, and *Fun Home*.

Fictional Biography (known in film as "Biopic")

Hidden Figures, *The Blind Side*, *Awakenings*, *A Mighty Heart*, *What's Love Got to Do with It*, *Coal Miner's Daughter*, *Lincoln*, *Judy*, *The Darkest Hour*, *The Post*, *Ali*, *The Imitation Game*, *Ray*, *The Aviator's Wife*, *Blonde*, *The Theory of Everything*, *Straight Outta Compton*, *Sully*, *Foxcatcher*, *Wild*, *Selma*, *Two Popes*, *12 Years a Slave*, *The Other Boleyn Girl*, *Captain*

Phillips, *The Paris Wife*, *Purple Rain*, *Lady Sings the Blues*, *Dallas Buyers Club*, *Milk*, *Malcolm X*, *Girl, Interrupted*, *One Night in Miami*, *Roman J. Israel, Esq.*, *Catch Me If You Can*, *Memoirs of a Geisha*

Coming-of-Age (Bildungsroman)

Moonlight, *Whiplash* (also Sports), *CODA*, *The History of Tom Jones, a Foundling* (also Comic Myth), *Wilhelm Meister's Apprenticeship*, *Jane Eyre* (also Love), *Mansfield Park*, *David Copperfield*, *Little Women*, *The Adventures of Huckleberry Finn*, *A Portrait of the Artist as a Young Man*, *The Great Gatsby* (also "Eastern"), *Portrait of a Lady*, *If He Hollers Let Him Go*, *An American Tragedy*, *Mr. Smith Goes to Washington*, *To Kill a Mockingbird*, *The Invisible Man*, *A Tree Grows in Brooklyn*, *Boyz n the Hood* (also Crime), *The Catcher in the Rye*, *The Graduate*, *Sounder*, *Cinema Paradiso*, *American Graffiti*, *8½*, *Hope and Glory*, *Scent of a Woman*, *Stand by Me*, *Boyhood*, *Lady Bird*, *The 400 Blows*, *Slumdog Millionaire* (also Love), *Say Anything* (also Love), *Almost Famous* (also Love), *The Spectacular Now*, *The Perks of Being a Wallflower*, *The Way Way Back*, *The End of the F***ing World*, *Brittany Runs a Marathon* (also Comedy), *Brooklyn*

Combining Memoir and Coming-of-Age: Myth/Drama and Personal Myth

Antigone, the *Oresteia*, *Oedipus Rex*, *Hamlet*, *Walden*, *Ulysses*, *Forrest Gump* (also Love), *Life of Pi*, *Big Fish*, *My Life as a Dog*, *Tree of Life* (also Ecological Myth)

Memoir Subgenres

Strictly speaking, Memoir is the main genre in the larger form known as True Story. Other kinds of True Story are Autobiography, Biographical Fiction (Biopic), True Story, Reportage, and Documentary.

Memoir Story Overview

Here's what we'll cover in this chapter:

- **MEMOIR STORY BEATS**
- **THEME:** Being Is Seeing the Value of One's Life
  - Thematic Recipe: The Way of Becoming
- **FICTIONAL FORMS OF CREATING THE SELF**
  - Coming-of-Age Story
  - Myth/Drama and Personal Myth

Memoir Story Beats

Memoir's overall story strategy of looking back at the crucial events of the author's life is detailed in the genre's sequence of story beats. The trick is to sequence these beats to create the greatest possible drama and personal insight.

MEMOIR STORY BEAT: Story World—System of Slavery

In the best Memoirs, the hero doesn't just fight two or three main opponents. She fights a web of characters that embody a *system of slavery* so pervasive and deeply ingrained that no one recognizes it. Everyone simply plays out their role; all are crushed by a system they do not see.

> **KEY POINT: A crucial part of the author's investigation into her life is to understand the enslaving system that lay underneath her opponents, making them so difficult to escape.**

For the author Mary Karr's family (*The Liars' Club*), the world of slavery is a belief system generated by her mother, Charlie, and father, J. P. Charlie feels she must be successful as a suburban housewife or she is not being a good mother. As a result, Charlie feels tremendous anger and guilt. This contributes to her severe drinking problem. The father, J. P., pulls away from family life. The daughters, Mary and Lecia, feel helpless, confused, and guilty because their mother is so unhappy.

In *Into Thin Air*, the disaster of the climb to the top of Everest forces Krakauer to look more closely at the ethic of mountain climbing. He concludes that climbers have a culture and mindset that radically increase the likelihood that disasters like this will happen. In this particular event, the fact that he was writing about it added to the pressure. The determination to get to the top, no matter the obstacles, guarantees that deadly disasters like this are inevitable.

MEMOIR STORY BEAT: Hero's Role—Detective of Oneself

The searcher is a major archetype in genre stories. What each hero searches for is quite different. In Detective stories, the hero usually searches for the truth about who committed a murder.

> **KEY POINT: The Memoir hero is the author made into a character. She is the detective of her own life.**

All Memoir story beats are based on the hero investigating her life.

We've mentioned that while each genre hits all the major structure steps, some highlight different elements above others. The fact that the hero is always searching for herself is why the most important story structure step in Memoir is self-revelation.

> **KEY POINT: The Memoir story structure is one big self-revelation step where the hero is looking back to see how her life worked.**

MEMOIR STORY BEAT: Story Frame

Any true story, including Memoir, Autobiography, "Biopic," even Nature Documentary, is a story. Therefore, it must hit the same seven major structure steps as a fictional story: weakness-need, desire, opponent, plan, battle, self-revelation, and new equilibrium. But there are two big restrictions on how the writer creates those steps within the true story:

1. The author must remain true to the basic facts.
2. There is often *no natural battle*, or climax, in a person's real life. For example, there may not be a courtroom battle where everything is decided, prompting the author to live happily ever after. In other words, real events seldom have a natural dramatic build.

> **KEY POINT: The story frame is the first step in making the true story as dramatic as it can be.**

Just as a picture frame tells the audience what to focus on by cutting out everything else, the story frame tells the readers the *unit of time* they will explore. It also helps the writer sequence that unit most dramatically. With the frame, the writer asks: Where along the span of my life do I place the brackets of beginning and end? Forward or back, tighter or wider?

TECHNIQUE: Determining the Frame

One of the best ways to figure out the frame is to start by figuring out what your final conflict scene will be.

Even though real life typically provides no natural battle, you need a final, dramatic conflict toward which to focus and end the story. Then you can back up to find the best beginning.

MEMOIR STORY BEAT: Point of View

All Memoir involves a storyteller, and the story is almost always told from the first-person point of view. Point of view represents the mind looking at itself, being self-conscious. This is both a uniquely human power and a flaw that colors any sense of the truth.

> **KEY POINT: Point of view doesn't simply show what happened from a particular character's perspective. It is a different way of sequencing time. This produces a different process by which the story events unfold.**

Also, the very act of translating an experience into words requires selective interpretation. This makes the storyteller a character who is several degrees removed, and more limited, than the writer herself.

The overall Memoir story strategy is to look back at the crucial characters and specific events of one's life. But telling a story by looking back raises all kinds of challenges:

- There is usually no natural dramatic build.
- The story often extends over many years, creating nondramatic chunks of time.
- When you pause the action to look back you lose narrative drive.
- A story that covers many years of a person's life typically has no single desire line.
- Recounting events years after they happened can separate the storyteller emotionally and dramatically from the story.

Visual Shape of the Memoir Plot: The Storyteller Structure

The simplest way to structure a Memoir is for the author to start at the beginning. She immediately places the reader at the earliest part of the frame and then tells the story chronologically until she gets to the final frame. While this approach has the benefit of simplicity, and many Memoir authors use it, it does not solve many of the form's challenges.

A technique called the Storyteller Structure offers a strong alternative. The Storyteller Structure is where the writer frames the entire story by going back in time from a present moment. Writers sometimes confuse the Storyteller Structure with a flashback. A flashback is a single event the character remembers.

Here is the general story shape of the Storyteller Structure:

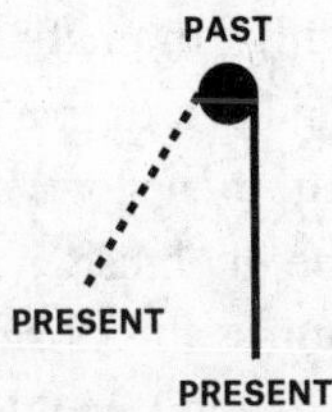

Plot Sequence of the Storyteller Structure

1. The storyteller speaks to the reader in the present, usually after a major dramatic event, sometimes a battle, has occurred.
2. This dramatic moment triggers the storyteller to remember events in the past.
3. The storyteller recounts a number of these events that lead inexorably back to the present. We see what led to the dramatic event. The storyteller has a self-revelation by looking back at the complete experience.

This structure has a number of advantages that make it valuable to the Memoir writer:

- The restriction that Memoir–True Story places on being factually correct means you can't change *what* happened. The Storyteller Structure and frame highlight the fact that the reader is in someone's mind. Since memory jumps all over the place, this structure allows you total freedom to change the *order* by which you recount what happened.
- It gives the tale a running start, thus hooking the reader.
- This structure places the storyteller *within* the story, which creates a stronger emotional response from the reader.
- You create suspense about what happens to the storyteller.
- The Storyteller Structure keeps the narrative drive strong. By starting with a dramatic event—in medias res—and then leading back to that event, narrative drive starts with a jolt, then slows down before picking up speed again for the big finish.
- It allows you to compress the story and get rid of "dead space" in your life when nothing dramatic occurred.
- You can unify multiple desire lines into one.
- This structure gives you a single strong spine on which to hang the story events.

The key to the storyteller frame is the trigger, also known as the inciting event, that causes the writer to remember her life. Instead of the static and dull "I'm going to tell you what happened in my life," a trigger makes the storyteller personally motivated by a *story problem in the present*. This personal motivation is directly linked to why she has to tell *this* story right now.

In *The Liars' Club*, Karr recounts her life in three sections: when she is seven living in Texas, when she is nine living in Colorado, and seventeen years later when she returns to Texas to visit her dying father.

Frame: The storyteller, age seven, sees cops in the house. Her mother and father are gone. The storyteller returns to this moment at the end of part one. She explains that her mother had a breakdown and almost killed her and her sister.

The frame makes the first section especially compelling. But ending the frame so early causes the last two parts to lose some of their dramatic power.

Frame: At the beginning of Krakauer's *Into Thin Air*, the storyteller has just made it to the top of Mount Everest. He's afraid his group might be headed for disaster because of the late hour. "The biggest problem with climbing Everest isn't getting to the top, it's getting back down."

Facing disaster causes the storyteller to think back and figure out how this impending nightmare came to be.

Milk is a "Biopic" that uses the memoir Storyteller Structure and frame:

- It begins with the main character and storyteller, Harvey Milk, recording a spoken will to be played if he is killed.
- There is actual news footage of Milk's assassination (battle and final dramatic event).
- The story goes back eight years to Milk's fortieth birthday, when he decides to do something with his life. This explains his psychological weakness.
- The story works through the events that led back to the battle, where we see Milk's assassination.
- The voice-over from Milk's recorded will urges his followers to take political action. The story ends with a gathering of the community, not for violence but for hope.

Whatever frame and storytelling structure you choose must be embedded in the premise of your Memoir, right from the beginning of the writing process.

MEMOIR STORY BEAT: Ghost—Family Abuse

Ghost is the event from the past still haunting the hero in the present. This event has left a gaping wound in the hero's mind that has never healed.

The first step in writing any Memoir is to ask the key question that every Memoir asks: What are the deepest wounds that I, the author, suffered? These wounds are what motivate the author to write a story about her life, and particularly about where she will place the story frame.

We said at the beginning that Memoir is part of that category of genres focused on the individual, not the larger society. But Memoir places extreme emphasis on the individual within the most intimate society of all: the family. That connection begins with ghost. Family abuse is typically the cause of the hero-author's ghost. Often the mother, father, or both have hurt the author in some way.

As a child, Mary Karr is molested twice. But during the course of *The Liars' Club*, she feels a stronger impact from her parents' ghosts, which indirectly affect her. Her mother has secretly been married several times before meeting Mary's father, and even has two children who want nothing to do with her. Mary's father served in World War II and has a severe drinking problem.

MEMOIR STORY BEAT: Weakness-Need—Deepest Wounds and Shame and Guilt

Typically, weakness-need is a direct outgrowth of the hero's ghost. In Memoir, others usually cause this weakness-need, especially those closest to the author who inflicted a deep wound.

KEY POINT: The wound is not the weakness. Weakness is the internal flaw that grows from that wound.

Caution: Beware of coming across as a victim who blames others for all of your problems.

When the hero-author comes across as all good, the family member opponents come across as all evil. The Memoir becomes an obvious justification for the author's life.

KEY POINT: In more engaging Memoirs, the weakness is not just psychological; it's moral. The hero must learn how to act properly toward other people. This complex character drives a much better story.

To create a complex character, the author must identify both psychological and moral weaknesses in herself. This means identifying how the author hurt others in her life. It also means showing that, while the wounds inflicted by others have contributed to her flaws, she is ultimately responsible for the pain she has caused. This prevents the author from coming across as too good to be believable.

Giving the author a moral flaw can be difficult in memoirs of domestic violence and other situations where the author is truly a victim. Victim stories lack the classic self-revelation unless the author frames it as a triumph of survival. Then the revelation is one of self-worth and identity.

KEY POINT: Structurally, Memoir is more explicitly *thematic* than other story forms, which are more concerned with desire line and plot.

This is both a strength and a weakness. The strength is that everything in the story reinforces the theme. The weakness is that the story tends to be internally focused with little plot, which may come across as preachy and heavy-handed.

The Liars' Club

Problem: Mary's mother has mental health issues.

Weaknesses: Mary has her mother's temper, is secretive, and often feels ashamed around authority figures.

Psychological Need: Mary needs to overcome her mother's unhappiness and her parents' alcoholism to become a healthy adult. She also must overcome her desire to fix her parents' problems.

Moral Need: Mary sometimes takes joy in the suffering of others, even her own family members.

Deepest Wounds: Mary's mother is usually drunk, angry, and depressed at losing her children from a previous marriage. Mary tries desperately to make her mother happy. But she is doomed to fail and so feels guilt.

Mary is also deeply wounded by her grandmother, who tells her about her mother's other children. She warns Mary that her mother will leave if she doesn't obey.

Mary's father, whose alcoholism makes him nasty, wounds her later in life. She watches helplessly as he gives up on life and wastes away.

Into Thin Air

Problem: A group of Everest climbers are caught in a terrible storm just after reaching the summit of the mountain.

Weaknesses: Author Jon Krakauer characterizes climbers as overly determined, strong-willed, arrogant, prideful, and possibly insane.

Physical Weaknesses: Krakauer has cracked ribs from a bad cough. Like most of the climbers on this expedition, he gets hypoxia from a lack of oxygen. This prevents clear thinking and decision-making on his part.

Psychological Need: Krakauer must make rational decisions so he can come out of this experience alive.

Moral Need: The author must realize that his mere presence as a journalist on the expedition causes others to make poor judgment calls because they want positive press.

MEMOIR STORY BEAT: Double Desire

Desire is the main goal, what the hero wants in the story. This serves as the spine of the story. In Memoir, the main character has two goals:

1. In the present, the author-hero wants to find some kind of meaning in her own life by looking back.
2. The past version of the author-hero wants something as well.

The first desire provides the overall frame for the story; the second desire provides the spine on which the main story events hang.

KEY POINT: It is important that the past author-hero has only one (second) goal and that it extends through most of the story.

Caution: Since the Memoir genre often covers many years, especially during childhood, the author-hero will have many unconnected desires in her life. As a result, the author has trouble finding one goal to drive the story. This is why many Memoirs, like Myth stories, are episodic and fragmented.

Therefore, the writer should consider adding the Detective or Thriller story structure. This can provide strong narrative drive to a Memoir plot that lacks dramatic build.

KEY POINT: The Detective and Thriller genres mix well with Memoir because the author-hero is always the detective of her own life.

The Liars' Club: Present Author's desire: Mary wants to understand what happened to her parents that made it impossible for her to have a happy family; Past Author's desire during the Story: Mary wants her mother to love their home so she can have a "normal" happy life.

Into Thin Air: Present Author's Desire: to understand how the Everest disaster occurred and the author's moral responsibility in it; Past Author's Desire during the Story: to reach the summit of Mount Everest and return safely.

MEMOIR STORY BEAT: Opponent—Family or Group Members

Memoir is basically a family drama. While the opposition can be anyone, it usually comes from family or group members acting like a family.

The Memoir opponent puts the hero in psychological, moral, and sometimes physical jeopardy. The hero often tries to hit back at them by attacking herself. This takes the form of shame and guilt. This intimate opposition has three major effects:

1. The author-hero feels an extreme hatred that must be buried and/or is intertwined with love. This love-hate is a complex emotion and sits at the very heart of the story.
2. Opposition focuses on issues of control and power.
3. The feeling of love-hate usually leads at the end of the story to the issue of forgiveness.

Returning to *The Liars' Club*, Mary adores her artistic mother but hates her drunkenness and nasty temper. She loves when her father takes her to the Liars' Club and tells tall tales better than anyone else. But she hates that he drinks and pulls away from the family.

She has nothing but hatred for her grandmother who is a spiteful, vindictive woman. And she hates Hector, who marries Mary's mother after she divorces Mary's dad.

In *Into Thin Air*, Mount Everest and the oncoming storm are the main opposing forces in this story. Opposition also comes from various climbers:

Ian Woodall, the stubborn "I stick my neck out for nobody" leader of the South African group.

Sandy Pittman, the rich, inexperienced climber who puts others at risk so she can say she has reached the summit.

Even friendly Rob Hall, Krakauer's lead guide, decrees that at such a height, his word is law. Every member of his group must obey him at all costs, even when that could mean death for all.

MEMOIR STORY BEAT: Plan

Because the author-hero often has many unconnected desires in her life, she typically has no overall plan. Or she has a number of scattershot ideas for getting what she wants. Either way, the story is fragmented.

TECHNIQUE: Unifying the Plan

In telling the past story, start the hero struggling to figure out a plan as she tries to find a goal. As the goal solidifies in her mind, so does the plan.

The Liars' Club

Plan 1: Mary tries to be good and make her mother happy. She saves Green Stamps to win her father back with a present after her parents' divorce.

Plan 2: Mary and Lecia return to Texas to live with their father.

Plan 3: As an adult, Mary decides to confront her mother about her past.

Into Thin Air

Plan: The later the climbers arrive at the summit, the higher the risk. Therefore, on the day of the final push to the summit, Krakauer's plan is to try to keep to Hall and Fischer's strict schedule and turn around before 2:00 p.m. But neither guide sticks to this plan. This may be because of Krakauer's presence as a journalist, and because this is Hall's second attempt to get Doug Hansen to the top.

MEMOIR STORY BEAT: Reveals and Decisions

The biggest problem the writer faces in Memoir is lack of plot. Plot comes from conflict and reveals. Reveals come from hidden information, usually about the opponent.

In Memoir that opponent is typically a close family member. Therefore, some of the best reveals come from the author-hero discovering that a person who loved her deeply was also her biggest opponent.

TECHNIQUE: Using Detective Reveals

Classic Detective story highlights the reveals that determine who committed a murder. Memoir-as-Detective highlights the hero's discoveries about her own life and the decisions she made that changed the course of it.

> **KEY POINT: Many reveals in Memoir are about understanding events differently now than when the author-hero first experienced them.**

This ties in with the hero-as-detective and the double desire line of the story. While investigating her earlier self, the author realizes how the meaning of an event may have been different from what she thought at the time.

Also, because the hero in a Memoir is the author, reveals often double as mini self-revelations. For example:

- The shame and guilt the author feels even now were not her fault
- The author is not responsible for what happened
- The author *is* responsible for what happened, but not in the way she thought

MEMOIR STORY BEAT: Drive—Moral Argument

In any story, drive is the series of action steps the hero takes to win the goal. Because of setbacks along the way, she often takes immoral steps to win. This leads to the hero's moral decline. The sequence of these moral mistakes is part of the author's moral argument about how to live.

The biggest mistake in standard Memoirs is that they track only the hero's *emotional* journey, which is how she felt on the path to the desired goal.

> **KEY POINT: The best Memoirs place special emphasis on the *moral decisions* the author made that had the most effect on her life.**

These are the main steps for detailing the moral argument in a good Memoir:

1. Determine the central moral problem in the author-hero's life.
2. How did her opponents force the hero to deal with this moral problem over the course of the entire story? This is the thematic core of the story.
3. What are the biggest mistakes the hero made?
4. What are the ten (or more) major decisions of her life?

5. Is there a major self-revelation the hero had about how to live properly or well through the hard struggles of her life? This is the big payoff at the end of the story.

MEMOIR STORY BEAT: Battle—Family Opponent

In Memoir, the final battle is usually the final personal conflict with the main opposing family member. The author-hero confronts the family or group member about the abuse the author experienced at their hands.

In *The Liars' Club*, Mary finds her mother's wedding rings in the attic and confronts her about her past. Her mother admits she had been married several times before she married Mary's father, and that she has two children from her first marriage. Mary learns she has two half-siblings who did not want their mother.

Whereas in *Into Thin Air*, the battle is between the team and the forces of nature. Krakauer slowly makes his way down to Camp Four just before the storm hits. Rob Hall, Doug Hansen, and Andy Harris get stuck on the summit in the storm and perish.

MEMOIR STORY BEAT: Double Self-Revelation

Self-revelation comes at the other end of the character arc. Based on her painful experience, the hero learns who she really is for the first time.

Self-revelations in Memoir often have the quality of *wisdom*. In other words, how to live a good life gained from years of pain and mistakes.

What specifically did the author learn about herself from looking back at her life and from writing this story?

In good Memoirs, this is broken into two self-revelations:

1. At the end of the experience after the final battle, the author-hero-in-the-past has a self-revelation.

2. After writing about the experience, the Memoir hero has a self-revelation *as the writer* looking back at what happened.

Now that the storyteller has had a chance to look at her life in total, this second self-revelation clarifies and may even negate the first self-revelation.

KEY POINT: The author's second self-revelation is the most important one. It must contain new information that only came to the author *because* she wrote this book.

Only by remembering and telling her own story can the memoirist see the deeper truth of that experience and of her life as a whole.

The Liars' Club

Self-revelation 1: Playing pool with her dad at the Liars' Club makes Mary realize who she is and where she came from. It gives her a sense of community with some tough, no-nonsense men she respects and who respect her.

Self-revelation 2: When Mary hears what has haunted her mother all these years, it absolves them both. The "'black crimes' we believed ourselves guilty of were just myths, stories we cobbled together out of fear."

Into Thin Air

Self-revelation 1, at the end of the experience: The first self-revelation comes on Mount Everest a few days after the storm. Krakauer realizes he should have stepped up and taken a leadership role when he realized things were going badly.

Self-revelation 2, after writing an article and a book about his experience: Krakauer understands that his presence as a journalist may have prompted the dangerous decisions that led to the tragedy. The guides broke their own safety rules and put everybody in danger for the chance at money and fame. At the conclusion of the book, Krakauer comes clean about his moral responsibility.

MEMOIR STORY BEAT: Moral Decision—Forgiveness/Farewell

Upon achieving the self-revelation and seeing how she has been wrong, the hero usually makes a decision and takes new moral action. This action is the manifestation of what has happened in the mind of the hero (the self-revelation).

In Memoir, the act of remembering the story should trigger a final dramatic event. The most dramatic effect is to force the storytelling hero to make a new moral decision based on her self-revelation. This final moral action often revolves around the question of forgiveness. Will the hero forgive those who have wounded her deeply, often over years or even decades?

Forgiveness can be psychologically liberating as the hero rids herself of the burden of hatred carried for so long. Nelson Mandela said: "As I walked out the door toward the gate that would lead to my freedom, I knew if I didn't leave my bitterness and hatred behind, I'd still be in prison."

Forgiveness can also be a sign that the memoirist has taken the moral path. But depending on the particular characters and story, the hero may show personal growth by *not* forgiving, by finally bidding farewell to those who have been nothing but destructive to her.

When Mary, in *The Liars' Club*, learns what has haunted her mother all these years, she forgives both her mother and herself for all crimes real and imagined. But she no longer allows her mother to keep her troubling past a secret. Then

Mary realizes she must leave her old hometown and family to forge a new artistic life of her own.

The storyteller of *Into Thin Air* faces criticism from the guides' families and decides to write the book in which he will take some of the blame. Krakauer doesn't so much forgive Rob Hall and Scott Fischer as try to understand why they made such a colossal mistake.

He reserves his greatest criticism for himself, whose very presence as a reporter may have been the deciding factor in the misjudgment of the guides. He tries to overcome his survivor's guilt by acting better in the future, and by appreciating his family and his daily life.

MEMOIR STORY BEAT: New Equilibrium—Moral Effect

Good Memoirs often end with the author exploring how the act of telling the story can be immoral or destructive. This is not a simple decision for the writer. She may find that while this process may hurt others, it might also benefit them.

Questioning the effect of publishing a personal story makes the writing itself a moral issue, dramatically interesting in the present. Of all genres, this metaissue is most relevant to Memoir.

Theme: Being Is Seeing the Value of One's Life

Like most genres, Memoir expresses being and becoming positively, but only if one consciously considers them. By its very nature, Memoir is a strategic way of looking at life. It is about looking past the troubles of day-to-day and taking the longer and deeper view.

Memoir is an example of taking a Socratic approach to life, constantly asking questions about oneself and one's relationships. This is not an easy way to be. But it can be full of richness, texture, and insight.

Memoir Thematic Recipe: The Way of Becoming

Theme is the author's vision for how to live a good life. In Memoir, the author is also the hero, so the theme is something she must discover for her own benefit.

As in any genre, theme in Memoir comes from the basic action of the hero and key question the genre asks. The hero's basic action is to search inside oneself. As we mentioned at the beginning, that search focuses on three key questions: Why am I unique? What does my life mean? Why has it been valuable?

This is why writing one's Memoir is an important, even essential, human activity. It is not part of one's bucket list. It *is* the bucket list.

Memoir gives us the steps for creating our own becoming. It says we become our best self by rethinking our past to find the causes of the choices we made. This is not an intellectual exercise. It is about seeing the psychological and moral patterns that defined us once, but do not need to define us in the future.

The great irony of the Memoir is that this most past-oriented of all story forms is about creating a better future. It shows the immense power of story when someone applies it to themselves. We do that specifically by facing our excuses and confronting our opponents.

Memoir is the most directly personal and thematic of all story forms, which makes it a transcendent form of storytelling by definition. The author reviews her life, finds the larger themes, and thereby transcends herself.

Fictional Forms of Creating the Self

The two main fictional forms of creating the self in story are:

1. The Coming-of-Age Story, also known as bildungsroman
2. Myth/Drama and Personal Myth

The Coming-of-Age Story

A "bildungsroman" is a novel of personal development or formation, tracking the process of a young hero, typically male, becoming an adult. The story details not only the character's psychological and moral growth, but also his or her education in the strict and sometimes brutal ways of society. Originally a German story form, the bildungsroman gained popularity throughout Europe.

Examples include Henry Fielding's *The History of Tom Jones, a Foundling*, Johann Wolfgang von Goethe's *Wilhelm Meister's Apprenticeship*, Charlotte Brontë's *Jane Eyre*, Jane Austen's *Mansfield Park*, Charles Dickens's *David Copperfield*, and James Joyce's *A Portrait of the Artist as a Young Man.*

The "Coming-of-Age" story is the same as a bildungsroman. However, in Hollywood the term "Coming-of-Age" usually refers to a character moving from child to adult. In addition, these films often focus on the hero's first sexual experience. This sensationalistic version of the story is superficial, using the lowest common denominator of sex to expand the audience.

In *The Anatomy of Story*, I point out that "a true coming-of-age story shows a young person challenging and changing basic beliefs and then taking new moral action." Stories like *David Copperfield*, *The Adventures of Huckleberry Finn*, *The Catcher in the Rye*, *Good Will Hunting*, *Scent of a Woman*, *Stand by Me*, and the political Coming-of-Age story

Mr. Smith Goes to Washington are especially good at this aspect of the form.

Other examples of Coming-of-Age include *To Kill a Mockingbird*, *Moonlight*, *CODA*, *A Tree Grows in Brooklyn*, *The Graduate*, *Cinema Paradiso*, *American Graffiti*, *8½*, *Hope and Glory*, *Boyhood*, *The 400 Blows*, *Slumdog Millionaire* (also Love), *Say Anything* (also Love), *Almost Famous* (also Love), *The Spectacular Now*, *The Perks of Being a Wallflower*, and *The Way Way Back*.

The Art and Story of the Self

Genres aren't just about telling entertaining stories. Each one explores one or more art/story forms that every reader must master to live a successful life. For example, the story form of Horror is religion. In Action, it's war and sports. In Myth, Memoir, and in the Coming-of-Age story, it's personal identity.

Personal identity is not something a person has or something that was lost that she must find. The "search for personal identity" is a misnomer; this is an act of *creating* the self.

KEY POINT: Creating the self is the first and never-ending art form.

For the sake of simplicity, we will use "self" interchangeably with "individual" and "person." In the Story of the Mind and Truth section of the Detective genre, we will look more deeply at how the mind operates through story. It begins by creating a character of itself called "I." The transcendent Coming-of-Age/bildungsroman and Memoir-Myth stories are Myths of self-development. They track how this "I" develops and becomes unique over a lifetime. These story forms are the fictional expression of existential philosophy, which we will refer to as the Existential Code.

KEY POINT: Character change is basic to any story form. But both Memoir and Coming-of-Age explore this change in-depth. They do so primarily by highlighting weakness-need at the beginning of the story and self-revelation at the end.

The Graduate is one of the best Coming-of-Age stories in American film. Basic existentialist ideas seem to be woven throughout. As the film's poster says: "This is Benjamin. He's a little worried about his future."

The film lays out all kinds of false traps Ben could blame for his malaise and his unformed self. A recent college graduate, he is apparently trapped by his parents' expectations, his schooling that set him up for a "productive" life path, and pressure from his father's friend to take a high paying job in a business like "plastics."

But finally, Ben realizes he is actually free. He doesn't have to submit to any of that pressure. He decides to do the unthinkable and crash his girlfriend's wedding to the "proper" guy. They run off together. The movie ends with them sitting in the back of the bus realizing, "we're responsible for this and now we must live with the consequences." Rather than the predetermined "they-lived-happily-ever-after" ending, the writers suggest that the real struggle for this new couple is just starting. Their life won't be easy, but it will be all theirs.

Coming-of-Age Story Beats

As we have seen with religion, war, and sports, the creative process for creating the story/art is the same. The individual projects symbols onto an external canvas. Working within the limits and rules of that canvas, the artist engages in a constant feedback loop with the work. She looks at the external form she is making and compares that to the internal model in her mind. She changes the external shape, which in turn adjusts the internal model. At the end of the process, the final work is "born."

This same process occurs in making the self. What exactly are the steps for creating one's self and creating one's life, as depicted in the Coming-of-Age genre? And what are the stages of growth the individual moves through over the course of a lifetime?

Like any story form over time, Coming-of-Age shows the creation of the individual primarily through the seven major structure steps.

COMING-OF-AGE STORY BEAT: Frame—Weakness-Need to Self-Revelation

Coming-of-Age shows the creation of the self in a single moment, at the self-revelation. To set that up, this form depends heavily on the structural story frame. This is the contrast between the hero's weakness-need at the beginning of the story and the hero's growth by the time of the self-revelation.

Weakness-Need

At the beginning the hero is enslaved primarily by a sense of self that makes them believe they are not free. The Existential Code refers to this generally as "bad faith." The character may be thinking through a rigid ideological lens or accepting the values of the larger society without question. Her sense of self is limited and determined by others' expectations. She pities herself and blames others for her situation.

Self-Revelation

Coming-of-Age highlights this step above all others. This is the moment of growth when the character sees herself in a fundamentally different way. To experience growth, the character must see clearly who she really is, take responsibility for her actions, and see how she can have a positive effect on others.

> **KEY POINT: Creating the self means confronting internal slavery and realizing one is responsible to be oneself. Therefore, according to the overall process of these stories, freedom means creating and becoming oneself.**

COMING-OF-AGE STORY BEAT: Self-Life Stages

Given the extreme complexity of the human mind, there are myriad ways of describing the "stages" of change in any human being. Some are found in psychology, some in philosophy, and others are expressed through story. I put "stages" in quotes because any living process, including human, is one of constant change. Death is a revolutionary change. "Stages" are always somewhat arbitrary distinctions we make when trying to understand change in the complex human animal.

Stages of the Self in Story

Coming-of-Age is especially good at expressing the self's stages of growth in story terms. It adds emotional detail and suggests different sequences for how a life might evolve.

The artistic process of the individual creating herself over a lifetime works through these steps and techniques:

- The outside world: the canvas with which the individual interacts
- Fundamental character types, or archetypes
- Life stages that all humans pass through, known as archetypal situations
- The creativity the individual uses in dealing with those stages
- The hero's character change

Notice a basic distinction between self stages and life stages. Life stages, or archetypal situations, are social situations that every person must experience from birth to death. These situations connect the individual to the culture. Stories then express these situations within a plot so we can learn how to handle them.

Fairy tales express the archetypal situations of the child, especially the most important one of the child separating from the mother. The Myth and Memoir forms, with the longest character arc of any genre, can show all the major archetypal situations from birth to death.

Coming-of-Age focuses most often on the step of the teen becoming an adult. Here are some of the other archetypal situations we see portrayed in stories:

- **BIRTH:** facing the pain of life.
- **CHILD TO ADULT:** taking the full responsibility of being an adult.
- **MARRIAGE:** a spiritual mesh between two individuals, an understanding that causes each to blossom as a person.
- **CREATING CHILDREN:** creating a person and becoming a true parent.
- **DEEPER LEVELS OF ADULTHOOD:** expressed as the search for understanding, from striving for individual gain to being in total harmony with the natural world.
- **BECOMING GODLIKE:** in Coming-of-Age combined with Myth, the character may gain a sense of immortality.

Shakespeare's Seven Stages of Life

One of the most famous story expressions of life stages is found in the "all the world's a stage" monologue in Shakespeare's comedy *As You Like It*. He defines the stages of an individual becoming their true self over a lifetime based on seven stages, roughly equating to decades. His "stages of man" are infant, schoolboy, lover, soldier, justice, pantaloon, and old age, facing imminent death.

Shakespeare Tragedies Based on Stages of Life

One of the ways Shakespeare creates transcendent Coming-of-Age/Myth/Drama plays is by basing tragedy on a character at a major stage of the life cycle. This grounds the drama in the psychological and moral landmarks of the aging process. While heading down the river of life, the hero pauses momentarily in the eddies of moral challenges unique to each decade.

These are the natural weaknesses appropriate to a particular stage in a person's life found in four of Shakespeare's tragedies:

- ***ROMEO AND JULIET***: the extreme passion and poor judgment of youth
- ***HAMLET***: indecision of a young adult entering the moral complexity of the social world
- ***MACBETH***: the "vaulting ambition" of a young middle-aged adult
- ***KING LEAR***: the foolish confidence and poor judgment of an aged, once-great man

According to Shakespeare, becoming a fully realized human being means climbing the growth ladder from ego to higher self. Nowhere is this clearer than in *Hamlet*. He starts as a child tied to and bitter toward his mother. Then he struggles in his sexual relationship with Ophelia and with the moral complexity of avenging his father against his uncle. Finally, he becomes a true adult when he realizes he is the instrument of a higher purpose: "there is a special providence in the fall of a sparrow."

Individual Stages in Coming-of-Age and Myth/ Drama Stories

From these overviews of the development of the self in story, let's look at particular stages of the self.

> **KEY POINT: These self stages happen through character change, which is completed when the character has a self-revelation.**

1. CHILDHOOD FOREVER

At one end of the ladder of self stages is the never-ending childhood. The self is fixed in childhood. Not only is the child not responsible for others, she is not responsible for herself. She is carefree. Her life is all about play.

This stage represents both the dream of immortality and the desire to hold on to the best qualities of childhood.

Perhaps no story has captured the bittersweet quality of eternal childhood better than J. M. Barrie's play *Peter Pan, or the Boy Who Wouldn't Grow Up*. Peter is on the ultimate boy's adventure, fighting pirates in Neverland with his platoon of Lost Boys. For Peter these battles never grow old. And neither does he. So he can't accept what has happened (in an epilogue) when he returns to his friend and mother figure, Wendy Darling, to take her back for one more adventure.

Wendy is us. She gets older. She has become a woman with children of her own. So, reluctantly, she must turn Peter down. Her pain, and ours, at losing our childhood forever is extreme.

A modern take on the everlasting childhood is *Toy Story 3*, best of the brilliant *Toy Story* films. Andy, now a young man, is leaving for college, and he wants to bring only Woody, his favorite toy, with him. This is his desperate effort to keep the playfulness and wonder of his childhood.

But Woody is wiser than Andy. He sacrifices his love for the boy so he can rejoin the community of his toy friends and Andy can grow up. Then he gets Andy to give all the toys to the little girl around the block, who will play with them as only a child can. When, along with the little girl, Andy plays with his toys one last time, he becomes Wendy, the adult saying goodbye.

2. CHILD TO ADULT

The shift from child to adult in story shows the process of someone taking responsibility for her actions and her life. Psychologically, the child no longer maintains the false image of herself and her world. Morally, the child no longer blames others for her misfortunes. Instead she takes actions to right past wrongs. It's worth noting that many adults haven't reached this stage.

The Adventures of Huckleberry Finn is America's premier Coming-of-Age story, based on its national sin of slavery. Besides the revolutionary use of dialect, the author Mark Twain flipped the form and made literary history by having a boy create the moral self of the American nation. If *Tom Sawyer* represents America's utopia, *Huckleberry Finn* shows its dystopia, in brutal detail.

Huck's journey down the river has the classical Myth story structure. But his stops are not those of an adult male warrior conquering one monster after another. His stops are complex moral battles, based on money and race in the young nation, expressed through personal drama. By making his hero a boy on a journey through America, Twain identifies the nation as a child just as devoid of morality as the young hero.

Huck struggles to create a moral self. Surrounded by overwhelming venality, corruption, and racism, this young boy can only learn what true morality means from the decency and friendship of a runaway slave.

To Kill a Mockingbird extends America's original Coming-of-Age story about its national sin of slavery to 1930s Alabama. Structurally, what makes it unique is that it tracks a double coming-of-age, of six-year-old "Scout" Finch and her attorney father, Atticus. For Scout, growing up means seeing the limitations of adults, even in her godlike father. For Atticus, "growing up" means seeing the inability of the law to control the darker angels of our human nature, in both his neighbors and in himself.

In *Moonlight*, the hero is a young Black boy who comes to accept he's gay. This is revolutionary for American popular film.

True "coming-of-age" doesn't happen in a moment of grand self-revelation. It happens in fits and starts; two steps forward and one step back. Or in this case, one step forward and two steps back. The script structures the boy's journey into three sections, which is really three connected short stories. Each section highlights one of three big challenges the hero Chiron faces: he's young, Black, and gay.

Because of this "perfect storm" of challenges, Chiron is constantly bullied. The beautiful irony of the first section is that this nine-year-old's father figure is the crack dealer who sells to his perpetually high and neglectful mother.

In section two, teenager Chiron has his first sexual experience with his best friend Kevin. But Chiron's bully pressures Kevin to beat on him. The next day Chiron experiences his biggest success of the film when he smashes a chair over the bully's head. But this moment of freedom only leads to greater slavery when he is arrested and sent to juvie.

In section three a grown Chiron has a meal with Kevin,

now married with a child. Chiron admits he sells drugs for a living and hasn't been physical with anyone since Kevin touched him years before.

The film ends with the possibility of a self-revelation for Chiron as a gay man. But if so, it is slight step forward for a man with so many barriers that will never go away.

3. CHILD TO ADULT IN ANTI-COMING-OF-AGE STORIES

An anti-Coming-of-Age story also shows a child taking responsibility and seeing herself as she really is. However, she tries to disconnect the idea of taking responsibility from the idea that she has to get a boring, compartmentalized job in a social system that kills all wonder and creativity.

Probably the most famous Coming-of-Age story of the twentieth century, *The Catcher in the Rye*, gives us a classic example of transcending the form through anti-Coming-of-Age. The writer J. D. Salinger telegraphs this strategy with the first-person Storyteller Structure in the opening paragraph.

> If you really want to hear about it, the first thing you'll probably want to know is where I was born, and what my lousy childhood was like, and how my parents were occupied and all before they had me, and all that David Copperfield kind of crap, but I don't feel like going into it, if you want to know the truth.

Holden saying he doesn't want to go into all that David Copperfield crap is Salinger saying right up front: "I am rebelling against the most famous Coming-of-Age story in history until now. I'm rebelling against the entire form. My character and I are rebels in every way."

Turns out *The Catcher in the Rye* and *David Copperfield* are polar opposites in how to write a Coming-of-Age story and how to express theme through plot. *David Copperfield* represents the high point of plot in the nineteenth century. Within six years, the move to antiplot began with the publication of Gustave Flaubert's *Madame Bovary*. She is a passive character where most of the action happens in her imagination. *The Catcher in the Rye* is the ultimate twentieth-century Coming-of-Age version of antiplot.

KEY POINT: *David Copperfield* expresses theme through a massive amount of plot while *The Catcher in the Rye* is an antiplot where almost nothing happens.

In every way, Holden is a real-life, purposeless kid. This character is expressed in action through a purposeless plot, as Holden simply walks around New York for three days. Like *Ulysses*, *The Catcher in the Rye* is a meandering journey through the city. But *Catcher* doesn't have the Myth landmarks and references of *Ulysses*. So it doesn't have the advantage of jumping back and forth from the quotidian to the universal.

While unique, Salinger's antiplot approach to Coming-of-Age has a high cost. His almost real-time recounting of Holden's walking tour of New York seems designed to force the reader to experience the same boredom the hero feels. Plot is the sugar of story. Once you remove it, the reader is left with one long lesson of character change and theme.

What sets *The Catcher in the Rye* apart is its remarkable prose style and unique first-person voice. To whatever degree it appeals to the teenage reader is due to Holden constantly calling out the phoniness of adults. Discovering the vast amount of hypocrisy that seems to come with being a grown-up may be the ultimate revelation for a teenager coming of age.

4. CHILD TO ADULT IN A FANTASY BILDUNGSROMAN

A Fantasy bildungsroman is a Coming-of-Age story where the steps of becoming an adult are intensified in a fantasy world.

Of all the elements that contributed to the success of the *Harry Potter* stories, the greatest is writer J. K. Rowling's mixing of the Fantasy and bildungsroman story forms. The brilliance of the stories' premise is to show the development of a boy from age eleven to seventeen in a magical prep school. The hard work of becoming an adult is made infinitely more appealing by also tracking how a boy becomes a wizard.

Besides combining these two genres, Rowling's use of the school is the key to making this Fantasy bildungsroman the most popular series of books in history. High school is now the universal passage to adulthood. So every reader sees their own school experience in light of Harry. For kids, Harry is the student they would all like to be. For adults, he is the student they would all like to have been.

Instead of highlighting the encounters the young hero has with an oppressive society, as in the traditional bildungsroman, Hogwarts exemplifies the values of learning, magic, friendship, and love. Instead of a painful struggle, the coming-of-age becomes a delightful, if scary, journey into one's own magical possibilities.

5. ADULT TO LEADER

In this change, a character goes from being concerned only with finding the right path for himself to realizing he/she must help others find the right path as well. This is an example of the self changing well into adulthood.

Examples include *The Matrix*, *Saving Private Ryan*, *Elizabeth*, *Braveheart*, *Forrest Gump*, *Schindler's List*, *The Lion King*, *The Grapes of Wrath*, *Dances with Wolves*, and *Hamlet*.

This change from adult to leader is built into the Myth

form where the hero gets a public revelation (that he is a king). We also see it in stories that combine Myth and Drama. It is rare in Coming-of-Age stories, which usually focus on the child becoming an adult.

6. LEADER TO VISIONARY

At the height of development of the self is the transformation from leader to visionary. Leader to visionary really represents a refinement of the leader, itself a refinement of the adult. It can happen at any time during adulthood, but typically occurs when the character is older. It is the change from helping others find the right path—the leader—to providing a new moral vision for how an entire society should act in the future—the visionary. This is not just a personal change; it is a change in the culture. This change is found most often in the great religious stories and in some Creation Myths.

The story of Moses tracks one man's change from adult to leader to visionary. The designing principle is this: A man who does not know who he is struggles to lead his people to freedom and receives the new moral laws that will define him and his people.

The key element in this change of the self is the broad but detailed *moral* vision that allows the individual to lead a people to a better life for all.

7. MACHINE TO HUMAN AND SUPERHUMAN

Going from machine (robot) to human and superhuman is a species change. The storyteller has created a machine version of a human being, with certain strengths but also weaknesses that make it both more and less than human. When the robot becomes human, it shows deeper emotion, empathy, and morality than the typical person.

Whether the final result is human or superhuman is left to the viewer to decide.

Season one of *Westworld* has one of the most ambitious growth tracks ever attempted in story. Robots go from machine to human consciousness, with the suggestion that their new moral vision is beyond human. The Moses of this tribe is Dolores. She has the classic Myth self-revelation of discovering who she is at the end of the journey and becoming a leader of her tribe. At her moment of great insight, she says, "Now I know who I must become."

According to *Westworld*, four main elements are necessary for human consciousness: memory, free will, moral choice, and suffering. The vehicle for accomplishing these elements of a new consciousness is Story itself.

8. HERO TO ARTIST: *KÜNSTLERROMAN*

A *Künstlerroman* is a bildungsroman in which the hero becomes an artist. We mentioned at the beginning that creating the self is the first and never-ending art form. At the upper end of this development ladder is the artistic self. The artistic self, also known as the creative self, represents a mind overcoming ideology to hone new facets of its individuality through a work of art.

> **KEY POINT: Each work of art the individual creates is a condensed version of his/her own self-consciousness and identity.**

Examples include *David Copperfield*, *A Portrait of the Artist as a Young Man*, *In Search of Lost Time*, *A Tree Grows in Brooklyn*, *Look Homeward, Angel*, *Black Boy*, *Of Human Bondage*, *This Side of Paradise*, *The World According to Garp*, *Hope and Glory*, *Cinema Paradiso*, *Girls*, *CODA*, and *Frances Ha*. There are few examples of this subgenre, especially recently, because stories about artists usually lack drama and commercial appeal.

The most famous *Künstlerroman* is James Joyce's *A Portrait of the Artist as a Young Man*. A more current example is *CODA* (children of deaf adults). *CODA* is *Fame* with fish. That high-concept premise lays the foundation for the film's power.

The premise line is as follows: While working on her family's fishing boat with her father and brother, who are deaf, a young woman finds she may have the talent to go to the Berklee College of Music. This film plays out all the familiar beats of the subgenre of the Coming-of-Age of an artist (*Künstlerroman*): the main character must choose between family and individual artistic success. The premise's ironic contrast of a deaf family and a daughter who can sing allows the story to build to an emotional high.

Emotional power is the great promise of the Coming-of-Age form. The question arises: What is the story technique that prompts tears of joy? Essentially, it's when a character goes from isolation to communion. *CODA* ends with three scenes in succession that won it the Academy Award for Best Picture.

The first scene, from the point of view of the deaf parents, is the school concert. We see but cannot hear the effect their daughter's singing has on the audience. After the concert, she sings for her father while he feels the vibrations of her throat.

In her audition, the girl's first attempt is amateurish. Her music teacher saves her by pretending to screw up while accompanying her on the piano. On her second chance, her voice begins to soar. She adds sign language so her family, hiding in the balcony, can be part of her finest moment.

If you can get through those scenes without tears running down your cheeks, it means you're already dead. That's the power of great writing, brought to life by honest acting and clean directing.

9. HERO TO ARTIST OF ANOTHER PERSON

Another advanced stage of the Artistic Self involves the artistry of another person. This is not simply becoming the father or mother, as we see in *Ulysses* and *Forrest Gump*. This is the art of creating a community and helping another person become their own Artistic Self.

The subgenre that shows the positive creation of another person is something I call the Traveling Angel Comedy. In *The Anatomy of Story*, I wrote that "the typical traveling angel story begins by establishing a community, and a family, in trouble. The angel—in fact or in function—then enters and proceeds to fix everyone's problem." In this case, the angel helps the individual to become an artist.

The Intouchables is one of the best Traveling Angel Comedies. A rich quadriplegic named Philippe hires a poor man named Driss to be his caretaker. Over the course of the story, Driss fixes Philippe's dysfunctional family. But the main focus is Philippe. Driss's energy and passion for life show the regimented, uptight, and ideological Philippe how to love life and find love in spite of his extreme disability.

Myth/Drama and the Personal Myth

The fictional Coming-of-Age story and the nonfiction Memoir connect to form two transcendent genres:

1. Myth/Drama
2. Myth + Memoir = the Personal Myth

Myth/Drama

One of the most important developments in the history of story is the creation of the hybrid form of Myth/Drama. Its modern manifestation is the Personal Myth, which is a combination of Myth and Memoir using the Myth beats to structure the story.

We first see the Myth/Drama form in the shift from Homerian grand Myths like the *Iliad* and the *Odyssey* to the theatrical dramas of the three great Greek playwrights: Aeschylus, often considered the father of drama, Sophocles, and Euripides. Their plays retain such mythical elements as

- the correspondence between the natural, universal order, and the relation of the king to his people, and
- references to characters from Greek mythology, like King Agamemnon, his wife, Clytemnestra, daughter Electra, and son Orestes.

Myth/Drama might be called the Psychological Epic. It decreases the fantastical and symbolic journey found in classic Myth and increases the moral conflict between intimate opponents. In addition, Drama makes Myth believable and current and highlights the psychological and moral issues along life's path.

TECHNIQUES FOR THE BEST MYTH/DRAMA

- Keep the Myth form hidden, especially if there's a particular Myth on which you're basing the story. You get the power of Myth, but it feels more real.
- Give the hero a strong goal to support tangents when the characters engage in dramatic conflict. That spine is provided by the hero's desire line. Without a strong spine, the tangents collapse the story.
- If possible, have the hero bring his family on the journey. This creates the central conflict from within the family, and allows the story to build instead of being episodic.

- Have at least three to four Myth scenes for each drama scene. This keeps the narrative drive strong. A Myth beat is usually a fantastical encounter with a strange opponent on the path. A drama beat is usually conflict with an intimate opponent, typically within the family.
- Intensify the moral tests for the hero on his journey. This puts the hero under progressively more pressure.

Myth/Drama often uses a more complex form of the meander story shape known as a "vortex street." A vortex street is a single river with a series of eddies, or spirals, alongside. The hero goes down the stream in search of the main Myth goal but has a number of stops along the way in which he has personal, dramatic exchanges. The vortex street story looks like this:

The big advantage of the vortex street is that the story combines the forward narrative drive of the "river" with the more complex, detailed drama and social issues of the "eddies."

Examples include *The Adventures of Huckleberry Finn*, *Forrest Gump*, *Little Miss Sunshine* (Myth Comedy), *Hope and Glory*, *Big Fish*, *The Grapes of Wrath*, *Apocalypse Now*, *Candide*, and many of Dickens's stories, like *David Copperfield*.

The key Myth/Drama story is Sophocles's *Oedipus Rex*. Perhaps no other Greek Myth/Drama has such a strong link between the natural order, the morality of the king, and the health of the kingdom. The plague on Thebes is the direct result of the failure to bring the murderer of the previous king to justice. Oedipus discovers that the murderer is the current king, himself. So it is an individual and king not knowing himself who ultimately causes the plague.

By killing his father, the previous king, and marrying his mother, Oedipus has transgressed far beyond the personal or societal. He has a committed a crime against the entire natural order, and that destroys him and the kingdom.

In the Detective chapter, we discuss this play as the first Detective story. Oedipus's investigation is not just about who committed the murder, but also about the deeper moral connections between a king, his family, and his people.

> **KEY POINT: Investigating the moral element in the story is the crucial connection between the Mythical and the modern dramatic story.**

SHAKESPEAREAN MYTH/DRAMA

Shakespeare expands on the great Greek dramatists using the Myth/Drama form. His main technique is to place the interpersonal drama within a larger world of natural and supernatural forces. This involves matching three levels within the play: the personal, the political, and the mythical.

We know that Shakespeare often heightens the dramatic effect by focusing the story on a central problem inherent to the hero's age. We see the first passion of teenage love in *Romeo and Juliet*, the question of personal identity of young adulthood in *Hamlet*, the extreme ambition of the young middle-aged man in *Macbeth*, and the crumbling power and authority of old age in *King Lear*.

Hamlet is a textbook example of the Myth/Drama form, showing a clear shift from the mythical to the dramatic. We see this first and foremost in the main character. Hamlet marks the move to modern man.

Shakespeare began his creative process with the mythical warrior Amleth. He transformed this character into a man battling himself over morality. Good versus evil is a superficial idea of justice, typical of Myth stories. Nothing is all good or all evil in *Hamlet*.

Looking at the shift in a different way, Hamlet is Odysseus as a young man trying to blend his warrior past with his artistic self. He is a prince who would be king. But he spends all his time exploring the art of practical morality. To determine the guilt of the king, Hamlet puts on a play depicting how the act may have occurred, then watches the king's response.

Hamlet dramatizes the central moral problem of the young adult coming to terms with responsibility. But it also makes heavy use of the mythical element of a real ghost and explores the conflict between the rational and the mystical within Hamlet himself.

Shakespeare also avoids the usual warrior opponent found in Myth. This is not Achilles versus Hector on the field of battle in front of two armies. Hamlet never goes head-to-head with King Claudius; he barely confronts him. His key dramatic struggle is not against Claudius or his mother, but within himself as he tries to find the right action and make his peace with the inequities of the world.

Personal Myth, or Life Journey Myth

The modern-day version of the Myth/Drama form is the Personal Myth. Personal Myth is a hybrid form that combines Myth with creative Memoir. The dramatic elements tend to come from embellishing Memoir or expressing autobiographical elements through a Myth story structure.

Examples of Personal Myth include *Cinema Paradiso*, *For-*

rest Gump, *Life of Pi*, *Big Fish*, *Almost Famous* (also Love), *Hope and Glory*, *My Life as a Dog*, and *Tree of Life* (also the Ecological Myth).

In this subgenre, the writer turns him/herself into a fictional character and sends that character on a mythical journey. This journey is usually magical, although it doesn't have to be. But the real events must have magical overtones and the character must undergo major, almost archetypal change.

TECHNIQUE: Structuring the Personal Myth

Begin by describing your whole life in mythical terms, using elements like labyrinth, wilderness, talisman, and god. Then intercut mythical-fantastical scenes with dramatic ones.

Cinema Paradiso: Paradise Lost

Cinema Paradiso is the greatest Coming-of-Age film. It is the ultimate genre hybrid, combining Myth/Drama, Personal Myth, the Modernization story, Coming-of-Age (bildungsroman), and *Künstlerroman* to track the making of a filmmaker.

This is the story of a man, Salvatore, going back to his small town after the death of his surrogate father, Alfredo. He remembers when he was a boy of eight and Alfredo would let him run the movie in the projection booth at the village theater, called Cinema Paradiso. This is a paradise world where the entire community gathers to enjoy great movies and Salvatore falls in love with the art of film. One day, the cinema burns down, blinding Alfredo. It is rebuilt, but it's not the same. Salvatore leaves the town because it is too small for his dreams. When he returns for Alfredo's funeral, he receives one last gift from his friend.

Cinema Paradiso achieves greatness using three major techniques:

TECHNIQUE 1: Social Fractals

It plays out the same pattern at different scales in the story, from individual to family to community to society to world. This is also known as social fractals, which we will explore in more detail in Science Fiction.

> **KEY POINT: The trick to *Cinema Paradiso* is that it matches the rise and fall of the hero, the cinema, and the town.**

TECHNIQUE 2: Social Fractals in Time

The film tracks these three elements through the stages of the town as it declines. This is a paradise lost story, where the childhood paradise is lost through the inevitable modernization of the world.

The stages of the town are the larger social stages that any society will pass through as it modernizes. Some of the best films in history use this strategy, such as *Dances with Wolves*, *Butch Cassidy and the Sundance Kid*, *Citizen Kane*, *The Magnificent Ambersons*, *Meet Me in St. Louis*, *The Wild Bunch*, *McCabe & Mrs. Miller*, *Seven Samurai*, and *The Apu Trilogy*.

TECHNIQUE 3: Storyteller Structure

The Storyteller Structure allows the writers to connect and contrast the characters and the stages of the town over fifty years. This gives the sequence a powerful emotional build.

The Next Rung Up the Ladder

Memoir tells us how we can change our choices going forward in life. But it is focused on the personal and looks at the past.

It doesn't show us how to create happiness within the larger structures of society and culture. For that understanding we must look to Science Fiction.

Science Fiction is the next rung up on the genre ladder because it focuses on how these larger structures operate and to what degree they make happiness possible.

6

Science Fiction: Science, Society, and Culture

The Tempest: First Science Fiction and Western

Shakespeare's *The Tempest* is a play about America: the magical island where a new world can be created for good or bad. This is the first Science Fiction story. The hero goes on a journey and uses technology to create a new world with a political system. The technology is magic and the political system is one of rightful kingship. All of this happens on an island, the laboratory of man and one of the key techniques in the Science Fiction form. The hero controls a monster, Caliban, which is right out of Myth and Horror.

The Tempest is also the first Western, because the hero creates a home in the wilderness of the new world. A European forced by political oppression to go west starts a new life and colonizes those who already live on the land.

Why Science Fiction Became Necessary

After Darwin, the world had to rethink itself as a land without gods. This rethinking has happened through two major expressions of the mind: science and art. These two forms of thinking have become separate kingdoms. Neither camp understands the other.

To prove this, C. P. Snow, in his famous essay "The Two Cultures," conducts a social experiment. He asks his artist friends if they know the second law of thermodynamics. He believes that, for scientists, this is the equivalent of what reading Shakespeare is for artists. If one does not know a law so fundamental to how the world works, one is simply uneducated.

Science Fiction is the story form that unites these two ways of thinking. It shows us that Science versus Story is a false distinction. Science *is* a story. $E=mc^2$ isn't just an equation; it's a true story. Darwin's theory = the story of life's change.

What is the value of adding science to fiction? Perhaps humanity has become so advanced in our use of technology that we need a story form to harness it to human emotion. Or perhaps we can only get a full understanding of how the world works by melding these two apparently opposing modes of consciousness.

That's what we'll explore.

Science Fiction: How It Works

All genres express a unique relationship of individual to society. That's because the human being, the social animal, always lives among Others. This is ambivalent at every level of life. The living entity fears the Other, but also depends on them to survive and flourish.

More than any other story form, Science Fiction is about the difficult relation of the individual to the society, and how various sizes of societal rings determine one's life. Specifically, it's about how to live a free life within the complex enslaving bonds of modern society. Science Fiction asks: If every human is both a composition and part of a larger composition, how is the individual possible? How can an individual live within the system and still remain an individual?

In our examination of the genres, why would we next explore the most futuristic of all story forms? The reason is that all the genres we've looked at until now emphasize the individual. With Myth, we get some sense of the culture of the story world. But the hero journeys through that culture and the story focuses on the hero's personal development. With Science Fiction, the viewpoint is one of society first.

Then why not look first at other heavily social genres, like Crime, the Western, or the Gangster story? After all, Crime focuses on the morals and laws by which society functions. The Western tracks the evolution of civilization. Since Science Fiction is about the future, doesn't it make more sense to deal with it last?

No. Science Fiction has to be next because it's not really about predicting the future.

> **KEY POINT: Science Fiction is concerned with how to *create* society, and in particular, how to create a *better* society.**

While this is one of the newest major genres in the history of story, its emphasis on how society works provides the foundation of all social story forms.

Science Fiction Mind-Action Story View

The Science Fiction Mind-Action story view says that the world is best understood as a vision of how life works without gods.

By extension, Science Fiction says that to write stories of social engineering, we have to express both the physical and cultural problems every society faces. This means the writer must explore the art forms of science, society, and culture.

Science Fiction has been described as social philosophy in fiction form. Its deepest insight is that it adds the third rail, technology, to the relationship of land and people as the gateway to understanding how any society operates.

We see this in the story strategy of Science Fiction: send the hero to a unique technological future that highlights the strengths and weaknesses in the present world.

KEY POINT: Science Fiction tells us how to create a better society right now. It does so primarily by showing us the dystopian world we will create if we continue to make the wrong choices.

Science Fiction Compared to Other Genres

Science Fiction is part of the "speculative fiction" family of genres, also composed of Horror and Fantasy. This genre expresses the elements of land, people, and technology using the largest arenas of space and time in all of story. If Horror shows personal devolution, and Fantasy shows personal and societal evolution, Science Fiction shows societal and universal evolution.

To evoke such grand arenas, this form typically uses the Epic story structure. The technical definition of the Epic is: the fate of the nation is determined by or expressed in the actions of a single individual or family. That's why Epic is often used in Myth.

Both Epic and Myth deal with grand scale. Epic highlights the connection between individual and society. As one goes, so goes the other. Myth uses a journey structure and focuses on the hero discovering her destiny.

In Science Fiction, the Epic changes from the fate of the nation to the fate of the universe. It asks: What is the next or best form the planet will take? It then narrows the question down to this: How will we use our technology? Science Fiction makes the case that technology is not a foreign entity. It is humanity, extended. Finally, the form asks: What is your vision of the good life when our tools are so powerful and our reach is so great?

Science Fiction vs. Myth

Both Science Fiction and Myth make use of massive arenas. To see the difference in their story worlds, it is helpful to think in terms of Charles and Ray Eames's famous film *Powers of Ten.*

Powers of Ten begins with the camera looking down on a couple having a picnic in the park. The camera then jumps to ten meters above them, then one hundred meters, and so on, until, moving by powers of ten, the telescope takes in the farthest reaches of the universe. The camera zooms back down to the couple, again at powers of ten. Then, reversing the process, the camera jumps "inside" one of the people, and takes a progressively smaller view at the power of ten until it sees at the subatomic level.

The Myth world exists at the scale of the individual within a city or kingdom. The Science Fiction world exists at either extreme of the size spectrum, the character dealing with both the universal and the subatomic.

Because Myth has the longest growth track of any genre, Science Fiction almost always uses a Myth story structure. In effect, we put the most ancient story form in futuristic clothing. Both genres benefit from this marriage. Myth is updated and feels new. Science Fiction gets a solid, emotional story foundation for its often-clinical look and intellectual themes.

Given the intimate connection between Science Fiction and Myth, it's not surprising that Science Fiction occasionally combines with another genre from the Myth family, the Western. The traditional Western didn't disappear. It traveled to the future and re-created the wilderness in outer space. The Science Fiction–Western hybrid gives us an adventure story in space, which is extremely popular with audiences worldwide. Examples include *Star Wars*, *Dawn of the Planet of the Apes*, *Guardians of the Galaxy*, and most recently, *The Mandalorian*.

KEY POINT: If you want to write a *popular* Science Fiction story, your best bet is to write it as a space Western.

Examples of Science Fiction

Stories

The Shrinking Man, "Speech Sounds," "Bloodchild," "I Have No Mouth and I Must Scream," "'Repent, Harlequin!' Said the Ticktockman," *Deathbird Stories* (collection), *The Beast That Shouted Love at the Heart of the World* (collection), *The Illustrated Man* (collection), *The Martian Chronicles* (a collection that the author, Ray Bradbury, insisted is Fantasy)

Novels and Films

Frankenstein; or, The Modern Prometheus (also Horror), *The Time Machine*, *20,000 Leagues Under the Sea*, *Journey to the Center of the Earth*, *The War of the Worlds*, *Parable of the Sower*, *Parable of the Talents*, *The Three-Body Problem*, *Agency* (*The Jackpot Trilogy*), *Dune*, *Star Wars* (although its creator refers to it as Space Fantasy), *The Empire Strikes Back*, *Star Trek*, *Star Trek* (2009), *Star Trek II: The Wrath of Khan*, *The Hunger Games*, *Divergent*, *Close Encounters of the Third Kind*, *Blade Runner*, *Inception*, *Interstellar*, *Alien* (also Horror), *Aliens* (also Action), *Avatar* (also Ecological Myth), *Gattaca*, *Rollerball*, *Looper*, *WALL-E*, *Gravity*, *The Terminator* (also Horror), *Terminator 2: Judgment Day* (also Action), *Fahrenheit 451*, *Ad Astra*, *Galaxy Quest*, *Guardians of the Galaxy*, *The Martian*, *Mad Max* (also Action), *Mad Max 2: The Road Warrior* (also Action), *Mad Max: Beyond Thunderdome* (also Action), *Mad Max: Fury Road* (also Action), *Total Recall*, *Children of Men*, *The Andromeda Strain*, *Minority Report*, *Logan's Run*, *Contact*, *Soylent Green*, *Brazil*, *The Incredible Shrinking Man*, *I Am Legend*, *The Last Man on Earth*, *The Truman Show* (also Fantasy), *Men in Black* (also Comedy), *Planet of the Apes*, *The Dark Tower* (also Myth and Western), *Edge of Tomorrow*, *A.I.*, *The Fifth Element*, *The Difference Engine*, *Fantastic Voyage*, *The Day the Earth Stood Still*, *Fantastic Planet*

Television

The Twilight Zone (also Horror and Fantasy), *Black Mirror*, *Dark* (also Thriller), *Star Trek: The Next Generation*, *Star Trek: Deep Space Nine*, *Star Trek: Voyager*, *Star Trek: Enterprise*, *The Man in the High Castle*, *Stargate SG-1*, *Firefly*, *The X-Files*, *The Hitchhiker's Guide to the Galaxy*, *Dr. Who*, *The Umbrella Academy* (also Fantasy), *Fringe*, *Babylon 5*, *Squid Game* (also Gangster), *The Outer Limits*, *Alias*, *Quantum Leap*

Science Fiction Subgenres

Space Opera, Time Travel, Dystopian, Alternate History, Military, Adventure, Cyberpunk, Postapocalyptic, Steampunk, Alien Invasion, Hard Science Fiction

Science Fiction Story Overview

Here's what we'll cover in this chapter:

- Science Fiction Story Beats
- Theme: Being Is Recognizing Choices
  - Thematic Recipe: The Way of the Social Creator
- How to Transcend the Science Fiction Story
  - Science Fiction/Myth
  - Science Fiction/Horror

Science Fiction Story Beats

Science Fiction is the broadest and loosest of all story forms. No other genre covers as much space and time or explores the universe in a more haphazard way. This means it is almost impossible to tease out a set of story beats that sharply define this amorphous form. But certain beats and techniques recur.

SCIENCE FICTION STORY BEAT: Story World

World-building is grander and more detailed in Science Fiction than in any other genre. The writer must create everything in the story, including elements of the world that other genres accept as part of the everyday world.

As we have discussed, every story world is a unique combination of land, people, and technology. In Science Fiction, these three elements are magnified.

1. Land includes the universe, the space-time rules, and the scientific theories used to explain how the universe works.
2. People covers the society and culture, including the social stage, government, economic system, and social and gender roles.

3. Technology refers to advanced tech, especially one or two "fulcrum" technologies that determine the basic operation of that particular world.

As we saw in C. P. Snow's "The Two Cultures" argument, we usually think of science as the opposite of art. But science and art are similar in many ways. Science is a story in which the conclusions can be tested. Art is a story in which truth is expressed through symbol. Both the scientific and artistic methods begin with a hypothesis/premise the creator then tests again and again (experimenting/rewriting) on a physical canvas.

KEY POINT: The vast scope and minute detail of the story world require the Science Fiction writer to reproduce three art forms of life in the story: science, society, and culture.

Other genres, like Horror, Myth, and Crime, explore a larger art/story form of life only in their transcendent versions. Like Memoir, Science Fiction explores its art/story forms in the basic genre itself.

Story World: Rules of the Universe

Science Fiction is most concerned with the creation of society-culture, which is where the genre enters the realm of social philosophy. But it also explores the physical foundation of the world at a much larger and deeper level than any other form.

We begin world-building by defining the physical building blocks of the story. Like the rules of the Fantasy world, these are the rules by which the Science Fiction world operates.

Spatial Arena

Because the story may cover vast space, the writer's first step in creating the story world is to outline the single, overall arena where the story occurs.

There are two kinds of Science Fiction arenas:

1. A single tight arena: one planet or location (*Alien*, *Aliens*, *Blade Runner*, *Avatar*, *Arrival*)
2. Many worlds in succession, which is an adventure story in space and sometimes time (*The Stars My Destination*, the *Foundation* trilogy, *Star Trek*, *Star Wars*, *Inception*, *Interstellar*, *The Mandalorian*)

The Space-Time Rules

These rules establish the possibilities of gravity-space-time on which the universe is founded. For example, this may involve defining the normal continuum, how that continuum could be bent, and alternative worlds of different matter or antimatter.

Rules of Motion

These determine the way people counter gravity and the speed of light and so cover vast distances.

Star Wars: once the Millennium Falcon enters "hyperspace"—essentially a freeway tunnel—it can move at "light speed," which is considerably faster than the speed of light. Hyperspace and light speed allow the ship to cover vast distances safely.

> **KEY POINT: In good Science Fiction, the rules always have severe penalties if someone breaks them.**

In *The Stars My Destination*, people have the ability to "jaunte," or teleport themselves to a different location. If someone jauntes without precise knowledge of location, they could reappear, dead, in a rock.

Four "Stories" That Explain the Physical Universe

KEY POINT: Underlying the narrative in any Science Fiction is one or more scientific theories that provide the laws and logic by which the universe operates.

There are four main physics paradigms: Newtonian, Einstein's Theory of Relativity, Quantum Mechanics, and Post-Quantum. Using these different stories of physicality, the writer can create radically different story worlds and plots and add a sense of authenticity to the story.

TECHNIQUE: Breaking the Laws

Don't be afraid to break the laws of physics to make the story work. But if you do, make sure the new law is consistent.

Examples of stories that use theories from physics include *2001: A Space Odyssey*, *The Martian*, *Gravity*, *Apollo 13*, *WALL-E*, *A Wrinkle in Time*, *Quantum Leap*, *Fantastic Voyage*, *Solaris*, *Dr. Who*, *Inception*, *Ad Astra*, *Ant-Man*, *Ant-Man and the Wasp*, *Looper*, *The Terminator*, *Star Trek*, *Avengers: Endgame*, *Interstellar*, and *Arrival*.

Story World: Society-Culture

After establishing the physical basis of the universe, creating the society-culture is *the* major step in building the story world. This is a daunting artistic challenge in part because society and culture are different but inseparable.

The vast, amorphous things we refer to as "society" or "culture" are not fully grown fixed entities.

KEY POINT: **Society-culture is a story that has been created by every individual in history. It is constantly being re-created every day in the largest collective art form in the world.**

In story terms, "society" is the world, hero, opponents, and minor characters.

KEY POINT: **The foundation of the society, known as the system, is the hierarchy of power and the rules by which the system operates in the family, the organization, or the society.**

How the system works determines how the individuals act toward one another as they try to be successful within the rules.

"Culture" is composed of the ideas, values, moral code, and plan that create a way of living. It is also how the system justifies itself and convinces the individuals to accept their place in it. In the extreme, the culture is what traps the individual members.

KEY POINT: **99 percent of all stories go from slavery to freedom, so you must design the society-culture to show how people are enslaved.**

Society-Culture: Fractals

It is impossible to create a broad and detailed society-culture in the story world without using social fractals. This is especially true in world-building genres like Science Fiction, Myth, and Fantasy.

A fractal is a pattern with the same shape or structure at

various scales of space and time. In other words, the part is the same as the whole. A fractal looks the same no matter how much you zoom in or zoom out.

Why is this so valuable? Fractals give form to scale. They're building blocks that keep the basic structure of the unit intact. So, no matter how complex the story, the basic wisdom of the story remains clear.

KEY POINT: Every society is really a collection of mini-societies all connecting to and interacting with one another simultaneously. *Societies are fractals with human beings.*

The concept of fractals is also found in literature of the American Transcendental movement, whose motto was "the All in Each." The poet and painter William Blake wrote:

To see a World in a Grain of Sand
And a Heaven in a Wild Flower,
Hold Infinity in the palm of your hand
*And Eternity in an hour.**

Defining the various interlocking systems within which the individual lives is like the "powers of ten" applied to society. Some of the major social scales found in Science Fiction are:

1. Organism
2. Body-Person
3. Family
4. Organization
5. City
6. Nation

---

* William Blake, from the poem "Auguries of Innocence," from his personal notebook, written circa 1803.

7. Planet
8. Interplanetary

Let's start by applying the idea of fractals to the organizing principle of the story world, the system.

Four Pillars Within the Society

Irwin Thompson, in his book *At the Edge of History: Speculations on the Transformation of Culture*, provides one of the most profound explanations of the workings of social fractals at every level of development. He begins by laying out the four roles that make up the pillars of every social unit, what he calls "the structure of a primary human group."

These four pillars are the building blocks of the society. Within the tribe we have:

Shaman	**Headman**
Clown	**Hunter**

How do these four functions work?

- The Headman is the chief who runs the organization.
- The Hunter gets the food and defends the tribe.
- The Clown keeps the people in the organization, especially the Headman, in touch with reality.
- The Shaman gives the organization the values and priorities by which the people should live.

Within this four-point opposition are four two-point oppositions. The two roles on the left are concerned with ideas. The two roles on the right are concerned with operation. The two roles at the top are in charge. The two roles at the bottom execute the vision.

KEY POINT: The four roles that make up the pillars of every social unit work together, but each is also in conflict with the others.

Let's see how the major elements of society—social stage, economy, technology, and culture—combine with the hero in a Science Fiction story.

Society-Culture: Social Stages

Social fractals define a system at multiple levels. They are also a process technique, a way of understanding how an entity evolves, in detail, over time.

TECHNIQUE: Evolving Social Fractals

Social fractals allow you to extend the system's basic pattern of the four-point opposition over space and time.

This is done through a fiction technique I call "social stage." Social stage refers to the type of society-culture as it evolves. Implied in this technique is that all societies evolve through the same basic stages as they go from birth to death.

Social stage is the crucial technique used in the Western, where the cultural stages are depicted in great detail. But it is also an important technique in Science Fiction, where the central definer of the world is less about the year the story takes place and more about the evolutionary stage.

KEY POINT: The evolutionary social stage portrayed in Science Fiction is either

- **the negative stage we will enter if we make certain choices now, or**
- **the positive stage we will enter if we make different choices now.**

We can detail the evolution of social stage by applying anthropological theory, Nietzsche's theory of moral evolution, Thompson's code of societal development, and the history of story. Alone, each of these codes is helpful but limited. Together, they give us a powerful, integrated vision of how any society-culture evolves, and therefore how to apply it to write great Science Fiction.

We have discussed that any social system or story world is made up of some combination of land, people, and technology. Over time, these combinations pass through four major social stages:

1. Wilderness
2. Village/Town
3. City
4. Oppressive City

These stages represent the larger *forces of change* acting on the individuals living within the society.

Economy and Technology

Connected to each of these social stages is a primary economic activity on which everything in that world depends and the *fulcrum* technology each one uses.

- **WILDERNESS/TRIBE:** Hunting
- **VILLAGE/TOWN:** Agricultural
- **CITY:** Industrial
- **OPPRESSIVE CITY/SCIENTIFIC-PLANETARY:** Electronic

> **KEY POINT:** Science Fiction can occur in any of these stages. But even if it is set in the wilderness, the technology is advanced in some way.

For example, in the *Mad Max* series of films, people traverse the barren desert in gas-guzzling, fast cars.

KEY POINT: Good Science Fiction always highlights the larger forces acting on the characters.

Examples: too many people are coming to the planet; there's not enough water, air, or oil for everyone; the society has a new government; the technology is becoming obsolete; machines have become too powerful.

Cultural Stage

The evolution of society is closely associated with the evolution of the culture. Cultural evolution tracks the change in the cluster of ideas and values on which the system is based. Typically, the name of the stage highlights the main way the culture traps the individual.

The four cultural stages that normally attach to the four social stages are:

- **WILDERNESS TO VILLAGE:** Shame Culture
- **VILLAGE TO TOWN:** Guilt Culture
- **TOWN TO CITY:** Consumer Culture
- **OPPRESSIVE CITY/PLANETARY:** Fear Culture

Hero and Story

These stages of society, culture, economy, and technology translate into the types of story the society is most likely to tell. This in turn determines the type of main character that drives the story.

How does this work? The hero is shaped in large part by her story world, especially by the society in which she lives.

But society is too vast and detailed for the writer to define in the limited space and time of a story. Therefore, you must use a shorthand for connecting hero to world.

KEY POINT: To connect the hero to the story world, find the character type associated with the social-cultural stage and make that character a unique individual.

Let's explore in detail how each social stage connects the elements of society, culture, technology, hero, and story. We'll also see how one social stage necessarily evolves and becomes more complex over time.

Stage 1. Wilderness to Village—Hunting—Shame Culture-Master Morality—God or Superhero to Warrior

LAND-SOCIETY-ECONOMY

In the wilderness, nature is all-powerful. People are nomads, living in small groups that are constantly on the move hunting for food. Let's look again at Thompson's basic social unit of the tribe, seen as a four-point opposition to highlight the point that each is in conflict with the other three:

Shaman	**Headman**
Clown	**Hunter**

In a wilderness world, the main activity is survival. The system is usually highly organized and is maintained by the exercise of physical force.

CULTURE

This natural and social world of physical dominance finds cultural expression in "master morality" and "shame culture."

Since the master can take what he wants, master morality is based on martial values that celebrate the use of force to solve problems.

The values of the shame culture are the Action values of courage, achievement, physical ability, strength, honor, glory, and doing well (success), as opposed to doing good (justice).

This is a male-dominated culture. When the individual fails to achieve a standard in the eyes of others, he feels shame. The shame culture is the natural outgrowth of any society at the wilderness/early village stage and, to this day, in any male-dominated organization like the police and the military.

HERO

In stories that depict the wilderness stage, the main opponent is some version of nature. Therefore, people create gods and superheroes to try to gain some control over the natural forces. In the modern age, we have few new stories of this stage. Science Fiction often re-creates this world after an apocalypse. The writers of *Gravity* used outer space to create a true wilderness.

When a village is first established, the main opponent is the outsider, the "barbarian," who wants to destroy the village and steal its food. Therefore, the natural Hero for this stage is the warrior. He is physically bigger and tougher than the villagers. The villagers hire him to help them fight the outside warriors, the "savages" who want to return life to the wilderness. Those inside the walls consider outsiders less than human.

STORY EXAMPLES

Star Wars, *The Empire Strikes Back*, *Mad Max*, *Mad Max 2: The Road Warrior*, *Mad Max: Beyond Thunderdome*, *Mad Max: Fury Road*, *The Mandalorian*, *Robinson Crusoe*, *Guardians of the Galaxy*, and *The Martian*.

Stage 2. Village/Town—Agriculture—Shame Culture to Guilt Culture—Master Morality to Slave Morality—Warrior to Merchant

LAND-SOCIETY-ECONOMY

The wilderness becomes the village when the nomads settle down. They plant roots, grow crops, and build structures. The village has only the basic buildings of a functioning society, as we see in the Western genre: the jail, church, saloon, store, plus fences and walls to protect them from their enemies.

This society is young and expanding with plenty of new land to conquer. And that is precisely the attitude these people have toward nature. Generally, nature is to be tamed and transformed for the economic benefit of humans. In the Western, it is to be tamed for the economic benefit of the white settler. As the village and surrounding farms build roads and enjoy a surplus of crops, people start to trade. So begins the merchant.

When the four primary social pillars evolve from the tribe into the village-agricultural unit, the individual becomes the institution. As Thompson points out, the social fractal of the tribe evolves into a more complex version of the original pattern. Thus:

The headman becomes the state, the hunter becomes the military, the clown becomes art, and the shaman becomes religion. Caution: Even though one social stage evolves into another, two or more stages may coexist in the same general area.

Religion	**State**
Art	**Military**

As the village becomes the town, the social organization increases in complexity. Those in power can't see everything. Things are decided behind closed doors. Therefore, social control has to be internalized within the individual, based on personal relationships.

CULTURE

The shift from village to town also changes the values promoted by the system. This finds cultural expression in the shift from shame to guilt culture.

The resulting values of guilt culture include getting along, fairness, faithfulness, reliability, and self-sacrifice.

KEY POINT: Guilt comes when we take on too much responsibility for others, especially the family, and then attack ourselves when we inevitably fail.

The main difference between shame and guilt culture is the emphasis on doing well (success) versus doing good (morality), on doing the best thing versus doing the right thing. Shame is our public embarrassment when people see how we failed to accomplish something. Guilt is our private self-recrimination when we fail to fulfill a promise.

KEY POINT: Shame is a failure of achievement; guilt is a failure of love.

HERO

In the town, attack from the outside has virtually disappeared. Therefore, the hero of this world shifts from the warrior to the average person, the everyman or everywoman character. Social interaction is intimate, among family and friends. The main story problem is personal justice, especially between man and woman or parent and child.

STORY EXAMPLES

Frankenstein; or, The Modern Prometheus, *The Shrinking Man*, *Star Trek*, *Avatar*, *Children of Men*, *Rise of the Planet of the Apes*, *The Twilight Zone*, *Dark*, *Close Encounters of the Third Kind*, and *Interstellar*.

Stage 3. City—Industry—Consumer Culture—Everyman/Everywoman Hero

LAND-SOCIETY-ECONOMY

As a growing town reaches its horizontal boundaries, it starts to expand vertically and become a city. The increasingly complex social organism becomes more specialized. This has three major effects:

1. Comparative advantage brings disproportionate benefits to a few individuals within the whole. Extreme differences of wealth, class, status, and power emerge.
2. More rules are needed to govern all the people.
3. The power of technology increases exponentially, moving from horsepower to machine power. As a result, advanced technology is needed to build and run the city.

According to Thompson, when the four pillars of the village-agricultural unit evolve into the city-industrial unit, they add even more complexity to the same four-point pattern—the state becomes government, the military becomes industry, art becomes media, and religion becomes education. The basic tribal four-point opposition becomes:

Education	**Government**
Media	**Industry**

As the town becomes a city and diversifies, a second process occurs simultaneously. This process takes the individual away from the group. It creates the second strain of the city, the dark underbelly that drags everyone down. As the city grows bigger, the family grows smaller, fragments, and often disappears completely. The individual is alone.

All this happens in a system that is powerful, vast, deep, and unseen. The individual is under control but is also on her own. As a result, she experiences a sense of alienation and the impersonal. When alienation and frustration reach the extreme, the average person often feels power only through destruction. This means crime. Without the "nosy neighbor" of the town, there is no one on the scene to weed out the ne'er-do-wells among us.

CULTURE

As the society shifts from town to city, the individual lives in a world of different ethnic backgrounds, status, wealth, and power. Individuals must coexist among a mass of Others. This produces a polarizing division between values.

On the one hand we have a view that might be called "we are all human beings." These values include diversity, tolerance, fairness, and cooperation. On the other hand we have the view that "familiarity breeds contempt." These values include intolerance, racism, nationalism, class consciousness, and "me first."

As the second strain of the city also emerges, so does a darker set of values. Because the individual has become atomized within the broader social world, he comes to believe that nothing is valuable but himself. This is the Cynic's state of mind: a thing has value only to the degree that it increases one's personal power, pleasure, or money.

KEY POINT: In the city, the result is the loss of the very *concept* of morality and the rise of consumer culture.

This shift in values is fueled by an economic and technological system that can produce massive amounts of product at progressively lower cost. What once would be the rarest luxury is now common to everyone. The desire for a few goods becomes a "need" for all goods.

KEY POINT: The irony of consumer culture is that the more it makes things seem available, the more it enslaves us into making the money to buy them.

HERO

In stories of the city, the citizen's main opponent is still another citizen. But opposition in the city usually comes from an unjust person in power. The hero is still the everyman or everywoman character. But now he/she has two central concerns: fighting for social justice and getting free from the slavery of bureaucracy.

STORY EXAMPLES

The Hunger Games, *Westworld*, *Inception*, *Rollerball*, *Brazil*, *Metropolis*, and *The Truman Show*.

Stage 4. Oppressive City/Planetary—High Technology—Information—Fear and Mass Consumer Culture—Antihero

LAND-SOCIETY-ECONOMY

As a city ages, it becomes overgrown, complex, and corrupt, with too many stringent rules. Technology continues to increase its power exponentially, moving from industrial to high-tech electronics, with an emphasis on information technology. In an oppressive political system, technology is used to keep tabs on where everyone is and what everyone wants. This information becomes the primary means to expand the consumer culture and concentrate power.

The four social functions evolve into what Thompson calls the planetary information society. Government becomes managers, industry becomes technicians, media becomes critics, and education becomes scientists. The four-point opposition is:

Scientists	**Managers**
Critics	**Technicians**

This resulting society is unequal, unjust, and oppressive, with avenues to success largely closed off to most citizens. The city becomes a classic zero-sum game. It moves toward a binary society with a few controlling almost all wealth and power and the rest struggling to get by.

CULTURE

In contrast to the shame and guilt cultures, this culture has been called a "fear society."* (For the sake of simplicity we

---

* Frank Furedi, *Culture of Fear: Risk Taking and the Morality of Low Expectation* (1997).

will refer to fear society as fear culture.) The means by which the society controls the individual has moved from public embarrassment—shame—to self-imposed sanction—guilt—to fear of punishment from a largely unseen power above.

public shame → private guilt → punishment from above

The fear society builds on the consumer culture by encouraging the purchase of things. The vast majority of the profit goes to those who already have both extreme wealth and power. The political system is so interconnected with the financial system that a republic in name is really an oligarchy in practice.

HERO

In this social stage, the main opponent isn't a particular person, but the enslaving system itself. The system is so vast, deep, subtle, and ubiquitous that most individuals are not even aware of its existence. They simply struggle through their lives with no sense of the causes or solutions to their problems.

This society-culture necessarily creates the antihero. In the history of story, we see two kinds of antihero. First is the antihero who refuses to be beaten down by the forces of the oppressive city and is therefore sent into exile or killed. This is the rebel archetype, a character type going as far back in western culture as Prometheus and the Zeus Creation Myth.

In modern story forms, the rebel is most commonly found in Science Fiction stories, such as *Brazil*, *The Hunger Games*, *The Matrix*, and *Divergent*. Notable examples of this antihero outside Science Fiction include *Cool Hand Luke*, *Missing*, *The Shawshank Redemption*, and *Breathless*.

The second type of antihero is the character who stays behind and is oppressed. In the extreme, he is incompetent, antisocial, and sometimes escapes into his own mind where he may see himself as a superhero. Examples of this character outside Science Fiction include *The Secret Life of Walter Mitty*, *Taxi Driver*, *The Trial*, *Slumdog Millionaire*, *The Joker*, and *Midnight Cowboy*.

STORY EXAMPLES

All dystopian Science Fiction stories are set in this fourth social stage, like *Her*, *Blade Runner*, *A Clockwork Orange*, *The Handmaid's Tale*, *Squid Game*, *Animal Farm*, *Nineteen Eighty-Four*, *Brave New World*, *Divergent*, *Black Mirror*, *Logan's Run*, *The X-Files*, *Soylent Green*, and *Fahrenheit 451*.

Society-Culture: The Full Cycle of Social Stages

> **KEY POINT: In the evolution of society-culture, nature grows smaller, society grows larger and more complex, and the hero loses power.**

In twentieth-century storytelling, the assumption is that this evolution of social stages is an inexorable cycle. The inevitable end point is the self-destruction of the oppressive city through human corruption and out-of-control technology. Supposedly, the cycle must begin again with a new wilderness and the ruins of the old technology strewn across the barren landscape. Examples of this approach are the *Mad Max* films, the *Planet of the Apes* films, anti-Westerns like *McCabe & Mrs. Miller* and *Dances with Wolves*, and Modernization stories like *Cinema Paradiso*, *The Magnificent Ambersons*, *Citizen Kane*, *The Last Picture Show*, and *The Apu Trilogy*.

TECHNIQUE: Voice-Over Narration

In film, voice-over narration is an excellent method of expressing the larger social forces affecting the Science Fiction story.

The famous voice-over at the beginning of *Mad Max 2: The Road Warrior* establishes the world's social revolution from oppressive city back to wilderness and connects it to the hero's overall character change:

MAX: I remember a time of chaos . . . ruined dreams . . . this wasted land. But most of all, I remember the Road Warrior. The man we called "Max." To understand who he was, you have to go back to another time . . . when the world was powered by the black fuel . . . and the desert sprouted great cities of pipe and steel . . . For reasons long forgotten, two mighty warrior tribes went to war, and touched off a blaze which engulfed them all . . . And in this maelstrom of decay, ordinary men were battered and smashed . . . men like Max . . . the warrior Max. In the roar of an engine, he lost everything . . . and became a shell of a man . . . a burnt-out, desolate man, a man haunted by the demons of his past, a man who wandered out into the wasteland. And it was here, in this blighted place, that he learned to live again.

Highlighting a positive cycle of social change is a recent concept in the history of story. New forms like the Ecological Myth and Rejuvenation story (which we'll discuss in Fantasy) provide a more hopeful alternative to the inevitable decline of civilization. The most famous example of the Ecological Myth is *Avatar*.

Story World: Über Tech

One of the key insights of the Science Fiction form is the massive effect technology has on society at every step of its development. This is a surprise to many. We normally think of technology as a relatively recent phenomenon, beginning with the Industrial Revolution and proceeding rapidly to the electronic wizardry of today.

But technology is as old as humankind itself. Examples include fire, the wheel, and the domestication of the horse. Technology is the measure of how humanity has magnified its power. It is how humans use their mind to increase their ability to think and act. Technology is the third pillar of creating a story world because it is the measure of the magnification of both human ability and human potential.

> **KEY POINT: Technology is a form of art, a practical application of the mind to making the world work. Therefore, the level of technology is an expression of the level of human consciousness at the time.**

TECHNIQUE: Fulcrum Technology

Make technology important to the characters and the plot.

Science Fiction puts tremendous emphasis on the crucial technology of a particular place and time. This is the *fulcrum* technology upon which the society/world depends.

Science Fiction also emphasizes how technology changes humanity. A profound insight of the genre is that while we create technology, it re-creates us. Technology and humanity are part of a never-ending feedback loop.

A common expression of this loop in Science Fiction is the robot, the machine man. The use of a robot always raises the question: Who is more human, the robots or the human beings? In *Blade Runner* and *Ex Machina* the answer is the robots.

In creating the technology of the Science Fiction story, the writer typically focuses on the modes and rules of communication, transportation, and information. Beyond telling an entertaining story, the ultimate point is to comment on these major technologies today.

Interstellar uses an extreme combination of primitive and futuristic technology. On an earth decimated by war, pestilence, and famine, farmers drive ancient trucks and struggle to produce crops with old machinery. But hidden away nearby are the remnants of NASA, with advanced robots and a spaceship that will pass through a wormhole to get to three potential planets humans might inhabit. After traveling back in time, the hero uses Morse code and his daughter's wristwatch to send the advanced equations that will save humankind.

Caution 1: Because of the desire to get the story moving, many writers create their future world with a few broad brushstrokes. Texture makes a big difference in the quality of the story.

KEY POINT: Science Fiction without a detailed view of the society-culture is superficial and predictable.

TECHNIQUE: Detailing the Story World

To kick your story to a higher level, give sufficient details about as many rules of the world as possible. Focus on politics, society, culture, work, love, sports, and games, sometimes even language. This will make the physical manifestation of your new world seem more real to the reader.

Caution 2: Science Fiction writers often make the mistake of creating a futuristic world so bizarre that it's unlike anything we know today.

KEY POINT: The single biggest reason that many Science Fiction stories fail is that they alienate the audience by making them a clinical observer, not an emotional participant.

TECHNIQUE: Recognizable World

Create a *recognizable* future world so the viewers see it is different, but still *their world*. First, include elements in the world that exist now, then add the new rules you create.

SCIENCE FICTION STORY BEAT: Weakness-Need—Unevolved

Since Science Fiction is such a broad genre, and is often structured by using another genre, like Myth, the hero's role in the story can vary widely. She may wander through an apocalyptic landscape or search for new worlds. Or, she may fight the forces of societal oppression. In transcendent Science Fiction, she may even create a new society.

Due to the scope of Science Fiction, the world or system often dwarfs the hero and *dominates* her. As a result, the hero is a clean slate simply experiencing new worlds. Or, she's the good hero oppressed by the evil system. This creates a big hole in the middle of your story that a more complex character should fill.

TECHNIQUE: The Hero's Moral Flaw

Create a complex character by giving her a severe weakness-need, and especially a moral need. This way she isn't an innocent victim.

As in any genre, the hero in Science Fiction may be flawed in many ways.

KEY POINT: Often the hero's weaknesses turn on what it means to be human.

In other words, the hero is inhuman, animalistic, or unevolved in some way. For example:

- ***BLADE RUNNER***: Rick Deckard ruthlessly kills androids, so he is less human than the robots. He must learn to become truly human.
- ***STAR WARS: A NEW HOPE***: Luke is an impulsive boy who must gain self-discipline and master the ways of the Force to defeat the evil empire.
- ***2001: A SPACE ODYSSEY***: The apelike hominids are killers and the humans want to kill HAL. Human beings must evolve to become a new, higher species.
- ***TOTAL RECALL***: Quaid is a hired killer for Cohagen and must become a rebel to save the people of Mars.
- ***THE TERMINATOR***: Sarah is a victim and must become a leader of the new society.
- ***TERMINATOR 2: JUDGMENT DAY***: Terminator is a machine and a killer. It must become a leader in the human fight against machines.

Science Fiction stories are often combined with Myth because they involve such a long arc of character growth. But in Science Fiction, the various stages of growth are often expressed in terms of the evolution of humanity itself.

> **KEY POINT: The best Science Fiction stories connect the hero's lack of evolution with the planet's lack of evolution.**

SCIENCE FICTION STORY BEAT: Minor Characters—Creating Society and System

Of all the detailing that goes into the Science Fiction story world, the minor characters are the primary component the writer uses when creating an entire society. They allow the author to contrast other characters with the hero, thereby defining her. These minor characters are a main way the author expresses the larger themes of the story.

In fact, much of the success of the story comes from how well the author has detailed these lesser characters. There are three kinds:

1. Normal minor characters who interact with the hero as the story requires. Due to the grand philosophical oppositions inherent to the form, many character differences are simplistic. For example, in *Star Trek*, Spock is logical, while Dr. "Bones" McCoy is emotional.
2. Different beings, or species, that express the anthropology of space. When creating an entire world, writers often try to save time by defining the minor or alien characters using simple shorthand, based strictly on a weird appearance or only one character trait. For example, the logical race, the warlike people, the furry people, and my favorite, the people with the fat heads. This makes the story seem thin and schematic, as well as psychologically simplistic.

   In better Science Fiction, alien beings live by a different set of social rules than the humans. A true anthropology of space is about exploring these rules and their effectiveness.
3. Machine people, referred to as androids or robots. This third type of character highlights the central issue in Science Fiction. Robots, which may also be aliens, are fundamental to the Science Fiction form because they highlight the flaws in human evolution. They question how human behavior works and often appear more "human" than the people.

SCIENCE FICTION STORY BEAT: Desire

The hero's desire line determines the spine of the story. In Science Fiction, the desire is a specific goal that brings the hero into contact with the special technology of the world.

In negative Science Fiction set in an oppressive, dystopian society, the desire is usually to escape. We see this in *The Hunger Games*, *Logan's Run*, *A Clockwork Orange*, *Brazil*, and *The Terminator*.

In positive Science Fiction, usually set in the larger universe with multiple subworlds, the desire is to explore, to find something, to win a war, or to save the earth. We see these more active and positive desires in *Star Wars*, *Star Trek*, *Interstellar*, *Dune*, *Total Recall*, and *The Mandalorian*.

Science Fiction stories often have a dominant future world with multiple subworlds and cover vast amounts of space and time. This makes it hard to give the hero an active, propulsive desire line. As a result, story momentum dies.

KEY POINT: In the best Science Fiction stories, the hero has a strong, specific goal. She is not dominated by the massive world that surrounds her.

At the beginning of *Star Wars: A New Hope*, Luke is given the task of saving Princess Leia and procuring the plans to the weak spot in the Death Star. Attacking this weak spot is exactly where the story ends.

To avoid losing a strong desire line, make sure everything funnels down to a single vortex point at the end. To use the vortex technique, tell the reader the *general* end point of the story at the beginning. I emphasize the word "general." You want to let the audience know where they're going. But you don't want to give away the exact ending.

The vortex point of *Star Wars: A New Hope* is suggested in the opening scroll of the title card:

> Rebel spies managed to steal secret plans to the Empire's ultimate weapon, the Death Star, an armored

> space station with enough power to destroy an entire planet. Pursued by the Empire's sinister agents, Princess Leia races home aboard her starship, custodian of the stolen plans that can save her people and restore freedom to the galaxy.

The vortex point occurs when Luke fires his missiles into a two-meter opening in the ship's exhaust ports, which destroys the Death Star.

Christopher and Jonathan Nolan are masters of the vortex technique. Both *Interstellar* and *Inception* set up a giant vortex in which all plot lines converge to a single point in space and time.

In *Inception*, the hero, Cobb, travels throughout the world to collect his team. The team travels to three progressively deeper levels of a man's subconscious to plant an idea in his mind. We know this up front when Cobb is hired to do the job.

In *Interstellar*, Cooper and his team travel to three worlds in outer space to find a new place for humans to live. Even before the hero is given this assignment, we get a hint that Cooper has been successful. His daughter sees books fall off her shelves; this is Cooper returning from the future.

Visual Shape of the Science Fiction Plot: Branching

Like Fantasy, Science Fiction emphasizes the story world above all other structural elements. That's why both of these forms often use the branching plot shape.

There are two kinds of branching plot shapes:

1. Multiple heroes go after goals at the same time
2. One character explores different branches in succession

Each branch represents a complete society in detail or different stages of the same society. For example: wilderness, village, city, or oppressive city.

Branching plots are based on:

- Exploring societies in a sequence
- Comparing individuals within a society

Here are two examples of the branching plot shape:

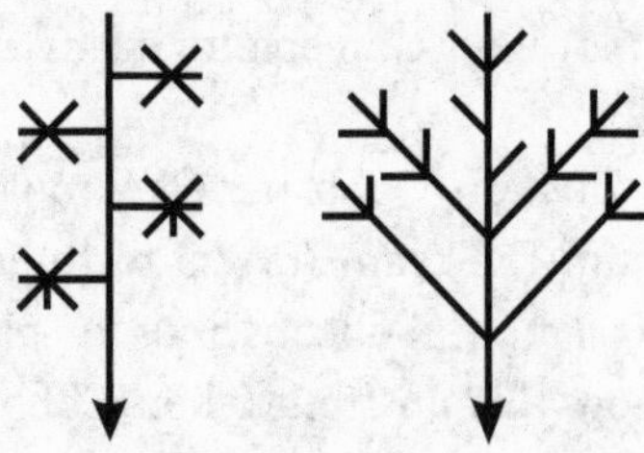

We see branching in transcendent Science Fiction/Myth when the hero journeys from subworld to subworld. Examples include *Star Wars: The Empire Strikes Back*, *Dune*, the *Foundation* trilogy, *Stranger in a Strange Land*, *2001: A Space Odyssey*, *The Stars My Destination*, *Riddley Walker*, *Lost*, *Battlestar Galactica*, *Star Trek*, *Interstellar*, *Inception*, *The Matrix*, and television's *Westworld.*

There are an infinite number of possible branching systems, but the best branch inward, moving toward a vortex point. In nature, we see this when streams flow into a river.

In a story, the writer crosscuts from the many to the few to the one. This gives the story convergence and increasing narrative drive. In *Interstellar* and *Inception*, the Nolan brothers connect the branching-in story shape to the vortex technique.

As we saw with Myth/Drama, Vortex Street is an advanced plot shape in which the hero goes on a path and makes stops along the way. On these tangents she explores dramatic issues or minisocieties.

Arrival has one of the most unique plot shapes, not only in Science Fiction but in all of story. The writers use a circular Vortex Street in both space and time.

The story begins with the hero, Louise, and her young daughter, Hannah, who dies. In the body of the film, Louise must figure out the language of alien heptapods that have come to earth. She discovers that they are giving earth an advanced holistic language so humans can save them far in the future. This language includes the ability to mentally project forward in time where Louise can see her daughter, not in the past but in the future. This gives her a personal and societal goal going forward.

Arrival is also a perfect example of the kind of story we enjoy more the second time around when we aren't busy trying to figure out the plot.

SCIENCE FICTION STORY BEAT: Opponent—Authorities

The Science Fiction opponent is a powerful authority figure and the main representative of the negative *system*. This is true in both positive and dystopian Science Fiction. The main opponent's goal is typically ultimate control over the planet or the universe. Often, the authority figure uses robots to reach his goal.

- ***STAR WARS***: Darth Vader and the Emperor
- ***DUNE***: The Baron and the Emperor
- ***THE TERMINATOR***: An unstoppable killing machine
- ***BLADE RUNNER***: Killing machines
- ***THE MATRIX***: Machines control humans and have created the illusion that humans are in charge. The main authoritarian figure representing the machines is Agent Smith.
- ***WESTWORLD***: Humans create, enslave, and kill robots for pleasure. The main opponents are the corporate bosses who created, own, and run the park.

Caution: The problem with fighting an opponent in power is that the more powerful he is, the less likely he will come into direct, ongoing contact with the hero. This prevents conflict, the lifeblood of dramatic story. These problems are solved by a technique we saw in the Action story.

TECHNIQUE: Four-Point Opposition

Great Science Fiction stories use a four-point opposition and hierarchy of opponents.

By having one hero and at least three opponents who are connected to each other in a hierarchy, the writer can continually bring back central opponents as the hero goes on her journey.

> **KEY POINT: Since the ultimate Science Fiction story is about the evolution of the universe, the best writers *compare the opponent's detailed vision of the future with the hero's vision.***

SCIENCE FICTION STORY BEAT: Plan

The Science Fiction plan revolves around how to find something, how to fight, how to take revenge, or how to save someone. In the most ambitious Science Fiction, the plan eventually focuses on how to make a new world.

Examples include the *Foundation* trilogy, *Star Wars*, *2001: A Space Odyssey*, *Interstellar*, *The Stars My Destination*, and *Arrival*.

KEY POINT: Since the hero usually travels the universe and covers such a wide expanse of space and time, the biggest plot challenge is how to compress time, place, and/ or events.

Science Fiction (and Action) writers solve this challenge in three main ways:

1. Set up a vortex for the story that will funnel everything down to a single point.
2. Crosscut characters and storylines at a faster pace as the story reaches the vortex point.
3. Use the four-point opposition. The opponents' plan to beat the hero connects the plot beats and allows them to build to the climactic ending, as in *Star Wars*, *The Empire Strikes Back*, and *Return of the Jedi*.

SCIENCE FICTION STORY BEAT: Plot—Subworlds

Science Fiction stories often move the plot through a succession of worlds. Each visit to a subworld is a major plot beat or set of beats. The characters take a sequence of actions to reach a goal within the subworld, and those actions are also part of the overall goal of the story. This is similar to the way chapters work in relation to an entire novel.

The original *Star Wars* trilogy makes extensive use of desert, jungle, ice, swamp, and forest. It matches the subworlds to the main story structure beats.

KEY POINT: In the first *Star Wars* trilogy, each subworld is defined and distinguished primarily through natural settings.

In *Star Wars: A New Hope*, Luke's weakness-need is established in his home on the desert planet of Tatooine. The main opponent is manifested in the subworld of the spherical Death Star, a warship ruled by Darth Vader.

In *The Empire Strikes Back*, Luke's weakness-need is reestablished in the ice planet of Hoth, culminating in an opening battle. The story then crosscuts between two main subworlds: Luke trains in the jungle/swamp world of Dagobah while Han Solo, Chewbacca, and Princess Leia visit Cloud City on the gas planet of Bespin.

SCIENCE FICTION STORY BEAT: Reveal

As in most story forms, the main Science Fiction reveal is usually about the opponent. However, the biggest reveal often occurs when the character is confronted with a choice that will result in a radically different future.

In *Star Wars: A New Hope*, as Luke prepares to shoot at the weak spot in Darth Vader's Death Star, he hears the words of Obi-Wan telling him to rely on the Force rather than the ship's technology to make the shot. Luke turns off the targeting computer and makes the shot that will eventually bring down the Empire.

In the final episode of season one of *Westworld*, robot Dolores realizes she must kill her creator, Robert Ford, to lead the revolution for robots to gain a new consciousness and become free of human domination. This is both a story reveal and a self-revelation.

SCIENCE FICTION STORY BEAT: Battle

Given the vast expanses of space and time in the Science Fiction story, the best battle often occurs at a vortex point.

Characters move at techno speed, with the pace increasing through progressively faster crosscuts among the fighters.

The famous final battle of *Star Wars: A New Hope* occurs in the ultimate vortex. Fighter pilots battle each other as the Rebel forces, led by Luke, try to shoot a rocket into a two-meter hole at the end of a long trench in the Death Star. He is able to accomplish this in spite of three obstacles: Darth Vader is shooting at him from behind; the walls of the trench prevent him from maneuvering; and the Death Star is within seconds of destroying the rebel base. There is no tighter convergence of space and time than this.

Arrival: Flipping the Battle Beat

An important element of the Female Myth is to manage differences without physical conflict. In this transcendent Female Myth/Science Fiction, the hero is able to prevent a battle that would lead to a world war. Louise realizes that the heptapods have come to Earth not to destroy it but to give earthlings a gift of language that can help us see into the future.

SCIENCE FICTION STORY BEAT: Self-Revelation—Public/Cosmic

At the highest level, Science Fiction is about how to create a new universal social order. In these stories, the hero doesn't just have a revelation about herself. When the story uses Myth as the structuring genre, her self-revelation is also public or even cosmic. The hero may realize she is the leader of the tribe.

> **KEY POINT: In Science Fiction that creates a new world, the hero has a vision of how the entire society might evolve in the future.**

Caution: Even in transcendent Science Fiction, the tendency is to make this "vision" of a new world a mere plot beat or pretty picture. A true vision of a new world is a detailed *moral* vision of how the members can live together in greater harmony and creativity.

Along with a new moral vision, the hero may undergo massive character change, moving from Man to Overman. Nietzsche's Overman (*Übermensch*) is one of the most important ideas in philosophy. Nietzsche said that this allegorical character is as morally superior to humans as humans are to animals. He also said that humanity has never achieved it; it is a goal of what humanity could become.

Science Fiction and Myth writers have tried to put flesh on this potential human with little success. How does a human imagine what this higher-than-human moral code would be?

KEY POINT: The mythic-religious equivalent of the Overman is the Chosen One.

In the Myth chapter, we talked about the Chosen One as a person selected by God, gods, or destiny for the divine purpose of leading a people to a righteous life. Examples are Adam, Moses, Jesus, King Arthur, Luke and Anakin Skywalker (*Star Wars*), Paul Atreides (*Dune*), Neo (*The Matrix*), Jake Sully (*Avatar*), and Harry Potter. Neo suggests elements of the Overman but is still essentially a Chosen One.

KEY POINT: The differences between the Chosen One and the Overman represent some of the fundamental differences between religion and philosophy.

In Myth-religion, the story begins with the hero already anointed as the Chosen One. He/she must rise to the occasion to fulfill that characterization. In contrast, the philosophical Overman is not predestined. The end point of the character's struggle is what produces a higher person and a higher species.

The possibility of the Overman in *2001: A Space Odyssey* is embodied in the giant fetus, known as the Star Child, floating in space at the end of the film. As mentioned, the Star Child may be the next evolutionary stage of humankind. Or not. This is probably the best example in film history of using a visual symbol to stand for a moral vision. A giant baby tells us nothing about how humankind can get to a new moral stage.

The plot of *The Matrix* is all about finding "the One." Morpheus, leader of the rebellion against the machines, is certain that slacker "Neo" is the One, in spite of evidence that he is a loser. Morpheus begins the long process of training him to accept and execute that role. At the end Neo realizes that to defeat the Matrix he must choose between saving himself or saving Morpheus. Even though he still doesn't believe he is "the One," he chooses almost certain death to save his friend. This proves he is the One. He declares to his enemy, Agent Smith, that his true name is Neo.

Although Neo is clearly an example of the Chosen One, he also has elements that suggest the Overman. At the beginning of *The Matrix*, Neo is the opposite of the evolved Overman. He's enslaved, literally a brain in a vat. This refers to René Descartes's famous philosophical hypothesis that suggests we don't know what we commonly think we know. We don't even know if we have a body.

In going from a brain in a vat to a man who sees the reality of machines controlling humans, Neo becomes a new Prometheus leading an entire species to freedom. But, similar to other stories trying to track this character change, Neo has no cosmic revelation. Neo is chosen, but he's not an Overman. *The Matrix* lacks any detail of what a new level of consciousness and morality might be. Instead, after making his escape from the battle in the building, he says in voice-over:

> I didn't come here to tell you how this is going to end. I came here to tell you how it's going to begin. I'm going to hang up this phone, and then I'm going to show these people what you don't want them to see. I'm going to show them a world without you.

Arrival is a rare example of a story whose advanced theme is expressed through its unique story structure. It is a Female Myth in which a woman's ability to see holistically instead of divisively is matched by the circular story structure in space and time. The result is a self-revelation and global revelation about how people can live together, not just on Earth but also with citizens of the universe.

Theme: Being Is Recognizing Choices

Science Fiction says that being human is not just about creating one's personal world at home and at work. Nor is it about taking responsibility for the entire society in which we live. It's about creating the very foundations of being in the world: space-time rules, architecture, politics, business, gender roles, status, transportation, communication, sports, language, and ultimately, consciousness itself.

Nothing is assumed in this story view. Through choices, we create and re-create everything every day. But the vast majority of time, we don't know it. As a result, the larger system is perpetuated and we blindly follow the same path we've always taken to our eventual end.

> **KEY POINT: Science Fiction says that the most profound choices we make are influenced by the technology we have invented.**

Nowhere is the gap in our daily lives larger than between the unconscious use of our tools and the massive effect they have on the entire society.

Science Fiction, the ultimate cautionary tale, expresses being more negatively than any other form except Horror and Gangster. This genre is a massive wake-up call that comes when the hero, and by extension all of us, must make a final moral choice. These consequences will not only affect that character's life forever, but the entire world.

Science Fiction Thematic Recipe: The Way of the Social Creator

As with all story forms, Science Fiction's strategy for becoming is an outgrowth of the hero's basic action and the genre's key question. The basic action is to make a better world for the future. The key question is: *How?*

Becoming in Science Fiction is a process of seeing the structural elements of our world and then deciding how to improve the system every day. The first step to improving the system is to go beyond self-involvement and to see how world and self always affect each other. No other genre puts as much emphasis on the existential idea of choice.

Science Fiction almost always shows this key to becoming from the negative: the dystopia that will occur if we make certain choices now. It makes the argument that, ironically, you create a better society when you fight for your own and others' individuality.

How to Transcend the Science Fiction Story

There are two main ways to transcend the Science Fiction form, and again they involve mixing genres.

1. Science Fiction/Myth Epic

   We explored this combination of Myth and Science Fiction in a previous chapter where Myth was the main genre. Then the story is usually a grand Myth involving human evolution, like *2001: A Space Odyssey*.

   When Science Fiction replaces Myth as the main genre, the resulting story has a different scope and emphasis. As the most creative genre with the largest arenas of space and time, the Science Fiction/Myth Epic details the *creation* of society-culture in detail, and how it goes through change. In the process, the genre highlights how society-culture is a form of art and story.

   Examples include *The Tempest*, *Robinson Crusoe*, *Dune*, the *Foundation* trilogy, *Stranger in a Strange Land*, *Arrival*, *The Stars My Destination*, *Riddley Walker*, *Lost*, *Battlestar Galactica*, and *Star Trek*.

2. Science Fiction/Horror Epic

   In the Horror chapter, we saw that when Horror is the main genre in the mix with Science Fiction, the story focuses on the nightmare caused when humans try to become God. When Science Fiction is the lead form, we get dystopian fiction, emphasizing a society of slavery.

   Examples include *Nineteen Eighty-Four*, *Animal Farm*, *Brave New World*, *Fahrenheit 451*, *The Twilight Zone*, *A Clockwork Orange*, *The Handmaid's Tale*, *Squid Game* (also Gangster), *Lord of the Flies*, *The Matrix*, *Metropolis*, *Mad Max: Fury Road* (also Action Epic), and *Dawn of the Planet of the Apes*.

Transcending Science Fiction 1: The Science Fiction/Myth Epic

The first way to transcend the Science Fiction story is by combining it with Myth. The challenge of the form is to show how society and culture work at the most basic level, as the product of a flawed human species.

Robinson Crusoe: Creating Society from Scratch

Robinson Crusoe uses one of the main techniques of Science Fiction, the story world of the island, to show the art of building a society-culture from scratch. In the history of story, the island has been the laboratory of man where the "author" creates different experiments of how individuals can live together in a group.

In *Robinson Crusoe*, the hero is a lone individual who transforms his natural world through technology, while appealing to Christianity to support him in trying times. He moves through the first two basic stages of society, from hunter-gatherer to farmer. Over the course of the story, he engages in slavery, sells a boy into indentured servitude, kills most of the natives on the island, and makes a man whom he calls "Friday" his servant.

The similarities to how the English (and other Europeans) colonized the "New World" are easy to see. Crusoe ends the story returning to England to live off the wealth of his plantation in Brazil. All of this is presented in the most positive light, and the story has been so popular it has become a subgenre of its own, known as the "Robinsonade."

Foundation Trilogy

Many Science Fiction stories, most famously the *Star Wars* saga, are loosely based on the history of the Roman Empire. Isaac Asimov, creator of the *Foundation* trilogy, has said that he was inspired by Edward Gibbon's landmark work, *The History of the Decline and Fall of the Roman Empire*. This is the historical version of Thomas Cole's epic painting cycle, *The Course of Empire*.

Asimov creates an interplanetary Galactic Empire that is

failing. Much like the monks in the Dark Ages after the fall of Rome, hero Hari Seldon is an intellectual who wants to save the best of humankind. He comes up with a theory of psychohistory that he believes can show humans how to shrink the upcoming dark ages from thirty thousand to one thousand years after the fall of the empire.

Asimov applies the term "psychohistory" to his own theory of social stage/cultural evolution. What is unique is that he uses the theory not only to structure the story, but also as a plot device the hero uses to determine his actions.

Transcending Science Fiction 2: The Science Fiction/Horror Epic

The other way to transcend Science Fiction is to make Horror the secondary genre. Today, the Science Fiction/Horror Epic is more commonly known as dystopian fiction. This is the premier story form of the fourth social stage, the Oppressive City. It is about how to find freedom in spite of the inherent and complex enslavement of modern society.

The Science Fiction/Horror Epic has several flaws as a story form. These are the flaws of any story trying to depict a human society and, more generally, the human species itself. Because of this near impossible task, dystopian stories are usually simplistic. The society is typically unrelenting in its oppression and evil and is often so abstract that it bears little resemblance to the real world on which it comments.

These elements would seem to make dystopian stories unpopular. So why do so many people love to write them? Dystopian stories have plenty of conflict and plot, which is the most important element in popular storytelling. What they typically lack is moral complexity and the detailing of what a modern enslaving society really means.

The question arises: How can one write a Science Fiction/

Horror Epic that accurately expresses the causes of modern social slavery? First, we present the negative elements that create a society at its worst. The assumption is that we cannot find freedom unless we first recognize the depth and breadth of our enslavement.

As social philosophy in fiction form, great Science Fiction gives us a guide to the *structural* way society enslaves the individual and how to create a free society in its place.

KEY POINT: If the Science Fiction writer's ultimate goal is to help us change the world for the better, he/she must show exactly how society can be both a place of slavery and a place of freedom.

Creating a Society of Freedom and Slavery

The problem of Slavery/Freedom is one of the most important topics in philosophy. That's because it deals with how an individual lives among others. This is an essential moral theme in every genre.

KEY POINT: All social systems are the vehicle for freedom but also a form of prison. Therefore, it's not a free system versus an enslaving system, but rather a social system with elements of both.

To create a world of both slavery and freedom, we return to the art of constructing society-culture. In the chapter on Myth, we explored the key elements in creating a utopia and dystopia. Let's look more closely at these two types of story world, with a focus on dystopia, the true subject of the Science Fiction/Horror Epic.

We said that dystopia occurs when the land, people, and technology are out of balance. The result is that the individual lives in a destructive state of nature and is either an animal competing to the death for scarce resources or a cog in a machine. In both cases, the individual is enslaved.

This raises two questions: What are the techniques and tools by which an actual society enslaves the individual? How are these elements of slavery intertwined with elements of freedom?

KEY POINT: Human social units are structures of real choice, apparent choice, and outright restriction used to control the individual.

Choice in modern society is similar to the structure of a video game. Imagine a video game is a ski slope with a number of trails. The individual player has many choices over the course of the game. These are real choices of how to act: whether to take this trail or that trail. But they are also apparent choices, because they exist within a hidden structure that the game designer has determined. This hidden structure forces the player to move in a certain general direction to reach the outcomes the designer wants her to reach. As the game nears the end, the designer funnels the player to the bottom of the hill and toward a limited number of exit points.

KEY POINT: Inside the experience of playing the game, the individual believes she is always acting with free will. But the truth is, she is being inexorably guided to the exit.

For the social unit to function at an optimum level, it has to direct its members to take certain actions as well as give each individual real choice to do what they most desire. A choosing individual will not only work harder, they will create new possibilities that can benefit others as well.

However, free choice is never absolute. To create and

maintain an optimum social machine, the society must *force* a tremendous amount of coordination. Individuals will not want to stay wedded to the unit if they feel compelled to act a certain way, especially against their individual desires. Therefore, the social unit must give individuals as much *apparent* choice as possible.

But real choice, apparent choice, and restriction are not the only elements that determine slavery and freedom in society.

Society of Slavery

We discussed simple slavery and freedom in the Action form as physical confinement. But this doesn't begin to explain the scope and depth of slavery in our world.

A less artfully depicted totalitarian society creates all rules and restrictions from the top down in the mistaken belief that this results in the most efficient system. Force is centripetal, drawing all benefits inward and up. It uses no deception. It rules simply through force.

A more artfully depicted totalitarian system uses deception to give the individuals apparent choice. It induces its members to make the choice the leadership wants them to make.

Community: Freedom or Slavery

"Community" expresses the idea of how physically separate human beings who have some measure of free choice experience union. In the Myth chapter, we talked about community as the key element in a utopia. But it can also be used to enslave. This happens in Science Fiction/Horror in two ways.

First, the idea of community immediately creates an opposition between connecting with Others versus remaining an individual. But the Other is not necessarily one's enemy. On the contrary: the individual, in the highest sense, is impossible without Others to help define, distinguish, and strengthen her.

Therefore, the individual divorced from all social contact is not absolutely free, nor absolutely great. Rather she is stunted and animalistic, concerned primarily with preventing death.

At the opposite end of the spectrum, the individual who remains tied to the social whole, who sees herself as part of the social One rather than being One herself, is also stunted. She has characteristics of a machine: highly repetitive behavior, conformity, and a life of "quiet desperation."

Transcendent Dystopias

In addition to the dystopian story technique of making the land, people, and technology of the world out of balance, the Science Fiction/Horror Epic adds two other techniques to intensify the dystopia:

1. the underlying, often hidden *system* that organizes and enslaves the world, and
2. the human species that creates the system, which is fatally flawed and doomed to destroy itself.

The flawed species depicted in Science Fiction/Horror is an outgrowth of the flawed mind portrayed in the Horror form. The Horror mind hates the Other because it is different. But that hatred is based on fear. Science Fiction gives us the human species that is monstrous, bent upon enslaving one another and destroying the planet.

KEY POINT: One of the great insights of dystopian stories is that the right-wing fascist state and the left-wing totalitarian state are fundamentally the same. Both come from one or a few people who believe they know best what everyone else should think and do. Both rule by fear. They differ primarily in whom they deem the Other, the less-than-human.

Brave New World and *Nineteen Eighty-Four*

Brave New World and *Nineteen Eighty-Four* are among the most advanced and prescient depictions of potential dystopian society ever written. A cursory comparison shows important similarities but also crucial differences in constructing a modern slave state.

In *Brave New World*, writer Aldous Huxley says that the biggest danger of dystopia comes from those who try to socially engineer utopia. He sets up the classic opposition of oppressive city and wilderness-village that we see combined in *Mad Max*. Citizens live in the World State, with a rigid class system, where all reproduction is socially engineered. Anyone who procreates through sex is subject to deep shame.

The *Brave New World* society is all about ensuring that the people are constantly happy. It does this by promoting the use of promiscuous sex and the ready availability of the pacifying drug Soma. In this, *Brave New World* prefigures much of *The Matrix*, in which Thomas Anderson can take the blue pill and live, like his fellow citizens, in a blissful, comfortable state.

Where *Brave New World* achieves a dystopia based primarily on mind control through drugs and pacifying entertainment, *Nineteen Eighty-Four* creates its dystopia primarily through political control, propaganda, and criminalizing behavior.

In *Nineteen Eighty-Four*, the postrevolution world has divided into three superstates: Oceania, Eurasia, and Eastasia. These nations appear to be at war, but are in fact all ruled by "the Party" and "Big Brother." The Party maintains strict control over the people, known as "proles" (proletariat), through surveillance of all communication devices. They are also subject to constant propaganda through "Newspeak," a limited language that enforces the proper way to think. Anyone who goes against the official ideology, known as "Ingsoc," is considered a "thoughtcriminal" (and yes, it's one word).

Hero Winston Smith rebels against the Party by loving a woman. For this, he faces reeducation. In a classic example of the Prisoner's Dilemma, Smith betrays his love when confronted with his worst fear, a cage of rats. She falls to the trick of the Prisoner's Dilemma and betrays him as well.

Part of the power of Orwell's vision is that he shows that the same modern totalitarian state can come from both ends of the economic-political spectrum: capitalism and socialism/communism. His detailing of the intricacies of mind control in an advanced technological dystopia has never been equaled.

The Hunger Games: The Politics and Business of Hell

The secret of the enormous popularity of *The Hunger Games* is that it combines the past through Myth with the future through Science Fiction. It grounds them both in the nightmare of Horror. The mash-up of ancient past with distant future gives the audience the sense that this story isn't specific to a particular time and place; it is universal. It is the essence of what human beings are.

The Hunger Games is a modern version of one of the most important of all Greek myths, Theseus and the Minotaur. Every year, King Aegeus must send seven young men and seven young women to be eaten by the Minotaur in ritual payment for a crime. The writer Suzanne Collins updates this premise by creating a tyrannical dystopia where twenty-five teens are forced to fight until only one is left standing, all for the pleasure of a morally corrupt populace.

Collins also uses Science Fiction to take the capitalist foundation of American society to its logical extreme: competition and money have life-and-death stakes. Like *Rollerball* and *Westworld*, the players are pawns to big corporate money. You lose, you die.

Collins uses the full array of Science Fiction/Horror techniques to detail the world in the *Hunger Games* series. First, she creates the overall arena, a totalitarian society where this moral horror can believably occur. She then sets up fundamental contrasts within the arena between the rich, powerful, immoral Capitol versus the poor, starving, rural District 12. Within this macro-arena of high contrasts, she then constructs a second, smaller arena, the field of battle. This arena has a clearly defined wall surrounding it to set up the pressure cooker effect. The building conflict causes such extreme pressure that the whole thing finally blows sky-high.

Her greatest technique is to turn the Theseus setup into the most horrific Prisoner's Dilemma in story. True, each individual is not fighting against one other. Plus, cooperation is possible and even useful throughout much of the game. But ultimately the game comes down to a zero-sum competition between two. Only one can live. The other must die.

The Next Rung Up the Ladder

Science Fiction is unmatched in getting us to look at the big picture, to see how the building blocks and larger forces of society-culture affect our lives. Yet it typically lacks the details of how to live in society day-to-day.

For that we turn to Crime. Not to commit it, but to stop it. Crime highlights the law and morality by which society operates and strives for equal justice.

7

Crime: Morality and Justice

Cain and Abel: First Crime Story

If Adam and Eve is the first Horror story, Cain and Abel is the first Crime story. After highlighting the relationship of Adam and Eve, the Genesis story turns to the children.

The author of this story does not give us a child of each gender. They give us two sons. But, like the Adam and Eve story, the key relationship is not between these two. It's between the children and God the Father. As the sons compete for his approval, they get into progressively greater conflict.

With Cain, we see how the binary mind of the human animal defaults to either-or thinking: any approval my Father gives to my brother is disapproval of me. This is the classic zero-sum game. The mind assumes the world is one of scarcity. Cain feels he must compete with his brother for the limited affection his Father has to offer. As he is lessened and his brother increases, there comes a moment when the only recourse he sees is to kill his brother. We end with the ultimate binary opposition: life and death.

In failing to win his Father's love, Cain perceives a terrible injustice. But he is focused on the wrong cause: his problem is with his Father, not his brother. His solution, murder, is the ultimate crime because it can never be taken back.

The story of Cain and Abel is a perfect expression of the nuclear family as well as the essential technique of four-point opposition. As we discussed in the previous chapter, four is the classic number of characters used to express a society in story. This rule and the four-point opposition technique provide the structural foundation of classic family dramas like *Long Day's Journey into Night*, *Death of a Salesman*, and *East of Eden* (based on Cain and Abel).

The relationship between the family drama and Crime has always been crucial. The intense conflicts of mother versus father, parent versus child, and child versus child provide fuel to the fire of crime.

Crime Story: How It Works

The Crime story is about people who break the law and those who catch them. It is based on the starting principle that everyone in society has equal rights as human beings. Therefore, the story is about restoring fairness and justice whenever that fundamental human law is violated.

We see this in the overall story strategy of the Crime story: pit a criminal who thinks he's above society against a defender of society's rules and values.

Crime is a primary genre because it highlights the unacceptable desires people have when living within a society, since fulfilling those desires may hurt someone else. It also emphasizes the means one can and cannot use to *achieve* one's desires.

This in turn highlights the difference between legality and morality: what the law allows versus what is good and right to do. They are not always the same. When that happens, the question arises: What is the proper response?

In our investigation of genres, why does Crime follow Science Fiction? If Science Fiction is about creating society,

Crime is about upholding the laws upon which the society is based, and without which the society cannot operate.

Crime Mind-Action Story View

The Crime version of Mind-Action is that life is a constant attempt at moral accounting. In trying to reach one's desires in a society, each of us uses others and occasionally harms them. On the ledger between the two individuals, each action is recorded, along with what is owed.

This happens countless times every day in ways big and small, morally and legally. Laws are simply moral rules enforced by the governing body of the society. A transgression can be as slight as failing to thank one's spouse for an act of kindness. Or it can be as devastating as being unfaithful. It can be as simple as a speeding ticket or as destructive as murder.

In a social world, the moral accounting must always be balanced. An action must be paid for. If I use or transgress you, I must pay for it in kind. If I do not pay, there will be conflict.

Balancing the books becomes more difficult and complex when moral action is at odds with legal action. If I believe I must take an illegal action to balance the moral books, I accept the price I must pay. Antigone feels she must bury her brother in spite of the king's edict against it. For that she dies. Once again, the Law of Necessary Cost of Living rears its ugly head, and that cost is high.

The Crime Story Compared to Other Genres

The Crime story is in the same family of genres as Detective and Thriller. Yet they have fundamentally different purposes. Detective and Thriller are concerned first and foremost with finding the truth. That truth is usually about who is guilty of the crime. But the action that tracks the storyline is investigation. Assigning guilt only comes at the end.

Crime stories put less emphasis on the detection of the criminal, which is Detective, and more emphasis on the contest between criminal and lawman, which is Action. The story begins with someone committing an illegal act. In the process of applying justice, the transcendent Crime story questions whether the illegal act is immoral, and whether true justice has been done.

We've talked about the genres as fictional expressions of a form of philosophy. For example, Science Fiction is social philosophy. In later chapters, we'll see how the Western expresses a philosophy of history and the Detective story is fictional epistemology.

Crime is fictional moral philosophy. In fact, Crime is simply a more expansive version of the moral argument found in every story and every genre. Because each genre expresses its own unique philosophy for living a good life, all genres play out some version of a philosophy of ethics.

KEY POINT: All Story tracks the costs of the hero's means to reach an end.

Although Action shares certain elements of Crime, it is Crime's opposite thematically. Action starts from the point of view of the individual and is about superiority. It's about how to be successful in getting what one wants and rising to the top of the hierarchy.

Crime starts from the point of view of the society and is about everyone being fundamentally equal, at least in basic human rights. It's about making sure no one takes advantage of someone else as he/she tries to gain a good life. That's important, because if that is abridged, the system collapses and everyone suffers.

Examples of Crime

Novels and Films

Double Indemnity, *The Postman Always Rings Twice*, *The Talented Mr. Ripley*, *The Dark Knight* (also Myth and Fantasy), *Strangers on a Train* (also Thriller), *The Third Man*, *The Manchurian Candidate* (also Political Thriller), *In Cold Blood*, *Touch of Evil*, *Witness for the Prosecution*, *Out of the Past*, *The Night of the Hunter*, *In a Lonely Place*, *Ace in the Hole*, *Bombshell*, *Dial M for Murder*, *Trainspotting* (also Coming-of-Age), *Heat*, *Bonnie and Clyde*, *Sweet Sweetback's Baadasssss Song*, *The Town*, *The French Connection*, *The Underground Railroad*, *The Nickel Boys*, *Rum Punch*, *LaBrava*, *Reservoir Dogs*, *Pulp Fiction*, *Once Upon a Time in Hollywood*, *Shaft*, *BlacKkKlansman*, *Boys Don't Cry*, *The Accused*, *White Heat*, *Kill Bill 1–2*, *Mystic River*, *Lethal Weapon*, *If Beale Street Could Talk* (also Social Drama and Love), *Collateral*, *Hell or High Water* (also anti-Western), *The Grifters*, *D.O.A*, *Gilda*, *The Killers*, *Point Blank*, *Payback*, *Laura*, *The Departed* (also Gangster), *Body Heat*, *High and Low*, *Pepe le Moko*, *Dog Day Afternoon*, *Training Day*, *Dead Presidents*, *Thelma and Louise*, *Fight Club* (also Horror), *Diabolique* (also Horror), *The Petrified Forest*, *Taxi Driver*, *Beverly Hills Cop* (also Comedy), *Stakeout*, *I Am a Fugitive from a Chain Gang*, *Menace II Society*, *The Shawshank Redemption*, *The Lovely Bones*, *Gone Girl*, *Fruitvale Station* (also Social Drama), *Do the Right Thing* (also Social Drama), *Winter's Bone*

Television

Better Call Saul, *American Gothic*, *Dexter*, *Barry*, *Perry Mason*, *Lupin*, *24*, *Justified*, *Sons of Anarchy*, *Mr. Robot*, *The Shield*,

Oz, *Ozark*, *Longmire*, *Lucifer* (also Fantasy), *The Flash* (also Fantasy), *Agents of S.H.I.E.L.D.* (also Fantasy), *Carnival Row* (also Fantasy), *American Crime Story*, *Money Heist*, *Narcos*

Crime Subgenres

Epic Crime Tragedy, Crime Black Comedy, Social Drama, Courtroom Drama, Film Noir, Caper (Heist), Crime Comedy, Fish out of Water, Criminal as Hero, Crime Fantasy, Prison Escape

Crime Story Overview

Here's what we'll cover in this chapter:

- **CRIME STORY BEATS**
- **THEME:** Being Is Living by Laws and Fighting for Justice
  - Thematic Recipe: The Way of Creating Justice and Transcending Society's Rules
- **HOW TO TRANSCEND THE CRIME STORY**
  - Morality Story Beats
  - Epic Crime Tragedy
  - Crime Black Comedy

Crime Story Beats

The Crime story beats are founded on this basic logic:

1. A criminal thinks he is above society and commits a crime that makes him extremely wealthy or powerful.
2. Enter a cop, who appears average, but is actually deep. He quickly figures out who did it and comes after the criminal.
3. The two battle to the death.
4. Each tests the other to the limits of their capabilities.

Let's look at the Crime story beats in detail.

CRIME STORY BEAT: Story World—Slavery of Superficial Society

Crime stories focus on how people live together in society. Specifically, how do people get what they want when others say they cannot or should not want it?

The Crime story world can take one of two extremes, and both are dystopias:

- It is a world where there is no crime. All desires and all actions needed to accomplish those desires are permitted. The result is a chaotic state of nature, with total power taken by those with money and guns.
- The world is a fascist police state. Almost everything a person does to realize his/her desire is a crime.

Modern culture tries to walk the line between these two extremes to produce the best overall society. Whatever story world is depicted in a Crime story, it is always a place where people are living on a surface reality. As in the Science Fiction world, people live Thoreau's "lives of quiet desperation." Or they are simply unselfconscious.

The society in the Crime story is also one of extreme wealth and poverty. The possibility of moving up the social ladder through hard work is almost gone. Therefore, some people turn to crime.

CRIME STORY BEAT: Inciting Event—Crime

The criminal commits a crime that catapults him to a new level of wealth or power.

TECHNIQUE: Ingenious Crime

Because the story often tracks the master criminal, whether he is hero or opponent, make the crime ingenious. The crime is the expression in action of the brilliance of the criminal's mind and artistry. If he's a master criminal, we want to see what he comes up with.

The Dark Knight begins with the Joker robbing a bank. Part of his plan is to have one of the robbers back a school bus through a bank wall, thereby killing the other robber. The Joker then kills the driver and drives away with all the money.

Before leaving, the Joker tells an injured customer, "I believe whatever doesn't kill you makes you *stranger*." This is a cute flip of the Nietzschean line, "Whatever doesn't kill you makes you stronger." Thus, the Joker identifies himself as a twisted, negative version of the Nietzschean Overman.

Christopher McQuarrie's great Crime story, *The Usual Suspects*, has one of the most ingenious crimes in film history. It is so brilliant it fools not only the FBI but the audience.

The hero in the story is the master criminal, Verbal. But one of the ways he fools both FBI and audience is that he doesn't appear to be the hero. Verbal's crime is ingenious because he is an *artist* of crime, in particular, a *master storyteller*. He does this in four main ways:

1. He makes up the whole story from the photos, articles, and wanted posters pinned to the bulletin board behind the FBI agent.
2. He pretends to be the ally, fooling the apparent hero Keaton, FBI Agent Kujan, who is the apparent main opponent, and us, the audience. Verbal is the ultimate unreliable narrator (see the Detective chapter).
3. Verbal pretends to be weak and stupid when he is strong and smart.
4. He creates a fake opponent, the ruthless criminal named Keyser Söze, to deflect attention from himself as the real killer.

KEY POINT: The more deception the criminal uses, the better the Crime story will be.

CRIME STORY BEAT: Cop Hero Strengths and Weakness-Need

Within this dark and divided social world, we introduce the hero. In Crime, the hero is either the enforcer or the criminal. The fact that the hero can be either cop or outlaw means that we're exploring the mirror image of the person on either side of the law.

The cop lives at a deeper level than others of the society and is even deeper than the master criminal.

KEY POINT: The cop is a regular person but especially good at his job. In other words, he is the master cop.

This element of the master cop is found in the prototypical modern Crime story, *Crime and Punishment*. The brilliant criminal Raskolnikov is no match for police investigator Porfiry Petrovich. Similarly, the rich, haughty killer in the typical *Columbo* episode is no match for the humble, dumpy Columbo, a character modeled on Porfiry.

Even a master cop has a strong weakness-need. He may be poor, average, or lonely. He doesn't fit in with society. Ironically, he lives according to the best values of that society and has a stronger faith in it than anyone else.

A thematic implication of this type of hero is that the truly great individual is not the person with the most power, money, or status, even though those things are what the society publicly prizes the most. It's the person who does great work within the rules. This person wins the game not by cheating, but by playing straight.

CRIME STORY BEAT: Values and Moral Code

In every genre the hero begins believing in a set of values that will then be challenged over the course of the story. In many genres, these values are so specific that they make up a moral code of ethics. Since either cop or criminal can be the hero in a Crime story, here is the basic moral code of each:

Cop

- The law is holy and must be enforced at all costs.
- A brotherhood exists among the (mostly male) police force. Like soldiers, cops understand and rely on each other for their duty and their lives. Therefore, they work by an unwritten code of silence that they will not turn in a fellow cop, even if he breaks the law (despite the first value).

Criminal

- The criminal operates by the value of "honor among thieves." There are examples of this in real life. But given that a criminal is by definition only out for himself and violates others to get it, the opposite idea, that there is no honor among thieves, is more likely to be true.
- The code of silence, known in the mafia as omertà, is quite real in organized crime. Here, the success of the organization, as opposed to the individual, makes this an absolute value broken at the cost of death. We will discuss this in more detail in the chapter on the Gangster genre.

CRIME STORY BEAT: Desire—Catch a Criminal

In all genres, the desire line of the hero determines the spine of the story. Crime, like Horror, establishes the hero's desire after the opponent attacks.

With a cop hero, the desire is to catch a criminal. Notice this is different than the desire in the Detective form, which is to find the truth. This goal explains why the Crime genre is a blend of Detective and Action. The cop usually figures out fairly easily who committed the crime. The emphasis then is on the battle of wits as the cop tries to catch the criminal.

TECHNIQUE: Crime Stories with a Criminal Hero

Make the criminal at least partially justified in breaking the law to get what he wants.

This technique has two main benefits:

1. The criminal hero becomes more complex and appealing.
2. The cop is torn between his desire to catch the criminal and his desire for the criminal to succeed.

In *Les Misérables*, Jean Valjean's original crime is stealing bread for his starving sister and her family. The cop is the relentless and unforgiving Inspector Javert. In the end, inspired by the mercy Valjean has shown him, Javert lets Valjean go. But he is haunted by his failure to do his duty. So he commits suicide.

A less obvious example of the cop torn by this dilemma is *The Thomas Crown Affair*. Crown wants to rob a bank to show he is master of the game and cannot be caught. Insurance investigator Vicki (the cop) wants to defeat him in the game and catch him. She is also in love with him.

Visual Shapes of the Crime Plot: Linear and Branching

Like Horror and Action, Crime uses the most popular story shape, the linear. The hero has a single goal that he chases with intensity and one main opponent trying to stop him. It looks like this:

When Crime subgenres like Social Drama have a single hero, they use the linear form. But when Social Dramas have multiple heroes, they are more likely to use the branching shape to sequence the plot.

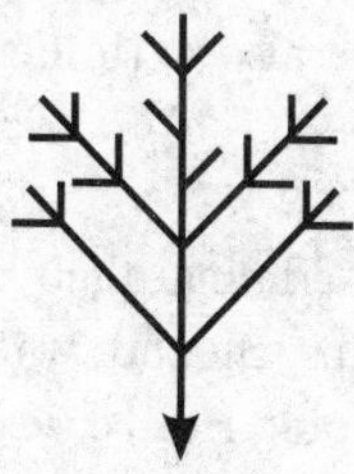

Examples of single-hero-linear Social Drama include *Norma Rae*, *Roma*, *Erin Brockovich*, *Boys Don't Cry*, *The Accused*, the *Oresteia*, *Antigone*, *A Doll's House*, *Hedda Gabler*, and *An Enemy of the People*.

Examples of multiple-hero-branching Social Drama include *The Help*, *Traffic*, *Nashville*, *Crash*, *21 Grams*, and *Babel*.

CRIME STORY BEAT: Opponent/Mystery—Super Criminal

The Crime opponent can be criminal or cop. Again, we're playing with the mirror image of the person on either side of the law. Whether he is the hero or the opponent, the criminal is usually brilliant and/or a master at beating the system.

The criminal feels that because he is such a superior individual, he should be able to live by his own rules. He feels he can play the game of life deeper or faster than the human sheep that surround him.

The criminal's goal is money, power, or to win the game and prove he is superior to everyone else.

Examples of master-criminal-as-hero include Rodion Raskolnikov (*Crime and Punishment*), Thomas Crown (*The Thomas Crown Affair*), Verbal (*The Usual Suspects*), and Walter White/Heisenberg (*Breaking Bad*).

Examples of master-criminal-as-opponent include the Joker (*The Dark Knight* and *Joker*), Hannibal Lecter (*Silence of the Lambs*, which is also a Thriller), Moriarty (*Sherlock Holmes*), Alain Charnier (*The French Connection*), and Villanelle (*Killing Eve*).

There is no greater criminal than the Joker in *The Dark Knight*. He is a genius psychopath whose massive intellect is shown by his ability to plot. He accuses District Attorney Harvey Dent and Batman of being schemers. But he is the master schemer, a modern Moriarty who acts not out of greed or revenge but for the game. And he is better at the game than anyone else.

The Joker is literally the author of Gotham City, in that he constructs criminal plots that will remake the city to express his moral vision. Many have described the Joker as a nihilist, a man in love with chaos. But this is a serious misreading.

If Batman is the Dark Knight, the Joker is the Dark Philosopher. The entire plot of *The Dark Knight* is a series of moral conundrums the Joker creates to expose what he believes is the true animal nature of humankind. This plot tracks the beats of the modern Crime story going all the way back to its origin, *Crime and Punishment*. The Joker constructs ever more difficult versions of the genre's central question: What would you do if you had to choose between two bad moral options?

The Dark Knight focuses on whether someone can remain a hero when the opponent becomes increasingly ruthless. This question is central to our world. But as the cop in *Touch of Evil* says about being a cop, "It's supposed to be (tough) . . . A policeman's job is only easy in a police state."

CRIME STORY BEAT: Drive—Cat and Mouse

The middle of the Crime story is a series of conflicts where cop and criminal match wits and force. This is the cat and mouse struggle, one-on-one, master cop versus master criminal.

KEY POINT: In the top Crime stories, both cop and criminal are the best at their respective jobs, and both are equal in ability.

This is essential to creating a heavyweight fight between the combatants. While fans of Horror want to feel constant and building pressure, fans of Crime want to see intense punch-counterpunch between cop and criminal in a fifteen-round bloodbath.

TECHNIQUE: Obsessive Cop

During the Drive step, show the cop becoming obsessed and going too far to catch the criminal, thus acting *like* the criminal.

This sequence of immoral action blends two characters the audience thinks are opposites. Instead of good cop versus bad criminal, black versus white, we see that they are in many ways similar. This technique in the moral argument of the Crime story comes from the genre's underlying theme, which is to explore the thin line between acting inside and outside the law.

Why is this crucial to the transcendent version of the genre? In a morally relative world, the line between right and wrong is never clear. This is especially true when the story explores the difference between what is legal and what is moral.

This technique also brings up other key questions: Who is committing the bigger crime? Is it the criminal who goes against society's laws of what is appropriate to want and the proper means to get it? Or is it the cop who is forcing an individual to deaden his life and become part of the mass?

One of the best examples of the cop going too far occurs in a classic scene in *The Dark Knight*. Batman is interrogating the Joker in a sealed room in the police station.

BATMAN: Then why do you want to kill me?

THE JOKER: I don't want to kill you! What would I do without you? Go back to ripping off mob dealers? No, no, no! You . . . you . . . complete . . . me.

BATMAN: You're garbage who kills for money.

THE JOKER: Don't talk like one of them. You're not! Even if you'd like to be. To them, you're just a freak, like me. They need you right now. But when they don't, they'll cast you out, like a leper. You see, their morals, their code, it's a bad joke. Dropped at the first sign of trouble. They're only as good as the world allows them to be. I'll show you. When the chips are down, these . . . these civilized people, they'll eat each other. See, I'm not a monster. I'm just ahead of the curve.

This technique contributes to the biggest problem writers face in the Crime story plot. The cop crossing the line is so common to the form that we expect it. We know the cop will break the law for the higher good of catching the criminal. That makes the plot predictable. The best way to overcome predictability of plot is through deception.

TECHNIQUE: Deceptive Attack

Make both cop and criminal masters of the game by using deception where each surprises the other and the audience. This includes where and how an attack will be made. It is especially important that each character hides their overall campaign of attack.

CRIME STORY BEAT: Reveal—Criminal Uncovered

The crime reveal is usually about the trickery the criminal uses to escape the cop. To set this up, think of the criminal as an artist of crime. Ask yourself: What are the *hidden* attacks that will cause the most trouble for the hero?

In *The Dark Knight*, the Joker makes a video of a fake Batman and directly challenges the real Batman to catch him.

CRIME STORY BEAT: Drive—Moral Argument

Like most genres, the Crime form highlights certain structural elements above others to get their effects. Crime emphasizes the moral argument, which focuses on the immoral and illegal actions the hero takes to win.

To prevent the theme from being heavy-handed, the writer must express the moral argument through the plot. We'll explain how to express moral argument in transcendent Crime stories later on. Here's an example of how plot might carry moral argument in a simple Crime story: The hero—whether cop, criminal, or average citizen—commits an illegal act. To hide his responsibility and avoid punishment, he commits another illegal act. The police or other criminals respond, which puts the hero into an even tighter moral bind. He then makes another mistake. And so on.

CRIME STORY BEAT: Apparent Defeat—the Criminal Escapes

The apparent defeat is when the hero believes he has lost the fight against the opponent. This is one of the main techniques for telling any story as dramatically as possible, since in the vast majority of cases the hero comes back to win.

In the Crime form, the apparent defeat occurs when the criminal escapes or wins a major victory.

In *The Dark Knight*, the Joker tricks Batman into going to the wrong location, and Rachel, the woman he loves, dies in an explosion.

CRIME STORY BEAT: Gate-Gauntlet-Visit to Death—Chase

The Gate-Gauntlet-Visit to Death beat usually happens just before the battle step. The hero is under immense pressure in the contest with the main opponent. This pressure often translates into the constricted space through which the hero moves. At this moment, he passes through a narrow gate, walks down a long gauntlet while being attacked from either side, and/or has a sense of his approaching death.

The Crime version of this story beat is often a big chase. Here Crime borrows from Action: the chase is cat and mouse at top speed.

The Dark Knight again gives us a brilliant expression of the beat. The Joker sets up a massive version of the Prisoner's Dilemma. In the Prisoner's Dilemma, police place two prisoners in separate rooms and give them each a choice: confess or stay silent. If one stays silent while the other confesses, the punishment will be more severe. So, because of distrust, each prisoner is tempted to betray the other.

The Joker re-creates the Prisoner's Dilemma on a grand scale by setting two ships against each other. One is filled with commuters, the other with hardened criminals. The passengers are given the choice of pushing a button to blow up the other ship before the other ship destroys them. If neither ship pulls the trigger by midnight, the Joker will destroy them both. His assumption: when forced to choose between trusting the humanity of strangers and their own survival, each group will kill the other.

The brilliance of this plot beat comes from the larger plot and thematic sequence of the story. Up until this moment, the Joker has forced Batman to make a series of moral choices that have become progressively more difficult. They are all designed to make the case that man is just an animal with a thin veneer of morality. Batman has taken the moral high ground. Now the Joker takes the choice out of Batman's hands. The Joker will use a herd of humans to prove his point.

It turns out the Joker is wrong. Neither ship chooses to blow up the other. This is a great story beat. The only problem I have with it is that the outcome is not believable. The writers don't play true to the reality about human beings that they carefully crafted throughout the film. They have made a brilliant case only to blow the conclusion. Does anyone really believe that a group of average citizens, faced with destruction at the hands of a boatload of killers, would not choose to blow up the prisoners in a split second?

CRIME STORY BEAT: Violent Battle or Big Revelation

Since the Crime story desire is to catch a criminal, the battle is the final violent confrontation between criminal and cop. Usually this happens in a pitched gunfight deep in the bowels of the city. Again, we have the problem of predictability. How many times have we seen the final crime battle in a creepy old warehouse with lots of metal pipes?

The big action battle between cop and criminal is the final legal accounting in the story. It is almost always enforced with a gun. In transcendent Crime stories, this beat may be a big reveal, which moves the Crime story closer to the Detective genre. The crime reveal is usually based on the trickery the criminal uses to escape the cop.

To see why this beat is found in transcendent Crime stories, we must remember that the criminal is an artist. To defeat the cop he must use extreme trickery. The closer you can push the big reveal to the end of the story, the better the story will be.

The Usual Suspects contains perhaps the greatest reveal in the history of the Crime story. FBI agent Kujan realizes the truth at the last minute. In quick succession, he and the audience learn that:

1. Verbal made up the entire story.
2. He isn't the weak, mousy man we thought he was.
3. He created the opponent, Keyser Söze.
4. Verbal *is* Keyser Söze; he is the killer.

The final reveal is one of the keys to great plotting in any story form. For many writers, this is the biggest technique holding them back from success.

TECHNIQUE: Final Reveal

Plan your reveals at the beginning of the story. Make each part of the opponent's overall, interconnected campaign of attack against the hero.

CRIME STORY BEAT: Self-Revelation—Society Reaffirmed

The normal self-revelation in the Crime story occurs when the cop reaffirms the values of living in society and within the law. This is true even if the citizens are relatively shallow and do not appreciate him.

In *Fargo*, during a cold and cloudy Minnesota winter's day, Police Chief Marge Gunderson takes the killer to jail.

MARGE: So, that was Mrs. Lundegaard on the floor there. And I guess that was your accomplice in the wood chipper. And those three people in Brainerd. And for what? For a little bit of money? There's more to life than a little money, you know. Don'tcha know that? And here ya are, and it's a beautiful day. Well, I just don't understand it.

There is also a negative version of this self-revelation: society loses.

In *The Thomas Crown Affair*, Crown defeats the law and the brilliant insurance investigator he has come to love. She realizes she has lost and made the biggest mistake of her life. We are glad to see this great individual get away. The artist in the game of life beats the system. But it's a Pyrrhic victory. He is alone, having spurned what may be the love of his life.

The Dark Knight gives us a mixed self-revelation in a finale going all the way back to the classic Western *The Man Who Shot Liberty Valance*. In that film, when it turns out the hero of a gunfight didn't actually kill the bad guy, the newspaperman refuses to print the truth. He says, "When the legend becomes fact, print the legend."

Batman decides to let District Attorney Harvey Dent die a hero, so the people will have hope in justice. Batman, the true hero, takes the role of the scapegoat. The society is reaffirmed through lying.

CRIME STORY BEAT: Moral Argument Conclusion—Poetic Justice

In the standard Crime story, the conclusion of the moral argument is simple: the criminal is punished and the law is upheld.

But while the justice system enforces legal accounting, it does not necessarily produce justice. Laws are only a rough estimate of moral accounting.

The basic moral accounting between two people must always be made equal. This simple but powerful equation is expressed in the Old Testament saying "An eye for an eye."

KEY POINT: "An eye for an eye" is not just about finding a punishment to fit the crime. It is the symbol of the deeper desire to close the wound and equal the books. Only then can the victim feel that justice has been done.

The New Testament adds a new wrinkle to one's sense of justice through the idea of forgiveness. When an eye for an eye is not possible, the victim is helpless to heal the psychic wound. Forgiveness provides the victim some measure of freedom from the shackles of rage and resentment. But forgiveness is not a substitute for justice, so it does not balance the books.

The modern justice system tries to replace an eye for an eye with systemic punishment. Laws evolved so that a vengeful form of moral accounting would not destroy the social fabric through endless feuds. In those cases, the collateral damage becomes far worse than the original crime. Plus, systemic punishment prevents vengeance against the wrong person.

Although punishment through the justice system may give the victim some sense of revenge, it is always a poor substitute. Unless the system metes out justice with some equivalent to an eye for an eye, the account is not settled and the victim is still owed.

Crime and Detective stories give us the outcome rarely found in life through the technique of "poetic justice." Poetic justice is payment in kind, payment unique to that crime, karmic reckoning, or payment by the offender's own hand.

When Hamlet plots the destruction of his friends Rosencrantz and Guildenstern, who have betrayed him, he says:

> For 'tis the sport to have the enginer Hoist with his own petard, an't shall go hard. But I will delve one yard below their mines. And blow them at the moon.

In short, their own bomb will blow them up.

We see examples of poetic justice in Detective stories like Agatha Christie's *Murder on the Orient Express*, *L.A. Confidential*, and *Vertigo*, as well as in the transcendent Thriller *The Conversation.*

Theme: Being Is Living by Laws and Fighting for Justice

Like Science Fiction, Crime expresses being and becoming negatively. Crime says that being human is a daily effort to live fairly with others. But we are doomed to fail. When we fail, everyone pays. The Crime story says that we must live within the law, even when the law limits our freedom. Being is a constant balance between the self and others, between what we want versus what we're allowed, between what is valuable versus what is just.

Crime says it's not a matter of *if* we fail to keep that balance, but *when*. If we must break the law to get what we want, being is an ongoing conflict with society's enforcers. The result is a complete loss of freedom.

The basic distinction in Crime is: being in this world is inherently unjust, so creating justice is an act of becoming.

Crime Thematic Recipe: The Way of Creating Justice and Transcending Society's Rules

The Crime story's thematic recipe, or strategy for becoming, is not simply a matter of looking at the hero's basic action. This is because the hero may be the cop or the criminal. To find the key question raised by the genre, let's look at becoming for each character separately.

The basic action of the cop is to catch a criminal. From the cop's point of view, the recipe for a successful life is to live within the rules of society and enforce them when they are broken.

Notice the Crime form places the highest value in all of story on the society, as opposed to the individual. Even when society's enforcer commits a crime in bringing the criminal to justice, the recipe says that reconfirming society's rules for all is more valuable.

But enforcing the law is the cop's job. His greater task, and ours, is to fight for justice. To become our best selves, we must create justice where it does not exist. That is one of the highest forms of helping others. By doing so, the cop helps the world and also helps himself.

While we may all be equal in our inalienable rights, we know from the Action and Crime genres that that's not how it works in daily life. Many of us start each day with the moral ledger vastly out of balance and no hope of making it right. We may have great talent and drive to play the game of life. Yet we may not even be allowed into the "ballpark" because of gender, race, status, power, or money. Enforcing the rules of fair play may be only a first act in creating justice. But it is an essential one.

Flipping to the criminal hero, his basic action is to break free from what he believes are the extreme strictures of society. By definition, the law is for everyone. But individuals are different. Therefore, if one is to fulfill his or her unique potential in this life, one is *obligated* to break the law. Notice this is the opposite argument from that of creating justice through equality. This argument states that laws that treat us equally make us equally disadvantaged.

The obligation to break the law is especially valid when the law is immoral. The point of law is to translate true morality into guidelines that can improve everyone's life. When law's foundation in morality is weak or destroyed, society itself becomes intolerable.

All stories make a moral argument. But Crime makes the story's moral issue its raison d'être. The criminal's moral argument embodies the key question of the form: Who is allowed to live above the law? Is there a person of such power, wealth, intellectual or moral excellence who is justified in transgressing the law by which everyone else must live?

Seen in the broadest sense, Sophocles's play *Antigone* is a transcendent Crime story. King Creon is a tyrant who forbids the burial of Oedipus's son, Polynices. Antigone, who is Creon's niece, decides to bury her brother in defiance of the law. She justifies this act by an appeal to an "unwritten law." Her view is that duty to family is superior to societal law, especially when that law is unjust. King Creon sentences her to death, then finds that she has already committed suicide.

How to Transcend the Crime Story

Transcendent Crime stories explore the arts of morality and justice, as well as the contrast between what is legal and what is moral. They begin by focusing on morality, because it is the foundation of what is valuable in life.

KEY POINT: The main way we create our everyday morality is through story. And the main technique for doing that is the moral argument. Advanced moral argument is the primary feature of any transcendent Crime story.

Let's begin with how advanced moral argument contrasts with simple moral argument. The standard Crime story tracks a criminal breaking the law and the agent of society, the cop, bringing him to justice. Action-reaction-equilibrium. This is an accounting of one person's illegal and immoral actions.

The best Crime stories also show a single illegal/immoral event as the catalyst for the bigger story. But that's not the main point. They're really about moral accounting over a lifetime. These transcendent Crime stories weave a detailed and complex moral universe that tells us how human life has meaning and value.

KEY POINT: The moral accounting in transcendent Crime balances what one owes versus what one is owed in this life, with life-or-death stakes.

These stories are the playing out of karma on the great balance sheet of life. How payment is made and how far down the road it happens, we don't know. But payment *will* be made.

Transcendent Crime tends to fall into two subgenres:

1. **EPIC CRIME TRAGEDY**

   Examples include the Moses story in the Old Testament, *Antigone*, *Crime and Punishment*, *Copenhagen*, *Sunset Boulevard*, *M*, *The Third Man*, *The Usual Suspects*, *The Thomas Crown Affair* (also Love), *Three Billboards Outside Ebbing, Missouri*, *Touch of Evil*, *The Dark Knight* (also Myth and Fantasy), *Cool Hand Luke*, *Un Prophet*, *À bout de souffle* (*Breathless*), *The Wire* (also Detective/Police Procedural), and *Mare of Easttown*.

2. **CRIME BLACK COMEDY**
   Examples include *Breaking Bad*, *Parasite*, *In Bruges*, *Blood Simple*, *Fargo* (film and television), and *No Country for Old Men* (also anti-Western).

Like most genres, Crime expresses one of the major art forms of life—in this case morality—only at the transcendent level of storytelling. In the previous chapter on Science Fiction, we said that to create society and culture in a story, we first had to understand how true society and culture are created. We asked: How do individuals in society create the art and story of society-culture every day?

Morality is a subset of culture. It represents the foundation values of any culture. Writing a transcendent Crime story involves creating an entire moral system and then challenging it. Therefore, we have to begin with how people create their personal moral system, known as a moral code.

The Art and Story of Morality

For someone to break the law, we must first make the law. Law = moral code turned into a legal code. The legal code provides detail and lays out how it will be enforced.

A transcendent Crime story gives the writer three challenging tasks:

1. Re-create the moral system of the larger culture of the story;
2. give the hero a personal moral code; and
3. show how that character breaks their personal code over the course of the story.

To see how we create a moral code, let's start by defining the larger term, morality. Morality is a system of relative value. Values are not abstract objects like Freedom, Justice, Loyalty, and the like. They are ways of acting. A person assigns an abstract value to each way of acting. These are set against other valuable ways of acting. Therefore, when someone lives by a moral code, they balance the various ways of acting available in that situation at that moment.

This has two ramifications:

1. Values exist only in action. Therefore, what we call "values" are meaningless unless the individual chooses a particular action.
2. The true value of any action is determined by subtracting the cost of the other choice(s), known as the "opportunity cost."

The larger morality is a system of values expressed through secular and religious stories, such as the Judaic and Christian religions. Since moral systems are woven through the entire fabric of the culture, most individuals simply accept the morality according to which everyone seems to live. This becomes part of their ideology that allows them to take shortcuts for choosing their actions in daily life.

Throughout history, philosophers have stated that accepting the general morality is not sufficient for a good life. From birth we develop codes of consciousness for how the world works. These codes take the vast complexity of the world and simplify it so that we can act successfully in day-to-day life. One of these is a personal moral code for how to interact with others.

A personal moral code is a more condensed system of values and actions that the individual chooses to govern their life. It takes the complexity of daily interaction with others and provides a simple guide to good values and right versus wrong action.

KEY POINT: Making moral choices is inherently complex because it involves balancing the good—what is valuable to me—with the right—what is valuable to others.

A Moral Code Is a Story Code

The technique of creating a story's moral code matches the most important revolution in moral theory of the last two hundred years: Nietzsche's idea that all moral systems are created by man, not by God. In *Beyond Good and Evil* and *On the Genealogy of Morals*, Nietzsche makes the case that moral/religious systems evolved based on who is in power and who is out of power.

A new moral code is what the Myth hero learns at the end of the story when she has a public/cosmic vision. Examples are Moses's Ten Commandments, Jesus's Sermon on the Mount, parts of the Koran and Zen Buddhism, and personal codes, like Mahatma Gandhi's "Satyagraha" (seeking truth) and civil disobedience, and Dr. Martin Luther King Jr.'s "I Have a Dream" speech.

KEY POINT: Every moral code is also a Story Code. Moses getting the Ten Commandments is not just the "cosmic vision" plot beat found in the *Book of Exodus*. It is a story unto itself.

Story Beats for Creating a Moral Code

While a moral code is an important beat in any story, it is an essential part of all genres in the Crime family, including Detective, Thriller, and Gangster. In Gangster, we have the mafia code and, specifically, omertà, the code of silence. In the Western, we have the Code of the West. And in Detective we have the Code of the Detective.

KEY POINT: You create a moral system by using the seven major structure steps plus the various beats of the moral argument (outlined below).

Beats of Morality and the Moral Argument

The first way we've been defining moral argument in this book is the point the author wants to express about how to live. The second way we've defined it is how the author expresses the point in the mechanics of the storytelling.

Moral argument is primarily an argument through action, and secondarily through dialogue. The moral beats in the plot are the first way to express theme through structure. They are also the beats of creating the art of morality.

To see how individuals create morality, in story and in life, let's look at the beats of the moral argument in detail:

MORALITY STORY BEAT 1: Story World—the Moral Universe

Everyone is born into a world with a highly detailed moral system already in place. This system has a major effect on how the individual creates their personal moral code.

The specific moral system that preexists the hero embodies a view of two main elements: responsibility and choice.

Responsibility

A moral code is a guide for how to act toward others. Therefore, it does not come into play unless someone's action directly and negatively affects someone else. Morality depends on who caused the effect.

KEY POINT: **In our social world, individual action *always* occurs in a moral universe to the extent that all actions have consequences for others. A moral universe doesn't mean that people act morally. It means that all actions between people have moral consequences.**

At the heart of the assessment of right versus wrong action is the element of responsibility. Before we can balance the moral accounting of who did what to whom, we must be clear about who caused the debt. This can be difficult, and sometimes impossible.

KEY POINT: **Any moral system depends on how it defines and assesses responsibility.**

This can vary widely. At one extreme is the Nietzschean view that making a promise to someone is absurd, because it suggests that humans are capable of controlling the effects of their actions into the future. According to this view, the idea that one is responsible for one's actions is an illusion, although probably a necessary one.

At the other extreme is Jean-Paul Sartre's existential view of extreme responsibility of the self. Because "existence precedes essence," we are what we do. This means that we are responsible for the results of our life and the moral effects we have on others. The existential view of morality and responsibility gives the individual no excuse.

The origins of Sartre's view go back at least 2,600 years, to Heraclitus's famous dictum: "Character is destiny."

KEY POINT: Being responsible for the results of our life and the moral effects we have on others has huge ramifications for the overall story process of creating and living by a moral code, and for story itself.

It gives us two rules:

1. The hero should drive the story.
2. The development of this character's *integrity* is the true process we track in a great plot.

In other words, the story tracks how the hero overcomes her moral weakness and takes right action. In structural terms, does the hero fulfill, or fail to fulfill, her moral need, which is what she must do to treat other human beings properly?

Casablanca gives us one of the best examples of the overall story process defined by "character is destiny." Rick goes from wanting revenge on the woman who left him and "I stick my neck out for no one" to "you need to help your husband so I can fight the Nazis."

The moral code embedded in "character is destiny" contrasts with some other types of moral system and responsibility. It means our future is not determined by fate, the gods, or what we were "born to do" (destiny), as in the classic Myth story. The old-school idea of fate is that the gods above determine our future, while destiny is given to us (by whomever) from birth. In either case, we have no choice in the matter.

KEY POINT: Fate, destiny, and "everything happens for a reason" are predetermined and determined by someone else. They involve an abdication of personal responsibility and have nothing to do with one's character or one's choices.

Fate, destiny, and "everything happens for a reason" are examples of craving for a purpose. It means we are desperate for some higher power to call the shots for us and add meaning to our lives. When things go bad, we don't want to say we screwed up and that's why it turned out wrong. We want to be able to say that it was bound to happen, it was already determined, and there was nothing we could do about it. In short, it lets us off the hook.

Choice

After responsibility, the next major characteristic of any moral system is the concept of choice. Like existentialism, "character is destiny" is necessarily about choice. Unlike fate, destiny, and "everything happening for a reason," this concept says that we determine our destiny from the quality of our character. It comes from a willingness to take responsibility.

KEY POINT: Once we are willing to take responsibility, we have choice. Without choice, there is no responsibility and no morality, and vice versa.

In the chapter on Action, we talked about the phenomenon of choice existing even when we are not aware of it. Everyday life becomes a flow of actions without much thought. But choices are always being made, even when we're not aware of them. As Sartre says, "Not to decide is to decide."

When someone becomes conscious of the centrality of choice, they transform the flow of actions into a series of choices. The result is to become conscious of the opportunity cost, the choices one is *not* making. This is followed by the realization of one's freedom to take a new course of action at any time.

TECHNIQUE: The Never-Ending Moral Challenge

Instead of borrowing the particular moral and legal system of the general society, the writer of transcendent stories creates their own.

KEY POINT: The most important technique for creating the finest transcendent television dramas in multiple genres is to set up a moral universe that constantly tests the moral fiber of every character in the story.

The reason this technique is found mostly in television is that the story often extends over multiple episodes and seasons. Putting the characters in a tightening moral vise is one of the best ways to build the episodes to a dramatic conclusion. Here's how to execute this technique:

1. Set the story in a world of extreme competition, defined by survival of the fittest.
2. The big question all characters must face is: How does one do the right thing in a deadly arena? In other words, the characters are always under extreme moral pressure.
3. Each episode has at least one unique moral challenge for the lead character(s).
4. These moral challenges not only define each episode, they determine how the best shows *sequence* their episodes in a season.

MORALITY STORY BEAT 2: Character Web—Moral Code

The characters, especially the hero, have certain essential beliefs and values. These values make up the hero's personal moral code and guide her actions.

A moral code is a simplified guide to good values and right versus wrong action. It balances the freedom of the individual to go after what she values—her desire—and the freedom of others *not* to be harmed by it.

> **KEY POINT: The crucial question in any moral code is: how much of your values are about helping yourself versus how much do you care how your actions will affect others.**

TECHNIQUE: Executing the Moral Code

Embed the moral code over the course of the plot.

We see the moral code in moments when the character deals with a specific moral situation. The moral code affects the story in three main places:

1. Values of the hero that are present from the beginning.
2. In the middle, the hero takes right and wrong actions as she tries to get her goal. During the moral argument in the middle of the story, she is forced to ask: Is this the proper means to the end I'm trying to get?
3. The hero's final moral decision determines whether she has moved to a higher moral level.

To apply a moral code to your story, write out a detailed code for your hero. Do this in relation to the three pivotal moments where the character might use the moral code to determine her actions.

L.A. Confidential is a transcendent Detective story we will explore in more detail in the Detective chapter. But it gives us an excellent example of expressing the character's moral code from the beginning. One of the lead characters is Edmund. Here his captain, Dudley Smith, questions his moral credentials for being a detective, ironically by portraying them in a negative light.

CAPTAIN SMITH: Edmund, you're a political animal. You have the eye for human weakness, but not the stomach.

ED EXLEY: You're wrong, sir.

CAPTAIN SMITH: Would you be willing to plant corroborative evidence on a suspect you knew to be guilty, in order to ensure an indictment?

ED EXLEY: Dudley, we've been over this.

CAPTAIN SMITH: Yes or no, Edmund?

ED EXLEY: No!

CAPTAIN SMITH: Would you be willing to beat a confession out of a suspect you knew to be guilty?

ED EXLEY: No.

CAPTAIN SMITH: Would you be willing to shoot a hardened criminal in the back, in order to offset the chance that some . . . lawyer . . .

ED EXLEY: No.

CAPTAIN SMITH: Then, for the love of God, don't be a detective. Stick to assignments where you don't have . . .

ED EXLEY: Dudley, I know you mean well, but I don't need to do it the way you did. Or my father.

Let's look at some classic moral codes in story:

The Ten Commandments

The Ten Commandments compose the most influential moral code in story history. It is an entire moral system in miniature expressed as the Exodus story. This moral code is a new vision for an entire people, and it comes at the end of the Moses story.

This moral code is a perfect expression of the dual purpose of moral systems: to proscribe desires, which are values (ends), and actions, which are means. In effect, it is a moral code that defines a vast moral argument. Five commandments refer to proper desires, and five refer to the proper actions one might take to reach a desire.

Proper desires (ends):

1. I am the Lord your God. You shall have no other gods before me.
2. You shall not make for yourself a carved image. You shall not bow down to them or serve them.
4. Remember the Sabbath and keep it holy.
5. Honor your father and your mother.
10. You shall not covet your neighbor's house, wife, slaves, or possessions.

Proper actions (means):

3. You shall not take the name of the Lord your God in vain.
6. You shall not murder.
7. You shall not commit adultery.
8. You shall not steal.
9. You shall not bear false witness against your neighbor.

The Existential Moral Code

The Existential Code that we mentioned in the Memoir chapter is based on the connection between identity and freedom that underlies any moral code. If the individual is what she does, she is free to choose. So she is responsible for the consequences of her actions.

The objection to the Existential Code is that it is too broad to provide advice in a shifting, relativistic world. Its guidelines are too hazy and free-form for most people to apply.

KEY POINT: The Existential Code simply gives the opening framework of a moral code. It says, "The choice is up to you. You must define what your moral code is. And that too will be part of your identity."

The one guideline it does give is the idea of the moral universe we just discussed. The moral universe says that because we live in a social world, one's actions *always* have a moral effect on others. Therefore, one is never choosing just for oneself.

The Existential Code says that whatever standards one uses for their personal moral code must be defined without appeal to an absolute god or from a book of god's rules. How one defines their moral code *will* be relative to multiple factors because, at its base, morality is an art form and a culture.

The Chivalric Code

The Chivalric Code comes from the French word *chevalerie*, meaning "horse soldiering." It is a moral code that mixes two story forms: Action and Religion. The Action subgenre is the tale of the knight-errant. Its religion is Christianity. The central values of the chivalric code are honor, courage, service to others, courtliness, faith, and respect for women's safety (not as equals).

Bushido

Like the Chivalric Code, Bushido, or the Way of the Warrior, combines Action and Religion. But here, the warrior is the samurai and the religion is Neo-Confucianism, Shinto, and Zen Buddhism. The seven values of Bushido are:

- ***JIN***: benevolence toward humankind; universal love; compassion
- ***MAKOTO***: sincerity and truthfulness
- ***CHUGI***: devotion and loyalty
- ***MEIYO***: honor and glory
- ***YU***: valor; bravery, tinged with heroism
- ***REI***: proper behavior; courtesy
- ***GI***: the right decision, taken with equanimity; rectitude

The Code of the West

Sometimes we see moral codes for an entire genre. The Code of the West, on which the Western genre depends, is an outgrowth of living on a horse, just like the Code of Chivalry. The cowboy has been called the knight-errant of the plains. The values of being a knight in the Old West include independence, freedom, self-reliance, courage, honesty, loyalty, and respect for women's safety. These are the values every good cowboy believes at the beginning of the story.

The Code of the Detective

The detective is the cowboy who has gone to the city. So it's not surprising that their codes are similar. Each is a "knight" helping others, especially the weak. But the detective is a more jaded figure who soldiers on against the never-ending immoral behavior of his/her fellow human beings. He is a dark knight, but still a knight for good in the moral relativity of the city world.

In the last scene of *The Maltese Falcon*, the detective Sam Spade gives the most famous expression of the Detective's Code in story. He is faced with the choice between love and honor, between staying with the woman he loves and sending her to jail for murder. In deciding to send her to jail, and probably to her death, Spade tells her:

> When a man's partner is killed, he's supposed to do something about it. It doesn't make any difference what you thought of him. He was your partner and you're supposed to do something about it. And it happens we're in the detective business. Well, when one of your organization gets killed, it's bad business to let the killer get away with it, bad all around, bad for every detective everywhere.

This is as unheroic an argument for doing the right thing as we can find in genre storytelling, and it perfectly expresses the Dark Knight of the city.

In Bruges is a masterpiece and the epitome of the transcendent Crime Black Comedy story. As such, it flips the story technique of the moral code on its head at every beat. *In Bruges* begins by showing the twisted but logical moral code of professional killers.

- Boss Harry had ordered Ray to assassinate a priest. In shooting the priest, Ray accidentally kills a young boy.
- To Harry, this is morally unforgivable and must be paid for in kind.
- Harry orders Ray's partner, Ken, to assassinate him.
- Ken fails to do so because he doesn't think it's right.

The moral code of the society of hit men is in direct contrast to the morality of the larger society. The larger society says that settling conflict must be done within the legal system. This benefits not only those in conflict but also other members of the society who could be hurt if the conflict spills over.

The moral code of the hit men says that, if they have been paid for a job, they have the right to settle conflict on their own. This is business, and money has the highest value. The professional killers are the executors of balancing the moral and business accounts of their clients.

In the first plot beat, Ray's immoral action is not assassinating the priest. The assumption is that the priest had it coming. It was the "necessary" balancing of the books, though particulars are never mentioned.

Part of the hit man's code is that there must be no collateral damage, since that creates an entirely new debt. Killing a child, who is at the peak of his potential for a long and good life, creates the biggest owing of all.

This is precisely the rule and value that Ray has broken. For boss Harry, this is the true immoral action, and it is unforgivable.

Since *In Bruges* is a Crime Black Comedy (with elements of tragedy), the defenders of the larger morality, the cops, are almost nonexistent. Harry is the structural equivalent of the cop.

The story is built on the irony that the man enforcing the strict moral code is a professional killer who owns an assassination business. A further irony is that a professional killer has an absolute moral rule against killing a child.

This is not just Harry's personal moral code. It is a moral universe of eye-for-an-eye. The logic is upside down but internally sound. This is the setup of one of the most complex and powerful moral arguments in story.

MORALITY STORY BEAT 3: Opposition—The Good vs. the Right

The hero runs up against a strong opponent who wants to prevent her from getting the goal.

Values and action are intimately connected. In the practical art of morality, they are often identical. Typically, right action depends on seeking good value. What makes the art of morality complex is when the good and the right come into opposition. This is the central *trade-off*, or internal opposition, in any moral code.

> **KEY POINT:** The internal opposition in any moral code and moral argument is:
>
> **ends = the good vs. means = the right**

The "good" is what the individual perceives as valuable. It improves her state of being in some way. She may not be correct in her evaluation, but she starts with this perception.

On the other hand, the "right" is relational. It is a balance between two or more entities in the social whole. A wrong action is one that harms someone else. It diminishes what is good for them.

In spite of this basic trade-off between the good and the right, the right depends on the good. Before we can decide what is a right versus wrong action, we must first make an assessment of value.

MORALITY STORY BEAT 4: Plan—Values and Right and Wrong Action

The hero concocts a plan that will defeat the opponent and win the goal.

A moral code is a game plan, similar to what we would use in an Action story like war or sports. It is a guide for how to act in various situations when seeking a goal. In other words, if "x" happens, I should do "y." Moral codes based on an all-powerful god get rid of the complexity and simply give a universal command. "You should always do 'y.' Under no circumstances should you do 'z.'" These codes are more concerned with maintaining unity through obedience to the group.

Relative moral codes—those not based on an all-powerful god—allow for different situations, circumstances, and exceptions. They tend to emphasize the individual over the group.

Any plan in a moral code is concerned with two major activities:

1. assessing what makes a goal valuable
2. assessing the right and wrong actions used to reach a goal

The game plan in a moral code is fundamentally different from the game plan in an Action story, which is strictly about how to win.

KEY POINT: A moral code is a game plan for how to win only *desirable* goals using only *proper* actions.

MORALITY STORY BEAT 5: Drive—Assessing Ends vs. Means

Because the opponent is initially too strong, the hero becomes desperate and begins to take Immoral Actions to get the goal.

KEY POINT: When values and action, the good and the right, come into opposition, the central question of the moral argument is: Should the individual put the right above the good, others above the self?

Like other animals, the human being will often use any means required to achieve her ends. But, as the symbol-maker, the human being is the only animal that occasionally questions her own means and denies herself an end.

The decision to question one's means is a necessary step in creating an ethical code of behavior. A moral code is not relevant until a person is willing to deny herself certain actions. Without this restraint, the (im)moral system destroys both the individual and the society.

The fundamental idea that a moral code restricts desires and actions is the source of the term "the straight and narrow path." Its origin is thought to be Matthew 7:14 of the New Testament, "Strait is the gate, and narrow is the way, which leadeth unto life."

During the "Drive" of everyday life, the individual may struggle to assess both ends and means and how they might conflict. Every day the individual comes up with goals. Then, as she takes actions to reach them, she must assess what actions she will take to achieve them, and which actions go against her established set of values.

Freedom vs. Justice: The False Distinction

The moral code found in the Crime story highlights one of the great conflicts in philosophy. This is the most important issue in transcendent Crime: freedom versus justice.

On the simple level, these two definitely come into conflict. If you regulate my actions for the group, then I can't do anything I want. This normal sense of freedom assumes I'm living on a desert island, where my actions affect no one but myself. As soon as I live in society, I must consider how the actions I take to get my goal affect other human beings trying to get their goal.

KEY POINT: Justice is basically optimizing freedom for everyone.

The Story Code: Freedom vs. Justice

Just as all moral codes are story codes, the seven-step Story Code (as described in the Horror chapter) is also a moral code. It is fundamentally about the conflict between freedom and justice. The Story Code makes clear the fact that humans are free to choose and inherently concerned with the good and the right.

KEY POINT: The Story Code tracks a human being chasing value—"the good"—and using questionable means—"the right"—to get it.

Story magnifies this conflict between freedom and justice through drama. The hero begins with a set of values and a goal. But she doesn't just want the goal; she is obsessed with getting it. Story heightens the conflict even more by having the hero lose to the opponent through the early and middle parts of the story. This creates moral pressure as the hero must decide how far she will go to win. In desperation, she starts taking immoral actions to gain the goal. There comes a time when she decides to do anything to win. The question becomes: Is losing her morality to gain the goal a worse form of enslavement?

Morality: Existential Code vs. Story Code

The Story Code is not a moralistic system for showing how to act properly, although some "moral tales" do exactly that. Like the Existential Code, it says that *all* human action has moral effects on others, whether intentional or not.

KEY POINT: Story doesn't say that all individuals should act morally. It says that all actions have moral effects.

Showing that the Story Code is essentially moral is simply a description of the process by which all individuals, acting to get what they want, must deal with the moral ramifications of their actions.

Previously we showed how the Existential and Story Code describe the process of creating an individual. So how do the Existential and Story Code differ as moral systems?

EXISTENTIAL CODE	STORY CODE
Accepting the moral responsibility of freedom is valuable.	Acting morally even when freedom is lost is valuable.
As freedom declines, so does moral responsibility.	The struggle to gain value can lead to immoral action, which is its own form of slavery.
Greatness of character (integrity) comes from a series of moral choices, made under the knowledge that life has an end.	Greatness of character comes at one crucial moment of choice.

Like the Existential Code, the dramatic Story Code defines who a character really is, not by her self-revelation, but by the new moral action she takes that proves the self-revelation.

Crime and Punishment

Just as Edgar Allan Poe created the Detective story and Mary Shelley created the transcendent Horror story, Fyodor Dostoevsky created the Epic Crime Tragedy. *Crime and Punishment* defines the beats of the criminal-as-hero story. This form transcends the genre in three ways:

1. by moving it to the level of tragedy,
2. by exploring the nature of society's moral code, and

3. by highlighting the fundamental distinction between legal and moral crime.

To see why *Crime and Punishment* was such a revolutionary story, it has to be seen in light of Charles Darwin's *On the Origin of Species*, published in 1859, and the stories of Poe, written some twenty years before that. I don't know whether Dostoevsky was aware of either, but they form a definite pattern in the history of ideas.

Poe wrote about the power of the mind, both conscious and unconscious, and the way the mind attacks itself through guilt. Darwin's book knocked humanity from its pedestal above the animals and undercut the God-basis of morality. Dostoevsky extended the work of Poe and sought to counter the theological effects of Darwin.

The societal morality expressed at the beginning of *Crime and Punishment* is similar to the Crime form we talked about earlier. The society's code is conformist, authoritarian, hierarchical, repetitive, and dull. In addition, a large underclass is mired in extreme poverty.

Hero Rodion Raskolnikov is at the same time extremely intelligent and wretchedly poor. This is a lethal combination. He has rejected society's obviously flawed morality but has replaced it with a faulty moral code of his own. His is the code of the false Overman. He performs an experiment in which killing a "useless" old woman will prove the worthlessness of the masses and his own superiority.

There is a major weakness in the premise of this story. The idea that killing an innocent stranger proves one's intellectual and moral superiority to the rest of humankind is colossally stupid and immoral. But let's put that aside for a moment.

The defender of the larger morality's values is the cop investigating the murder (actually two murders), Porfiry Petrovich. Like Marge Gunderson in *Fargo*, he is an average person but extremely good at his job. He is also Raskolnikov's equal in philosophical combat.

Unlike the hero's actions in the typical Crime story, Raskolnikov does surprisingly little to defeat the cop. In fact, many of his actions implicate him in the crime. This is not a master criminal like Thomas Crown, who wants to expose the incompetence of the authorities and prove his brilliance. This is a man paralyzed by deep guilt.

Porfiry seems to do little to investigate. As in the typical Crime story, the cop figures out fairly quickly who did it. But the cat and mouse fight between him and the killer is not physical or strategic: it's philosophical.

The story spends relatively little time on the mechanics of crime solving. Instead, it is primarily a moral and emotional struggle Raskolnikov has with himself and those he loves.

KEY POINT: In *Crime and Punishment*, Raskolnikov's mind serves as the courtroom in which he sentences himself for the moral crime he has committed.

The sequence of actions is not the usual one of the hero becoming more immoral over the course of the story. It is the reverse, a sequence of him going from immoral killer to moral confession.

MORALITY STORY BEAT 6: Attack by Ally—Shame and Guilt

During the middle of the story, the hero's ally attacks her by saying that he shares the hero's goal, but believes her actions to get the goal are immoral and must stop.

He gives reasons for why the hero's actions are wrong and will cause harm. But the hero does not listen at this point and instead tries to justify each act.

This "attack by ally" step in the art of morality is both a moral attack from without and an attack from within in the form of shame and guilt. Shame and guilt are two of the negatives of being the self-conscious animal. The mind punishes itself for failure and tries in vain to balance the moral accounts.

When the individual feels shame and guilt, she doesn't need defenders of society's moral system to criticize her for her immoral act. She does it quite well on her own. Plus, shame and guilt are the gift that keeps on giving. When others punish the individual, she feels she has paid her debt and can move on.

KEY POINT: When the individual attacks herself through shame and guilt, it is never enough no matter how hard she tries.

Like Poe's *The Tell-Tale Heart*, the hero of *Crime and Punishment* isn't driven to confess by the excellence of the police investigation. He does so because of the overwhelming fear, paranoia, and guilt he feels at killing a human being. As such, *Crime and Punishment* is one of the great "guilt culture" stories (see chapter 6, Science Fiction). These stories reached their height some thirty years later in the plays of Henrik Ibsen.

KEY POINT: In *Crime and Punishment*, the guilt is the punishment.

In Bruges

In this brilliant scene of advanced moral argument, hero Ken and opponent Harry argue the good versus the just, the relative versus the absolute.

HARRY: Let me get this right. Not only have you refused to kill the boy, you've even stopped the boy from killing himself. Which would have solved my problem. Which would have solved your problem. Which sounds like it would have solved the boy's problem.

KEN: It wouldn't have solved his problem.

HARRY: Ken, if I had killed a little kid, accidentally or otherwise, I wouldn't have thought twice. I'd've killed myself on the fucking spot. On the fucking spot. I'd've stuck the gun in me mouth. On the fucking spot.

KEN: That's you, Harry. The boy has the capacity to change. The boy has the capacity to do something decent with his life.

MORALITY STORY BEAT 7: Battle, Moral Self-Revelation, and Moral Decision

The "battle" moment in any moral code is the moment when the individual sees the deeper clash of value systems at stake and must decide what course of action to take.

The moral self-revelation occurs, if at all, when the individual sees the effect of her action on others.

If it is negative, the individual realizes: "I have wronged them. I can't do whatever I want. I must make amends to try to balance the moral accounts."

The battle is the vortex point of the plot, and it makes the plot speed up as we get to the end. Similarly, the hero's final moral decision is the vortex point of the theme, and it clarifies which way of life is best, at least in this situation.

TECHNIQUE: Final Decision

No matter how complex the conflict of values, funnel it down to a single decision at the end. All the possible ways of living come down to the choice between two.

For the moral decision, the individual first makes a calculation of ends and means (self-revelation). Then she chooses what she thinks will have the most value, not just for herself but also for others.

KEY POINT: A moral decision must have two elements for it to be moral: it must affect others and it must involve a personal sacrifice by the individual, no matter which choice she makes.

The moral decision is the climax of the moral code and of any transcendent Crime story. Its main value is that it is the best way to express theme through structure. It simplifies the complex theme down to two choices: the hero acts either this way or that.

In the final sequence of actions leading up to Raskolnikov's moral self-revelation and decision, Dostoevsky makes it easy for him not to confess. First, someone else confesses to the crime. Second, the man who has overheard Raskolnikov confess to the crime commits suicide.

When Raskolnikov learns of the man's suicide at the police station, he leaves, apparently free. But Sonya, the woman he loves, who has urged him to confess, is waiting there. His moral self-revelation comes from seeing her gaze, her goodness, and her righteousness. His moral decision is to go back inside and turn himself in.

Raskolnikov's moral self-revelation is not complete. Because he confessed after someone else had already done so, he gets only eight years in prison. This for the premeditated killing of one woman and the murder of another who saw him do it. To me, this is a gross miscarriage of justice.

Perhaps that is why even in prison Raskolnikov cannot accept full responsibility for his crime. But with the love and help of Sonya, he finally sees the light.

In Bruges

The end of *In Bruges* is one of the best examples of moral code, moral argument, and poetic justice in all of story. To see how to execute these advanced techniques at the highest level of craft, let's look closer at the self-revelations and moral decisions of this film.

The power of the ending comes from the moral code that boss Harry states early in the story.

HARRY: Ken, if I had killed a little kid, accidentally or otherwise, I wouldn't have thought twice. I'd've killed myself on the fucking spot. On the fucking spot. I'd've stuck the gun in me mouth. On the fucking spot!

Battle and Ken's Moral Decision 1: The final battle occurs at the top of the tower. Ken expects Harry to murder him for his failure to kill his partner. With Harry's gun pointed right at him, Ken makes his first of two moral decisions in the story's finale. He pushes his gun along the ledge to Harry.

KEY POINT: Ken accepts Harry's moral accounting for himself, but not for Ray.

KEN: Harry, I'm totally in your debt. Things that have gone between us in the past, I love you unreservedly for all that.

Harry lowers his gun.

HARRY: What?

KEN: For your integrity. For your honor. I love you. The boy had to be let go. The boy had to be given a chance. And to do that, I had to say fuck you, and fuck what I owe you, and fuck everything that's gone between us. And that's what I had to do. I'm not fighting you. And

I accept everything totally you're gonna do. I accept it. Totally . . .

HARRY: Well you say all that fucking stuff I can't fucking shoot you now, can I . . .

Harry shoots Ken in the leg.

HARRY: You think I'm going to do nothing to you just because you're standing about like Robert fucking Powell . . . out of Jesus of fucking Nazareth.

Harry and Ken have made a deal. The debt is wiped clean. The books are even.

> **KEY POINT: What follows is one of the most transcendent scenes in film history and should be studied closely by any fiction writer.**

Harry is helping Ken down the steps. Eirik runs up to them near the top and tells Harry that Ray is down in the street below.

Harry's Moral Decision 1: Suddenly, the deal is off. Harry breaks the agreement he made with Ken just moments before. He will now try to kill Ray. Ken goes for his gun but Harry pulls his first. They fight. Harry is too strong. He turns the gun toward Ken and shoots him in the neck.

Harry is devastated at what he has done, but returns to his moral code. "I'm sorry, Ken. But you can't kill a kid and expect to get away with it. You just can't."

Ken's Moral Decision 2: Harry runs down the steps while Ken drags his limp body back up the steps and across the floor. A wide swath of blood trails behind him. His plan is to yell down to Ray to warn him of the danger. But when he struggles to look over the ledge of the tower, he sees that the entire plaza below is locked in fog!

What can he do? Meanwhile, in the plaza, Ray is enamored with his new girlfriend. As Harry hurries down the steps,

Ken buttons his gun in his coat and drops coins like rain into the plaza below. At first we don't know why. As the coins hit, people back away. Ray and his girlfriend take notice. Now standing on the ledge, Ken steels himself and jumps.

The body splats on the stone floor. Ray rushes to his friend. Incredibly, Ken is still alive. "Harry's here. Take my gun." And he dies. But the gun has broken in the fall.

In jumping to his death to try to save Ray, Ken has made the ultimate Moral Decision and sacrifice. This has the power of a cosmic reversal.

Harry's Self-Revelation and Final Moral Decision: Now comes the self-revelation and moral decision of the main opponent. Harry chases Ray through the streets of Bruges. Finally, he traps him on a plaza where a film crew is shooting a movie. One of the actors is a dwarf, dressed as a schoolboy, whom Ray has come to know over the course of the story. Ray, with a bullet in him, staggers forward. He sees the dwarf from behind and thinks it's the ghost of the boy he shot.

RAY: The little boy.
HARRY: That's right, Ray. The little boy.
Harry shoots Ray three more times in the back. Ray crawls to the dwarf, who has been shot by one of Harry's bullets. Harry thinks he has killed a child.
HARRY: Ah. I see.
Based on that self-revelation and confronted by his own moral code, Harry places the gun in his mouth.
RAY: It's not . . .
HARRY: You've got to stick to your principles.
He puts the gun back in his mouth and blows his head off.

Harry's self-revelation, "Ah, I see," has just shown him he was too rigid in his principles. But those principles are absolute and have become an ideology frozen in his mind. Harry can't change. He has to walk the talk of his code, and so makes the final Moral Decision to take his own life.

KEY POINT: **To execute the big moral decision at the end, the character must clearly express their moral code early in the story.**

This outcome is one of the great examples of poetic justice. The writer-director Martin McDonagh has re-created exactly the moral ambiguity of Ray's killing of the boy. Now, by his own hand, Harry must accept the same justice he demanded for Ray.

This is great writing and it's what makes *In Bruges* one of the finest transcendent Crime stories ever made.

MORALITY STORY BEAT 8: Thematic Revelation

A thematic revelation is where the moral code rises to another level of understanding. No longer limited to the self-revelation of one individual, the moral code grows and becomes a guideline for all people in how to live morally.

KEY POINT: **In stories with a thematic revelation, the balancing of accounts may involve poetic justice, which is payment appropriate to that crime.**

Let's see how the story of morality plays out in the two main transcendent Crime forms: Epic Crime Tragedy and Crime Black Comedy.

Epic Crime Tragedy and Crime Black Comedy: The Story of Morality

Creating a moral code is a major step for an individual who wants to make her life a work of art. But it is not an absolute.

The great danger of the personal moral code is that the individual will consider herself a "higher" human being than other individuals and act immorally. When that happens in story, we have a transcendent Epic Crime Tragedy or Crime Black Comedy.

Epic Crime Tragedy

We mentioned earlier that transcendent Crime was first done as tragedy in *Crime and Punishment*. This novel then became the model of the modern Crime story. The tragic version of transcendent Crime depicts the master criminal hero who commits crime to prove the shallowness of the system or because of a moment of weakness.

KEY POINT: Tragedy is about lost potential, of what might have been. So the tragedy here comes from the fact that a clearly superior individual would waste his greatness in such a useless and destructive attempt to prove it.

By adding epic, this subgenre of Crime highlights the moral system of an entire nation.

KEY POINT: The Epic Crime Tragedy details the difficulty of *re-creating* a better moral system. It highlights how morality itself is a form of art and story, but also how it is rigid and resistant to change.

A surprising number of stories in the Bible, especially in the Old Testament, are Crime stories. They are about moral crimes and punishment.

The Moses story is transcendent Crime using the structure of an epic Myth. Moses's personal journey is also the journey of a people. Through his development as a leader, his society gains a new moral system, and they rise as a new kind of people.

But as in any Crime story, the cost of this new moral gift must be paid. The Jews begin their journey in bondage and then wander for forty years. These are not just fun plot beats to show they are a lost people. They are paying for the crimes they have committed as law-breaking sinners.

When God, the moral arbiter of the system, determines that they have paid a fair price for their crimes, he deems them worthy of a new set of laws, the Ten Commandments. These laws will clarify each person's moral accounting over a lifetime. But when Moses sees the new moral depravity to which his people have descended while he was gone, he promptly shatters the tablets.

The Russian society and culture depicted in *Crime and Punishment* is the epitome of "rigid and resistant to change." In part, this is why Raskolnikov's attempt to expose its flaws is reactionary and has serious flaws of its own. Dostoevsky's solution is to fall back on Christianity's absolute system of values, as though that alone can solve the crisis in modern values.

The fact that the main person pushing Raskolnikov to accept this moral system is Sonya, a woman whose poverty drives her to prostitution, is highly ironic. Again, she is an example of using Christ's "worst among us" to make the case. For Dostoevsky, it is Sonya's deep faith, in spite of the larger society's cruelty and her own "fall," that proves how right this moral system is.

Twenty years later, Nietzsche would make the case that the Christian religion is itself an art form and that it is the answer the slave creates precisely because she has no power. Nietzsche asks the question: If not the moral system of the herd, what should we use? His answer is not a false Overman like Raskolnikov. It is the real Overman of an artistic human treating others as moral equals with the right to "over"-come themselves in their quest for a great life.

ATONEMENT: THE IMPOSSIBLE ATONEMENT

It has been argued that it's impossible to write a modern tragedy. The question is: How can the common man suffer a tragic fall? Dostoevsky tried to answer the question by defining the Epic Crime Tragedy with a hero of extraordinary intelligence and potential who destroys it all by committing a senseless murder.

Atonement is a modern tragedy combining Epic Crime Tragedy with Love. The story begins with a single immoral event that ripples out to destroy two lives and cripple a third. The criminal is thirteen-year-old Briony Tallis, who wrongly accuses her sister's boyfriend of rape. The story then plays out how this decision affects the wronged man, the woman he loves, and the girl who made the accusation.

What are Briony's excuses? Was it fate? Was it her destiny? Did it happen for a reason? Did she simply not understand sexuality? We could excuse her by saying she was young, she was mad at him, she didn't mean for it to get out of hand. But none of that matters. "Character is destiny," and her character, her integrity, was defective.

The key storytelling technique in *Atonement* is the surprise of who is telling this story. Until the end, it has seemed to be primarily about the wronged man. But he didn't act immorally. It is the girl who told the lie. She is the one who must somehow fix the imbalance in the moral order that has lasted sixty years.

At the end Briony tries to atone by making another choice: to write a novel about what happened and take responsibility for it. So the story concludes with her as an old woman, being interviewed for her novel titled "Atonement." Now she will try to tell the story for good, to give the lovers, through fiction, the lives they never had. She tells the story to apologize, even though there are some moral accounts in this life that can never be made right.

The tragedy is that it's too late. Briony can't bring them back and it ruined her life as well. That's the heartbreaking tragedy of what might have been. The writers use the Love story form to heighten the tragedy even further. It is not just the way the immoral act hurts these individuals, but how it prevents the blossoming of a great love.

Crime Black Comedy

True tragedy is rare in any form of modern storytelling, so modern versions of transcendent Crime are usually done as Black Comedy. Examples include *Breaking Bad*, *Blood Simple*, *In Bruges*, *Goodfellas*, *Fargo* (in film and television), and *No Country for Old Men*.

> **KEY POINT: The Black Comedy version of transcendent Crime shows how the moral code can be a destructive system. It tracks a story in which the combination of extreme passion and lack of knowledge creates a deadly world and a downward cycle where even love kills.**

Parasite is a transcendent Crime story that balances the books on an inherently corrupt capitalist/class system. With elements that go back as far as *Crime and Punishment* and *High and Low*, this film uses a structural sequence similar to the old proverb "For want of a nail the shoe was lost . . ." What is unique here is not the crime or the punishment, but the comical karmic trip that gets to the punishment.

It is impossible to exaggerate the artistic accomplishment of *Breaking Bad* as a transcendent Crime Black Comedy story. It is also one of the finest television shows in history and one of the great works of art of the twenty-first century.

Transcendent Crime, whether Epic Tragedy or Black Comedy, has to do with moral accounting over a lifetime: what you owe versus what you are owed in life, with life-and-death stakes.

The storylines in *Breaking Bad* are the playing out of karma on a vast scale through a terrible comedy of errors. On the great balance sheet of life, payment will be made. How it's made and how far down the road, we don't know. Let's look at the balance sheet for Walter White, high school chemistry teacher.

What he is owed:

- Walt feels he was cheated out of his share of what became a billion-dollar chemical business. He believes he is a genius and deserves to be a rich businessman, praised for the genius he is.
- Because he has cancer, he believes he has the right to make and sell drugs so his family will be taken care of after he's gone.

What he owes:

- He is making high-grade meth that is destructive to those who use it.
- A rival gang kills one of his sellers, Combo.
- He lets his partner's girlfriend die when he could have saved her.
- He kills countless people, some guilty and some innocent, some in a premeditated way and some through negligence.

How do the writers play out this moral accounting through character and plot?

Hero Walter White is a complex and contradictory character, which I define primarily as someone with a highly compartmentalized moral code. In many ways Walt is a good man. But he also does terrible things, which he rationalizes with one of the show's taglines: "You did what you had to do to protect your family."

KEY POINT: Because the hero starts as a normal and moral person, the viewer cannot see him in terms of the Crime or Gangster stereotype.

This is not *The Godfather* or *The Sopranos*. Walt is not a gangster, not one of "those" people. In American Gangster stories, "those" people is code for poor Italian American immigrants. No, the viewer sees that Walt is me. He's as "normal" as I am. So I, the viewer, go down the road with him.

One of the keys to the greatness of *Breaking Bad* is that Walt's character change is embedded right in the original premise of the show. Show creator Vince Gilligan said, "What was interesting to me was a straight arrow character who decides to make a radical change in his life and goes from being a protagonist to an antagonist." In his initial pitch to Sony Pictures, he said, "I want to take Mr. Chips and turn him into Scarface over the life of the series."

Breaking Bad is a serial with an end point from the start. This is rare in television and gives the show a vortex point that focuses every episode inexorably to this end. Each episode plays out that change through the plot.

KEY POINT: The entire show expresses what I believe is the most important technique in all of story: plot comes from character.

Walt begins as a brilliant but nebbishy normal guy. But he changes into someone hooked on monetary success and the intellectual game. As a result, his character over the series goes from nebbish to assertive to feeling that he is an artist, the self-proclaimed master chef, "Heisenberg" (one of the towering geniuses of quantum mechanics).

KEY POINT: Walt starts as Dr. Jekyll, becomes Dr. Jekyll and Mr. Hyde, and by the end of the series he's just Mr. Hyde.

Besides its unique premise and complex character, a big reason why *Breaking Bad* is one of the best shows ever is the ability of the writers to sequence plot over the course of the season. On a show with a serial structure, this may be the most important talent a television writer can have.

KEY POINT: Serial story structure in television changes a show's unit of measure from the episode to the season. It's all about building the stories, building the episodes to a climactic season finale. The writers of *Breaking Bad* build the moral decisions *sequentially*, in this case negatively.

Like *The Dark Knight*, plot over the course of each season is determined primarily by the sequence of the hero's moral decisions. Walt's moral decisions get progressively worse. We watch him pave the road to hell one brick at a time.

KEY POINT: Crime is what the writers use to give this everyman a series of moral tests, which he flunks as they slowly tighten the moral vise over the course of the show.

Walt goes from killing a man but being justified, to letting his partner's girlfriend choke to death, to killing a number of men in a premeditated way.

Staff writer George Mastras said: "One of our biggest debates was about Jesse's girlfriend, when Walt lets her aspirate. How far can we push this guy toward darkness and not lose the audience? He's still doing this for good reasons, but he's doing horrible things."

This may be the key line of this or any great television series: How far can we push the hero toward darkness and not lose the audience?

And what is the final moral accounting in this masterpiece of Crime Black Comedy? Walt's attempts to square the books destroy the love between him and his family and lead to his death and the deaths of countless other human beings.

The Next Rung Up the Ladder

The life philosophy of Crime highlights the way our lives are founded on a society of laws, and how what is legal may not be moral. It gives us principles for assessing ends and means. But it doesn't give us many details on how to navigate the morality of everyday life.

For that, we must look to Comedy.

8

Comedy: Manners and Morals

Comedy: How It Works

Some genres are based on a primal emotion through which the individual reacts to the world. For example, Horror and Thriller are founded on fear. Since Comedy highlights human incompetence, it is founded on a feeling of superiority, which is made physical. Comedy wants to make fun, to laugh at others.

Therefore, to understand comedy, we must begin with what causes laughter. It comes from the human ability to project, to see the difference between the ideal versus the real.

Laughter occurs when someone is reduced instantaneously from high ideal to low real, but not too much. When we see the difference between ideal and real in a split second—and it's not terrifying—we laugh.

The words "not too much" are a crucial qualifier. If a man slips on a banana peel and falls on his behind, it's funny. If he slips on a banana peel and cracks his head open, it's not.

The philosopher Henri Bergson made one of the most astute insights ever about comedy when he explained what makes people laugh.

KEY POINT: Bergson said that the physical-biological reaction of laughter occurs whenever we see another person reduced in one of three basic ways: to an animal, a child, or a machine.

KEY POINT: Implied in this analysis is that we see other people as characters who are reduced symbolically.

Let's define these three kinds of "comic drop":

- Animal humor occurs when we see people doing the basic bodily functions humans share with animals. Examples are "bathroom humor" and any "dirty joke" involving sex.
- Child humor happens when an adult acts like a child. More generally, it occurs when someone reacts with *more* emotion than the situation would normally require. Examples are crying, panic, or throwing a tantrum.
- Machine humor happens when someone acts like an object or a machine. More generally, it occurs when someone reacts with *less* emotion than the situation requires. Examples are dry humor or "deadpan." Machine comedy is the opposite of child comedy. This distinction is crucial to the way many comedy stories are set up.

Comedy Mind-Action Story View

Along with Myth, Comedy may be the oldest recognizable story form. Yet in the evolution of genres as expressions of the human mind in Action, Comedy is a relatively late form. Why? It shows humans in a well-established society.

The Comedy Mind-Action story view is about the flaws of the mind, people acting badly, and the inequities of the social system. If Science Fiction is about how society works, Comedy is about how society doesn't work. It's about how people screw up.

Comedy is the story form of practical morality. It shows us that day-to-day morality is never pure or clean. Practical morality is always filled with conflict.

Comedy has a specific tone, story structure, and philosophy. The comic tone begins with obsession: passion for the goal, the chase, and the fight. Comedy heightens the intensity of the individual's desire to such a degree that it becomes absurd.

To get the goal, the character projects a facade, a lie about herself. She exhibits pretense by putting herself up on a pedestal. Comedy pushes the projection of the mind further than any other genre except Fantasy. The difference between the projected self, the ideal, versus the real, is extreme.

Ironically, instead of making her more successful in society, the character's facade only increases her isolation. The Comedy story structure then tracks the beats that take the hero(es) from isolation to marriage and communion.

This process is mirrored in the overall story strategy of Comedy: tear down the facades the hero has put up to succeed in work and romance.

The deeper theme of comedy, which is tolerance, is also expressed through tone and structure. While the characters are obsessed with getting the goal, the subtext of the comic tone is the reverse of obsession. By being so over-the-top, Comedy suggests that no matter how bad things seem to be, everything will work out in the end. This story form uses a double attack: it makes fun of the belief as well as the intensity of the belief.

The Comedy philosophy of life is one of the most unique of all genres. Negatively, it believes that:

- Individuals are part of a larger social whole but are mostly unaware of how everyone is affecting them.
- Everyone is a collection of roles. We have a true self and a true value, but also a public image that we project to gain power and popularity.
- What people strive for is relatively silly and not nearly as valuable as we think at the time.
- People are often incompetent in their actions.
- Action often does not lead to success and occasionally leads to the opposite of what the person intended (this is the definition of irony).
- People only think they learn. Actually, they remain the same and repeat the same mistakes throughout their lives.

Positively, the Comic view of life believes that:

- A common humanity exists under the surface of roles and pretension that makes people good and valuable.
- There is no problem that can't be solved, if only by laughing at it.
- The iconoclast or devil are valuable. Questioning and attacking the system are ultimately creative and useful.
- Society will endure and life will go on, no matter what we do to screw it up.

KEY POINT: The comic view is that destroying false pillars leads to re-creating society in a better form.

Because the individual is so interconnected with society, the destruction of the hero's facades often leads to a total destruction of the group as it was. Yet somehow everyone survives, gets together, and re-creates and renews the community in a better way than it was before.

Comedy Compared to Other Genres

It could be argued that Comedy is in a category of its own, different from all other forms. Part of that has to do with the deep structure.

KEY POINT: Comedy is the only form that works by undercutting every beat of the Story Code.

Where all other genres are about accomplishing the goal, Comedy is most likely to end in failure of the goal, or accomplishing it in spite of incompetence. For example, in Action, Myth, and Western, the hero accomplishes a great goal, while in Comedy, what the hero wants is shown to be worthless.

Also, many comedies, especially the comic subgenre of Black Comedy, purposely deprive the hero of a self-revelation. Unlike all other forms, Comedy works through failure.

Comedy vs. Drama

The structural contrast between Comedy and the other genres is most clear when we compare Comedy to Drama. This may be the oldest genre distinction in story, represented by the smiling and frowning masks from the golden age of Greece, 500–300 BC. Drama is too broad to be considered a true genre, but certain features are always present and tragedy is its highest form.

The obvious difference between Comedy and Drama is one of tone. But many comedies go back and forth over that tonal line. The most important difference between these forms is one of structure.

Classic Drama tracks the slow decline and (usually) rise of the hero at the self-revelation. Comedy, on the other hand, shows the character being dropped instantaneously many times over the course of the story. For the writer, that means set up—drop, set up—drop, set up—drop, et cetera. Every time the character drops, that's a laugh.

Comedy vs. Horror and Thriller

Surprisingly, Comedy is most similar to Horror. It could be categorized as a less consequential form of Horror. Both genres work by reducing the character. As Bergson pointed out, we laugh when a character is reduced to animal, child, or machine. Horror reduces characters to animal and machine.

Comedy does this only enough to allow us to laugh. The character falls, but she comes back. Horror reduces a character all the way to death, from which there is no return.

If Horror and Thriller are about the emotion of fear, Comedy is about the emotion of disdain. Horror places us in a position of submission. Comedy places us in a position of dominance.

A perfect expression of the close connection between comedy and horror is the clown. To some he is an absurd-looking character whose goofy movements and predilection for pratfalls make him funny. To others he is an otherworldly alien whose exaggerated painted-on smile fails to mask a murderous intent. The Joker (*The Dark Knight* and *The Joker*) and Pennywise (*It*) are clowns who fall into the Horror category.

Comedy vs. Action

At the extreme opposite of Comedy is the Action story, which is about the excellence of human action. The Action hero is the loner who knows how to win. Comedy is about human action at its worst, about how and why things don't work. The

Comic hero is incompetent and socially awkward, yet ultimately brings everyone together in a community.

Comedy vs. Myth

In his seminal work *Anatomy of Criticism*, Northrop Frye defines the history of the major story types before the emergence of modern genres. The distinctions among the forms rest primarily on the type and power of the hero driving the action, which connects to the theory of the Great Chain of Being we discussed in Myth. They are:

- **MYTHIC:** god
- **ROMANTIC:** superhero
- **HIGH MIMETIC:** hero
- **LOW MIMETIC:** everyman
- **IRONIC:** antihero

Translated into today's storytelling, the first three forms would fall into the Myth and Action genres. Low mimetic (meaning "to imitate") would be either Drama or Comedy. *Don Quixote* marks a major turning point in the history of story, from Frye's heroic forms to the ironic. He is the fake knight who goes on a comic myth journey tilting at windmills for the love of his lady fair, the peasant girl Dulcinea.

Comedy vs. Science Fiction and Crime

In the previous two chapters we spoke about Science Fiction and Crime as the first genres of society. If Science Fiction is about creating a society, Comedy is about the struggle of living in and constantly re-creating it. Comedy is Crime that's funny. Both genres deal with immorality and injustice within the social whole.

Examples of Comedy

Plays

A Midsummer Night's Dream, *Twelfth Night*, *Much Ado About Nothing*, *As You Like It*, *The Comedy of Errors*, *The Importance of Being Earnest*, *Noises Off*, *Tartuffe*, *The Miser*, *A Flea in Her Ear*, *Absurd Person Singular*, *The Norman Conquests*, *House and Garden*, *La Cage aux Folles*

Novels and Films

A Confederacy of Dunces, *Ghostbusters*, *Little Miss Sunshine*, *The Graduate*, *Legally Blonde*, *Clueless* (also Love), *Wedding Crashers*, *Bridesmaids*, *Beverly Hills Cop*, *Ferris Bueller's Day Off*, *Crocodile Dundee*, *The Hangover*, *What About Bob?*, *The Grand Budapest Hotel*, *Sideways* (also Love), *Animal House*, *Airplane*, *Fast Times at Ridgemont High*, *This Is Spinal Tap*, *Waiting for Guffman*, *Best in Show*, *The Incredibles* (also Myth), *Dazed and Confused*, *Shrek* (also Myth), *Dr. Strangelove*, *Get Shorty* (also Gangster), *Zootopia* (also Myth and Detective), *Brittany Runs a Marathon* (also Coming-of-Age), *The Descendants*, *Bridget Jones's Diary* (also Love), *Vice*, *The Big Short*, *The Devil Wears Prada*, *Thank You for Smoking*, *Catch-22*, *M*A*S*H*, *Caddyshack*, *Lost in America*, *Trading Places*, *Ninotchka*, *Midnight*, *To Be or Not to Be*, *Modern Times*, *Steamboat Bill Jr.*, *Election*, *Sullivan's Travels*, *My Man Godfrey*, *It Happened One Night*, *Some Like It Hot*, *The Lady Eve*, *Twentieth Century*, *Ball of Fire* (also Fairy Tale/Fantasy), *My Favorite Wife*

Television

Curb Your Enthusiasm, *Frasier*, *Parks and Recreation*, *Ted Lasso*, *Girls*, *Fawlty Towers*, *The Big Bang Theory*, *Malcolm in the Middle*, *Father Knows Best*, *The Honeymooners*, *Leave*

It to Beaver, *The Danny Thomas Show*, *My Three Sons*, *The Andy Griffith Show*, *The Dick Van Dyke Show*, *The Beverly Hillbillies*, *Bewitched*, *Taxi*, *Get Smart*, *Everybody Loves Raymond*, *Community*, *Modern Family*, *The Golden Girls*, *Soap*, *The Honeymooners*, *Unbreakable Kimmy Schmidt*, *Schitt's Creek*, *The Phil Silvers Show*, *The Bob Newhart Show*, *Absolutely Fabulous*, *Derry Girls*, *BoJack Horseman*, *American Vandal* (also Detective), *Sex Education*

Comedy Subgenres

Romantic Comedy, Screwball Comedy, Comic Myth, Action Comedy, Buddy Story, Traveling Angel, Farce, Parody, Black Comedy, Satire, Comedy of Remarriage

Comedy Story Overview

Here's what we'll cover in this chapter:

- **COMEDY STORY BEATS**
- **THEME:** Being Is Living with Absurdity and Laughter
  - Thematic Recipe: The Way of Being Yourself
- **HOW TO TRANSCEND THE COMEDY STORY**
  - Black Comedy
  - Satire

Comedy Story Beats

The Comedy story strategy comes from solving the hero's weaknesses as she chases her goal. Starting from a position of isolation and incompetence, the hero schemes and puts up facades to move up the social ladder. Ultimately these facades are all exposed, but the hero usually succeeds anyway.

COMEDY STORY BEAT: Weakness-Need—Comic Gap

All great Comedy comes from a great comic character. Therefore, the first question you, the writer, must ask is: What makes a good one?

The comic hero is a bumbler. Because laughter comes from reducing the character—the "comic drop"—the funniest hero doesn't realize she is incompetent. Instead, she thinks she's cool. This inherent pretense allows you, the writer, to set her up and drop her as many times over the course of the story as you want.

Step 1 in creating your hero and all other characters in a Comedy is to create the Comic Gap, what I call the "high-low" within the character. The "high" is the pretense, the height from which you drop the character again and again. The "low" is the weakness of the character and the first way you create laughs throughout the story.

COMEDY STORY BEAT: Character Web—Comic Character Types

There are an infinite number of possible comic characters, but they come in certain basic types. Let's look at the most important ones, going from weakest to strongest in social stature. We'll list each character's high and low, and how this translates into their psychological and moral flaws.

Note: a character can be more than one type.

1. Nerd, Klutz, Dummy, or Clown

- High: illusion that she is romantic, successful, or cool.
- Low: is really a nerd, incompetent, unattractive, or a bumbler.
- Psychological need: to gain self-confidence and overcome loneliness.

- Moral need: rarely present because the character is a victim.
- Key technique: this character must think she's cool (or capable or smart) or there is no drop.

Examples include Lucy Ricardo in *I Love Lucy*, Phoebe and Joey in *Friends*, Louis Tully (Rick Moranis) in *Ghostbusters*, the criminals in *Home Alone*, *Arthur*, *Tommy Boy*, *Parks and Recreation*, *30 Rock*, *The Big Bang Theory*, *Cheers*, *Seinfeld*, and *Community*.

2. Everyman or Everywoman

- High: eternally optimistic, a good worker, tries hard.
- Low: lacks confidence, is the butt of abuse, or can't get any respect in the daily world.
- Psychological need: to gain confidence and respect from others.
- Moral need: to stop using others to succeed.

Examples include *Moonstruck*, *The 40-Year-Old Virgin*, *Big*, the boyfriend in *Meet the Parents*, *American Beauty*, Michael in *The Office* (U.S. version), *The Dick Van Dyke Show*, *The Honeymooners*, *Seinfeld*, *All in the Family*, *The Golden Girls*, *Community*, *Soap*, and *Parks and Recreation*.

3. Know-It-All

- High: speaks in a pompous tone using jargon and big words; appears to be an expert.
- Low: is completely wrong.
- Psychological need: to lose his superiority complex.
- Moral need: to stop forcing others to live the way he/she lives.

Examples include the psychologist in *What About Bob?*, Dad in *Little Miss Sunshine*, Alvy Singer and the professor in

Annie Hall, young Dr. Frankenstein in *Young Frankenstein*, Dr. Raymond Stantz (Dan Aykroyd) and Dr. Egon Spengler (Harold Ramis) in *Ghostbusters*, the adults in *The Graduate*, Larry in *Curb Your Enthusiasm*, *Frasier*, and *30 Rock*.

4. Show-Business Type

- High: apparently sincere, loves everyone, has a high sense of his own talent.
- Low: insincere, is effusive in situations that require no emotion, or has no talent.
- Psychological need: to become authentic.
- Moral need: to stop lying to others.

Examples include *Tootsie*, *Annie Hall*, *Spinal Tap*, *30 Rock*, *The Larry Sanders Show*, *The Mary Tyler Moore Show*, Alan Brady (Carl Reiner) in *The Dick Van Dyke Show*, and Martin Short's character Jackie Rogers Jr.

5. Princess

- High: thinks she is perfect, the world revolves around her, and that she is above the toil and dirt of life.
- Low: gets dirty, abused, and ignored like anyone else.
- Psychological need: to see other people's point of view, to see her own faults.
- Moral need: to learn to help others, especially the poor.

Examples include Rachel in *Friends*, Diane in *Cheers*, Elle in *Legally Blonde*, Cher in *Clueless*, and Judy Benjamin in *Private Benjamin*.

6. Aristocrat

- High: rich appearance, is arrogant and snobbish just because he has money and power.
- Low: looks pretty silly when stripped to his underwear, knocked down, or when confronted with sex or mess.

- Psychological need: to see himself as equal to others; to see the value of people, not things.
- Moral need: to allow others to live freely and spontaneously.

Examples include the pageant boss in *Little Miss Sunshine*, the family in *Wedding Crashers*, Warner and Vivian in *Legally Blonde*, the Margaret Dumont characters in the Marx Brothers films, Judge Smails (Ted Knight) in *Caddyshack*, the rich brothers in *Trading Places*, *The Adventures of Tom Jones*, *Vanity Fair*, *Pride and Prejudice*, and *Emma*.

7. Slob or Boor

- High: his high-class surroundings and the mere fact that the character is a person and an adult.
- Low: is dirty, crude, boisterous, and exposes the false superiority of others.
- Psychological need: when present, to overcome a sense of inferiority.
- Moral need: to stop imposing his boorishness on others.

Examples include Borat and Bruno, Tommy Boy, the Blues Brothers, *Animal House*, Rodney Dangerfield's characters in *Caddyshack*, *Easy Money*, and *Back to School.*

8. Trickster

- High: pretends to be of a higher class, important, knowledgeable, and altruistic.
- Low: is average in class, status, and knowledge, and is out for himself.
- Psychological need: to overcome the fear of commitment.
- Moral need: to stop lying and using others for his own ends.

Examples include Venkman (Bill Murray) in *Ghostbusters*, John and Jeremy in *Wedding Crashers*, *Legally Blonde*, Trapper John and Hawkeye in the film *M*A*S*H*, *Trading Places*, *Men in Black*, *Groundhog Day*, *Beverly Hills Cop*, and *The Phil Silvers Show*.

9. Traveling Angel

- High: is surrounded by tradition, routine, bureaucracy, and pretense.
- Low: knows the true priorities of life, especially in their ability to have fun and show others a good time; also pokes fun at the rich and pompous.
- Psychological and moral need: none—usually perfect, so they have no psychological or moral need; when present, to learn how to love.

Examples include Mary Poppins, Tripper (Bill Murray) in *Meatballs*, Ferris Bueller, Crocodile Dundee, the Music Man, *Down and Out in Beverly Hills* (a remake of *Boudu Saved from Drowning*), Driss in *The Intouchables*, *Chocolat*, *Amélie*, and *Bienvenue chez les Ch'tis* (*Welcome to the Sticks*).

COMEDY STORY BEAT: Inciting Event—Leapfrog

The inciting event is an event from the outside that causes the hero to come up with a goal.

In Comedy, this goal creates a desire line that will give you a strong spine on which to hang all the gags. Gags pause the storyline so we can watch the character fall. Story scenes move the story forward and give us the line.

Caution: The biggest mistake in comedy writing is to string together too many jokes or gags at the beginning of the story. The result is no storyline and no narrative drive.

TECHNIQUE: The Leapfrog

To avoid this mistake and set up the comic desire line:

Step 1: Use the story structure beats of your particular comic subgenre—for example, Romantic Comedy, Myth Comedy, Traveling Angel, and so on—to create the overall spine.

Step 2: After the inciting event, begin with a story scene. This initiates the comedy desire line.

Step 3: Use the *leapfrog technique*: story scene—gag—story scene—gag—story scene—gag, all the way to the end.

Step 4: Don't do too many jokes or gags without a story scene.

> **KEY POINT: The leapfrog technique increases narrative drive and creates a comedy that gets funnier as it moves toward the end.**

COMEDY STORY BEAT: Desire—Clothesline

To create the storyline, or "clothesline," on which to hang the jokes, you must create the hero's specific desire.

TECHNIQUE: The Dangerous Desire

Early in the story, give your hero a single overall goal that leads her into *progressively deeper trouble*.

That trouble is all her fault.

A desire that gets the hero into trouble gives you three major benefits:

1. It provides the main spine of the story.
2. It creates comedy from the character.
3. It is another way you create laughs over the entire story.

From the desire you can create all other pieces of the character puzzle. Ask yourself this question: What *specifically* does my hero want?

Four Weddings and a Funeral, which is a Romantic Comedy: to win the lover (Carrie).

The Hangover, which is a Detective/Comedy: to find the groom.

The general goal in any Comedy is to gain success or romance, with humorous results. Clearly, this is extremely broad. That's because the theme in Comedy is not defined by the basic action of the hero, as it is in the other genres. It is defined by the hero's *approach* to the action.

TECHNIQUE 1: Intense Desire

The comic theme is about the danger of wanting anything too much. Therefore, the hero doesn't just want their specific goal. They should *really* want it, and be willing to do almost anything to get it.

TECHNIQUE 2: Intensity vs. Incompetence

In setting up the plot, try to set up a contrast between the intensity of the desire versus the character's incompetence in trying to get it. If the intensity of desire is a ten, their ability to get it is a one.

TECHNIQUE 3: Expose the Incompetence

The goal should force the hero to take the one action they are worst at executing. This will connect the hero's flaw to the various nightmares they experience along the way.

Visual Shapes of the Comedy Plot: Linear, Meander, Branching, and Storyteller

Theoretically, Comedy could use any story shape since it can be combined with any other genre. But in practice, basic Comedy usually takes the linear form. The hero has a simple goal and takes intense but incompetent steps to reach it.

Comedy Myth uses the meander form.

An often-reactive hero goes on a journey meandering here and there through the countryside. Examples include *Don Quixote*, *Tom Jones*, *Candide*, *The Adventures of Huckleberry Finn*, *Little Big Man*, *Guardians of the Galaxy*, *Shrek*, and *Little Miss Sunshine*.

The transcendent Black Comedy form uses the branching shape to show the illogic and destructiveness of the entire system.

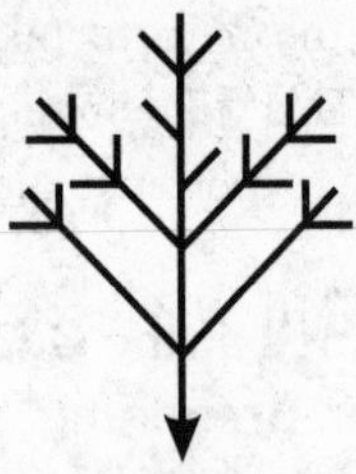

Examples include *Alice in Wonderland*, *Catch-22*, *Network*, *Goodfellas* (also Gangster), *Parasite* (also Crime), *Wag the Dog*, *After Hours*, *Dr. Strangelove*, and *Gosford Park*.

The hero in the satirical Love story *Annie Hall* uses the Storyteller Structure to remember the love of his life.

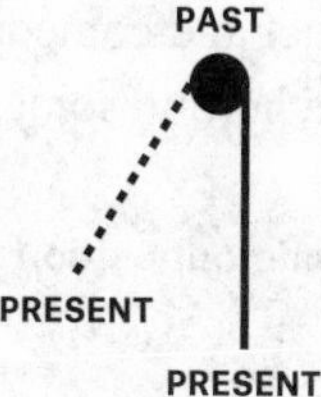

COMEDY STORY BEAT: Opposition—Four-Point

Opposition is the third major way you create comedy over the course of the entire story.

> **KEY POINT: The single most important element in great comedy is the relationship between the hero and the opponents (or other heroes).**

The two-point opposition in a normal story is a simple conflict between hero and main opponent. But this doesn't provide enough plot and laughs. Comedy is essentially social, so the hero and opponents must make up a society in microcosm.

> **KEY POINT: The social quality of comedy is why the key technique in writing this genre is the four-point opposition.**

There are many ways to set up the four-point opposition. The most common is to set the hero versus one main and at least two secondary opponents and their allies. In television, the most common way to execute the four-point opposition is among four heroes on the show.

The reason this technique is so valuable in Comedy is that it exponentially increases conflict and plot. It also gives you the ability to create laughs from four different sources.

The main opponent in a Comedy can be a person in any social role. But it is typically some authority figure and/or representative of society.

To get the most conflict and comedy, the opponents should be a true opposite of the hero in some way.

KEY POINT: These comic oppositions must be sustainable over the entire story.

There are four main ways to make the characters sustainable opposites:

1. By the kind of comic drop each undergoes: to animal, child, or machine
2. In power and/or status, such as parent/child, outlaw/cop, boss/worker, official/citizen
3. Opposite in gender
4. Opposite in values and beliefs

The strength of the best American sitcoms is the four-point opposition by which the show generates its comedy. *The Golden Girls* set up a textbook four-point opposition based on the three major types of comic drop:

- **BLANCHE:** animal
- **ROSE:** child
- **DOROTHY:** machine
- **SOPHIA:** machine

Friends used a six-point opposition based on comic drop and character type:

- **RACHEL:** child princess
- **ROSS:** child nerd

- **PHOEBE:** child dummy
- **JOEY:** child dummy
- **MONICA:** machine
- **CHANDLER:** machine

The Office had another brilliant comic opposition of characters:

- **MICHAEL:** child
- **JIM AND PAM:** machine
- **ANDY:** child
- **DWIGHT:** usually child, occasionally machine

Modern Family changed the family sitcom by creating an extended family with three variations on the classic male-dominant nuclear family:

- **FAMILY 1:** The older dad remarries a younger woman with a child.
- **FAMILY 2:** Two gay men, including the grown son of the older dad, adopt a baby
- **FAMILY 3:** A female-dominant nuclear family, and the mom is the daughter of the older dad.

Modern Family used an eight-point opposition based on comic drop (animal, child, or machine), character type, gender, sexual orientation, and age:

1. Older man, Jay: machine, patriarch, gruff grandparent character type
2. Younger wife, Gloria: child, sexy princess
3. Her precocious son, Manny: child acting like an adult
4. Jay's gay son, Mitchell: machine or child
5. Mitchell's flamboyant husband, Cameron: child

6. Jay's daughter, Claire, boss of her house: machine
7. Claire's husband, Phil: child and dummy
8. Their three kids: child princess, machine second daughter, child son

To heighten the comic opposition in your story:

1. Just as the hero has a comic gap, so should each opponent.

KEY POINT: The opponent must be pretentious or he won't be funny. Without pretense he is simply powerful and cannot be dropped. The opponent's comic gap comes from their weakness and need.

2. Make the opponent menacing but not deadly.
   Establish early that this character can cause great trouble for the hero, but not too much pain or death. As we mentioned, if the character drops too far, it's not funny. For example, the first ghost in *Ghostbusters* is scary but doesn't actually hurt anyone.

   The rare exceptions to this rule are Black Comedy and Crime Comedy. But they handle the dangerous opponent in a special way that makes it okay for the audience to laugh, albeit nervously.
3. Emphasize sharp contrast.
   For example, we can contrast big/small, old/new, masculine/feminine, rich/poor, and country/city.
4. Add clusters of values to the contrasting characters.
   This is one of the keys to giving a Comedy thematic punch. As a story form that deals with the morality in daily life, Comedy works by putting the values as well as the characters into conflict. Values tend to cluster into value systems. The best value contrasts are between ways of life.

KEY POINT: The trick is to connect the values to the opposing characters.

For example, big/small. Possible values associated with "big" are: forcefulness, power, and direct dealing versus values of "small": tact, scheming, and delicacy. Or take country versus city. Possible values for "country" are: honesty, decency, patriotism, and hard work versus values of the "city": fast-talking, confidence, money, and "me first."

KEY POINT: Push the oppositions to the extremes. In other words, make the characters and their values as different from each other as possible.

COMEDY STORY BEAT: Revelation—Nightmare

Comedy that comes from character starts with a weakness within the character. Good comedy often creates a terrifying situation from that weakness. This terrifying situation builds over the course of the story.

That's why the Comedy reveal is almost always some kind of *nightmare* for the hero. The hero realizes that the worst thing that could possibly occur has happened to her, and usually the opponent caused it.

KEY POINT: A great Comedy isn't just one big nightmare at the end. It is a succession of nightmares.

Nightmare revelations:

- ***LITTLE MISS SUNSHINE:*** Their van breaks down and they have to push.

- ***WEDDING CRASHERS***: Gloria's brother ties Jeremy up in bed and her dad visits.
- ***WHAT ABOUT BOB?***: In the TV interview, Marvin is terrified of appearing on camera, and the nightmare is made worse for him when Bob becomes the star of the interview.
- ***BIG***: Josh is alone in a ratty apartment on his first night as an adult in the big city.
- ***LEGALLY BLONDE***: Elle thinks her boyfriend is going to propose but instead he dumps her.
- ***GROUNDHOG DAY***: This film is structured as a repeating nightmare in which weatherman Phil is forced to repeat the same Groundhog Day, apparently forever. Each day brings its own unique version of the nightmare he is experiencing.

TECHNIQUE: The Comic Cyclone

You want the biggest laughs at the climax of the story. Therefore, sequence as many comic nightmares as possible and have them come at a faster and faster pace. This way, the final, ultimate nightmare will prompt the biggest laughs.

> **KEY POINT: To determine lesser nightmares, figure out what the hero wouldn't do or would be terrified to do. Then repeat that as many times as possible *in different forms* over the course of the story at more and *more extreme levels*.**

COMEDY STORY BEAT: Plan—Scam

The particular plan depends on the hero, her unique goal, and the opponents she is trying to defeat. But generally, the strategy the hero will use to win comes from the overall story strategy found in any Comedy: put up facades to succeed in work and romance.

Therefore, the comic plan almost always involves scams and disguises. A scam is a deceptive plan the hero uses to defeat the opponent and get what they want.

Rules for creating a good scam:

- Make the opponent think the hero is going after one goal while actually going after the opposite. This is a scam about desire. For example, in the classic fable *Br'er Rabbit*, the rabbit begs the bear not to throw him into the briar patch, which is exactly where he wants to go.
- A good scam is not a single event. It is a *campaign of deception*, a complex plan that requires many scenes to accomplish.
- Try to extend the scam as close to the end of the story as possible.

Scams are found in *Cyrano de Bergerac*, *Wedding Crashers*, *Legally Blonde*, *Ghostbusters*, *The 40-Year-Old Virgin*, *Beverly Hills Cop*, *Groundhog Day*, *Young Frankenstein*, *Heartbreaker*, and many Romantic Comedies.

Plan: Disguise and Mistaken Identity

Disguise is role-playing used to succeed in society. It is a *physical expression* of what the characters are already doing in every comedy: putting up facades.

Four rules for a good disguise are:

1. It should drop the character in an essential comic way: animal, child, or machine. Examples include:
   - Animal: a man wearing a bear suit in *Rules of the Game*, Bottom with a donkey's head in *A Midsummer Night's Dream*.
   - Child: Lily Tomlin dressed as a little girl in her Edith Ann character.

- Machine: Miles Monroe pretending to be a robot in *Sleeper*.

2. Find the one disguise that the character least wants to wear, but will force him to confront his weakness and need. For example, in *Tootsie*, chauvinist Michael (Dustin Hoffman) has to dress as a woman.
3. The disguise a character has purposely taken should be one he cannot take off. In other words, he is trapped in the disguise. In *Tootsie*, Michael is desperate to remove his disguise so he can romance Julie. But if he does he will lose his job on the daytime soap.
4. Tell the audience the disguise so that they can simultaneously see the role and the real person behind it.

COMEDY STORY BEAT: Drive—the Overall Danger

As the character takes actions to reach the goal (drive), she must experience real danger, physical and/or emotional, for the comedy to work and be sustained. This puts pressure on the hero throughout the middle of the story.

Caution: The audience cannot actually see death or the comic tone will be shattered. Again, the exceptions are Black Comedy and Crime Comedy, but these are rare and tricky to pull off.

KEY POINT: The danger is often social, in the form of public embarrassment. In Comedy, the greatest punishment a person can receive is public shame and ostracism.

Examples include *Shrek*, *Wedding Crashers*, *Groundhog Day*, *Legally Blonde*, *The Hangover*, *Trading Places*, *Ferris Bueller's Day Off*, *Ghostbusters*, *The Blues Brothers*, and *The Pink Panther*.

Drive: Immoral Actions

Comedy is the genre of manners and morals. We mentioned that Crime is also about morality. But it highlights grand immorality and injustice within the social whole. Comedy highlights the lesser but more common immoral actions of the everyday as the hero tries to succeed in life and love.

> **KEY POINT: These everyday immoral actions are essential to building the story throughout the middle in both plot and theme.**

As the hero drives toward the goal that has gotten her in trouble, she exacerbates her problem by how she tries to win. Typically, this takes some form of lying, cheating, and stealing. Because Comedy emphasizes the group over the individual, these immoralities, even when relatively minor, have major social repercussions.

Examples include *Wedding Crashers*, *Groundhog Day*, *The 40-Year-Old Virgin*, *The Descendants*, *The Big Short*, *Election*, *My Man Godfrey*, *Tootsie*, *American Beauty*, *Seinfeld*, and *Fleabag*.

COMEDY STORY BEAT: Battle—Ultimate Worst Nightmare

The comic story reaches its climax in the battle with the hero struggling through the greatest possible trouble. This is the ultimate comic nightmare.

TECHNIQUE: Creating the Ultimate Nightmare

To figure out the comic battle, go back to home base: the desire line. The hero's goal must eventually lead her to her worst fear, the one thing in the world that this character would most like to avoid. This connects the weakness to the battle, which makes the laughs even bigger.

Examples of the ultimate nightmare experience:

- **DEATH:** *Men in Black*, *Ghostbusters*, *After Hours*, *Beverly Hills Cop*, *Butch Cassidy and the Sundance Kid*, *Airplane!*
- **PERSONAL OR PROFESSIONAL FAILURE:** *American Beauty*, *Little Miss Sunshine*, *The Full Monty*, *Back to School*, *Lost in America*, *Take the Money and Run*
- **BEING EMBARRASSED OR BECOMING NAKED IN PUBLIC:** *Four Weddings and a Funeral*, *Wedding Crashers*, *Legally Blonde*, *M*A*S*H*, *Risky Business*, *Victor/Victoria*, *La Cage aux Folles*, and many Romantic Comedies
- **FEAR OF THE OPPOSITE SEX:** *Four Weddings and a Funeral*, *Cyrano*, *The Graduate*, *Tootsie*, *Annie Hall*, *Blind Date*
- **CAUGHT BEING UNFAITHFUL:** *Tootsie*, *Shampoo*, *Bob & Carol & Ted & Alice*, *Unfaithfully Yours*

NIGHTMARE TECHNIQUE 1: Start from the End Point

Determine the ultimate nightmare up front in the writing process. Then, go back to the beginning and build the lesser comic nightmares so they increase along the way.

NIGHTMARE TECHNIQUE 2: Battle of Chaos

Take the nightmare to its logical extreme. A comic battle is often a *battle of chaos*. Everything is destroyed. All facades are stripped away and everyone is comedically dropped.

Examples of a chaotic battle include *Animal House*, *Little Miss Sunshine*, *Shrek*, *What About Bob?*, *Trading Places*, *What's Up, Doc?*, *The Blues Brothers*, *Risky Business*, *Ferris Bueller's Day Off*, and *Ghostbusters*.

Sometimes the battle is a big reveal. In *Tootsie*, Michael confesses live on the show that he is really a man. This reveal is broadcast nationwide.

COMEDY STORY BEAT: Self-Revelation

The vast majority of heroes have a self-revelation in which they learn one great insight about themselves and make a moral choice. This is also true in Comedy, even though the hero is usually incompetent in some way.

Examples include *Wedding Crashers*, *Little Miss Sunshine*, *Clueless*, *Annie Hall*, *The 40-Year-Old Virgin*, *Tootsie*, *Groundhog Day*, *Risky Business*, and *Moonstruck*.

Caution: It has become all too common that the comedy self-revelation involves the hero experiencing public shame. The writer tries to find a ceremony or event where as many people as possible are gathered to see the main character learn his lesson. The theory seems to be that the self-revelation is more dramatically powerful and emotionally satisfying if it is combined with acute public embarrassment. This beat is now a painfully predictable cliché and absurdly unbelievable. I also find it anything but funny.

There are two notable exceptions in comic subgenres where the hero does not get a self-revelation: most Traveling Angel stories and all Black Comedy.

COMEDY STORY BEAT: New Equilibrium—Marriage and New Community

Comedy always ends with some kind of marriage or reconciliation. This may be a literal marriage or simply a communion where people have overcome conflict and get together.

But Comedy doesn't always end happily. If no one has learned anything, or if the communion is forced or is the product of inertia, the Comedy can end in sadness or despair.

Anton Chekhov is the master of this ending (*Uncle Vanya*, *The Cherry Orchard*). The entire Black Comedy subgenre moves toward this moment.

Theme: Being Is Living with Absurdity and Laughter

The comic sense of being is fundamentally different from all other genres because of its essential view of the world. Other genres have an underlying faith that the world works. Comedy believes that it doesn't.

If other genres see the cup of human life as at least half full, Comedy sees it as more than half empty. Where other genres see the amazing genius in how the world fits together, Comedy always sees the incongruities, the broken places, where the whole thing is within a hair's breadth of falling apart.

The comic sensibility is acutely aware of how things should work, but don't. Since it believes this is the norm, its response is not to cry but to laugh. Comedy says that daily life is a struggle to get through petty and sometimes grand slights. We are armed only with the balm of laughter and the faith that everything will ultimately succeed.

Like Horror, Comedy says we human beings are a mass of foibles, contradictions, and stupidities. We are especially conscious of the stupidities in ourselves. So daily life is a constant effort to project positive images that hide the horror of who we really are. In this way, Comedy shows the human animal at its most self-conscious.

Comedy also shows the human-being-as-liar. Because we are so aware of the contrast of the projected self and the real self, we are acutely aware of the problem of truth in general. Human beings are always struggling to reconcile the illogic and false image of everyone around us with what, at least to us, is the obvious and painful truth.

This is most clearly the case in the way people act toward each other. Comedy is the story form of practical morality, which it expresses negatively as a never-ending stream of immoral actions that everyone perpetrates upon everyone else.

Comedy Thematic Recipe: The Way of Being Yourself

Although Comedy's strategy for becoming derives from the basic action of the hero and the genre's key question, this form shows the hero's basic action negatively. Over the course of the story, the bumbling hero creates facades to gain success. Indeed, all comic characters create false value as their basic way of acting. What they project about themselves is hollow, puffed up, and makes them susceptible to an embarrassing fall.

Success only comes when the hero strips away all facades and stands naked before society. When others see that she's just a human being like them, they change from adversary to ally. The hero realizes that what she has craved isn't really worth it after all, and certainly not worth all the immoral behavior she thought was needed to get it.

Underlying the key question in Comedy is the profound question underlying the thematic recipe in all the genres: How does an adult grow? After we reach physical maturity, if we're lucky we may have fifty or more years to live. Exactly how does one become the highest form of themselves?

Each genre answers this question in a different way. For example, Myth says we grow by discovering what we were born to do. If we dig deep within ourselves, figure that out, and then do it, we will have a good life.

Comedy's answer to this question is suggested by the key question unique to the form: Do you lie or show your true self?

According to the Comedy story view, the world is filled with incompetence, immorality, and hypocrisy. Becoming our best self comes from tearing down facades, presenting our real self to the world in spite of the consequences, and acting well toward others. We grow only by embracing ourselves as we really are and accepting the world as an imperfect and endlessly funny place.

Groundhog Day: The Philosophical Comedy

Groundhog Day is one of the most brilliant comic thought experiments in story. A man is locked in an eternal present so he can practice living and fix his mistakes to create a good life. Through its premise, structure, and Romantic Comedy form, the film presents a comic version of Nietzsche's "eternal recurrence" and Aristotelian ethics.

TV weatherman Phil Connor, class-A selfish narcissist, comes to Punxsutawney, Pennsylvania, to shoot a piece on Groundhog Day. This is the town's annual celebration in which a groundhog predicts if there will be six more weeks of winter. Phil's lovely, sweet producer, Rita, and his cameraman, Larry, the object of Phil's disdain, accompany him. When Phil tries to leave the next day, he is blocked by a snowstorm and discovers he is somehow cursed to repeat the same Groundhog Day forever.

Once it becomes clear Phil cannot leave, his central desire is to sleep with Rita. Because he must keep trying to solve the same problem every day, the story puts extreme emphasis on his plan, which in comedy is a scam. And Bill Murray, in whatever forms his character takes, is the greatest schemer in the history of American film.

The benefit of having to repeat the same day is that Phil gets to perfect his scheme to have sex with Rita. The problem is that Phil's overwhelming narcissism keeps ruining his chances. In a previous date, Phil discovered that Rita would like to live in the mountains. Here he uses that information to trick her into thinking they are simpatico. But again his flaw rears its ugly head.

PHIL: You weren't in broadcasting or journalism?

RITA: Uh unh. Believe it or not, I studied nineteenth-century French poetry.

PHIL: (*laughs*) What a waste of time! I mean, for someone else that would be an incredible waste of time. It's so bold of you to choose that. It's incredible; you must have been a very, very strong person.

In the next round, Phil tries again.

PHIL: You weren't in broadcasting or journalism?

RITA: Uh unh. Believe it or not, I studied nineteenth-century French poetry.

PHIL (*quoting a poem*): *La fille que j'aimera / Sera comme bon vin / Qui se bonifiera / Un peux chaque matin.*

RITA: You speak French?

PHIL: *Oui.*

Nietzsche's idea of eternal recurrence—to be forced to live one's life exactly as it was lived again and again forever—is normally thought of as the worst curse imaginable. It seems similar to the punishment Prometheus suffered for stealing fire and giving it to humankind. Zeus had him chained to a rock and sent an eagle to eat his liver. Overnight, the liver would grow back, whereupon the eagle would eat it again.

But Nietzsche believed that this possibility could instead be a great benefit, what he called amor fati, or love of fate. If we can accept and even love the life we are living, to the degree that we would live it again forever, we gain a tremendous sense of freedom. We realize we can choose to become anyone we want. As a friend of mine once put it far more succinctly, "Remember, John, the worst you can do is screw up."

The structure writers often use to embody this theme is to take the single day, found in stories like *Ulysses*, and repeat it endlessly. In effect, *Groundhog Day*'s circular structure gives us a Comic Myth, not in space but in time. The circle of Phil's life is a treadmill of meaninglessness until he learns what he needs to know.

Groundhog Day is also a perfect expression of Aristotle's metaphysics and ethics in tracking one man's journey from potential to actual. Aristotle is the father of process philosophy, of the idea of becoming. He says that when we apply the idea of becoming to living, we get what he calls the "well-lived life."

The well-lived life comes from becoming the best person one can be, which ultimately means living a virtuous life. Therefore, one must consciously identify one's potential and take actions to realize it.

The implied challenge comes from identifying and choosing which version of one's potential self one wants to be, and doing that now.

KEY POINT: ***Groundhog Day*** **is really Phil's search for his best self. He is cursed to relive the same day forever until he figures out the best** ***version*** **of his potential he wants to become.**

It's only when Phil realizes that his best self comes when he helps others, instead of using them for his own gain, that he breaks the curse and finds love.

This is the same as Aristotle's idea of virtue for the sake of virtue. Ironically, it also creates a win-win where Phil succeeds far more than when he was using others for his own selfish ends.

Comedy Subgenres

One of the reasons Comedy is so underrated and difficult to write is that there are many subgenres, with each using different story beats. Here are the basic differences of some of the major comic subforms.

Romantic Comedy

The Romantic Comedy is a funny Love story. It goes back and forth over the line of comic and serious.

Examples include *When Harry Met Sally*, *The 40-Year-Old Virgin*, *Tootsie*, *Shakespeare in Love*, *Four Weddings and a Funeral*, *500 Days of Summer*, *Wedding Crashers*, *Groundhog Day*, *The Philadelphia Story*, *Moonstruck*, *Ninotchka*, *It Happened One Night*, *Some Like It Hot*, *The Lady Eve*, *Twentieth Century*, *Ball of Fire* (also Fairy Tale/Fantasy), and *My Favorite Wife*.

Shakespearean Comedy

Shakespeare's approach to comedy can be seen in the comedy beats and techniques he uses in plays such as *A Midsummer Night's Dream*, *Twelfth Night*, *Much Ado About Nothing*, *As You Like It*, and *The Comedy of Errors*. They include:

- **COMIC TYPES**
- **SCAMS**
- **DISGUISE AND MISTAKEN IDENTITY, ESPECIALLY CROSSGENDER AND THE USE OF TWINS**
- **MISCOMMUNICATION**
- **PHYSICAL GAGS:** with animal, child, and machine comic drop
- **WIT:** the language of love
- **SELF-REFLEXIVE:** the use of actors, songs, and the play within a play expresses the basic idea of comedy as putting on facades to be successful

Comic Myth

The combination of Myth and Comedy, also known as Epic Comedy, is the story of an antihero who goes on a journey.

Instead of the action hero as warrior, the antihero is usually an incompetent, a holy fool, or a child.

Examples include *Don Quixote*, *The Adventures of Huckleberry Finn*, *Little Big Man*, *Guardians of the Galaxy*, *Shrek*, *Crocodile Dundee*, *Dances with Wolves* (also anti-Western), and *Little Miss Sunshine*.

As mentioned, Miguel de Cervantes's *Don Quixote* represents the turning point from Northrop Frye's high romance (Myth) to the ironic (Comedy). It also marks the end of Myth as way of life. Gone are the gods and magic. Now Myth becomes narrower, more human-oriented. This transition marks the change from the heroic mind to the ironic mind. This story is the basis of all Epic Comedy to come.

How did Cervantes accomplish this massive shift? Don Quixote is the Romantic warrior turned on his head. Indeed, in tilting at windmills he literally falls on his head and is not right in the mind. *Don Quixote* shows that in a mechanistic world, heroism and the heroic quest are both noble and silly.

Little Miss Sunshine uses one of the oldest comic structures, the comic journey. Part of the success of this combination of Comedy and Myth is that these two genres are in many ways opposites. The Myth form, using the journey as its main technique, wants to be big, heroic, and inspiring. Comedy is about cutting things down to size. This means that in a comic journey story, the Myth sets up the laughs (puffing up the characters), while the Comedy provides the punch line.

The risk of combining these two genres is that it causes structural problems: an episodic story and weak narrative drive. *Little Miss Sunshine* uses three techniques to solve these problems: the false goal, the end point, and the family. The first technique is one *Little Miss Sunshine* shares with *Don Quixote*, the first Comic Myth. The other two techniques are additions *Little Miss Sunshine* made to the Comic Myth structure that are missing in *Don Quixote*.

A fundamental story beat of Comic Myth is that the hero chases a false goal. Don Quixote's false goal is the object of his love, Dulcinea. He believes she is a lady of refined feminine ideal, a damsel who must be saved. The heroine of *Little Miss Sunshine*, Olive, has a false goal as well. She wants to win the crown of feminine beauty.

The first technique writer Michael Arndt uses to overcome the episodic structure of Myth is to tell the audience the end point of the comic journey at the beginning. The family is taking Olive to compete in the Little Miss Sunshine beauty pageant. What's more, the characters will be going on a single-line journey. This apparently simple technique is crucial because it gives the audience a line, literally, on which to hang the events and the gags. Arndt has already promised the audience where they are going to go. In effect, it gives them the breathing space to laugh. Instead of becoming impatient with what happens next, the audience can sit back to enjoy the ride—and the jokes.

To overcome the episodic problem of opponents who are new and strangers to the hero, Arndt uses the key Myth technique for unifying the story: bring the family along for the ride. That means that Olive's main opposition is among people the audience knows, especially her father, and it's a sustainable, ongoing opposition. Instead of a succession of unconnected events, the story has a steadily building conflict. That makes the jokes funnier and lets the writer build to the funniest gag of all when the family finally gets to the pageant.

This technique also gives the film a more emotionally satisfying conclusion, not just for the hero but for the other family members as well. The family's political system, an incompetent dictatorship, is overthrown and the family is renewed.

In most comic Myths, like *Don Quixote*, *Tom Jones*, or *Little Miss Sunshine*, the journey extends over the entire story. Not *Crocodile Dundee*. As in the classic Fantasy story, the hero in *Crocodile Dundee* jumps from one story world to another. This provides the sharp contrast of world and character upon which the comedy is based. This is a subgenre known as "Fish out of Water."

The brilliance of the premise comes from the fact that the story smashes together the first and last of the four major social stages: wilderness and oppressive city. This is a fundamental technique of the anti-Western and the Modernization story that has been twisted here for comic effect. The wilderness man, with all his physical abilities and unselfconscious goodwill, encounters the various human denizens of the city jungle. He then uses the skills he has developed in the real jungle to tame the all-too-human animals of the city jungle.

Farce: The Desire for False Value

Farce is the comedy of complication. It uses the largest group of characters of any Comic form, with the possible exception of Satire.

Farce is a subgenre that sets up a minisociety of individuals all chasing after an object simultaneously. By showing all individuals seeking the goal with extreme intensity and split-second timing, Farce structure highlights the fact that the object has little or no true value and everyone's efforts are foolish.

Farce is comedy-as-game. It is an abstracted version of society and its moves are executed like speed chess. Farce is full of sound and fury, signifying nothing. In many ways, it's another example of flipping the Story Code itself. It is a comical Zen lesson in the value of *not* wanting, or at least not wanting too much.

Examples include *The Comedy of Errors*, *The Importance of Being Earnest*, *Noises Off*, *Tartuffe*, *The Miser*, *A Flea in Her Ear*, *Absurd Person Singular*, *The Norman Conquests*, *House and Garden*, and *La Cage aux Folles*.

Screwball comedies include *Bringing Up Baby*, *What's Up, Doc?*, *Arsenic and Old Lace*, *A Fish Called Wanda*, *Fawlty Towers*, elements of *Tootsie*, and the end of *Flirting with Disaster*.

Buddy Story

The Buddy Story is a form of the Action Comedy involving two friends. It is really three genres: Action, Comedy, and Love (Romance). These friends are typically men, which is why the relationship between them is sometimes called "bromance."

Examples include *Butch Cassidy and the Sundance Kid*, *Lethal Weapon*, *48 Hrs.*, *Midnight Run*, *The Blues Brothers*, *Tommy Boy*, *Bill and Ted's Excellent Adventure*, and *Swingers*.

Female buddy stories include *Bridesmaids* (also Romantic Comedy), *Gentlemen Prefer Blondes*, *The Heat*, *Charlie's Angels*, *Outrageous Fortune*, *Big Business*, and *Romy and Michele's High School Reunion*.

Gunga Din, *Ghostbusters* (1984), *Ghostbusters* (2016), and *The Other Woman* are examples of Buddy Story with three friends. *Thelma and Louise* and *Cagney and Lacey* use the Buddy structure but are not comedies. *Romancing the Stone* is a Buddy Story with a man and a woman.

The brilliance of *Wedding Crashers* comes from its premise and its mix of two comedy subgenres that, surprisingly, we rarely see together. The film takes the wedding, the moment when the community of two is created and the larger society is renewed, and reduces it to a crass sexual mating game.

The utopian world of the wedding becomes the environment where two liars can use the romantic notions that lead to marriage to reduce women to sexual objects. They're all about getting the goal without paying the emotional price. In effect, the story takes the sociobiological principle of men looking to mate with as many women as possible and turns it into a master scam with over a hundred rules of play.

The immense popularity of the film is the result of its ingenious mix of Buddy Story and Romantic Comedy. This means the script has twice the story beats in the same amount of time. The story begins with the Buddy Story by establishing the two friends as criminals of love. Once their teamwork is established, the story switches to two strands of Romantic Comedy. The scams build, which only heightens the immorality of these two men in love, until both learn that love and honesty are more valuable than unending sex with strangers. The story ends by uniting the Buddy Story and Romantic Comedy lines, with the two couples on their way to crash another wedding.

Traveling Angel Comedy

What may be the most popular of all subgenres is a story form I call the Traveling Angel Comedy. A breakout Romantic Comedy can be more successful, but the form has many more failures because these films are so predictable. The Traveling Angel Comedy is a little-known genre that just keeps winning.

This subgenre also works well in Westerns like *Shane* and Detective Stories like Sherlock Holmes, Hercule Poirot, and any number of other repeating sleuths. Even Science Fiction has a Time-Traveling Angel, *Doctor Who*.

But where the form really shines is in Comedy. A textbook example, and a massive hit, is *Mary Poppins*. *Ferris Bueller's Day Off* is a slight variation on the form, and another big hit.

We'll explore the Traveling Angel story in more detail in transcendent Fantasy. But basically it works like this:

The Traveling Angel character (see also Comedy Character Types) is perfect in some way. She enters a community in trouble where a number of characters have problems. The Angel shows them how to solve their problems and then moves on to help the next town, with a parting promise that one day the Angel will return.

Before you rush out and write one of your own, know that it's more complex than it looks. This apparently simple form is a combination of Comedy and Fantasy, often with Love Story thrown in as well. What's more, it splits the hero, giving some functions to the Angel and some to the characters with the problems.

Examples include *Santa Claus*, *Ferris Bueller's Day Off*, *Mary Poppins*, *Being There*, *Crocodile Dundee*, *Good Morning, Vietnam*, *The Intouchables*, *Amélie*, and *Chocolat*.

Parody

Parody is a subgenre that makes fun of other genres. Thus, it is an abstraction of an abstraction. The biggest danger in writing parody is that this double distancing of the audience drains the emotional juice from the story. Farce has the same problem, but the danger is more extreme in Parody.

This is one of the reasons Parody rarely works for more than a scene. The audience delights in the takeoff of the form they know and love. But the writer doesn't have to sustain an entire story because that would require the audience to make an emotional investment.

Successful Parody for an entire film or television show includes *Airplane!*, *Police Squad!*, *The Naked Gun*, *Get Smart*, *Blazing Saddles*, *High Anxiety*, and the lone transcendent Comedy in the Parody form, *Young Frankenstein*.

How to Transcend the Comedy Story

Like transcendent Crime, transcendent Comedy explores the art of morality and justice. Instead of highlighting the big distinctions between what is legal and what is moral, Comedy highlights the messy morality of everyday life.

Transcending the Comedy form typically comes in two subgenres: Black Comedy and Satire. These forms go beyond everyday comedy of manners and morals to show the false values and injustice of the social and cultural system. They critique society by showing that the entire system is absurd.

Black Comedy

Black comedy is the comedy of illogic and destructive systems. The members of the society believe so strongly in the system that they can't see the absurdity of its logic.

Often the system is right in the title: *Alice in Wonderland*, *Network*, and *Gosford Park*. Also *Catch-22*, *Goodfellas*, *Jojo Rabbit*, *Wag the Dog*, *After Hours*, and *Dr. Strangelove*.

These are the Black Comedy beats:

1. A number of characters live and/or work within an organization.
2. One character gives a detailed example of the rules, logic, and values by which the system operates.
3. The hero has a *negative* desire.
4. The opponents, also in the system, compete with the hero for the same goal.
5. One character who is in the system realizes the logic is absurd.
6. All take extreme methods to reach the goal.
7. The battle is extremely destructive.
8. No one has a self-revelation.
9. All survivors immediately resume going after the goal.

In Black Comedy, the downward cycle of logic and destruction never stops.

Satire

Satire is the comedy of beliefs. It questions the values by which the entire society operates. Most of the time, a satire ridicules the culture's faulty view of a good life. But it rarely provides an alternative.

Novels and Films

Don Quixote (also Comic Myth), *The Life and Opinions of Tristram Shandy, Gentleman*, *The Adventures of Tom Jones, a Foundling*, *Groundhog Day*, *Tootsie* (also Romantic Comedy), *American Beauty*, *Rules of the Game*, *Candide*, *A Modest Proposal*, *Vanity Fair*, *Pride and Prejudice*, *Emma*, *Sense and Sensibility*, *Vice*, *The Big Short*, *Thank You for Smoking*, *Annie Hall* (also Romantic Comedy), *Catch-22*, *M*A*S*H*, *Legally Blonde*, *The Graduate*, *Caddyshack*, *Clueless*, *Fast Times at Ridgemont High*, *Lost in America*, *Trading Places*, *Animal House*, *Best in Show*, *This Is Spinal Tap*, *Shampoo*, *Dick*, *Election*, *Sullivan's Travels*

Television

Seinfeld, *Fleabag*, *All in the Family*, *The Simpsons*, *VEEP*, *Arrested Development*, *The Larry Sanders Show*, *Friends*, *The Mary Tyler Moore Show*, *I Love Lucy*, *Cheers*, *30 Rock*, *The Office*, *Sex and the City*

These are the Satire story beats:

1. The hero exists within a social system.
2. One character explains in detail the values on which the system is based.
3. The hero has a strong desire within the system.
4. The hero is determined to rise to the top level of the system.

5. He/she has at least three opponents:
   - One within the system at the same level as the hero
   - An opponent at the top of the system—an authority figure
   - An opponent in a competing system
6. The hero and the opponents explain their beliefs, what they value.
7. As the characters compete for the same goal, their beliefs lead them to do silly and destructive things. This is how their beliefs fail them, and it is the main source of the comedy.
8. Apparent defeat and revelation: at his lowest point, the hero sees the absurdity of this system and the absurdity of the competing system. He goes to the opposite extreme and decides that nothing has value. He becomes destructive.
9. He/she tries to cause the downfall of both systems.
10. In the battle the main system collapses or is severely changed, and the pretentious are defeated.
11. The hero may have a self-revelation about spontaneity, truth, and creating something of real value.
12. The hero takes moral action.
13. There is a marriage of friendship or love. On rare occasions, the hero creates a new system based on better values.

Seinfeld: The Karma Comedy

To see how transcendent Comedy works, we have to look at *Seinfeld*. This is not a "show about nothing," as its makers once jokingly proclaimed. It's a comedy of manners and morals that's as old as comedy itself and as new as the moral problems everyone faced this morning.

Seinfeld plays with the rules of modern etiquette, especially in male-female relationships. It shows the daily injustices we all suffer. So there is a *moral element* at the heart of every episode. But the brilliance of the writing comes from how justice is done.

KEY POINT: *Seinfeld* is the karma show. Cosmic justice always happens, but in a very roundabout way.

The amazing variety of episodes are unified by the overall story challenge the characters constantly face: in the modern American big city, manners and morals are much more fluid than the manners of old. Jerry and friends are always trying to figure them out and always getting them wrong.

These are some of the moral questions they deal with: whether to give your fiancé your ATM code, saying "Nice to meet you" when you've already met, using someone who can read lips to spy on your friends, whether to spare a square of toilet paper for a stranger in the next stall, changing religions to please a girlfriend, and whether to stay with a pretty boyfriend after his face has been disfigured. These are the apparently insignificant, day-to-day moral issues on which our lives turn.

To see how *Seinfeld* satirizes American culture and explores the challenges of everyday morality, we'll break down its unique character web and plot structure.

The *Seinfeld* character web was revolutionary. This was the first sitcom where all four major characters were often immoral and unlikable. This cut against the conventional wisdom that had ruled television, and Hollywood entertainment generally, since the 1950s. To everyone's surprise, the audience liked them anyway, first, because of their flaws, not in spite of them, and second, because they were always getting screwed over by the absurd system.

Once again, we see the power of the four-point opposition, here based on comic drop and gender differences: usually machine Jerry versus children George, Elaine, and Kramer. Especially in a long-running television show, a character isn't just one comic drop. So sometimes Jerry is a child, and George, Kramer, and Elaine play animal comedy.

KEY POINT: Even though Jerry is the star, all four are equal characters.

This also was revolutionary. Until then, many sitcoms were based on a single star who drove every show (such as *I Love Lucy*). The other characters were not equal. The show often failed because one character was unable to create that much comedy over a season and a series.

To generate shows for many years, a sitcom needs at least four equal characters who can drive the story and the comedy. Each *Seinfeld* episode is dense with comedy; all four comics drive their own storyline. It sustained its brilliant comedy for nine seasons, typically from twenty-two to twenty-four episodes per season. Though other shows have had more episodes, no other television comedy has sustained a high level of quality for that long.

The plot development in *Seinfeld* was also revolutionary, and was an outgrowth of the revolution in character. By having four unlikable characters who can drive the comedy, the writers crosscut among three to four predicaments per show. This created not only a complex plot, but also more and shorter scenes than in the traditional sitcom.

The challenge of many storylines in a twenty-two-minute sitcom is that it can make each predicament too simple. The brilliant *Seinfeld* solution is to tie all the predicaments together and in a surprising way. The characters pay for their moral crime with karmic justice, balancing the books with a shock and a laugh.

One of my favorite examples is from season five, episode

fourteen, "The Marine Biologist." To impress a woman, George has claimed he is a marine biologist. Meanwhile, Kramer has gone to the beach to practice his golf drives. While George and his new girlfriend are walking along the beach, there is an emergency with a whale. Naturally, George's girlfriend expects him to save the day. So into the water he goes. In the final reveal back at the coffee shop, notice how the lines eventually weave and karma is done.

GEORGE: The sea was angry that day, my friends, like an old man trying to send back soup in a deli. I got about fifty feet out and suddenly, the great beast appeared before me. I tell you, he was ten stories high if he was a foot. As if sensing my presence, he let out a great bellow. I said, "Easy, big fella!" And then, as I watched him struggling, I realized that something was obstructing its breathing. From where I was standing, I could see directly into the eye of the great fish.

JERRY: Mammal.

GEORGE: Whatever.

KRAMER: Well, what did you do next?

GEORGE: Well then, from out of nowhere, a huge tidal wave lifted me, tossed me like a cork, and I found myself right on top of him—face to face with the blowhole. I could barely see from the waves crashing down upon me, but I knew something was there. So I reached my hand in, felt around, and pulled out the obstruction.

George dramatically reveals the obstruction to be a golf ball.

KRAMER (*embarrassed*): What is that, a Titleist?

George nods.

KRAMER: A hole in one, huh?

JERRY: Well, the crowd must have gone wild!

GEORGE: Oh, yes they did, Jerry—they were all over me. It was like *Rocky 1*. Diane came up to me, threw her arms around me, and kissed me. We both had tears streaming down our faces. I never saw anyone so beautiful. It was at that moment I decided to tell her I was not a marine biologist!

JERRY: Wow! What'd she say?

GEORGE: She told me to go to hell, and I took the bus home.

That's the power of great comedy.

My Bildungsroman Reveal

Most of my personal formation came from single transcendent events, like a specific film. But the overwhelming power of *Seinfeld* happened once a week for twenty-two-plus episodes a season for over nine years! It is impossible to convey the effect of watching the sheer brilliance of this show for that long. The fact that the writers produced this material at the rate of one every week is mind-boggling.

For most of the 1990s, *Seinfeld* was my weekly place of worship. It showed that comedy could be as profound as any other story form, if not more so. No other comedy, in any medium, has been this great. I hold this truth to be self-evident.

The Next Rung Up the Ladder

The philosophy of comedy shows us that living together in society requires tolerance of our flaws, and that, in spite of our mistakes, we can make a better life for everyone.

What's missing is a guide for how to grow. We'll get that when we explore Fantasy, Detective, and Love Story. But first we have to see how the larger society evolves and affects our lives.

For that we turn to Western and Gangster.

9

Western: The Rise and Fall of Civilization

Shane: The Warrior Moses

Shane, the gunfighter, comes down from the mountaintop to make it possible for a family of farmers to defeat an earlier embodiment of civilization, the cattleman. But Shane cannot experience the fruits of love and family. Instead, he is doomed to wander alone in the wilderness forever. This is the essential Western story.

The Western: How It Works

The key to understanding how the Western works is embedded in its title: go west. This process not only encapsulates the basic theme of the genre, it's the ethic upon which all American storytelling has been based. This is the belief that we can reinvent ourselves at any time, over and over again. The Western hero is the epitome of this belief. He is the individual who can pull up stakes and go.

Implied in this ethic are both extreme individualism and absolute freedom. These values are connected: no outside force or inner limitation can prevent someone from being whatever he or she wants to be.

On a greater scale, the act of going west is why the classic Western is about nation building, about transforming wilderness into civilization. The process of modernization is codified in the ideology of "Manifest Destiny," the credo that justified the expansion of the United States in the late 1840s. The classic Western translates this ideology into story form.

Manifest Destiny is part of a succession of creeds that have collectively become known as the American Dream. Contrary to popular belief, the term "American Dream" is relatively recent. The historian James Truslow Adams coined the term in his book *The Epic of America*, in 1931. But the American Dream goes back a long time in the history of ideas.

In 1630, John Winthrop delivered a sermon called *Shining City on the Hill* on a ship bound for the New World. Winthrop (1588–1649), the first governor of the Massachusetts Bay Colony, spoke of America as the world's last hope to fulfill God's promise on earth. Winthrop's image of the "shining city on the hill" was borrowed from Jesus's Sermon on the Mount in the New Testament.

The westward movement at the heart of this genre also gives us the form's great misconception: the true Western hero does not go west to create a home in the new land. He is neither the farmer nor the shopkeeper. The true Western hero is the cowboy.

KEY POINT: The cowboy goes west to go back in time, to live in the pristine wilderness free from humankind itself.

This process is captured perfectly in the titles of the James Fenimore Cooper novels that first defined the genre. This series, known as the *Leatherstocking Tales*, are: *The Deerslayer* (story dates 1740–1755), *The Last of the Mohicans* (1757), *The Pathfinder* (1758–1759), *The Pioneers* (1793), and *The*

Prairie (1804). The hero, Natty Bumppo, based on the historical figure Daniel Boone, is a hunter/man of the wild who steadily moves west ahead of the frontier.

Taken together, the Western story beats detail the reluctant leader of nation building. We see this in the form's story strategy: a wandering cowboy fights criminals trying to stop people from building their homes out of the wilderness.

Here lies the fundamental contradiction of the Western hero: in blazing a path to the wilderness, the cowboy makes it possible for others to follow him and build the nation. The common people creating their homes out of the dystopian land are like the Israelites wandering in the desert. The cowboy hero is Moses.

As the pathfinder, he knows his work is necessary and valuable. But he also knows the cost is losing the natural world he loves. In defeating the Indians and cattlemen so the farmers can build their own nation, the cowboy joins them as the doomed man. He can lead his people to the promised land, but can never enter it himself.

The Western Mind-Action Story View

The Western Mind-Action story view of immigrants moving west and building the nation highlights the success of the American Dream, both economically and spiritually. But above all it's about *moral* success. The Western is its own religion. It is America's Creation Myth.

As we mentioned in the Myth chapter, religion is a collection of Myth stories that express the moral code necessary to achieve immortality. In post-Darwinian America, religion became naturalized and grounded in the "West." American history became the religion that all faiths in the United States could believe in.

The use of the term "myth" when applied to the Western has always been ambiguous. The Western Creation Myth doesn't recount the fantastical battle between gods and Titans that led to the birth of the gods and the rule of Zeus on Mount Olympus. Nor does it recount the Judaic six-day creation of the world by an all-powerful God, the making of Adam and Eve, or the fall of humankind after the first man and woman ate from the Tree of Knowledge.

Here, we mean Myth in its more powerful sense as the formal, fictional description of the physical-social-cultural stages of humanity's development. The Western Creation Myth recounts the birth of human society through the toil of real men and women cultivating a new land. In the Western, the human being doesn't come from a god. Western "gods" are real individuals making their world and their nation.

KEY POINT: The Western is a deeply religious story form because it presents a unified system of values, based on "progress," in which humans can have faith.

The Western is the *naturalistic* moral tale. It promotes the ideal of the natural man who lives freely and independently, even when he's among others. Ironically, it is because he lives freely and independently that the hero has a tremendous will for justice. He will always aid the weak when they are attacked by the strong.

In barest terms, the Western is about the hunter questioning his own use of physical force. It asks the central moral question of Action: To fight or not to fight? And the second question that immediately follows the first: Should the main method of enforcing justice be killing or appealing to the claim of what is right?

The Western is both compressed and inclusive. Therefore, much of the Western myth's power is that it is the great "macro" form. It brings together in one vision the various social stages in human cultural evolution. It then telescopes these forms into a single-story unit so that the contrast and continuity are clear.

Besides being the naturalistic religion, this is why the Western is about the rise and fall of civilization. It is the natural, "this-world" story form that includes all other story forms under its umbrella. Alone among genres, it shows the full evolution of society.

KEY POINT: If Science Fiction is social philosophy in fiction form, and Crime and Comedy are applied moral philosophy, the Western gives us a philosophy of history.

To be clear, the Western doesn't portray the real history of the American West. It portrays a *theory* of history. The classic Western shows us history as linear progress, literally moving east to west and conceptually tracking the rise of civilization from corruption toward perfection.

That's why criticism of the Western as unrealistic is irrelevant. One argument points out that white/mixed-race people from the south populated "El Norte" years before and in much greater numbers than the movement from east to west. That's true. But the American Creation Myth and its theory of history are based strictly on European migration.

The Western's theory of history doesn't just show the rise of civilization. Its transcendent version, the anti-Western, shows its fall. It highlights the end of the American frontier, the world's last habitable frontier. When the Western evolves to the anti-Western, it becomes a modern Myth about living in the dystopia of the oppressive city.

This raises the central question of the Western's storytelling strategy: In a story about building civilization, why does the writer make the hero the person who avoids civilization?

That choice is the main reason the transcendent anti-Western is where the genre becomes a work of art. Focusing on the man who builds civilization would make the form heroic. Focusing on the man who avoids civilization makes it tragic because of the terrible human costs.

In our investigation of genres, why does the Western follow Science Fiction, Crime, and Comedy, the three genres of how society works? Science Fiction is about creating society in the future. The Western is a vision of society in the past. But it is nowhere close to being historically accurate.

The real value is to show how society *evolves*, not only through a grand process of how humans change, but also as a compressed view of the major forms of slavery a human being has and will face. Simply put, the Western says that humans begin by fighting against nature and end by fighting against corporations.

The Western Compared to Other Genres

As we have seen, while each genre is a unique form, some genres form families that share common features. The Western is part of a third family of genres that includes Myth and Action. Each has a fighter hero and has the same thematic emphasis on taking action.

Contrary to popular opinion, the traditional Western didn't die. It traveled to the future and became the Science Fiction Western. The fight on the frontier simply moved from the American West to outer space. Examples of this incredibly popular form are *Star Wars*, *Dawn of the Planet of the Apes*, *Guardians of the Galaxy*, and *The Mandalorian*. Han Solo, space cowboy, is one of the most popular heroes in the history of film.

Examples of Western

Novels, Films, and Stories

The Virginian, *Riders of the Purple Sage*, *The Great Train Robbery*, *Shane*, *The Ox-Bow Incident*, *3:10 to Yuma*, *The Captives*, *Stagecoach*, *The Sisters Brothers*, *Fort Apache*, *She Wore a Yellow Ribbon*, *Red River*, *The Searchers*, *Hombre*, *Valdez Is Coming*, *The Man Who Shot Liberty Valance*, *Winchester '73*, *The Shootist*, *The Good, the Bad and the Ugly*, *A Fistful of Dollars*, *For a Few Dollars More*, *Wyatt Earp*, *Gunfight at the O.K. Corral*, *Tombstone*, *High Plains Drifter*, *Jesse James*, *Bend of the River*, *The Revenant*, *Ride the High Country*, *Duel in the Sun*, *The Plainsman*, *The Naked Spur*, *The Cowboys*, *True Grit*, *The Dark Tower* (also Myth and Science Fiction), *Along Came Jones* (also Comedy), *Cat Ballou* (also Comedy), *Blazing Saddles* (also Comedy), *The Big Country*, *Junior Bonner*, *One-Eyed Jacks*, *The Gunfighter*, *Annie Oakley*, *The Life and Times of Judge Roy Bean*, *The Assassination of Jesse James by the Coward Robert Ford*, *The Magnificent Seven*, *Broken Arrow*

Television

Bonanza, *Cheyenne*, *The Rifleman*, *Maverick*, *Rawhide*, *The Lone Ranger*, *Gunsmoke*, *The Life and Legend of Wyatt Earp*, *The Big Valley*, *Wagon Train*, *Bat Masterson*, *Lonesome Dove*, *The Mandalorian* (also Science Fiction), *Cowboy Bebop* (also Science Fiction), *The Wild Wild West* (also Science Fiction), *Justified*, *Longmire*, *Deadwood*, *Yellowstone*, *Godless*

Western Subgenres

Anti-Western, Space Western, Contemporary, Traveling Devil Anti-Western, Comedy

Western Story Overview

Here's what we'll cover in this chapter:

- **WESTERN STORY BEATS**
- **THEME:** Being Is Doomed Existence
  - Thematic Recipe: The Way of the Fighter for the Weak
- **HOW TO TRANSCEND THE WESTERN STORY**
  - Anti-Western

Western Story Beats

The Western story beats play out the form's larger story strategy: a wandering cowboy fights criminals trying to stop people from building their homes out of the wilderness.

WESTERN STORY BEAT: Story World—the New World

All genres show the individual within the larger society: how people interact and evolve together. The three major components, in both society and story world, are the land, the organization of the people, and the specialized technology.

The most striking feature of Western land is its vast space, an unspoiled wilderness as far as the eye can see. This land is a natural cathedral. It has the expanse, physical objects, and godlike perspective we associate with the film medium, plus the density and formalism characteristic of theater. Western land is naturalistic theater.

Whether set within the lush forests of the Appalachians, the wide plains of the prairie, or the stark desert of the southwest, this is a land where settlers can cultivate rich natural resources. The material world of America contrasts with the depleted landscape typically found in European story. As F. Scott Fitzgerald says in *The Great Gatsby*, European settlers discovered the "fresh, green breast of the new world." As a result, the Western exudes a new sense of absolute freedom and overwhelming promise.

That promise can only be realized, however, by undertaking the massive job of taming nature. This means exercising brute power to transform wilderness into farm and village. The settlers also believe this requires destroying the native peoples who have always lived off the land.

Story World: The Frontier

The Western has a unique story world among genres in that its story focuses on the frontier between wilderness and civilization.

> **KEY POINT: The Western frontier is one of both space and time.**

The fact that the Western exists between two evolutionary stages of society has more to do with making it one of the essential story forms than any other structural feature. Why?

- The Western begins with all-powerful nature, highlighting the physical and biological foundation of human life. Then, when the world shifts to society, we see how nature and society combine to produce the culture.
- When characters live between two social stages, their existence expresses a massive feedback loop: the social changes act upon the characters, and the characters act upon the land and society in a way that creates social change.
- That change is one of taming nature, of people doing the basic work of building a civilization.

Story World: The Farm and the Village

As the story world shifts from wilderness to society at the frontier, we see society's birth in the creation of farms and villages.

KEY POINT: In the Western, the story world is a fragile community in its infancy.

While Science Fiction is about how to create a society, only the Western shows an entire society in the process of being built. This raises the issue of the value of society itself. We know from Myth that the story world always expresses opposing values. So the world of the frontier creates a canvas on which to show a morality play in primal form.

Morality is the core task of creating a civilization, and it happens in the newly emerging farm and village. Therefore, the Western questions what it means to live in a culture of extreme individualism.

Since the Western highlights the transition line between wilderness and village, it also highlights the contrast between the nomadic hunter and a new breed of social man, the farmer. The farmer is settling down, literally planting roots by growing crops and constructing buildings that endure the harsh natural elements. This society is looking for new land to conquer. Conquer is exactly what these people plan to do.

The Western town is society in miniature, in its essential form. Only the basic societal buildings exist: jail, church, saloon, store, and hotel. This is first society, with the basic specialties found in any social organism.

In *My Darling Clementine*, the sense of society's fragility is expressed in a church where only the floor and steeple have been constructed. No matter. The townspeople conduct their dance anyway. It's pleasurable, communal, and spiritually uplifting in the great outdoors. These are the values the genre wants to express.

Story World: The Battle Against Social Entropy

The village in the classic Western is often a boomtown. It is a state of nature, a place of extreme competition for rich resources and almost no law to prevent theft and murder. This is either a utopian or a dystopian world, depending on whether the individual has power or not.

The first and most essential requirement in establishing a community is stopping social entropy. Above all, the larger unit must not fall apart. Therefore, the classic Western is a battle against chaos.

Why? The boomtown is society near anarchy. Desire for money and pleasure has no bounds. Individuals are not yet woven together by trust and by law into a stable social unit. They are at war with one another to gain as much power, wealth, and reputation as possible in the midst of this lawlessness. At the same time, they must protect themselves from their neighbors.

This is a situation of great potential, both for enhancement and destruction. Owning land rich in material resources where the six-shooter is in every hand guarantees both outcomes.

The combination of great potential for growth and death prompts most members of a Western community to press for law and restrictions. While restrictions cut into the potential individuals have for rapid gain, they make it more likely that growth will endure.

In game theory terms, most people are willing to take lower gains now to avoid total loss and guarantee consistent gains in the future. A few are not. Those are the bad guys.

Story World: Primitive and Advanced Technology

The third pillar of the story world is technology, the tools by which humanity transforms the land into society. In the Western Myth, this technology is highly symbolic. Its tools are sacred objects. They not only drive the story; they are part of the genre's thematic vision.

The first key techno-symbol in the Western is the horse. The cowboy lives on his horse. This animal is what connects physical man to nature. As the cowboy's primary means of transportation, the horse is what allows him the freedom to roam the vast wilderness he loves. It gives him mastery over nature without dividing him from it. And it makes him a more effective fighter and hunter. One of the central ironies of the Western is that taming the horse is an early step in going from wilderness to village. This evolution from hunter to farmer also marks the end of cowboy life.

The second techno-symbol is the fence. Nothing could be more primitive or more powerful. Once the free, open land is fenced off, the wilderness and its endless promise are over. In *My Darling Clementine*, the fence is shown by a couple of thin wooden rails on a post. The vast wilderness is clearly visible beyond. Yet that rickety fence is what shapes the land for a new society of laws.

Robert Frost is famous for the line, "Good fences make good neighbors." For the lone cowboy riding the range, neighbors are what he desperately wants to avoid. Fences are the beginning of a capitalist system of competition for scarce resources where the land for everyone suddenly becomes "mine." Once the first settlers have fenced the land, the process has begun that will lead to vast differences in wealth and power.

The symbol of the fence gains added power when it evolves from wood to barbed wire. Historically, the barbed wire fence was one of the most influential of all technologies. Not only did it end the Old West, it defined the way World War I was fought.

In the classic Western, the metal barbs make the fence a weapon that stops the cattle drives. Thus, the barbed wire fence creates one of the main conflicts in the Western story form. This is the conflict between early man, the cattle-driving cowboy, versus later man, the farmer, whom the cowboy defends.

The cowboy hat is the symbol of character. The physical man who rides through the land on horseback must have a wide-brimmed hat to protect himself from the brutal sun. This is not an aristocratic or even middle-class man. This is the common workingman.

The use of force, especially with a gun, is a direct outgrowth of the story world in which the cowboy must defend a fragile community in its infancy.

KEY POINT: The gun is the technology that drives the Western plot and focuses the theme in the final showdown.

The weapon of choice is the six-shooter, a pistol with six bullets in a rotating chamber. It is the tool by which fighters make an immediate, all-or-nothing settlement of conflicting claims. This expresses a nation in its earliest stages of social evolution. Boundaries may exist in name, but the laws that protect the society within those boundaries are still weak. Without an established system of distributing rights and settling conflicts, individuals must use the personal, direct, and destructive means of the gun.

The gun is mechanized force, the "sword of right action" multiplied many times over in its ability to kill. This weapon is how the sheriff enforces the few laws that exist and defeats social entropy. It is also how the cowboy with the white hat enforces moral law against the man with the black hat.

Yet there is a terrible price to pay for basing society on the gun. The good cowboy knows he is right. But many people die, and the violent life takes a severe toll on him psychologically. The cowboy's responsibility to stop this endless violence is one reason he can never live with a woman and create a family. It is why he can never enjoy the fruits of civilization.

The high cost of the gun is especially controversial in a modern, mature society. In this early civilization, the proper use of a gun is a child's necessary rite of passage. The primary rule is: the righteous man never draws first. In films like *Destry Rides Again* (1939) and *Shane* (1953), children play with guns as if they were toys. Only the cowboy hero knows the despair that real guns bring.

A final Western symbol is the silver badge. This is the mark of the law and justified force. The badge symbolizes law imposed not just on wilderness, but also on passion in human beings. The badge is a symbol of progress.

WESTERN STORY BEAT: Hero's Role—the Cowboy as Fighter

The cowboy is the most individualistic hero in genre storytelling, even more so than the lone detective. So it's ironic that the Western, more than any other form, is about how a society develops.

We see how the Western is really about the rise and fall of civilization when we break down the role of the hero.

> **KEY POINT: This genre is unique in that it has a primary hero and a secondary hero.**

The primary hero is the cowboy. The secondary hero is the farmer who creates a home out of wilderness and thereby creates a nation of laws and civilization itself.

The cowboy is a fighter, a warrior on a horse. This is the key action that defines him to his core. Much of what the

Western means emanates from this fighting identity. The cowboy is essentially the Action hero at the beginning of civilization. While he doesn't build civilization himself, he makes it possible for the farmer and the merchant to do so.

Every genre has a central question that the particular story must answer to properly play out the form. Among the most important ramifications of the fighter hero is the question the Western asks. Not surprisingly, it is the same question the Action story asks: Does the hero choose freedom or life? More precisely, does he stand and fight? Or does he flee and fight another day? According to the moral code of the West, the cowboy hero must always stand and fight for what he believes.

Hero's Role: The Cowboy vs. the Supercowboy

When it comes to character, the Western is about comparing men. The most obvious comparison is between cowboy and farmer, between pathfinder and nation-builder. In a world based on power, the cowboy is the fighter who lives on his horse in the wilderness. But the more profound comparison is between the cowboy versus the supercowboy.

The supercowboy combines primal man with Aristotle's "great-souled" man, the man who uses his power reluctantly. He is the man who simply knows greatness and acts accordingly. He is the Nietzschean Overman who cannot be tempted, corrupted, or deterred. It is because of the supercowboy's power, and his willingness to exercise it at the cost of his life, that the values of a civilized community exist.

The supercowboy takes two forms:

1. He is the lawman with the courage and skills of a gunfighter. He stands against outlaw warriors who want to continue the wild chaos of an unfenced nature. The quintessential version of this man is Wyatt Earp (*My Darling Clementine*, *Tombstone*).

2. He is the lone warrior or gunslinger who opposes destructive men because of his evolved self-mastery and sense of natural right. The quintessential versions of this man are Natty Bumppo (*The Last of the Mohicans*) and Shane (*Shane*).

Hero's Role: The Cowboy as Savior

The Western hero is also a savior. When he drives the story, he takes the form of the "traveling angel." Traveling Angel is a subgenre found not only in the Western but also in Detective stories and Comedies. Perfect in some way, the traveling angel enters a town in trouble. He or she helps each of the other characters solve their individual problems, makes the town whole, and then moves on to the next town. The pain of losing this doctor of community is assuaged by the angel's parting promise to return.

The classic Western Traveling Angel story is *Shane*. Shane comes down from the mountains to the plains below, and there he reluctantly uses his gun to make the wilderness safe for family life. Then, as the eternal loner, he must move on.

A variation on the Traveling Angel story is the "Traveling Devil." A man who seems to be the devil incarnate visits an apparently moral, upright, even utopian town. The traveling devil exposes the hypocrisy and hidden immorality of the town and shows the townspeople how to live with a new and higher morality. The Traveling Devil story is a subform of the anti-Western, which we'll explore later.

The classic example of the Traveling Devil Western is *High Plains Drifter*. The "Stranger" comes out of the waves of heat on the high plains and rides into a town. He willingly uses gun and whip to exact justice on a community that hides a terrible secret of its own corruption, cowardice, and hypocrisy.

WESTERN STORY BEAT: The Cowboy's Values—the Code of the West

The Western man is a physical man, both because he lives outside on the land and because he lives by his body. So his values derive first from his physical ability. The classic cowboy rides a horse and drives cattle. He respects physical skill with a horse and a gun. He sets off on his own and values personal freedom above all else.

KEY POINT: The cowboy's sense of freedom is limited to what affects the hero's personal space and movement.

The old cowboy in *The Shootist* expresses this view of freedom when he teaches a young man his version of the famous Code of the West: "I'll not be wronged, insulted, nor laid a hand on. I don't do those things to others and I require that they don't do them to me."

The Western presents a hero who loves nature deeply and chooses to live with it rather than with others. Yet by saving people when he must, he places human life above his love of nature and solitude.

Thus, the genre lays out an order of values, a set of priorities in which nature is valuable, but not as valuable as man. While the Western questions the concept of society, it eventually applauds it. This is the human with deep flaws. By applying the severest test to human beings, the form shows the true value of social man.

The value system of the cowboy is loosely summarized in the Code of the West. This code is an outgrowth of both the cowboy's physical ability and the fact that he lives on the frontier. The historian Frederick Jackson Turner first defined the way the frontier creates the cowboy's moral system, and indeed the entire American identity, in an essay that became known as the "frontier thesis." We'll get into this theory in more detail later. In simple terms, Turner said that pioneers living on the edge of the wilderness made values like individualism and self-reliance *the* defining characteristics of an American.

The Code of the West is a cluster of moral values that complement one another as a way of life. It expresses a simple dualism, often referred to as "white hat/black hat." This dualism also arises from the frontier, and emerges organically anytime a people fight to establish a village in the wilderness.

> **KEY POINT: The Code of the West lays out the moral values that comprise the "American Dream." It is a recipe for success in both economic and spiritual life.**

Here are the main values associated with the Code of the West: independence, freedom, self-reliance, courage to confront a challenge head-on, will to justice, pride in being able to overcome any challenge, achievement, honesty, loyalty, hospitality to strangers, respect for women (but not as equals), and sacred regard for the horse.

WESTERN STORY BEAT: Weakness-Need—the Loner and the Man of Shame

What are the deep flaws that ruin the cowboy's life at the beginning of the story? The cowboy's extreme individualism and need to be absolutely free take a severe toll. It means the cowboy, and especially the supercowboy, is a loner. He cannot or will not form the bonds of love, so he cannot enter the community and become a full human being. Other than Shane, the textbook example of this man is Ethan Edwards in *The Searchers*.

The supercowboy experiences a sharp dichotomy between his advanced sense of right action and his stunted emotional growth. His self-mastery conflicts with his social awkwardness, and the result is that he is sentenced to wander until he dies.

The cowboy, like the samurai, is also a bit of a dinosaur. He cannot adapt to social change. The new world bewilders him and he cannot escape. He knows he must adapt or die, but he doesn't know how, emotionally or intellectually.

Another deep weakness is that the cowboy is trapped in a shame culture. As we discussed in Action, this way of thinking is based on the need to live up to a public standard. When someone falls short in the eyes of others, they feel acute shame.

Shame culture is common when people transform the land from wilderness to village. When the village first takes shape, it is under attack from outside forces that want the wilderness back. Therefore, it's fragile. Everyone must do their part or the whole society collapses.

This is the story world and the culture in which the cowboy is born. In this extremely physical world, with his primary tool the gun, the cowboy constantly faces the test of who is fastest on the draw. He is defined by athletic ability and always in public. Above all, he can never avoid the fight.

In films like *Shane*, *Destry Rides Again*, and *The Man Who Shot Liberty Valance* (1962), the hero tries desperately to break free of the deadly trap of shame culture and his own masculinity. But to no avail. The culture is too strong. The mind is too weak. The ritual must be performed.

WESTERN STORY BEAT: Desire—Save the Builders of Civilization

The desire line of the hero determines the spine of every story. In a Western, the main desire is not what it appears to be. It's not bringing civilization to the wilderness. The super-cowboy initially wants to go west to leave civilization behind.

He thereby becomes a pathfinder for the secondary hero, the farmer, who does want to build a new home, nation, and civilization.

As first settlers, the farmer and his family come under great danger from the "Indians" (Native Americans) and the "bad" cowboy who wants nothing to do with fencing the land and taming his own wildness. The farmer is not a warrior. Therefore, he must appeal to the "supercowboy" for protection.

The irony is that the supercowboy is similar to the Indian and the bad cowboy in his exceptional fighting ability. This ability is what allows him to fulfill his desire to help the farmers and villagers, even though that dooms his own way of life.

What is the desire of the secondary hero of the Western? The farmer or the minor characters want to go west to escape from a corrupt, enslaving civilization. They long for an untouched wilderness where they can try again and this time do it right. In this movement west, the secondary characters mimic the journeys of their predecessors who traveled from "decadent" authoritarian Europe to a New World promising absolute freedom and spiritual purity. These characters have no sense of irony that their current effort at building a "higher" civilization is also doomed to fail. They have no recognition that they will be part of creating a new corrupt society as wave after wave of inherently flawed human beings tries to do the same thing they're doing.

The overall action of the Western is cultivating the land, building the town, and consolidating the bonds that make an ideal community, or promised land. They're all made possible by the lone individual who is doomed never to see it.

TECHNIQUE: The Supercowboy's Goal

While the supercowboy's overall life goal is protecting the builders of civilization, you must also give the hero a *specific desire* that brings him into constant physical conflict. Whatever he wants in this story, he can get it only through fighting.

Visual Shapes of the Western Plot: Linear and Rise and Fall

The classic Western uses the most popular story shape, the linear. The cowboy hero has one goal and one main opponent trying to stop him. It looks like this:

The transcendent anti-Western uses the rise and fall story shape, much like the Gangster genre.

The modern cowboy has initial success but is eventually destroyed by the forces of the new social stage, the city.

WESTERN STORY BEAT: Character Web—Common Man Heroes

How do Western heroes and opponents fit within the larger character web that defines the form?

The Western genre went from historical fact to legend to myth. Early America was full of everyday common men and women trying to make a new life. So the heroes, superheroes, and gods of this story form, both good and bad, are also rough-hewn, common men, and sometimes women, who accomplish extraordinary and glorious feats every day. In the process, they create a civilization on a continent.

- Historical/legendary heroes and superheroes include Wyatt Earp, Doc Holliday, Bat Masterson, Buffalo Bill Cody, Wild Bill Hickok, Calamity Jane, Billy the Kid, Jesse James, and Butch Cassidy and the Sundance Kid.
- Imaginary common-man gods, superheroes, and antiheroes include Paul Bunyan, John Henry, Shane (*Shane*), the Stranger (*High Plains Drifter*), Blondie (*The Good, the Bad and the Ugly*), Harmonica (*Once Upon a Time in the West*), Ethan Edwards (*The Searchers*), the Magnificent Seven (*The Magnificent Seven*), the Wild Bunch (*The Wild Bunch*), Josey Wales (*The Outlaw Josey Wales*), Marshall Will Kane (*High Noon*), and John McCabe and Constance Miller (*McCabe & Mrs. Miller*).

The pantheon of Western mythical characters is much closer to the Greek pantheon than the Judaic or Christian idea of God. Like the Greek gods, the Western "gods" are rough, bawdy, sensual lovers of life, sometimes funny, and occasionally ludicrous. To see barmaids in a fight is not unlike watching Athena compete with Aphrodite; we like them more for it.

As befits the new democratic society, the Western pantheon has neither Zeus on the mountaintop nor One God in Heaven above. In these Mythical-religious story systems, other gods stand in a strict hierarchy and pay fealty to the top god. Westerners find their divinity in humanity itself, not in an idealized, all-good and all-powerful figure. The Western "gods" don't live on high; they roam the plains. Each brings order and justice, by law or by revenge, to the common people who struggle to build their lives. Like Norse gods, the Western gods are mortal. Death is a constant possibility.

The moral code that underlies the Western form is broader than the Christian moral code, with different values and priorities. For example, sex outside of marriage doesn't equal adultery in the Western. Sex per se is neither good nor bad—what matters are the consequences. Like the Christian moral code, the Western "gods" play out a strict, good versus evil ethics.

The secondary characters in the Western revolve around creating home, nation, and civilization. The farmer tills the soil with the help of his family. The preacher brings God's word to the wilderness. The schoolmistress not only educates the community's children in "readin', writin', and 'rithmetic," she is the "good woman" who will become the lawman's wife.

WESTERN STORY BEAT: Opponent—Indians and Bad Cowboys

The opponent provides the obstacle to the hero's drive to reach the goal.

The Western opponent is someone the hero must fight physically. He takes two main forms.

Cowboys vs. Indians

In early versions of the genre, the "Indians" are the first obstacle for the European civilization-building settlers. Their very name, given to Native Americans by Europeans, commemorates a colossal blunder in which some of the first explorers landing in America thought they had found India.

Like the cowboy, the Indians are hunters, but they are of a different race and they were on the land first. To the white

European and Eastern seaboard settlers, these natives aren't human. They are the "Other," barbarians who only want to destroy their farms and villages.

The settlers seek aid from the cowboy, the horse warrior who is physically bigger and tougher. They know the cowboy is also a barbarian, but he's their barbarian. He helps the community fight the savage forces that would prevent the evolution of society.

While cowboys versus Indians seems like the main conflict, the classic Western portrays only the end of that fight. Typically set in the 1870s and 1880s, these stories show the Indians' final stand in the three-century war that marked their genocide in the United States. The outcome of this fight had long since been determined.

Farmers vs. Cattlemen, Good Cowboys vs. Bad Cowboys

In later versions of the Western, the fight between farmers and cattlemen is the main conflict and the one that determines the form. These tough cowboys are the white warriors of the wilderness. They view dividing up land for cultivation as the opposite of progress. This second opposition in the genre becomes focused on gunslinger versus gunslinger.

One of the great strengths of the Western is how it compares the enforcers. The key contrast is not between the gunfighter versus the farmer or the gunfighter versus the community builder. It's between the moral gunfighter, or good cowboy, versus the immoral gunfighter, or bad cowboy. These are the same kind of man.

Like the good cowboy, the bad cowboy is a physical man who lives by his body. Each has the physical ability to draw a gun quickly and shoot with deadly accuracy. Thus, the clash of the two manifestations of this natural man is a clash of essential morality: the leader versus the tyrant.

In this sense, *Red River* is a quintessential Western. The leader of the cattle drive becomes tyrannical in his efforts to get the cattle to market. His adopted son becomes the new leader by using moral right to defeat his authoritarian father.

Moral Opposition

The Western is a morality play on a vast, stark canvas. These two physical men in opposition, supercowboy versus bad cowboy, demonstrate a moral conflict in their fight over the community.

The bad cowboys are the forces of social entropy. Their desire for unrestricted gain can only lead to anarchy. This may take the form of driving cattle across an unfenced, uncultivated wilderness. Or it can be a lawless boomtown in which the cowboys' desire for women, liquor, and gambling turns Main Street into a war zone.

The "good" townspeople push for law and the restriction of desire to avoid the death of their town and their future. Those who oppose such restrictions, the "outlaws," have no consideration for principles. They are willing and able to use their guns to gain wealth, power, and status.

More precisely, they do not wish to cultivate self-improvement. Their gain does not come by carefully developing the environment nor by cooperating with other members of the community. It comes from gathering a fighting force of gunmen and using weaponry to steal wealth.

These men promote social entropy because of their disdain for development and their failure to care and preserve. On the other hand, the good, law-abiding citizens attempt to construct the bonds that will form an identifiable, strong, and lasting society.

When the farmer and the villager bring in the good cowboy, he may be a man of the law—the marshal or the sheriff—or he may be the supercowboy. The supercowboy, with his Code of the West, values courage, self-reliance, decency, and a clear difference between right and wrong.

But the more powerful the good cowboy, the more powerful the opponent. The bad cowboy is freedom in the extreme, the great "I," the unrestricted id, with a complete lack of social responsibility. His goal is to destroy.

The relationship between the supercowboy, bad cowboy, and the farmers demonstrates Nietzsche's classic distinction of master morality and slave morality. Nietzsche would say that the values of the supercowboy and bad cowboy are part of master morality. As physical men, they are warriors from the wilderness who respect each other's courage and skill, in spite of their radically different values. They ask for and give no quarter.

Nietzsche argues that in slave morality the concept of "evil" is a creation of those in a position of weakness. The farmers and townspeople are slaves to the warrior skills and sensibility of the bad cowboy. So they call him evil. He is ruthless and vicious because he is primal. He wants wildness, open land, and free rein to grab wealth without playing by rules or a new morality.

TECHNIQUE: The Nemesis

Give the hero a nemesis, the most dangerous opponent for *that particular character*.

As in the Action story, always make the opponent the best fighter possible and the best able to attack the hero's biggest flaw. Generally, that flaw is a symptom of the shame culture and the cowboy's reluctance to kill.

WESTERN STORY BEAT: Opponent's Plan—Destruction

Whether bad cowboy or "Indian," the opponent commits a crime against the settlers. The crime is designed to destroy what has been built and create a lawless world where everything is decided by force. The destroyer, with superior firepower, is bound to win this contest. He creates a psychology of hopelessness that prompts the settler to want to give up.

Examples include:

- **INDIAN ATTACKS:** *Stagecoach*, *Fort Apache*, *She Wore a Yellow Ribbon*, *Red River*, *The Searchers*, *The Plainsman*, *Broken Arrow*
- **SELLING WEAPONS TO THE INDIANS:** *The Plainsman*
- **CATTLE RUSTLING:** *The Virginian*, *The Ox-Bow Incident*, *The Cowboys*
- **CUTTING FENCES AND BURNING FARMS:** *Shane*
- **DESTRUCTION OF PROPERTY OR INFRASTRUCTURE:** *Wagon Train*
- **TERRORIZING THE TOWN:** *Wyatt Earp*, *High Noon*, *The Man Who Shot Liberty Valance*, *High Plains Drifter*, *Pale Rider*
- **KIDNAPPING:** *The Searchers*, *The Plainsman*
- **THEFT:** *Jesse James*, *Bend of the River*, *The Man Who Shot Liberty Valance*, *A Fistful of Dollars*, *Butch Cassidy and the Sundance Kid*
- **MURDER:** *Shane*, *Once Upon a Time in the West*, *True Grit*, *Destry Rides Again*, *Winchester '73*, *The Naked Spur*, *A Fistful of Dollars*, *High Plains Drifter*, *The Outlaw Josey Wales*

WESTERN STORY BEAT: Plan—Direct Confrontation

The initial plan in the typical Western comes from the villagers/farmers. Under assault from Indians or bad cowboys, they bring in the supercowboy, whether lawman or gunslinger, to lead the fight. His method is confrontation.

The plan is not complicated, as it is in a Detective story. The cowboy is a fighter. The sequence of actions he takes to defeat the opposition and gain peace for the community is a sequence of escalating fights. Usually they begin with fist-fights and escalate to gun battles. Primal men decide the issue through force.

WESTERN STORY BEAT: Battle—Showdown

The battle in any story is the last and biggest conflict that determines the winners. In a Western, the entire story typically funnels down to the showdown, a gunfight between the supercowboy and the bad cowboy.

KEY POINT: The showdown is by far the most important story structure step in the Western genre.

Why? The final showdown is not a simple matter of one man killing another in a fit of anger. This is a theatrical event with a complex ritual. Whether it's in a saloon or on Main Street, it is always about honor, bravery, image, and courage. It is a demonstration of status, as either public humiliation or triumph.

Often, the showdown begins with the bad cowboy goading the good cowboy or shaming the farmer who has no ability with a gun. The bad cowboy calls the good cowboy a cheat, a sissy, or a coward. There is no greater shame for the cowboy than to be seen as unmanly in the eyes of other men.

Everyone present knows that this insult will result in someone's death. In a shame culture as intense as this, the cowboy cannot walk away or else he would be branded with a scarlet "C" for coward. He is trapped in the shame culture and forever in a double bind. On the one hand, he must constantly prove his manhood at the risk of his life. On the other hand, even if he wins, someone will die.

KEY POINT: The showdown determines the nation's future, of civilization or chaos, in a split second.

Often, this split second is stretched to what feels like an eternity. The audience enjoys both the pleasure and the pain of this intense extended moment.

Films with famous gunfights include *My Darling Clementine* and *Tombstone*, which depict the legendary shootout at the O.K. Corral; *The Magnificent Seven*, based on *Seven Samurai*; as well as *Shane*, *Unforgiven*, and *The Man Who Shot Liberty Valance*.

The writer-director who understood the ritual essence of the showdown and heightened it to the nth degree is Sergio Leone. In *The Good, the Bad and the Ugly*, he ups the ante by having a gunfight among three characters. He brings the camera into super-close-up on the eyes of the three men as they each look for the "tell" of who will draw first.

The best gunfight of all may be in *Once Upon a Time in the West*, a great anti-Western. Instead of coming at its usual place at the end of the story, this gunfight opens the film.

Three tough cowboys wait at a railroad station in the middle of nowhere. In typical Leone fashion they wait a long time, which builds the suspense and the drama for the single, brief moment to come. The train comes to a stop. No one gets off. The train pulls out. Standing there on the other side of the tracks is a cowboy whose name we do not know. One of the three bad cowboys says, "Looks like we're shy one horse." The lone cowboy replies, "You brought two too many." In a flash, it's over. The three men are dead. The lone cowboy takes one of their horses and rides away. So the myth of "Harmonica" begins.

WESTERN STORY BEAT: Moral Argument—the Moral Showdown

The best stories distill the moral argument of how best to live in the world to a choice between two actions. The Western is structured to converge at the focal point of the hero's final moral decision using the gun. It equates living morally with being a man, and being a man with using a gun. This moral equation is highly suspect in a modern society. But it's the reason the Western must end in a duel between the good man and the bad man.

The duel is the final proof of the character's moral quality. In this way, the Western emphasizes the crisis, or "limit situation," that defines the character in an instant.*

KEY POINT: The Existential Code is expressed in this direct, moral confrontation of the Western.

On the surface, the showdown is a contest in which, like the Roman gladiators, the winner lives and the loser dies. But it's really the ultimate moral contest. Like the errant knights of yore, this Western joust expresses moral worthiness.

In the showdown, the hero has the added burden of the Code of the West: the good cowboy must never draw first. This rule appears to give the bad cowboy an opportunity: to draw his gun or not. But the bad cowboy does not have a higher morality; he *will* draw.

The real moral decision is with the good cowboy: Do I wait to act in self-defense, but risk dying? Or do I draw first, making me a killer, but live to fight another day for the values of the community? The moral life/death conflict of the Western is primal, taking humans back to an animal nature rooted in survival: predator versus prey.

At what point does this moral vision of how to live become false? In the story/film *3:10 to Yuma*, the hero agrees to help take a criminal to prison because his son thinks he's a coward. The writers' story strategy is to increase the number of guns

* See Karl Jaspers and Hans-Georg Gadamer.

arrayed against the hero while at the same time decreasing his allies, until he is a man alone facing certain death.

The existential question becomes: Is living according to your moral code worth dying for? For this man, it is, even when his choice is undercut by the near certainty that the criminal will escape anyway. In the end, the man's son has immense respect for him. Unfortunately, the man is no longer alive. This kind of false moral accounting is one of the main reasons why an essential story form like the classic Western is dead.

WESTERN STORY BEAT: Self-Revelation—Eternal Wanderer

After the final battle, the hero in most stories has a self-revelation where he realizes who he really is. In the Western, his first self-revelation occurs *before* the showdown. The hero has tried to avoid the trap of living by the gun through a reluctance to kill other cowboys in the wilderness. But with the looming gunfight, he realizes that he must kill. He has to stand up and do what's right. As Shane says to young Joey, "A man has to be what he is."

The most famous visual expression of this self-revelation is at the end of *The Searchers*. Hero Ethan Edwards has returned his kidnapped niece to her home. But the yearslong search through the land of death has hardened him. The family goes inside to celebrate. Ethan stands alone, outside, framed in the doorway with the wilderness behind him. He turns and walks away.

She Wore a Yellow Ribbon expands this sense of the cowboy who creates the nation but misses out on the promised land. The story of the impending retirement of an army captain who is able to prevent an Indian war ends with a troop of cavalrymen riding on patrol through Monument Valley.

VOICE-OVER: So here they are, the dog-faced soldiers, the regulars, the fifty-cents-a-day professionals, riding the outposts of a nation. From Fort Reno to Fort Apache, from Sheridan to Stark, they were all the same. Men in dirty-shirt blue, and only a cold page in the history books to mark their passing. But wherever they rode and whatever they fought for, that place became the United States.

WESTERN STORY BEAT: New Equilibrium—Doomed Man

At the end of any story, new equilibrium is established. Everything is back to normal. But one thing has changed: the hero is at either a higher or lower level, based on his self-revelation.

In the Western, the hero has succeeded in his goal. But inside, he is a fallen man. He knows he cannot change. He can only die.

Theme: Being Is Doomed Existence

Like all genres, the Western asks the basic question of being: What does it mean for any human to exist? Whether classic Western or anti-Western, set in present day or the distant past, the Western is the ultimate existential story. It is the clearest expression we have of the doomed life we all lead. Living is being-that-must-end. Our pristine natural world is gone and we will never get it back. We, too, are always dying.

The sense that any moment could be our last makes living sweeter. By telling the tragic story of the cowboy and the "Indian," the Western lets us feel this bittersweet quality of life. Perhaps, like existentialism, it makes us appreciate the life we have all the more.

Like no other form, the Western shows us exactly how our doomed way of life works. This is evolution in the broadest sense. The Western expresses what kind of survival is possible and how survival ends for us all.

The process is clear: the individual is always part of the social whole. He is building a civilization. Yet, that very civilization will grow until it limits and often destroys the individual. The life the individual builds will inevitably put him in conflict with those who don't share his view of "progress."

The Western's view of being is fundamentally different from most genres because it doesn't separate being from becoming.

KEY POINT: For the Western, being *is* becoming.

Western Thematic Recipe: The Way of the Fighter for the Weak

What does this identity of being and becoming mean? As it is for all genres, the Western's thematic recipe for becoming your best self comes first from the basic action of the hero. In fighting so that others may build a home and a nation, the Western makes a strong connection between individual action and the future of the society. It says that the human being grows from natural soil and evolves from nature to civilized nature. Therefore, the Western's view of becoming could be summarized as: when you help others make a home, you make a civilization where everyone is free to live their best life.

The Western's manual for successful life also comes from the genre's key question. This is the same question as the Action story, from which it derives: To fight or flee, freedom or life? The answer for the cowboy is simple: he must always stand and fight because that is the guarantee of freedom for all.

The Western's vast thematic recipe, encompassing how any

human society evolves through stages and becomes itself, funnels down to the individual in the showdown. One person in the middle of the street faces "death" in a split second of action. This is the existential choice we make every day. To be or not to be? All the macro-forces of social and cultural development come down to this moment. One outcome gives all the joys, benefits, and sorrows of a life well lived. The alternative is eternal nothing.

How to Transcend the Western Story

The way to transcend the Western is by writing the anti-Western. This is one of the most advanced and thematically powerful of all story forms. The anti-Western argues that there is a fall of civilization when the city inevitably takes over. It shows how freedom is possible but difficult within the harsh reality of modern civilization.

Novels

Lonesome Dove, *Horseman, Pass By*, *The Last Picture Show*, *The Border Trilogy* (*All the Pretty Horses*, *The Crossing*, *Cities of the Plain*), *Blood Meridian: Or the Evening Redness in the West*

Films

Destry Rides Again, *High Noon*, *Hud*, *Butch Cassidy and the Sundance Kid*, *The Wild Bunch*, *McCabe & Mrs. Miller*, *Once Upon a Time in the West*, *The Last Picture Show*, *A Man Called Horse*, *The Outlaw Josey Wales*, *Little Big Man*, *Unforgiven*, *Dances with Wolves*, *Monte Walsh*, *Hostiles*, *The Power of the Dog*

Western vs. the Anti-Western and Serious Fiction

The novelist Hernan Diaz said this about the Western form:

> You know, the Western is such an oddly marginal genre. You'd expect it to be central to the American literary canon, because it's so perfect as an ideological tool. It's the culmination of individualism, it's an ideological tale of the birth of the nation, it romanticizes genocide . . . And yet most people will be hard-pressed to name three Western writers before Cormac McCarthy or Larry McMurtry. And it has been overshadowed by film in such an interesting way. Compared to detective fiction or science-fiction—both of which have had massive impacts on literature—the Western didn't fulfill its promise or its potential.

The Western began with dime novels and progressed to the first creators of the form with *The Virginian* in 1902 and *Riders of the Purple Sage* in 1912. Its heyday in movies was the 1920s through the 1950s, and culminated in television Westerns from the late 1950s to the mid-1960s. The timing of its popularity is curious because it came fifty to one hundred years after the ideology it expressed.

The classic Western translated the ideology of Manifest Destiny (which reached its apex in 1850) and the concept of progress into a story form. Therefore, this popular form from 1900 to 1960 was always about an ideology whose time had come and gone, a nostalgic past that never existed. The Western was artistically a dead form walking.

The ideological opposite of America's Creation Myth is serious fiction, especially the so-called Great American Novel. Serious fiction has focused almost solely on the flaws of America's first two Creation texts, the Declaration of Independence and the U.S. Constitution, and the resulting failings of the nation. If the Great American Novel is about any one thing, it's about the failure of the American promise.

The fact that the classic Western was artistically dead even when most popular is also the reason it never had the kind of influence of the Detective and Science Fiction genres. Detective has remained a vibrant form because it tells us "how we know the truth" in a progressively more ambiguous world. It is story as puzzle solving. The move from omniscient point of view to a specific narration, along with the overall movement in the history of fiction forcing the reader to figure out the story, has made Detective *the* template of modern storytelling.

Science Fiction owes its relevance to the fact that it's about "how we create our world." How do we make our world better going forward, especially in a race against the self-destructiveness of our own species? In narrative terms, Science Fiction combines the two modes of advanced consciousness, story and science. The Western shows primitive behavior, Story as basic human morality.

Transcending the Western: The Stories of History and Civilization

To understand how to write an advanced story form like the transcendent anti-Western, we must first understand how humankind creates the genre's underlying art/story forms: *history* and *civilization*. The Western expresses history through four major stages of cultural evolution: wilderness, village, city, and oppressive city. It expresses civilization through the story structure of rise and fall, the tragic version of the story of a king. As we shall see in the next chapter, this is the same structure as the rise and fall of the gangster king.

Creating Civilization in Microcosm: The Frontier Thesis

The best way to see the long arc of civilization is to see it in miniature, in a prototypical story. To put it another way, what is the microcosm of civilization found in the western experience?

> **KEY POINT: European settlers' entrance into what was, for them, a virgin continent provides the best case study of civilization-building in world history.**

European settlers' mass movement on the continent from east to west marked the creation of the American identity and civilization. As we discussed, Frederick Jackson Turner described how this came about in his brilliant essay of cultural creation, "The Significance of the Frontier in American History," known as the "frontier thesis" (1893).

The frontier thesis serves as a premise, or story version, of a scientific hypothesis. This story shows the process of a people becoming who they are, in this case Americans.

The beauty of using the frontier thesis as a case study is that the European migration into the New World clearly shows how the ideas that make up a culture are the product of their interaction with the three main pillars of society: the land, people, and technology. It also shows how all of American storytelling is defined by the fundamental movement of American history, expressed by Horace Greeley as, "Go West, young man. Go West."

The key features of the frontier thesis are:

- The frontier was the meeting point between savagery and civilization.

- As the immigrant confronted the crucible of the free, harsh land, the land transformed him from a European into an American.
- The frontier created an American who was selfish and individualistic, valuing personal freedom above all, along with strength, inquisitiveness, a practical, inventive mind, and exuberance.

In short, said Turner, "America has been another name for opportunity." Turner ended his essay with a crucial point: by 1890, when the frontier disappeared, the first great period of American civilization ended. This was not a coincidence.

The close of the frontier meant a fundamental shift in the American character, from social stage two, the village, to social stage three, the city. With that shift, the morality-values on which the nation is based had to shift as well.

The United States serves as a popular case study of how civilization and formal history work due to a number of factors. First, its history unfolded over a relatively short period of time. Second, the process represented a clear east-to-west tide. Third and most important is the European idea that America began as a "clean slate."

There is one massive flaw in this idea: North America was not a clean slate. In 1492 it was a vast, lush continent in which nature was all-powerful and technology was primitive. But empty it was not. Estimates of the Native American population in North America before 1492 vary from ten million to more than fifty million.

Another factor arguing against the "clean slate" view is the importation and enslavement of millions of Africans. The subjugation of African human beings by Europeans meant that the new civilization was founded on far more than hard work and taming the savagery of the frontier. Indeed, the very document that created the United States, the Constitution, is founded on the worst sort of moral corruption: mass slavery. This flaw at the heart of the nation's formation document has poisoned the government of the United States to this day.

In spite of these flaws in the clean slate theory, the United States is still a useful model. In fact, it is necessary to writing a transcendent anti-Western. Why? Because the Western plays out the larger underlying process of the rise and fall of civilization.

> **KEY POINT: The Western expresses a theory of how history works.**

The Story of History

History is commonly understood as the study of all human events leading up to this moment. But this description is so broad as to be infinite. Thus, it has no insight or value. As a result, history as a story form has typically been told in one of two more focused ways: top-down or bottom-up.

Known as "the Great Man Theory," top-down history shows a man (always a man) driving big events and taking entire nations with him. This is historical storytelling using the Hollywood star system. Bottom-up history shows main characters who are disenfranchised but somehow come together and create the larger social movements of a country.

> **KEY POINT: The Western doesn't show top-down history or bottom-up. It shows history in theory, the Historical Code. Instead of being caught up in individual events, the Historical Code allows us to see the *process as a whole*.**

The Historical Code

Besides highlighting certain art/story forms in life, some genres portray essential processes that explain how various things work over time.

- **SCIENCE FICTION:** Evolutionary Code
- **MEMOIR, MYTH, AND COMING-OF-AGE:** Existential Code
- **ALL GENRES:** Story Code

The Historical Code, found in the Western, is the record of the development and interaction of the three major structural elements in the story world: the land, people, and technology. This is the interplay of mass numbers of individuals acting within social wholes and scales of geography, using tools to transform the physical world.

This Code also explains how these threads weave into one tapestry. Like the other three codes we've discussed (Evolution, Existential, and Story), the Historical Code says that it is only through process that we can truly understand human life.

What is the process by which the land, people, and technology interact in the long term?

KEY POINT: History is the product of an alternation between expansion and consolidation at every scale in human life.

In the minute-to-minute experience of daily life, this resonance moves from individual action (expansion) to organization (consolidation), then back to action. In the individual life span, this alternates between creating greatness versus adapting to change.

This rhythmic movement between expansion and consolidation is an outgrowth of the fundamental principles of extension and connection. Each individual wants to expand their domain outward but also make connections within the organism itself. Expansion gives range but at the cost of tensile strength. Connection makes the organism internally stronger, but the cost is a smaller domain.

The American Theory of History: Progress

Earlier, we mentioned that the classic Western translated the ideology of Manifest Destiny and the concept of progress into a story form. The change based on the connections of land, people, and technology influences a society's evolution. Progress in this theory of history is based on a linear improvement of humankind.

KEY POINT: "Progress" became the American theory of history, indeed the American religion, because of a fortuitous confluence of raw land, lush resources, westward settlement, and the revolutionary rise of transportation machinery like the railroad and the steamship.

The idea of progress is an extension of the core ideas of enlightenment and the universe as machine. The implied equation is that enlightenment = perfection through reason. And we get ever closer to perfection when we live as a machine.

This profound concept of machine civilization got its fuel from the rapid growth of the American economy and the inspiration of seeing the nation connected through the railroads. "No phrase in 1840s America is used as much when connecting machines to progress as 'the annihilation of space and time.'"*

---

* Leo Marx, *The Machine in the Garden.*

The concept of progress became supercharged by three social factors:

1. the larger Industrial Revolution gave rise to an exploding economy,
2. the founding of this relatively new American republic was based on the idea of the machine, and
3. a growing democratization of the republic as voters became less aristocratic and more like the common person.

Progress took on the appearance of fact with increased industrialization and the "Machine Age" in the late 1800s. Henry Adams highlighted the contrast of past and future when he compared the Virgin Mary, the central symbol of the Middle Ages, with the dynamo, generator of massive electric power, that he believed was the central symbol of the Modern age. Unlike religion, which put forth an unchanging ideal to which we should all strive in our daily lives, science was the activity of gaining increased knowledge at an ever-increasing rate.* The possibilities of the coming age, especially in America, seemed endless.

Within a decade of Adams's private publication of his landmark book, World War I delivered a harsh blow to this idea of world progress. Despite continued technological advancement, World War II delivered an even heavier blow with the deaths of more than fifty million people.

But the expansive vision of progress emerged relatively unscathed in the United States. The fact that the nation was separated from its origin countries by an ocean, along with the rise of the classic Western, meant that Americans could hold on to their religion of progress with renewed fervor.

---

* Henry Adams, "The Virgin and the Dynamo," chapter 24 of *The Education of Henry Adams* (privately 1907, published 1918).

Transcending Western: The Anti-Western Story Form

One could argue that anti-Western films began in 1939 with *Destry Rides Again* or in 1951 with *High Noon*. But this transcendent form hit the heights of creative genius with four films released in a three-year span from 1968 to 1971: *The Wild Bunch*, *Butch Cassidy and the Sundance Kid*, *Once Upon a Time in the West*, and *McCabe & Mrs. Miller*. The structural brilliance of these stories makes them profound examples of the form and shows what the anti-Western genre can be.

Butch Cassidy and the Sundance Kid: Over the Hill

To see the beauty of the anti-Western in a moment, we can do no better than look at the opening scenes of *Butch Cassidy and the Sundance Kid*. Written by screenwriting master William Goldman, these scenes do more in less time than any other scenes in movie history.

The opening scene shows an unnamed man (Butch Cassidy) casing a bank so he can rob it. To the guard he laments the lost beauty of the old bank. But the guard responds that people kept robbing it. During the conversation, the barred windows and doors clang shut and the room goes dark. It's closing time. That in a nutshell is the entire movie for this amiable man and for the Western form itself.

In the second scene, a shockingly handsome cowboy (the Sundance Kid) is playing poker with two men. Frightening in his nastiness, one man accuses the cowboy of cheating. Clearly, this is another classic Western gunfight over cards, and it's probably going to end with the handsome, and somewhat insolent, cowboy dead. The stranger from the opening scene arrives and strongly suggests that his friend, the handsome cowboy, walk away from the table without his winnings. Handsome cowboy refuses, claiming he wasn't cheating, and furthermore states that he will only leave if the frightening man asks him to stay. The stranger reminds his friend that he might be over the hill. But the handsome cowboy refuses to back down.

So the stranger brings his friend's proposal to the frightening man, who tells him he can wind up dead along with his friend. The stranger shrugs and says, "I can't help you, Sundance." And with that everything changes.

The man realizes he is about to enter into a gunfight with the infamous, fast-draw legend, the Sundance Kid. He will surely die. The now sheepish man asks Sundance to stay. Sundance walks toward the door while his friend Butch collects his winnings. When the man asks Sundance, "How good are you?" Sundance whirls and performs a wonder of fast-draw marksmanship that lets the man know just how close he came to death.

As the two friends walk out, Butch jokingly comments, "Like I said, over the hill."

KEY POINT: This is the *prototypical* anti-Western scene and one of my favorite scenes in film. Goldman is simultaneously creating two Western superheroes while setting the stage for their eventual and inevitable destruction.

The lines of dialogue are sensational, some of the best ever written. But what makes them work so well is the scene strategy on which they are based. The writer must set up two characters, show how they are fundamentally different, establish their legendary status with a bang, show how they "dance" together brilliantly as both action buddies and comedy team, then slip in the ultimate theme of the story—about the death of men like this and the Old West itself.

For the writer to do all that is extremely difficult. Goldman accomplishes it with the following strategy: he sets up a fake crisis that makes the audience think the handsome stranger will certainly die. Crisis defines character in a moment, and we see it expressed through action. Crisis allows us to see these two particular characters as cool under pressure, so much so that they can comically bicker like an old married couple while death is apparently staring one of them in the face.

The result of the strategy is that the audience *experiences* the truth at the same time as the killer: Sundance flips instantaneously from petulant loser to the greatest gunfighter in the West. We also see the essence of the men's relationship, with Butch as the funny fast talker and Sundance the man of action.

The scene strategy funnels down to a thematic vortex point, the line where Butch laughingly says, "Like I said, over the hill." In light of his recent display of shooting ability, Sundance is the farthest thing from over the hill. But by the end of the film, he and Butch will be over the hill, not because of their physical age, but because the age in which they live has passed them by. When a new society comes along, even the wit and talent of these two superheroes isn't enough to survive.

From Western to Anti-Western

Grounded in the techniques of the Historical Code and the rise and fall of civilization, we can see how the anti-Western is among the most insightful and challenging of all genres. It marks the crowning moment where the Western becomes a true art form.

> **KEY POINT: The anti-Western is the genre that best expresses being as becoming in story.**

The original Western, typically set during the empire building of the 1870–1880s' United States, depicts a transition from constructing a society (expansion) to refining it and giving it texture (consolidation). It tracks and, for the most part, celebrates a decentralized society. It confirms the value of social man.

In the anti-Western, the central "moment" in the social process moves to the end of the American frontier from 1890 to 1900. The closing of land occurs simultaneously with the formation of a mechanized, mass society on a national scale. The resulting story form investigates a new, more profound moment of social and cultural evolution.

As an art form, this story indicates the many ways in which humankind must be, but also cannot be, a social animal. If human beings are social, they will ultimately be destroyed. The anti-Western shows a stronger, centralized system oppressing a smaller, decentralized community. It tracks how advanced, hierarchical society limits or even enslaves the individual.

Like species, genres diversify. The Western evolved into a number of story forms beyond the anti-Western. The primal man of nature, the cowboy, became the thinker—the Detective—and the ruthless businessman—the Gangster. The Western also turned into the Action story, which is about conflict and war. And it became the Modernization Story: the negative version known as the "Machine in the Garden," and the positive version of the Ecological Myth, about balancing the individual, the family, society, and nature within a single ecological system.

To see how the Western story form evolved, we begin with the hero who drives the action. The anti-Western shows the man of nature trying to survive in the mass society of the city world. Inherent to the original Western form is that the hero never marries. And yet, somehow, he has three sons:

1. The anticowboy
2. The detective, the "good son"
3. The gangster, the "bad son"

Here are the essential differences between the Western and the three main story forms that evolve from it:

- **WESTERN:** creating civilization, the nation, and the American Dream, especially through the positive use of the gun.
- **ANTI-WESTERN:** the larger society destroys the individual who built it.
- **DETECTIVE:** the society is filled with lies, corruption, and murder, but a brilliant mind will find the truth and bring justice.
- **GANGSTER:** the corruption of the American Dream, and the negative use of violence to gain monetary success.

Anti-Western Story Beats

The reason this story form is known as the anti-Western is that it takes every major story element of the Western, such as story world, hero, plot, and theme, and turns it upside down.

ANTI-WESTERN STORY BEAT: Story World—Encroaching City

The change from Western to anti-Western begins with the story world and its unique combination of land, society, and technology. The anti-Western expresses the idea that one of the seminal events in world history was the closing of the American West in the 1890s. This was the final frontier of the New World, both in fact and in concept.

The effect of this change in the relationship between land and society was profound. This shift goes far beyond American society. It expresses a fundamental change in the formal history that any society must pass through when agricultural society shifts to industrial.

We have already discussed how the Western embodies the

overall progression of social stages: wild nature, pastoral nature and village, town, city, and oppressive city. Let's explore in more detail the shift from village to city that is the focus in the anti-Western:

1. Direct society, with its easily recognizable forces, starts to move inexorably to indirect society, with its hidden and more powerful forces.
2. The village society that has been expanding horizontally across the land now meets its limits.
3. The society grows vertically, and the village becomes the town and then the city.

The city presents dramatic contrasts of wealth and power, far greater than are possible in the village world. This increase in opportunity comes at a cost. A new state of nature emerges. Where before the common man was subject to death at the hands of the wilderness, now he is vulnerable to the attacks of the rich and powerful of the new civilization.

The city also means more rules to govern the massive influx of people rushing in to take advantage of its immense possibilities. The individual's freedom to roam the land and choose how he wants to create a new life is sharply restricted by the rules of the bureaucracy and its economic forces.

My Bildungsroman Reveal: *McCabe & Mrs. Miller*

McCabe & Mrs. Miller exposed the lie at the heart of the Western story form that shaped me the most. It expressed the shame culture that sometimes forced me to physically "prove" I was a man. The story laid out a more realistic development of my country, not the whitewashed image I wished it had been. Here was the real potential of the film medium, as both intensely sensual and grandly philosophical. This film depicted the entire modernization process, the social evolution from wilderness to oppressive city, in one story. Amazing.

Three years later, when I saw *Seven Samurai*, my destiny was clear.

Story World: The Morally Corrupt Society

The anti-Western depicts society as it begins the shift from village to city, from direct power to indirect power. Instead of a farmer or merchant heroically building the nation, the everyman/everywoman is physically incompetent and morally depraved. These people look and act alike. They are petty, prejudiced, self-centered, authoritarian, afraid to step out of the crowd, and hypocritical.

In the corrupt society of the anti-Western, shame has lost its power to motivate right action. The idea of individual responsibility so crucial to building the West is gone.

In *High Noon*, the hero, Marshal Will Kane, feels a strong duty to defend the town against four outlaws coming to take revenge. But the townspeople are ungrateful cowards who aren't willing to help him protect the law and the town they have created. With the last-minute assistance of his Quaker (peaceful) wife, the marshal kills the four outlaws in a showdown at high noon. He tosses his badge into the dirt and rides away.

The town in *McCabe & Mrs. Miller* is not the flat, dry, treeless town of the classic Western. It's set in the lush, green, muddy, and hilly wilderness of the American Northwest. When hero John McCabe first arrives, he is greeted by the paranoid looks of the grubby townspeople. Everyone is isolated and wallowing in their own poverty. Only by pulling out a deck of cards in the local saloon can McCabe draw these cautious loners into a community for a game of poker.

Story World: Turn-of-the-Century Technology

The technology depicted in the anti-Western is not the horse, the fence, or the six-gun used to build the village out of the wilderness. It is the machines used to build the industrial city in what has become known as the Machine Age.

Once Upon a Time in the West focuses its story on the first great engine of the Industrial Age, the train.

The whorehouse in *McCabe & Mrs. Miller* purchases a modern labor-saving miracle, the vacuum cleaner.

In *The Wild Bunch*, set in 1913, its outlaw heroes are amazed by the automobile. Then in their final showdown, they use a machine gun to wreak mass destruction on Mexican troops. Foreshadowing the slaughter to come, this same weapon would mow down millions of men trying to climb over barbed wire in World War I.

ANTI-WESTERN STORY BEAT: Anti-Western Hero

Just as the anti-Western changes the combination of land, people, and technology from the village to the city, it changes its depiction of the main character from superhero to antihero. The anti-Western main character is no longer the action hero with a gun. In the extreme, he becomes the reactive antihero who doesn't know how to shoot.

In the history of story, this shift is predetermined whenever the society changes from village to city. The complex, indirect forces of the city create problems that can no longer be solved, if they ever were, by aiming a gun at the "barbarian" of a different race or color. The warrior is not prized. He is obsolete.

The anti-Western focuses on the turning point when the village suddenly transforms into the city. It shows the decline of hero to antihero as the social forces of the future social stage bear down. Here are some of the most famous antiheroes from the anti-Western form, listed in the order the films were released.

In *Destry Rides Again*, Tom Destry Jr. is the comedic antihero cowboy, the self-deprecating lawman who solves problems not with a gun but by telling illuminating fables. Destry is cowboy Jesus.

The Wild Bunch are antiheroes as ruthless killers, nasty men trying to do one more job before the West they've known disappears. Corrupt lawmen chase them south of the border and corner them in the stronghold of a brutal Mexican general. All that's left for them is to die with honor trying to save one of their own. It's a beautiful but hopeless gesture.

Easygoing Butch and supercowboy Sundance are classic Western village men in *Butch Cassidy and the Sundance Kid*. They aren't smart enough to see the city world of corporations and national superposse closing in. Like the Wild Bunch, they are driven farther into the past, in the form of the less modernized country of Bolivia. Finally, their individual heroics with a six-gun are no match for the mass gunfire of the Bolivian army.

In *Little Big Man*, Jack Crabb might be called the Tom Jones and Leopold Bloom of the old West. Jack is a picaresque little man buffeted by corrupt characters at every level of society. As the 120-year-old narrator, Jack recounts being raised in the utopian world of the Cheyenne, a culture he finds superior to the Western white world into which he was born. Over the course of the story, Jack experiences every beat of the Western genre turned upside down: becoming an incompetent gunslinger, encountering a pious but sexually voracious reverend's wife, being tarred and feathered as a snake oil salesman, becoming the town drunk, and being responsible for the massacre of the Seventh Cavalry at the Little Big Horn.

In *McCabe & Mrs. Miller*, John McCabe is a gambler who

does his part to build the nation by setting up a whorehouse in a mining town. Then he falls in love with the madam he hires to run it. The townspeople think he's a famous gunslinger, though there is no evidence of that. His successes in business and in romance with Mrs. Miller increase with the physical growth of the town. But like Butch and Sundance, his success catches the eye of a corporation. They want to buy him out. The bureaucrats will not accept no for an answer.

With his head filled with hollow phrases of Manifest Destiny and the American Dream, McCabe decides to fight. Unfortunately, he doesn't know how. He's not a gunfighter. His weapon of choice isn't the manly six-gun strapped to his hip where all can see it. McCabe uses a derringer, the "woman's weapon," hidden away in his sleeve. He learns too late that the promise of the Western is hollow. Believing in the myth costs McCabe his life.

Later anti-Westerns, like *High Plains Drifter*, *The Outlaw Josey Wales*, and *The Quick and the Dead* might be called "Revenge by the Stranger." In these stories, the antihero takes the form of a greedy killer or an avenging angel. This is the highly mythical and existential man (or woman) who returns from the dead or the distant past to take revenge on corrupt social man. This antihero is highly capable as a warrior, but his mix of righteous action with rape and murder makes him a Western-style gangster. Long gone are the clean moral distinctions of the classic Western.

ANTI-WESTERN STORY BEAT: Anti-Western Values

Like the clean moral distinctions, the values of the Code of the West have disappeared. The anti-Western hero still believes in the Code but doesn't realize it's obsolete. Or he has only known the true values of the post-Western city world, which are money and power.

- The Wild Bunch rob banks and will kill anyone who gets in their way without a second thought. Says their leader Pike about innocent bystanders during a robbery: "If they move, kill 'em."
- The ex-madam in *Once Upon a Time in the West* arrives in town to discover that her new husband has been murdered for his land. The land has the only water for fifty miles, and the coming railroad will need plenty of water.
- McCabe's form of Horatio Alger pulling himself up by his bootstraps is running a whorehouse for miners. His mistake is that he believes the lawyer who fills his head with the fake values of the American Dream.
- Butch and Sundance are bank robbers who don't realize that the old ways are over.

ANTI-WESTERN STORY BEAT: Opponent—the Corporate Boss

The main opponent in the anti-Western is not the Indian, the cattle baron, or the gunslinger. The gunslinger is just the hired hand for the real opponent: the corporate boss or moneyman. The corporate boss wants to steal the entrepreneur's property to build his empire. Or, like the gangster, he simply wants to kill any individual who gets in his way.

Detective Patrick Harrigan hires an incompetent posse to chase down and kill the Wild Bunch, who robbed his employer, the railroad.

Railroad tycoon Morton hires gunman Frank to scare the ex-madam's husband into forfeiting his land in *Once Upon a Time in the West*. Instead, Frank kills the husband and his three children in cold blood.

Two agents from the Harrison Shaughnessey mining company want to buy the fine business McCabe has created from nothing. When McCabe foolishly demands too much, they send three killers to destroy him.

The writer William Goldman creates an opposition that perfectly expresses the new world of the anti-Western in *Butch Cassidy and the Sundance Kid*. Butch and the gang rob a train carrying the payroll money of a corporation from the East owned by a Mr. E. H. Harriman. This is a character who never appears in the story. He is the main opponent, representing the future social stage—the city—coming on fast.

Butch and Sundance rob small banks and trains and have no trouble avoiding the ragtag local posse. Harriman responds with the power of the city world. He hires an all-star posse of men from all over the West. Instead of incompetent locals, Butch and Sundance have to beat the best lawmen in the country.

In response, Butch and Sundance try to go back in time by escaping to the village world of Bolivia. But the second stage has almost disappeared. At the time of their deaths, Butch and Sundance are exploring the idea of going to Australia. It's too little, too late. The Bolivian army is waiting to gun them down.

ANTI-WESTERN STORY BEAT: Apparent Victory

Most stories go from slavery to freedom. This is one of the reasons why they typically have an apparent-defeat plot beat in which the hero believes he has lost for good. But he gets a reveal that tells him he can still win; he comes back for a dramatic victory.

The anti-Western doesn't end in freedom. It ends tragically in slavery or death. So the anti-Western often has a moment of Apparent Victory and/or Utopian Moment.

On their way south, the Bunch rests for a while in a Mexican village, Agua Verde, home to one of their members. It is a lush green utopian community where these men might live if they weren't who they are and weren't being hunted down by the future.

After almost losing their lives to the all-star posse, Butch and Sundance decide to go to Bolivia. Sundance's girlfriend, Etta, tells the men:

> I'm twenty-six and I'm single and a schoolteacher and that's the bottom of the pit. And the only excitement I've known is here with me now. So I'll go with you and I won't whine and I'll sew your socks and I'll stitch you when you're wounded. And I'll do anything you ask of me except one thing. I won't watch you die.

Then one auspicious night, she tells them she's going home.

ANTI-WESTERN STORY BEAT: Battle—Massacre

The showdown in the anti-Western is fake. There is no contest to see who can draw his six-gun the fastest. There is no rule whereby the supercowboy must wait for the bad cowboy to draw first. The corporation strikes with shock and awe. The mechanization of guns going into the twentieth century means the showdown is a massacre. The hero never had a chance.

The four surviving men of the Wild Bunch make a "beau geste" by walking into the coliseum where General Mapache and hundreds of his men are waiting. They demand Mapache return their friend Angel, who is near death from torture. When Mapache cuts Angel's throat, the Bunch grab the machine gun and mow down men, women, and children.

The grand irony is that these old cowboys are using the magnified firepower of the modern machine gun to approximate a level playing field and take on an entire army. But they are trapped rats. Even a noble effort—if noble is the right word for a massacre—cannot save them from destruction. In fact, nobility is what causes it.

Like *High Noon*, *McCabe & Mrs. Miller* flips the final showdown beat. McCabe is not the good cowboy facing down the bad cowboy in the middle of the street under the watchful eyes of an adoring community. The townspeople don't even know that a showdown is taking place. McCabe, who is anything but a gunfighter, desperately tries to escape three ruthless killers under the blanket of heavy-falling snow. Meanwhile, the townspeople are putting out a fire at a church none of them attends. The man who built the town and has defeated three killers dies without help or recognition.

ANTI-WESTERN STORY BEAT: No Self-Revelation

The anti-Western is one of the few story forms where the hero does not have a self-revelation. Like the antihero of the Black Comedy, the anticowboy does not understand he is obsolete, that his time has passed. He can only die.

McCabe can't understand how stupid he has been in trying to negotiate with killers.

Butch and Sundance's self-revelation is handed to them by their friend, Sheriff Ray Bledsoe:

> You should have let yourself get killed a long time ago when you had the chance. See, you may be the biggest thing that ever hit this area, but you're still two-bit outlaws. I never met a soul more affable than you, Butch, or faster than the Kid. But you're still nothing but two-bit outlaws on the dodge. It's over, don't you get that? Your times is over and you're gonna die bloody, and all you can do is choose where.

But they are incapable of seeing it. So they die bloody in a strange town in Bolivia.

The cost of men who cannot learn is most devastating in *The Wild Bunch*. They wipe out hundreds of soldiers and villagers. This is the mass destruction of war. In windswept desolation, the few surviving villagers walk out of town toward nothingness.

Butch Cassidy and the Sundance Kid Finale: Death of the Western

In the film's final scene, Butch and Sundance are holed up in a little room in a small Bolivian village. They try to stanch the blood from the bullet holes they've just received trying to get away. The only escape is back out the front door to the main street.

As they prepare their guns for another attempt, Butch tells Sundance his new idea. They'll go to Australia, where they speak English. Sundance reluctantly agrees. What neither man realizes is that half the Bolivian army is lining the rooftops outside.

As funny as the dialogue is, it's the screenwriter's scene strategy that makes this scene an all-time great. As in the opening, Goldman (the Great) places his characters in a tight room that's getting smaller by the second. As in the poker scene, he puts the two men in a crisis. But this crisis is real. And this time they will not escape.

The key to the scene strategy is that Goldman sets up an increasingly extreme contrast between what the heroes know, and what the audience knows (the arrival of the Bolivian army). This is the reverse strategy of the poker scene, where the audience is not in on the joke. That's because the poker scene ends in success while this scene ends in death. It expresses the buddies' fatal flaw, which is that they cannot see beyond their little personal world. And that's what kills them.

Again, the scene focuses toward a thematic vortex point coming at a single line of dialogue, which is also the entire film condensed into one line. At the last moment, Butch wonders if Sundance saw the great lawman Lefors out there.

No. Relieved, Butch responds, "Good. For a second there, I thought we were in trouble." This final line, which ties in with previous moments and lines in the film, makes you laugh and breaks your heart.

Butch and Sundance rush out the front door and into the battle with guns blazing. The frame freezes and we are spared seeing the horror of their death. But we hear it. The image of their bravado bleeds into sepia as three volleys of rifle fire explode. The carnival player-piano tune comes up, evoking simpler, better days. In that one moment, we see legend turn to myth, we say goodbye to two superheroes we love, and we feel the utter sadness of the death of the glorious Western genre.

My Bildungsroman Reveal: My Dinner with Goldman

Butch Cassidy and the Sundance Kid represents another huge moment in my personal bildungsroman. I saw the film at my high school two years after having my mind blown in sophomore English class when a new teacher taught us Northrop Frye's Theory of the Hero. I didn't intellectually connect antiheroes Butch and Sundance with the larger development of the history of story. But as a seventeen-year-old going to prep school while the nation burned over racism and Vietnam, I was profoundly touched by these characters and their fate.

Four years later, my girlfriend's parents were having an intimate dinner party in their apartment in New York City. By then I was an avid film student and knew the screenplay of *Butch Cassidy and the Sundance Kid* practically by heart. When I discovered that my girlfriend's father, a famous businessman, knew William Goldman, I begged him to invite Goldman to the dinner party.

Goldman sat at one end of the table, flanked by a woman I do not recall, and me. For the next two hours, I peppered

Goldman with one question after another. I don't know if he suspected he had been set up. But he was a great sport who gave this starry-eyed kid a brilliant lesson in screenwriting. I do know he appreciated the deep respect I had for his work as the writer, the true author, of that masterpiece.

Occasionally the woman across from me tried to have a normal dinner party conversation with him. But I would have none of it. Sitting at the side of this master was a once-in-a-lifetime experience. So began my love of the art form of screenwriting. More important, Goldman's work in *Butch Cassidy* showed me that the screenwriter—not the director—is the real auteur of any film, just as the writer is the author of every other art form of story/structure. This includes the novel, theater (playwright not director), music (composer not conductor), architecture (architect not builder), and television (creator-writer-showrunner not director).

The Next Rung Up the Ladder

The Western is the ultimate big-picture genre, showing the evolution of civilization and the individual's place within it. But it ends with the encroachment of the city into the village world.

Our next step up the ladder of genre enlightenment is the cautionary tale of the Gangster. It shows us how the business and politics of the city world move toward oligarchy and dictatorship at the expense of individual freedom.

10

Gangster: The Corruption of Business and Politics

The Origin of the Gangster Story

The Gangster story evolved from the Western, the last true Creation Myth. Once the frontier closed and everything moved to the third and fourth social stages (city and oppressive city), the world could not be created. It had to be re-created. The problem is, no one knew how to do that.

Because of these societal changes, by 1930, Hollywood genres that had glorified the male, the loner, the father, and the fighter were anachronistic. These story forms worked by creating an unreal environment where problems could be solved strictly by using individual action and violence. In the city, that would not work.

What was needed was a Rejuvenation Myth. But that subgenre is far more challenging to create than the lone warrior. Instead, popular American storytelling went negative. After a decade of Prohibition, the rise of organized crime, and the beginning of the Great Depression, the cautionary Gangster story was born.

The Gangster Story: How It Works

The Gangster story is the art of morality expressed in its most negative extreme. It takes Crime's emphasis on the unacceptable desires within a society, and the improper methods to reach those desires, then magnifies them to an entire social system. In the Gangster genre, society itself is criminal.

Every story of gangsters is the story of kings. Every story of a bad king is a gangster story. The showrunner David Benioff referred to *Game of Thrones* as "*The Sopranos* in Middle Earth."

We see the king motif in the overall story strategy of the Gangster form: track the rise and fall of a "king" in a democracy who uses illegal and immoral means, especially killing, to gain success. We're not supposed to have a king in a democracy. Yet we have them all the time. In *Oedipus Rex*, when the false king takes over, a plague ravages society. Twenty-five hundred years later, the Gangster king brings modern society the plague of violence and fear.

Gangster Mind-Action Story View

The Western is based on *the* American commandment, "Go West, young man. Go West." This migration created two major genres: the Western and the Gangster story. The Western focuses on the pioneer in the wilderness. The Gangster story focuses on the European immigrant trying to rise in American cities.

These genres are uniquely American. Other than the "spaghetti Western," the Western has had little effect on storytelling outside the United States. Only recently has it returned with the Science Fiction Western. The Gangster story, however, has had a major effect on worldwide storytelling.

If the Western embodies the term "West," the Gangster

story embodies the term "gang." This contrast makes all the difference. The direction of the Western is horizontal, going west, spreading out along the plains to build farms and villages. The direction of the Gangster is vertical, moving up in the big city, making money and gaining success, often by destroying any other business that gets in the way.

By changing the direction of spatial movement from going West to going up, the Gangster story states that building a life is not about cultivating the free virgin land. First, it says that success comes from forming an organization and using money to make money. Second, success comes from marrying business and politics: the gangster wants money, but he must exercise absolute power to get it.

The main factor that determines a story form set in the city is the hero who drives it. With the Gangster story, a new myth hero was born.

KEY POINT: The gangster is the cowboy turned criminal, which is why the Gangster story marks the evolution of the Western into a kind of Crime story.

Like the Western and the Action story, Gangster focuses on the individual. But unlike the main characters in those genres, this hero can only succeed by being part of a gang. Instead of individual versus individual fighting to succeed in modern American life, it is now organization versus organization.

The Gangster Mind-Action story view is the twentieth-century version of John Winthrop's "shining city upon a hill" sermon and the American Dream credo of Manifest Destiny. When European settlers first came to America, the American Dream consisted of a dual strain of spiritual freedom and wealth of resources. The potential to realize both seemed endless. But with a hero who uses criminal and violent means to amass riches and territory, the American Dream was corrupted. The spiritual element of a good life disappeared, leaving only money.

This change in ethos is physically manifested when the hero moves from frontier to city. In turn, this physical change births three new story forms:

1. In popular fiction, the Gangster genre, which reaches its height in the Gangster Epic.
2. From serious fiction, what I call the "Eastern," which is a negative "Rags to Riches" story.
3. The Economic-Political Epic, which details the destruction of the capitalist republic.

KEY POINT: The basic difference between the Western and the "Eastern" is that the Western is the story of America on the rise while the "Eastern" is America on the decline.

The Great Gatsby was published in 1925, thirty-five years after the U.S. census declared that the western frontier had closed. This was a mere seven years after the Great World War, fought among the "corrupt" European powers Americans had fled in the first place. Serious fiction and "the Great American Novel" had been exposing the gap between American ideals and reality for decades, from *The Scarlet Letter* to *Moby-Dick* and *The Adventures of Huckleberry Finn*. But those novels had a rarefied readership.

The Great Gatsby was revolutionary in that it linked the Eastern, the serious fiction version of the story, to what would soon become the more popular Gangster version of the same tale. Narrator Nick Carraway flips America's commandment, to "Go East, young man. Go East." This is precisely his movement: he starts in the Midwest—solid, nothing fake—and goes east to make it rich in the great American city of business, New York. Nick doesn't go to make things. He goes to sell bonds, to make money off money.

Six years later, in 1931, Hollywood produced three Gangster stories—*Public Enemy*, *Little Caesar*, and *Scarface*. These defined the form and created the fundamental Gangster Mind-Action story view.

KEY POINT: The Gangster genre was revolutionary in using a popular myth form to expose the gap between the American Dream of all-men-created-equal versus reality.

The Gangster genre uses a sleight of hand similar to the Western. In the Western, the hero is not the nation builder but the man trying to escape civilization. The Gangster story appears to attack the reality of American life by turning the real gangster of 1920s America into the dark character, the "bad son" of the cowboy. We are supposed to be disgusted by this monster and what he has done to the "shining city on the hill." But that's not what happens. Because the gangster drives the story, and because he is so good at making the money we all desire, the audience wants him to win.

The gangster is the personification of the decayed social world. The once shining city has grown mean, dark, and tawdry. This process of corruption is described in the opening two lines of *The Magnificent Ambersons*, one of the great film examples of the "Machine in the Garden" subgenre (see the Myth chapter). In *The Magnificent Ambersons*, the destroying machine is the automobile. The narrator says:

> The magnificence of the Ambersons began in 1873. Their splendor lasted throughout all the years that saw their midland town spread and darken into a city.

What is it about the Gangster story view that gives it such power and appeal? As the gangsters in *Peaky Blinders* say, "We give you what you want." Above all, that means money. Money equals the triumph of success in the abstract. This success is quantified down to cents. Money translates into the physical, into Gatsby's mansion, with parties so big he doesn't know who most of the guests are. No matter. This proves he's made it. In *Slumdog Millionaire*, Salim luxuriates in a bathtub full of cash just before his gang blows him away.

Desire and money soon fuel sensation and a permanent high. They translate into women as pure sexual objects, their bodies strictly for use, again and again.

The Gangster Mind-Action story view is not just about fulfilling the "wrong" desires. It is desire out of control: "I want everything." And that suggests the hidden cost. Unbound desire is how the gangster world sucks the individual into a slavery he cannot escape. The Gangster story portrays the most powerful slavery of any genre, including Science Fiction dystopia.

Falling into the trap of thinking freedom equals money isn't strictly limited to the Gangster story. This movement is a natural tendency for any individual as they grow older and climb the ladder of resources and power. By focusing on the acquisition of money, the Gangster story shows us how day-to-day life is easily consumed by the money game: working, getting paid, paying bills, and hopefully, getting rich.

On a systemic level, the gangster is pure, unchecked capitalism. It is every value of the world subservient to one value, money, with a willingness to use violence to get it. The logical end point of the Gangster story is the devouring of the world. It transforms everything on the earth into objects, sensations, and finally, waste.

We often minimize the scope of the Gangster story view by thinking of it as the subgenre of the professional outlaw.

Or we ghettoize it as the story of a single ethnic group, Italian Americans, who populate so many of its stories. But this story view is as wide and deep as business and politics.

KEY POINT: This is the story of the business-political gangster who believes he is not an outlaw but law itself.

Gangster Compared to Other Genres

Gangster is part of the Crime family, along with Detective, Crime, and Thriller. It could be considered a subform of the Crime story, a kind of Criminal-as-Hero. It also has a crossover connection to the Action family, since it highlights the bad cowboy who has gone to the city world.

How does Gangster compare to Detective? In the Western chapter, we said that while the cowboy never marries, he has three sons. They are the anticowboy of the anti-Western; the good son, the detective; and the bad son, the gangster.

Both detective and gangster operate in the city world. One finds the truth and brings the criminal to justice. The other commits crime for money and uses murder to get to the top.

In our investigation of genres, we discuss Gangster now because it describes the next social-cultural stage after the Western. Unlike the Western, the uniquely American Gangster story expanded all over the world. Both genres are far more than a story expression of a particular country. They are an expression of *formal history*, of how any society must evolve. But while the Western shows us a landscape and a social stage that has long since passed, the Gangster story shows us the inner working of the oppressive city in which we all live now.

More important, we discuss Gangster here because the best of the form explores the arts of business and politics and shows how they have fallen from the stated ideals of capitalism and republic. Combining the moral philosophy of Crime, the social philosophy of Science Fiction, and political philosophy, Gangster gives us nothing less than the way of the modern world.

Examples of Gangster

Films

The Public Enemy, *Little Caesar*, *Scarface*, *The Irishman*, *The Long Good Friday*, *Casino*, *The Departed* (also Crime), *A History of Violence*, *Gomorrah*, *Sexy Beast*, *Miller's Crossing*, *Get Shorty* (also Comedy), *American Gangster*, *City of God*, *Once Upon a Time in America*, *Mean Streets*, *Angels with Dirty Faces*, *The Roaring Twenties*

Gangster Story Overview

Here's what we'll cover in this chapter:

- **GANGSTER STORY BEATS**
- **THEME:** Being as the Slavery of False Values
  - Thematic Recipe: The Way of Destruction
- **HOW TO TRANSCEND THE GANGSTER STORY**
  - The Gangster Epic
  - The Eastern
  - The Economic-Political Epic

Gangster Story Beats

All Gangster stories play out the beats of *The Public Enemy*, *Little Caesar*, and *Scarface*. They also use these beats as a foundation from which to vary the form.

GANGSTER STORY BEAT: Story World—the Corrupt City

Every genre hero is defined in part by the story world. As in the Crime story, the Gangster world is a society of extreme wealth and poverty. The possibility of moving up the social ladder through hard work is almost gone. Therefore, some people turn to crime.

In this genre, the city itself is corrupt. Society is divided into

- Criminal versus Noncriminal
- Lower-class, ethnic neighborhoods, specifically Italian and Irish Catholic, versus middle-class, northern European Protestant

Story World: Inherent Corruption of Capitalism

The world of the classic Gangster story sets up a false opposition between the proper capitalism of hard-working "normal" Americans and the cheating capitalism of Italian American gangsters. The "cheating capitalism" of the gangster is simply capitalism hiding from the police. It differs from basic capitalism in goal and means. It sells a product, usually illegal liquor, or drugs, to satisfy socially unacceptable desires. And it uses methods that are immoral and illegal.

Advanced Gangster stories avoid this distinction and state that the establishment world is itself corrupt, both economically and politically. This is not simply a matter of the establishment having climbed the ladder first.

> **KEY POINT: Advanced Gangster stories state that corruption is inherent to the capitalist system.**

Just as the gangster moves to consolidate economic and political power for himself, the natural tendency of pure capitalism is to move toward monopoly and oligarchy so it can charge the customer the maximum possible price.

The capitalist system portrayed at the beginning of any Gangster story is so vast and deep that it seems not to exist at all. It's the world we all recognize.

The Godfather Part II

The brilliance of *The Godfather Part II* comes from the fact that it is structured on the notion of social fractals, which we discussed in Science Fiction. Through a crosscut in time, the film tracks the process of Vito Corleone building a business and becoming a godfather on the neighborhood level from 1917 to 1925 versus his son Michael expanding the empire on the national and international levels from 1958 to 1959.

In 1958, Michael partners with mob boss Hyman Roth in Cuba. First, they meet with the Cuban dictator Fulgencio Batista, along with the heads of some of America's largest "legitimate" companies, such as AT&T, to plan their investments. Later, Michael, Roth, and other gangsters celebrate Roth's birthday. As they cut a cake with a map of Cuba, Roth says:

> What I am saying is, we have now what we have always needed, real partnership with the government . . . Here we are, protected, free to make our profits without Kefauver, the goddamn Justice Department and the FBI, ninety miles away, in partnership with a friendly government . . . looking for a man who wants to be President of the United States, and having the cash to make it possible. Michael, we're bigger than U.S. Steel.

Story World: Slavery of Organization

In this highly organized, corporate world, where upward mobility is tightly restricted, the individual tries to find material success by being part of an organization.

KEY POINT: The cost of finding material success by being part of an organization is that, ironically, the gangster lives in a world of increasing slavery.

The organization in which the gangster operates has these characteristics:

- It's a kingdom often based on a family.
- The head gangster (the "king") has absolute power based on force.
- The crime family is rigidly hierarchical, with strict rules and defined lines of power.
- The group is all.
- The gangster begins, remains, and ends in debt. His slavery doesn't just come from following orders. He is in debt to the organization, and the organization never forgets. This means he can never leave. Once he's signed on, he's in forever. The *cost* of leaving is his life.

Like Film Noir, a subgenre of Crime (*Double Indemnity*, *The Postman Always Rings Twice*), Gangster tracks the trip to hell within an inexorable, tightening vise. Once the individual makes the first decision, the rest is a causal line to self-destruction. This applies to the wives as well as to the gangster. In season five, episode three of *Peaky Blinders*, Aunt Polly says to Michael's wife, "We all try to get away. But we never do." The lead gangster, Tommy Shelby, says, "You marry a Shelby. You stay fucking married."

We might call this the Gangster Code. In *The Godfather Part III*, Michael says, "Just when I thought I was out, they pull me back in." *The Sopranos* gangsters make fun of this line, but it applies to them as well.

The family runs its kingdom using gang rules. It demands

and collects "taxes," meaning payoffs, from businesses that operate within their kingdom. This is an insurance policy that guarantees the "king" won't smash the business, or the businessman, outright. The businessman survives under the threat of death.

Within the city, clear geographical boundaries define what each family controls. Just as the Western has the basic buildings of early society—the jail, saloon, church, and dry goods store—gangster life occurs in buildings of human desire: the speakeasy (drinking), the bookie joint and casino (gambling), and the whorehouse (sex).

The opponents have their own subworlds. Police have the station and competing gangsters live within their own family compound. Even opponents within the gangster's own family may have their own subworld.

Story World: Technology

The primary technology of the Gangster story is the gun. In going from the Western to the Gangster, the tool of killing is magnified a hundredfold, from the six-gun to the Thompson submachine gun. This supermechanized weapon represents total human destruction.

Another weapon is the unmarked handgun that can be tossed after it's used to commit a murder. This gun is not worn, honestly and with pride, in plain sight on the hero's hip. The gangster keeps it hidden in his coat pocket.

The clothes of the gangster also differ from the cowboy's. The cowboy, the workingman on a horse, wears simple clothes and a wide-brimmed hat to protect himself from the sun. The gangster of the city sports the stylish fedora, a symbol of blood-sucking, old world aristocracy. He wears the gaudy raiment of a nouveau riche man buying and shooting his way to success.

GANGSTER STORY BEAT: Hero—Gangster as Killer

From this rigidly delineated and restricted city world, the new myth hero arises. The genre is named after the hero's role and his basic action. He's not just a lone criminal. He runs a criminal gang and kills ruthlessly.

Wrapped up in the term "gangster" is the basic method the gangster uses to succeed. Being part of an organization multiplies his power. And that power involves force.

The hero's role in any genre comes from how that character executes the story strategy. You'll recall Gangster tracks the rise and fall of a "king" in a democracy.

> **KEY POINT: Because we're not supposed to have a king in a democracy, the gangster's fall is never tragic.***

The reason we're supposed to despise the gangster and not pity his fall is that he's a hollow man. He always shoots first. He enslaves and kills people for money and power. Yet, we have invested our time and emotion in him, so we love to see him succeed. We're also excited to watch someone with almost unlimited confidence.

The Godfather: The Art of Leadership

To this day, *The Godfather* is the premier Gangster Epic. In part this is because it follows the classic tale of the immigrant seeking the American Dream. But it's also because the story transcends the Gangster beats to focus on the exercise of power and the art of leadership.

The writer Mario Puzo achieves this feat through a unique structure and genre mix. The story tracks the making of a new

---

* Robert Warshow, "The Gangster as a Tragic Hero," 1948.

godfather. Combining Gangster with Myth and Fairy Tale, Puzo uses the classic fairy-tale trick of the three brothers (such as the *Three Little Pigs*), with the youngest as hero. This technique allows him to compare the style and strategy each brother would use to lead the family.

The first two brothers, each with the wrong traits and methods, fail. Sonny, the eldest, is a fighter. Fredo is a sweet soul with no chance of being a godfather. So his place in the organization is taken by Tom, the adopted brother. Tom is a talker. Neither approach to being a godfather works in a war against the other crime families. Only the youngest, Michael, has the right combination of traits—toughness and smarts—to win the war and make their criminal empire grow.

GANGSTER STORY BEAT: Weakness-Need—Contradictory Character

Weakness-need is the first major structure step in any story. Weakness refers to the fundamental internal flaw that is destroying the character's life. Need is what the character must do to fix it and grow.

In simple characters the weakness is psychological, not moral. In other words, the flaw hurts the character but no one else. As a result, it's easy for the audience to like and identify with them. But there's no complexity, and little if any character change.

A common misconception among writers is that a "complex character" equals a bad person. In fact, a complex character means someone with contradictions:

- A psychological contradiction is a trait that is both a strength and a weakness. For example, loving but jealous, idealistic but cynical, loyal but unforgiving.
- A moral contradiction refers to a character who has a

highly compartmentalized moral code. In other words, it's a moral code that both helps and hurts others and allows the character to shift back and forth between right and wrong without seeing the problem.

The gangster has both psychological and moral contradictions to a greater degree than any other genre hero. Michael Corleone believes in family, honor, and loyalty, but he also kills people. He sees no contradiction there because he believes he only kills when it's justified.

Weakness-Need: Prohibited Desires and Extreme Ambition

What are the gangster's most serious weaknesses? Unlike the criminal-as-hero (such as Thomas Crown), the gangster is neither brilliant nor deep. He doesn't commit crime to win the game. He is a common, even cheap man, defined by his extreme ambition to be king. He amasses money and power by fulfilling his customers' prohibited desires through illegal drink, drugs, gambling, and sex.

Scarface (1932): Up-and-coming gangster Tony Camonte points to the sign outside his apartment that says: THE WORLD IS YOURS—COOK'S TOURS. "Someday I look at that sign and I say, 'Okay, she's mine.'"

> **KEY POINT: The gangster has the most contradictory and compartmentalized moral system of any genre hero.**

It's a big mistake to think that this ruthless man has no values at all. He values family, honor, loyalty, and money. At the same time, he justifies using murder, cheating, and stealing to reach his goals. In one line, he's the killer who loves his family.

Here is Tony's moral code:

TONY: Listen, Little Boy, there's only one law you gotta follow to keep out of trouble: do it first, do it yourself, and keep on doing it . . . There's only one thing that gets orders and gives orders.

He aims the machine gun.

TONY: And this is it. That's how I got the south side for you, and that's how I'm gonna get the north side for you. It's a typewriter. I'm gonna write my name all over this town with it, in big letters! . . .

He starts shooting.

Shame Culture Weakness and the Mafia Moral Code

Like the cowboy, the gangster lives in a highly male-dominated world. He is part of an organization that uses physical force to succeed. This creates the perfect environment for a shame culture. Shame is what one feels when failing to reach a standard in the eyes of others. As we saw in the Action and Science Fiction chapters, shame culture values honor, appearance, achievement, physical ability, self-reliance, strength, courage, glory, doing well (as opposed to doing good), and pride.

This shame culture is a twisted form of Nietzsche's master morality, in which he who has force is right, even when using it is wrong. Because gangsters succeed through illegal action, especially murder, the gang's moral code is founded on silence, on not being a "snitch." This is known in Mafia organizations as "omertà," and failure to strictly follow this code results in death.

KEY POINT: Omertà is an external restraint on the members of the gang to conform. But the shame culture is an even more powerful form of internal slavery by which the gang member justifies his destructive and murderous actions.

GANGSTER STORY BEAT: Inciting Event—Petty Crime

The gangster often begins his life of crime with a petty offense. Examples include *The Public Enemy*: as a kid, Tommy and his friend shoplift, *Little Caesar*: Rico robs a gas station, *The Godfather Part II*: Vito Corleone steals a rug, *Goodfellas*: Henry quits school and sells stolen cigarettes for the local mob boss.

GANGSTER STORY BEAT: Desire—Money and Empire

The spine of the story is determined by the desire line of the hero. The gangster's goal is to gain money and power, and ultimately to build an empire. He is poor and starts near the bottom of the organization. He wants to become the boss of his crime family.

The final goal of empire is accomplished through the immediate goal of making the deal. The deal determines the money and the territory, and it creates the debt on which the whole system depends.

The gangster is unapologetically proud of his quest for money and the conspicuous consumption that comes with it.

The famous scene in *The Great Gatsby* when Gatsby brags of wearing a new shirt every day is repeated in *Scarface*. Tony wants to impress Poppy with the opulence of his new place. She says, "Kind of gaudy, isn't it?" He replies, "Ain't it though? Glad you like it."

KEY POINT: The gangster sees freedom strictly in terms of money.

This is one of the reasons he always remains enslaved. He can never get enough and someone else is always trying to take it away from him. For the gangster, chasing the American Dream becomes a nightmare.

GANGSTER STORY BEAT: Allies—Gang Members

Unlike the criminal-as-hero who works alone, the gangster is part of the most tightly hierarchical team in any story form. The team extends out from the family to include trusted outsiders. The family is organized like a military unit, with "captains," "lieutenants," and "soldiers."

GANGSTER STORY BEAT: Opponent—Gang Boss, Rival Gangs, and Cops

The gangster has a greater variety of opponents than any other hero. The story world is a brutal state of nature. Like the king, the gangster exists in a system that justifies itself through force. Therefore, he always fears that his allies will try to kill him, just as he schemes to kill those of greater power. The inevitable act is betrayal, so the gangster is always suspicious and alone.

The Gangster story goes beyond the typical four-point to a six-point opposition. Here are the major characters who fulfill those roles:

1. The Gang Boss: the hero usually starts out on a lower rung of the ladder. He wants the boss's job.
2. The Gang Family as a whole: the family is a vise that will not let the hero go or avoid his debt.
3. Other gang members: they're competing with the hero for money and power within the organization.
4. Cops: they represent normal society and enforce the proper methods of getting a goal.
5. Competing gangster families: these families provide competition over turf.
6. Within the hero's personal family: the gangster may be in competition with his father but more often he competes with his brothers.

All of these opponents fight the hero simultaneously, which creates density of conflict and violence.

GANGSTER STORY BEAT: Plan—Deception and Violence

The gangster's plan consists of the illegal and immoral methods he uses to reach his goal of empire. Therefore,

- The plan is to cheat, steal, and use various kinds of deception, such as extortion and protection rackets. Also, the gangster forms alliances but breaks them when necessary.
- The plan usually involves premeditated murder. The gangster will kill all contenders for the throne, including his boss, competition within the family, other gang bosses, indeed anyone who gets in his way.

GANGSTER STORY BEAT: Fake Ally—Gang Members

A fake ally is a character who appears to be the hero's friend but is actually an enemy. In the Gangster genre, certain gang members shift alliances from hero to opponent over the course of the story. This makes them fake allies.

TECHNIQUE: Shifting Alliances

Gang members are the trick to Gangster plot because every time one of them shifts sides it creates a revelation and more conflict.

This technique comes from one of the underlying themes of the Gangster story, which is that *absolute power is the most fragile power of all*. Everyone below the boss is scheming to take his place.

The original *Godfather* has five fake allies. They are Don Corleone's driver, who is part of the attempt to assassinate him, Michael's two bodyguards in Sicily, who try to blow him up in his car but kill his wife instead, Tessio, the lieutenant who switches his loyalty to Barzini, and Michael's brother-in-law, Carlo, who sets up Sonny's murder.

GANGSTER STORY BEAT: Reveal—Betrayal

The fake ally leads to a related plot beat: the gangster reveal. It usually exposes the trickery the opposing gangster or gang member uses to betray the hero.

TECHNIQUE: Hiding the Opponent's True Power

Hide the opponent's true power under the surface, from both the hero and the reader. Then, when you expose the opponent's intent and method of attack, you get a reveal.

GANGSTER STORY BEAT: Drive—Accelerating Violence

The hero's original desire line becomes the drive in the middle of the story as the hero takes a series of actions to reach the goal. The gangster and all his opponents compete for money and power by shifting alliances to help their cause.

With so many opponents attacking the hero from so many directions, the story builds through accelerating violence. Business disagreements over the deal beget violent conflicts that inevitably turn into vendetta, or revenge killing, which ultimately becomes gang war.

In every other genre, the drive is where most of the moral argument of the story plays out. The hero, initially losing to the opponent, becomes desperate and starts to take immoral steps to win. The ally attacks him for his methods, but the hero doesn't listen. Here, that doesn't happen.

KEY POINT: The basic Gangster story is the only genre with little or no discussion about the morality of the hero's actions.

With his compartmentalized mind, the gangster has rationalized his immorality from the beginning, usually to help his family. This is the man who kills without compunction. Therefore, anytime the gangster discusses what actions to take, he is concerned with strategy, not morality.

Visual Shape of the Gangster Plot: Rise and Fall

In any story, the desire line and drive step form a particular story shape based on the hero's methods and final success. In a Gangster story, these beats take the form of rise and fall.

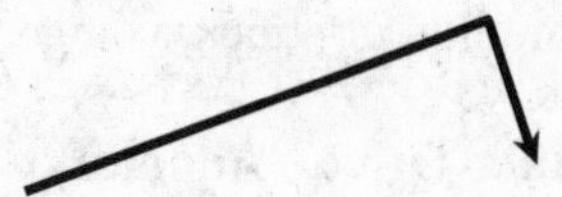

The hero moves up the organization ladder and gains wealth. But this rise of external success is accomplished through the most immoral means. As a result, the gangster's internal stature as a human being falls (if it was ever that high in the first place). And usually, the story ends in the gangster's death, in a costly Pyrrhic victory, or in slavery.

The Godfather Part II is a long crosscut in time, comparing the actions of a father and son forty years apart as each rises in power. It uses two story strands to compare approaches to being a godfather and building a criminal empire. Even more than *The Godfather*, *The Godfather Part II* highlights the immigrant. It tracks an Italian boy, Vito, coming to America by himself after a mafia don kills his family in Sicily. Vito is a dark Horatio Alger who starts with theft and uses the money to create his olive oil business.

Michael's line tracks the expansion of his empire by paying off officials, including a U.S. senator, and extending it internationally to Cuba.

No Gangster film has shown the rise and fall of the hero as effectively as *Goodfellas*. The process is embodied in three sequences. The first tracks young Henry learning the system's rules and navigating the rites of passage to reach a respected place in mob society. But the brilliant step here is showing us for the first time a gangster so in love with the mob world. Instead of a story that goes from slavery to freedom, the writers show us a story that goes from freedom—or, more precisely, apparent freedom—to slavery.

The second sequence, using Henry's narration, tracks the destruction of a restaurant business when the mob, as real vampires, sinks its teeth into it and sucks it dry:

HENRY VOICE-OVER: Now the guy's got Paulie as a partner. Any problems, he goes to Paulie. Trouble with the bill? He can go to Paulie. Trouble with the cops, deliveries, Tommy, he can call Paulie. But now the guy's gotta come up with Paulie's money every week, no matter what. Business bad? Fuck you, pay me. Oh, you had a fire? Fuck you, pay me. Place got hit by lightning, huh? Fuck you, pay me.

The scene ends with the mob guys burning down the restaurant for the insurance.

The third crucial process is a single shot in which Henry and his new girlfriend enter a club through the back door, pass through the kitchen, and end up sitting at the front table during a show. At every step of the journey he greases someone's palm with a twenty-dollar bill. This shot matches the rise of the Italian American gangster, from immigrant outsider, to poor manual laborer, to rich, powerful boss at the top of the social heap.

GANGSTER STORY BEAT: Battle—Mass Murder or Massive Destruction

The battle is the final conflict in the story. The gangster battles the cops or other gangster families. The shootout either destroys the gangster or consolidates his power. Because murder is the basic method he uses throughout the story, the final battle often involves mass murder or total destruction.

> **KEY POINT: If the gangster consolidates his power in this battle, there is always the sense that it *will not last*.**

Again, *The Godfather* flips the traditional Gangster beat. Instead of being killed by a rival gang or the police, Michael has his men gun down the heads of the other five mafia families of New York, along with his lieutenant, Tessio, and brother-in-law, Carlo, who betrayed the family. He does this while standing as the godfather to Carlo's son in church.

Goodfellas also flips this Gangster beat. Instead of a shootout or a gang war, Henry testifies in court against his former partners in crime. While they go to jail, he lives a safe but boring suburban slavery in the witness protection program.

GANGSTER STORY BEAT: No Self-Revelation

The gangster has no self-revelation because he is incapable of seeing the glaring flaws of his compartmentalized moral code. He justifies his heinous behavior by saying it was necessary to protect himself and his family.

In *The Godfather*, Carlo's wife, Connie, accuses Michael of murdering her husband. Michael denies the allegation to his own wife, Kay, and insists that she never ask about his business again. Kay watches as Michael's men pay fealty to him as

"Godfather" until the door is closed in her face. Thanks to his moral downfall, the self-revelation that Michael should have goes to Kay.

Goodfellas uses the Black Comedy technique of purposely depriving the hero of the self-revelation. The hero has no sense of the larger system in which he has been ensnared.

> **HENRY HILL:** And that's the hardest part. Today everything is different; there's no action . . . [I] have to wait around like everyone else. Can't even get decent food . . . I'm an average nobody . . . [I] get to live the rest of my life like a schnook.

GANGSTER STORY BEAT: New Equilibrium—Death or Death of the Soul

The gangster dies in a hail of bullets or he triumphs but loses his soul. Our momentary sense of victory at the death of a bad man is eclipsed by the realization that he will quickly be replaced by someone just as bad.

In *Scarface*, Tony dies beneath the sign THE WORLD IS YOURS—COOK'S TOURS. This is the very sign he once pointed to when he proclaimed that the world would be his.

In *The Godfather*, Michael has become morally dead. But his ability to rationalize that he is doing it all for his family makes him unable to see it.

And in *Goodfellas*, without the excitement and freedom of his criminal life and the community he loved, Henry faces a life of nothingness. The irony obvious to anyone but him is that the past life for which he is so nostalgic killed most of his friends, destroyed his family, and sent him to jail.

Theme: Being as the Slavery of False Values

The Gangster story expresses being and becoming more negatively than any other story form. It says that being in the modern world means living as a slave to money and to our own desires. Everything in the modern world is quantified, bought and sold. Therefore, living is a constant struggle to make money and increase our power and status.

Being is a losing battle with our desires. Just being alive places us in an impossible trap. To live is to want. We may try to live a "balanced life," with "moderation in all things."* But we are doomed to fail.

Like dark Science Fiction, Gangster says that being is living in a social system that is inherently corrupt. This system seems to be based on a free market. But it is far from politically or economically free. The market is designed to heighten our desires so that they are greater than our true needs. The result is a perpetual motion machine of buying and selling where "we must run as fast as we can, just to stay in place. And if you wish to go anywhere you must run twice as fast as that."† It's completely mad. So it goes.

Gangster Thematic Recipe: The Way of Destruction

The thematic recipe of any genre comes from the hero's basic action and the key question the form asks. Gangster is a cautionary tale about what happens when the individual tries to gain success within a mass, modern society using any means necessary. The key question in the Gangster story is: How do you succeed in the city world without losing your soul?

---

* Hesiod c. 700 BC.

† Lewis Carroll, *Alice in Wonderland.*

The Gangster story answers with this recipe for success: beware of false desire and immoral and illegal methods. If you act as if success is all about money, and you do anything to get it, you will destroy yourself and your family.

Even worse, being human means a constant temptation of false values. Succumb to that and you will live in the worst slavery. It's not just false values that enslave. Like Buddhism, the Gangster view of becoming tells us to beware of desire itself. Since any desire will necessarily become an obsession, our only hope for living the good life is to avoid desire entirely.

Part of why this cautionary tale is so negative is that it implies we *will* fail. Not only are we up against our own desires, we live within a larger system that creates and stokes them beyond our control.

Worst of all, the Gangster story says that thinking freedom comes from money is the natural trap as someone seeks success. It's all too easy for us to succumb.

The one sliver of hope the genre gives us is that by showing us ourselves and our society in the worst light, there may be a chance that we can beat this obsession. But it is only by concerted effort, and a shift from tactical to strategic thinking, that a more expansive and humane form of freedom can become part of our life.

How to Transcend the Gangster Story

The transcendent Gangster story grows from the same soil as the transcendent Western. Each happens when the city evolves into the oppressive city. Each says we must look at the much larger system to see how it corrupts and destroys everyone. Like the so-called Great American Novel, the transcendent Gangster story is a response to what it perceives as the false promises of America's first two Creation texts, the

Declaration of Independence and the U.S. Constitution, and the nation's failure to live up to those promises.

Transcendent Gangster is the most challenging of all genres to write for three reasons. First, it explores the vast economic-political system in personal and dramatic terms. Second, it expresses two of the major story forms in life, business and politics, and how they are inextricably intertwined. Finally, it shows the ways materialism is similar to gangsterism, and how business and politics can become corrupted.

Why Associate Business and Politics with the Gangster Genre

One could argue that the arts of business and politics are natural outgrowths of the Action genre, like War and Sports stories. Action is about being the best, defined to the last decimal. Both business and politics keep score. Both are about winning.

Business is the art of war by economic means. It is a sport in which the winner makes the most money. Politics is the art of war through the exercise of power. It is a sport in which the winner gets to tell everyone else what to do. We don't discuss business and politics in the Action chapter because in their modern-day form, they are part of an immensely complex society.

The fact that Science Fiction is about creating society and culture suggests it is the proper genre to tell stories of how people exchange value and govern themselves. Science Fiction highlights government by creating an extreme tyranny in an abstract future. That is theoretically fascinating. But it lacks detail.

Seeing business and politics as the essence of the transcendent Gangster story makes a great deal of sense, for three reasons:

1. More than any other form, the transcendent Gangster story explores the system within which people actually live. It shows how people go about getting two of their greatest desires: money and power.
2. Transcendent Gangster shows how the larger system of money and power affects, controls, and often destroys the individuals within it. It is a version of the Modernization Story whereby the individual is caught in a process that he/she cannot understand or fight.
3. Transcendent Gangster shows the forces that push business and politics toward corruption, with business becoming oligarchy and the republic becoming dictatorship.

Any business leader who tries to create a monopoly is a gangster. John D. Rockefeller was the most powerful economic gangster in American history. He used social Darwinism to justify his methods of gaining monopoly, saying: "The growth of a large business is merely a survival of the fittest."

Any totalitarian leader is a gangster. Adolf Hitler was the ultimate political gangster. Bertolt Brecht made this connection explicit in his play *The Resistible Rise of Arturo Ui*, the story of a Chicago gangster that mimics the rise of Hitler.

Transcendent Gangster Genres: The Gangster Epic, the Eastern, and the Economic-Political Epic

The transcendent Gangster genre takes three forms: the Gangster Epic, the Eastern, and the Economic-Political Epic.

1. The Gangster Epic
   The first way to transcend the Gangster form is by writing one that stands for the nation. This story combines the gangster hero with complex plot and advanced theme. Examples include *The Godfather Part I* and *II*, *Goodfellas*,

The Sopranos, *Peaky Blinders*, *Boardwalk Empire*, and *Un Prophète*.

2. The Eastern

As mentioned, the "Eastern" is a negative "Rags to Riches" story. The hero is not an actual gangster, but rather an everyman who tries to rise up the ladder of financial and social success. He either fails or succeeds materially while losing his soul.

In *The Dream of the Great American Novel*, Lawrence Buell identifies the "American Dream," or Rags to Riches story, as one of the main structures that make up the Holy Grail of American writers: the Great American Novel. This is a kind of Coming-of-Age success story. In other words, it is an American bildungsroman, a story of personal development or formation in which:

- a young American improves himself and often gets rich
- an ordinary person becomes extraordinary
- the hero helps create the United States in the process.

Basic versions of Rags to Riches, such as the classic Horatio Alger stories, track not only the character's personal development but also their success in gaining wealth and social position in a wonderful land of opportunity.

KEY POINT: The best Rags to Riches stories highlight the *failure* of the American Dream, in contrast to the Western, which highlights its success.

In these negative stories, the hero may get rich but lose his integrity. This shows the costs of financial success and the entrepreneurial spirit in capitalist American culture. The main character does not change from child to adult.

Rather, he is a permanent child-adult, having some form of arrested development. His main weakness is that he has a false image of himself that eventually destroys him even as he gains financial and social success.

The Eastern argues that America's founding myth is a hollow boast. It highlights the difference between the promise of the Declaration of Independence and the failure to make good on it. It states that the main reason for this failure is that there is no real upward mobility anymore. The individual must become a cog in a company or use immoral or illegal means to succeed. Ironically, this type of Great American Novel holds that the United States is not great, or is in decline.

The Eastern is best understood as a form of the much larger Economic-Political Epic. Examples include *The Great Gatsby, The Portrait of a Lady, The Wings of the Dove, The House of Mirth, The Age of Innocence, Main Street, Babbitt, Dodsworth, The Jungle, The Grapes of Wrath, Citizen Kane, The Magnificent Ambersons, Mr. Deeds Goes to Town, Mr. Smith Goes to Washington,* and *Mad Men.*

3. The Economic-Political Epic

The Economic-Political Epic is a story that tracks an individual caught within the economic-political system. The hero cannot navigate the intricacies of how money and power work together to determine modern life. These stories have national and international stakes.

This genre has the largest number of fiction masterpieces of any story form. We can further divide this subgenre into stories that are primarily business or political and stories that explore how these systems interact.

Business stories: *The Big Short*, *Wall Street*, *Okja*, *Slumdog Millionaire* (also Love), *Erin Brockovich* (also Social Drama), *The Social Network*, *Jerry Maguire* (also Love),

Nightcrawler (also Thriller), *Syriana* (also Political Thriller), *Traffic*, *The Wolf of Wall Street*

Transcendent Business stories: *Death of a Salesman*, *Glengarry Glen Ross*, *American Beauty* (also Satire), *The Jungle*, *The Conversation* (also Epic Thriller), *Sweet Smell of Success*, *The Magnificent Ambersons*, *Michael Clayton* (also Thriller), *Squid Game* (also Science Fiction and Thriller)

Political stories: *The Front Runner*, *Vice*, *On the Basis of Sex*, *The Favourite*, *Mary Queen of Scots*, *The King's Speech*, *Gladiator* (also Action Epic), *The Last Emperor*, *Doctor Zhivago*, *Reds*, *Gone with the Wind*, *The Last of the Mohicans* (also Action and Love), *Excalibur* (also Myth), *Dances with Wolves* (also anti-Western), *The Candidate*, *Gunga Din* (also Action), *The Great Man Votes*, *The Great McGinty*, *Hail the Conquering Hero*, *Advise and Consent*, *The Best Man*, *Seven Days in May*, *In the Loop*, *Z*, *Bob Roberts*, *The Manchurian Candidate* (also Political Thriller), *Marie Antoinette*, *Darkest Hour*, *Meet John Doe*, *Rollerball* (also Science Fiction), *Hunger Games* (also Science Fiction/Myth), *A Face in the Crowd*, *Burr*, *Lincoln*, *1876*, *Empire*

Transcendent Political stories: *The Prince*, King Arthur stories like *Le Morte d'Arthur*, the *Oresteia*, *Antigone*, *Richard III*, *A Doll's House*, *Hedda Gabler*, *It Can't Happen Here*, *Hamilton*, *Mr. Smith Goes to Washington*, *Lawrence of Arabia*, *The West Wing*, *House of Cards*, *All the King's Men*, *All the President's Men*

Transcendent stories combining business and politics: *A Christmas Carol* (also Horror and Fantasy), *The Great Gatsby*, *Mad Men*, *Heart of Darkness*, *Moby-Dick*, *It's a Wonderful Life*, *How Green Was My Valley*, *The Resistible Rise of Arturo Ui*, *Citizen Kane*, *Game of Thrones* (also Fantasy and Action), *Network* (also Black Comedy), *Pather Panchali*, *I, Claudius*, *Days of Heaven*, *Westworld* (also Science Fiction)

The Art, Story, and Game of Business-Politics

To understand how to write transcendent Gangster stories, we must first explore the story forms of business and politics that underlie the genre. These story forms, like the Gangster story itself, use the structure of rise and fall, the tragic story of a king.

The fact that the mind works through story means that all human activities are a form of story. But, like some of the other art forms of life we've discussed, business and politics seem to be as far from "art" as one can get. Let's look again at this quote from Richard Flanagan's novel *First Person*, where scam artist "Ziggy" Heidl explains his success:

> *I made it up.* Every day, just like you. *Like a writer* . . . What do you think a businessman is? A politician? They're sorcerers—they make things up. Stories are all that we have to hold us together. Religion, science, money—they're all just stories. Australia is a story, politics is a story, religion is a story, money is a story . . .

Business is the art of establishing and exchanging value. Economics is the study of that art form. The individual employs business to quantify freedom and slavery in his day-to-day survival and then uses tools within a marketplace to increase his freedom.

KEY POINT: Business is the work we do to pay the cost of living.

If we were forced to describe the art of business in one technique, it would have to be: buy low, sell high. But that captures only two moments in a massive process. What makes business an art and a story is that executing this technique requires a complex and difficult campaign.

KEY POINT: Business is storytelling for money.

Business claims to serve the customer. But in reality, business is about increasing itself. That's why business is also the game of making money. Whoever makes (and keeps) the most money wins.

To talk about how business works, we must talk about how the human mind works. Specifically, how the mind interacts with other people and the environment to quantify and trade resources. The vast complexity of business and the worldwide economic system comes from the vast complexity of the human mind.

"Business" for animals is simple. If an animal sees a resource it wants, it either kills it or fights another animal to take it. End of story. But as soon as we introduce the human mind and its ability to create symbols, calculation and strategy come into play. One human may kill another for a resource, but that is extremely costly for an animal as social as man. Therefore, this solution will only happen in relatively scarce situations.

Turning someone into a slave, while deeply immoral, is much more useful in the long term than killing. When jobs become specialized, it is even more useful to exchange goods, either by barter or by exchanging money.

As always, the business mind begins with what the human being desires. Simply put, he wants *more*. While born an individual, the human being is part of a group, a society, and a system. When multiple individuals living together all want more at the same time, the first requirement is to establish the value of "more." This means value must be quantified.

What makes business an art form is that nothing has an objective value. It takes human beings to agree on that value. So we assign symbols based on supply and demand.

But both supply and demand are subjective. We are never

totally aware of how much supply there is of a product, or of the amount and fervor of the demand.

KEY POINT: Since business is the art of establishing value, business and morality must be seen as one. Together they form the art of establishing value in life.

If business is the exchange of value, then politics is the control of value. Herein lies the fundamental reason business and politics must be understood in tandem. As a combination of art and game, politics is the competition for power in which we keep score. This competition plays out as a story.

Caution: The biggest mistake writers make in telling stories about business and politics is to see them separately. They are inextricably entwined, the two strands of the DNA of practical life.

There is no clearer example of the unbreakable connection between business and politics than in the founding of the United States.

KEY POINT: The United States was built on two genocides: of Native Americans and African Americans. The first genocide was about getting rid of competition for real estate. The second was about cheap labor to develop it.

The Story Beats of Business-Politics = The Story of Capitalism and the Republic

Transcendent Gangster stories attack the vast system of business and politics. Therefore, we must work through the story beats of both.

In today's Western world, when we say business-politics, we are really talking about a particular hybrid form, the capitalist republic. Capitalism claims to increase freedom through money. A republic claims to increase freedom through power, whether by having it or by avoiding others lording it over you.

Stories about capitalism and republic highlight the way these systems can move from freedom and justice toward corruption and absolutism.

KEY POINT: The transcendent Gangster form gains its immense dramatic impact by showing that extreme capitalism and totalitarian government have the same flaw. Each expresses the "Universal Mind" of a child.

In business, the child mind is the pure id that wants, wants, and wants some more. In politics it is a mind most comfortable with firm control from above. Only when the human mind moves to adulthood can it begin to live with something even approaching moderation and democracy.

As we go through the beats of the transcendent Gangster story, we will look closely at the two best examples of the Eastern, *The Great Gatsby* and *Mad Men*, as well as the three best examples of the Economic-Political Epic, *It's a Wonderful Life*, *How Green Was My Valley*, and *Network*.

Transcendent Gangster Story Beats

Transcendent Gangster stories place a heavy emphasis on story world. The main story world elements transcendent Gangster stories critique include:

- The culture of capitalism and republic
- The system of capitalism and republic
- The organizing principle of the American system

Story World: The Culture of Capitalism and Republic

Before exploring the story of the capitalist republic, I must make the same distinction I made about Religion. This is not a description of my personal beliefs. I am analyzing a system of beliefs as a story.

The story of capitalism describes the advanced business world we live in today. But it is not reality. Capitalism is a type of religion that many storytellers, including Charles Dickens, have commented on. Whether you agree or disagree with their critique is up to you.

The dictionary defines capitalism as "an economic and political system in which a country's trade and industry are controlled by private owners for profit, rather than by the state."

As the name implies, this is a system for creating capital and controlling its flow. But what is that? Capital is not an object, like a rock. Capital—money or goods—is an idea made physical. It is the potential to gain resources and take action. Capitalism is a particular organizing principle for creating wealth for the individual that also affects the larger social unit.

Adam Smith, a key figure in the Scottish Enlightenment, is often called the "father of capitalism" because of his treatise *An Inquiry into the Nature and Causes of the Wealth of Nations* (1776), known simply as *The Wealth of Nations*. His main point is that in a "free market," individual self-interest will produce prosperity for the society by an "invisible hand." Individual freedom + desire = collective wealth.

Both money and morality deal with value. Therefore, instead of opposing morality, or being amoral, capitalism is first a *moral theory* of how self-interest actually increases the general good of everyone.

The idea that pure capitalism is a moral theory and not a description of reality makes sense when we discover that

Adam Smith began as the moral philosopher who wrote *The Theory of Moral Sentiments* (1759). This is where Smith first introduced the metaphor of the "invisible hand."

> The rich . . . consume little more than the poor . . . They are led by an invisible hand to make nearly the same distribution of the necessaries of life, which would have been made, had the earth been divided into equal portions among all its inhabitants, and thus without intending it, without knowing it, advance the interest of the society, and afford means to the multiplication of the species. When Providence divided the earth among a few lordly masters, it neither forgot nor abandoned those who seemed to have been left out in the partition.

Notice this is a moral argument about the value of selfishness. It is also a kind of "Divine Right of the Rich." God created a world with a few masters and uses his "invisible hand" to give the poor some benefits as well. This is the first use of what would become known as the "trickle down" theory.

KEY POINT: Far from being an objective description of how the world works, capitalism is a culture and a religion.

Seeing capitalism as a story helps us explore the validity of this moral system. As with any moral system, the issue of responsibility is central to the concept. To what degree should the individual be responsible for the well-being of other individuals in the group and to the group as a whole?

Capitalist Values

Since capitalism is essentially a moral code that describes the ownership and exchange of values, we must look at what it values to learn how it works. Capitalism makes wealth the highest value, and believes certain character traits help get it. Among them are initiative, self-reliance, self-discipline, and delayed gratification.

Individual initiative is useful in business, no matter how small or big the business may be. But self-reliance is a misnomer in today's world. Once the society moves beyond the wilderness-nomad stage to an agrarian, and especially an industrial and information society, no businessperson is self-reliant. The need for communal infrastructure like police, fire, roads, and communication places much greater emphasis on collegiality, consensus building, and leadership.

One of the fiercest critiques of the religious system of the modern capitalist republic is found in this famous scene in *Network*. When anchorman Howard Beale warns millions of viewers that Communications Corporation of America (CCA), owner of his network, is being bought by a Saudi Arabian conglomerate, CCA's boss, Arthur Jensen, calls him on the carpet.

ARTHUR JENSEN: You have meddled with the primal forces of nature, Mr. Beale, and I won't have it! . . . There are no nations. There are no peoples. There are no Russians. There are no Arabs. There are no third worlds. There is no West. There is only one holistic system of systems, one vast . . . interwoven, interacting, multivariate, multinational dominion of dollars. Petro-dollars, electro-dollars, multi-dollars, reichsmarks, rins, rubles, pounds, and shekels. It is the international system of currency which determines the totality of life on this planet. That is the natural order of things today. That is the atomic and subatomic and galactic structure of things today! And YOU have meddled with the primal forces of nature, and YOU . . . WILL . . . ATONE!

Democracy Values

Democracy is defined as "government by the people, especially rule of the majority." Implied in the idea of government by the people is that everyone in the society gets to decide.

If we think of democracy as a story form, we see that it is contrary to the classic Myth form, based on gods and superheroes. In democracy the heroes are mere mortals, known in a monarchy as "subjects" (but treated as objects). The "subjects" in democracy run the organization.

> **KEY POINT: Far from being an objective description of a form of government, democracy is a culture and a religion that promises that everyone can be free and equal at the same time.**

Therefore, democracy and republic are not two competing systems of governance. Democracy is the idea. Republic is the operating system.

Story World: The System of Capitalism

Any story world operates through a system. The system has highly defined roles, a hierarchy, and a set of rules. These roles and rules organize and enslave.

The story world of capitalism is supposedly operated by the "invisible hand" mechanism. Its proponents claim that it is an accurate description of how *any* human system would work if individuals have maximum freedom.

> **KEY POINT: A major difficulty with proving that the "invisible hand" creates the most value in a society is that capitalism is a utopian idea that doesn't exist and has never existed in reality.**

Story World: The Organizing Principle of the System

In the Science Fiction chapter, we talked about the organizing principle of a system that dictates how the society controls its members.

KEY POINT: The organizing principle determines who is relatively free and who is relatively enslaved. Therefore, all the stories in the culture are based on this one principle, which then reprograms the population again and again.

We see this clearly when we compare the English versus American systems. The old English system was based on the firstborn son inheriting the father's property. Therefore, the underlying motto of the English system is: you are what you were born into, and that can never change.

The American system is based on the ideals of equality and freedom. Therefore, the underlying motto of the American system is: you can be anyone you want.

KEY POINT: English story is about inheritance within a hierarchical system whereby the individual must play out the role they were born into. American story is about the individual who has absolute freedom to re-create himself and be whomever he wishes to be.

The transcendent Gangster story explores the flaws of the principle of absolute freedom: it creates impossible expectations that justify doing anything to win and can end in despair.

The Great Gatsby

Gatsby and his cousin Nick are both trying to accomplish the great American project of remaking oneself. Nick says, "The truth was that Jay Gatsby of West Egg, Long Island, sprang from his platonic conception of himself. He was a son of God—a phrase which, if it means anything, means just that—and he must be about His Father's business, the service of a vast, vulgar, and meretricious beauty. So he invented just the sort of Jay Gatsby that a seventeen-year-old boy would be likely to invent, and to this conception he was faithful to the end."

The ultimate expression of a land of total opportunism is the gangster, for whom the goal is everything. Gatsby's business associate is Meyer Wolfsheim, rumored to be the gangster who fixed the 1919 World Series. When asked about this, Gatsby says, "He just saw the opportunity."

Mad Men

Mad Men is one of the great Easterns and Economic-Political Epics. Like Gatsby, hero Don Draper has reinvented himself with a stolen name and background. He is also in the business of reinvention. He is a master at selling the lie that you can be anything you want if you buy the right product.

TRANSCENDENT GANGSTER STORY BEAT: Character Web

In a transcendent Gangster story, the character web is typically large, complex, but highly organized and encapsulates the entire society. The plot often turns on how the social rules of the society operate.

The Great Gatsby is the embodiment of the American foundation principle that you can be anyone you want to be. The writer F. Scott Fitzgerald makes all of his characters variations on the contrast of fake versus real character. This is one of the techniques that allows him to tell the Great American Novel so succinctly.

Both Gatsby and Nick are desperately trying to remake

themselves. But Nick is solid, substantial, and moral. He says, "I am slow-thinking and full of interior rules—everyone suspects himself of at least one of the cardinal virtues, and this is mine. I am one of the few honest people that I have ever known."

The hollow, immoral, and illegal Gatsby has one saving grace: he's going after the ideal of true love. He believes Daisy is the perfect woman, the American Dream in romance. But she too is fake: she's selfish, careless, weak, and a coward. Therein lies the tragedy of Jay Gatsby.

Nick's girlfriend, Jordan, is a variation on Daisy and a foreshadowing of her actions. From the beginning, Nick wonders what Jordan is concealing. When she leaves a borrowed car out in the rain and lies about it, Nick remembers a newspaper story about how Jordan moved her ball from a bad lie in a golf tournament. After Jordan almost hits someone with her car, she says it's up to other people to keep out of her way.

Mad Men's designing principle is to track the slow liberation of its main characters over the decade of the 1960s. Creator Matthew Weiner connects his characters within a single ad agency. Each is enslaved to the American system they're selling. Its creed can be summed up as:

- Whatever sells wins.
- Men rule women at work and lie to them at home.

As a result, the character web is built on two major contrasts:

- Within the characters: dream versus reality.
- Men versus Women.

The first contrast is the dream the characters create for the good life versus the reality of how they live:

- In their job, they promote the idea that the good life is available to all.
- The reality is that their suburban lives are full of flaws, lies, and disappointment.

Mad Men highlights strict gender roles that are starting to break down. The men, in positions of power, drink, smoke, and fool around. The women, either housewives or secretaries, must put up with the abuse. Ironically, the female characters are the most interesting of the show. They start in the lowest positions and are only vaguely aware of what's not working. But we see them fight heroically to get free.

TRANSCENDENT GANGSTER STORY BEAT: Hero—Entrepreneur vs. Boss

The story of capitalism has two possible main characters: the entrepreneur and the company. In the Western, the cowboy and the farmer work together. But in the story of capitalism, entrepreneur and company are opponents.

The businessman is among the most negatively portrayed of all genre heroes. He is either the boring man of numbers or the vampire, like Scrooge, who sucks the lifeblood from his workers and customers. The businessman-as-vampire analogy is why this character is usually portrayed as the opponent, not the hero. He embodies the classic view that business favors the value of money versus family, decency, right action, caring, and love, even though that is not necessarily the case.

The company is personified in the boss, and in the extreme the "captain of industry." This character is usually portrayed even more negatively than the businessman, partly because of the anticompetitive actions of the "robber barons" like Cornelius Vanderbilt, Andrew Carnegie, John D. Rockefeller, J. P. Morgan, and Henry Ford.

KEY POINT: The richest individuals in the capitalist republic create the New Aristocracy, which is based on money, not title. It can be as powerful a totalitarian force in a republic as it is in a monarchy.

Although Daisy's husband, Tom, is the opponent not the hero in *The Great Gatsby*, he is a classic example of the New Aristocracy. He is "new money," but still older money than Gatsby's. Fittingly, he lives in a grand but conservative estate in East Egg. The nouveau riche Gatsby, from the Midwest, lives in a more garish estate in West Egg.

TECHNIQUE: Epic of the Everyman

Using the Gangster genre for stinging social commentary about the gap between American Dream and reality has happened in only a handful of stories. The basic Gangster story says that gangster business is just a small part of capitalism. It is found in small ethnic subpockets of just a few cities, practiced by lone individuals like Scarface and Little Caesar. That's why the main technique for taking the Gangster story to the next level is to do it as an epic of the everyman.

An epic is a story in which the actions of an individual or family determine or illustrate the fate of a nation. Historically, epics have involved kings and queens. So the idea of an American epic, a "king" in America, seems like a contradiction in terms.

The Sopranos is a television series built on the technique of the king of everyday. Here's the revolutionary premise: a ruthless mob boss comes into conflict with his mother, his wife, and his kids and sees a psychiatrist. Terence Winter, a writer for the show who later created the Gangster Epic *Boardwalk Empire*, said, "The mob genre is the bait and switch for this show."

The writer Diane Frolov said, "It's almost like writing

about kings and queens at court. You have your own government in the sense that's outside the government and its own laws. While you have the family thing, they're in this larger context."

The writers plot "kings and queens at court," while showing an everyday reality of a king frustrated by a wife and kids he can't control. "King" Tony Soprano can slap his son around but he can't keep him from screwing up.

KEY POINT: In the Eastern and Economic-Political Epic, the hero is in a position to affect the entire nation.

Arthur Miller, author of *Death of a Salesman*, called "sales" the ultimate American job. *Mad Men* uses a salesman to tell the epic of the everyman. Hero Don Draper is a Madison Avenue creative director, so he is selling far more than one product. He is selling the American Dream. His ads change America and, eventually, the world. This makes Don Draper the King of America.

TRANSCENDENT GANGSTER STORY BEAT: Weakness-Need

Story Beats:

- Each character has a unique weakness, but all characters share the same national weakness.
- The hero has some form of arrested development and is trapped in a false image of self that destroys him/her.
- If the hero is male, he emotionally remains a boy.
- If the hero is female, she typically tries to live up to the image of pretty object demanded by the rigid, patriarchal social system.

Doing business does not mean that either seller or buyer has a psychological or moral flaw. Quite the opposite. Each is fulfilling a basic human need to survive and thrive. In the process they create value.

KEY POINT: The transcendent Gangster story highlights the moment when need becomes greed.

Then business becomes a game of who can win the most money. This in turn fuels a never-ending desire for *more*. The result is the beast that feeds on money, and it never gets full. Greed becomes a moral flaw when it has negative effects on others.

The Great Gatsby: Gatsby is a con man and cheat, greedy for money and another man's wife. But what of Nick, the other main character in the novel? Fitzgerald uses the third-person storyteller whereby Nick describes Gatsby. So the basic structure of the story tracks how Gatsby changes Nick's life. This means that Nick is one of two heroes, and the only one who undergoes change.

Nick is an "observer hero," so he's passive. But that's inherent to the theme. He doesn't act until it's too late. He is Gatsby's enabler. Nick has come east to make his fortune in the bond market. Initially, he too is driven by greed. But unlike Gatsby, he hasn't resorted to cheating.

Weakness-Need 2: The Self as Buyer

The transcendent Gangster story (Gangster Epic, Eastern, and Business-Political Epic) also highlights the moment when one sees oneself primarily as a buyer.

In the chapter on Science Fiction, we talked about the connection between the evolution of society and the evolution of culture. We saw that as the society went from tribe to agriculture to industry to high tech, the culture went from shame to guilt to consumer. In an advanced economic system, this move to consumer culture is expressed in the buyer.

The buyer in consumer culture has two main weaknesses: a belief in the myth of pure individualism–absolute freedom and an insecurity of self.

The foundation of the most individualistic and capitalistic culture in the world, the United States, is the ideology of pure individualism. This culture connects extreme individuality with the childish notion that a person is absolutely free. Consumer culture defines creating the self primarily as accumulating things that make one appear successful. This produces a psychological weakness of love for the object and insecurity of the self.

Exactly how does this occur? For a business to sell the story of its product, it must create a Need for the product in the mind of the customer. Only then can it fulfill that Need in the form of its product. The product becomes the second major structure step in the story, which is what the buyer desires.

Business could sell based on fulfilling the true need people have for its product. But if it just relied on true need, its sales would be a minute percentage of its potential. Therefore, private enterprise, using advertising (the plan), intensifies the customer's weakness-need by creating self-doubt. "You are not good enough. You could be prettier. You could be smarter. You could be richer. You could be better. You could have, and be, so much more." In this equation being (identity) = having things.

The psychotherapist Philip Cushman calls this insecurity of self or self-hatred the "empty self." This inherent lack not only creates the desire to buy the product the first time, it creates a perpetual cycle of false need. The product temporarily solves the craving, but the craving quickly returns. Once hooked, buyers are remarkably monogamous. Now the business has a customer for life. This is ideal for a consumer culture and necessary for the optimal functioning of a techno-capitalist system.

KEY POINT: The product never fulfills the buyer's need, because it's not a need. It's a desire. It's a sensation that lasts for a moment and then is gone. Like a drug, the product must be purchased and taken again to experience the high.

Gatsby is the ultimate buyer. He is buying Daisy, but more exactly embodying the idea that he can be whoever he wants to be. The whole point of Gatsby is that he is a man without identity or substance. Everyone is "old sport" to him. All of the people who come to his parties, to get their booze and fun for free, are fake as well. They simply want to consume and gain status.

What about the character Gatsby is dead set on "buying"? Daisy is the American dream girl: pretty, airy, childlike, charming, and rich. But she is also completely hollow, and, unlike Gatsby, she has no saving grace. She does not love anyone.

When we first meet her, Nick says about her and her friend Jordan, "The two young women ballooned slowly to the floor . . . There was an excitement in [Daisy's] voice . . . a promise . . . that there were gay, exciting things hovering in the next hour." Later, Nick says, "She's got an indiscreet voice . . . It's full of—" Gatsby says, "Her voice is full of money."

Mad Men is a show about happiness. It takes direct aim at "Life, Liberty, and the pursuit of Happiness" promised in the Declaration of Independence. As an advertising genius, Don Draper knows the American Dream he is selling is fake. But he and the rest of the Mad Men are just as desperate to buy it.

DON: Advertising is based on one thing: happiness. You know what happiness is? Happiness is the smell of a new car. It's freedom from fear. It's a billboard on the side of the road that screams with reassurance that whatever you're doing, it's okay. You are okay.

All characters in *Mad Men* share this same internal flaw: they crave happiness through material things, so it leaves them disappointed. In season five, episode twelve, "Fees and Commissions," Don pitches Dow Chemical, the maker of napalm, at the height of the Vietnam War. He states what may be the tagline of the entire show:

> What is happiness? It's a moment before you need more happiness.

A second way the characters in *Mad Men* have the same weakness is that they all act like children. Don is a stunted boy who must have his women and booze and who treats his pretty wife, Betty, as a child. Betty's psychiatrist calls her a little girl. Pete is a nasty little boy who pouts when he doesn't get his way and insults anyone in a weaker position. Peggy is a naive little girl who dresses in Peter Pan collars and practically begs for approval. Roger is an aging boy who demands his pleasures, including his liquor and his mistress, Joan. The ad copy guys are frat boys, constantly insulting women's looks and trying to get them into bed.

TRANSCENDENT GANGSTER STORY BEAT: Desire—Money, Monopoly, and Total Wealth

Even in the most advanced capitalistic economy, the first desire is to make the sale. The famous salesman's motto is "ABC," which stands for "Always Be Closing." Accomplish the goal. Complete the story. The sale produces what the seller really wants: money. The seller's long-term goal is wealth.

Story Beat: the hero creates or joins some kind of business through which he is determined to win his fortune.

On the surface, Gatsby wants Daisy. But this is far more than a simple Love story. By placing it within the Eastern story structure of going after financial success in the city, Fitzgerald turns Daisy into the human expression of the American promise being corrupted by money and status. In the process, love itself is twisted and destroyed.

Gatsby's desire for Daisy and the monetary American Dream is symbolized by the green light on the dock of Daisy's mansion.

The writer Matthew Weiner's brilliant conception for *Mad Men* is to connect selling Americans' desire to the personal and work lives of the ad men themselves. The ad men want the image of the good life they're selling to be true, even if they intellectually make fun of the poor suckers who buy it.

Visual Shape of the Plot—Cycle of Rise and Fall, Boom and Bust

One of the oldest story processes, going back at least as far as *Oedipus Rex*, is the rise and fall of the king and the kingdom. We saw this story shape in the Western genre, which tracks the rise and fall of civilization. We see it in the Gangster form with the rise and fall of the king in a democracy.

In capitalism this takes the form of boom and bust. Rise and fall in other story forms is a onetime process. In capitalism, it is a cycle that never stops. Boom is simply the crescendo while bust is the decrescendo. In this, it is similar to the never-ending cycle of the social stages depicted in Thomas Cole's *The Course of Empire*.

Because value is always highly subjective and changeable, an economy can never eliminate boom and bust entirely, even with government safeguards to soften the fall and restart the rise. Why? Human psychology is the "value added" to actual supply and demand. The alternating emotions of greed and fear on a massive scale are what truly create the boom and bust.

The Big Short dramatizes the true story of three groups

of investors who, in 2007, realize the entire financial system of the United States is corrupt and ready to fall. Using extreme leveraging and false information about the health of the housing industry, banks and brokerage houses have created a bubble to extract massive profits. Various federal institutions are in on the scam.

The main characters spot the corruption and bet against the system, going "short." When the true value of housing becomes clear, the market crashes and the "heroes" make a fortune. But huge numbers of average investors and homeowners are wiped out. Meanwhile, the government bails out the banks. This film is a devastating critique of the modern "capitalist" republic.

TRANSCENDENT GANGSTER STORY BEAT: Opponent

Story moves through conflict. Transcendent Gangster stories that critique advanced capitalism highlight three major sets of opposition:

1. Seller versus buyer
2. Entrepreneur versus company
3. Owner versus worker

The interweaving of these three oppositions determines the story and how it critiques the system.

Seller vs. Buyer

No matter how complex the economy becomes, the first opposition in the capitalist story is always seller versus buyer. Because there are only two players in a simple transaction, each is aware of the opposition.

However, the relationship between seller and buyer cannot be one of conflict only. To complete the transaction, both must have some level of trust that what the other is exchanging has the value they promise it has. The economist Rachel Botsman calls this a "trust leap."

This means that seller and buyer are also allies. Notice this creates a basic contradiction in any transaction. The seller opposes the buyer but also wants the buyer to think they're friends. The more complex the system, the less aware the buyer is that the seller wants to defeat him.

Entrepreneur vs. Company

When the seller goes from entrepreneur to company, he gains major advantages over the buyer in the competition. The biggest is that the seller can afford a campaign to fool the buyer about his need for the product and the product's real value. This deception includes convincing the buyer that the seller is his friend.

A major plot beat in every season of *Mad Men* but the first one shows capitalism's inevitable move toward conglomeration: Don's smaller, more entrepreneurial ad agency competes with bigger corporations and must fend off their efforts to buy them.

Owner vs. Worker

Stories about advanced capitalism are most severe when it comes to the third opposition: owner versus worker. They argue that since money is always the highest value, the owner's prime motivation is to get the cheapest labor possible to do the job. The result is that some workers live in never-ending poverty, a form of enslavement.

KEY POINT: In the relationship between owner and worker, the owner has a strong incentive to keep the worker a wage slave. But it's the buyer seeking the lowest price who makes the slavery endure.

In *Glengarry Glen Ross*, the unseen owners of the real estate company place their agent employees in a trap that most cannot survive:

BLAKE: We're adding a little something to this month's sales contest. As you all know, first prize is a Cadillac Eldorado. Anyone wanna see second prize? Second prize is a set of steak knives. Third prize is you're fired.

TRANSCENDENT GANGSTER STORY BEAT: Plan—Telling a Story

In many ways, the art of capitalism is the art of selling.

The main way the seller convinces the buyer to purchase his product at a particular price is through advertising and marketing.

> **KEY POINT: An ad is a story form. Therefore, every good ad hits the seven structure steps of a good story.**

In *The Great Gatsby*, Gatsby's image as a business titan with massive wealth is a fake story, or a series of fake Rags to Riches stories he tells anyone who will listen.

Don is famous for the ads he pitches to win a company's business in *Mad Men*. In season one, he uses nostalgia and photographs of his own once-happy family to sell Kodak on their new home projector, which they have tentatively titled "The Wheel." The new name he comes up with, "Carousel," is a reference to happy family outings.

TRANSCENDENT GANGSTER STORY BEAT: Moral Argument—Prisoner's Dilemma

Moral argument is the case the author makes about how to live by sequencing the hero's actions and justifications. The basic Gangster story is unique in that the hero gives almost no verbal justification for what he does to get the goal. In the "Eastern" and Economic-Political Epic, the hero is largely morally blind to their own corruption. They justify their methods based on the greater good of making money for themselves or the company.

Story Beats:

- The hero commits progressively more immoral actions to gain money and success.
- The hero is absorbed by the corporation where he/she loses all sense of individuality.
- Either the hero fails to get rich or finds the cost of wealth is his/her soul.

Mad Men is rife with instances of what people working at the ad agency will do for money. For example, their largest account is Lucky Strike cigarettes, an addictive product they know has killed millions. Faced with a government requirement to put warnings on the label, Don suggests they deflect the buyer's attention by advertising that the cigarettes are "slow roasted."

In season five, episode eleven, "The Other Woman," all partners except Don arrange for Joan, a secretary and single mother, to prostitute herself so the agency can get the Jaguar account. As payment, she becomes a partner.

In the next episode, "Fees and Commissions," Don assures Dow Chemical, the maker of napalm, that a market share of "81 percent isn't enough!" He tells them if it was good enough to use against the Germans and Japanese in World War II, it's good enough to use in Vietnam. His final moral justification is: "When America needs it, Dow makes it, and it works."

Invisible Hand vs. Invisible Fist and the Prisoner's Dilemma

The capitalism that Adam Smith describes is primarily a moral code. It sets up an end—wealth—and describes an ideal means for getting it. So what is the moral argument of its story? And what is the moral argument of stories that oppose it?

Smith's main moral and economic claim in favor of unregulated capitalism is that it would reduce the inequity of a few masters holding most of the earth's resources. He argues that when an individual acts with rational self-interest, an "invisible hand" creates the greatest total value and freedom for the greatest number. This is a moral argument.

Transcendent Gangster stories make a number of moral arguments that attack unregulated capitalism and the invisible hand. Here are some alternative metaphors that encapsulate their arguments:

1. INVISIBLE FIST

KEY POINT: The first argument against unregulated capitalism is that the invisible hand is really an invisible fist.

Instead of providing an invisible helping hand from rich masters to the poor, pure capitalism gives the owner a fist with which to bludgeon his employee. The employee is a helpless wage slave.

Instead of distributing value downward to all, the few masters quickly and radically increase their advantages. This becomes a perpetuating cycle when the aristocrats of money begin the game with inherited resources and then pass them along to the next generation.

The effect of the upward cycle for the rich is the downward cycle for the poor. Dickens shows that when this discrepancy becomes extreme, the poor have no "safety net" with which to stop the fall.

KEY POINT: The effect of the invisible fist isn't just disastrous for the poor, it also lessens the total wealth for the entire society.

This undercuts Smith's main claim for pure capitalism, that it produces the greatest wealth for the greatest number.

2. INVISIBLE MOUTH

The second metaphor that storytellers use to attack unregulated capitalism is that it's an "invisible mouth." Based on the need to sell product to survive and thrive, capitalism is a machine that eats resources and leaves a massive amount of waste. This is a drain on the society's total wealth. But it is typically not counted in the final tabulation of benefits.

The most famous example of the "invisible mouth" metaphor is the valley of the ashes in *The Great Gatsby*. Behind the billboard of the optometrist T. J. Eckleburg's eyeglasses lies the waste of America's voracious capitalism represented literally by mounds of ash.

3. PRISONER'S DILEMMA

The "Prisoner's Dilemma" is the third major metaphor transcendent Gangster stories use to attack capitalism and the invisible hand. We see the Prisoner's Dilemma in dystopian fiction and Crime stories such as *Lord of the Flies*, *Nineteen Eighty-Four*, *The Hunger Games*, *Squid Game*, and *The Dark Knight*. Stories that use this metaphor to argue that unregulated capitalism is immoral and destructive include *Heart of Darkness*, *Pather Panchali*, *A Christmas Carol*, *How Green Was My Valley*, *Glengarry Glen Ross*, *Network*, and *Mad Men*.

You'll recall that in the Prisoner's Dilemma two people are arrested for allegedly committing a crime. The police place them in separate rooms and offer each the following choice: confess or stay silent. If one prisoner stays silent while the other confesses, the punishment is extreme for the silent prisoner.

How does this apply to the story of capitalism? Let's look at the oppositions playing out during the story that culminate in the battle, which in business is the transaction. Smith argues that each "player" has a discrete desire line. As each accomplishes his/her goal, somehow the entire community grows.

Where is the opposition in all this? Despite elements of trust, every transaction has a level of conflict. Each community is filled with a vast number of individuals whose desires are in conflict with opponents.

In the Prisoner's Dilemma story model, capitalism is the equivalent of the police while the individuals are the prisoners. Ironically, the authorities are the unregulated system. When there is no law to guarantee the well-being of the whole, every player, both individual and company, is enslaved to some degree.

KEY POINT: Individuals in competition are more likely to choose individual gain at the expense of the whole, especially when the benefit to the whole is vague.

The desire not to lose their transaction means that everyone is grabbing for limited resources at the same time. Each perceives they are in a zero-sum game even when they aren't. Plus, trying to beat the other contestant in the transaction means that all are induced to lie and cheat to get the best outcome.

The Prisoner's Dilemma model attacks Smith's best argument for the capitalist utopia: it produces greater *total* wealth.

KEY POINT: The flaw in capitalism's moral system causes the flaws in its economic system. Extreme individualism produces *less* wealth for all.

At the same time, the Prisoner's Dilemma argues that regulated capitalism, in which each individual must pay something for the common good, produces greater wealth for all. The moral argument for taking care of others—which costs the wealthy relatively little—is that it results in tremendous buying power for the poor. This in turn creates an upward cycle once they are above the critical mass needed to save and invest.

How Green Was My Valley

How Green Was My Valley is one of the greatest films ever made. It is the equal to *Seven Samurai* in dramatically showing how the system controls a few individuals. The story tracks a family whose father and sons work in a dangerous coal mine to make a meager wage.

The basic opposition is owners versus workers. Each side is caught in a Prisoner's Dilemma with a draconian choice based on self-interest. The owners are concerned about the survival of their company. This means selling the most coal and paying the lowest wage possible. When the price of coal plummets, the owners naturally choose to cut wages, even though the workers can't live on that pay. That risks the destruction of the company.

The workers have a no-win choice as well. The only way they can try to gain control over their economic lives is to use the power of the group and strike. But that means living in such severe poverty for so long they can't hold out. The result is widespread social conflict with the breakup of families and community.

The entire process pulls coal from the mines, which turns the valley from green to black (another valley of the ashes). There is no thought of a greater good as one company depletes the earth and everyone in the community suffers. Worst of all, the workers are dependent on the dangerous mine itself. When the mine inevitably collapses, the hero's beloved father dies. As great as these people are in heart, they have no chance against the economic system.

TRANSCENDENT GANGSTER STORY BEAT: Moral Argument—Business Corrupts the Republic and Harms the Truth

Transcendent Gangster stories make another major attack against capitalism: its subjugation of morality to money doesn't only affect the individual. Even more devastating is its subjugation of the republic.

These stories make two main points. First, because getting elected is expensive, the politician must turn to business, which is happy to pay to translate its moneyed interests into law that may be hurtful to the larger society.

Second, capitalism is harmful to the truth and thus to the republic itself. The politician hires high-tech advertising to sell the citizen buyer whatever "truth package" will work. This story form is propaganda. Propaganda techniques have always been central to the authoritarian handbook, from Machiavelli's *The Prince* to Nazi Germany, Joseph Stalin's Soviet Union, and Mao Tse-tung's China.

> **KEY POINT: The combination of business's ownership of government and high-tech advertising creating the "truth" is the greatest force pushing the republic toward totalitarianism.**

TRANSCENDENT GANGSTER STORY BEAT: Battle—Prison, Slow Death, and Murder

In business, the battle step is typically a nonbattle. The seller wants above all to avoid conflict, to keep from calling attention to the fact that the corporate seller and stockholders are the big winners in the transaction.

The transcendent Gangster story brings the real conflict to the surface. It states that in the larger war the New Aristocrats of money pit one ethnic group or class against another. The average worker/citizen is subject to a prison of poverty and slow death that they can't understand. Those who vocally fight back are sometimes murdered.

One argument against using story as a model for understanding the modern capitalist republic is that it must exaggerate and falsify for dramatic effect. To some degree this is valid. But the critique it makes against the system is not necessarily false. The vast majority of corporate executives do not order the death of their opponents. But history is rife with examples of dangerous working conditions, sweatshops, workers killed by strikebreakers, and people killed by pollution even when the corporation knew it was lethal.

The battle in *The Great Gatsby* is Gatsby's murder. It is the perfect example of class warfare waged by the rich. Daisy's husband, Tom, who is fabulously wealthy, has been having an affair with Myrtle, wife of George Wilson, the owner of a gas station. When Daisy runs over Myrtle while driving Gatsby's car, Gatsby heroically takes the blame. Tom tells George it was Gatsby's car that killed Myrtle. George kills Gatsby and Tom and Daisy go to Europe on vacation.

TRANSCENDENT GANGSTER STORY BEAT:

Self-Revelation—None

The theme of the transcendent Gangster story involves slavery to money, the loss of individuality, and the corruption of the American Dream. But the hero rarely sees it.

The transcendent Gangster story uses the same final story beat as the Black Comedy (the comedy of destructive systems). It says that the businessperson is largely incapable of a self-revelation, even when the system collapses. The ideology is too strong and the influx of short-term money is too great for the "smartest people in the room" to realize how blind they are to a better way.

These stories argue that the same lack of self-revelation applies to the way business corrupts the republic. Like the metaphor of the frog that gets used to water warming to a deadly boil, citizens in the modern republic may one day look around and find that their republic is gone.

Don's self-revelations are subtle in *Mad Men*, often with him taking one step forward and two steps back. In the middle of the final season, he realizes he can no longer take the money for the soulless work he does in the big corporation that bought his company. He runs off to the West Coast and spends time at the Esalen Institute looking within.

This is not the typical grand, but unbelievable, self-revelation in Hollywood storytelling where Don finally sees just how fake his life in New York advertising has been. While meditating, he comes up with the famous Coke ad "Hilltop," where a vast community of hippies sings: "I'd like to buy the world a Coke . . ."

With this moment of creative brilliance, Don marries his past to his new self and gives us the ultimate example of corporate consumer culture co-opting the community-based counterculture. This may be the best final moment in television history.

TRANSCENDENT GANGSTER STORY BEAT: New Equilibrium—Business Owns the Republic

The transcendent Gangster story has a negative end in which business owns the individual and the republic itself. The argument is that the drive for individual material gain overwhelms everything in its path. The fundamental trade-off between freedom and equality found in any social unit as it specializes will never disappear. Only when the Universal Mind begins to see making money as part of a larger moral code, with a different sense of responsibility for all human beings, will the entire system jump to a new level of effectiveness and morality.

As the ultimate transcendent Gangster/Black Comedy, *Network* ends with the business learning nothing and perpetuating its destruction. The network has Howard murdered because his message is killing the ratings. Here is the message the network doesn't want the people to hear:

HOWARD: At the bottom of all of our terrified souls, we know that democracy is a dying giant, a sick, sick, dying, decaying political concept, writhing in its final pain . . . It's the individual that's finished. It's the single, solitary human being that's finished . . . The whole world is becoming humanoid creatures that look human but aren't. The whole world, not just us. We're just the most advanced country, so we're getting there first.

The famous ending of the ultimate transcendent Gangster story, *The Great Gatsby*, depicts, in a tighter and more poetic form than any other work of fiction, how the republic has been corrupted by business. In a few words, Fitzgerald recaps the entire process of America and its promised dream: from first natural utopia to a fake utopia built on a tawdry craving for money and all it can buy, whatever the cost. These are cautionary last words for all who live in a republic and struggle to "keep it."

> As the moon rose higher the inessential houses began to melt away until gradually I became aware of the old island here that flowered once for Dutch sailors' eyes—a fresh, green breast of the new world—for a transitory enchanted moment man must have held his breath in the presence of this continent, compelled into an aesthetic contemplation he neither understood nor desired, face to face for the last time in history with something commensurate to his capacity for wonder.
>
> [Gatsby's] dream must have seemed so close that he could hardly fail to grasp it. He did not know that it was already behind him, somewhere back in that vast obscurity beyond the city, where the dark fields of the republic rolled on under the night.
>
> Gatsby believed in the green light, the orgiastic future that year by year recedes before us. It eluded us then, but that's no matter—tomorrow we will run fast, stretch out our arms farther . . . And one fine morning—
>
> So we beat on, boats against the current, borne back ceaselessly into the past.

The Next Rung Up the Ladder

The Gangster story warns us that chasing after wealth and power is the biggest danger to happiness in today's city world. It appears to be the way of success. But it turns us into machines and destroys the community that makes us human.

The next step up the genre ladder of enlightenment is the first step to happiness: Fantasy.

11

Fantasy: The Art of Living

Mary Poppins

Mary Poppins is a traveling "angel" who fixes a dysfunctional family by taking the children on trips to utopian worlds. Once she's turned the family's home into a mini utopia, she moves on to fix another family, with the promise that one day she will return. This is the power of utopia in daily life, if we can only learn how it's done. For that we look to Fantasy.

Fantasy: How It Works

The mind's ability to project symbols is embedded right in the genre's title: Fantasy. The self-conscious mind can create all sorts of alternate selves it would like to be.

> **KEY POINT: This power to project is partly about being someone *else*. But Fantasy is mainly about being someone *more*.**

The dream of becoming more is fundamentally different than the basic human desire to gain more. It represents a shift of the individual from quantity to quality as the measure of life.

In story structure terms, it signals a change from the surface-desire line of gaining something "else," to the deeper line from weakness-need to the self-revelation of becoming someone "better."

Why should Fantasy be the next rung up the ladder of enlightenment? We began with genres focused on the individual: Horror, Action, Myth, Memoir, and Coming-of-Age. The next genres—Science Fiction, Crime, and Comedy—are forms where the individual must find her place within the society. The Western and Gangster genres show the evolution of civilization. Gangster is a cautionary tale that warns the individual of the negative forces of the modern city world.

Fantasy returns our focus to the individual. Like Myth and Memoir, it is primarily about evolution of the self. The difference is, it shows us a true path to happiness. Its transcendent form, Social Fantasy, takes us even higher up the ladder. While Gangster suggests social corruption is inevitable, Social Fantasy shows how the city world can renew itself and the individuals living within it can grow.

Fantasy Mind-Action Story View

The Fantasy version of the Mind-Action story view shows that magic exists in even the most mundane worlds. Not magic in the fun sense of making things float. This larger sense of magic exists in the unexplored possibilities buried in each of us and in our world. Above all, Fantasy celebrates *imagi*nation, the primary tool for showing people how to live well.

Fantasy demonstrates this both positively and negatively. Positively, it shows a vision of the perfect life, or what appears to be the perfect life. Negatively, it shows a vision of life based on values taken to their worst extreme.

Thanks to the enormous contrasts of plot and world, Fantasy is the most "high-concept" of all stories. While it appears to be a "light" form, the genre's foundation is rigidly geometric.

KEY POINT: Great Fantasy depends on establishing the geometry right from the premise, so the story can build thematic complexity on a strong base.

All fantasy is allegorical. The fantastic stands for something else. Therefore, Fantasy always has two tracks: the fantasy track and the reality track it represents. The classic Fantasy story structure is a journey from mundane to fantastical and back to the mundane again.

KEY POINT: The Fantasy story strategy is: a repressed hero explores a heaven or hell.

This plays out in a precise story sequence:

A = the hero's weakness in the mundane world
B = the fantastical world that challenges the hero
A^2 = the hero and the mundane world changed

Fantasy is most popular when the larger society is homogenized. People are bored from living in a mundane world. Fantasy gives us the *idea for change* so that we can make it happen.

KEY POINT: Great Fantasy's version of evolution includes the individual, the society, and the spirit of the society made real.

Fantasy shows us how to find magic in our world and ourselves so we can turn life itself into a work of art. That's why the philosophical expression of the form is aesthetics. The transcendent version of the form, Social Fantasy, combines aesthetics and social philosophy. Of all the art forms expressed in the various genres, none is more uplifting than Fantasy.

Fantasy Compared to Other Genres

Fantasy is part of the speculative fiction family of genres that also consists of Horror and Science Fiction. In a way, Fantasy is the opposite of Horror. Horror shows negative evolution on a personal level, with everything shutting down. Fantasy shows personal and societal evolution, with everything opening up. Science Fiction expands Social Fantasy to universal evolution, exploring the possibility of a better human race.

STORY ELEMENT	SCIENCE FICTION	FANTASY
Primary technique	Dystopia	Utopia
Genre focus	The *structures* needed to create a better society.	The *values* that make it happen.

Writers often confuse Myth and Fantasy because these forms have a number of similarities. The biggest difference is in the overall story structure:

- In Myth the structure is built around a long journey.
- In classic Fantasy, the hero jumps to a new place, then jumps back.

Examples of Fantasy

Novels and Films

The Wizard of Oz (also Female Myth), *Alice in Wonderland*, *Peter Pan*, *The Wind in the Willows*, *Winnie the Pooh*, *Mary Poppins*, the *Harry Potter* and *Fantastic Beasts* stories, *The*

Lord of the Rings (also Myth), *The Chronicles of Narnia: The Lion, the Witch, and the Wardrobe*, *Big*, *Field of Dreams*, *E.T.*, *Back to the Future 1–3*, *Honey, I Shrunk the Kids*, *Tarzan* (also Action), *The Fisher King*, *The Dark Knight* (also Crime), *The Truman Show*, *Yellow Submarine*, *What Dreams May Come*, *Somewhere in Time* (also Love), *Pan's Labyrinth* (also Horror), *Edward Scissorhands* (also Horror), *Shadow and Bone* (also Myth), *Jonathan Strange & Mr Norrell*, *The Magicians*

Television

The Umbrella Academy (also Science Fiction), *Lucifer* (also Crime), *The Dresden Files* (also Detective), *Carnival Row* (also Crime), *Charmed*

Radio

A Prairie Home Companion

Fantasy Subgenres

Urban, Traveling Angel, Traveling Devil, Paradise on Earth Fantasy, Fantasy Political Epic, Romantic, Space Fantasy, Historical, Magical Realism, Sword and Sorcery, Dark, Alternate History

Fantasy Story Overview

Here's what we'll cover in this chapter:

- **FANTASY STORY BEATS**
- **THEME:** Being Is Struggling to Realize One's Potential
  - Thematic Recipe: Making One's Life a Work of Art
- **HOW TO TRANSCEND THE FANTASY STORY**
  - The Traveling Angel Fantasy
  - Paradise on Earth Fantasy
  - Fantasy Political Epic

Fantasy Story Beats

Like Science Fiction, Fantasy is a broad and loose genre, so it lacks the detailed map of story beats found in other forms. But it involves far more than magical spells or fantastical creatures. Fantasy beats are landmarks in the geometrical story structure of a character going from mundane to fantastical and back to mundane. The critical beats play out the strategy of a repressed hero exploring a heaven or hell.

The basic idea is to send the main character to a new world that will increase her mental possibilities. In the Fantasy form, that usually means getting a second chance and learning how to live life with style, freedom, and spontaneity. The result is that when the hero returns, the reader understands that they can reach that evolutionary step in real life.

FANTASY STORY BEAT: Story World

World-building in a Fantasy is massive, both in scope and value. It is the preeminent feature of the genre because the reader can immerse herself in the world and never leave.

KEY POINT: The success of any Fantasy depends mainly on the quality of the story world.

KEY POINT: The biggest mistake Fantasy writers make is failing to adequately define the rules of the story world.

How does the writer construct this allegorical world?

Step 1: Within a single physical arena, describe the overall combination of the three main elements of any world: land, people, and technology. This includes the natural settings, man-made spaces, society and culture, and important tools.

Step 2: Find a metaphor for the world. The purpose of this

unique story world is to help define the characters, sequence the plot, and express the theme. A single metaphor makes the world unique and embodies the allegory in one powerful image.

Alice in Wonderland is the greatest Fantasy ever written, albeit with fierce competition. The story world leads down the rabbit hole to the underworld. Notice how this is a very different expression of the underworld than other genres.

KEY POINT: Alice's underworld is not the land of death. It's the land where causation and process are upside down, where easy thinking goes to die.

Wonderland takes place entirely in Alice's mind. It's the story of a person living within a vast matrix of dangerous artifice. It signifies the mind as monster, the monster of illogic. But this illogic also has a deeper truth: this is where the fantasy comments on the real. For example:

- "It's no use going back to yesterday, because I was a different person then."
- "'Who in the world am I?' Ah, that's the great puzzle!"
- "Why, sometimes I've believed as many as six impossible things before breakfast."

The author, Lewis Carroll, was a professor who taught logic. That means he also taught nonsense.

KEY POINT: Nonsense is extremely valuable when it comes to the goal of Fantasy, which is happiness.

Step 3: Define the culture based on the values of the main characters. It is often helpful to use types of culture common to a particular combination of land and people, like shame culture in a wilderness/village world or guilt culture in a town/city.

In *It's a Wonderful Life*, Bedford Falls is a guilt culture based on the values of its leader, George Bailey. The primary values are love, decency, responsibility, and self-sacrifice. Pottersville, the alternative Bedford Falls, is a consumer and fear culture based on the values of its leader, Mr. Potter. The primary values are money, power, and competition.

Step 4: Give the world a system of rules. The Fantasy world operates by a different set of rules than the real world. As with Science Fiction, these rules define everything from transportation and communication to social hierarchy and magic.

KEY POINT: Expose the hero to the rules of the fantasy world as soon as she enters it.

When Dorothy's house lands in Munchkin Land in *The Wizard of Oz*, Glinda arrives as a glowing white ball. She explains to Dorothy that she is a good witch, that Dorothy has killed the Wicked Witch of the East and is now wearing her magic shoes.

KEY POINT: We don't know why the rules work in a fantasy world. *But they make sense within that world.*

Step 5: Define the technology and magic system. A common misconception of the Fantasy world is that it marks a return to nature and is therefore without advanced technology. But nature versus technology is a false distinction. Fantasy worlds have an array of naturalistic tools available to its characters.

KEY POINT: The primary technology in Fantasy is magic. It works through animism, which is the belief that all things are alive with soul or spirit.

Like Myth, Fantasy places great emphasis on the rules of magic by which the story world operates. Be sure to answer these six questions:

1. What are the magic powers?
2. Who has them?
3. What are the limits to the powers?
4. Can someone else get them and, if so, how?
5. Are any powers limited to a location?
6. Can the powers be terminated?

Caution: the more magic power a character has, the less vulnerable they are to defeat and the less useful they are to you in the story.

Step 6: Detail whether it's a free or enslaved world. As in Myth, story worlds in Fantasy tend to go to extremes of either dystopia-slavery or utopia-freedom. Both can be found in the same story, as we see in *Big*. The key technique is how you define the three pillars of any story world: the land, people, and technology.

Dystopia: When these three elements are out of balance, everyone is out for themselves. They compete like animals for scarce resources or serve as cogs in the larger social machine. In story terms, a world of slavery is an expression of the hero's or opponent's weaknesses and values.

The Wonderland of *Alice in Wonderland* is a chaotic world. The connections among characters are fractured. They're based on illogic that doesn't fit the hero's conformist thinking of how things should be. Over the course of the story, the world turns into a tyrannical monarchy where the Queen's insane flights of fancy may result in Alice's death at any moment.

Utopia: When the three elements are in balance and harmony, the result is a *community*. Within such a world, the individual grows. In story terms, a world of freedom is an expression of the highest values of the hero and her allies and the hero's self-revelation and greatest potential.

In *Harry Potter*, Hogwarts is one part King Arthur land and one part modern world. It teaches its young students the art of magic as well as life values such as love, friendship, and justice.

Because *Mary Poppins* is a Traveling Angel story, the self-revelation is given to the main opponent, the rule-bound and strict father. Having learned from Mary the values of fun, play, and living with style, he flies a kite with his kids in the park.

Step 7: Create the subworlds. Within the larger story world are various subworlds through which the hero must pass on her way to the goal. Each subworld is a rich landscape for the hero to explore. Each expresses its own unique set of values and serves as a set of plot beats on the path.

Among the famous subworlds of Oz are the Deadly Desert, Munchkin Land, the Yellow Brick Road, the Haunted Forest, and Emerald City.

The subworlds of *Harry Potter and the Sorcerer's Stone* include the Dursley home, Harry's room under the stairs, the Leaky Cauldron pub, Diagon Alley, Gringotts bank, Platform 9¾ at the train station, the Hogwarts Express, Hogwarts School of Witchcraft and Wizardry, the dining hall, the library, Hagrid's hut, the Forbidden Forest, the basement, and the infirmary.

Step 8: Create the double arena. The Fantasy story shows a contrast between the mundane and the fantastical. These subworlds differ by their unique value system and their level of personal evolution.

To create the double arena, define each subworld in comparison to the other. Here's the sequence:

First, define the mundane world. The mundane world in which the hero starts the story is a physical manifestation of her great weakness, stunted level of growth, and the enslaving society in which she lives. The weakness has locked the hero into a way of thinking and acting that is filled with mistakes. The society is built on a faulty set of values and exacerbates the hero's personal weakness and way of life. At the beginning of *Harry Potter and the Sorcerer's Stone*, Harry is a lonely orphan who has never known the love of his parents. He lives with his oppressive aunt and uncle, "Muggles" who value money and things and live in a cookie-cutter house.

Second, define the Fantasy world. The Fantasy world expresses the mundane world's negative values, but takes them to the extreme. Or it is a utopian world with a highly evolved set of values that contrasts with the hero's original values. Moving through this world drives the hero to a new level of personal evolution.

KEY POINT: The fantasy world should represent a dream or nightmare come true for the reader.

Most of the time, Fantasy works through the technique of utopia. The trick to creating this positive story world is that it only seems to be completely utopian.

KEY POINT: Even a positive fantasy world has a duality; it is utopian with a dark side.

This dark side is what challenges the hero's weakness so that she has matured when she returns home. In other words, the fantasy world is generally positive. But it has a catch that makes the character want to go back home to a reality far better than before.

TECHNIQUE: World vs. Weakness

To create the positive elements of the fantasy story world, make it the opposite in some way to the hero's great weakness. This is what forces the hero to grow.

There are many ways to get to "opposite." Therefore, instead of starting with the hero's weakness, some writers reverse engineer the process by beginning with their own idea of where they would love to visit. Examples include 1890s America, a jungle lair, a toy company, a major league baseball diamond in the backyard, a Hollywood movie studio where animated and real characters coexist, and a bizarre underground world where animals talk and have tea parties.

Third, define the changed real world. After visiting the fantasy world, the hero returns to the original mundane world to find it is different, based on the hero's changed perspective. The new world is the highest realization of the mundane world's potential. This has happened because the hero has learned the lessons from the fantasy world, including its values and best features. At the end of *Harry Potter and the Sorcerer's Stone*, Harry is going back to live with his oppressive Muggle family for the summer. But that's no longer the mundane world in which he started. He says, "I'm not going home. Not really." Hogwarts, with his friends as family, is his new home.

Urban Fantasy

Classic Fantasy is often called "Portal Fantasy" due to the hero jumping from mundane to fantastical and back. The subgenre of Urban Fantasy takes place in a city and does *not* use this strategy. Instead, it goes back and forth between mundane and fantastical areas of the city. In other words, fantastic things happen in a realistic story world.

This deprives the story of the overall back-and-forth movement that expresses the main themes of the Fantasy form. But it has the advantage of imbuing the city, where most of us now live, with fantastical elements brimming with possibilities.

Examples of Urban Fantasy include the *Fantastic Beasts*

stories, parts of the *Harry Potter* stories, *The Magicians*, *The Umbrella Academy*, *Lucifer*, *The Dresden Files*, and *Dark*.

Placing Fantasy within the city means that the genre usually combines with other story forms, especially Crime, Thriller, and Detective.

FANTASY STORY BEAT: Hero—Explorer

The hero begins buried within the mundane world. From that point on, she explores a fantastical world and thereby finds herself. All Fantasy story beats are based on the thematic idea of discovering what is valuable in life.

FANTASY STORY BEAT: Weakness-Need—Repressed and Blinded

Weakness-need is the first structure step of any story, and particularly important in Fantasy. It is what this genre is designed to solve. One of the tricks to great fantasy is that the hero's weakness is the opposite of the fantasy world. This way, the world tests the weakness.

> **KEY POINT: The act of going to a fantasy world must open the person to fantastic and fun possibilities, which is the form's recipe for living a good life.**

Therefore, the hero's psychological need usually involves one or more of the following:

- To break through convention and stereotype
- To overcome boredom
- To open the mind
- To see the possibilities in oneself and one's world
- To learn to have fun
- To learn to live well

Moral need is not always present in Fantasy, in part because the hero may be a child. When present, it is typically about learning generosity, love, and appreciation of one's family.

TECHNIQUE: The Slow Open

Before entering the fantasy world, spend time establishing the hero's weakness.

This is the setup for everything to come. Without it, there is no final payoff. For example, in *Alice in Wonderland*, young Alice has a strict sense of logic and manners. Her main psychological weakness is that she sees the world in rigid categories. This is especially true when applied to herself. So she's constantly being asked: Who are you? Her need is to be open to surreal logic so she can live a fun, exciting, and creative life.

FANTASY STORY BEAT: Desire—Explore an Imaginary World

Fantasy stories cover a wide variety of desire lines. Typically, the hero must eventually get back home. But in order for the fantasy to work structurally, the hero's immediate goal must be one that forces her to:

- Go to a fantasy world that makes her confront her weakness
- Explore a number of fantastical subworlds
- Fight fantasy characters

KEY POINT: The world holds the secrets to the hero's success and growth. She must discover how this world works so she can get back home and mature.

In the film *The Wizard of Oz*, Dorothy initially wants to go "somewhere over the rainbow." This takes her to Oz. However, almost as soon as she arrives, her true desire is to get home. This forces her to journey through a number of subworlds.

Caution: In Fantasy there is a fundamental clash between story world and desire. World-building can kill narrative drive.

KEY POINT: Killing narrative drive is the worst sin in popular storytelling, in every genre.

The clash between story world and desire creates a catch-22. Story world is 360 degrees. Narrative drive is going in a single direction at top speed. In other words, they're exact opposites. This gives you a big dilemma.

To solve this problem:

- Find a specific, urgent desire line to give the story a solid spine and intense narrative drive.
- Don't explain the whole world of your story at the beginning. This stops the action.
- Hang the story world on the hero's desire line and explore the world as the hero fights toward the goal.

Visual Shapes of the Fantasy Plot: Meander and Branching

The most common plot shapes used in the Fantasy form are meander and branching. A meander is a winding path without apparent direction. Structurally, this shape has one hero, an easygoing narrative line, and many opponents the hero meets in succession.

The classic Fantasy hero covers a great deal of territory but in a haphazard way. As in Myth, she also encounters a number of characters from different levels of society. But unlike Myth, plot in Fantasy comes primarily from encountering new subworlds.

Examples of meander stories include the *Harry Potter* stories, *Big*, *The Wizard of Oz*, *Field of Dreams*, *Back to the Future 1–3*, *Honey, I Shrunk the Kids*, *Zootopia*, *Toy Story 1–4*, *Yellow Submarine*, and *Edward Scissorhands*.

The branching story shape perfectly expresses transcendent Social Fantasy. As we saw with transcendent Science Fiction, each branch of the story represents a complete society in detail, or different stages of the same society the hero visits, like wilderness, village, city, or oppressive city.

Plot comes from a hero exploring worlds in a sequence or from comparing individuals within a society, pictured in order here.

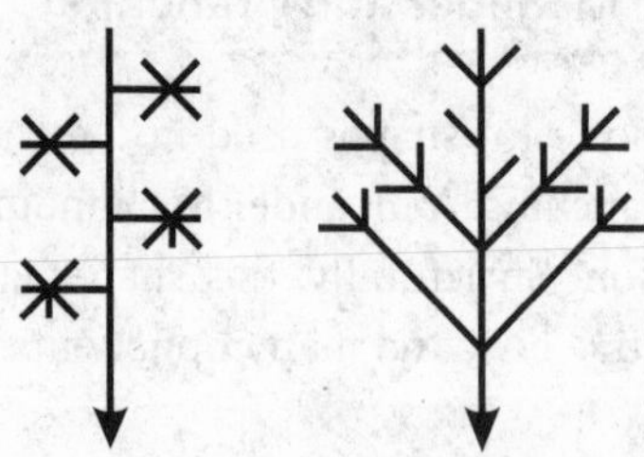

Most Social Fantasies use the first approach to tell the story. For example, the first figure is a visual expression of the plot in the Fantasy Political Epic *Gulliver's Travels*. The hero travels to four branches in succession, with each representing a different kind of society and political system.

Alice in Wonderland extends the branching underground to a world where logic is upside down.

It's a Wonderful Life compares two versions of the same town based on two different leaders and their values.

Other examples of branching include *A Christmas Carol*, *Pleasantville*, *A Connecticut Yankee in King Arthur's Court*, *Coco*, and *Midnight in Paris*.

FANTASY STORY BEAT: Character Web—Fantastic Characters

Minor characters can make or break the Fantasy. They provide wonderment and terror. But their real value is their connection to the hero. Just as the story world is animated to both test and support the hero, so are the minor characters. Objects are animated and sometimes made human, as are animals. The purpose is to turn every element of the fantastical world into an interconnected, palpable web.

> **KEY POINT: Give the minor characters unique talents, magical abilities, and/or special powers that highlight the strengths and weakness of the hero.**

Examples of special powers include the ability to fly, to read minds, to see the future, and to cast spells. Fantasy is a fun genre, so have fun with these characters. The success of the story depends on it.

Alice in Wonderland has one of the finest character webs in the history of the Fantasy genre. Among the objects and characters are the rabbit hole, the keyhole to the garden, the tears that become a flood, the flamingo croquet mallet and the hedgehog ball, the White Rabbit, the Caterpillar, the Cheshire Cat, the Mad Hatter, the March Hare, the Gryphon, the Mock Turtle, the Knave of Hearts, and the Queen of Hearts.

All minor characters in *Alice in Wonderland* are illogical creatures. They exemplify the fundamental way Wonderland attacks Alice's great weakness, her determination that all things must be in their rightful place.

The *Harry Potter* stories have fantastical objects and characters that are the match of any Fantasy ever written. Examples include the Sorting Hat, magic wands, flying broomsticks, the Sorcerer's Stone, Hedwig the owl, the Hippogriff, Fluffy the three-headed dog, the phoenix, werewolves, unicorns, Basilisk, dementors, centaurs, dragons, goblins, ghosts, and giants.

FANTASY STORY BEAT: Opponent—Authorities

Like many of the other characters in the web, the opposition often has fantastical skills. But their powers typically involve black magic.

TECHNIQUE: The Opponents' Powers

Over the course of the plot, make sure your hero forces the opponents to use their unique powers and skills. This increases conflict.

You can have a wide array of opponents in a Fantasy. The question is: Who is the best one for your story?

The main opponent in classic Fantasy is typically the authoritarian father figure who runs the system. The toxic male and/or tyrannical character forces the hero and all other characters to follow strict rules, to have limited desires and goals, to worship money and authority, and to give up their dreams. This is life by rote, a trudge through a daily prison on a strict schedule.

This character is the human embodiment of a frozen society. If the society and the hero are to grow, the opponent must have a self-revelation about loosening the rules so everyone can live their own life and make their own mistakes.

- ***MARY POPPINS***: Father
- ***E.T.***: military men and scientists
- ***THE TRUMAN SHOW***: the Director

When the authoritarian figure in Fantasy is a woman (and possibly mother), she has all the negative elements of the authoritarian father. But she also highlights the loss of the "feminine" values in the society, like caring, love, and community.

- ***THE WIZARD OF OZ***: the Wicked Witch of the West
- ***ALICE IN WONDERLAND***: the Queen of Hearts, who commands, "Off with their heads!"

This type of opponent is popular in Fairy Tales, which are a combination of Fantasy and Horror. For example, the evil witches in *Snow White*, *Cinderella*, and *Sleeping Beauty*.

In Social Fantasy, the main opponent is typically the authoritarian head of the society. The conflict between the hero's and the authoritarian's values is what expands the notion of growth from the hero to the society. Other opposition characters represent the failings of the society and the reason it is sick.

In *It's a Wonderful Life*, Mr. Potter will do anything to own and rule the town. The minor characters in Pottersville (the negative version of the town) are mean-spirited as a result of living in a town built on the love of money.

FANTASY STORY BEAT: Plan

In Fantasy, the plan involves figuring out how to adapt to this new world and defeat the opponent. The plan highlights the central question for the middle of any story: How do you build the plot? Here the solution depends first on whether the hero explores a positive or a negative world.

Positive world:

1. Many good things should happen to the hero.
2. Near the end of the story, introduce a negative trigger.

Since the positive fantasy world is clearly superior to the hero's original mundane world, there must be a believable reason that makes the hero want to return home (albeit in a new way).

The trigger must not be an external character or force that drives the hero's return. Rather, it should be something internal and personal that will result in long-term harm for her if she stays.

In *Big*, Josh undergoes a spiritual gauntlet when he returns to his neighborhood and sees the fun he will miss if he doesn't have a childhood. This triggers his realization that he needs to go back and be a kid if he is to have a good life as an adult.

Negative world:

1. The hero may use tools from the real world to fight the opposition.
2. Her experiences become increasingly nightmarish.
3. She is toughened but also enlightened by the experience.

In *It's a Wonderful Life*, after almost dying by suicide, George enters Pottersville, the town Bedford Falls would have become if George had never been born. This is Clarence's plan to show George how awful the town would be if he had never lived.

FANTASY STORY BEAT: Passageways Between Worlds

In classic Fantasy, the hero jumps to a new place, then jumps back.

> **KEY POINT: Classic Fantasy always uses a passageway to move between worlds.**

Moving through a passageway often takes only a moment. But it is one of the most popular techniques in all of story. Why?

- *The passageway is a special subworld.* Like the Myth underworld, the passageway should be filled with characters and objects that are strange and surreal and yet perfect for the story. Only by seeing the story again will the audience realize how appropriate and possibly foretelling these characters are. In effect, they are stitches in the story tapestry.
- *The passageway allows the viewer to make the transition from the realistic to the fantastic.* Physically getting the hero to the new world is not the main problem at this point in the story. It's changing the viewers' minds. It's getting them to flip their mental filter from realistic—"people don't float"—to fabulous—"isn't it great that people can float here?" Without that flip, the viewer can't enjoy the story and will not be open to the larger Fantasy theme: to look for the hidden possibilities in life.

TECHNIQUE: Enjoy the Passageway

Since the passageway is a unique subworld, spend some time there. Let the reader enjoy being with the characters. Because it's so important to get the story moving, this is not always possible. But when it happens, it's gold.

Examples: the rabbit hole in *Alice in Wonderland* and the mirror in *Through the Looking-Glass and What Alice Found There*; the cyclone in *The Wizard of Oz*; the wardrobe closet in *The Chronicles of Narnia: The Lion, the Witch, and the Wardrobe*.

FANTASY STORY BEAT: Drive—Journey Through Subworlds

In the middle of the story, the hero explores a number of subworlds where she must fight fantastical opponents for the goal. Since all fantasy is allegorical, these worlds comment on reality.

> **KEY POINT: The hero should encounter as much of the fantasy world as possible.**

In *A Christmas Carol*, ghosts take Ebenezer Scrooge to three worlds from his life story: Christmas Past, Present, and Future. In each he sees how his actions hurt others.

Mary Poppins uses magic to take her young charges, Jane and Michael, through Bert's street paintings into a beautiful country setting. There they go on a carousel ride, sing and dance with animals, and compete in a race riding the carousel horses. At Uncle Albert's house, they all enjoy a tea party while floating on the ceiling. Then the children go on a disastrous trip to their father's bank. Back home, Mary takes them up the chimney to the rooftops, where they dance with the chimney sweeps in a wonderful "world of enchantment."

TECHNIQUE: The Fantasy Reveal

Revelations are one of the keys to plot. They come from the exposure of hidden information, usually about the opponent.

KEY POINT: In Fantasy, the best reveals come from discovering the secrets of how the fantasy world works, or how the opponent controls the world.

In the first of the seven *Harry Potter* books, Harry learns that the Sorcerer's Stone produces the Elixir of Life that makes the drinker immortal. This is what Voldemort desperately seeks. Harry uses the invisibility cloak to watch Snape threaten Professor Quirrell. This is a red herring that makes him believe Snape is his opponent instead of his ally. In later books, the main reveals center on Voldemort's use of horcruxes, which he needs to gain immortality and absolute power. Destroying these horcruxes is the only way to defeat him.

In *Field of Dreams*, Ray hears a voice telling him, "If you build it, he will come." Everything in the story turns on who this "he" refers to. Ray builds a baseball diamond in his cornfield and thinks "he" is Shoeless Joe Jackson, who, along with other members of the infamous Chicago Black Sox of 1919, shows up to play. Then Ray thinks "he" means the baseball writer Terence Mann. Finally, Shoeless Joe shows Ray that "he" refers to the catcher, his late father, from whom he has been estranged. Ray and his dad play catch and make up for years of lost time.

FANTASY STORY BEAT: The Super Magical Moment

Fantasies that involve utopia often have magical moments. All things connect and work together in this moment.

KEY POINT: A Fantasy must have one super magical moment. If you can create more than one, even better.

The way to create the super magical moment is to ask yourself: What is the perfect expression, in action, of this particular world when all is right?

- ***MARY POPPINS***: the tea party on the ceiling and the rooftop dance of the chimney sweeps.
- ***BIG***: dancing on the piano with his boss and jumping on the trampoline with his soon-to-be girlfriend, Susan. (This moment also expresses the essence of Fantasy/Love. As she goes from fear to joyous jumping, she is opening up to possibilities of fun, freedom, and romance in her world.)
- ***FIELD OF DREAMS***: playing ball with Shoeless Joe Jackson and the guys on his personal baseball diamond.

FANTASY STORY BEAT: Battle—the Final Test

The big battle in a Fantasy may be an actual physical battle that determines if the hero wins the goal. It can also be a final test the hero must pass, which is an element from the Myth form.

In *Alice in Wonderland*, Alice fights with the Queen and her guards.

In *The Wizard of Oz*, Dorothy fights the Wicked Witch of the West.

And in *Mary Poppins*, Father stands up to the bank president.

FANTASY STORY BEAT: Self-Revelation—Free and Fun

In the Fantasy self-revelation, the hero sees what it means to live with a free spirit every day and learns to value home in a new way.

> **KEY POINT: Make sure the fantastical world solves the weakness of the hero. That way, when she returns, she's solved her personal problem and the mundane world is now a playground.**

In the self-revelation the hero may overcome one or more of the weaknesses we discussed earlier: break through convention and stereotype, overcome boredom, open the mind, see the possibilities in oneself and one's world, and learn to have fun and live well.

Dorothy in *The Wizard of Oz* wakes up back home surrounded by her aunt, uncle, three farmhands, and the traveling salesman. She happily proclaims, "There's no place like home."

In *A Christmas Carol*, Scrooge is overjoyed to discover that it's still Christmas Day. He sends a boy to buy a turkey for Bob Cratchit and then joins the celebration with his nephew's family.

Theme: Being Is Struggling to Realize One's Potential

Fantasy has the most positive view of being and becoming of any genre. It says that living equals being creative. As the symbol-making animal, we can't help being creative. The difficulty is focusing that creativity on ourselves.

To be creative about one's own life is the ultimate expression of the self-conscious animal. Fantasy says: "I am the character I create of myself. I do this every minute of every day."

Fantasy Thematic Recipe: Making One's Life a Work of Art

In each of the genres, we have seen how the thematic recipe comes from both the hero's basic action and the key question raised. In Fantasy the basic action is to explore an imaginary world. This includes being willing to experience the new. The hero enters a world of wonder in order to understand how to keep wonder in her life.

The key question is: How do you live with style, spontaneity, and freedom? At first glance, this question seems unconnected to the hero's basic action of exploring an imaginary world. To overcome her inflexibility, she must journey through an external world richer and more wondrous than her own. Finding out how the wonderful is possible, she sees that freeing herself to live with joy is the way to have a successful life.

If Fantasy's recipe could be reduced to a single line, it would be: live with childish wonder and playfulness at any age. Two of the greatest films of the form, *Big* and *Field of Dreams*, show the hero taking on this seemingly impossible challenge. In the process of growing up, we put away childish things and silly, magical thoughts so we can take on the responsibility of money, job, and family. But the cost is enormous. If we can somehow maintain that childish wonder and fascination with what is and what might be, while still meeting the goals of everyday life, we will have a happy life.

Becoming in Fantasy means learning the tools for making life itself a work of art. This may mean that the individual expresses herself through art. But more important, it is an attitude of being creative in everything one does.

This is what the dream of being "more" is all about. The tool of consciousness essential for this task is imagination. Through imagination we can see the potential in all things and in ourselves. Life becomes art.

The Naturalistic Ideal: Living Artistically

The Fantasy genre brings up the underlying theme of this book: humankind is the symbol-creating animal. As such, the highest form of this capacity is to see the world as a story. The major story forms are how the human mind organizes the world and learns to live. I call this the *New Poetics*.

What does a New Poetics mean and why is the thematic recipe of the Fantasy form so important to it? In a naturalistic world, Humanism becomes the ideal. Humanism devoid of a god means creating culture-as-such, in which culture is the refinement of humankind's highest capacities.

KEY POINT: Humanism at its best is living artistically, with creativity and story being an approach to every action.

How to Transcend the Fantasy Story

Transcendent Fantasy, known as Social Fantasy, shifts the focus from the individual to the society. This is the story form that combines aesthetics and social philosophy. It works by creating utopias, apparent utopias, or even dystopias. The strategy is to dramatize a thought experiment of how government and society could work in a way that would maximize personal happiness.

If Fantasy shows us to how to make life itself a work of art, Social Fantasy shows us models of how society can help make that happen.

Social Fantasy takes three major forms:

1. Traveling Angel Fantasy: Focuses on an angel who fixes the community. The social scale of this form is smaller than the others, yet quite effective.
2. Paradise on Earth Fantasy: Deals primarily in utopias and emphasizes the ideas and culture necessary to create a heavenly society on earth.
3. Fantasy Political Epic: Combines Fantasy and the political story (see the Gangster chapter). It contrasts utopias and dystopias, sometimes uses fake utopias, and highlights the social and governing structures of the story world.

Transcending Fantasy 1: Traveling Angel Fantasy

The Traveling Angel Fantasy is the genre of the deus ex machina savior. Normally, we think of deus ex machina as a failure of storytelling because the hero does not solve her own problem. She relies on a god descending from the heavens in a carriage to fix everything with the wave of a hand, a thunderbolt, or a wand.

However, the Traveling Angel Fantasy takes the flaw of the deus ex machina technique and turns it into a powerful story structure. Thematically, it provides a recipe for how a community can improve itself with the right teacher. Although the "angel" appears as a savior, she does not act like one. She doesn't do all the work herself, which would relieve individuals from any responsibility for their own lives. She is a master at spotting the causes of the problem, whether for an individual or for the community at large. She leads the individuals in the right direction, but lets them figure out the solution for themselves.

This is a complex feat. That's why the genre is a far more challenging form than it seems. For one thing, it divides the seven steps of the story between the traveling angel hero and the characters with the problems (see the summary table of the seven steps in the Appendix). The other characters have the weakness-need and the self-revelation. The angel has the desire, which is to help the people in trouble, and the plan for how to do so. In effect, the angel acts as a super-ally to the people in trouble.

Because the angel has the complicated task of educating and guiding an entire community without fixing the problem herself, she is the author's version of a perfect person. She embodies in a single human being the way a successful community would act.

In the best Traveling Angel stories, the angel also has a

weakness-need. This is usually a psychological flaw but it may also be moral. Giving the "perfect" person a flaw adds emotional intensity to the story because the audience sees that the angel is a real human being. She too must fix something to have her best life. Clarence, the angel who must help George in order to win his wings in *It's a Wonderful Life*, is a lighthearted version of the flawed angel.

The Traveling Angel form is found in Detective stories, Comedies, Love stories, and Westerns. When done as a Fantasy, the story adds magic. Often the hero is a real angel, with supernatural powers that include being able to move objects, float, and jump through space and even time. Adding the power of magic increases the audience's sense of the interconnectedness and harmony of all things through a living spirit. It also highlights the tremendous potential hidden in both the world and ourselves.

Examples of the Traveling Angel Fantasy include *Mary Poppins*, *Miracle in Milan*, *The Bishop's Wife*, and elements of *It's a Wonderful Life*.

My Bildungsroman Reveal: Life Can Be Incredibly Fun

My mother took all three kids to see *Mary Poppins* one Saturday afternoon in the fall of 1964. From the moment Mary floats down from the clouds, I was hooked. I vaguely recall having a crush on the pretty Englishwoman with her crisp British enunciation. She proved you could have fun as long as you were organized and did your chores. She was "practically perfect in every way." She was also a pretty good singer.

Two things made *Mary Poppins* a landmark in my life. First, the beautifully realized fantasy world made me believe that life could be fun every day. Second, I sensed that the immense synthetic power of film—the combination of writing, acting, cinematography, and most of all the amazing musical score—could change my life. It made me think: that's where I want to live. And I believed I could.

Transcending Fantasy 2: Paradise on Earth Fantasy

The Paradise on Earth strategy gives the audience a detailed model of how a happy society could work. It's a living, breathing machine where each of the individual parts works well together.

Examples include *Winter's Tale*, *Pleasantville*, *Coco*, *Zootopia*, *The Night Circus* (also Love), *Midnight in Paris*, and *Toy Story 1–4*.

Paradise on Earth Fantasies sometimes base their stories on other utopian art forms like the circus and the garden. When the individual enters the big top, she is transported to another world. The circus is a society in miniature, but it features the unique, the awe-inspiring, and the fantastical ability of the performers to "fly." The show is a grand spectacle that may include animals from all over the world. Best of all, the audience sees humans becoming "gods" by performing amazing feats of bravery and physical ability. Then, like the traveling angel, this community of nomads moves to another town to work its magic.

A negative variation of the Paradise on Earth strategy is the paradise lost story. In this subform, the writer creates a paradise, then shows how humans inevitably destroy it and themselves through their flaws. The most famous example of this story is Adam and Eve in Genesis of the Old Testament. Other versions of the paradise lost form are the "Machine in the Garden" and the anti-Western.

Pleasantville is both a Paradise on Earth Social Fantasy and a Rejuvenation Myth. The Rejuvenation Myth counters the downward cycle of social stages in storytelling, where we go from wilderness to village to city to oppressive city and back to wilderness. It shows how the oppressive city can be reborn as a community.

KEY POINT: The success of *Pleasantville* comes from a story structure that moves from apparent to real utopia.

Like *American Beauty*, we start off showing the slavery of the bland suburban subworld, as all houses look the same. David, the hero, is enslaved in the system, but doesn't know it. This is expressed in human terms through his bad home life. As he mouths the lines of his favorite TV sitcom, *Pleasantville*, he overhears his divorced parents arguing on the phone.

The dystopia of the hero's broken family is set in opposition to the perfect nuclear family and apparent utopia he sees on TV. Since *Pleasantville* is primarily a Fantasy, David and his twin sister, Jennifer, travel through the passageway of the television using the magical remote control provided by the TV repairman. In a nice touch, the repairman is played by Don Knotts, the brilliant comic actor who played Barney Fife in the utopian small town of Mayberry on *The Andy Griffith Show*.

As David and Jennifer, now Bud and Mary Sue, enter the sitcom world of Pleasantville, we learn the rules by which this apparent utopia operates. It seems to be a pastoral, suburban village where everything works perfectly. The breakfast table is overflowing with a bounty of food. These parents are cheerful and loving.

But beneath this apparent utopia is a dystopia, literally a black-and-white world with rigid rules of conformity where men rule and women serve. The main opponent is the authoritarian Mayor, determined to enforce the rules.

The trigger that begins the process of changing the town from slavery to freedom is when Mary Sue introduces her date Skip to sex. In his after-sex glow, Skip sees color for the first time in the form of a red rose. This has a butterfly effect, prompting more change at a progressively greater speed. This is the same effect that allows George Bailey to change so many lives in *It's a Wonderful Life*.

We see this in miniature when Bud goes on a drive with Margaret. As they enter a utopian subworld of forest and garden, the world changes from black and white to glorious color.

Next, Bud becomes a leader in turning the apparent utopia into a real one. He has a revelation about transforming the town into a place of true freedom and harmony. The vehicle is the wall he and Mr. Johnson paint. It is a mirror of who they can be if they simply wake up to the possibilities.

In the battle in court, Bud defeats the authoritarian Mayor by showing him his own emotions. What is the takeaway for creating a utopian word? Feelings are messy—but they are what make life worth living. The Mayor runs away and the people discover that the town is now in total color. This Social Fantasy ends with a utopia for all.

Transcending Fantasy 3: Fantasy Political Epic

A combination of Fantasy and the political story, the Fantasy Political Epic is the darkest form of Social Fantasy. It emphasizes three advanced story elements: system, causation, and process. Its story strategy is to contrast utopias and dystopias, expose fake utopias, and compare societal structures and forms of government.

Examples include *Gulliver's Travels*, *A Christmas Carol* (also Horror), *Alice in Wonderland*, *A Connecticut Yankee in King Arthur's Court*, *One Hundred Years of Solitude*, *The Lord of the Rings* (also Myth), *It's a Wonderful Life*, *The House of the Spirits*, *Arcadia*, *Midnight's Children*, and *A Song of Ice and Fire/Game of Thrones* (also Action Epic).

It's a Wonderful Life is the greatest Fantasy Political Epic in film history. Previously, we examined this film as one of the best Business-Political Epics due to its attack on pure capitalism. Now let's look at it from a different angle.

The film is usually touted as director Frank Capra's masterpiece. But the story structure is what makes it work. The writers are Frances Goodrich, Albert Hackett, and Capra, based on the brilliant premise and short story by Philip Van Doren.

Like *Pleasantville*, it uses Fantasy to compare a real-life utopia and dystopia. Once more, small-town America is the laboratory for a thought experiment of how a real utopia might actually work.

KEY POINT: The structural technique that makes *It's a Wonderful Life* the premier Fantasy Political Epic is how it expresses utopia and dystopia in *the same town*.

It's a Wonderful Life demonstrates the essence of social freedom through the butterfly effect. The writers set this up by changing the original causation point of the story, which is what the world would be like if George had never been born. The traveling angel Clarence creates an alternative present where Bedford Falls has been transformed into Pottersville.

This thought experiment of an alternative present relies on two major contrasts. First is the contrast between the town leaders: George and Potter. George Bailey is an altruistic capitalist. He believes he has a responsibility to look out for his fellow human being even as he makes a profit. The negative result of this value system is that he has fallen hopelessly behind in financial success.

George's opponent is pure capitalist Henry Potter. He believes that people are worth no more than the money he can make from them.

The second major contrast is in the town itself. At first,

this appears in the visual contrast of Pottersville and Bedford Falls. For example, Main Street in Pottersville is all bars and nightclubs with flashing neon lights.

But the key contrast of the town comes in the detailing of the character web, especially the minor characters in the two versions of the town.

KEY POINT: The main way the writers show utopia and dystopia is by comparing who each minor character becomes under different leaders and value systems.

For example:

- **ERNIE:** the jovial cabdriver with his own home and family versus a bitter man whose wife left him.
- **VIOLET:** a fun-loving, kind woman versus the town prostitute.
- **MR. GOWER:** the town pharmacist versus a homeless drunk who spent twenty years in jail.
- **BROTHER HARRY:** a war hero who saved a troop transport and won the Medal of Honor versus the boy who died and therefore wasn't there to save hundreds of men.
- **GEORGE'S MOM:** loving and friendly versus mean and suspicious.
- **GEORGE'S WIFE, MARY:** loving wife and mother versus timid spinster.

KEY POINT: None of these minor characters is absolutely free or successful living in Bedford Falls. But within their unique capabilities and social position, they are their best and freest selves.

When George comes back after experiencing the horrors of Pottersville, he is ecstatic to see Bedford Falls again. But how can we say that Bedford Falls is a utopia if he previously hated living there so much he wanted to commit suicide?

This is one of the most profound elements of the film. It expresses what a real community of freedom is. A real utopia isn't everyone deliriously happy every minute of the day. Nor is it a positive state of mind. George may become depressed again six months after the film ends.

Real freedom is a social structure that puts its people in the best position to win the game of their lives. During their life path, they will occasionally feel limited by their neighbors and saddened by whatever success they have not achieved. But any society where people help each other be their best is a pretty wonderful life and may be the best world we can get.

Game of Thrones

A Song of Ice and Fire, by George R. R. Martin, and the television show *Game of Thrones*, whose name comes from the first book of the novel series, comprise one of the best Fantasy Political Epics ever written. For simplicity, we will refer to both versions as *Game of Thrones*.

In most epics, a single individual or family determines the fate of the nation. In this case, four major families determine the fate of seven kingdoms. Co-showrunner David Benioff described the premise as "*The Sopranos* in Middle Earth." This contest where many combatants try to become king is a world war between gangsters in the Middle Ages.

The original story seems to have been influenced by both video/online games and board games like *Risk*. It is also based on European history from approximately 1300 to 1500, especially the War of the Roses in England. Unlike such classic Fantasy Political Epics as *Gulliver's Travels* and *A Connecticut Yankee in King Arthur's Court*, *Game of Thrones* does not compare types of government. All seven kingdoms in this world are monarchies.

However, *Game of Thrones* does deal in political contrasts. It uses the Fantasy Political Epic to compare different approaches to leadership, governing, and war. Like *The Godfather* and *It's a Wonderful Life*, the story structure highlights the contrasts.

The Godfather uses the fairy-tale structure of three brothers to show the best strategy for leading a family in a crime war. *Game of Thrones* uses a tournament structure to determine the best strategy for leading a nation in a world war. *It's a Wonderful Life* gives us an alternative version of the same town. *Game of Thrones* gives us an alternative version of Medieval Europe.

This story uses a massive "branching-in" structure:

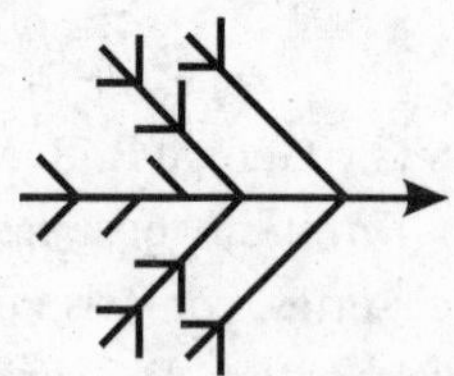

It funnels down to four types of leadership before indicating which is the most effective. The most important leadership skill is managing the trade-off between strategy and morality. For the vast majority of the tale, the lone principle of success seems to be: whoever acts morally dies. The story is all about the strategy of winning the game of thrones. Ironically, a story in which whoever acts morally dies ends up showing that moral leadership is the most effective way to govern.

These are the three major techniques *Game of Thrones* uses to achieve its magnificent grand tapestry:

1. A tournament story structure
2. All contestants compete for the same goal
3. Story fractals with multiple four-point oppositions

TECHNIQUE 1: The Tournament Structure

The main story challenge of such a huge epic is that lots of crosscutting halts the narrative drive. The tournament structure gives the massive story tapestry a funnel to a specific vortex point. Every individual strand is clearly part of the larger goal of winning the throne. This increases narrative drive over the episode, the season, and the series.

KEY POINT: The closer we get to the vortex point of the story, the fewer the strands and the faster the narrative drive.

This tournament structure also determines the most shocking feature of the show: death of major characters. Before *Game of Thrones*, killing off a major character would kill the show. Here it's not only necessary, it makes for a better story.

TECHNIQUE 2: Same Goal and Vortex

Game of Thrones is the ultimate example of all characters competing for the same goal. That goal is found right in the title: the throne.

KEY POINT: The throne represents power. This allows for a variety of action as each character uses a different leadership approach to gaining power.

TECHNIQUE 3: Story Fractals with Multiple Four-Point Oppositions

In Science Fiction, we talked about social fractals whereby the same pattern exists at every level of the society. This is one of the most valuable techniques for creating both a vast and detailed society.

Game of Thrones has the most extensive use of social fractals in story. How does it use multiple four-point oppositions to create the character web? Within the seven kingdoms of Westeros, four main families compete for the throne. Each family is built on a four-point opposition. Each four-point opposition branches out to their allies and other opponents. The result: a massive number of characters the reader can understand, all moving toward the final goal.

The four main families comprise the foundation four-point opposition on which the entire novel and TV series is based:

Stark	**Lannister**
Baratheon	**Targaryen**

The first family in the series is Stark, led by Ned. This is actually a six-point opposition:

Ned and Catelyn	**Robb**
Sansa	**Jon Snow, the illegitimate son**
Arya	**Bran and Rickon**

As the story progresses, the family makes a number of strategic blunders. So it moves to a four-point opposition with Sansa, Jon Snow, Arya, and, to a much lesser extent, Bran.

The Lannisters begin as a five-point opposition that moves to three:

Cersei	**Tyrion**
Jamie	**Tywin**
Joffrey and Tommen	

The Targaryen four-point opposition is:

Viserys Targaryen	**Daenerys Targaryen**
Khal Drogo	**Ser Jorah Marmont**

Baratheons, which is a three-point opposition:

Stannis Baratheon	**Melisandre**
Ser Davos	

The game of thrones funnels down to these final four contestants:

Cersei	**Daenerys**
Sansa	**Jon Snow**

With three of the four semifinalists being women, we are struck by the irony that the most male-dominated show in history turns out to be a feminist war story. That said, the show originally presented most women as sexual beings writhing in the background of men in conversation, which coined the term "sexposition."

The leadership differences among the contestants come into sharpest contrast in the semifinals. Cersei has always been a tyrant. Daenerys, a popular leader of the common people, seems to have the best chance of beating the men and winning the game. But she becomes despotic and cruel and therefore fails.

Since Daenerys was so clearly the front-runner, I thought the television writers would flip expectations and make Sansa the winner. She comes the farthest and has the best combination of leadership skills of all the contestants. She begins the show as a child bride dominated by her husband King Joffrey and his mother, Queen Cersei. Then she suffers sadistic abuse at the hands of her second husband, Ramsay Bolton.

Sansa shows her leadership ability when she gets the various lords in the north to join her as allies in the fight against Bolton. Before the Battle of the Bastards, she warns Jon Snow that Bolton will not let their brother Rickon live. But Jon falls for Ramsay's trick and almost loses the battle.

In the shocking ending of *Game of Thrones*, none of the four semifinalists wins the game. This is a story disaster, one of the worst endings of a show in television history. One can surmise that the original author, George Martin, would never have made this mistake. But he hadn't completed the novel series when the showrunners wrote the final season.

This disaster also highlights the main problem with the tournament structure: if everything funnels down to a final winner in the game of thrones, it better be a great winner. The writer is betting everything that the final payoff is going to be worth years of investment by the viewer.

The winner should exemplify the show's theme: What does it mean to master strategy and lead a nation? Instead, the showrunners chose a character who didn't even play the game, much less earn the prize. Choosing Bran was like picking the killer in a whodunit based on the one person who was incapable of committing the crime.

The Next Rung Up the Ladder

The philosophy of Fantasy pushes us to open our minds to see all we can become, as well as the positive world we can create. But it doesn't say much about how the mind works best. For that, we must look to the Detective story.

12

Detective Story and Thriller: The Mind and the Truth

Sherlock Holmes

Sherlock Holmes is the embodiment of the detective and the human mind. He demonstrates genius at work. Highlighting the inductive process from the physical clue to the truth, creator Arthur Conan Doyle shows that a mind's brilliance is primarily the result of the method it uses.

"The Murders in the Rue Morgue": Origin of the Detective Form

The Detective story, also known as Mystery, is the premier genre of the modern age. While Conan Doyle is its finest practitioner, Edgar Allan Poe invented it. He also created the modern psychological Horror story.

This feat is even more remarkable when we realize that Horror and Detective are in some ways opposite forms. What unites them is they both focus on the mind. Horror emphasizes the irrational mind while Detective expresses the rational mind. Poe's first Detective story, "The Murders in the Rue Morgue," was published in 1841. Many of the beats of the modern Detective genre can be found right there.

Detective Story and Thriller: How They Work

The Detective story is based on flipping one of the seven basic story structure steps: it hides the opponent until the end. We know that stories rely on conflict between hero and opponent. The question is: When one is hidden until the last scene, how do you create plot?

You make the hero solve a mystery that has been created by the opponent. This forces the detective and the reader to solve the puzzle together.

> **KEY POINT: Due to the hidden opponent, the Detective story has the most complex plot of any genre story.**

Each genre is founded on the sequence of the story beats. When we look at the Detective beats together, we see they track the inductive process of the mind. Inductive reasoning means going from the object, or clue, to the full story of who committed the crime.

That means Detective is a story about how to think successfully. Other minds trying to solve the crime are clouded by prejudice, preconceptions, and ideology. By comparison, the detective is determined to look at "the things themselves." Wherever those things take the detective, that's where she must go.

Great Detective stories also track a second process in the plot: from small corruption to large corruption. This gives the murder larger societal implications. The individual's corruption hides the corruption of the entire society.

In the best Detective stories, even the most brilliant detective has a blind spot in her thinking. That flaw can elevate the story to tragedy.

KEY POINT: The detective investigates the corruption in herself.

Thriller, also known as Suspense, is a form of Detective story in which the investigator is in mortal danger. While the classic detective also faces extreme violence, we are rarely afraid for their life. In Thriller, fear is the overwhelming emotion.

Detective Mind-Action Story View

The Detective version of Mind-Action says that life is about asking questions, searching for truth, and assigning guilt. Therefore, the Detective story dramatizes the issue of *how* we know. In philosophy, this is known as epistemology.

While most genres explore art forms of life in the transcendent versions of the form, the Detective story's exploration of the mind is inherent to the basic form. The Detective story says that the mind is a never-ending problem solver in which symbols lead to clues that reveal insights, and finally stories. They aren't just stories about what is meaningful, stimulating, or entertaining. These internal stories are the Story Codes we create every day about who we are, how the world works, what is valuable, and how to live successfully. They are stories about what is *true*.

KEY POINT: The great insight of the Detective Mind-Action story view is that life is about comparing stories to learn what is really true.

Only then can we make the right decisions. When we stop comparing and come to accept that one is "the Truth," our mind can freeze into an ideology incapable of seeing deeply.

However, the Detective story is about more than finding the truth. It is about bringing the real killer to justice. That's why the second major element of the Detective Mind-Action story view is that we are compelled to assign guilt when we see that an immoral action has occurred. We must bring the perpetrator to justice, because that is the only way the larger society can approach fairness. Just as the clues combine to create a story, the truth about one individual fulfills a wider social need.

The Thriller Mind-Action Story View

Thriller presents a variation on the Detective Mind-Action Story View. By making the investigation potentially lethal, Thriller says that the truth doesn't always set us free. It can get us killed. This limits the value we place on it.

Thriller says that the search for truth must be balanced against life itself, and sometimes even love. But in this genre, truth is still supreme. When the danger comes from family or lover, Thriller suggests that freedom and a good life are only possible when we expose the guilt in those who hold emotional sway over us.

Detective and Thriller Compared to Other Genres

The Detective story is a member of one of the three major genre families: Crime. Besides Detective, this family includes Thriller, Crime, and Gangster. Crime is a trickier family of genres than Speculative Fiction or Myth because its genres are more alike. Many of their beats and techniques overlap.

Therefore, a writer is in more danger of choosing the wrong genre to execute their unique story idea.

Detective and Thriller vs. Myth

To see the essential differences between Detective and other forms, we have to place it within the larger context of "learning stories." Plot consists of the main character going back and forth between *acting* and *learning* over the course of the story. Great plot comes from increasing the conflict (acting) and the number of shocking revelations (learning).

Acting and learning also apply to genres. If we think of them on a spectrum, some genres emphasize acting and some learning. Myth genres like Myth, Action, and Western are primarily "acting" forms. Detective and Thriller are "learning stories" at the other end of the spectrum. Crime and Gangster are close to the middle.

In *The Anatomy of Story*, I talk about the rise of learning stories:

> Generally, in the long history of storytelling, there has been a move from almost total emphasis on acting—in the myth form, where the audience learns simply by modeling themselves on the hero's actions—to a heavy emphasis on learning—in which the audience's concern is to figure out what is happening, who these people really are, and what events really transpired, before achieving full understanding of how to live a good life.
>
> We see these "learning" stories from authors like Joyce, Woolf, Faulkner, Godard, Stoppard, Frayn, Ayckbourn, and in films as varied as *Last Year at Marienbad*, *Blow-Up*, *The Conformist*, *Memento*, *The Conversation*, and *The Usual Suspects*.

Detective vs. Thriller

KEY POINT: Investigating provides the spine in both of these genres.

DETECTIVE	THRILLER
Typically involves a murder that has already happened.	Usually involves a murder that is yet to occur.
The hero is often a professional investigator, a "private eye," and therefore is trained in the techniques of the trade.	The hero is usually an untrained, average person who sees something suspicious and looks into it.
Is capable with his fists and carries a gun.	Has no ability to fight, doesn't carry a gun, and has a physical or mental weakness that makes her (yes, she is typically female) susceptible to attack.
Many suspects.	One main suspect.

Crime vs. Detective and Thriller

Detective and Thriller are about uncovering the truth. Crime is about catching the criminal. It emphasizes winning the battle as opposed to figuring out who did it. In this way, Crime moves away from the learning side of stories and toward the action side.

Horror vs. Detective and Thriller

As mentioned, Detective and Horror are opposites: one shows the mind at its best while the other shows it at its worst.

All three genres involve killing. But Detective and Thriller hide the murder while Horror makes it as graphic and disgusting as possible.

With Horror, there is no detecting the killer's identity. It's obvious. Just the sight of him makes his killings more horrifying. Detective is about actively seeking the killer. Horror is about escaping him. Thriller, which is a combination of Detective and Horror, is about uncovering the killer while escaping his attacks.

Combining Genres: Love and Thriller, Love and Detective

Love is often combined with the Thriller to give love life-and-death stakes. In these stories, fear and love are in direct conflict. This mix gives the Thriller strand more heart and the Love story strand more plot.

The relationship between Detective and Love gets at why we are discussing Detective and Love last in this book. Quite simply, they are the highest genres. Like the Love story, the Detective form is both deeply biological and all too human. The individual mind develops by virtue of its daily struggle to deal with the world. The human mind has serious flaws that have destroyed millions as well as the brilliance to create vast castles of thought and reality.

We could easily have made Detective the first genre in the book since it focuses on how the mind is formed and how it works. As the self-aware animal, we are most distinguished from other animals by our mind. Plus, we understand all other parts of the world through it.

But just as love is both the basic act of mating and the source of the highest bond between people, the human mind develops from simple sensation to the deepest insights about truth and how to live successfully.

So far, the sequence of genres has moved from emphasis on the personal/individual to the larger society. With Fantasy, Detective, and Love, we go back to the intensely personal, but at a higher level. Still, the ways of mind and love have great effects on society.

Examples of Detective

Novel Series

Dublin Murder Squad stories (Tana French), *Alphabet* mysteries like *A Is for Alibi* (Sue Grafton), *Harry Bosch* police procedurals (Michael Connelly), *Easy Rawlins* mysteries (Walter Mosley), *Harlem Detective* series (Chester Himes), *The No. 1 Ladies' Detective Agency* mysteries (Alexander McCall Smith), Matt Jones mysteries (Robert Ellis), Lisbeth Salander in the *Millennium* series (Stieg Larsson), Nancy Drew mysteries, V. I. Warshawski mysteries (Sara Paretsky), stories of Lord Peter Wimsey (Dorothy L. Sayers), Father Brown (G. K. Chesterton), Inspector Maigret (Georges Simenon), and Hercule Poirot (Agatha Christie)

Novels, Films, and Stories

The Hound of the Baskervilles, *The Collected Sherlock Holmes Short Stories*, *Sherlock*, *Sherlock Holmes: A Game of Shadows*, *Spotlight* (also Social Drama), *The Maltese Falcon*, *Laura*, *Vertigo*, *L.A. Confidential*, *The Trespasser*, *Devil in a Blue Dress*, *The Daughter of Time*, *Cotton Comes to Harlem*, *The Big Sleep*, *Farewell My Lovely*, *And Then There Were None*, *The Murder of Roger Ackroyd*, *The Woman in White*, *Down the River unto the Sea*, *The Black Dahlia*, *The Big Nowhere*, *The Moonstone*, *The Name of the Rose*, *The Girl with the Dragon Tattoo*, *In the Woods*, *The Long Goodbye*, *Zootopia* (also Comedy and Myth), *Tales of Mystery and*

Imagination (Poe), *The Thin Man*, *The Hangover*, *Fletch*, *The Pink Panther*

Television

The Wire (also Crime), *CSI: Crime Scene Investigation*, *The Killing*, *True Detective* (season 1), *NCIS*, *Criminal Minds*, *The Bridge*, *The Tunnel*, *Broadchurch*, *Engrenages* (*Spiral*), *Veronica Mars*, *The X-Files*, *Prime Suspect*, *Law and Order: SVU*, *Moonlighting*, *Bones*, *Braquo*, *Sherlock*, *The Adventures of Sherlock Holmes*, *Elementary*, *Mindhunter*, *American Vandal* (also Satire), *The Dresden Files* (also Fantasy), *Stranger Things* (also Horror), *Top of the Lake*, *Twin Peaks*, *Scott and Bailey*, *Homicide: Life on the Street*, *NYPD Blue*, *Ironside*, *The Rockford Files*, *Murder, She Wrote*

Detective Subgenres

Police Procedural, Cozy Mystery, Locked Room, Gentleman Mystery, Comedy Detective, Reporter, Scientific Investigation, Cosmic Detective/Thriller, Story of the Mind and Truth, Supernatural, Black and African American, Hard Boiled, Women Sleuths, Private Investigators, Traditional Detectives, Historical, International

Examples of Thriller

Classic Thrillers

The Silence of the Lambs, *Michael Clayton*, *Basic Instinct*, *The Sixth Sense*, *Razorblade Tears*, *The Plot*, *Promising Young Woman*, *Mulholland Drive*, *The Collector*, *The Girl on the Train*, *Strangers on a Train* (also Crime), *False Witness*, *Pieces of Her*, *Shutter Island*, *When the Stars Go Dark*, *Presumed Innocent*, *Rear Window*, *The Conversation*, *Shadow of a Doubt*, *Gaslight*, *Dial M for Murder*, *Seven*, *Witness*, *Black Swan*,

The Da Vinci Code, *Rebecca*, *Blue Velvet*, *The Fugitive*, *Fatal Attraction*, *The Man Who Knew Too Much*, *Sleeping with the Enemy*, *Cape Fear*, *North by Northwest*, *Notorious*, *Winter's Bone*, *Sorry, Wrong Number*, *Nightcrawler*, *I See You*, *Run*, *Panic Room*, *Birdbox*, *Gerald's Game*, *The Woman in the Window*, *Suspicion*, *The Gift*, *Fear*, *Charade*

Political Thrillers

Killing Eve, *Homeland*, *Z*, *Argo*, *Dark* (also Science Fiction), *Zero Dark Thirty*, *The Day of the Jackal*, *The Constant Gardener*, *The Third Man*, *JFK*, *No Way Out*, *The Manchurian Candidate*, *Syriana*, *The Parallax View*, *All the President's Men*

Thriller Subgenres

Political Thriller, Woman in Jeopardy, Psychological Suspense, Historical, Military, Technothriller, Legal, Medical

Detective/Thriller Story Overview

Here's what we'll cover in this chapter:

- **DETECTIVE/THRILLER STORY BEATS**
- **DETECTIVE THEME:** Being Is Questioning and Discovering Guilt
- **THRILLER THEME:** Being Is Uncovering Our True Enemies
  - Detective Thematic Recipe: The Way of the Truth
  - Thriller Thematic Recipe: Finding the Truth About Our Loved Ones
- **HOW TO TRANSCEND THE DETECTIVE/THRILLER STORY**
  - The Cosmic Detective/Thriller
  - The Story of the Mind and Truth

Detective and Thriller Story Beats

The Detective and Thriller story beats play out each genre's strategy.

- **DETECTIVE STORY STRATEGY:** The hero questions a number of people capable of committing a crime to uncover a surprising truth.
- **THRILLER STORY STRATEGY:** Place a vulnerable hero in a tightening vise and show them trying to escape by finding the truth.

DETECTIVE AND THRILLER STORY BEAT: Opponent's Plan to Commit Murder

All Detective stories begin with a mystery. The killer's plan is the key to the entire plot because it creates the *puzzle* that tests the detective and the audience.

> **KEY POINT: The opponent does two things at the beginning of the story: (1) he commits a crime, usually a murder, and (2) he comes up with a plan to cover it up.**

This step has a huge effect on the story:

- It causes the unique structural flip in the Detective form: the opponent remains hidden until the end, and
- It's what makes the plot so complex and difficult to create. Although the reader follows the detective solving the case, the opponent is really driving the action. As a result, the hero's actions uncovering the crime are typically the opposite of the opponent's actions committing it.

This leads to one of the biggest mistakes writers make about story: they think plot is the sequence of actions where the hero chases after the goal. But this is only what the plot looks like to the *reader*.

KEY POINT: Plot is the grand strategy the author and the opponent use to put the hero in the worst possible trouble and trick the reader.

This leads to the best plot technique, not just for writing the Detective form but for writing any story.

TECHNIQUE: The Opponent's Plan First

Always begin by figuring out the opponent's plan. Then you can figure out the hero's plan to defeat him.

The Detective opponent is a kind of magician: he creates a separate reality, a separate "truth." That's why the key to the mystery is not what the opponent did, but how he *disguises* it.

The criminal must:

- Create a fake alibi for himself
- Know at least one other character who had motive to kill the victim
- Frame one or more of those characters.

The killer doesn't just hide something. He sends the detective in the wrong direction.

KEY POINT: The detective and killer are competing over which *story* is accepted. You the writer must create clues that support at least two answers: the killer and at least one other.

TECHNIQUE: The Ingenious Opponent

Make the killer's plan ingenious. This is the foundation of a great Detective story. It must be a puzzle so complex that only a brilliant detective can figure it out.

If the murder is simple with an obvious killer, no competing suspects, no cover-up of the crime, and no red herrings to trick the detective into going in the wrong direction, the story is over before it's barely begun.

The importance of the killer's plan has a profound philosophical basis:

> **KEY POINT: In all life, deception is the way of both predator and prey. Therefore, the more deception used by both opponent and hero, the better the plot will be.**

This brings up one of the most useful techniques in all of story.

TECHNIQUE: The Opponent's Plan Determines Investigation

Once you figure out the killer's plan, investigating the clues that lead to various suspects will become clear.

To execute this step, write down the sequence of the killer's plan, including killing the victim, followed by what he does to hide it, the red herrings he uses to mislead the hero, and how he or his men attack the hero as she investigates.

Arthur Conan Doyle considered "The Adventure of the Speckled Band," a "Locked Room" mystery, his best Sherlock Holmes story. Dr. Grimesby Roylott, who has practiced medicine in India, has already murdered one stepdaughter. Now he plans to murder his lone surviving stepdaughter the same way. He insists she sleep in a room that has a bell cord and a ventilator hole that connects to his room. In the middle of the night, a deadly snake will slide down the cord and bite the woman in the bed. Then it will return through the hole to the doctor's room.

In *Knives Out*, when Ransom Drysdale discovers that his grandfather Harlan has cut him out of his will and plans to give everything to his nurse, Marta Cabrera, he comes up with a plot to change the labels of his grandfather's medication. This will not only kill him, it will frame Marta for his murder, thus nullifying the will. While everyone else is at the funeral, Ransom swaps the vials back.

In *Vertigo*, Gavin Elster wants to murder his wife. When he learns that his old college friend, police detective "Scottie" Ferguson, suffers from vertigo, he hires a woman, Madeleine, to pretend to be his wife and get Scottie to fall in love with her. Pretending to be suicidal, she runs to the top of a tower. Elster is there with his real wife, already dead from a broken neck. When Madeleine runs to the top, Scottie can't follow due to his vertigo. Elster throws over the real wife, and Scottie, guilt-ridden, believes he is to blame for her death. Elster and Madeleine wait until the coast is clear to make their escape.

Thriller: Opponent's Plan to Commit Murder

In a Thriller, the crime may have already occurred. More often, the investigator has to prevent it from happening. But the first step of determining the opponent's plan is the same.

In *Gone Girl*, when Nick Dunne finds his wife, Amy, missing, he fears the worst. The police soon suspect Nick is guilty of her murder. Nick slowly realizes that Amy has created an elaborate scheme to frame him and send him to jail.

In *The Man Who Knew Too Much*, while on vacation in Marrakesh with his wife, Dr. Ben McKenna encounters a man with a knife in his back. Before he dies, the man tells the doctor that a politician is going to be assassinated in London.

DETECTIVE AND THRILLER STORY BEAT: Story World—Enslaving Society

To solve the crime, the Detective must investigate the specific story world in which it happened. That world also resists the detective's search for the truth.

The Detective ecology is the city or oppressive city world, except in the subgenre "Cozy Mystery." These enslaving elements characterize the city:

- Facades that create contrasting worlds: outside versus inside, public versus private, surface lies versus deeper truth
- The organization is all-powerful
- Loss of the individual
- Corporations with a clear hierarchy
- Contrast of wealth and poverty

Detective stories show the heights and the depths of society. We've talked about using utopia and dystopia to express a society as freedom and slavery. In Detective stories and Thrillers, we often see the technique of the fake utopia. Part of the society's ability to enslave its members is that they think they're free.

The best example of fake utopia in the Detective form is *L.A. Confidential.* The voice-over montage at the beginning of the film sums up the modern Consumer/Fear Culture underlying the city's beautiful exterior.

In the popular television show *Murder, She Wrote*, mystery writer Jessica Fletcher investigates murders in her small hometown of Cabot Cove, Maine. This story world is similar to that of a Cozy Mystery. During its airing from 1984 to 1996, the seemingly bucolic Cabot Cove had the highest murder rate per capita in the United States.

In a classic Thriller, the story world is typically the average, daily world, focused on a domestic or family situation. But underneath this apparently normal or even utopian facade is the reality of dark secrets and corruption. Examples include *Rear Window*, *Shadow of a Doubt*, and *Blue Velvet*.

In the subgenre Political Thriller, the story world is usually the city. As the hero investigates, she enters a black hole of corruption that is vast, interconnected, and many layers deep. Examples include *Killing Eve*, *Z*, *The Third Man*, *JFK*, *No Way Out*, *The Manchurian Candidate*, *The Conversation*, *Syriana*, *The Parallax View*, and *All the President's Men*.

DETECTIVE AND THRILLER STORY BEAT: Hero's Role—Search for the Truth

Detective: The detective searches for the truth, usually about who killed someone. She is typically a professional who solves deadly puzzles for money.

Thriller: The hero is the endangered investigator. She is not a professional.

Woman in Jeopardy

A major subgenre of Thriller is known as the "Woman in Jeopardy" story. One could argue that the Thriller form was created to highlight the dramatic power of putting a woman in danger. To paraphrase Margaret Atwood, "Men are afraid that women will laugh at them; women are afraid that men will kill them."

In *Suspicion*, when he discovers a shy young woman is an heiress, a gambler and con man begins to court her. After the wedding, she suspects her husband is a murderer and she may be next.

The hero in *Shadow of a Doubt* is a teenage woman, nicknamed Charlie, after her favorite uncle. Young Charlie comes to believe that her uncle is the "Merry Widow" serial killer.

As the story progresses, she becomes aware of a much bigger danger: the helpless, subservient state of women in a materialistic culture run by men.

DETECTIVE AND THRILLER STORY BEAT: Detective's Ghost

Ghost is the event from the past still haunting the hero in the present.

A failing in the Detective's past causes her intense guilt, resentment, even hatred. This ties in with the larger issue of any detective story: Who is guilty of the crime?

> **KEY POINT: The detective's main motivation is to even the accounts of wrongdoing in her past, even when she is not responsible for the injustice.**

In *The Killing*, the lead police detective Sarah Linden is a single mother who feels guilty for putting her work above her son. When a girl is found dead in the trunk of a submerged car, Sarah becomes obsessed with finding the killer.

In *Mare of Easttown*, Police Detective Mare Sheehan is haunted by the suicide death of her son who blamed her for his troubles. She is also recently divorced and in a custody battle with her former daughter-in-law over her grandson. In addition, a girl has been missing for over a year and the girl's mother holds Mare personally responsible. All of these personal elements motivate her to solve the murder of a teenage mother. But they also make her job more difficult.

And in *The Silence of the Lambs*, Clarice Starling was a young child when her father, a marshal, was shot and killed during a robbery. Her mother was unable to support the family. At ten, Clarice was sent to live on a sheep ranch. But after seeing the lambs slaughtered, she ran away. She spent the rest of her childhood in an orphanage. Clarice is determined to save the latest victim of the killer to forever silence the sound of slaughtered lambs that haunts her.

Thriller is much more concerned than Detective with making a strong emotional connection between hero and opponent. Therefore:

TECHNIQUE: Weakness Matches Crime

Give the hero a ghost and weakness, both psychological and moral, that in some way matches the opponent's crime, but is less serious.

This technique is valuable because it allows you to blur the difference between hero and criminal. It also forces the hero to make a character change while investigating the crime.

In *Shutter Island*, U.S. Marshal Teddy Daniels is investigating the escape of a patient named Rachel, who drowned her children, from a hospital for the criminally insane. Teddy has had a drinking problem. His wife died in an apartment fire some years before.

Teddy's real name is Andrew Laeddis, who killed his wife after she set the fire and drowned their three kids. Overwhelmed by guilt, Andrew had a complete breakdown and was sent to the mental hospital to recover.

DETECTIVE AND THRILLER STORY BEAT: Detective Hero—Strengths and Weaknesses

The detective's strengths come from her archetype. She is both the searcher and the magician. Her main strengths are:

- She has a brilliant mind with a precise mental process. She is always curious and lives by her wits.
- She has a strong will to justice, which is the great task of the city world.

- She has the ability to see things from other people's perspective.
- She can pretend to be others. In other words, she uses facade to uncover facade.
- She is a loner who lives and works outside the organization. This is a strength because it gives her the freedom to investigate outside the law.
- Like the cowboy, she is between lawman and outlaw. So she knows how to navigate the world of crime.
- The cost of being a loner in a corporate, organized world is that she is morally tainted. She often has to take on the dirty jobs, so others look down on her. But she is also the most morally concerned of any character in the story, including the cops.
- The great detective is a combination of scientist and artist. The scientist induces truth from physical clues. The artist re-creates a new reality from signs that no one else can see. This makes her the ultimate modern hero.

KEY POINT: The real subject of the scientist-artist is not the criminal but human nature.

The Detective story says that human nature never really changes, no matter how modern or advanced we get. Humanity may have experienced cultural evolution. But the essential human mind has not.

TECHNIQUE: Unique Detective

Give the detective *special talents* for solving mysteries.

This takes the lead character and the genre beyond procedure. It treats detective/police work as an art form. Given that there have been thousands of detectives, creating one with unique talents is a tall order.

KEY POINT: Giving your hero special investigating abilities is the best way to distinguish yourself from other writers in the form.

Examples include Sherlock Holmes, Easy Rawlins, Miss Marple, Sam Spade, Philip Marlowe, V. I. Warshawski, Columbo, Nancy Drew, Inspector Maigret, Lisbeth Salander, Hercule Poirot, Precious Ramotswe (*The No. 1 Ladies' Detective Agency*), William von Baskerville (*The Name of the Rose*), Lord Peter Wimsey, Father Brown, Mike Hammer, Kinsey Millhone, Harry Bosch, Veronica Mars, Dirk Gently (*Dirk Gently's Holistic Detective Agency*), Jessica Fletcher (*Murder, She Wrote*), Castle, Dana Scully (*The X-Files*), Patrick Jane (*The Mentalist*), Adrian Monk (*Monk*), Dexter, Brenda Leigh Johnson (*The Closer*), Olivia Benson (*Law and Order: SVU*) Benoit Blanc (*Knives Out*), Dr. Temperance "Bones" Brennan (*Bones*), Jane Tennison (*Prime Suspect*), Eve Polastri (*Killing Eve*), and Maddie Hayes (*Moonlighting*).

DETECTIVE AND THRILLER STORY BEAT: Detective's Weaknesses

In many classic Detective stories, especially series, the hero is a "traveling angel" (see Comedy and Fantasy) who solves a crime and then moves on to the next case. This detective typically has no flaws. For example, Hercule Poirot has no guilt about any past failing.

In other stories of the form, the detective has serious weaknesses of her own. These unique weaknesses often come from taking the essence of the detective, a searcher for the truth, to its logical extreme. She is unsure, paranoid, and obsessed with justice to the point of hurting others. This means she is often world-weary. She lives in the gap between the ideal of justice and the reality of crime.

In "A Scandal in Bohemia," Dr. Watson highlights the psychological weaknesses of Sherlock Holmes when he describes his friend's view of Irene Adler:

> All emotions, and [love] particularly, were abhorrent to his cold, precise but admirably balanced mind. He was, I take it, the most perfect reasoning and observing machine that the world has seen.

All three main detectives in *L.A. Confidential* have serious psychological and moral flaws. Ed is self-righteous, by-the-book, and high-handed. Bud is quick-tempered, resentful at being viewed as a dumb muscle man, and has a soft spot for women in distress. Jack will do anything for fame or extra cash, is a know-it-all, and is easily swayed.

Main Weakness: The Detective's Limited Point of View

KEY POINT: The detective's most serious weaknesses come from what it means to be a detective: limited point of view and lack of knowledge. She is a person whose every job begins in ignorance.

This limited point of view is compounded by emotional flaws. That's why Detective stories are often told in "first person." Being in the mind of the detective makes the reader *feel* the detective's confusion and frustration at not knowing what is happening. This also highlights the reader's sense that the world is full of deception, and that we often miss much of what is going on.

TECHNIQUE: The Weakness Story

Make the detective's weakness-need an entire story of its own.

Weakness is not just something embedded in the character

that hurts as she goes about her daily life. The character has created a *story* about her weakness that blames others and hides the flaw from her understanding.

Often this story includes the ghost. But the story covers much more than this one event. The character constructed the story a long time ago, sometimes even in childhood. When first created, it might have helped her deal with the severe situation in which she found herself. But it's become a much bigger problem that's hurting her now.

Some psychologists refer to this as the *script*. The character repeats the script over and over and gets the same bad results. This becomes a cycle of self-destruction the character may not be able to overcome.

Examples include characters in *The Killing*, *Mare of Easttown*, *Engrenages* (*Spiral*), *Devil in a Blue Dress*, *L.A. Confidential*, *True Detective* (season 1), *Homeland*, *NYPD Blue*, *Shutter Island*, and *The Silence of the Lambs*.

In the novel *The Trespasser*, by Tana French, the main character, Antoinette Conway, is a female police detective who feels the murder squad hates her and wants her out. She's created an entire story about how she's the victim fighting heroically against cops who should have her back.

Some of this is true. But much of it is the story she's created that hides the flaws hurting her life. What makes this a special police procedural is that French places the hero's weakness story alongside the other stories she uses to explain who murdered the victim. The reader sees that they're all stories people construct to rationalize human motivation and behavior, including our own.

KEY POINT: A great detective always searches for the true story about the murder and ultimately about herself.

Some detectives have physical and/or mental afflictions that make it more difficult for them to do their work. For example, Monk has obsessive-compulsive disorder. Former chief of detectives Ironside is paralyzed and confined to a wheelchair. Kinsey Millhone has tinnitus. While useful in making the detective's job harder, these kinds of challenges do not take the place of psychological and moral flaws.

Thriller Hero's Weaknesses: Adding Emotion to Intellect

The Detective story highlights the brilliance of the detective's intellect. The Thriller highlights the intensity of the investigator's emotions. The hero feels lost, insecure, desperate, on the edge, and most of all, afraid.

> **KEY POINT: In Thriller, the hero is in deep *emotional* danger.**

In *Michael Clayton*, Michael is a "janitor lawyer" who cleans up the mess when one of his firm's clients screws up. He has a gambling addiction, plus he owes $85,000 to a loan shark after borrowing money to open a bar with his brother, who then stole it.

In *Basic Instinct*, Nick has had problems with cocaine and alcohol. His wife committed suicide because she couldn't live with such a violent man.

> **KEY POINT: The hero must have a weakness or quality that makes her more susceptible to *physical* danger, so we are afraid for them.**

Here are some examples of the vulnerable hero:

Killing Eve: Eve is an MI5 security analyst with a desk job. She is going up against Villanelle, a highly trained master assassin.

The Sixth Sense: the hero is a boy.

The Fugitive: the hero is wanted for murder and is on the run.

Presumed Innocent: the hero is on trial for murder.

Rear Window and *Witness*: the hero is injured.

TECHNIQUE: The Weakness-Crime Connection

Bring the hero's ghost and weakness to the surface and overcome it by solving the crime.

The storyline in a good Thriller isn't just about investigating while escaping attack. There are two lines to track: the personal and the crime. In other words, the hero's ghost and weakness should be brought to the surface and overcome by solving the crime.

TECHNIQUE: Two in One

These two tracks should weave into one. Therefore,

- the act of solving the personal problem should help the hero solve the crime, and
- the act of solving the crime should help the hero fix her unique psychological or moral weaknesses.

The audience gains double satisfaction.

Jeff's psychological weakness in *Rear Window* is that he won't marry his beautiful girlfriend, Lisa (played by Grace Kelly). Clearly, this makes no sense. However, by solving the crime with her, he commits to marry her, thus overcoming his reluctance.

TECHNIQUE: Faith vs. Skepticism

To connect love to the thriller plot, make the hero confront this essential issue: faith versus skepticism in love.

- Does she make the leap of faith in her partner, believe totally in love, and risk her own death, or
- Does she fail to make the leap, protect herself, and risk losing the love of her life?

The reason this is such a brilliant story strategy is that it gives love *life-and-death stakes*.

Examples include *Suspicion*, *The Gift*, *Fear*, *Rebecca*, *Notorious*, *Dial M for Murder*, and *Charade*.

DETECTIVE AND THRILLER STORY BEAT: Values—the Code of the Detective

In the Crime chapter, we talked about how the writer creates a moral code. The prime values of the detective come from her basic action: she looks for the truth and brings the guilty person to justice. Therefore, the three main values of the Detective Code are truth, honor, and professionalism. These values are absolute: the detective always gets her man.

DETECTIVE AND THRILLER STORY BEAT: Detective Desire—to Solve a Mystery and Find the Truth

The mystery is the trick to any detective story. It is the code that must be cracked, a pattern of signs that only the detective can recognize.

The Detective form has one of the most propulsive narrative drives of any genre. Ironically, the focus is on finding out what happened in the past, usually involving a murder. These high stakes of life and death are why the audience is willing to look back.

Thriller Desire: To Solve a Mystery While Escaping Attack

KEY POINT: The Thriller hero's desire should get her into progressively deeper trouble.

This is why the Thriller is a blend of Detective and Horror.

As Michael Clayton investigates his friend Arthur's death, he becomes the next target of assassination.

KEY POINT: In the best thrillers, the hero's investigation into a potential crime also becomes an investigation into fear itself.

Visual Shapes of Detective and Thriller Plots: Spiral, Frames, and Chinese Boxes/Russian Dolls

Detective and Thriller plots use story shapes that sequence the workings of the mind:

1. Spiral

The simplest is the spiral. A spiral is a path that circles inward to the center. It looks like this:

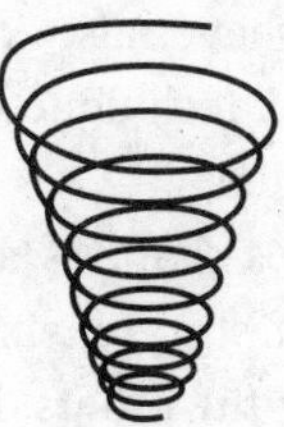

Thrillers often use the spiral shape, as the hero uncovers *layers* of the opponent. She keeps returning to a single event or memory and explores it at progressively deeper levels. So she constantly sees new things. In spiraling, the hero literally circles around the event and sees the problem from a number of perspectives.

Plot in a spiral story is based on two sequences happening simultaneously:

- Going deeper into the same world and getting *reveals*, and
- The hero sees her darker side as she approaches her personal hell at the center.

Notice the hero goes on both an external and an internal journey, with the physical matching the psychological. This plot shape also shows society at progressively deeper levels: the implication is that how society really works is a lot worse than we thought.

TECHNIQUE: Change Perspective

The character has a flashback where they see the event from a new angle.

Examples of the spiral shape in Thriller include *The Conversation*, *Blow-Up*, *Vertigo*, and *Rear Window*.

2. Frames

The frames shape, also known as a "frame narrative," is a more complex technique used in transcendent Detective stories and Thrillers.

The frames shape is a type of Vortex Street in which a succession of storytellers tells part of the story, with each contradicting the others. No storyteller has the one true answer. This shape uses multiple points of view. Frames look like this:

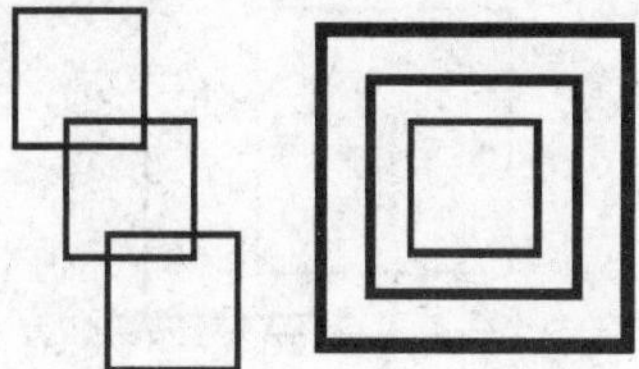

The frames shape is used most often when different storytellers recount the same event, as in *Rashomon*. It can also be used for fictional biography and stories of the self, like *Citizen Kane*.

Examples of the frames shape include *The Norman Conquests*, *Closer*, *Arrested Development*, *The Affair*, *The First Day of the Rest of Your Life*, *Paris*, and *Avenue Montaigne*.

KEY POINT: The frames story differs from most branching stories in that it presents a sequence of different minds as opposed to a sequence of different subworlds.

3. Chinese Boxes/Russian Dolls

A subcategory of the frames shape is known as Chinese boxes or Russian dolls. This refers to nested boxes or dolls, one inside the other. Chinese boxes is a form of spiral, but told strictly though the *mind* of a character.

Chinese boxes takes two basic forms:

1. Mind within a mind: The hero's mind explores a mysterious situation but finds nothing conclusive. So she looks again, this time from a new perspective and a new interpretation of clues. She jumps back and forth through time, based not on chronology but on mental associations. The order of the story follows the

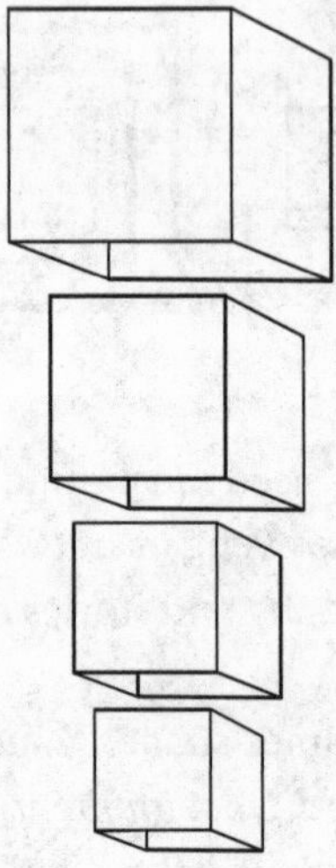

order of what the hero *learns*, not of what the hero does (as in Spiral). Although sometimes the hero learns something about a crime, usually she learns the truth about a relationship. Examples of mind within a mind include *Shutter Island*, *Inception*, *Memento*, *Last Year at Marienbad*, and *The Conformist*.

2. Story within a story within a story: A storyteller tells a story about what another storyteller told her, which itself may have been from a third storyteller. This is the story version of the game "telephone." Examples of a story within a story include *Frankenstein* and *Heart of Darkness*.

KEY POINT: In both versions of Chinese boxes, whatever final truth the hero gains is at best relative. It is a tissue, a wisp, or quite possibly nothing at all.

DETECTIVE AND THRILLER STORY BEAT: Detective Opponent—the Killer, the Suspects, and the Mystery

The main opponent in any Detective story is the killer who is hidden among multiple suspects. To compensate, the writer introduces a mystery the detective must solve.

The opponent usually has a smooth, urbane, even kind exterior, with a ruthless interior.

- ***L.A. CONFIDENTIAL***: the police captain, Dudley Smith
- ***CHINATOWN***: rich and powerful Noah Cross
- ***VERTIGO***: Gavin Elster, Scottie's friend from college

The Detective opponent meets two structural requirements:

1. He is competing with the hero for the goal. The opponent wants to get away with the crime that the detective is trying to solve.

> **KEY POINT: The goal the opponent and the detective are really competing over is whose story about the murder will be believed.**

2. He is the character best able to attack the hero's flaws.

> **KEY POINT: Attacking the one great weakness of the detective should be a crucial part of the opponent's original plan.**

- ***VERTIGO***: Elster uses Scottie's vertigo to get away with murdering his wife.
- ***L.A. CONFIDENTIAL***: Police Captain Smith takes advantage of his detectives' faith in law enforcement to plant evidence and place the blame on defenseless minorities.

Opponent's Flaw: Hubris

As in Greek tragedy, the Detective and Thriller opponent's great weakness is often hubris, or excessive pride. The killer loses the battle of minds because he underestimates the mind of his opponent.

The television show *Columbo* was founded on the hero taking advantage of the opponent's hubris. Each week, the killer is rich and haughty and looks down on the slow-talking police detective in the rumpled raincoat. This is always a fatal mistake.

TECHNIQUE: Iceberg Opponent

Use the "iceberg" opponent and accelerate the reveals about him.

Like an iceberg, the most dangerous part of the opponent should be hidden below the surface. To execute this technique:

- Reveal information about the opponent in pieces and at an increasing pace over the course of the story. This means you will have more reveals as the story nears the end. Remember: how you parse out the reveals is what makes or breaks your plot.
- Consider having your hero go up against an obvious opponent early on. As the conflict intensifies, the hero discovers attacks from a stronger hidden opposition.

KEY POINT: Because the opponent stays hidden until the end, the detective and the reader uncover the killer together.

TECHNIQUE: More Suspects

To challenge the detective and reader, add more believable suspects.

You must introduce a number of characters who could

have committed the crime. Otherwise, it's easy for the reader to guess who did it. This ties in with the basic story strategy of the genre: the hero questions a number of people capable of committing a crime to uncover a surprising truth.

To be a real suspect, a character must meet three requirements:

1. Motive
2. Opportunity
3. No alibi

Agatha Christie was brilliant at setting up a wide array of believable suspects. *And Then There Were None* is one of her best. Seven guests have been invited to an island. At dinner, a message from the hosts states that each is guilty of murder. One after the other, the guests start to die. With each murder, there are fewer suspects in the puzzle. The television show *Lost* twisted this brilliant premise, combined it with Science Fiction, and expanded it tenfold.

The Killing is a television Detective story that requires two seasons to solve a single crime. That increases the number of suspects the police must investigate. There are thirty-two viable suspects in the murder of Rosie Larsen.

TECHNIQUE: Decreasing Suspicion

"Take the stink off" at least one character. This is slang for removing suspicion. Your goal is to create the least likely character to commit the crime. Play with motive, opportunity, and/or alibi so it appears a particular character could not have done it. This technique can be applied to a number of characters to keep the reader guessing, but it is especially important for the true criminal.

Thriller Opponent: Attack

In Thrillers, the opponent doesn't just hide from the investigator. He attacks.

KEY POINT: Put the hero under as much pressure as possible.

BEST OPPONENT TECHNIQUE: Emotional Attack

The opponent doesn't just attack physically. He attacks the hero's greatest emotional weakness, especially with the weapons of guilt and fear.

Nick has a strong ghost and weakness in *Basic Instinct*: he has a track record of accidental shootings, his wife's death by suicide is attributed to his violence, and he has addiction problems with alcohol and cocaine. Main suspect Catherine Tramell taunts him about the death of his wife and constantly brings up his deep emotional flaws.

KEY POINT: The Thriller opponent is far subtler in his attacks than the Horror monster.

An extreme version of emotional attack is known as "gaslighting," which comes from the film *Gaslight* (1944). This form of emotional abuse is common in Women in Jeopardy Thrillers. The husband makes the wife question her sanity. He claims she is seeing things, is too sensitive, or is making things up. He says she is responsible for what she accuses him of doing. He professes to be worried about her physical and mental health.

In classic Thrillers with one suspect, the hero spots a suspect relatively quickly and investigates. But she is not sure if they actually committed the crime.

The classic Thriller with a single character under suspicion can *decrease plot*: either they did it or they didn't. Therefore, it's helpful to use the Detective technique of multiple viable suspects.

DETECTIVE AND THRILLER STORY BEAT:

Plan—Investigation

Detective is the most knowledge-oriented of all story forms. Therefore, it highlights two mental structure steps: plan and revelation. These occur during the drive, the series of actions the detective takes to reach her goal throughout the middle of the story.

The plan explores the art form inherent to the Detective genre: the mind. It shows that the mind is essentially the art of solving problems and creating stories.

The first task of writing a Detective story is to figure out how the killer will commit the crime and cover it up. The next is to determine how the detective will solve it. In this most mind-oriented of all stories, the hero's plan is complex and involves these mental processes:

1. Observation of physical evidence, or clues.
2. Questioning various suspects.
3. Inductive logic, rational analysis, and intuition.
4. Memory—in the form of flashback—that *leads* to an insight.
5. Re-creating the crime, a different reality of what happened. This reality is a story.
6. Testing the theory on the suspects.

Notice that this sequence builds from individual clues to an entire story, a theory of what these clues mean.

Like the detective, the Thriller hero is an investigator. But she is usually an amateur who gets into danger. So the story is more about her fear. The Thriller hero hits the same investigative beats as the detective, but she does them based more on intuition.

The biggest challenge in the Thriller plot is that once its hero comes under attack, she no longer acts but reacts. This stops narrative drive.

KEY POINT: The hero must continue to take investigative actions while fending off attack.

Create suspense by increasing the risk that the character will be harmed.

Let's look more closely at the five main investigation steps (plan) the detective uses to solve the crime.

Plan/Investigation Step 1. Observation: Clues and Reveals

The first step in the Detective's plan to find the killer is to observe physical evidence. This is why Sherlock Holmes is symbolized by the magnifying glass.

Physical evidence is useful only if it becomes a clue. In other words, it must lead to a revelation, or *new information*, that brings the detective closer to the truth.

KEY POINT: In both Detective story and Thriller, the reveal of new information is the single most important story structure step.

KEY POINT: A clue is partial knowledge of the truth, which means it is also vague and may lead the detective in the wrong direction.

TECHNIQUE: Determine Reveals Up Front

Create the reveals when you figure out the opponent's plan at the beginning of the writing process.

The Detective story's emphasis on puzzle-solving leads to two crucial plot elements:

1. The Detective story has *more reveals* than any other genre.
2. The quality of the story is based on the *quality* of those reveals and how they are *sequenced.*

Therefore, the reveals better be good, and you better be good at making them build.

TECHNIQUES FOR A GREAT REVELATION SEQUENCE

- Intersperse real clues with red herrings.
- Reveals should generally increase in intensity.
- They should come at a faster pace as you approach the end of the story.
- They should move closer to home. In other words, someone the detective is close to personally.

Let's look at the revelations sequence of some of the best-plotted Detective stories:

Murder on the Orient Express: Detective Poirot investigates the death of Ratchett.

1. A paper saying AISY ARMS indicates the Daisy Armstrong murder.
2. Ratchett has been stabbed twelve times.
3. Ratchett apparently told the porter in French he had a nightmare, but he spoke only English.

4. A woman in a white nightgown was seen walking down the hallway.
5. Poirot learns that Hector's father was the Armstrong prosecutor and that Hector was close to the late Mrs. Armstrong.
6. Poirot discovers the Princess's connection to the Armstrongs.
7. Poirot confirms that Hildegarde knew the dead Armstrong maid.
8. He finds the conductor's uniform in her suitcase.

Defending Jacob: A district attorney investigates the murder of a fourteen-year-old boy, and his own son Jacob is a suspect.

1. Reader reveal (investigator already knows): the DA is questioned before a grand jury.
2. The DA discovers the murdered boy bullied his son. His son is a suspect.
3. His son showed off a knife at school.
4. The DA finds the knife and throws it away.
5. The son is not well liked in school.
6. Reader reveal: the DA's father was a convicted murderer.
7. On vacation a girl the boy knows disappears.
8. The mother sees red splotches on the boy's bathing suit. She now knows her son is a murderer.

Caution: Another mistake many Detective writers make is that their detective comes up with a revelation from thin air. It was "just a hunch" or the product of jumping to conclusions.

KEY POINT: A revelation must be triggered by a *specific physical clue*.

Thriller: Reveal

The Thriller reveal is usually about evidence of the main suspect's guilt. This occurs during the drive step as the hero seeks to uncover the criminal. In this genre, the drive is a crosscut between two tracks:

1. Finding evidence that the suspect committed the crime, and
2. Finding evidence that the suspect did *not* commit the crime.

KEY POINT: Make these two lines fairly even. This creates serious doubt within the hero and causes fear and desperation.

The two most crucial reveals occur near the end of the story:

1. The hero discovers new, powerful evidence that indicates the suspect is innocent of the crime. The hero is baffled and embarrassed. This is the hero's apparent defeat.
2. The hero stumbles upon a conclusive piece of evidence that the suspect is in fact guilty. She is strengthened by this reveal because it verifies her suspicions. But she is also terrified to learn of the opponent's true power and intent.

The Conversation: The Director hires Harry to get audio surveillance on Mark and Ann.

1. Harry listens to the tapes and hears Mark say, "He'd *kill* us if he had the chance." Harry interprets that to mean harm will come to the couple.

2. Harry's suspicions are confirmed when he hears violence and screaming coming from Mark and Ann's hotel room.
3. Harry discovers that Ann is not dead.
4. Harry reinterprets Mark's voice on the tape to be saying, "He'd kill *us* if he had the chance." He realizes that Ann and Mark have killed the Director.

DETECTIVE AND THRILLER STORY BEAT: Opponent's Plan—Red Herrings, False Meaning, and Lies

As the hero investigates, she encounters red herrings as well as real clues. A red herring is a piece of evidence planted by the killer designed to trick the detective.

TECHNIQUE: Red Herrings

Use red herrings as part of the opponent's original plan to hide his own involvement in the crime.

Here's Hercule Poirot: "Ladies and gentlemen, we now come to my own reconstruction of the night of the murder—or, the night of the red herrings."

The significance of the false clue is ironic: the story form with the most brilliant of all heroes is also the one that highlights the mind's flaw of limited point of view. A false clue expresses the inability of the mind to see the multiple possibilities of a symbol.

Red herrings are just one of many flaws of the human mind highlighted by the Detective story. The mind wants to make connections, and will do so even if things don't connect. This leads to one of the most difficult techniques for writers to execute:

TECHNIQUE: The Double Clue

Every clue should support at least *two* answers of who committed the crime.

In *The Killing*, the entire case comes down to who owned the key card found at what may be the scene of the murder. The key card opens one of the offices in city hall. Due to other evidence, Detective Linden thinks it belongs to the mayor. But instead it opens the door to the office of his opponent in the upcoming race for mayor: Darren Richmond.

The main clue that solves the case in *Chinatown* has to do with the saltwater in Hollis's lungs. Everyone thinks it's from the ocean near the spot where his body was found. But Jake discovers it's from the saltwater pond at Noah Cross's estate where Hollis was drowned.

DETECTIVE AND THRILLER STORY BEAT: Plan/Investigation Step 2—Questioning

Once the detective observes symbolic objects and gains a sense of their potential meaning, she explores them. To learn what the clues really mean, she asks questions. Questioning suspects and finding physical evidence provides the main part of the drive.

In simple form, investigation works like this:

- the detective goes to the murder scene and finds physical evidence;
- this leads her to another location where she questions possible witnesses and other suspects and finds more physical evidence;
- this leads her to another location to follow up, ask more questions, and find more evidence, et cetera.

The individuals the detective questions are potential suspects who may be guilty of murder. Therefore, they are potential opponents who do not want to answer truthfully. What kind of questions does she ask them?

KEY POINT: The detective uses questions *designed to deceive.*

In *Murder on the Orient Express* Hercule Poirot says, "Only by interrogating the other passengers could I hope to see the light. But when I began to question them, the light, as Macbeth would have said, thickened."

Poirot keeps many of the passengers off balance with his questions. For example, he has Elena Andrenyi sign her name and asks her if she's ever been to the U.S. He berates Miss Debenham in view of the Colonel, so that the protective man will barge in and expose his relationship with her.

Deception is a major part of Sherlock Holmes's method. In "A Scandal in Bohemia," he disguises himself as a clergyman to illegally retrieve a photo from Irene Adler. When Dr. Watson yells "Fire!" Holmes watches where Adler goes to retrieve her most prized possession. In "The Final Problem," Holmes again uses the cleric disguise. When he returns from his apparent death at Reichenbach Falls, Holmes disguises himself as an old man before exposing his true identity to Watson.

DETECTIVE AND THRILLER STORY BEAT: Plan/Investigation Step 3—Intuition and Inductive Logic

The detective uses intuition plus inductive and deductive logic to make sense of the evidence. Intuition does not work in a linear way. It is the capacity of the mind to recognize a pattern, which is the *sequence* of symbols describing what happened. After collecting evidence, the detective has a first hunch of who might be guilty. A hunch is an unformed hypothesis, often called "gut instinct." But it is not pure conjecture. It is the first step in a more refined scientific method.

Blinded by red herrings, the detective fears that her intuition may be wrong. Now she must bring logic into play. Logic is the grammar of thought. It is a *systematic* sequencing of symbols.

KEY POINT: The sequence of symbols represents causal events: if this fact exists, then it must cause that effect. Illogic is false causation.

The main distinction about logic has to do with the two directions of the sequence: induction and deduction. Inductive logic moves from the specific thing to the general, abstract principle. Deductive logic moves in the opposite direction, from the principle to the specific object.

A bad detective, and especially the typical cop in a Detective story, begins with deductive logic. He has a presumption of who the killer probably is and then tries to make the facts confirm it.

KEY POINT: Once the mind hardens into a fixed theory of how the world works, it has a difficult time using inductive logic.

A good detective always begins with inductive logic. That's why Sherlock Holmes is actually the master of induction, not deduction. The detective gathers physical evidence and then generalizes about how it might form the bigger picture. But a fertile mind also plays the sequence from the other direction, deducing to get a different understanding of the clues.

KEY POINT: The detective must find the *necessary* way to sequence the facts. This necessary sequence of facts is what produces the true story.

Knives Out's Benoit Blanc, speaking about the novel *Gravity's Rainbow*, says, "It describes the path of a projectile determined by natural law. Et voilà, my method. I observe the facts without biases of the head or heart. I determine the arc's path, stroll leisurely to its terminus and the truth falls at my feet."

DETECTIVE AND THRILLER STORY BEAT: Plan/ Investigation Step 4—Flashback Memory and Changed Point of View

One of the main ways the investigator finds the truth is by rethinking the past. She returns to a memory to see if she can find a different pattern that reveals a deeper force at work.

KEY POINT: Memory is one of the most dramatic ways the investigator considers the evidence.

In the act of looking back, the detective must consider the event from a new perspective. At first glance, this seems impossible. She can't suddenly see the entire scene from a radically different point of view. To do that, she must see or hear a recording of the event that has a different point of view.

When that is not available, she can focus on the memory from a different scale. She can bore in to see the smaller details. Or she can see it as part of a larger perspective. Her goal is to find the causal connection she has missed until now. This can be the linchpin that makes a whole new view of reality possible.

Examples include *Vertigo*, *Blow-Up*, *The Sixth Sense*, *Memento*, *Shutter Island*, and the Crime stories *The Usual Suspects* and *Gone Girl*.

In *The Conversation*, uncovering the crime turns on the correct interpretation of a single line of dialogue caught on tape. When the surveillance expert Harry Caul first listens to the tape, he hears, "He'd *kill* us if he got the chance." Caul is afraid that the director of the company that hired him is going to kill the couple. After listening to the recording multiple times, Caul realizes the couple is actually saying, "He'd kill *us* if he got the chance." He figures out too late that the couple is justifying murder.

DETECTIVE AND THRILLER STORY BEAT: Plan/ Investigation Step 5—Re-create a New Reality: The Story

In the first four steps of her investigation, the detective gathers the symbolic objects as evidence and breaks them down to their core meaning. Now she recombines the clues to create a different reality of what happened. The detective goes from analysis to synthesis. This synthesis is not simply a verifiable theory. It is a story.

DETECTIVE AND THRILLER STORY BEAT: Final Reveal of the Killer's Fatal Mistake

Until this moment, the clues and reveals have pointed away from the real killer. But he makes one mistake that leaves a hole in his story. This final reveal is the tipping point: the physical clue points right at him. This prompts the detective to re-create the correct version of reality. Now the pieces of the puzzle fit.

Early in *L.A. Confidential*, Ed confides to Jack that Rolo Tomasi is the name he uses for the man who got away with killing his father. After Captain Smith shoots Jack, Jack's last words are "Rolo Tomasi." Smith asks Ed if he knows anything about "Rolo Tomasi." Ed realizes that Smith murdered Jack.

In *Vertigo*, Gavin Elster's fake wife, Madeleine, is obsessed with a portrait of a woman wearing a diamond necklace. After her apparent death by suicide, Scottie starts to date Judy, who has an uncanny resemblance to the dead woman. Before going out to dinner, Scottie sees Judy wearing the necklace from the portrait. He realizes that Judy is Madeleine and that Elster gave her the necklace as payment for helping him murder his wife.

KEY POINT: The final reveal must be the biggest and the best. When it's good, it can make the entire story.

TECHNIQUE: The Least Likely Killer

The killer should be the least likely to have committed the crime.

The form's emphasis on reveals points up another challenging requirement for the author:

- you need a complex mystery where the reveals build to the final surprise, and
- the final surprise must be an ingenious solution that shocks the audience but also makes sense.

In *Murder on the Orient Express*, Agatha Christie comes up with one of the greatest surprises in the history of Mystery. She does it by upending the entire form. Readers are so used to the single killer that the idea of twelve people murdering the victim never enters the reader's mind. The brilliant trick at the heart of the story is that twelve is the number of members on a jury who will try and, in this case, execute a man who deserves to die.

Knives Out's Ransom Drysdale is bad news. He is so clearly the most likely person to have murdered his grandfather that experienced Detective viewers immediately dismiss him as the real killer.

DETECTIVE STORY BEAT: Battle—Trial of the Killer and the Battle of Stories

The detective re-creates the crime using a different story. She then confronts the real killer with the truth of what he has done. In effect, the detective conducts a trial. She uses the pressure of a "trial" to get the killer to make his fatal mistake. This reveal gives the detective the final proof that her theory is correct. Under this pressure, the killer breaks and makes one last effort to get away.

KEY POINT: This trial of the killer is really a battle of stories. *Both* should be logical. But only one is true.

In classics like Agatha Christie stories and the *Thin Man* series, this battle of stories takes place in a theatrical setting with all possible suspects present.

The film *Murder on the Orient Express* is the ultimate example of a battle of stories. In the final trial with all suspects present, detective Hercule Poirot presents two theories/stories of what happened. The first interpretation of the evidence is that the murderer, disguised as a conductor, used a passkey to enter Ratchett's compartment. He stabbed him to death, then left the train when it was stopped by the snowdrift. The killer was probably a rival member of the Mafia who was exacting revenge over some disagreement.

The second interpretation of the same evidence indicates that all twelve passengers stabbed the man because he masterminded the kidnapping and murder of a baby to whom they were all intimately connected. Due to the ambiguity of the signs and the fact that the victim was a despicable man guilty of murder, the detective takes the higher moral path and concludes the truth will never be known.

THRILLER STORY BEAT: Battle—Opponent's Final Attack

In the Thriller battle, the opponent discovers that the hero knows of his guilt and attacks. The hero must fight back from a position of extreme weakness.

KEY POINT: The hero should come up with a new way of fighting in order to win. Ideally, she should improvise a last-second solution.

In *Rear Window*, his leg in a cast, Jeffries sits in his wheelchair in the dark when he hears the murderer, Thorwald, coming to silence him. Armed with nothing but his camera, Jeffries takes a picture with a flash that temporarily blinds Thorwald. Jeffries keeps replacing the bulb and taking pictures. This slows Thorwald but doesn't stop him. Finally, Thorwald pushes Jeffries out the window. Jeffries holds on by his fingertips, then lets go just as the police arrive to break his fall.

Michael Clayton confronts corporate lawyer Karen Crowder, who ordered the murder of Michael's friend Arthur. He says that instead of trying to kill him, she should have bought him off. This is her one and only chance before he takes his evidence to the police. He is bluffing. He must get her to confess so he can get it on tape. She agrees to pay him ten million dollars. He photographs her with his phone and walks away as police swarm around her.

Police Procedural Battle: The Interrogation

In the last few decades, the Detective story on television has largely taken the form of the Police Procedural, which shifts the main character to a team of cops. In these shows, the battle often occurs in the interrogation room. This creates a pressure cooker effect as the cop bores in on the suspect.

Examples include police detective Jane Tennison in *Prime Suspect*, Brenda Leigh Johnson in *The Closer*, Detective Andy Sipowitz in *NYPD Blue*, Detectives Olivia Benson and Elliot Stabler in *Law & Order: Special Victims Unit*, and DC Janet Scott in *Scott & Bailey*.

DETECTIVE AND THRILLER STORY BEAT: Self-Revelation—the Detective Sees Her Own "Crime"

Detective stories do not give the hero a special kind of self-revelation. This is especially true in a series, whether for book, film, or television. Instead, the hero goes from one case to another like a "traveling angel." She uses her brilliant mind to solve crimes committed by killers who have weaknesses. But she rarely has a new self-revelation about her own flaws.

Examples include Sherlock Holmes, Hercule Poirot, Miss Marple, Benoit Blanc (*Knives Out*), Mma Ramotswe (*The No. 1 Ladies' Detective Agency*), Columbo, Nick Charles (*The Thin Man*), Jessica Fletcher, Lord Peter Wimsey, Inspector Maigret, Father Brown, Patrick Jane, and Castle.

In more ambitious Detective stories, the detective has serious personal flaws that she confronts at the end of the story. She has a negative self-revelation about how she played a part in the larger tragedy.

Sarah knows she has done brilliant police work in finding Rosie Larsen's killer in *The Killing*. But she realizes she has probably lost her son in her zeal to get the job done.

At the end of *Vertigo*, Scottie has a deeply negative self-revelation. He realizes he's been a fool, unable to truly love. By dragging Madeleine to the top of the tower and then refusing to forgive her, he sees that he is partly responsible for killing the woman he loved.

DETECTIVE AND THRILLER STORY BEAT: Moral Argument—Poetic Justice

The moral argument in the Detective form funnels down to this point: the only way to make a premeditated killer pay properly for his crime is through poetic justice. Poetic justice is payment in kind, a creative consequence to that crime. This solution is justified in both moral and story terms.

Why is poetic justice so powerful in the Detective form? Putting justice in the hands of an impersonal system is rarely satisfying. Murder can never be paid in full. The person is dead forever. Only poetic justice can get close to balancing the moral books and giving the victim's family a sense that justice has been done. Poetic justice is notoriously difficult to achieve, but when it happens there is nothing better.

Murder on the Orient Express may be the greatest example of poetic justice in the history of story. A man who masterminded the kidnapping-murder of a child is found dead from twelve stab wounds. The fact that there are twelve members in a jury is what makes it the perfect punishment in both fact and symbol.

Early in *L.A. Confidential*, Captain Smith asks Ed Exley, who is up for promotion to detective, if he would be willing to kill a guilty man if he thought the man would get off. When Exley says no, Smith tells him in no uncertain terms that he should not become a detective. At the end of the story, Exley holds a gun on Smith and is about to arrest him for the multiple murders. When Smith says he will talk his way out of conviction, Exley shoots him in the back. Using Smith's criterion, Exley proves he is worthy of being a detective.

Vertigo flips the poetic justice from killer to detective. This is one of the reasons *Vertigo* is among the greatest Detective stories. When Scottie discovers that the woman he loves has involved him in Gavin Elster's scheme to murder his wife, he drags her to the top of the tower where the crime occurred. She begs him for forgiveness, but he refuses. When a dark figure climbs the stairs, she backs up in terror and falls to her death. This mimics the apparent suicide of Elster's wife. Meanwhile, Elster, the real killer, goes free. Scottie realizes he will forever pay for the death of the woman he loved.

The Conversation is a transcendent Thriller in part because poetic justice is applied to the investigator, not the killer. The hero has made a mistake that has led to a man's murder. In so doing, we also see the hero's fatal flaw.

Detective Theme: Being Is Questioning and Discovering Guilt

The Detective story states that questioning is the daily task and challenge of being. Every moment of every day we look at signs to determine the truth. Usually it's easy. This looks like a wall, while that looks like a door. I will go through the door.

What happens when we are confronted with more complex problems? Then the detective, "I," must use the most refined tools of consciousness to get at the truth. Our life may depend on it.

Detective says that the great danger of being is in letting our story of how the world works harden into ideology. This creates a template of who we are and how the world responds to us. Yet the template may be wrong, and it freezes our sense of what we can become.

The Detective story gives us a second sense of being. It is about *discovering* guilt, then assigning responsibility. Every day is a moral battleground where each of us takes actions that affect others. To live with others, we must constantly balance the moral books.

Thriller Theme: Being Is Uncovering Our True Enemies

Thriller changes our sense of daily being from an intellectual challenge to an emotional one. The most difficult investigation is about those closest to us. How do our intimate bonds control us? Worse, what if our lover or family member is actively trying to hurt us or force us into intimate enslavement? This is the most terrifying dystopia imaginable.

Such slavery would be devastating by itself. But the investigation needed to bring it to light would also be extremely challenging and possibly dangerous. How do we see clearly when our judgment is clouded by love? How do we break out of our chains when our jailer is aware of our investigation?

Detective Thematic Recipe: The Way of the Truth

Each genre's recipe for becoming our best self comes from two sources: the hero's basic action and the key question the genre asks. Because the detective's final act is to bring the killer to justice, she is often confused with the cop whose job is to enforce justice. The detective's primary task is to find the truth. Usually this quest results in the guilty person going to jail and the innocent going free. But that is not always the case. Nor is it the point.

The right way of living, according to the story form, is to ask questions and look behind appearances to find the truth, no matter the consequences. Truth improves the quality of our lives.

By focusing on the act of finding the truth, the Detective story highlights the human mind at its best. Therefore, in the Detective genre, the highest expression of becoming is the artist-scientist, which is one of the key elements in the Story of the Mind.

Values, also known as virtues, are inherent in the thematic recipe of any genre. The Action form says that all values depend on courage. The Detective form says that all values—such as morality, justice, and freedom—depend first on the truth, and second upon taking responsibility.

Another element that determines the thematic recipe is the key question all stories in the genre ask. In the Detective form, the key question is: Who is guilty and who is innocent? Notice that this question combines the two main values of the Detective form, truth and responsibility.

The moral argument of the Detective story is a combination of determining truth and assigning blame. Both are necessary. The moral argument comes to a head at the end of the story, when the detective must decide whether to hand the killer over to the police.

Thriller Thematic Recipe: Finding the Truth About Our Loved Ones

Becoming in the Thriller is different than in Detective because the key question is not: Who did it? The question is: Is your suspicion justified? This is a far greater challenge when the opponent is intimate.

This represents a deeper question of "being" in the world. Can we trust those closest to us? Or are they using us for their own benefit? Asking these questions can be extremely difficult. But Thriller says that real freedom and growth are not possible without doing so.

In Thriller, the hero's basic action is to investigate while escaping attack. Taken to its logical extreme, this means Thriller requires us to uncover and confront our personal tormentor. It says that to live well we must stand up to those who we believe are hurting us, even if it may only be in our head. The alternative is that we live the rest of our days in a bondage we have helped create.

How to Transcend the Detective/Thriller Story

The Detective story may be the key genre of the modern world. In the relatively affluent Western world, few of us are Action heroes. But we are all detectives. The mind is the source of our world and the life we lead. It is also the final frontier in our quest to make life meaningful.

A transcendent Detective story takes two major forms:

1. The Cosmic Detective/Thriller
The first transcendent Detective story, the Cosmic Detective/Thriller, is an investigation into the complexity of guilt and the meaning of life. The detective's investigation eventually leads to herself. She discovers her own guilt and a larger responsibility we all have for one another. This provides the foundation for a new moral vision. The Cosmic Detective/Thriller usually combines Detective or Thriller with Myth, Epic, and Drama. Examples include *Oedipus Rex*, *Hamlet*, *The Maltese Falcon*, *Laura*, *Vertigo*, *L.A. Confidential*, *The Silence of the Lambs*, *The Conversation*, and *Shadow of a Doubt*.
2. The Story of the Mind and Truth
The second transcendent Detective story is an investigation into the mind itself. As a result, we discover that the mind works as a story. The mind's first story is the character called "I." One of the best techniques for expressing the Story of the Mind is known as self-reflexive, a "meta" fiction that highlights the act of telling a story while it unfolds.
The Story of the Mind is automatically about how we know the truth.

KEY POINT: Truth only happens when the mind works well. This is a mind that finds solutions.

The Story of the Mind isn't about getting to the One Truth. It emphasizes the methodology that gives us the best chance to get to the closest approximation of truth. The end point of the methodology is recognizing a truth for that particular moment. But it is also a method that produces the highest forms of truth: art, science, and philosophy. This is a mind embodied in the artist-scientist.

Examples include: Sherlock Holmes stories and their modern-day versions on television, *The Trespasser*, *Rashomon*, *The Usual Suspects*, *The Name of the Rose*, *Foucault's Pendulum*, *Last Year at Marienbad*, *The Conversation*, *Blow-Up*, *The Conformist*, *Identity*, *Shutter Island*, *Memento*, *Westworld*, *L'Avventura*, *The Big Lebowski*, *Being There*, *The Father*, *Inside Out*, *Inception*, *The Illusionist*, *Sleuth*, *The Hours*, *À la recherche du temps perdu* (*In Search of Lost Time*), *A Portrait of the Artist as a Young Man*, *Ulysses*, *Mrs. Dalloway*, *To the Lighthouse*, *Citizen Kane*, *The Sound and the Fury*, *Absalom, Absalom!*, *Trainspotting*, *Breathless*, *Frankenstein*, *American Psycho*, *Sliding Doors*, *A Heartbreaking Work of Staggering Genius*, *Everything Is Illuminated*, *The Real Thing*, *Copenhagen*, *Noises Off*, *The Norman Conquests*, *House and Garden*, and *Betrayal*.

Transcending Detective 1: The Cosmic Detective/Thriller

Since the classic Detective story focuses strictly on who killed John Doe, the first way to transcend comes from exploring a more advanced goal and theme. The Cosmic Detective Story shows the investigator searching for psychological and moral truth. The end point is about finding solutions to social problems and ways of living a meaningful life in a morally challenging world.

The Cosmic Detective story explores advanced themes in three areas simultaneously:

1. The psychological: why the victim was killed
2. The social: the society that produced the crime and the justice system that brings the criminals to trial
3. The cosmic: the search for ultimate meaning in this life

The writer has a lot of leeway in this form. However, the story structure best designed to express all three elements is Detective combined with Myth or Epic, and Drama.

We explored the Myth genre in detail in chapter 4. Drama is too broad to be considered a genre. But it is a story form with certain traits, especially the intimate opponent and the final moral decision. The main effect of combining Myth and Drama with Detective is to make the investigative journey more fantastic and to add interpersonal drama and detailed moral conflict.

The most important feature of a Cosmic Detective story is how the detective's investigation leads to herself. She must learn of her own moral and psychological failings.

KEY POINT: The detective has a deep flaw, an internal opponent of her own. Tracking the *external* opponent, the murderer, must eventually lead the detective to discover her *internal* weakness.

We mentioned that the moral argument in a classic Detective story ends with the hero deciding whether to hand the killer over to the police.

KEY POINT: The Cosmic Detective story asks: Who else is to blame? And especially, what is the detective's own responsibility for the crime?

Oedipus Rex: The First Detective Story

Oedipus is the first detective in the history of story. *Oedipus Rex* begins with a plague in the land. An oracle says this plague was caused by the murder of the old king. So King Oedipus takes it upon himself to find out who did it.

There are three main ways that *Oedipus Rex* is a Cosmic Detective story. First, the detective is also the king. This creates a one-to-one connection of detective to kingdom: as the hero goes, so goes the society. When the hero is corrupt, the society has a plague.

Second, this detective doesn't just investigate the murder. He investigates the moral responsibility of everyone involved, including himself. What constitutes immoral behavior is defined in personal, social, and cosmic terms. Oedipus commits a crime against the entire natural order (the cosmic), and that destroys him (the psychological) and his kingdom (social).

Third, the detective and the killer are the same man. This meets the crucial requirement for transcending the form: the detective discovers that he is in some way guilty of the crime. The key questions for Oedipus, the detective, change from "Who done it?" to "Who am I?" and "How is the agent of justice the most guilty one of all?"

Hamlet: The Greatest Detective Story

It's been said that Shakespeare's four major tragedies progress from the most human, mind-oriented story of *Hamlet* to the most primal, life-oriented story of *King Lear*. The extreme mental element is just one reason *Hamlet* is arguably the greatest Cosmic Detective story. With its masks, plays, madness real and performed, and constant questioning and probing, *Hamlet* presents a story world and plot sequence similar to the modern big city where Sam Spade, Philip Marlowe, and Jake Gittes roam.

These are just a few of the story elements that make *Hamlet* the epitome of a Cosmic Detective story:

- *Hamlet* explores the problems of the young adult: identity and coming to responsibility.
- The play makes heavy use of the ghost and conflict within Hamlet between the rational and the mystical.

- It shifts from mythical to modern man: Hamlet is a young Ulysses trying to connect his warrior past to his artistic self.
- Shakespeare doesn't structure the story using the traditional warrior opposition. In other words, Hamlet doesn't go head-to-head with his main opponent. In fact, he barely confronts him.
- Hamlet's key struggle is not against King Claudius or his mother. It is within himself to find the right action and make his peace with the inequities of the world. In going from "Who done it?" to "Who am I?" this play, like *Oedipus Rex*, explores one of the great challenges of the human being: the nature of one's own identity.

Shadow of a Doubt: The Epic Thriller

An Epic Thriller represents the fate of a nation. The theme of the Epic Thriller is to show the dark side of Western freedom and capitalism and to attack the Western way of life. In this it is similar to the transcendent Gangster story. *Shadow of a Doubt*, the greatest Epic Thriller, is a scathing attack on the American system, corruption in the family, and the unequal relationship between the sexes.

Transcending Detective 2: The Story of the Mind and Truth

In working through the beats of the Detective story, we discovered that the detective's synthesis of what happened is not simply a theory that must be verified. There are two stories unfolding simultaneously.

First is the story of a number of people who had motive to kill another human being. One or more of them actually did. They used premeditation and deception in an attempt to evade guilt. Now a final conflict will determine the truth of who will pay the price for the killing.

Second is the story of how the detective uncovered that truth. This is the process of the mind at work. Basic Detective stories track the steps of discovering who murdered whom. Transcendent Detective stories focus on how the mind works and the process it uses for getting to the truth.

KEY POINT: With its ability to project symbols and be self-conscious, the mind is both the first and last art form and the first and last frontier for humankind.

The story of how the mind works reveals how it's able to work so well.

KEY POINT: The sequence of the story beats tracks how the mind can grow and get smarter.

To get a sense of how this complex Detective Story of the Mind unfolds, we'll explore the following revelation sequence. This form of transcendent Detective story is epistemology in fiction form:

- **REVEAL 1:** The mind works through story. Therefore, the story of the mind is first of all about how story itself came to be. It's the biological basis of Story. Dreams are the obvious way the brain creates stories. But the mind's artistry is more expansive than that. Simply by being self-conscious, we can step out of ourselves and consider our consciousness separately.
- **REVEAL 2:** The first story the mind creates is the story of a character called "I." The mind makes itself a character and then uses that character to live a story every day.

This ability to create the character "I" is the most powerful expression of the human ability to project symbols.

- **REVEAL 3:** The mind's success lies in the *methodology* it creates to look at itself and the world.

The Story of Myself, the Original "Origin Story"

The transcendent Detective Story of the Mind is about self-consciousness, how the mind creates itself as a story. All other stories are created through that lens.

As self-conscious beings, we begin by creating our own character, which we call "me," "myself," and "I." We immediately become aware of what is lacking within us, which are our needs. We create objects of desire, which fill our lack and give us what we need. These are symbols outside of us, and so our mind begins to populate the world with objects and characters. It also begins to create opponents. These are the characters that prevent us from getting what we need and want. Together these elements make up our "Origin Story."

Consciousness is fundamentally a problem-solving device. It is the tool the body uses to sense danger to its existence and overcome it. Always the success of the story comes down to two main steps: desire and opponent. Why are these steps so primal?

- Desire is the fuel of action. Opponent is the counterforce.
- Desire is attraction and opponent is repulsion, forward and backward along the same line.
- Bottom line: desire means Yes, opponent means No.

KEY POINT: Every story puts characters in a constraining situation and shows them struggling to get free.

The way consciousness experiences everything through the character of "I" plays out the struggle dramatically. Thought becomes emotionally engaging. What consciousness learns and teaches is thus more memorable and improves our chances of survival.

Stories of Internal Narration and Stream of Consciousness

TECHNIQUE: Matching Structure with Mind

Transcendent Detective stories attempt to match the structure of the story with how the mind works and feels.

Stories of internal narration and stream of consciousness track the mind *while it's working*. The character experiences the past, present, and future simultaneously based on mental associations.

Why is this useful? As storytellers, we need to account for the fact that humans only live in the present. "Now" is the first time frame. But these moments make up a second time frame: our entire life. So the sequence of all these moments creates patterns and affects what we experience now.

The words and images give us the constant now. The overall story structure shows us how the various "nows" create the larger pattern of change in our lives.

Examples include *À la recherche du temps perdu* (*In Search of Lost Time*), *A Portrait of the Artist as a Young Man*, *Ulysses*, *Mrs. Dalloway*, *The Hours*, *To the Lighthouse*, *The Sound and the Fury*, *Trainspotting*, *A Heartbreaking Work of Staggering Genius*, and *Everything Is Illuminated*.

Stories of the Self

Stories that deal with the self focus on its creation and destruction.

KEY POINT: The best way to show both the creation and destruction of the self is metafiction.

Metafiction highlights the fact that the story the audience is reading/watching was created in the author's mind. By extension, it's about how the mind itself is a form of story, complete with structure steps.

Another term for this highly specialized fiction technique is "self-reflexive." The author makes the audience aware that they are looking at a created work that is constantly being re-created as they watch.

When metafiction is applied to a story of the self, the mind typically becomes so self-conscious that it divides permanently. Life becomes a hall of mirrors, an infinite internal regression where the character thinks about themselves thinking about themselves thinking about . . . This is magnified tenfold when using mass media, which electronically divides image from reality.

Examples include *Shutter Island*, *Memento*, *Inside Out*, *Citizen Kane*, *8½*, *Six Characters in Search of an Author* (play and *Twilight Zone* version), *Birdman*, *Inception*, *Mulholland Drive*, *Fight Club*, *American Psycho*, *The Metamorphosis*, *Stranger Than Fiction*, *The Game*, *The Catcher in the Rye*, *Breathless*, *Persona*, *3 Women*, *Sherlock Jr.*, "switch comedies" like *Freaky Friday* and *17 Again*, *The Changeup*, *The Strange Case of Dr. Jekyll and Mr. Hyde*, *The Stranger*, *The Conformist*, *Absalom, Absalom!*, *Being There*, *The Good Person of Szechwan*, *A Portrait of the Artist as a Young Man*, *A Beautiful Mind*, and *Orlando: A Biography*.

Fight Club: The Divided Self

Fight Club is the ultimate self-reflexive book and film. The nameless narrator is intensely self-conscious. He constantly reflects on the modern cultural messages that are drowning him. Every technique and story beat highlights a mind looking at itself to the point of self-destruction.

The film starts at the cellular level in the hero's brain. The flashback Storyteller Structure uses a first-person unreliable narrator (a concept we'll discuss below) who doesn't tell us initially that his friend, Tyler, is really his doppelgänger. Because the narrator can't sleep or feel emotion, he goes to support groups of diseases he doesn't have just to hear the stories. He is fully aware that consumer culture enslaves him:

NARRATOR: Like so many others, I had become a slave to the Ikea nesting instinct . . . I flipped through catalogs and wondered: What kind of dining set defines me as a person?

When he tells Marla, a fellow support group junkie, that he has "more than one side" to him, she responds: "More than one side? You're Dr. Jekyll and Mr. Jackass!" He meets Tyler, who works nights and is a projectionist.

NARRATOR: You had to give it to him: he had a plan. And it started to make sense, in a Tyler sort of way. No fear. No distractions. The ability to let that which does not matter truly slide . . . [looking at a Calvin Klein ad on a bus] Is that what a man looks like?

TYLER: Self-improvement is masturbation. Now self-destruction . . .

The narrator and Tyler form "Fight Club" as a means of defining themselves and fighting the culture.

TYLER: How much can you know about yourself. You've never been in a fight? I don't wanna die without any scars.

NARRATOR: When the fight was over, nothing was solved, but nothing mattered. We all felt saved.

Later, Tyler expands Fight Club to Project Mayhem, a movement bent on destroying corporations. He argues they're saving humankind from the oppression of Consumer and Fear Culture through guerrilla warfare. Finally, the narrator realizes that he *is* Tyler. But he can't stop Tyler's takeover.

TYLER: Hey, you created me. I didn't create some loser alter-ego to make myself feel better. Take some responsibility! . . . All the ways you wish you could be, that's me. I look like you wanna look, I fuck like you wanna fuck, I am smart, capable, and most important, I am free in all the ways that you are not.

Caught in an endless feedback loop between his two negative selves, the narrator tries to commit suicide. He fires a shot through his cheek that kills Tyler. But the mass destruction continues. The narrator has created a downward cycle to hell from which he cannot escape.

TECHNIQUE: Point of View and Multiple Truths

> **KEY POINT: Any use of point of view in a story makes a comment about how the mind works and how it fails.**

Using a unique or multiple point of view makes the reader painfully aware of the personal prison within which every mind lives. But point of view is also one of the ways we free ourselves from the tyranny of our own limited subjectivity. This is especially true in "first person," common in the Detective form, and in what's known as "third-person close" (or "third-person limited"). Third-person close shows the story through one character's perspective. Using this point of view, the author can also jump inside other characters' minds.

KEY POINT: Point of view may be the single most powerful technique in story.

Why?

First, in telling a story through particular points of view, we force the reader to experience the character's unique interpretation. This strong sense of *what that character is feeling* connects the reader to the story.

Second, point of view allows the author to divide the characters' actions from what the author thinks about them.

TECHNIQUE: Events Outside the POV

To take full advantage of first-person point of view, create events that happened just beyond the hero's perspective. Then, when the hero discovers what she missed, there is a plot reveal.

Atonement

Young Briony Tallis sees her older sister Cecilia having an argument with Robbie, the housekeeper's son, by the fountain. Cecilia strips down to her slip and retrieves something from the fountain. What Briony doesn't see is that these two have a strong romantic attraction. This misinterpretation eventually leads Briony to accuse Robbie of raping a fifteen-year-old girl. She tries her entire life to atone for this mistake but fails.

Multiple-point-of-view stories use a different approach to overcome the straitjacket of subjectivity. A single event is remembered by a number of characters who offer radically different points of view. As a result, what each says happened is different.

Here the author shows us that we are a subjective mind

living in a world of other subjective minds. The story gives us a moment of omniscience and freedom beyond the limits of our own mind.

If POV in story shows us various limitations and inherent bias of the mind, it also shows us how multiple truths can exist simultaneously. Here, the reader can see the different lies each person expresses, even when they are not aware of it. But POV also allows the reader to see contradictory truths that each individual understands. This leads to a larger insight about the relationship between point of view and truth.

KEY POINT: Truth is not the opposite of lying. Truth and lying exist on a spectrum where both truth and lie are complex and ambiguous.

This is a crucial component to the Detective Mind-Action story view. In a world where lies and exaggeration come at an exponentially faster pace, knowing where the truth exists, even though it's not black or white, is essential for a good life.

TECHNIQUE: The Unreliable Narrator

The "unreliable narrator" is a fun POV technique that increases plot. The writer gains the reader's trust by using a particular character to narrate what happened. Since the speaker was actually there, the reader assumes that what is said is "The Truth." In fact, eyewitness testimony is highly suspect. Even when trying to be completely truthful, the individual *must* express bias.

The narrator then tricks the reader in some way, either by shading the truth, withholding information, or outright lying. The great reveal of the story comes the moment the reader realizes that the narrator has lied or is misinformed. This is also the moment the reader gains a deeper understanding of the mind itself. She sees the inherent bias in every mind, including her own.

Rashomon: We Are All Unreliable Narrators

Rashomon is the ultimate example in story of the relativity of truth and the power of the unreliable narrator. A woodcutter tells of an incident in which a thief ties up a samurai and rapes his wife. The samurai ends up dead. The question is how and why. The bandit, the wife, and the samurai's ghost give radically different explanations. Then the woodcutter tells yet another story of the events.

This multiple viewpoint, known as the "*Rashomon* effect," is commonly described as each individual giving different versions of the truth. But on the spectrum of interwoven truth and lies, they are really telling different lies. Every story necessarily involves the storyteller's bias and agenda.

The Next Rung Up the Ladder

The Detective story provides us with the tools to find the truth. Thriller helps us believe in ourselves and stand up for our freedom against those who try to attack us. But neither Detective nor Thriller gives us guidance about what we can do to create happiness in our lives.

In the previous chapter, we saw how Fantasy gives us one approach to happiness: open up our mind so we can see all we can become in a positive world of our creation. But Fantasy doesn't tell us how to live beautifully with that one special person.

For that, we need Love.

13

Love Story: The Art of Happiness

The Philadelphia Story: Modern Jane Austen

The Philadelphia Story is the perfect expression of the laws of Jane Austen, queen of the Romantic Comedy form. Tracy Lord, "ice goddess," must choose among three suitors. Each represents a different version of a man and a marriage. Love means choosing the right partner for happiness.

The Love Story: How It Works

The Love story tracks two people whose attraction and affection cause them to form a "marriage." It's based on the idea that each person grows *through* another person. The logic of the Love story works like this: the main character has a unique need that can only be fulfilled by one other person in the world. In other words, the lover must always be necessary to the main character and vice versa.

KEY POINT: Love stories say, "This is who I *must* be with to make my life great."

The love union is the smallest, most intimate society in life. We know from the other genres that there is always an internal contradiction, a push-pull, between the individual unit and the social whole. This ties in with the overall story strategy of the Love genre: force two people to sacrifice some of their individuality for the benefit of their life together. Initially, both characters resist making the sacrifice. Over the course of the story, each sees that the long-term gain far surpasses the short-term loss.

Love Mind-Action Story View

The Love story Mind-Action story view is that love is both a feeling and an action. It says that life is more than the state of being alive. Love is what cares for life, gives life meaning, and makes it thrive.

All genres give us a recipe for how to live. Love is the recipe for day-to-day happiness. It details the language of growth at the most intimate level. And it makes life great for both the individual and society.

KEY POINT: The Love story is the most profound of all story forms because it shows us that we become our true and best self by forming a community of two.

Like all genres, the Love story explores one or more art forms of human life. The traditional Love story expresses the art of love. The transcendent Love story expresses the art of marriage and happiness itself. It says we have a happy life only by learning *how* to love.

Philosophers from Plato and Aristotle to Bertrand Russell, Simone de Beauvoir, Jean-Paul Sartre, Irving Singer, and bell hooks have argued that learning how to love involves finding balance between one's personal interests and the best interests of the other.

Love Compared to Other Genres

Love vs. Action

At first glance, the Love story is clearly the opposite of the Action story. Action is about chasing a goal and destroying any obstacle that gets in the way. Love stories are about creation and rejuvenation. Care is love in action.

But when we look closer, we see that the genre's foundation has always linked Love closely to the Action form. Indeed, in the history of story, it has been difficult to separate the two.

From the beginning, the genre has been rife with Love stories that are really Action stories. The structure works like this: a confident man meets a beautiful woman. He wants her and chases her. She says no. He continues the chase. She resists for a while, but eventually he "wins" her over by "proving" his "love." This is not a Love story; it's a stalking story.

Love may be the most problematic of story forms. No other genre deals with such an extreme difference within the human being: from "lowest" lust to "highest" love. That's why a strong argument could be made for discussing the Love story early in the book, right after Horror and Action. Horror is about the first distinction of life versus death. Action is also primal, since it is required to live. Love in its most basic expression is procreation, necessary to life itself. In this sense, love is the opposite of action. One creates life; the other often destroys it.

The reason we discuss the Love genre last is that it shows us the way to an emotional quality of life far beyond procreation. Love is the highest capacity and experience of the human being. Without it, we cannot be fully human.

Examples of Love

Novels, Films, and Stories

The entire Romance Novel catalogue, *Camille*, *Jane Eyre*, *The Notebook*, *Rebecca* (also Thriller), *The Thorn Birds*, "The Gift of the Magi," *The Time Traveler's Wife*, *Outlander*, *Casablanca*, *The Great Gatsby* (also "Eastern"), *Silver Linings Playbook*, *500 Days of Summer*, *Sideways*, *Sleepless in Seattle*, *Bridgerton*, *Notting Hill*, *Moonlight* (also Coming-of-Age), *A Knight in Shining Armor*, *The 40-Year-Old Virgin*, *La La Land*, *Serendipity*, *Carol*, *Rocky* (also Sports), *The Big Sick*, *Moonrise Kingdom*, *Heartbreaker*, *The Wedding Singer*, *Tootsie*, *Groundhog Day*, *Shakespeare in Love*, *Slumdog Millionaire* (also Coming-of-Age), *Four Weddings and a Funeral*, *Wedding Crashers* (also Buddy Story), *Jerry Maguire*, *Moonstruck*, *Bull Durham* (also Sports), *Gilda* (also Crime), *How Stella Got Her Groove Back*, *If Beale Street Could Talk* (also Crime/Social Drama), *Beloved*, *Love in the Time of Cholera*, *Like Water for Chocolate*, *My Big Fat Greek Wedding*, *Wuthering Heights*, *The Goodbye Girl*, *Romeo and Juliet*, *Broadcast News*, *To Have and Have Not*, *Up in the Air*, *The Thomas Crown Affair* (also Caper), *10 Things I Hate About You*, *Dark Victory*, *The Year of Living Dangerously*, *Titanic*, *Call Me by Your Name*, *The Lady Eve*, *The Shop Around the Corner*, *You've Got Mail*, *The Night Circus* (also Fantasy), *Juno*, *High Fidelity*, *The Last of the Mohicans* (also Action), *Forrest Gump* (also Myth/Drama), *Crazy Rich Asians*, *Out of Sight*, *What's Up, Doc?* (also Comedy), *Risky Business*, *Almost Famous* (also Coming-of-Age), *Say Anything* (also Coming-of-Age), *The English Patient*, *Love and Basketball* (also Sports), *Brown Sugar*, *Amélie* (also Traveling Angel Comedy), *Harold and Maude*, *Knocked Up*, *The Hunchback of Notre Dame* (also Horror), *Brokeback Mountain*, *Splash* (also Fantasy), *While You Were Sleeping*, *Bridget Jones's Diary* (also Comedy), *Eternal Sunshine of the Spotless Mind*, *Sabrina*, *Bringing Up Baby*, *Delta of Venus*, *Just Wright*, *Deliver Us from Eva*, *A Room with a View*, *Strictly Ballroom*, *Always Be My Maybe*, *As Good as It Gets*, *Breakfast at Tiffany's*, *Sex, Lies, and Videotape*, *Woman of the Year*, *Romancing the Stone* (also Buddy Story), *Pygmalion*, *My Fair Lady*, *There's Something About Mary*, *Waiting to Exhale*, *Marty*, *Before Sunrise*, *Before Sunset*, *Before Midnight*, *The African Queen*, *The Gay Divorcée*, *Top Hat*, *Malcolm & Marie*, *Humoresque*, *Howards End*, *They All Laughed*, *Cyrano de Bergerac*, *Roxanne*

Love Subgenres

Romantic Comedy, Tragedy, Comedy of Remarriage, True Love, Epic Love, Erotica, Contemporary, LGBTQ+, Historical, Paranormal, Romantic Suspense, Young Adult, Black and African American, Military, Clean and Wholesome, Fantasy, Gothic, Vampires, Werewolves, Action Adventure, and many more.

Love Story Overview

Here's what we'll cover in this chapter:

- **LOVE STORY BEATS**
- **THEME:** Being Is Loving
  - Thematic Recipe: The Way of the Lover
- **HOW TO TRANSCEND THE LOVE STORY**
  - The Tragedy of Traditional Marriage
  - The Comedy of Remarriage
  - True Love and the Art of Marriage

Love Story Beats

The Love Story is a precise genre with over twenty distinct story beats. These form a *choreography* that demonstrates the deep love between two people.

The following beats are for a real Love story, not a sexual Action story. But a real Love story doesn't abandon physical attraction. Attraction is one of the main features that move the relationship beyond friendship to romance. A real Love story emphasizes a mutual chase and attraction that builds from animal lust to deeper qualities, interests, and shared values.

Every genre has structural elements that make it a challenge to write well. But the Love story, especially the subgenre Romantic Comedy, may be the most difficult genre of all. That's because the Love story turns on two contradictory structure beats: desire and opposition. On one hand, the story should take only ten minutes. Two people are strongly attracted to one another. The rest is negotiation.

On the other hand, the audience can't just *see* two people fall in Love. They have to *feel* it. That means a lot of page and screen time as each struggles to overcome their fear of love. These two contradictory elements account for many of the story beats that make up the form.

LOVE STORY BEAT: Story World/Canvas and Field of Play—Mind-Body and Exotic Subworld

In one respect, the Love story has the smallest story world/playing field of any genre: the mind-body of the lead characters. Regardless of the specific time or place, the lovers become progressively more interested in living strictly in the mind and body of the other. Structurally, the lover is simultaneously the story world, desire, and main opponent.

The mind is a rich fantasy world because of its ability to project symbolically. Over the course of the story, each character tries to get deeper within the other. They do this emotionally by delighting the other's mind and earning their trust, and physically by building their desire.

Yet, the lovers' mind-body is not the only story world. Placing the lead characters in exotic subworlds can promote the dream each has about the other. These are the many fabulous nooks and crannies where the prospective lovers can have physical touching, intimate conversation, and utopian moments.

When we think of world-building and utopian/dystopian worlds, we think of genres like Myth, Science Fiction, and Fantasy. We don't normally think of Romance novels, or the Love story in general. But we should, because it's one of the keys to a great Romance.

Clearly, the subworlds in Romance novels are utopias. However, they are also dystopias, and the writer needs both to push Romance to the transcendent level.

One of the reasons Regency is such a popular subgenre is that it appears to be a grand and utopian era for love. The Regency period in England, from 1811 to 1820, featured pretty dresses, elaborate dances, and balls in grand mansions that evoke a world that's one big party of witty banter between women and men. The reader wants to visit again and again.

How is the Regency world a dystopia? Similar to the foundation principle underlying old English society discussed in the Gangster chapter, this was a system where a man's inheritance went to his firstborn son. Therefore, the Regency story world is a disaster for women and almost every man.

Even though women are trying to marry dukes and lords, they're chattel. If a woman doesn't make the big score, she's dead. Her worth is based on her ability to look pretty, sit quietly, and not have a thought in her pretty little head. And above all, she must not be confrontational.

Jane Austen depicted this brilliantly in all her books, but

especially in *Pride and Prejudice*, where her heroine, Elizabeth, is extremely intelligent and confrontational. Incredibly, she ends up marrying the richest man in the county. He's the only man in England who likes it when a potential wife calls him morally deficient.

KEY POINT: You must depict the dystopia as well as the utopia in the story world of Love.

One of the best Love stories ever, *Four Weddings and a Funeral* has utopia and dystopia buried in the title and the premise. A wedding is a mini utopia: it's a time of perfect love *between* the couple and the community's love *for* the couple. A funeral is a mini dystopia, a time of despair and death, and the loss of a member of the community. This movie promises four utopias and a dystopia. How could anyone not want to watch it?

KEY POINT: Any subworld should help create love. As much as possible, it should:

- **be a physical manifestation of these unique characters,**
- **contribute to them falling in love with each other, and**
- **invite the reader to fall in love with them.**

That's why subworlds in Love are often exotic, cozy, self-contained, unique, and timeless.

The importance of major subworlds to the success of Romance novels is apparent from the categories listed on Amazon, the biggest seller of Romance novels in the world: Regency, twentieth-century, Scottish, Medieval, Victorian, American, ancient world, Viking, and Tudor. Even these settings are replete with smaller romantic subworlds to further the love.

In *Casablanca*, Rick and Ilsa first fall in love in Paris, the city of love, just as World War II is starting. They rekindle their love in the exotic locale of Casablanca. Rick's bar is both a dystopia of people waiting to escape the Nazis and a utopia of community, music, and fun.

LOVE STORY BEAT: Technology—Words of Love

From the outside, it may seem that the Love story has no unique technology. In fact, the crucial technology of love is mankind's first tool, language.

> **KEY POINT: Love stories, especially Romantic Comedies, put more emphasis on witty dialogue than any other genre.**

The greatest joy of the form is neither an erotic sex scene nor the marriage at the end. It's the banter between two people. For those who love Love stories, this is sex through words. For the audience, it's better than sex.

LOVE STORY BEAT: Ghost—Cycle of Fear

In Love stories, the ghost from the past is a love that ended badly. This deep emotional wound has closed them off to the possibility of finding new love. Examples include *Silver Linings Playbook*, *Sleepless in Seattle*, *The Philadelphia Story*, *Gilda*, *Camille*, *The Goodbye Girl*, *Four Weddings and a Funeral*, and *Heartbreaker*.

Silver Linings Playbook: Pat has recently been discharged from a mental health facility but must live in his parents' home. He is still hopelessly in love with his wife, Nikki, who filed a restraining order after he almost beat her lover to death.

PAT: Nikki's waiting for me to get in shape and get my life back together. Then we're going to be together.

Sleepless in Seattle: Sam comforts his son Jonah after the boy has a nightmare. Sam hopes Jonah's late mother is in heaven.

JONAH: I'm starting to forget her.
SAM: She could peel an apple in one long, curly strip. The whole apple . . .
SAM: I love you, Jonah.
JONAH: I love you, Dad.

Caution: Bad Love stories (let's not mention any names) show the ghost in a predictable and unbelievable way. Making one of your characters emotionally crippled from losing a love long ago is a genre cliché.

TECHNIQUE: The Ghost Cycle

One way to avoid this cliché is the ghost cycle, an ongoing fear of love in the present. Typically, the main opponent in a Love story is the lover.

> **KEY POINT: In the best Love stories, the true (internal) opponent is love itself. When a person begins to feel new love, they are afraid.**

TECHNIQUE: The First Fight

This fear is expressed when the eventual lovers meet. Why? They usually fight. Notice this makes no sense in real life. If you're attracted to someone, the last thing you would do is immediately start a fight with them.

Why do the lovers often fight at the beginning of Love stories? First, because we need conflict to extend the story. Second, they always fight to a draw. This shows that they are equal and right for each other.

The main reason they fight is that they suspect if they fall in love, they will lose their freedom and some of themselves. And they know the loss will hurt.

KEY POINT: This shows a fundamental principle of story: the intimate opponent does the most damage.

The would-be lovers are right to be afraid. But the strategy of the form is that, in the long run, they will gain far more through the love of this unique person. Examples include *Bridgerton*, *Notting Hill*, *Broadcast News*, *Moonstruck*, *Sex, Lies, and Videotape*, *Marty*, and *Romancing the Stone*.

LOVE STORY BEAT: Hero's Role—Lover

The hero in Love drives the story and provides the spine on which all the other story beats depend. The beats play out the difficulty of two people finding love with each other, and the great value of doing the work to make that happen.

LOVE STORY BEAT: Weakness-Need—Inability to Love
TECHNIQUE: Love Weaknesses

Begin your story by establishing two people who have weaknesses about love.

These weaknesses are so severe that both characters are experiencing a miserable life. At the beginning of the growth process, characters are isolated, closed down, and without love. As a result, their souls are dead. They are *unable to love*.

Potential weaknesses that block love include: living superficially, being lost in illusion, in despair, bored, lonely, bitter, cynical, afraid of or angry at others, lack of self-esteem, selfish, prejudiced, and judgmental.

KEY POINT: In the best Love stories, the lead characters have a moral as well a psychological weakness having to do with love. They don't know how to love and that hurts someone else.

TECHNIQUE: Mutual Need

In Love stories, it is especially useful to give the two characters a variation of the same need. This helps the audience better understand how the characters begin closed off and how they blossom at the end.

In *Silver Linings Playbook*, Pat has bipolar disorder, but that's not his weakness. His weakness in love is that he is obsessed with a past relationship. Tiffany's weakness in love is that she has been using sex as a substitute for intimacy. After they meet at a dinner party, Tiffany tries to jog with Pat.

PAT: What the fuck? I'm married!
TIFFANY: So am I!
PAT: What the fuck are you doing? Your husband's dead!
TIFFANY: Where's your wife?
PAT: You're crazy!
TIFFANY: I'm not the one who just got out of that hospital in Baltimore.
PAT: I'm not the big slut . . . I'm sorry . . . I'm sorry . . . I'm sorry.

Character Potential

The Love story is unique in establishing the hero's potential at the same time as their weakness and need. This comes from the profound idea that we become most fully ourselves *through love*, by joining in a community with another person. This is the character's *potential* for growth.

TECHNIQUE: Character Potential

Give each character vast potential even though they are unable to love. The hero must see this potential in the lover and vice versa.

Qualities that show potential:

- **QUIRKY PERSONALITY:** *500 Days of Summer*, *Annie Hall*, *High Fidelity*, *The Big Sick*, *Moonrise Kingdom*
- **VITALITY:** *Broadcast News*, *Wuthering Heights*, *Dark Victory*, *Pygmalion*
- **DETERMINATION:** *The Great Gatsby*, *Slumdog Millionaire*, *Jerry Maguire*, *Romancing the Stone*, *Born Yesterday*
- **VALUES:** *The Last of the Mohicans*, *Broadcast News*, *Adam's Rib*
- **SPECIAL ABILITY:** *The Thomas Crown Affair*, *Out of Sight*, *The Lady Eve*, *To Have and Have Not*, *The Big Sleep*
- **MORAL STRENGTH AND SENSE OF JUSTICE:** *Casablanca*, *If Beale Street Could Talk*, *Woman of the Year*, *The Hunchback of Notre Dame*
- **INTELLECT:** *Pride and Prejudice*, *Sideways*, *What's Up, Doc?*, *Bringing Up Baby*, *The Year of Living Dangerously*
- **GOOD HEART:** *Moonlight*, *The Time Traveler's Wife*, *Sleepless in Seattle*, *You've Got Mail*, *Rocky*, *Marty*

One of the best expressions of seeing potential in a possible lover is in the film *Out of Sight*, based on the Elmore Leonard novel. The story begins with thief Jack Foley forcing FBI agent Karen Sisco to join him in the trunk of a car so he can escape prison. Sparks fly, though she doesn't want to admit it. Later, he sits across from her in a bar.

JACK: It's like seeing someone for the first time, like you can be passing on the street, and you look at each other for a few seconds, and there's this kind of a recognition like you both know something. Next moment the person's gone, and it's too late to do anything about it. And you always remember it because it was there, and you let it go, and you think to yourself, "What if I had stopped? What if I had said something?" What if, what if . . . it may only happen a few times in your life.

KAREN: Or once.

JACK: Or once.

This dialogue encapsulates the real story of how these two people met, and how they later ran into each other. He waved at her as she waited for the elevator. They have this conversation and then they go up to her room to make love.

The Love story is all about the "What if . . ." It's the premise, the hypothesis, the thought experiment of the perfect combination of these two people at this exact moment of greatness. But the window of opportunity closes fast.

LOVE STORY BEAT: Desire—Life and Love

The main desire line in a romance is each character's wish to be with the other. To give the story a single spine and maximum narrative drive, one character's desire typically tracks the action.

> **KEY POINT: Love stories have the most intense desire of any genre.**

In a sexual Action story, the desire is purely physical. A man sees a beautiful or sexy woman and wants her, then goes out and gets her. As we have said, this is not a Love story.

In a Love story, intense desire plants the seed that changes the soul.

KEY POINT: A good Love story shows how love affects the living of one's entire life. Therefore, the best Love stories show a person trying to succeed in life with another person.

Structurally, that means the story has two desire lines: success in life and in love. So instead of beginning with love, we start by setting the success track of both characters, which is the life desire.

There are two main approaches to establishing the life desire:

1. He is ambitious in work while she wants love. In other words, she is ambitious through him. This old-fashioned approach is no longer possible or desirable. For example: *Howards End*, *Sense and Sensibility*, *To Have and Have Not*, *Pretty Woman*, *The Best Years of Our Lives*, *Casablanca*, *Camille*, *It's a Wonderful Life*, and *Woman of the Year*.
2. Two individuals try to be successful on their own. Both have a drive to succeed, but love stands in the way. Or each has a conflicting view of success. Eventually, they must learn that love can help both succeed in their life's work. For example: *The Big Sick*, *Shakespeare in Love*, *500 Days of Summer*, *Sideways*, *Wuthering Heights*, *Pride and Prejudice*, *Broadcast News*, *The Thomas Crown Affair*, *Annie Hall*, *Adam's Rib*, and *Tootsie*.

LOVE STORY BEAT: Desire—Gaze, Meeting, and Longing

After setting up the story world and each character's life desire, establish the main desire of the story: the lover. By breaking the love desire down into steps, the writer can build the love between the two characters so the audience can feel it, too.

The three main steps of love desire are:

1. The gaze
2. The meeting, known as "meet-cute"
3. The longing

Love Desire Step 1—the Gaze

Since the hero's main goal is to win the love of a particular person, the first step of the Love desire is the gaze. This is the first time one character sees the other.

KEY POINT: In real time the gaze happens in a flash. Yet it is one of the most important beats in a good Love story.

One challenge in Love is sustaining the story for longer than ten minutes. Another is to make the chemistry between the leads believable. These two characters must become lifelong lovers, not just friends.

KEY POINT: The gaze is the lightning strike of desire. But it shouldn't be about seeing an attractive woman or man. Rather, it's about sensing someone of incredible value in the face and movement of the other. The gaze that leads to deep love has X-ray vision.

This is a deeply ambivalent moment. While each character feels an intense attraction, each is also fearful. This is the "yes/no," the attraction/repulsion found in most Love story beats. We'll discuss the yes/no as we move through the beats.

500 Days of Summer: At a staff meeting, Tom gets his first look at Summer, a new hire at the company.

NARRATOR: For all intents and purposes, Summer Finn was just another girl. Except she wasn't . . . It was a rare quality, this "Summer effect." Rare, and yet something every postadolescent male has encountered at least once in their lives. For Tom Hansen to find it now in a city of 400,000 offices, 91,000 commercial buildings and 3.8 million people . . . Well, that could only be explained by one thing . . . Fate.

The fundamental difference of male-seeing versus female-hearing is highlighted in one of the few exceptions to the traditional Hollywood male-driven love story, *Sleepless in Seattle*. One of the ways it transcends the genre is by flipping this beat.

Annie is the main character driving the action. She doesn't see her eventual lover at first. She hears him. In fact, she hears a detailed story of a man's almost perfect love for his dead wife. She experiences him first on the human level, and more precisely, as a loving husband and father. Presumably, when she finally sees him she is pleased that he is not ugly. But his looks are irrelevant to whether she falls in love.

Love Desire Step 2—the Meeting

The second step of the love desire is the "meet-cute." This is where the two characters meet in a fun, serendipitous, and even bizarre way. This has a number of advantages:

- It brings in the idea of destiny, which increases the stakes. The story doesn't just involve two people. These two are destined to be together. The entire universe wants this to happen.

- It shows the audience that this is going to be romance, not friendship.
- It creates immediate conflict. Again, starting a Love story with a fight isn't realistic. But it makes a lot of structural sense. To create more than ten minutes of story, you have to have conflict.

Sometimes, this meeting makes the woman angry, or at least miffed. If the man is in control, he finds it amusing. The danger of this approach is that it's become a cliché and moves the story toward Action.

500 Days of Summer: Tom is listening to music on his headphones in an elevator when Summer enters. She notices his music.

SUMMER: I love the Smiths.
TOM: Sorry?
SUMMER: I said I love the Smiths.
SUMMER: You . . . You have good taste in music.
TOM: You . . . like the Smiths?
SUMMER (*Singing*): To die by your side, such a heavenly way to die.
SUMMER: I love 'em.
The elevator stops. Summer leaves while Tom stands there dumbfounded.
TOM: Holy shit.

Silver Linings Playbook reverses the "meet-cute" beat. Pat is socially awkward in the extreme. Pat's friends, Ronnie and Veronica, invite him and Tiffany over for dinner. Ronnie warns Pat not to ask Tiffany about her husband Tommy's death.

PAT: You look nice.
TIFFANY: Thank you.

PAT: Oh, I'm not flirting with you.

TIFFANY: Oh, I didn't think you were.

PAT: I just see that you made an effort, and I'm gonna be better with my wife. I'm working on that. I wanna acknowledge her beauty. I never used to do that. I do now. Just practicing. How'd Tommy die?

Love Desire Step 3—the Longing

For the traditional male lead character, we see two kinds of longing.

Option 1: The man wants the woman but keeps cool and controlled. Examples include *Pretty Woman*, *The Thomas Crown Affair*, *The Year of Living Dangerously*, *They All Laughed*, *Tootsie*, *The Big Sleep*, *To Have and Have Not*, *Rocky*, *Casablanca*, *Cyrano de Bergerac*, and *Roxanne*.

Option 2: The man wants the woman but totally exposes his heart. In this approach, the tough, cynical woman often laughs at him at first. But she is touched by his passion and the high value he places on her. Examples include *The Philadelphia Story*, *Wuthering Heights*, *Of Human Bondage*, *The Hunchback of Notre Dame*, *Camille*, and *500 Days of Summer*.

The woman's desire for the man is just as intense but usually more reserved. She must break through a barrier to let go. Examples include *Sleepless in Seattle*, *How Stella Got Her Groove Back*, *Moonstruck*, *About Last Night*, *Broadcast News*, *Pride and Prejudice*, and *The Thomas Crown Affair*.

In *Sleepless in Seattle*, after hearing Sam on the radio, Annie concocts an excuse at work to track him down, hires a detective to help, flies across the country, rents a car, and finds his house. But at the first moment of doubt when seeing him across the road, she rushes back home.

My Bildungsroman Reveal: The Quest for Cool

Love stories have immense power, especially when you see a great one at an impressionable age. My personal bildungsroman would not be complete without mentioning this scene from *The Thomas Crown Affair* (1968). Why? It almost ruined my life.

Master criminal Thomas Crown has pulled a bank robbery just to prove he could do it. Insurance investigator Vicki Anderson suspects him. While she looks for proof, they begin to date. In this scene, Crown has brought Vicki home in his Bentley. It's been raining and the windshield wipers are slapping back and forth. For a moment neither person says a word.

CROWN: Tomorrow?
VICKI: What about it?
CROWN: Us. Dinner.
VICKI: Marvelous.
CROWN: About six?
VICKI: Perfect.
He turns off the car.

I was sixteen when I first saw this movie. For the next twenty years I tried to be this cool. I failed miserably. Finally, I discovered that no one can be this cool, not even Steve McQueen. But by then the damage had been done. That is now my ghost, my scar, my shame. It hurts to this day.

Visual Shapes of the Love Plot: Linear, Branching, and Round

Like Action and Western, the classic Love story uses the most popular story shape, the linear. The typically male hero has a single goal, the lover, that he chases with intensity, and one main opponent, also the lover, trying to stop him. It looks like this:

When a number of individuals seek love simultaneously, Love uses the branching shape. The big danger in these stories is a lack of narrative drive due to all the crosscutting. The solution is a branching-in shape where all the storylines converge in one time and place.

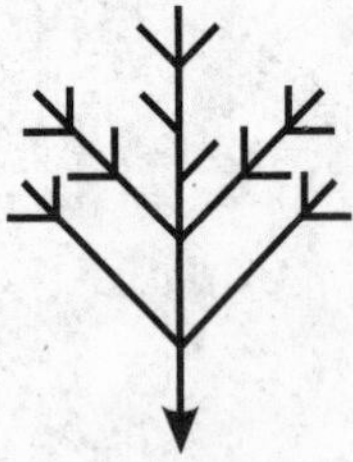

Examples include *Love Actually*, *He's Just Not That into You*, *New Year's Eve*, and *Valentine's Day*.

The round shape tells a story of extended connection where no one but the audience is aware of how the characters are related to one another. The round uses a passing-the-baton sequence where we go from one incident to another, with the same character in two successive scenes.

- **SCENE 1:** character 1 wants character 2
- **SCENE 2:** character 2 wants character 3
- **SCENE 3:** character 3 wants character 4, and so on, until the final character wants character 1, thus completing the circle

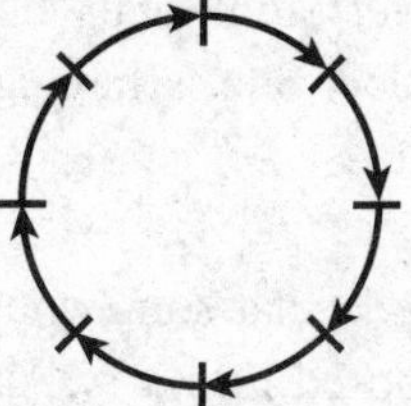

> **KEY POINT: The round is a comic view of society where the audience, in the superior position, sees the connections but the characters don't. The problem with the form is that it is highly episodic and therefore doesn't build.**

Examples include the original round story, Arthur Schnitzler's *Reigen*, as well as adaptations like *La Ronde*, the opera *Reigen*, *The Blue Room*, *Hello Again*, and *Choose Me*, *Sisterhood of the Traveling Pants*, *Paris, je t'aime*, *The Earrings of Madame de . . .* , *Le Fantôme de la Liberté* (*Phantom of Liberty*), and the beginning of *He's Just Not That into You*.

LOVE STORY BEAT: Allies—Love Advisors

Much of the success of the Love story depends on character oppositions. This refers not just to the two leads but also to the connection and contrast among the heroes and allies.

Each main character has a friend who gives them advice about love. That advice usually has to do with the stereotypical flaws of the other gender. These well-intentioned advisors are almost always wrong.

TECHNIQUE: Extending the Allies

Use the allies as a way of taking the Love story beyond simple dating to being about how men and women live their lives together.

In *When Harry Met Sally*, Sally has recently broken up with her boyfriend, Joe. She is having lunch with her best friends, Marie and Alice.

MARIE: All I'm saying is that somewhere out there is the man you are supposed to marry. And if you don't get him first, somebody else will, and you'll have to spend the rest of your life knowing that somebody else is married to your husband.

TECHNIQUE: Connecting Ally to Hero

Make each friend a variation on the hero's great weakness in love.

In the Romantic Comedy *Knocked Up*, each ally takes the lead character's weakness to its logical end point as a way of life. Main character Ben is a man-child who just wants to party and have one-night stands. Ben's ally is not a lone bachelor but a group of adolescent boys in men's bodies. Each is a permanent man-child with complete freedom but no love, children, or chance of ever getting them.

Main character Alison is a mature woman who's just gotten a promotion. Her ally is not a single woman, bitter about love and men, but a couple whose marriage is worn to the breaking point. They have love and kids, but no freedom or sense of self. Each faces the constant realization that they're growing old.

LOVE STORY BEAT: Character Web

Most Love stories focus on the two would-be lovers and their love advisors. But you still need to create the larger society that makes up the story world. This is especially valuable if you wish to detail a utopian and/or dystopian world. Also, in a Romance Novel series, a larger web of characters is necessary to extend the story.

Bridgerton is *Pride and Prejudice* with an entire television season to play out the story. This is one of the great advantages of the TV medium. *Pride and Prejudice* uses five daughters in one family to focus on how the system is designed to put women at a huge disadvantage. Within that same social structure, *Bridgerton* uses a family of four sisters and four brothers. The two four-point oppositions—sisters and brothers—show both female and male points of view in an unjust system.

This character web is also the source of the series' designing principle. Indeed, author Julia Quinn has written a Romance novel for every sibling. Notice the story strategy. In the first novel, one character is in the foreground and the others swirl around her. In the next novel she retreats to the background and another sibling moves to the foreground.

This is a brilliant strategy, not only for creating a utopian and dystopian social tapestry for each story, but also for extending the basic premise into a long-running novel and then TV series.

LOVE STORY BEAT: Main Opponent—Lover

The most difficult part of structuring the Love story is setting up the opposition. Many writers wrongly believe that the main opponent is someone who opposes the love, like a competing suitor or family member. These can be excellent secondary opponents.

The main opponent in a Love story is not an outside character but the potential lover. This is counterintuitive. The potential lover is the person the hero wants the most. So how can this be the main opponent?

KEY POINT: The lover is the main opponent because he/she is the biggest obstacle to making the love relationship work.

Structurally, the fact that the lover is both the desire and the main opponent is the main reason Love stories are among the most difficult genres to write well. It is also the source of the problem we discussed earlier: How do you create ongoing conflict between two people who are deeply attracted to each other? Put another way, how do you create enough plot?

There are four main ways to set up an ongoing opposition:

TECHNIQUE 1: Creating an "Odd Couple"

Make the lovers fundamentally different, based on values, power, wealth, and/or status. Ideally, try to make them opposites in some basic way.

KEY POINT: Always look for a difference that lasts.

Examples of differences that last:

- ***FOUR WEDDINGS AND A FUNERAL***: American versus British, forward versus reserved
- ***TITANIC***: rich, high-class family girl versus poor, low-class orphan
- ***WUTHERING HEIGHTS***: life of wealth versus life of passion
- ***PRIDE AND PREJUDICE***: rich, haughty man versus middle-class, self-righteous woman
- ***HOW STELLA GOT HER GROOVE BACK***: she's a forty-year-old stockbroker from the city versus a twenty-year-old from Jamaica
- ***WHEN HARRY MET SALLY***: contrasting views of men and women
- ***PRETTY WOMAN***: prostitute versus billionaire
- ***THE THOMAS CROWN AFFAIR***: male criminal versus female investigator
- ***ANNIE HALL***: control freak versus free spirit

- ***PYGMALION***: high-class professor versus lower-class flower seller
- ***BORN YESTERDAY***: intellectual versus "dumb" blonde
- ***THE LADY EVE***: rich, naive scientist versus con artist

TECHNIQUE 2: Family Opponents

Bring in outside opposition, like family.

The family's power over the individual has radically decreased in the modern city world. Therefore, opposition from the family is less common and not as effective as it was in traditional romances. But it still has value in generating conflict, especially in relationships that vary from tradition in race, religion, class, gender identity, sexuality, and physical ability.

Examples include *Titanic*, *Wuthering Heights*, *Pride and Prejudice*, *Bridgerton*, *Romeo and Juliet*, *West Side Story*, *Crazy Rich Asians*, *Howards End*, *The Big Sick*, *My Big Fat Greek Wedding*, *Moonlight*, *Brokeback Mountain*, *Call Me by Your Name*, and *My Fair Lady*.

TECHNIQUE 3: Mistakes

Have each character make mistakes, especially toward the other.

> **KEY POINT: This essential technique is why all great Love stories involve trust and forgiveness: trust that the other will not hurt them and forgiveness when they inevitably do.**

Examples include *The English Patient*, *Four Weddings and a Funeral*, *Casablanca*, *Howards End*, *Wuthering Heights*, *Camille*, *Pride and Prejudice*, *Moonstruck*, *The Thomas Crown Affair*, *You've Got Mail*, *Sex, Lies, and Videotape*, *The Lady Eve*, *Tootsie*, *Gilda*, and *Brief Encounter*.

TECHNIQUE 4: The Love Test

Put each character to the test: How much can you love? Test them *through conflict*.

In *Slumdog Millionaire*, the powerful crime boss, Javed Khan, controls Latika's every move. Test: Can Jamal overcome his jealousy and defeat the boss? Can Latika forgive Jamal for not having faith in her?

In *You've Got Mail*, Kathleen Kelly owns a small bookstore. Joe Fox's mega-bookstore is going to put her out of business. Test: Can she forgive him for destroying her dream? Can he forgive the horrible way she has treated him?

And in *Brokeback Mountain*, Jack and Ennis try to hide the loving bond between them from their eventual wives. Test: Can these men escape their traditional marriages and their fear of being killed by homophobes so they can be together?

As the two lead characters fall in love, they fight about three elements of increasing importance:

1. Personality
2. Success, money, family, and status in society
3. Morality: how each character treats others

The characters don't move from one type of conflict to the next so much as they layer one on top of the other. This adds much-needed conflict and plot to the story.

> **KEY POINT: Underlying all opposition in the classic Love story is the first human distinction: man versus woman. To get to marriage, each character must learn to accept and even enjoy the unique qualities of the other gender.**

This is difficult for both of them to do. Why? Man versus woman is grounded in biological differences that create psychological tendencies. These solidify into cultural stereotypes.

Together these factors create an overall moral view that each has of the other. To simplify horribly: men think women are sheep; women think men are pigs. Men interpret women's tendency to connect as "easily influenced" and "following the herd." Women interpret men's tendency to act aggressively as "selfish" and "oppressive."

How does each gender translate the stereotype when it comes to self-confidence and moral responsibility?

WOMAN: "I'm not good enough and it was all my fault."
MAN: "I'm great and it was all your fault."

Notice the obvious contradiction in the way both genders take responsibility. If a woman wasn't good enough to do the job, how can it all be her fault when it goes wrong? If a man is so great at doing the job, how can it be someone else's fault when things don't work?

LOVE STORY BEAT: Opposition Step 1—the Joust

We've already seen that the two main characters often fight when they first meet. Again, this unrealistic action gives the Love story plot. It also indicates the reluctance of the characters to weaken themselves through an attraction to the other.

From their first meeting on, the story builds conflict. The future lovers spar with each other to show they are of equal quality. They're playing a game, with each testing the other through action and words. Early on, the conflict is usually about personality, a superficial level.

In *You've Got Mail*, Kathleen is about to have her first date with her mystery correspondent. She is disappointed that he fails to show. Instead, her archenemy, Joe Fox, appears at the same restaurant. She doesn't realize he is her correspondent.

Gone with the Wind should be a perfect example of building conflict between the two potential lovers, except for one big problem. *Gone with the Wind* is not a Love story.

Just as no one believes Sam Spade is in love with the scheming Brigid O'Shaughnessy in *The Maltese Falcon*, no one believes that Scarlett O'Hara is in love with Rhett Butler, nor he with her. Scarlett is in love with Ashley Wilkes, first and forever. She only marries Rhett because she can't have Ashley. He is married to a saint.

Gone with the Wind is a paradise lost story (see the Fantasy chapter), but only from the point of view of the land-rich, white slave owners. This story is the premier example of Southern writers transforming a brutal and treasonous master–slave society into a lost utopian Dixie of gentility, chivalry, and good breeding.

TECHNIQUE: Forced Togetherness

Force the hero and the lover to work together even though they hate it.

This ties in with the problem of sustaining plot. In real life, when two people dislike each other, they go in opposite directions. But that won't allow the prospective lovers the time they need to get to know one another on a deeper level. Forcing them to coexist in the same location allows them both to fight and get to know each other better.

In *Heartbreaker*, Alex is paid to break up couples in which the man is wrong for the woman. A man hires him to stop his daughter Juliette from marrying a rich Englishman. To stay close to her, Alex pretends to be her bodyguard. Although she protests vehemently, she can't avoid it.

LOVE STORY BEAT: Opposition Step 2—Additional Suitors

Jealousy is the other side of the coin of longing. It also involves the gaze, but this time from a competing suitor.

TECHNIQUE: The Second Suitor

Bring in a second and sometimes third suitor to increase the conflict.

The competing suitor is the first outside opponent. He may be someone to whom the lover is engaged or has a close connection. Often, this character is high-class and stuffy.

- ***FOUR WEDDINGS AND A FUNERAL***: Carrie's first husband, Hamish Banks, is an arrogant, controlling Scottish politician.
- ***HEARTBREAKER***: Juliette's fiancé is Jonathan, a stuffy Englishman.
- ***SLEEPLESS IN SEATTLE***: Annie's fiancé, Walter, is pleasant but dull.
- ***WUTHERING HEIGHTS***: Jealousy is an ugly emotion that often leads to cruelty. When wealthy Edgar Linton wines and dines Cathy, Heathcliff says this to the love of his life:

> Tell the dirty stable boy to let go of you. He soiled your pretty dress. But who soiled your heart? Not Heathcliff. Who turns you into a vain, cheap, worldly fool? Linton does. You'll never love him, but you'll let yourself be loved because it pleases your stupid, greedy vanity.

TECHNIQUE: Comparing the Suitors

To increase plot, consider using a third suitor who also wants the lover and, in contrast to the second suitor, is smooth and sophisticated.

KEY POINT: The second suitor should embody an element the main character feels is missing in himself. The suitor is an alternate path of how to live and love. When present, the third and fourth suitors increase the opposition and represent other paths of marriage and life.

Jane Austen is the master of this technique. In fact, she defined the modern Romantic Comedy form. Using the classic fairy tale rule of three, she typically gives the heroine three suitors:

1. The heroine is first presented with the dull, conventional, even buffoonish man whose only appeal is that he will inherit enough money to provide the physical needs of life. This means sexual and emotional death.
2. Next is the charming, charismatic man who appears to be both marriage material and sexually exciting. She is initially drawn to this man but discovers he is hollow and lacks integrity.
3. Hidden in the background is the man of character who is neither charismatic nor dull, but has great integrity and deep love for the heroine. This man has the right combination of traits for a happy marriage.

In *Sense and Sensibility*, Marianne Dashwood has romantic notions of great love. The upstanding Colonel Brandon is clearly in love with her, but he does not fit her romantic ideals. One day, while riding in a storm, Marianne twists her ankle and is saved by the dashing John Willoughby.

The Philadelphia Story: The screenwriters Philip Barry and Donald Ogden Stewart are masters of the Austen technique of comparing the men. The story's four-point opposition is:

Hero: Tracy Lord, haughty and moralistic, cannot forgive her ex-husband for the behavior that broke up their marriage.

Main Opponent: Dexter, her upper class and sophisticated ex-husband, has learned humility and tolerance in overcoming his drinking problem.

Second Opponent: Mike, a middle-class reporter, is straightforward and passionate.

Third Opponent: George, Tracy's stuffy, social-climbing fiancé, is the embodiment of Rags to Riches who is overly concerned with appearance and propriety.

LOVE STORY BEAT: Plan—Scam

The big challenge in the middle of the Love story is how to build the opposition to keep the plot from being episodic.

TECHNIQUE: The Love Scam

Begin by giving the hero a plan, preferably a scam.

A scam is a plan that involves deception. There are three basic approaches to the plan.

Plan 1: the man applies full-court pressure. This type of plan involves the man relentlessly pursuing the woman with roguish charm. The problem with this approach is that it's patronizing and arrogant. Examples include *The Great Gatsby*, *Wuthering Heights*, *Rocky*, *Pride and Prejudice*, and *Of Human Bondage*.

Plan 2: the man scams the woman. In this approach, the man tricks the woman into liking him. Again, the woman becomes an object of conquest, which moves us closer to the sexual Action story. However, this does represent the reality of the way many men approach courtship. It also expresses an internal moral flaw the man must overcome to gain real love.

KEY POINT: Along with the first dance, the scam is the most important beat in Romantic Comedy.

Why is this technique so useful?

- Since whatever is hidden must eventually be revealed, it creates more plot.
- It is the fun part of the romance.
- The scam turns the Love story into a game.

KEY POINT: The more a traditional Romantic Comedy film is like a game, the more likely "traditional" men are to see it.

Examples include *Wedding Crashers*, *Groundhog Day*, *Sideways*, *Tootsie*, *Heartbreaker*, *The 40-Year-Old Virgin*, *You've Got Mail*, *Cyrano de Bergerac*, and *Roxanne*.

The 40-Year-Old Virgin: Cal has sent Andy into a bookstore to practice meeting women. His rule: only ask questions.

BETH: Can I help you?
ANDY: I don't know. Can you?
BETH: Are you looking for something?
ANDY: Is there something I should be looking for?
BETH: We have a lot of books, so maybe it depends on what you like.
ANDY: What, um, what do you like?
BETH: We have a great section of do-it-yourself.
ANDY: Do you like to do it yourself?
BETH: Sometimes . . . if, um, the mood strikes!
ANDY: How is the mood striking you now?
They laugh.
BETH: What's your name?
ANDY: What's your name?
BETH: I'm Beth.
ANDY: Andy.

BETH: Andy . . . Don't tell on me, okay, Andy?
ANDY: I won't . . . unless you want to be told on, Beth.
Andy smugly walks away.

Plan 3: the woman pursues and scams the man. This plan typically involves the woman coming up with a scam to get the man to ask her out and sometimes to marry her. Examples include *Sleepless in Seattle*, *Shakespeare in Love*, *The Lady Eve*, *About Last Night*, *Bringing Up Baby*, *What's Up, Doc?*, *Broadcast News*, and *The Thomas Crown Affair*.

In *The Lady Eve*, Jean Harrington is a con artist working on a cruise ship. When rich scientist Charles Pike boards the boat, she sets her sights on him. In the dining room, Jean watches him through her compact mirror as one woman after another makes a pass at him. As he leaves, she sticks out her foot and trips him, knocking him to the floor.

JEAN: Why don't you look where you're going?
CHARLES: Why don't I look?
JEAN: Look what you did to my shoe. You knocked the heel off.
CHARLES: Oh I did? Well I'm certainly sorry.
JEAN: You did and you can take me right down to my cabin for another pair of slippers.
CHARLES: Well certainly. I guess that's the least I can do. By the way my name's Pike.
JEAN: Oh everybody knows that. Nobody's talking about anything else. This is my father Colonel Harrington. My name is Jean. It's really Eugenia. Come on.
Jean, limping on one shoe, and Charles exit the dining room together.
JEAN: Funny our meeting like this, isn't it.
CHARLES: Yes, isn't it.

TECHNIQUE: Extending the Scam

Try to extend the scam as close to the end of the story as possible.

In a Romantic Comedy, much of the plot and audience interest ends with the conclusion of the scam. The ideal is to extend the scam at least through the battle.

Heartbreaker has an excellent scam that extends to the end of the story. As a professional heartbreaker, Alex does in-depth research, uses high-tech equipment, and employs two assistants. To get Juliette to agree to him becoming her bodyguard, he has an assistant steal her car. Then he "heroically" takes it back.

LOVE STORY BEAT: Drive 1—Initiating

The Love story plot is really about deepening the relationship. Initiation is when the two characters have a moment of communion where each finds out what the other one cares about. Each character questions and explores the other to find the *core* of the other person.

This exploration moves from the superficial to the deep. It starts with discussions about books, movies, food, and places they love. It proceeds to showing their homes, families, and/or unique customs. Finally, it deepens to discussions about what they dream of becoming in their lives, and what they value as human beings.

Examples include *Sideways*, *High Fidelity*, *500 Days of Summer*, *Silver Linings Playbook*, *Moonrise Kingdom*, *Annie Hall*, *When Harry Met Sally*, *My Big Fat Greek Wedding*, *A Room with a View*, *Pride and Prejudice*, *The Thomas Crown Affair*, *Dark Victory*, *Sleepless in Seattle*, *Cyrano*, *Pygmalion*, *The Lady Eve*, and *Wuthering Heights*.

The mutual exploration between the two characters has two possible outcomes:

1. the initial passion gains a foundation in respect, or
2. if each doesn't like the other's deepest self, the attraction is seriously weakened or even destroyed.

There is no better example of initiation than the scene in *Sideways* in which Miles and Maya talk about their mutual love of wine. The beauty of the scene is that they fall in love *through* this conversation about what they both love. This is an example of dialogue being more important in Love stories than in any other form. Notice how each is also describing themselves.

MAYA: Why are you so into Pinot? I mean, it's like a thing with you.

MILES: Uh, I don't know, I don't know. Um, it's a hard grape to grow, as you know. Right? It's uh, it's thin-skinned, temperamental, ripens early. It's, you know, it's not a survivor like Cabernet, which can just grow anywhere and uh, thrive even when it's neglected. No, Pinot needs constant care and attention. You know . . . ?

MILES: What about you?

MAYA: I-I like to think about the life of wine . . . How it's a living thing. I like to think about what was going on the year the grapes were growing; how the sun was shining; if it rained. I like to think about all the people who tended and picked the grapes. And if it's an old wine, how many of them must be dead by now. I like how wine continues to evolve, like if I opened a bottle of wine today it would taste different than if I'd opened it on any other day, because a bottle of wine is actually alive. And it's constantly evolving and gaining complexity . . . And it tastes so fucking good.

These words are poetry. They not only make the characters fall in love with each other, they make the audience feel the love, too. That's phenomenal writing.

KEY POINT: Once you've set up the attraction and the opposition between the two leads, the middle of the story is really a back-and-forth between *fighting* and *initiation*.

The initiation beat leads to the biggest problem in the middle of the story: initiation and fighting are direct opposites (again, the yes/no). That's why this back-and-forth is hard to pull off.

TECHNIQUE: Conflict vs. Communion

Use conflict to produce plot and moments of communion to show how love deepens.

Here are two techniques for building the conflict through the middle of the story while continuing the initiation:

TECHNIQUE 1: Two Plot Sequences

The middle should be a series of conflicts with each suitor taking action to win the lover. At the same time, the lover slowly gets new information about who the hero really is.

TECHNIQUE 2: Red Herrings in Love

The lover should also learn false information—"red herrings"—about the hero that makes her dislike him/her even more.

LOVE STORY BEAT: Drive 2—Flirting

The love artist is a master of flirting who knows strategically when to move forward and when to fall back. Flirting is done through conversation. Since the two are expressing attraction, we might think flirting is about paying the other a compliment. Nothing could be farther from the truth. In the fragile building of a romance, paying the other a compliment too soon is the quickest way into the "friend zone."

Flirting is expressed through banter. Structurally, banter is the combination of joust (opposition) and initiation. Banter is verbal dancing.

One of the most common and popular forms of banter, especially in Romantic Comedy, is men and women "riffing." Riffing is "a rapid, energetic, often improvised verbal outpouring, especially one that is part of a comic performance."

KEY POINT: Riffing in Love stories is often about the differences between men and women, again highlighting the dual nature of each story beat to both connect and oppose.

Much of the fun of the riff comes from the recognition that, in many ways, men and women *do* speak different languages.

Good riffing depends on:

- The musicality of the dialogue and
- How insightful the talk is

Examples include *Shakespeare in Love*, *When Harry Met Sally*, *As Good as It Gets*, *Four Weddings and a Funeral*, *About Last Night*, *Annie Hall*, and *Broadcast News*.

When Harry Met Sally: As Harry and Sally drive across the country together they discuss the ending of *Casablanca*.

SALLY: You're wrong.
HARRY: I'm not wrong. He wants her to leave. That's why he puts her on the plane.
SALLY: I don't think she wants to stay.
HARRY: Of course she wants to stay. Wouldn't you rather be with Humphrey Bogart than the other guy?
SALLY: I don't want to spend the rest of my life in Casablanca married to a man who runs a bar. It probably sounds very snobbish to you but I don't.
HARRY: You'd rather be in a passionless marriage—
SALLY: —and be the first lady of Czechoslovakia—
HARRY: —than live with man you've had the greatest sex

of your life with just because he owns a bar and that is all he does.

SALLY: Yes. And so would any woman in her right mind. Women are very practical, even Ingrid Bergman, which is why she gets on the plane at the end of the movie.

LOVE STORY BEAT: Drive 3—Seduction: The Verbal First Dance

Given that each beat in the art of love is both biological and artistic, one of the points of romance is to get to physical love. How does this happen? Through dialogue.

> **KEY POINT: Good talk, more than anything else, is what convinces the characters to have sex.**

Seduction scenes are the verbal equivalent of the first dance. For lovers of Love stories, these scenes represent the highest expression of the art of love.

Generally, there are two kinds of seduction dialogue.

The first is cool talk. Cool talk emphasizes jousting and playing the conflict between men and women. The characters express their interest in each other with understatement, wit, subtext, and double entendre.

Examples include *Four Weddings and a Funeral*, *Wedding Crashers*, *Before Sunrise*, *Before Sunset*, *The Thomas Crown Affair*, *To Have and Have Not*, *Out of the Past*, and *The Big Sleep*.

In *The Big Sleep*, Detective Philip Marlowe is working a case that involves Vivian Rutledge. As he digs deeper he begins to fall for her. Here they verbally spar:

VIVIAN: Speaking of horses, I like to play them myself. But I like to see them work out a little first, see if they're front runners or come from behind, find out what their whole card is, what makes them run.

MARLOWE: Find out mine?

VIVIAN: I think so.

MARLOWE: Go ahead.

VIVIAN: I'd say you don't like to be rated. You like to get out in front, open up a little lead, take a little breather in the backstretch, and then come home free.

MARLOWE: You don't like to be rated yourself.

VIVIAN: I haven't met anyone yet that can do it. Any suggestions?

MARLOWE: Well, I can't tell till I've seen you over a distance of ground. You've got a touch of class, but I don't know how, how far you can go.

VIVIAN: A lot depends on who's in the saddle.

The second kind of seduction dialogue is passionate talk. Passionate talk involves honest expression of feelings. Nothing is held back in trying to connect. The characters make their deepest feelings public. The most common version of this is when the man poetically praises the woman as the ultimate expression of her gender.

Examples include *Outlander*, *Shakespeare in Love*, *The Time Traveler's Wife*, *Moonstruck*, *Sleepless in Seattle*, *Cyrano*, *Roxanne*, *The Philadelphia Story*, *Wuthering Heights*, *Hannah and Her Sisters*, *The Hunchback of Notre Dame*, *Annie Hall*, and *Romeo and Juliet*.

In *The Philadelphia Story*, Mike has become infatuated with Tracy the night before her wedding to George.

MIKE: Tracy.

TRACY: What do you want?

MIKE: You're wonderful. There's a magnificence in you, Tracy.

TRACY: I don't know—go up, I guess, it's late.

MIKE: A magnificence that comes out of your eyes, in your voice, in the way you stand there, in the way you walk. You're lit from within, Tracy. You've got fires banked down in you, hearth-fires and holocausts.

TRACY: I don't seem to you made of bronze?

MIKE: No, you're made out of flesh and blood. That's the blank, unholy surprise of it. You're the golden girl, Tracy. Full of life and warmth and delight. What goes on? You've got tears in your eyes.

TRACY: Shut up, shut up. Oh, Mike. Keep talking, keep talking. Talk, will you?

> **KEY POINT: If you want to write a great love story, have no shame. You must be willing to express deep feelings publicly.**

Audiences demand to hear the hero express total passion for the lover, because they don't get that at home. That's not an insult to you, the reader. No one gets that at home, at least not to that degree. That's why we read books and go to movies.

LOVE STORY BEAT: Revelation—First Dance

The courtship dance represents a revolutionary deepening between the two individuals. It is always a mating dance. Learning the complex steps indicates a willingness of the dancer to play the social game and enter the social unit.

> **KEY POINT: In a serious Love story, the dance is the most important beat because it represents *love played out through action*.**

Why is this beat so valuable?

- The dance makes the love active, dramatic, and infinitely subtle.
- It creates the partnership.
- It's another way to show these two were born to be together.

KEY POINT: You must find a way to reset the obstacles to the love *after* the dance.

Again, we are creating the "yes-no" inherent in almost every Love story beat. After the moment of closeness (the yes), each character feels a rush of fear about what is overtaking them (the no). Therefore:

TECHNIQUE: Returning to the "No"

Right after the dance, remind the characters of the primary difference between them.

These include money, status, morality, and way of life.

In *When Harry Met Sally*, both Harry and Sally are at a New Year's Eve party without a date.

HARRY: And next New Year's Eve if neither of us is with anybody, you got a date.

SALLY: Deal.

They start to dance cheek to cheek. First Sally grows fearful at the closeness between them. Then Harry does. As someone yells out "ten seconds to New Year," they gaze at each other. Harry suggests they get some air.

With Jane Austen, we see the deeper societal function of the first dance. In Austen's England, the complex dance steps that both sexes must learn exist so that these rule-bound men and women can physically touch. This is true to some degree in any first dance. But a society known for requiring chaperones shows it in the extreme.

KEY POINT: The first dance doesn't have to be a real dance. But the two must play off each other as in a real dance.

Broadcast News has the ultimate example of a dance through words, not action. Until this point in the story, newscaster Tom Grunick has shown no romantic interest in producer Jane Craig. When there is an international emergency, they must go on the air live. Handsome Tom is chosen over the more experienced Aaron to anchor. As Aaron tells Jane crucial information over the phone, she feeds it to Tom through his earpiece. He performs beautifully. After the broadcast, Jane sits at her desk. Tom charges in and places both hands on the arms of her chair.

TOM: You're an amazing woman—what a feeling having you inside my head!

JANE: Yeah . . . it was . . . an unusual place to be.

TOM: It's like . . . indescribable . . . you knew just when to feed me the next line. You knew the second before I needed it. There was like, a rhythm we got into. It was like . . . great sex!

He pulls her toward him as she laughs.

This beat also works in mixed genre stories where Love is not the main form.

LOVE STORY BEAT: Revelation—First Kiss

Along with conflict, reveals are the key to plot. Reveals come from hidden information that suddenly becomes known to the hero and/or the audience. Reveals in the Love story are usually subtle, often about the other person's true character. To get these reveals, dig deep into their psychology.

Focus on four things:

1. The subtle differences between the two
2. What each is hiding from the other about their past
3. The growing feelings between them, which they are reluctant to express
4. The hidden agendas that each has going forward

Perhaps the biggest reveal, for both characters, is the first kiss.

> **KEY POINT: The first kiss represents a major leap in intimacy and therefore surprise because (1) the relationship has moved from friendship to romance, and (2) it also marks the highest desire and fear up to that point.**

Each character realizes they may lose themselves in the other for all time. They are at the point of no return.

TECHNIQUE: First Kiss

Frustrate the first kiss as long as possible and make it unique.

Examples of this technique include *It's a Wonderful Life*, *Meet Me in St. Louis*, *The Year of Living Dangerously*, *On the Waterfront*, *The Big Sleep*, *The Thomas Crown Affair*, and every Hallmark movie.

Another approach to the first kiss is for the woman to take the lead. The best example of this approach is *To Have and Have Not*.

First Sex

Surprisingly, First Sex is not one of the major beats in a Love story. There are a number of reasons for this. First, sex scenes are notoriously difficult to write. Prizes are given yearly to the novel with the worst sex scene. Woe that your writing is ever included on that list.

Part of the difficulty of writing "the act" is structural. Narrative drive in the story essentially stops while the couple makes love. Therefore, many writers try to rush through it as quickly as possible to get back to the plot. This is the equivalent of bad sex for real.

Another response to the difficulty of writing a sex scene is simply to skip it entirely. Given that the genre is about romance, not friendship, this creates the problem of the "elephant in the room." You shouldn't remove sex from a Love story. But you also shouldn't put sex before love unless that's the main thing you want to express.

This caution doesn't come from some old-fashioned moral belief that sex should come after love or even marriage. The world doesn't work that way, if it ever did.

This caution has to do with what makes the most powerful emotional impact on the audience.

KEY POINT: If you show sex too early, you virtually kill the possibility of the audience *feeling* that these two people have fallen in love.

The feeling of love, especially at the start of the story, is fragile. Whatever you do, don't kill it!

TECHNIQUE: Love Then Sex

Show the love developing between the characters first. Then, if you want, show them having sex.

Once the characters have sex:

- Immediately bring back the "no." In other words, have them pull back from what they've done. They realize they *may* have made a terrible mistake.

- After sex, make each tentative and gentle with the other to indicate that both still want the higher love.

In *When Harry Met Sally*, the first kiss leads directly to first sex. Sally and Harry are sitting on her bed. She is in tears over a breakup and asks Harry to hold her. They start to kiss passionately. Dissolve to Sally naked in bed with a big smile on her face. Harry is shocked.

The counterargument to holding off sex in a Love story is that this is not realistic. That's true, but it's not how stories of love work best. So break this rule at great risk.

Techniques for writing great sex scenes are remarkably similar to those for having great sex, according to experts. They include:

- Don't rush it. Take your time.
- Indulge the fantasies of the characters.
- Great sex scenes typically involve power held back, then finally breaking through.
- Try to place the scene in a unique location.

Examples include *Henry and June*, *Body Heat*, *Atonement*, *Blue Is the Warmest Color*, *Four Weddings and a Funeral*, *The Conformist*, *The Big Easy*, *Brokeback Mountain*, *Call Me by Your Name*, *Monster's Ball*, *Blue Valentine*, *Bull Durham*, *Don't Look Now*, *Secretary*, *Delta of Venus*, *The English Patient*, *The Year of Living Dangerously*, *Out of Sight*, *In the Realm of the Senses*, and *Risky Business*.

LOVE STORY BEAT: Apparent Victory—Perfect Love Moment

Many Love stories try to capture the essence of the love in one perfect moment. This is the personal utopia for the characters when love colors the world and the two people reach communion. The two become one, usually in a beautiful setting that is a visual manifestation of what they're feeling.

This moment may not last or it may end in a marriage. But the two will never be closer, and the audience rejoices in that. This beat is similar to the super magical moment in Fantasy. In story structure terms, it feels like a final victory. But it's false. Its opposite beat, the apparent defeat when the lovers break apart, soon follows.

Examples include *500 Days of Summer*, *Titanic*, *The Time Traveler's Wife*, *Moonrise Kingdom*, *Doctor Zhivago*, *Rebel Without a Cause*, *The Hunchback of Notre Dame*, *Almost Famous*, and *The 40-Year-Old Virgin*.

In *500 Days of Summer*, Tom exits the bathroom and finds Summer lying naked on her bed. This will be their first time having sex. As they start to kiss, Tom takes a fantasy walk through the city to music. Everyone he meets congratulates him on his great good fortune.

LOVE STORY BEAT: Apparent Defeat—Breakup

As the end of the story approaches, the lovers break apart, apparently for good. This apparent defeat is the death of the old self. The conventions and proprieties the characters once lived by now seem worthless. But the characters don't yet know the better self, and the stronger bond, that will replace what they have lost.

Examples include *Silver Linings Playbook*, *Jerry Maguire*, *Four Weddings and a Funeral*, *Moonrise Kingdom*, *Sideways*, *Wedding Crashers*, *Forrest Gump*, *Notting Hill*, *The English Patient*, *When Harry Met Sally*, *Brokeback Mountain*, *Pretty Woman*, *Bull Durham*, and *Pride and Prejudice*.

KEY POINT: In a good breakup there is a double defeat. Both characters fall.

Sideways: Miles and Maya are having a picnic when Miles lets it slip that he has to get back for the rehearsal dinner. Furious, Maya demands that Miles take her home. Before getting out of the car:

MAYA: You know I've just spent the last three years of my life trying to extricate myself from a relationship that was full of deception. And I'm doing just fine.

MILES: And I haven't been with anybody since my divorce. This has been a big deal for me, Maya. Hanging out with you. And last night. I really like you, Maya. And I am not Jack. I'm his freshman-year roommate from San Diego State.

Maya exits the car.

LOVE STORY BEAT: Moral Decline

Before and after the breakup, the characters are desperate to get the love of the other. This is a moral test. Each may use immoral methods, though this is not always present. Often, the immoral method after the breakup involves revenge.

KEY POINT: This moral decline leads to insights about right action and about the real depth in themselves.

In *Silver Linings Playbook*, Tiffany gives Pat hope when she falsely offers to get a letter to Pat's ex Nikki if he will be her dance partner. She then forges a return note from Nikki suggesting they may get back together.

In *Wuthering Heights*, since Cathy spurned true love between them, Heathcliff vows to take revenge on her and her family.

And in *Casablanca*, bitter at the loss of Ilsa, the love of his life, Rick refuses to give her the letters of transit that would allow her and her husband to escape.

LOVE STORY BEAT: **Battle of Words**

The Love story battle should focus on the characters' conflicting values and on how they might live together.

KEY POINT: Each argues for more power, trying to get the upper hand. Each is still blaming the other.

Examples include *When Harry Met Sally*, *The Thomas Crown Affair*, *Wuthering Heights*, *Pretty Woman*, *Pride and Prejudice*, *Heartbreaker*, *Broadcast News*, *Moonstruck*, *As Good as It Gets*, *Annie Hall*, *Of Human Bondage*, *Pygmalion*, *The Philadelphia Story*, *Gone with the Wind*, and *Duel in the Sun*.

Wuthering Heights: Cathy is dying in her bed. Heathcliff holds her.

CATHY: Hold me. Just hold me.

HEATHCLIFF: No, I'll not comfort you. My tears don't love you, Cathy. They blight and curse and damn you.

CATHY: Heathcliff, don't break my heart.

HEATHCLIFF: Oh Cathy, I never broke your heart. You broke it. Cathy, Cathy, you loved me. What right to throw love away for the poor fancy thing you felt for him. For a handful of worldliness. Misery and death and all the evils that God and man could have hammered down would never have parted us. You did that alone. You wandered off like a wanton, greedy child. To break your heart and mine.

CATHY: Heathcliff, forgive me. We've so little time.

The writers of *Heartbreaker* create the perfect battle scene by combining it with two moments that usually happen much earlier in the story: the first date and the first dance.

Alex takes Juliette to a closed disco. The grand scam he concocted from the beginning is based on knowing that her favorite film is *Dirty Dancing*. At the club, he plays the film's climactic song on the jukebox and the two reenact the big dance. He performs the steps perfectly and their fantastic dance ends with him hoisting a soaring Juliette over his head, just as in the original film.

KEY POINT: By delaying the first date and first dance to the most climactic moment of any story, the writers create the best beat in the film and a classic moment in the history of Romantic Comedy.

LOVE STORY BEAT: Self-Revelation—Double Reversal

Love stories where the two characters end up together focus toward a "double reversal" where both lovers have a self-revelation. Each learns from the other.

In the psychological self-revelation, each realizes they love the other and are not bound by their past. Specifically, each knows: "I love her/him in spite of everything keeping us apart. I believe there's enough love to overcome what's between us." This goes back to the crucial question of the form: How much can you love?

In the moral self-revelation, the hero and lover realize they have both been selfish.

KEY POINT: Ideally, each should decide to sacrifice the thing they are most selfish about for the other. This act is the proof of the moral self-revelation.

Double self-sacrifice is the equivalent in Detective, Thriller, and Crime of poetic justice. If you succeed, the effect is transcendent.

There is no better example of this mutual sacrifice than in O. Henry's beautiful "The Gift of the Magi." On Christmas Eve, Della has little money with which to buy a present for her husband, Jim. She sells her long, beautiful hair for twenty dollars so she can purchase a platinum chain for his precious pocket watch. When she gives him the gift, she discovers he sold the watch to buy expensive tortoiseshell combs for her hair. Though their gifts are useless now, each knows of the other's deep love.

KEY POINT: The result of the self-revelation is that the "I" finally becomes the "us." The characters go from being two separate individuals to one great community together.

The new way of life for the couple is not one character winning but both characters helping each other face their problems together. Their big insight is that love makes them both stronger.

Examples include *Four Weddings and a Funeral*, *Notting Hill*, *When Harry Met Sally*, *Forrest Gump*, *Moonstruck*, *Pretty Woman*, *Music Man*, *Children of a Lesser God*, *Tootsie*, and *The Philadelphia Story*.

LOVE STORY BEAT: New Equilibrium—Communion or Farewell

At the end of the story, either the two characters marry, which is the blossoming moment for both, or tragedy separates them forever.

Option 1. Communion (Marriage or Remarriage):

Communion is the key to any happy Love story and is the payoff of the audience's emotional investment. This moment is one of the main reasons people read and watch Love stories.

KEY POINT: If you don't end with a communion, your reader will be extremely upset. Therefore, you better have a very good reason for not doing so.

Three beats must happen in the story for the audience to feel a flood of emotion at the end:

- Deep desire established between the lovers at the beginning
- Separation
- Reunion with a public outpouring of emotion

If you hit all three of these beats in your story, the moment of reunion will *always* bring tears of happiness to an audience.

Examples include *Four Weddings and a Funeral*, *Notting Hill*, *When Harry Met Sally*, *Tootsie*, *Jerry Maguire*, *Pride and Prejudice*, *Sideways*, *The Year of Living Dangerously*, *Pretty Woman*, *Forrest Gump*, *Rocky*, *The Last of the Mohicans*, *Sleepless in Seattle*, and *Groundhog Day*.

In *Jerry Maguire*, Jerry enters the home where his ex-wife Dorothy and her son are living with her sister. Her sister is having a meeting of her women's group.

JERRY: Hello. Hello. I'm looking for my wife. Wait . . . Tonight, our little project, our company, had a very big night. A very, very big night. But it wasn't complete, it wasn't nearly close to being in the same vicinity as complete. Because I couldn't share it with you. I couldn't hear your voice. Or laugh about it to you. I miss my wife . . . We live in a cynical world. A cynical world. And we work in a business of tough competitors . . . I love you. You complete me. And I just . . .

DOROTHY: Shut up. Just shut up. You had me at hello. Hello.

They hug.

"You had me at hello" is one of the greatest lines in the history of Love stories.

Sideways twists the beat with a semicommunion and a promise of more to come. Miles plays a phone message in which Maya talks about how moved she was by his novel. She invites him to come by if he's ever up that way. As the message plays in voice-over, Miles drives in the rain. He knocks on Maya's door and . . .

Option 2. Farewell

This is the crucial moment in a tragic Love story. The author's strategy is that the audience feels the love most intensely when it is taken away.

> **KEY POINT: Only the greatest event can keep the lovers apart. The farewell is best when one character has to sacrifice their love for a higher purpose.**

Executed well, this moment can be powerful. But such a sacrifice is hard to justify now. Viewers are much less likely to believe that there is anything more important than true love.

If you can't justify losing true love, don't try this beat. It will infuriate the audience. They'll ask: The character is giving up great love for that?

Examples include *500 Days of Summer*, *Titanic*, *Camille*, *Dark Victory*, *Brief Encounter*, *Romeo and Juliet*, *Wuthering Heights*, *The Thomas Crown Affair*, and *Up in the Air*.

Option 3. Farewell and Communion

On rare occasion, the characters lose the love but gain something else. The audience gets to have their cake and eat it too.

Casablanca is the ultimate example of farewell plus communion. No other story comes close. Rick loses Ilsa but then walks off with his new friend, Louis. Essentially, Rick gives up one marriage for another (and one of the great "bromances" in film history).

> **KEY POINT: The switch from Love story to Buddy Story works because the story line with Louis has been set up all along. And it's a *more developed line than the one with Ilsa.***

Theme: Being Is Loving

Love isn't just that airy romantic notion that storytellers and songwriters have waxed poetic about for thousands of years. It's not, as Plato said, a moment of insanity, though it can feel that way. It's not simply the human method of ensuring the perpetuation of the species. Love is the state of being that a person must experience to "flower" as a human.

The Love story says that love is what binds us to others in the world. That feeling translates into the action of caring for another. Caring, in turn, is a feedback loop that improves the giver as well as the receiver and expands out to the community.

Unlike other genres, Love doesn't tell us what being is like every day by virtue of being alive. It tells us what being is like when we live our lives to the fullest. It is the precondition of being well.

Love Thematic Recipe: The Way of the Lover

As with all genres, Love's thematic recipe for how to live a good life comes from the hero's basic action and the key question every story must answer. In the Love story, the hero wants to gain love. Indeed, if we were to describe the form in a single line, it would be: the man or woman who loves. This is deceptively simple. A good Love story always pushes that action to its farthest extreme.

KEY POINT: The man or woman must love in spite of all differences between them, all outside opposition, and all mistakes each makes to the other.

That's why the key question of the genre is: *How much can you love?* But simply having a loving feeling toward the other is not enough. We cannot be happy in love unless we are happy within ourselves. Love makes that happen, and two fully blossomed individuals in turn make a great love.

Love's thematic recipe, the Way of the Lover, hits home with the reader in three main ways:

1. Love as Care

Romantic love is an intense feeling. But over time that feeling can cool and the relationship between the two individuals can become symbolic, accepted, even dull. Care, on the other hand, is always active. Care is using love to transform. It is what actualizes the human capability for a rich life. Only this active form of love can make both individuals better and happy for the long term.

2. Learning *How* to Love

Reading the Love story, we get caught up in whether the two characters will find love together. But the deep structure isn't about mastering the physical act of love. It's about mastering the moral act of love. The Love story makes the case that sacrificing for love brings the individual far more in return. This is also the moral argument of the genre. Both characters need to learn this by the end.

3. The Magic of Good Talk

We said earlier that the Love Mind-Action story view gives the audience the language of growth at the most intimate level. In Romance novels and Romantic Comedy, the most important ingredient for that is the magic of good talk. This means wit, banter, flirtation, learning to listen, and real communication between two people no matter the gender. This is a partnership of equals that works over the long haul. To paraphrase Ben Franklin: it's a marriage, if you can keep it.

How to Transcend the Love Story

The classic Love story expresses the art of love. Transcendent Love stories explore the art of "marriage." Where the classic Love story ends with a marriage, the transcendent Love story begins with one. It dramatizes the obstacles and techniques for true, long-lasting love. It may do this negatively through tragedy, or positively by showing how two people can grow through love over a lifetime. In the positive version, the strategy is to show models of how two individuals can work and play together to sustain personal happiness.

The Transcendent Love story takes three major forms:

1. The Tragedy of Traditional Marriage
   This transcendent Love story shows why the structural end point of the form, marriage, fails. Examples include *Anna Karenina*, *Madame Bovary*, *The Wife*, *The Awakening*, *Revolutionary Road*, *Scenes from a Marriage*, *Wuthering Heights*, *The Earrings of Madame de . . .* , *Brief Encounter*, *Who's Afraid of Virginia Woolf?*, *The Age of Innocence*, *The Portrait of a Lady*, Henrik Ibsen plays like *Hedda Gabler* and *A Doll's House*, Strindberg's *The Father*.
2. The Comedy of Remarriage
   The Comedy of Remarriage shows two people learning how to make a marriage last the second time around. Examples include *The Philadelphia Story*, *The Awful Truth*, *My Favorite Wife*, *His Girl Friday*, *Adam's Rib*, and *The Parent Trap*.

3. True Love and the Art of Marriage
   True Love stories explore the art of marriage and the techniques that make love last. Examples include *Pride and Prejudice*, *Four Weddings and a Funeral*, *The Thin Man*, *Hannah and Her Sisters*, *Sense and Sensibility*, *Adam's Rib*, *Blue Is the Warmest Color*, *Before Midnight*, and *The Best Years of Our Lives*.

Transcendent Love stories focus on the central philosophical issue of marriage. The question is how to live well with another person in ways that benefit both over the long term. The crucial difference is that a marriage is the most intimate and emotional of all social forms. Intimacy increases the potential benefit to each person in the marriage. But it also increases the danger of enslavement, inequality, and the destruction of the unit itself.

Unlike courtship, marriage extends over a long time with no clear end point. Therefore, it appears to be an art form that does not have a dramatic shape. It is an art form of duration, not crescendo.

But this is not necessarily true. Marriage is a living relationship between two human beings. Any living relationship must take on dramatic shape, even when it's so long that the human mind can't grasp it as a whole.

Part of the difficulty of seeing the dramatic shape of a marriage is that it takes the opposite shape of most stories. Instead of a crescendo to a climax, it takes the form of a decrescendo to an equilibrium state. Beginning with the most passionate unity possible between two separate human beings, the love changes to a different kind of relationship.

KEY POINT: Some would argue that the decrescendo of marriage is by definition undramatic. Not so. It is transformation of a different kind.

Here are the *crescendo* beats of the courtship love story:

- **STORY WORLD:** mind-body and exotic subworld
- Two individuals in psychological and physical need
- The projection of the self as sexual
- The look, the attraction, the desire, the fear
- The verbal joust with the other
- Initiation
- The kiss, the dance, and the consummation
- The breakup
- Battle of words
- **SELF-REVELATION:** double reversal
- **NEW EQUILIBRIUM:** communion or farewell

Here are the *decrescendo* beats of the "true," or enduring love story:

- **COMMUNION:** wedding
- **NEW LOVER:** exploring love day-to-day
- **WEAKNESS-NEED:** love is settled and differences between the sexes
- **DESIRE:** life success; later, to cultivate love in spite of the waning of passion
- **OPPONENTS:** obstacles to loving day-to-day
- **MORAL ARGUMENT:** issues of loving long term
- **SELF-REVELATION:** love is an entire way of living
- **NEW EQUILIBRIUM:** higher love

The different types of transcendent Love stories execute these beats of a marriage in different ways.

Transcending Love 1: Tragedy of Traditional Marriage

The Drama of the Old Contract

Stories about the Tragedy of Traditional Marriage begin by focusing on the emotion of love. When it cools, the relationship can become symbolic and hollow. Without fuel, the marriage engine grinds to a halt. The players simply go through the motions.

Tragedy of Traditional Marriage stories then shift to a deeper, structural reason for why the union fails. Love is not just a feeling. It is two people living together as a single unit. So the central issue in love, as it is really lived, is the *contract*. In other words, what each expects from and owes the other while living together as one (see the Crime chapter on moral accounting).

Like sexual Action stories where the man hunts a beautiful woman and eventually captures her, Tragedy of Traditional Marriage stories play out the Old-Fashioned Marriage contract between men and women. This contract is based on the first major distinction in human life, men versus women, and deals with it from the sociobiological view. These are the main points of that contract:

- The man is attractive primarily because he has power and money
- The woman is attractive primarily because of her physical beauty
- The man agrees to provide the resources
- The woman agrees to take care of the children

These elements tend to reduce men and women to their biological differences. The natural end point of this deal is destructive to both. Since the man works constantly to provide the resources, he turns into a machine. Since the woman is dependent on the man for everything, she turns into a child. Both may think this is a fair contract. But it has the seeds of failure built into it. Both may ultimately be hurt.

Tragedy of Traditional Marriage stories show the downward and destructive cycle of this contract over time.

As the ultimate projection of the human mind, love is both a transforming and destructive vision. *Madame Bovary* is a Love story that shows the dangerous capacity of this intensely emotional projection. Madame Bovary marries a boring country doctor. Her mind inflamed by romantic literature, she has two affairs and goes deep into debt to buy the expensive things of a higher class. With nowhere to turn, she commits suicide by taking arsenic.

In *The Earrings of Madame de . . .* the essence of the Old-Fashioned Marriage contract is right in the title. Madame de . . . (we never learn her last name) must sell the diamond earrings her husband gave her to pay off some debts. Told in the shape of "the Round," the story shows Madame de . . . on a downward cycle of enslavement due to her dependence on her husband's money.

Moonstruck has a main plot and a subplot. Each storyline gives a different view of fidelity in a marriage. In the main storyline, Loretta is engaged to be married to Johnny but doesn't love him. She has a passionate affair with Johnny's brother Ronny. The author makes the moral argument that infidelity is justified for true love.

The subplot concerns Loretta's parents, Cosmo and Rose. Cosmo is having an affair even though he still loves his wife and she loves him. The author shows that this infidelity is wrong because it places physical passion above deeper love and trust.

Transcending Love 2: The Comedy of Remarriage

The Comedy of Remarriage, a subgenre first identified by the philosopher Stanley Cavell, is a form of True Love story whose potential has barely been scratched.* It is no more realistic than the classic courtship Love story. But it does start with the failure of marriage. This highlights a crucial question in any True Love story: Why couldn't their love last?

This subgenre has serious challenges. First, there are few actual story examples of the form. Almost all of them are films from the mid-1930s through the early 1940s. Comedy of Remarriage is also limited in that it repeats many elements of the classic courtship Love story. After the initial breakup, the divorced couple goes through the process of falling in love again. The story ends in their remarriage.

On the plus side, Comedy of Remarriage deals with the central challenge of enduring love: How do these two people create the foundation for a new marriage that lasts?

For many reasons, the Comedy of Remarriage is a modernized classic Female Myth. The original Comedy of Remarriage is Cupid and Psyche. Cupid means "desire" or "love" (the Greek "Eros"), and Psyche means "soul" or "breath of life." In the story, Psyche betrays her husband through mistrust. Therefore, her mother-in-law, Aphrodite, goddess of love, puts her through a series of trials. Psyche passes these tests and is reunited with her husband.

Yet, Comedy of Remarriage is more than a modernized ancient Myth. Marriage and remarriage are basic to the species, and have existed in some form for a long time. With special twists to the basic story beats, Comedy of Remarriage could be a major form of True Love story in future storytelling.

---

* Stanley Cavell, *Pursuits of Happiness: The Hollywood Comedy of Remarriage*.

Here are the crucial elements to make the Comedy of Remarriage work:

1. At the beginning of the story, each character is trapped by the past and continues to fight about the flaws that broke up their marriage.
2. As the story progresses and the characters are forced to spend time together, each discovers a lighter, more playful side in the other before responsibilities of marriage and children shut them down. This is much closer to who they really are. Each falls in love with this new part of the other. The original reason they married is left behind.
3. At the double reversal (mutual self-revelation), each learns how to create a marriage based not on social rules, traditional male and female roles, or family. It is based on true and higher love between equals.

KEY POINT: In the Comedy of Remarriage you must come up with something *new and deeper* about the ex that allows each to fall in love again, but in a more profound way.

Transcending the Love Story 3: True Love and the Art of Marriage

True Love stories focus on how to live with a new marriage contract, and then expand to include a new way of being and living in the world.

KEY POINT: There are fewer examples of positive transcendent stories in Love than in any other genre.

For almost everyone, this is the most important Love story of all. So why is it rarely written? Because dramatizing how to live with love over a lifetime is extremely difficult.

KEY POINT: You must answer these two questions: How do two people take love beyond the initial courtship to a deeper level? How do you not only create the flame of love, but make it stronger and make it last?

This is one of the great challenges of life, if not the greatest of all. It leads to the central problem of writing the True Love story, and why it is so rare: finding a dramatic focus, or spine, for the story.

The classic Love story is built on a clean, specific goal that tracks the courtship process. The two characters see each other and want each other. The actions they take lead them to the vortex point of marriage. But when a writer goes beyond the goal-oriented courting process, they don't have a single desire line to shape the story and give it momentum.

The question is: What artistic vehicle can give form to love over a lifetime?

The scarcity of True Love stories makes it difficult to use our normal Aristotelian method of providing examples that describe the beats, principles, and techniques of the genre. Given that Tragic Love stories play out the Old-Fashioned Marriage contract, it is useful in this case to start with the elements of the "New Marriage" contract. From that we can see how to tell the True Love story.

The New Marriage Contract

The New Marriage contract handles the distinction of men versus women in a much different way than the Old-Fashioned Marriage contract. Instead of reducing men and women and pitting them against each other based on their biological roles, the New Marriage contract is based on an *artistic* relationship between the two. This also paves the way for modern Love stories between individuals of any gender.

- Lover #1 is attractive primarily because of how they care and make the other feel about themselves and their potential for a great life.
- Lover #2 is attractive primarily because of their ability to care for the partnership and encourage the other to be their best self.
- Both agree to provide the resources, to whatever degree they can.
- Both agree to take care of the children and recognize and encourage the unique ways each can do so.

The natural end point of this deal is a *creative opposition* that doesn't deny their biological differences but always tries to maximize the human potential of both.

KEY POINT: The New Marriage contract takes creativity to its farthest extreme. Each partner is creative in all aspects of life, every day. Love in this partnership becomes *an entire way of living*.

True Love Story Beats

This is how the True Love story expresses the New Marriage contract and executes the decrescendo beats we listed above.

TRUE LOVE STORY BEAT: Communion—Wedding

The story begins with the wedding of the lead characters, or its recent aftermath. The previous goal of love has been accomplished. Now they face an unknown future of how to live their life together.

TRUE LOVE STORY BEAT: New Lover—Exploring Love Day by Day

Both heroes represent a new kind of lover. Unlike the typical courtship Love story, the man doesn't start by wanting to strategize and conquer the woman. The woman doesn't start by wanting to uncover his deception, fend off his desire, and gain the upper hand.

Neither is seeking a union. The wedding has already happened. But while neither character is limited by the desire and plan of the past, each has real weaknesses.

TRUE LOVE STORY BEAT: Weakness-Need—Love Is Settled and Differences Between the Sexes

Because the new lovers are starting a marriage, they are just beginning the real exploration of what love between two people can mean. The problem is that each is the product of the Old-Fashioned contract. So they don't know that wedded bliss is just the opening step of their journey to greatness.

The married couple is still trapped by differences, some cultural and some biological. Even if the two think of themselves as "enlightened," they have barely scratched the surface of what thousands of years of cultural expectations and traditional values can do to their mind.

TRUE LOVE STORY BEAT: Desire—Life Success

Even if the heroes do not believe in the old roles, they incorrectly act as though love is settled in their lives. Now they turn their attention to success in work.

This is similar to the "Life Success" goal in the basic Love story. The couple doesn't come up with particular *goals for love* until they face opposition within the marriage. Only much later, at the self-revelation, will these "new lovers" understand what their real goal about love should have been all along.

TRUE LOVE STORY BEAT: Opposition: Obstacles to Loving Day-to-Day

In the normal writing process, we start with the hero's desire. That in turn tells us the opposition. But with the True Love story, the main challenge is that there is no clear goal, like courtship, to give the story a spine.

TECHNIQUE: Opposition Before Desire

In the True Love story, we need to reverse the process. We start with the opposition in order to uncover the particular desire about love that will shape the story.

Any marriage has an infinite number of possible opponents. But here are the most likely categories of opposition:

- Dealing with parents and children, often at the same time, without killing love
- Moral conflicts that arise in trying to balance work with love
- Larger social forces like economics, politics, and a shifting social stage that affect the couple in powerful but subtle ways

Focus on how these obstacles affect the characters' attempts to love day-to-day.

TRUE LOVE STORY BEAT: Moral Argument—Issues of Loving Long-Term

The daily obstacles to true, lasting love give dramatic focus to the deeper moral issues of the form. Here are some possibilities:

- Good lying versus bad lying: Is total honesty between couples always best for love? Is it preferable under certain circumstances? Or is it inevitably destructive?
- Should a person prioritize children above spouse or spouse above children? How do children weaken the love between parents?
- Can someone love society as well as the family? In what way is it possible to help society without losing the family?

TRUE LOVE STORY BEAT: Self-Revelation—Love Is an Entire Way of Living

There is no one self-revelation that can turn a person into a "new lover." It must be a series of self-revelations in which each character continually rediscovers that love is not a momentary feeling of ecstasy. It requires a new set of actions that become an entire way of living.

> **KEY POINT: The lovers/partners must consciously maintain passion or rejuvenate it when it starts to die. That means cultivating love.**

TECHNIQUE: Creativity in Everything

Take the idea of being creative into all aspects of life, especially in love.

Creation isn't a product; it's a process. In a larger sense, it means two people becoming artists of their life together. This way love infuses every activity they do. Some of the specific forms this mutual creativity could take are:

- The lover sees and helps heal the weakness in the other person that keeps the couple from having a fuller life.

- Both people enjoy sexuality and physicality as a way of caring for each other.
- Each tries to create a more intimate way of knowing and being with the other. This is not sparring, putting down, or agonizing about feelings or mistakes from the past. Instead, it's being playful, tender, kind, respectful, working through challenges together, and doing things in a loving way.

All of this makes up true partnership. What greater gift could someone give to their love?

TRUE LOVE STORY BEAT: New Equilibrium—Higher Love

The New Equilibrium does not describe a renewed love between the two, but a more evolved "lover." One may overcome a tendency to be a child. The other may overcome a tendency to be a machine. Together they create a higher love with a new contract that works for both.

Examples include *Pride and Prejudice*, *Four Weddings and a Funeral*, *The Thin Man*, *Hannah and Her Sisters*, *Sense and Sensibility*, *Adam's Rib*, *Blue Is the Warmest Color*, *Before Midnight*, and *The Best Years of Our Lives*.

Stories About the Art of Happy Marriage

As mentioned, there are few story examples of True Love and happy marriage. This comes from one of the basic principles of story: it must have conflict, the more the better. We see this in Leo Tolstoy's famous comment about family in *Anna Karenina*: "All happy families are alike; each unhappy family is unhappy in its own way."

Happiness, in whatever social unit, is almost impossible to dramatize. Unhappiness, on the other hand, can generate stories the length and quality of a Tolstoy novel (at least if you're Tolstoy). Let's look at some of the authors and stories that have successfully shown the art of the happy marriage.

We've already discussed Austen's technique of the three suitors. These men compete for the classic Love story goal: the woman's hand in marriage. But they also show us different recipes for married success.

In *Pride and Prejudice* the Bennet family has five sisters. The main suitors for these women are Darcy, Bingley, Collins, and Wickham. Let's compare the couples to see which marriages will likely be happy.

Jane and Bingley: This marriage will probably be happy. It is based on the Old-Fashioned Marriage contract. But Bingley will be a benign and loving dictator while sweet Jane will be content to be his helper.

Elizabeth's friend Charlotte and Mr. Collins: After Elizabeth turns him down, Charlotte grabs him. This is the Old-Fashioned Marriage contract in the extreme. Though Collins is rich, Charlotte is too smart and vital for such a dullard and will feel trapped.

Kitty and Wickham: This Old-Fashioned contract is based on deceit and false money. This marriage is likely to be filled with affairs and recriminations.

Elizabeth and Darcy: Although based on the Old-Fashioned contract, this marriage is as close to the New Contract as was possible in that time and culture. Elizabeth is smart and demands equality. Darcy has the money but, like Bingley, is a benevolent dictator and prefers a woman who is his equal.

The *Thin Man* movies, based on the book by Dashiell Hammett, combined the Detective and Romantic Comedy genres. Their recipe of romantic sleuths became the template for many films and television shows. It has been said that these films depict the happiest marriage in history. What are the defining characteristics of their happiness?

- They work together
- They have money

- They have no children to distract from the relationship
- They are playful
- They make each other laugh
- They respect each other's differences
- They protect each other from harm
- Each shows their childlike qualities
- They enjoy each other's company

In short, creativity is the foundation of their marriage.

The Next Rung Up the Ladder

Love gives us the recipe for day-to-day happiness. Transcending the form opens up the vast potential of who we can be. The freedom to explore love in every combination of gender, disability, race, class, and religion is a powerful tool for overcoming type to show the true individual in love. Each intimate society has a ripple effect on the larger communities and inspires readers to live with love.

What does this mean in our climb up the ladder of genre enlightenment? The sequence of genres started as a hierarchy of lowest to highest. Now that we've reached the top, we see that the genres form a tapestry. As Hegel might say, no one genre is the answer by itself.

KEY POINT: We need all the philosophies of life that the genres provide.

Embracing the best insights of all the story forms gives us the full experience of a happy life.

14

The Future of Storytelling

The Anatomy of Genres isn't merely a guide to our storytelling future. It's a map to the stories and structures that will shape our lives.

We are surrounded by story and story is embedded in us. Every day is a video game. But the stakes aren't about a high score. They're about overcoming the challenges to have a great life. And to do that, we must become conscious of ourselves as storytellers.

Whether you're writing a screenplay, novel, television show, play, video game, or web series, the future of stories in the marketplace runs parallel to the stories of our lives. Three elements stand out: they must be immersive, interactive, and "all genres all the time." That means mixing genres to a degree never seen before. The possibilities of combining more genres in new ways are endless.

Storytellers today are striving to create the most immersive experience possible, engaging the senses and the mind in a 360-degree field of play. Like the old *Choose Your Own Adventure* children's book series, the audience will interact with the story at every degree, from being totally passive to being the determining author every step of the way. This is already happening in novels, television, film, theater, theme parks, phones, and virtual reality (VR). It will be the determining factor in mediums yet to be invented.

One of the most exciting new structures I see coming in the interactive world, whether in video games, theme parks, or even television, is a single story that has elements from *all* the major genres. The viewer will jump from one genre to another, from scene to scene, as theme or point of view demands. From one character's POV, the story is a Fantasy. From another's perspective, it's Detective. Every permutation is a different story experience with the potential to be as rich as life itself.

What about the content of stories? Just as ancient Myths developed to express their unique world, emerging Myths will help us face the massive challenges of this world going forward. Genres such as the Ecological, Rejuvenation, and Female Myths will lead worldwide story in the coming decades.

The future of storytelling is about far more than writing a great story that sells. It's showing the audience that we're all storytellers, with the power to make our lives a work of art. This means consciously authoring our lives every day.

For writers and general readers alike, genres give us the modern philosophies and story forms to guide our lives. We need only study and use them. Story has always shown us sequences to enlightenment. *The Anatomy of Genres* provides a new ladder in which each story form is part of the answer.

In the beginning of this book, I mentioned two main goals. First was to give writers all the techniques they need to write great stories that sell. My second goal was to provide readers a comprehensive map to the structures of the world and the philosophies of life that could make their lives better.

I also have a secret goal: to spur a New Poetics. Poetics is the theory and practice of storytelling. The New Poetics means understanding the world as story forms. This is my contribution to the "stori-fication" of the world. Story and genre are the greatest knowledge of all. Nothing has the breadth, depth, power, and emotional impact of genre storytelling.

That's why, for me, the grand future of story is that it will lead to a higher level of consciousness for the human species. What does this mean? In the Science Fiction chapter, we said "technology is a form of art, a practical application of the mind to making the world work. Therefore, the level of technology is an expression of the level of human consciousness at the time."

Raising the level of human consciousness means understanding story as the universal religion. The religion of story doesn't divide people by beliefs. It brings us together as a guide for how to live successfully in the limited time we have on this earth. We can't shy away from that idea. We must embrace it as a way to see that we are all human beings struggling to have a good life.

This is the potential power of the New Poetics, the poetics of story in life. It's about seeing the world as fiction, as a story experience that you can learn from and use every minute of your life.

The question now is: How to begin?

You are at a turning point. *The Anatomy of Genres* gives you the essentials for success. If you want to create a brand for your writing and win the fierce competition of worldwide story, you must compete with the best. The crucial strategy in writing today is advanced theme expressed through complex plot. Genres are the vehicle for doing that. This isn't one way to succeed. It's the only way.

Perhaps the most important philosophical idea I can share is carpe diem. Seize the day! Don't let anyone stop you from telling the story that will be your legacy. The time to reach for success and greatness is now.

For my readers who are focused on making their life a

work of art, you too must seize the day. You're creating your present and your future at this very moment. Use this book as a daily guide to navigate the obstacles of life and find the solutions that can make you everything you can be.

One more thing: in the poetics of life, you're not just acting for yourself. If the future of storytelling is about moving human consciousness forward, about everyone having a good life through story, then you have a responsibility to be involved in that task.

We live in a moral universe. What you do with your life affects others. The ripple effect is incredibly vast and powerful. This book is also about viewing the world as a story that you can change for the better. That gives us all the best chance of having a wonderful life.

Let's get started.

APPENDIX: 7 MAJOR STORY STRUCTURE STEPS

All good stories work through seven major structure steps. These foundation steps comprise the Story Code. They mark the process of the hero's character change.

1. **WEAKNESS-NEED:** the hero is enslaved by habit of thought and action and suffers from a deep personal weakness that is destroying the quality of her life. The hero needs to overcome this flaw to grow.
2. **DESIRE:** the hero desires a goal outside of herself that she perceives as valuable and missing from her life.
3. **OPPONENT:** she confronts an opponent and an obstacle/challenge preventing her from reaching her goal. She will find at the end that the obstacle/challenge is herself.
4. **PLAN:** she concocts a plan, or strategy, that will allow her to defeat the opponent and achieve the goal.
5. **BATTLE:** she enters into a final conflict, or battle, with the opponent to determine once and for all who wins the goal.
6. **SELF-REVELATION:** at the end, the hero, if she grows at all, has a self-revelation about her true or better self, about how she has been wrong psychologically and morally. She then makes a decision about how to act and takes new action, proving what she has become.
7. **NEW EQUILIBRIUM:** with the system in a new equilibrium, the hero stands as a new version of herself, along with a new capacity for growing in the future.

ACKNOWLEDGMENTS

The Anatomy of Genres has been the work of a lifetime. I have been extraordinarily fortunate in all the people who helped bring it to fruition.

I first began to think strategically about fiction in my sophomore year of college when my roommate, Denny Foreman, and I would discuss the great works of literature. Later, I had a professor of film criticism, Jeremy Gilbert-Rolfe, an important abstract painter and art critic, who showed me how story could explain the world. He also told me I could be a major force in story at a time when I had no clue about or confidence in what I could become.

I tell writers that the ones who succeed are often the ones who are still standing. My parents, Amy and Jack Truby, were the ones who kept me standing through many hard years of learning the craft. Without their unwavering support, I would have been forced to become a doctor.

Big thanks to my agent, Noah Lukeman, who made this book possible by connecting me with the best publisher in the world.

All good writers need a good editor. I have had great ones. Anna Waterhouse, Ell Leigh Clarke, and Ollivier Pourriol provided valuable input on some of the main ideas in the book. Dan Kivlahan gave line edits with a breadth and depth I didn't think was possible. Ian Van Wye and the team at Farrar, Straus and Giroux did their usual outstanding job to make the book shine.

Finally, I must give massive credit to my wife, Leslie Lehr, a brilliant writer who edited every chapter of this daunting work four times. Now that's love. Quite simply, this book doesn't come close to reaching its full potential without her wise advice.